# *The* POWER *in* YOU

# *The* POWER *in* YOU

## The Definitive Thomas Troward

THOMAS TROWARD

JEREMY P. TARCHER/PENGUIN
AN IMPRINT OF PENGUIN RANDOM HOUSE
NEW YORK

JEREMY P. TARCHER/PENGUIN
An imprint of Penguin Random House LLC
375 Hudson Street
New York, New York 10014

*The Edinburgh Lectures on Mental Science* was originally published 1904, expanded 1909.
*The Doré Lectures on Mental Science* was originally published 1909.
*The Creative Process in the Individual* was originally published 1910, expanded 1915.
*Bible Mystery and Bible Meaning* was originally published 1913.
*The Law and the Word* was originally published 1917 (posthumous).
*The Hidden Power* was originally published 1921 (posthumous).
*Troward's Teachings in Condensed Form* was originally published 1958 in
*My Personal Reflections of Thomas Troward* (Booklet Three) by Harry Gaze.
These volumes first collected by Jeremy P. Tarcher/Penguin in 2015.



Library of Congress Cataloging-in-Publication Data

Troward, T. (Thomas), 1847–1916.
[Works. Selections]
The power in you : the definitive Thomas Troward / Thomas Troward.
p. cm.
ISBN 978-0-399-17479-7
1. New Thought. I. Title.
BF639.T746 2015 2015002865
299'.93—dc23

Printed in the United States of America
1 3 5 7 9 10 8 6 4 2

BOOK DESIGN BY TANYA MAIBORODA

This volume reproduces these works essentially as they appeared in their original editions. Except for adjustments that bring the text in line with contemporary typographic standards, the publisher has mostly retained the original spelling, usage, and style of the author. As these works were written in the first half of the twentieth century, they occasionally include an antiquated reference or word choice. For the purposes of historical accuracy, the publisher has left these intact, other than in cases of obvious error.

# CONTENTS

# The Edinburgh Lectures on Mental Science

1904, expanded 1909

*The Writer*

*Affectionately Dedicates*

*This Little Volume*

*To*

*His Wife*

# CONTENTS

# FOREWORD

THIS BOOK CONTAINS the substance of a course of lectures recently given by the writer in the Queen Street Hall, Edinburgh. Its purpose is to indicate the *Natural Principles* governing the relation between Mental Action and Material Conditions, and thus to afford the student an intelligible starting-point for the practical study of the subject.

T. T.
*March, 1904.*

# I

## SPIRIT AND MATTER

In commencing a course of lectures on Mental Science, it is somewhat difficult for the lecturer to fix upon the best method of opening the subject. It can be approached from many sides, each with some peculiar advantage of its own; but, after careful deliberation, it appears to me that, for the purpose of the present course, no better starting-point could be selected than the relation between Spirit and Matter. I select this starting-point because the distinction—or what we believe to be such—between them is one with which we are so familiar that I can safely assume its recognition by everybody; and I may, therefore, at once state this distinction by using the adjectives which we habitually apply as expressing the natural opposition between the two—*living* spirit and *dead* matter. These terms express our current impression of the opposition between spirit and matter with sufficient accuracy, and considered only from the point of view of outward appearances this impression is no doubt correct. The general consensus of mankind is right in trusting the evidence of our senses, and any system which tells us that we are not to do so will never obtain a permanent footing in a sane and healthy community. There is nothing wrong in the evidence conveyed to a healthy mind by the senses of a healthy body, but the point where error creeps in is when we come to judge of the meaning of this testimony. We are accustomed to judge only by external appearances and by certain limited significances which we attach to words; but when we begin to enquire into the real meaning of our words and to analyse the causes which give rise to the appearances, we find our old notions gradually falling off from us, until at last we wake up to the fact that we are living in an entirely different world to that we formerly recognized. The old limited mode of thought has imperceptibly slipped away, and we discover that we have stepped out into a new order of things where all is liberty and life. This is the work of an enlightened intelligence resulting from persistent determination to discover what truth really is irrespective of any preconceived notions from whatever source derived, the determination to think honestly for ourselves instead of endeavouring to get our thinking done for us. Let us then commence by enquiring what we really mean by the livingness which we attribute to spirit and the deadness which we attribute to matter.

At first we may be disposed to say that livingness consists in the power of motion and deadness in its absence; but a little enquiry into the most recent researches of science will soon show us that this distinction does not go deep enough. It is now one of the fully-established facts of physical science that no atom of what we call "dead matter" is without motion. On the table before me lies a solid lump of steel, but in the light of up-to-date science I know that the atoms of that seemingly inert mass are vibrating with the most intense energy, continually dashing hither and thither, impinging upon and rebounding from one another, or circling round like miniature solar systems, with a ceaseless rapidity whose complex activity is enough to bewilder the imagination. The mass, as a mass, may lie inert upon the table; but so far from being destitute of the element of motion it is the abode of the never-tiring energy moving the particles with a swiftness to which the speed of an express train is as nothing. It is, therefore, not the mere fact of motion that is at the root of the distinction which we draw instinctively between spirit and matter; we must go deeper than that. The solution of the problem will never be found by comparing Life with what we call deadness, and the reason for this will become apparent later on; but the true key is to be found by comparing one degree of livingness with another. There is, of course, one sense in which the quality of livingness does not admit of degrees; but there is another sense in which it is entirely a question of degree. We have no doubt as to the livingness of a plant, but we realize that it is something very different from the livingness of an animal. Again, what average boy would not prefer a fox-terrier to a goldfish for a pet? Or, again, why is it that the boy himself is an advance upon the dog? The plant, the fish, the dog, and the boy are all equally *alive;* but there is a difference in the quality of their livingness about which no one can have any doubt, and no one would hesitate to say that this difference is in the degree of intelligence. In whatever way we turn the subject we shall always find that what we call the "livingness" of any individual life is ultimately measured by its intelligence. It is the possession of greater intelligence that places the animal higher in the scale of being than the plant, the man higher than the animal, the intellectual man higher than the savage. The increased intelligence calls into activity modes of motion of a higher order corresponding to itself. The higher the intelligence, the more completely the mode of motion is under its control; and as we descend in the scale of intelligence, the descent is marked by a corresponding increase in *automatic* motion not subject to the control of a self-conscious intelligence. This descent is gradual from the expanded self-recognition of the highest human personality to that lowest order of visible forms which we speak of as "things," and from which self-recognition is entirely absent.

We see, then, that the livingness of Life consists in intelligence—in other words, in the power of Thought; and we may therefore say that the distinctive quality of spirit is Thought, and, as the opposite to this, we may say that the distinctive quality of matter is Form. We cannot conceive of matter without form. Some form there must be, even though invisible to the physical eye; for matter, to be matter at all, must occupy space, and to occupy any particular space necessarily implies a corresponding form. For these reasons we may lay it down as a fundamental proposition that the distinctive quality of spirit is Thought and the distinctive quality of matter is Form. This is a radical distinction from which important consequences follow, and should, therefore, be carefully noted by the student.

Form implies extension in space and also limitation within certain boundaries. Thought implies neither. When, therefore, we think of Life as existing in any particular *form* we associate it with the idea of extension in space, so that an elephant may be said to consist of a vastly larger amount of living substance than a mouse. But if we think of Life as the fact of livingness we do not associate it with any idea of extension, and we at once realize that the mouse is quite as much alive as the elephant, notwithstanding the difference in size. The important point of this distinction is that if we can conceive of anything as entirely devoid of the element of extension in space, it must be present in its entire totality anywhere and everywhere—that is to say, at every point of space simultaneously. The scientific definition of time is that it is the period occupied by a body in passing from one given point in space to another, and, therefore, according to this definition, when there is no space there can be no time; and hence that conception of spirit which realizes it as devoid of the element of space must realize it as being devoid of the element of time also; and we therefore find that the conception of spirit as pure Thought, and not as concrete Form, is the conception of it as subsisting perfectly independently of the elements of time and space. From this it follows that if the idea of anything is conceived as existing on this level it can only represent that thing as being actually present here and now. In this view of things nothing can be remote from us either in time or space: either the idea is entirely dissipated or it exists as an actual present entity, and not as something that *shall* be in the future, for where there is no sequence in time there can be no future. Similarly where there is no space there can be no conception of anything as being at a distance from us. When the elements of time and space are eliminated all our ideas of things must necessarily be as subsisting in a universal here and an everlasting now. This is, no doubt, a highly abstract conception, but I would ask the student to endeavour to grasp it thoroughly, since it is of vital importance in the practical application of Mental Science, as will appear further on.

The opposite conception is that of things expressing themselves through conditions of time and space and thus establishing a variety of *relations* to other things, as of bulk, distance, and direction, or of sequence in time. These two conceptions are respectively the conception of the abstract and the concrete, of the unconditioned and the conditioned, of the absolute and the relative. They are not opposed to each other in the sense of incompatibility, but are each the complement of the other, and the only reality is in the combination of the two. The error of the extreme idealist is in endeavouring to realize the absolute without the relative, and the error of the extreme materialist is in endeavouring to realize the relative without the absolute. On the one side the mistake is in trying to realize an inside without an outside, and on the other in trying to realize an outside without an inside; both are necessary to the formation of a substantial entity.

II

# THE HIGHER MODE OF INTELLIGENCE CONTROLS THE LOWER

We have seen that the descent from personality, as we know it in ourselves, to matter, as we know it under what we call inanimate forms, is a gradual descent in the scale of intelligence from that mode of being which is able to realize its own will-power as a capacity for originating new trains of causation to that mode of being which is incapable of recognizing itself at all. The higher the grade of life, the higher the intelligence; from which it follows that the supreme principle of Life must also be the ultimate principle of intelligence. This is clearly demonstrated by the grand natural order of the universe. In the light of modern science the principle of evolution is familiar to us all, and the accurate adjustment existing between all parts of the cosmic scheme is too self-evident to need insisting upon. Every advance in science consists in discovering new subtleties of connection in this magnificent universal order, which already exists and only needs our recognition to bring it into practical use. If, then, the highest work of the greatest minds consists in nothing else than the recognition of an already existing order, there is no getting away from the conclusion that a paramount intelligence must be inherent in the Life-Principle, which manifests itself *as* this order; and thus we see that there must be a great cosmic intelligence underlying the totality of things.

The physical history of our planet shows us first an incandescent nebula dispersed over vast infinitudes of space; later this condenses into a central sun surrounded by a family of glowing planets hardly yet consolidated from the plastic primordial matter; then succeed untold millenniums of slow geological formation; an earth peopled by the lowest forms of life, whether vegetable or animal; from which crude beginnings a majestic, unceasing, unhurried, forward movement brings things stage by stage to the condition in which we know them now. Looking at this steady progression it is clear that, however we may conceive the nature of the evolutionary principle, it unerringly provides for the continual advance of the race. But it does this by creating such numbers of each kind that, after allowing a wide margin for all possible accidents to individuals, the race shall still continue:—

> "So careful of the type it seems
> So careless of the single life."

In short, we may say that the cosmic intelligence works by a Law of Averages which allows a wide margin of accident and failure to the individual.

But the progress towards higher intelligence is always in the direction of narrowing down this margin of accident and taking the individual more and more out of the law of averages, and substituting the law of individual selection. In ordinary scientific language this is the survival of the fittest. The reproduction of fish is on a scale that would choke the sea with them if every individual survived; but the margin of destruction is correspondingly enormous, and thus the law of averages simply keeps up the normal proportion of the race. But at the other end of the scale, reproduction is by no means thus enormously in excess of survival. True, there is ample margin of accident and disease cutting off numbers of human beings before they have gone through the average duration of life, but still it is on a very different scale from the premature destruction of hundreds of thousands as against the survival of one. It may, therefore, be taken as an established fact that in proportion as intelligence advances the individual ceases to be subject to a mere law of averages and has a continually increasing power of controlling the conditions of his own survival.

We see, therefore, that there is a marked distinction between the cosmic intelligence and the individual intelligence, and that the factor which differentiates the latter from the former is the presence of *individual* volition. Now the business of Mental Science is to ascertain the relation of this individual power of volition to the great cosmic law which provides for the maintenance and advancement of the race; and the point to be carefully noted is that the power of individual volition is itself the outcome of the cosmic evolutionary principle at the point where it reaches its highest level. The effort of Nature has always been upwards from the time when only the lowest forms of life peopled the globe, and it has now culminated in the production of a being with a mind capable of abstract reasoning and a brain fitted to be the physical instrument of such a mind. At this stage the all-creating Life-principle reproduces itself in a form capable of recognizing the working of the evolutionary law, and the unity and continuity of purpose running through the whole progression until now indicates, beyond a doubt, that the place of such a being in the universal scheme must be to introduce the operation of that factor which, up to this point, has been conspicuous by its absence—the factor, namely, of intelligent individual volition. The evolution which has brought us up to this standpoint has worked by a cosmic law of averages; it has been a process in which the individual himself has not taken a conscious part. But because he is what he is, and leads the van of the evolutionary procession, if man is to evolve further, it can now only be by his own conscious cooperation with the law which has brought him up to the standpoint where he is able to realize that such a law exists. His evolution in the future must be by conscious participation in the great work, and this can only be effected by his own individual intelligence and effort. It is a process of intelligent growth. No one else can grow for us: we must each grow for ourselves; and this intelligent growth consists in our increasing recognition of the universal law, which has brought us as far as we have yet got, and of our own individual relation to that law, based upon the fact that we ourselves are the most advanced product of it. It is a great maxim that Nature obeys us precisely in proportion as we first obey Nature. Let the electrician try to go counter to the principle that electricity must always pass from a higher to a lower potential and he will effect nothing; but let him submit in all things to this one fundamental law, and he can make whatever particular applications of electrical power he will.

These considerations show us that what differentiates the higher from the lower degree of intelligence is the recognition of its own self-hood, and the more intelligent that recognition is, the greater will be the power. The lower degree of self-recognition is that which only realizes itself as an entity separate from all other entities, as the *ego* distinguished from the *non-*

*ego.* But the Higher degree of self-recognition is that which, realizing its own spiritual nature, sees in all other forms, not so much the *non-ego,* or that which is not itself, as the *alter-ego,* or that which is itself in a different mode of expression. Now, it is this higher degree of self-recognition that is the power by which the Mental Scientist produces his results. For this reason it is imperative that he should clearly understand the difference between Form and Being; that the one is the mode of the relative and the mark of subjection to conditions, and that the other is the truth of the absolute and is that which controls conditions.

Now this higher recognition of self as an individualization of pure spirit must of necessity control all modes of spirit which have not yet reached the same level of self-recognition. These lower modes of spirit are in bondage to the law of their own being because they do not know the law; and, therefore, the individual who has attained to this knowledge can control them through that law. But to understand this we must inquire a little further into the nature of spirit. I have already shown that the grand scale of adaptation and adjustment of all parts of the cosmic scheme to one another exhibits the presence *somewhere* of a marvellous intelligence underlying the whole, and the question is, where is this intelligence to be found? Ultimately we can only conceive of it as inherent in some primordial substance which is the root of all those grosser modes of matter which are known to us, whether visible to the physical eye, or necessarily inferred by science from their perceptible effects. It is that power which, in every species and in every individual, becomes that which that species or individual is; and thus we can only conceive of it as a self-forming intelligence inherent in the ultimate substance of which each thing is a particular manifestation. That this primordial substance must be considered as self-forming by an inherent intelligence abiding in itself becomes evident from the fact that intelligence is the essential quality of spirit; and if we were to conceive of the primordial substance as something apart from spirit, then we should have to postulate some other power which is neither spirit nor matter, and originates both; but this is only putting the idea of a self-evolving power a step further back and asserting the production of a lower grade of undifferentiated spirit by a higher, which is both a purely gratuitous assumption and a contradiction of any idea we can form of undifferentiated spirit at all. However far back, therefore, we may relegate the original starting-point, we cannot avoid the conclusion that, at that point, spirit contains the primary substance in itself, which brings us back to the common statement that it made everything out of nothing. We thus find two factors to the making of all things, Spirit and—Nothing; and the addition of Nothing to Spirit leaves *only* spirit: $x + 0 = x$.

From these considerations we see that the ultimate foundation of every form of matter is spirit, and hence that a universal intelligence subsists throughout Nature inherent in every one of its manifestations. But this cryptic intelligence does not belong to the particular *form* excepting in the measure in which it is physically fitted for its concentration into self-recognizing individuality: it lies hidden in that primordial substance of which the visible form is a grosser manifestation. This primordial substance is a philosophical necessity, and we can only picture it to ourselves as something infinitely finer than the atoms which are themselves a philosophical inference of physical science: still, for want of a better word, we may conveniently speak of this primary intelligence inherent in the very substance of things as the Atomic Intelligence. The term may, perhaps, be open to some objections, but it will serve our present purpose as distinguishing *this* mode of spirit's intelligence from that of the opposite pole, or Individual Intelligence. This distinction should be carefully noted because it is by the response of the atomic intelligence to the individual intelligence that thought-power is able to produce results on the material plane, as in the cure of disease by mental treatment, and the like. Intelligence manifests itself by responsiveness, and the whole action of the cosmic mind in bringing the evolutionary process from its first beginnings up to its present human stage is nothing else but a continual intelligent response to the demand which each stage in the progress has made for an adjustment between itself and its environment. Since, then, we have recognized the presence of a universal intelligence permeating all things, we must also recognize a corresponding responsiveness hidden deep down in their nature and ready to be called into action when appealed to. All mental treatment depends on this responsiveness of spirit in its lower degrees to higher degrees of itself. It is here that the difference between the mental scientist and the uninstructed person comes in; the former knows of this responsiveness and makes use of it, and the latter cannot use it because he does not know it.

III

## THE UNITY OF THE SPIRIT

WE HAVE NOW paved the way for understanding what is meant by "the unity of the spirit." In the first conception of spirit as the underlying origin of all things we see a universal substance which, at this stage, is not differentiated into any specific forms. This is not a question of some bygone time, but subsists at every moment of all time in the *innermost* nature of all being; and when we see this, we see that the division between one specific form and another has below it a deep essential unity, which acts as the supporter of all the several forms of individuality arising out of it. And as our thought penetrates deeper into the nature of this all-producing spiritual substance we see that it cannot be limited to any one portion of space, but must be limitless as space itself, and that the idea of any portion of space where it is not is inconceivable. It is one of those intuitive perceptions from which the human mind can never get away that this primordial, all-generating living spirit must be commensurate with infinitude, and we can therefore never think of it otherwise than as universal or infinite. Now it is a mathematical truth that the infinite must be a unity. You cannot have two infinites, for then neither would be infinite, each would be limited by the other, nor can you split the infinite up into fractions. The infinite is mathematically essential unity. This is a point on which too much stress cannot be laid, for there follow from it the most important consequences. Unity, as such, can be neither multiplied nor divided, for either operation destroys the unity. By multiplying, we produce a plurality of units of the same scale as the original; and by dividing, we produce a plurality of units of a smaller scale; and a plurality of units is not unity but multiplicity. Therefore if we would penetrate below the outward nature of the individual to that innermost principle of his being from which his individuality takes its rise, we can do so only by passing beyond the conception of individual existence into that of the unity of universal being. This may appear to be a merely philosophical abstraction, but the student who would produce practical results must realize that these abstract generalizations are the foundation of the practical work he is going to do.

Now the great fact to be recognized about a unity is that, *because* it is a single unit, wherever it is at all the *whole* of it must be. The moment we allow our mind to wander off to the idea of extension in space and say that one part of the unit is here and another there, we have descended from the idea of unity into that of parts or fractions of a single unit, which is to pass into the idea of a multiplicity of smaller units, and in that case we are dealing with the relative, or the relation subsisting between two or more entities which are therefore *limited by each other,* and so have passed out of the region of simple unity which is the absolute. It is, therefore, a mathematical necessity that, because the originating Life-principle is infinite, it is a single unit, and consequently, wherever it is at all, the *whole* of it must be present. But because it is *infinite,* or limitless, it is everywhere, and therefore it follows that the *whole* of spirit must be present at every point in space at the same moment. Spirit is thus omnipresent *in its entirety,* and it is accordingly logically correct that at every moment of time *all* spirit is concentrated at any point in space that we may choose to fix our thought upon. This is the fundamental fact of all being, and it is for this reason that I have prepared the way for it by laying down the relation between spirit and matter as that between idea and form, on the one hand the absolute from which the elements of time and space are entirely absent, and on the other the relative which is entirely dependent on those elements. This great fact is that pure spirit continually subsists in the absolute, whether in a corporeal body or not; and from it all the phenomena of being flow, whether on the mental plane or the physical. The knowledge of this fact regarding spirit is the basis of all conscious spiritual operation, and therefore in proportion to our increasing recognition of it our power of producing outward visible results by the action of our thought will grow. The whole is greater than its part, and therefore, if, by our recognition of this unity, we can concentrate *all* spirit into any given point at any moment, we thereby include any individualization of it that we may wish to deal with. The practical importance of this conclusion is too obvious to need enlarging upon.

Pure spirit is the Life-principle considered apart from the matrix in which it takes relation to time and space in a particular form. In this aspect it is pure intelligence undifferentiated into individuality. As pure intelligence it is infinite responsiveness and susceptibility. As devoid of relation to time and space it is devoid of individual personality. It is, therefore, in this aspect a purely impersonal element upon which, by reason of its inherent intelligence and susceptibility, we can impress any recognition of personality that we will. These are the great facts that the mental scientist works with, and the student will do well to ponder deeply on their significance and on the responsibilities which their realization must necessarily carry with it.

IV

# SUBJECTIVE AND OBJECTIVE MIND

UP TO THIS POINT it has been necessary to lay the foundations of the science by the statement of highly abstract general principles which we have reached by purely metaphysical reasoning. We now pass on to the consideration of certain natural laws which have been established by a long series of experiments and observations, the full meaning and importance of which will become clear when we see their application to the general principles which have hitherto occupied our attention. The phenomena of hypnosis are now so fully recognized as established scientific facts that it is quite superfluous to discuss the question of their credibility. Two great medical schools have been founded upon them, and in some countries they have become the subject of special legislation. The question before us at the present day is, not as to the credibility of the facts, but as to the proper inferences to be drawn from them, and a correct apprehension of these inferences is one of the most valuable aids to the mental scientist, for it confirms the conclusions of purely *a priori* reasoning by an array of experimental instances which places the correctness of those conclusions beyond doubt.

The great truth which the science of hypnotism has brought to light is the dual nature of the human mind. Much conflict exists between different writers as to whether this duality results from the presence of two actually separate minds in the one man, or in the action of the same mind in the employment of different functions. This is one of those distinctions without a difference which are so prolific a source of hindrance to the opening out of truth. A man must be a single individuality to be a man at all, and, so, the net result is the same whether we conceive of his varied modes of mental action as proceeding from a set of separate minds strung, so to speak, on the thread of his one individuality and each adapted to a particular use, or as varied functions of a single mind: in either case we are dealing with a single individuality, and how we may picture the wheel-work of the mental mechanism is merely a question of what picture will bring the nature of its action home to us most clearly. Therefore, as a matter of convenience, I shall in these lectures speak of this dual action as though it proceeded from two minds, an outer and an inner, and the inner mind we will call the subjective mind and the outer the objective, by which names the distinction is most frequently indicated in the literature of the subject.

A long series of careful experiments by highly-trained observers, some of them men of world-wide reputation, has fully established certain remarkable differences between the action of the subjective and that of the objective mind which may be briefly stated as follows. The subjective mind is only able to reason *deductively* and not inductively, while the objective mind can do both. Deductive reasoning is the pure syllogism which shows why a third proposition must necessarily result if two others are assumed, but which does not help us to determine whether the two initial statements are true or not. To determine this is the province of inductive reasoning which draws its conclusions from the observation of a series of facts. The relation of the two modes of reasoning is that, first by observing a sufficient number of instances, we inductively reach the conclusion that a certain principle is of general application, and then we enter upon the deductive process by assuming the truth of this principle and determining what result must follow in a particular case on the hypothesis of its truth. Thus deductive reasoning proceeds on the assumption of the correctness of certain hypotheses or suppositions with which it sets out: it is not concerned with the truth or falsity of those suppositions, but only with the question as to what results must necessarily follow supposing them to be true. Inductive reasoning, on the other hand, is the process by which we compare a number of separate instances with one another until we see the common factor that gives rise to them all. Induction proceeds by the comparison of facts, and deduction by the application of universal principles. Now it is the deductive method only which is followed by the subjective mind. Innumerable experiments on persons in the hypnotic state have shown that the subjective mind is utterly incapable of making the selection and comparison which are necessary to the inductive process, but will accept any suggestion, however false, but having once accepted any suggestion, it is strictly logical in deducing the proper conclusions from it, and works out every suggestion to the minutest fraction of the results which flow from it.

As a consequence of this it follows that the subjective mind is entirely under the control of the objective mind. With the utmost fidelity it reproduces and works out to its final consequences whatever the objective mind impresses upon it; and the facts of hypnotism show that ideas can be impressed on the subjective mind by the objective mind of another as well as by that of its own individuality. This is a most important point, for it is on this amenability to suggestion by the thought of another that all the phenomena of healing, whether present or absent, of telepathy and the like, depend. Under the control of the practised hypnotist the very personality of the subject becomes changed for the time being; he believes himself to be whatever the operator tells him he is: he is a swimmer breasting the waves, a bird flying in the air, a soldier in the tumult of battle, an Indian stealthily tracking his victim: in short, for the time being, he identifies himself with any personality that is impressed upon him by the will of the operator, and acts the part with inimitable accuracy. But the experiments of hypnotism go further than this, and show the existence in the subjective mind of powers far transcending any exercised by the objective mind through the medium of the physical senses; powers of thought-reading, of thought-transference, of clairvoyance, and the like, all of which are frequently manifested when the patient is brought into the higher mesmeric state; and we have thus experimental proof of the existence in ourselves of transcendental faculties the full development and conscious control of which would place us in a perfectly new sphere of life.

But it should be noted that the control must be *our own* and not that of any external intelligence whether in the flesh or out of it.

But perhaps the most important fact which hypnotic experiments have demonstrated is that the subjective mind is the builder of the body. The subjective entity in the patient is able to diagnose the character of the disease from which he is suffering and to point out suitable remedies, indicating a physiological knowledge exceeding that of the most highly trained physicians, and also a knowledge of the correspondences between diseased conditions of the bodily organs and the material remedies which can afford relief. And from this it is but a step further to those numerous instances in which it entirely dispenses with the use of material remedies and itself works directly on the organism, so that complete restoration to health follows as the result of the suggestions of perfect soundness made by the operator to the patient while in the hypnotic state.

Now these are facts fully established by hundreds of experiments conducted by a variety of investigators in different parts of the world, and from them we may draw two inferences of the highest importance: one, that the subjective mind is in itself absolutely impersonal, and the other that it is the builder of the body, or in other words it is the creative power in the individual. That it is impersonal in itself is shown by its readiness to assume any personality the hypnotist chooses to impress upon it; and the unavoidable inference is that its realization of personality proceeds from its association with the particular objective mind of its own individuality. Whatever personality the objective mind impresses upon it, that personality it assumes and acts up to; and since it is the builder of the body it will build up a body in correspondence with the personality thus impressed upon it. These two laws of the subjective mind form the foundation of the axiom that our body represents the aggregate of our beliefs. If our fixed belief is that the body is subject to all sorts of influences beyond our control, and that this, that, or the other symptom shows that such an uncontrollable influence is at work upon us, then this belief is impressed upon the subjective mind, which by the law of its nature accepts it without question and proceeds to fashion bodily conditions in accordance with this belief. Again, if our fixed belief is that certain material remedies are the only means of cure, then we find in this belief the foundation of all medicine. There is nothing unsound in the theory of medicine; it is the strictly logical correspondence with the measure of knowledge which those who rely on it are as yet able to assimilate, and it acts accurately in accordance with their belief that in a large number of cases medicine will do good, but also in many instances it fails. Therefore, for those who have not yet reached a more interior perception of the law of Nature, the healing agency of medicine is a most valuable aid to the alleviation of physical maladies. The error to be combated is not the belief that, in its own way, medicine is capable of doing good, but the belief that there is no higher or better way.

Then, on the same principle, if we realize that the subjective mind is the builder of the body, and that the body is subject to no influences except those which reach it through the subjective mind, then what we have to do is to impress *this* upon the subjective mind and habitually think of it as a fountain of perpetual Life, which is continually renovating the body by building in strong and healthy material, in the most complete independence of any influences of any sort, save those of our own desire impressed upon our own subjective mind by our own thought. When once we fully grasp these considerations we shall see that it is just as easy to externalize healthy conditions of body as the contrary. Practically the process amounts to a belief in our own power of life; and since this belief, if it be thoroughly domiciled within us, will necessarily produce a correspondingly healthy body, we should spare no pains to convince ourselves that there are sound and reasonable grounds for holding it. To afford a solid basis for this conviction is the purpose of Mental Science.

## V

# FURTHER CONSIDERATIONS REGARDING SUBJECTIVE AND OBJECTIVE MIND

An intelligent consideration of the phenomena of hypnotism will show us that what we call the hypnotic state is the *normal* state of the subjective mind. It *always* conceives of itself in accordance with some suggestion conveyed to it, either consciously or unconsciously to the mode of objective mind which governs it, and it gives rise to corresponding external results. The abnormal nature of the conditions induced by experimental hypnotism is in the removal of the normal control held by the individual's own objective mind over his subjective mind and the substitution of some other control for it, and thus we may say that the normal characteristic of the subjective mind is its perpetual action in accordance with some sort of suggestion. It becomes therefore a question of the highest importance to determine in every case what the nature of the suggestion shall be and from what source it shall proceed; but before considering the sources of suggestion we must realize more fully the place taken by subjective mind in the order of Nature.

If the student has followed what has been said regarding the presence of intelligent spirit pervading all space and permeating all matter, he will now have little difficulty in recognizing this all-pervading spirit as universal subjective mind. That it cannot *as universal mind* have the qualities of objective mind is very obvious. The universal mind is the creative power throughout Nature; and as the originating power it must first give rise to the various *forms* in which objective mind recognizes its own individuality, before these individual minds can re-act upon it; and hence, as pure spirit or *first cause,* it cannot possibly be anything else than subjective mind; and the fact which has been abundantly proved by experiment that the subjective mind is the builder of the body shows us that the power of creating by growth from within is the essential characteristic of the subjective mind. Hence, both from experiment and from *a priori* reasoning, we may say that where-ever we find creative power at work there we are in the presence of subjective mind, whether it be working on the grand scale of the cosmos, or on the miniature scale of the individual. We may therefore lay it down as a principle that the universal all-permeating intelligence, which has been considered in the second and third sections, is purely subjective mind, and therefore follows the law of subjective mind, namely that it is amenable to any suggestion, and will carry out any suggestion that is impressed upon it to its most rigorously logical consequences. The incalculable importance of this truth may not perhaps strike the student at first sight, but a little consideration will show him the enormous possibilities that are stored up in it, and in the concluding section I shall briefly touch upon the very serious conclusions resulting from it. For the present it will be sufficient to realize that the subjective mind in ourselves is *the same* subjective mind which is at work throughout the universe giving rise to the infinitude of natural forms with which we are surrounded, and in like manner giving rise *to ourselves also.* It may be called the supporter of our individuality; and we may loosely speak of our individual subjective mind as our personal share in the universal mind. This, of course, does not imply the splitting up of the universal mind into fractions, and it is to avoid this error that I have discussed the essential unity of spirit in the third section, but in order to avoid too highly abstract conceptions in the present stage of the student's progress we may conveniently employ the idea of a personal share in the universal subjective mind.

To realize our individual subjective mind in this manner will help us to get over the great metaphysical difficulty which meets us in our endeavour to make conscious use of first cause, in other words to create external results by the power of our own thought. Ultimately there can be only one first cause which is the universal mind, but because it is universal it cannot, *as universal,* act on the plane of the individual and particular. For it to do so would be for it to cease to be universal and therefore cease to be the creative power which we wish to employ. On the other hand, the fact that we are working for a specific definite object implies our intention to use this universal power in application to a particular purpose, and thus we find ourselves involved in the paradox of seeking to make the universal act on the plane of the particular. We want to effect a junction between the two extremes of the scale of Nature, the innermost creative spirit and a particular external form. Between these two is a great gulf, and the question is how is it to be bridged over. It is here, then, that the conception of our individual subjective mind as our personal share in the universal subjective mind affords the means of meeting the difficulty, for on the one hand it is in immediate connection with the universal mind, and on the other it is in immediate connection with the individual objective, or intellectual mind; and this in its turn is in immediate connection with the world of externalization, which is conditioned in time and space; and thus the relation between the subjective and objective minds in the individual forms the bridge which is needed to connect the two extremities of the scale.

The individual subjective mind may therefore be regarded as the organ of the Absolute in precisely the same way that the objective mind is the organ of the Relative, and it is in order to regulate our use of these two organs that it is necessary to understand what the terms "absolute" and "relative" actually mean. The absolute is that idea of a thing which contemplates it as existing *in itself* and not in relation to something else, that is to say, which contemplates the essence of it; and the relative is that idea of a thing which contemplates it as related to other things, that is to say as circumscribed by a certain environment. The absolute is the region of causes, and the relative is the region of conditions; and hence, if we wish to control conditions, this can only be done by our thought-power operating on the plane of the absolute, which it can do only through the medium of the subjective mind. The conscious use of the creative power of thought consists in the attainment of the power of Thinking in the Absolute, and this can only be attained by a clear conception of the interaction between our different mental functions. For this purpose the student cannot too strongly impress upon himself that subjective mind, on whatever scale, is intensely sensitive to suggestion, and as creative power works accurately to the externalization of that suggestion which is most deeply impressed upon it. If then, we would take any idea out of the realm of the relative, where it is limited and restricted by conditions imposed upon it through surrounding circumstances, and transfer it to the realm of the absolute where it is not thus limited, a right recognition of our mental constitution will enable us to do this by a clearly defined method.

The object of our desire is necessarily first conceived by us as bearing some relation to existing circumstances, which may, or may not, appear favourable to it; and what we want to do is to eliminate the element of contingency and attain something which is certain in itself. To do this is to work upon the plane of the absolute, and for this purpose we must endeavour to impress upon our subjective mind the idea of that which we desire quite apart from any conditions. This separation from the elements of condition implies the elimination of the idea of *time,* and consequently we must think of the thing as already in actual existence. Unless we do this we are not consciously operating upon the plane of the absolute, and are therefore not employing the creative power of our thought. The simplest practical method of gaining the habit of thinking in this manner is to conceive the existence in the spiritual world of a spiritual prototype of every existing thing, which becomes the root of the corresponding external existence. If we thus habituate ourselves to look on the spiritual prototype as the essential being of the thing, and the material form as the growth of this prototype into outward expression, then we shall see that the initial step to the production of any external fact must be the creation of its spiritual prototype. This prototype, being purely spiritual, can only be formed by the operation of *thought,* and in order to have substance on the spiritual plane it *must* be thought of as actually existing there. This conception has been elaborated by Plato in his doctrine of archetypal ideas, and by Swedenborg in his doctrine of correspondences; and a still greater teacher has said "All things whatsoever ye pray and ask for, believe that ye *have* received them, and ye *shall* receive them." (Mark xi. 24, R.V.) The difference of the tenses in this passage is remarkable. The speaker bids us first to believe that our desire *has* already been fulfilled, that it is a thing already accomplished, and then its accomplishment *will* follow as a thing in the future. This is nothing else than a concise direction for making use of the creative power of thought by impressing upon the universal subjective mind the particular thing which we desire as an already existing fact. In following this direction we are thinking on the plane of the absolute and eliminating from our minds all consideration of conditions, which imply limitation and the possibility of adverse contingencies; and we are thus planting a seed which, if left undisturbed, will infallibly germinate into external fruition.

By thus making intelligent use of our subjective mind, we, so to speak, create a *nucleus,* which is no sooner created than it begins to exercise an attractive force, drawing to itself material of a like character with its own, and if this process is allowed to go on undisturbed, it will continue until an external form corresponding to the nature of the nucleus comes out into manifestation on the plane of the objective and relative. This is the universal method of Nature on every plane. Some of the most advanced thinkers in modern physical science, in the endeavour to probe the great mystery of the first origin of the world, have postulated the formation of what they call "vortex rings" formed from an infinitely fine primordial substance. They tell us that if such a ring be once formed on the minutest scale and set rotating, then, since it would be moving in pure ether and subject to no friction, it must according to all known laws of physics be indestructible and its motion perpetual. Let two such rings approach each other, and by the law of attraction, they would coalesce into a whole, and so on until manifested matter as we apprehend it with our external senses, is at last formed. Of course no one has ever seen these rings with the physical eye. They are one of those abstractions which result if we follow out the observed law of physics and the unavoidable sequences of mathematics to their necessary consequences. We cannot account for the things that we *can* see unless we assume the existence of other things which we *cannot;* and the "vortex theory" is one of these assumptions. This theory has not been put forward by mental scientists but by purely physical scientists as the ultimate conclusion to which their researches have led them, and this conclusion is that all the innumerable forms of Nature have their origin in the infinitely minute nucleus of the vortex ring, by whatever means the vortex ring may have received its initial impulse, a question with which physical science, as such, is not concerned.

As the vortex theory accounts for the formation of the inorganic world, so does biology account for the formation of the living organism. That also has its origin in a primary nucleus which, as soon as it is established, operates as a centre of attraction for the formation of all those physical organs of which the perfect individual is composed. The science of embryology shows that this rule holds good without exception throughout the whole range of the animal world, including man; and botany shows the same principle at work throughout the vegetable world. All branches of physical science demonstrate the fact that every completed manifestation, of whatever kind and on whatever scale, is started by the establishment of a nucleus, infinitely small but endowed with an unquenchable energy of attraction, causing it to steadily increase in power and definiteness of purpose, until the process of growth is completed and the matured form stands out as an accomplished fact. Now if this be the universal method of Nature, there is nothing unnatural in supposing that it must begin its operation at a stage further back than the formation of the material nucleus. As soon as that is called into being it begins to operate by the law of attraction on the material plane; but what is the force which originates the material nucleus? Let a recent work on physical science give us the answer; "In its ultimate essence, energy may be incomprehensible by us except as an exhibition of the direct operation of that which we call Mind or Will." The quotation is from a course of lectures on "Waves in Water, Air and Æther," delivered in 1902, at the Royal Institution, by J. A. Fleming. Here, then, is the testimony of physical science that the originating energy is Mind or Will; and we are, therefore, not only making a logical deduction from certain unavoidable intuitions of the human mind, but are also following on the lines of the most advanced physical science, when we say that the action of Mind plants that nucleus which, if allowed to grow undisturbed, will eventually attract to itself all the conditions necessary for its manifestation in outward visible form. Now the only action of Mind is Thought; and it is for this reason that by our thoughts we create corresponding external conditions, because we thereby create the nucleus which attracts to itself its own correspondences in due order until the finished work is manifested on the external plane. This is according to the strictly scientific conception of the universal law of growth; and we may therefore briefly sum up the whole argument by saying that our thought of anything forms a spiritual prototype of it, thus constituting a nucleus or centre of attraction for all conditions necessary to its eventual externalization by a law of growth inherent in the prototype itself.

## VI

# THE LAW OF GROWTH

A CORRECT UNDERSTANDING OF the law of growth is of the highest importance to the student of Mental Science. The great fact to be realized regarding Nature is that it is natural. We may pervert the order of Nature, but it will prevail in the long run, returning, as Horace says, by the back door even though we drive it out with a pitchfork; and the beginning, the middle, and the end of the law of Nature is the principle of growth from a vitality inherent in the entity itself. If we realize this from the outset we shall not undo our own work by endeavouring to *force* things to become that which by their own nature they are not. For this reason when the Bible says that "he who believeth shall not make haste," it is enunciating a great natural principle that success depends on our using, and not opposing, the universal law of growth. No doubt the greater the vitality we put into the germ, which we have agreed to call the spiritual prototype, the quicker it will germinate; but this is simply because by a more realizing conception we put more growing-power into the seed than we do by a feebler conception. Our mistakes always eventually resolve themselves into distrusting the law of growth. Either we fancy we can hasten it by some exertion of our own from *without,* and are thus led into hurry and anxiety, not to say sometimes into the employment of grievously wrong methods; or else we give up all hope and so deny the germinating power of the seed we have planted. The result in either case is the same, for in either case we are in effect forming a fresh spiritual prototype of an opposite character to our desire, which therefore neutralizes the one first formed, and disintegrates it and usurps its place. The law is always the same, that our Thought forms a spiritual prototype which, if left undisturbed, will reproduce itself in external circumstances; the only difference is in the sort of prototype we form, and thus evil is brought to us by precisely the same law as good.

These considerations will greatly simplify our ideas of life. We have no longer to consider two forces, but only one, as being the cause of all things; the difference between good and evil resulting simply from the direction in which this force is made to flow. It is a universal law that if we reverse the action of a cause we at the same time reverse the effect. With the same apparatus we can commence by mechanical motion which will generate electricity, or we can commence with electricity which will generate mechanical motion; or to take a simple arithmetical instance: if $10 \div 2 = 5$, then $10 \div 5 = 2$; and therefore if we once recognize the power of thought to produce any results at all, we shall see that the law by which negative thought produces negative results is the same by which positive thought produces positive results. Therefore all our distrust of the law of growth, whether shown in the anxious endeavour to bring pressure to bear from without, or in allowing despair to take the place of cheerful expectation, is reversing the action of the original cause and consequently reversing the nature of the results. It is for this reason that the Bible, which is the most deeply occult of all books, continually lays so much stress upon the efficiency of faith and the destructive influence of unbelief; and in like manner, all books on every branch of spiritual science emphatically warn us against the admission of doubt or fear. They are the inversion of the principle which builds up, and they are therefore the principle which pulls down; but the Law itself never changes, and it is on the unchangeableness of the law that all Mental Science is founded. We are accustomed to realize the unchangeableness of natural law in our every day life, and it should therefore not be difficult to realize that the same unchangeableness of law which obtains on the visible side of nature obtains on the invisible side as well. The variable factor is, not the law, but our own volition; and it is by combining this variable factor with the invariable one that we can produce the various results we desire. The principle of growth is that of inherent vitality in the seed itself, and the operations of the gardener have their exact analogue in Mental Science. We do not *put* the self-expansive vitality into the seed, but we must sow it, and we may also, so to speak, water it by quiet concentrated contemplation of our desire as an actually accomplished fact. But we must carefully remove from such contemplation any idea of a strenuous effort on our part to *make* the seed grow. Its efficacy is in helping to keep out those negative thoughts of doubt which would plant tares among our wheat, and therefore, instead of anything of effort, such contemplation should be accompanied by a feeling of pleasure and restfulness in foreseeing the certain accomplishment of our desires. This is that making our requests known to God *with thanksgiving* which St. Paul recommends, and it has its reason in that perfect wholeness of the Law of Being which only needs our recognition of it to be used by us to any extent we wish.

Some people possess the power of visualization, or making mental pictures of things, in a greater degree than others, and by such this faculty may advantageously be employed to facilitate their realization of the working of the Law. But those who do not possess this faculty in any marked degree, need not be discouraged by their want of it, for visualization is not the only way of realizing that the law is at work on the invisible plane. Those whose mental bias is towards physical science should realize this Law of Growth as the creative force throughout all nature; and those who have a mathematical turn of mind may reflect that all solids are generated from the movement of a point, which, as our old friend Euclid tells us, is that which has no parts nor magnitude, and is therefore as complete an abstraction as any spiritual nucleus could be. To use the apostolic words, we are dealing with the substance of things not seen, and we have to attain that habit of mind by which we shall see its reality and feel that we are mentally manipulating the only substance there ultimately is, and of which all visible things are only different modes. We must therefore regard our mental creations as spiritual realities and then implicitly trust the Law of Growth to do the rest.

## VII

# RECEPTIVITY

IN ORDER TO LAY the foundations for practical work, the student must endeavour to get a clear conception of what is meant by the intelligence of undifferentiated spirit. We want to grasp the idea of intelligence apart from individuality, an idea which is rather apt to elude us until we grow accustomed to it. It is the failure to realize this quality of spirit that has given rise to all the theological errors that have brought bitterness into the world and has been prominent amongst the causes which have retarded the true development of mankind. To accurately convey this conception in words, is perhaps, impossible, and to attempt definition is to introduce that very idea of limitation which is our object to avoid. It is a matter of feeling rather than of definition; yet some endeavour must be made to indicate the direction in which we must feel for this great truth if we are to find it. The idea is that of realizing personality without that selfhood which differentiates one individual from another. "I am not that other because I am myself"—this is the definition of individual selfhood; but it necessarily imparts the idea of limitation, because the recognition of any other individuality at once affirms a point at which our own individuality ceases and the other begins. Now this mode of recognition cannot be attributed to the Universal Mind. For it to recognize a point where itself ceased and something else began would be to recognize itself as *not* universal; for the meaning of universality is the including of *all* things, and therefore for this intelligence to recognize anything as being *outside itself* would be a denial of its own being. We may therefore say without hesitation that, whatever may be the nature of its intelligence, it must be entirely devoid of the element of self-recognition *as an individual personality* on any scale whatever. Seen in this light it is at once clear that the originating all-pervading Spirit is the grand impersonal principle of Life which gives rise to all the particular manifestations of Nature. Its absolute impersonalness, in the sense of the entire absence of any consciousness of *individual* selfhood, is a point on which it is impossible to insist too strongly. The attributing of an impossible individuality to the Universal Mind is one of the two grand errors which we find sapping the foundations of religion and philosophy in all ages. The other consists in rushing to the opposite extreme and denying the quality of personal intelligence to the Universal Mind. The answer to this error remains, as of old, in the simple question, "He that made the eye shall He not see? He that planted the ear shall He not hear?"—or to use a popular proverb, "You cannot get out of a bag more than there is in it"; and consequently the fact that we ourselves are centres of personal intelligence is proof that the infinite, from which these centres are concentrated, must be infinite intelligence, and thus we cannot avoid attributing to it the two factors which constitute personality, namely, intelligence and volition. We are therefore brought to the conclusion that this universally diffused essence, which we might think of as a sort of spiritual protoplasm, must possess all the qualities of personality without that conscious recognition of self which constitutes separate individuality: and since the word "personality" has became so associated in our ordinary talk with the idea of "individuality" it will perhaps be better to coin a new word, and speak of the personalness of the Universal Mind as indicating its personal *quality,* apart from individuality. We must realize that this universal spirit permeates all space and all manifested substance, just as physical scientists tell us that the ether does, and that wherever it is, there it must carry with it all that it is in its own being; and we shall then see that we are in the midst of an ocean of undifferentiated yet intelligent Life, above, below, and all around, and permeating ourselves both mentally and corporeally, and all other beings as well.

Gradually as we come to realize the truth of this statement, our eyes will begin to open to its immense significance. It means that all Nature is pervaded by an interior personalness, infinite in its potentialities of intelligence, responsiveness, and power of expression, and only waiting to be called into activity by our recognition of it. By the terms of its nature it can respond to us only as we recognize it. If we are at that intellectual level where we can see nothing but chance governing the world, then this underlying universal mind will present to us nothing but a fortuitous confluence of forces without any intelligible order. If we are sufficiently advanced to see that such a confluence could only produce a chaos, and not a cosmos, then our conceptions expand to the idea of universal Law, and we find *this* to be the nature of the all-underlying principle. We have made an immense advance from the realm of mere accident into a world where there are definite principles on which we can calculate with certainty *when we know them.* But here is the crucial point. The laws of the universe are there, but we are ignorant of them, and only through experience gained by repeated failures can we get any insight into the laws with which we have to deal. How painful each step and how slow the progress! Æons upon æons would not suffice to grasp all the laws of the universe in their totality, not in the visible world only, but also in the world of the unseen; each failure to know the true law implies suffering arising from our ignorant breach of it; and thus, since Nature is infinite, we are met by the paradox that we must in some way contrive to compass the knowledge of the infinite with our individual intelligence, and we must perform a pilgrimage along an unceasing Via Dolorosa beneath the lash of the inexorable Law until we find the solution to the problem. But it will be asked, May we not go on until at last we attain the possession of all knowledge? People do not realize what is meant by "the infinite," or they would not ask such questions. The infinite is that which is limitless and exhaustless. Imagine the vastest capacity you will, and having filled it with the infinite, what remains of the infinite is just as infinite as before. To the mathematician this may be put very clearly. Raise $x$ to any power you will, and however vast may be the disparity between it and the lower powers of $x$, both are equally incommensurate with $x^n$. The universal reign of Law is a magnificent truth; it is one of the two great pillars of the universe symbolized by the two pillars that stood at the entrance to Solomon's temple: it is Jachin, but Jachin must be equilibrated by Boaz.

It is an enduring truth, which can never be altered, that every infraction of the Law of Nature must carry its punitive consequences with it. We can never get beyond the range of cause and effect. There is no escaping from the law of punishment, except by knowledge. If we know a law of Nature and work with it, we shall find it our unfailing friend, ever ready to serve us, and never rebuking us for past failures; but if we ignorantly or wilfully transgress it, it is our implacable enemy, until we again become obedient to it; and therefore the only redemption from perpetual pain and servitude is by a self-expansion which can grasp infinitude itself. How is this to be accomplished? By our progress to that kind and degree of intelligence by which we realize the inherent *personalness* of the divine all-pervading Life, which is at once the Law and the Substance of all that is. Well said the Jewish rabbis of old, "The Law is a Person." When we once realize that the universal Life and the universal Law are one with the universal Personalness, then we have established the pillar Boaz as the needed complement to Jachin; and when we find the common point in which these two unite, we have raised the Royal Arch through which we may triumphantly enter the Temple. We must dissociate the Universal Personalness from every conception of individuality. The universal can never be the individual: that would be a contradiction in terms. But because the universal personalness is the root of all individual personalities, it finds its highest expression in response to those who realize its personal nature. And it is this recognition that solves the seemingly insoluble paradox. The only way to attain that knowledge of the Infinite Law which will change the Via Dolorosa into the Path of Joy is to embody in ourselves a *principle* of knowledge commensurate with the infinitude of that which is to be known; and this is accomplished by realizing that, infinite as the law itself, is a universal Intelligence in the midst of which we float as in a living ocean. Intelligence without individual personality, but which, in producing us, concentrates itself into the personal individualities which we are. What should be the relation of such an intelligence towards us? Not one of favouritism: not any more than the Law can it respect one person above another, for itself is the root and support for each alike. Not one of refusal to our advances; for without individuality it can have no personal object of its own to conflict with ours; and since it is itself the origin of all individual intelligence, it cannot be shut off by inability to understand. By the very terms of its being, therefore, this infinite, underlying, all-producing Mind must be ready immediately to respond to all who realize their true relation to it. As the very principle of Life itself it must be infinitely susceptible to feeling, and consequently it will reproduce with absolute accuracy whatever conception of itself we impress upon it; and hence if we realize the human mind as that stage in the evolution of the cosmic order at which an individuality has arisen capable of expressing, not merely the livingness, but also the personalness of the universal underlying spirit, then we see that its most perfect mode of self-expression must be by identifying itself with these individual personalities.

The identification is, of course, limited by the measure of the individual intelligence, meaning, not merely the intellectual perception of the sequence of cause and effect, but also that indescribable reciprocity of *feeling* by which we instinctively recognize something in another making them akin to ourselves; and so it is that when we intelligently realize that the innermost principle of being, must by reason of its universality, have a common nature with our own, then we have solved the paradox of universal knowledge, for we have realized our identity of being with the Universal Mind, which is commensurate with the Universal Law. Thus we arrive at the truth of St. John's statement, "Ye know all things," only this knowledge is primarily on the spiritual plane. It is not brought out into intellectual statement whether needed or not; for it is not in itself the specific knowledge of particular facts, but it is the undifferentiated principle of knowledge which we may differentiate in any direction that we choose. This is a philosophical necessity of the case, for though the action of the individual mind consists in differentiating the universal into particular applications, to differentiate the *whole* universal would be a contradiction in terms; and so, because we cannot exhaust the infinite, our possession of it must consist in our power to differentiate it as the occasion may require, the only limit being that which we ourselves assign to the manifestation.

In this way, then, the recognition of the community of *personality* between ourselves and the universal undifferentiated Spirit, which is the root and substance of all things, solves the question of our release from the iron grasp of an inflexible Law, not by abrogating the Law, which would mean the annihilation of all things, but by producing in us an intelligence equal in affinity with the universal Law itself, and thus enabling us to apprehend and meet the requirements of the Law in each particular as it arises. In this way the Cosmic Intelligence becomes individualized, and the individual intelligence becomes universalized; the two became one, and in proportion as this unity is realized and acted on, it will be found that the Law, which gives rise to all outward conditions, whether of body or of circumstances, becomes more and more clearly understood, and can therefore be more freely made use of, so that by steady, intelligent endeavour to unfold upon these lines we may reach degrees of power to which it is impossible to assign any limits. The student who would understand the rationale of the unfoldment of his own possibilities must make no mistake here. He must realize that the whole process is that of bringing the universal within the grasp of the individual by raising the individual to the level of the universal and not vice-versa. It is a mathematical truism that you cannot contract the infinite, and that you *can* expand the individual; and it is precisely on these lines that evolution works. The laws of nature cannot be altered in the least degree; but we can come into such a realization of our own relation to the universal principle of Law that underlies them as to be able to press all particular laws, whether of the visible or invisible side of Nature, into our service and so find ourselves masters of the situation. This is to be accomplished by knowledge; and the only knowledge which will effect this purpose in all its measureless immensity is the knowledge of the personal element in Universal Spirit in its reciprocity to our own personality. Our recognition of this Spirit must therefore be twofold, as the principle of necessary sequence, order or Law, and also as the principle of Intelligence, responsive to our own recognition of it.

VIII

# RECIPROCAL ACTION OF THE UNIVERSAL AND INDIVIDUAL MINDS

It must be admitted that the foregoing considerations bring us to the borders of theological speculation, but the student must bear in mind that as a Mental Scientist it is his business to regard even the most exalted spiritual phenomena from a purely scientific standpoint, which is that of the working of a universal natural Law. If he thus simply deals with the facts as he finds them, there is little doubt that the true meaning of many theological statements will become clear to him: but he will do well to lay it down as a general rule that it is not necessary either to the use or understanding of any law, whether on the personal or the impersonal side of Nature, that we should give a theological explanation of it: although, therefore, the personal quality inherent in the universal underlying spirit, which is present in all things, cannot be too strongly insisted upon, we must remember that in dealing with it we are still dealing with a purely natural power which reappears at every point with protean variety of form, whether as person, animal, or thing. In each case what it becomes to any individual is exactly measured by that individual's recognition of it. To each and all it bears the relation of supporter of the race, and where the individual development is incapable of realizing anything more, this is the limit of the relation; but as the individual's power of recognition expands, he finds a reciprocal expansion on the part of this intelligent power which gradually develops into the consciousness of intimate companionship between the individualized mind and the unindividualized source of it.

Now this is exactly the relation which, on ordinary scientific principles, we should expect to find between the individual and the cosmic mind, on the supposition that the cosmic mind is subjective mind, and for reasons already given we can regard it in no other light. As subjective mind it must reproduce exactly the conception of itself which the objective mind of the individual, acting through his own subjective mind, impresses upon it; and at the same time, as creative mind, it builds up external facts in correspondence with this conception. "Quot homines tot sententiæ": each one externalizes in his outward circumstances precisely his idea of the Universal Mind; and the man who realizes that by the natural law of mind he can bring the Universal Mind into perfectly reciprocal action with its own, will on the one hand make it a source of infinite instruction, and on the other a source of infinite power. He will thus wisely alternate the personal and impersonal aspects respectively between his individual mind and the Universal Mind; when he is seeking for guidance or strength he will regard his own mind as the impersonal element which is to *receive personality* from the superior wisdom and force of the Greater Mind; and when, on the other hand, he is to give out the stores thus accumulated, he must reverse the position and consider his own mind as the personal element, and the Universal Mind as the impersonal, which he can therefore *direct* with certainty by impressing his own personal desire upon it. We need not be staggered at the greatness of this conclusion, for it follows necessarily from the natural relation between the subjective and the objective minds; and the only question is whether we will limit our view to the lower level of the latter, or expand it so as to take in the limitless possibilities which the subjective mind presents to us.

I have dealt with this question at some length because it affords the key to two very important subjects, the Law of Supply and the nature of Intuition. Students often find it easier to understand how the mind can influence the body with which it is so intimately associated, than how it can influence circumstances. If the operation of thought-power were confined exclusively to the individual mind this difficulty might arise; but if there is one lesson the student of Mental Science should take to heart more than another, it is that the action of thought-power is not limited to a circumscribed individuality. What the individual does is to *give direction* to something which is unlimited, to call into action a force infinitely greater than his own, which because it is in itself impersonal though intelligent, will receive the impress of his personality, and can therefore make its influence felt far beyond the limits which bound the individual's objective perception of the circumstances with which he has to deal. It is for this reason that I lay so much stress on the combination of two apparent opposites in the Universal Mind, the union of intelligence with impersonality. The intelligence not only enables it to receive the impress of our thought, but also causes it to devise exactly the right *means* for bringing it into accomplishment. This is only the logical result of the hypothesis that we are dealing with infinite Intelligence which is also infinite Life. Life means Power, and infinite life therefore means limitless power; and limitless power moved by limitless intelligence cannot be conceived of as ever stopping short of the accomplishment of its object; therefore, given the *intention* on the part of the Universal Mind, there can be no doubt as to its ultimate accomplishment. Then comes the question of intention. How do we know what the intention of the Universal Mind may be? Here comes in the element of impersonality. It has *no intention,* because it is *impersonal.* As I have already said, the Universal mind works by a law of averages for the advancement of the race, and is in no way concerned with the particular wishes of the individual. If his wishes are in line with the forward movement of the everlasting principle, there is nowhere in Nature any power to restrict him in their fulfilment. If they are opposed to the general forward movement, then they will bring him into collision with it, and it will crush him. From the relation between them it results that the same principle which shows itself in the individual mind as Will, becomes in the universal mind a Law of Tendency; and the direction of this tendency must always be to life-givingness, because the universal mind is the undifferentiated Life-spirit of the universe. Therefore in every case the test is whether our particular intention is in this same lifeward direction; and if it is, then we may be absolutely certain that there is no intention on the part of the Universal Mind to thwart the intention of our own individual mind; we are dealing with a purely impersonal force, and it will no more oppose us by specific plans of its own than will steam or electricity. Combining then, these two aspects of the Universal Mind, its utter impersonality and its perfect intelligence, we find precisely the sort of natural force we are in want of, something which will undertake whatever we put into its hands without asking questions or bargaining for terms, and which, having undertaken our business, will bring to bear on it an intelligence to which the united knowledge of the whole human race is as nothing, and a power equal to this intelligence. I may be using a rough and ready mode of expression, but my object is to bring home to the student the nature of the power he can employ and the method of employing it, and I may therefore state the whole position thus:—Your object is not to run the whole cosmos, but to draw particular benefits, physical, mental, moral, or financial into your own or someone else's life. From this individual point of view the universal creative power has no mind of its own, and therefore you can make up its mind for it. When its mind is thus made up for it, it never abrogates its place as the creative power, but at once sets to work to carry out the purpose for which it has thus been concentrated; and unless this concentration is dissipated by the same agency (yourself) which first produced it, it will work on by the law of growth to complete manifestation on the outward plane.

In dealing with this great impersonal intelligence, we are dealing with the infinite, and we must fully realize infinitude as that which touches all points, and if it does, there should be no difficulty in understanding that this intelligence can draw together the means requisite for its purpose even from the ends of the world; and therefore, realizing the Law according to which the result can be produced, we must resolutely put aside all questioning as to the specific means which will be employed in any case. To question this is to sow that very seed of doubt which it is our first object to eradicate, and our intellectual endeavour should therefore be directed, not to the attempt to foretell the various secondary causes which will eventually combine to produce the desired result, laying down beforehand what particular causes should be necessary, and from what quarter they should come; but we should direct our intellectual endeavour to seeing more clearly the rationale of the general law by which trains of secondary causes are set in motion. Employed in the former way our intellect becomes the greatest hindrance to our success, for it only helps to increase our doubts, since it is trying to grasp particulars which at the time are entirely outside its circle of vision; but employed in the latter it affords the most material aid in maintaining that nucleus without which there is no centre from which the principle of growth can assert itself. The intellect can only deduce consequences from facts which it is able to state, and consequently cannot deduce any assurance from facts of whose existence it cannot yet have any knowledge through the medium of the outward senses; but for the same reason it can realize the existence of a *Law* by which the as yet unmanifested circumstances may be brought into manifestation. Thus used in its right order, the intellect becomes the handmaid of that more interior power within us which manipulates the unseen substance of all things, and which we may call relative first cause.

## IX

# CAUSES AND CONDITIONS

THE EXPRESSION "*relative* first cause" has been used in the last section to distinguish the action of the creative principle in the *individual* mind from Universal First Cause on the one hand and from secondary causes on the other. As it exists in *us,* primary causation is the power to initiate a train of causation directed to an individual purpose. As the power of initiating a fresh sequence of cause and effect it is first cause, and as referring to an individual purpose it is relative, and it may therefore be spoken of as relative first cause, or the power of primary causation manifested by the individual. The understanding and use of this power is the whole object of Mental Science, and it is therefore necessary that the student should clearly see the relation between causes and conditions. A simple illustration will go further for this purpose than any elaborate explanation. If a lighted candle is brought into a room the room becomes illuminated, and if the candle is taken away it becomes dark again. Now the illumination and the darkness are both conditions, the one positive resulting from the presence of the light, and the other negative resulting from its absence: from this simple example we therefore see that every positive condition has an exactly opposite negative condition corresponding to it, and that this correspondence results from their being related to the *same cause,* the one positively and the other negatively; and hence we may lay down the rule that all positive conditions result from the active presence of a certain cause, and all negative conditions from the absence of such a cause. A condition, whether positive or negative, is never *primary* cause, and the *primary* cause of any series can never be negative, for negation is the condition which arises from the absence of active causation. This should be thoroughly understood as it is the philosophic basis of all those "denials" which play so important a part in Mental Science, and which may be summed up in the statement that evil being negative, or privation of good, has no substantive existence in itself. Conditions, however, whether positive or negative, are no sooner called into existence than they become causes in their turn and produce further conditions, and so on *ad infinitum,* thus giving rise to the whole train of secondary causes. So long as we judge only from the information conveyed to us by the outward senses, we are working on the plane of secondary causation and see nothing but a succession of conditions, forming part of an endless train of antecedent conditions coming out of the past and stretching away into the future, and from this point of view we are under the rule of an iron destiny from which there seems no possibility of escape. This is because the outward senses are only capable of dealing with the relations which one mode of limitation bears to another, for they are the instruments by which we take cognizance of the relative and the conditioned. Now the only way of escape is by rising out of the region of secondary causes into that of primary causation, where the originating energy is to be found before it has yet passed into manifestation as a condition. This region is to be found *within ourselves;* it is the region of pure ideas; and it is for this reason that I have laid stress on the two aspects of spirit as pure thought and manifested form. The thought-image or ideal pattern of a thing is the *first cause* relatively to that thing; it is the substance of that thing untrammelled by any antecedent conditions.

If we realize that all visible things *must* have their origin in spirit, then the whole creation around us is the standing evidence that the starting-point of all things is in thought-images or ideas, for no other action than the formation of such images can be conceived of spirit prior to its manifestation in matter. If, then, this is spirit's modus operandi for self-expression, we have only to transfer this conception from the scale of cosmic spirit working on the plane of the universal to that of individualized spirit working on the plane of the particular, to see that the formation of an ideal image by means of our thought is setting first cause in motion with regard to this specific object. There is no difference in kind between the operation of first cause in the universal and in the particular, the difference is only a difference of scale, but the power itself is identical. We must therefore always be very clear as to whether we are *consciously* using first cause or not. Note the word "consciously" because, whether consciously or unconsciously, we are always using first cause; and it was for this reason I emphasized the fact that the Universal Mind is purely subjective and therefore bound by the laws which apply to subjective mind on whatever scale. Hence we are *always* impressing some sort of ideas upon it, whether we are aware of the fact or not, and all our existing limitations result from our having habitually impressed upon it that idea of limitation which we have imbibed by restricting all possibility to the region of secondary causes. But now when investigation has shown us that conditions are never causes in *themselves,* but only the subsequent links of a chain started on the plane of the pure ideal, what we have to do is to reverse our method of thinking and regard the ideal as the real, and the outward manifestation as a mere reflection which must change with every change of the object which casts it. For these reasons it is essential to know whether we are consciously making use of first cause with a definite purpose or not, and the criterion is this. If we regard the fulfilment of our purpose as contingent upon any *circumstances,* past, present, or future, we are not making use of first cause; we have descended to the level of secondary causation, which is the region of doubts, fears, and limitations, all of which we are impressing upon the universal subjective mind with the inevitable result that it will build up corresponding external conditions. But if we realize that the region of secondary causes is the region of mere reflections we shall not think of our purpose as contingent on any conditions whatever, but shall know that by forming the idea of it in the absolute, and maintaining that idea, we have shaped the first cause into the desired form and can await the result with cheerful expectancy.

It is here that we find the importance of realizing spirit's independence of time and space. An ideal, as such, cannot be formed in the future. It must either be formed here and now or not be formed at all; and it is for this reason that every teacher, who has ever spoken with due knowledge of the subject, has impressed upon his followers the necessity of picturing to themselves the fulfilment of their desires as *already accomplished* on the spiritual plane, as the indispensable condition of fulfilment in the visible and concrete.

When this is properly understood, any anxious thought as to the *means* to be employed in the accomplishment of our purposes is seen to be quite unnecessary. If the end is already secured, then it follows that all the steps leading to it are secured also. The means will pass into the smaller circle of our conscious activities day by day in due order, and then we have to work upon them, not with fear, doubt, or feverish excitement, but calmly and joyously, because we *know* that the end is already secured, and that our reasonable use of such means as present themselves in the desired direction is only one portion of a much larger co-ordinated movement, the final result of which admits of no doubt. Mental Science does not offer a premium to idleness, but it takes all work out of the region of anxiety and toil by assuring the worker of the success of his labour, if not in the precise form he anticipated, then in some other still better suited to his requirements. But suppose, when we reach a point where some momentous decision has to be made, we happen to decide wrongly? On the hypothesis that the end is already secured you cannot decide wrongly. Your right decision is as much one of the necessary steps in the accomplishment of the end as any of the other conditions leading up to it, and therefore, while being careful to avoid rash action, we may make sure that the same Law which is controlling the rest of the circumstances in the right direction will influence our judgment in that direction also. To get good results we must properly understand our relation to the great impersonal power we are using. It is intelligent and we are intelligent, and the two intelligencies must co-operate. We must not fly in the face of the Law by expecting it to do *for* us what it can only do *through* us; and we must therefore use our intelligence with the knowledge that it is acting *as the instrument of a greater intelligence;* and because we have this knowledge we may, and should, cease from all anxiety as to the final result. In actual practice we must first form the ideal conception of our object with the definite intention of impressing it upon the universal mind—it is this intention which takes such thought out of the region of mere casual fancies—and then affirm that our knowledge of the Law is sufficient reason for a calm expectation of a corresponding result, and that therefore all necessary conditions will come to us in due order. We can then turn to the affairs of our daily life with the calm assurance that the initial conditions are either there already or will soon come into view. If we do not at once see them, let us rest content with the knowledge that the spiritual prototype is already in existence and wait till some circumstance pointing in the desired direction begins to show itself. It may be a very small circumstance, but it is the direction and not the magnitude which is to be taken into consideration. As soon as we see it we should regard it as the first sprouting of the seed we have sown in the Absolute, and do calmly, and without excitement, whatever the circumstances may seem to require, and then later on we shall see that this doing will in turn lead to further circumstances in the same direction until we find ourselves conducted step by step to the accomplishment of our object. In this way the understanding of the great principle of the Law of Supply will, by repeated experiences, deliver us more and more completely out of the region of anxious thought and toilsome labour and bring us into a new world where the useful employment of all our powers, whether mental or physical, will only be an unfolding of our individuality upon the lines of its own nature, and therefore a perpetual source of health and happiness; a sufficient inducement, surely, to the careful study of the laws governing the relation between the individual and the Universal Mind.

# X

# INTUITION

We have seen that the subjective mind is amenable to suggestion by the objective mind; but there is also an action of the subjective mind upon the objective. The individual's subjective mind is his own innermost self, and its first care is the maintenance of the individuality of which it is the foundation; and since it is pure spirit it has its continual existence in that plane of being where all things subsist in the universal here and the everlasting now, and consequently can inform the lower mind of things removed from its ken either by distance or futurity. As the absence of the conditions of time and space must logically concentrate all things into a present focus, we can assign no limit to the subjective mind's power of perception, and therefore the question arises, why does it not keep the objective mind continually informed on all points? And the answer is that it would do so if the objective mind were sufficiently trained to recognize the indications given, and to effect this training is one of the purposes of Mental Science. When once we recognize the position of the subjective mind as the supporter of the whole individuality we cannot doubt that much of what we take to be the spontaneous movement of the objective mind has its origin in the subjective mind prompting the objective mind in the right direction without our being consciously aware of it. But at times when the urgency of the case seems to demand it, or when, for some reason yet unknown, the objective mind is for a while more closely *en rapport* with the subjective mind, the interior voice is heard strongly and persistently; and when this is the case we do well to pay heed to it. Want of space forbids me to give examples, but doubtless such will not be wanting in the reader's experience.

The importance of understanding and following the intuition cannot be exaggerated, but I candidly admit the great practical difficulty of keeping the happy mean between the disregard of the interior voice and allowing ourselves to be run away with by groundless fancies. The best guide is the knowledge that comes of personal experience which gradually leads to the acquisition of a sort of inward sense of touch that enables us to distinguish the true from the false, and which appears to grow with the sincere desire for truth and with the recognition of the spirit as its source. The only general principles the writer can deduce from his own experience are that when, in spite of all appearances pointing in the direction of a certain line of conduct, there is still a persistent *feeling* that it should not be followed, in the majority of instances it will be found that the argument of the objective mind, however correct on the facts objectively known, was deficient from ignorance of facts which could not be objectively known at the time, but which were known to the intuitive faculty. Another principle is that our *very first* impression of feeling on any subject is generally correct. Before the objective mind has begun to argue on the subject it is like the surface of a smooth lake which clearly reflects the light from above; but as soon as it begins to argue from outside appearances these also throw their reflections upon its surface, so that the original image becomes blurred and is no longer recognizable. This first conception is very speedily lost, and it should therefore be carefully observed and registered in the memory with a view to testing the various arguments which will subsequently arise on the objective plane. It is however impossible to reduce so interior an action as that of the intuition to the form of hard and fast rules, and beyond carefully noting particular cases as they occur, probably the best plan for the student will be to include the whole subject of intuition in the general principle of the Law of Attraction, especially if he sees how this law interacts with that personal quality of universal spirit of which we have already spoken.

XI

# HEALING

THE SUBJECT OF healing has been elaborately treated by many writers and fully deserves all the attention that has been given to it, but the object of these lectures is rather to ground the student in those general principles on which *all* conscious use of the creative power of thought is based, than to lay down formal rules for specific applications of it. I will therefore examine the broad principles which appear to be common to the various methods of mental healing which are in use, each of which derives its efficacy, not from the peculiarity of the method, but from it being such a method as allows the higher laws of Nature to come into play. Now the principle universally laid down by all mental healers, in whatever various terms they may explain it, is that the basis of all healing is a change in belief. The sequence from which this results is as follows:—the subjective mind is the creative faculty within us, and creates whatever the objective mind impresses upon it; the objective mind, or intellect, impresses its thought upon it; the thought is the expression of the belief; hence whatever the subjective mind creates is the reproduction externally of our beliefs. Accordingly our whole object is to change our beliefs, and we cannot do this without some solid ground of conviction of the falsity of our old beliefs and of the truth of our new ones, and this ground we find in that law of causation which I have endeavoured to explain. The wrong belief which externalizes as sickness is the belief that some secondary cause, which is really only a condition, is a primary cause. The knowledge of the law shows that there is only *one* primary cause, and this is the factor which in our own individuality we call subjective or sub-conscious mind. For this reason I have insisted on the difference between placing an idea in the sub-conscious mind, that is, on the plane of the absolute and without reference to time and space, and placing the same idea in the conscious intellectual mind which only perceives things as related to time and space. Now the only conception you can have of *yourself* in the absolute, or unconditioned, is as *purely living Spirit,* not hampered by conditions of any sort, and therefore not subject to illness; and when this idea is firmly impressed on the sub-conscious mind, it will externalize it. The reason why this process is not always successful at the first attempt is that all our life we have been holding the false belief in sickness as a substantial entity in itself and thus being a primary cause, instead of being merely a negative *condition* resulting from the *absence* of a primary cause; and a belief which has become ingrained from childhood cannot be eradicated at a moment's notice. We often find, therefore, that for some time after a treatment there is an improvement in the patient's health, and then the old symptoms return. This is because the new belief in his own creative faculty has not yet had time to penetrate down to the innermost depths of the sub-conscious mind, but has only partially entered it. Each succeeding treatment strengthens the sub-conscious mind in its hold of the new belief until at last a permanent cure is effected. This is the method of self-treatment based on the patient's own knowledge of the law of his being.

But "there is not in all men this knowledge," or at any rate not such a full recognition of it as will enable them to give successful treatment to themselves, and in these cases the intervention of the healer becomes necessary. The only difference between the healer and the patient is that the healer has learnt how to control the less self-conscious modes of the spirit by the more self-conscious mode, while the patient has not yet attained to this knowledge; and what the healer does is to substitute his own objective or conscious mentality, which is will joined to intellect, for that of the patient, and in this way to find entrance to his sub-conscious mind and impress upon it the suggestion of perfect health.

The question then arises, how can the healer substitute his own conscious mind for that of the patient? and the answer shows the practical application of those very abstract principles which I have laid down in the earlier sections. Our ordinary conception of ourselves is that of an individual personality which ends where another personality begins, in other words that the two personalities are entirely separate. This is an error. There is no such hard and fast line of demarcation between personalities, and the boundaries between one and another can be increased or reduced in rigidity according to will, in fact they may be temporarily removed so completely that, for the time being, the two personalities become merged into one. Now the action which takes place between healer and patient depends on this principle. The patient is asked by the healer to put himself in a receptive mental attitude, which means that he is to exercise his volition for the purpose of removing the barrier of his own objective personality and thus affording entrance to the mental power of the healer. On his side also the healer does the same thing, only with this difference, that while the patient withdraws the barrier on his side with the intention of admitting a flowing-in, the healer does so with the intention of allowing a flowing-out: and thus by the joint action of the two minds the barriers of both personalities are removed and the direction of the flow of volition is determined, that is to say, it flows from the healer as actively willing to give, towards the patient as passively willing to receive, according to the universal law of Nature that the flow must always be from the *plenum* to the *vacuum.* This mutual removal of the external mental barrier between healer and patient is what is termed establishing a *rapport* between them, and here we find one most valuable practical application of the principle laid down earlier in this book, that pure spirit is present in its entirety at every point simultaneously. It is for this reason that as soon as the healer realizes that the barriers of external personality between himself and his patient have been removed, he can then speak to the sub-conscious mind of the patient as though it were his own, for both being pure spirit the *thought* of their identity *makes* them identical, and both are concentrated into a single entity at a single point upon which the conscious mind of the healer can be brought to bear, according to the universal principle of the control of the subjective mind by the objective mind through suggestion. It is for this reason I have insisted on the distinction between *pure* spirit, or spirit conceived of apart from extension in any matrix, and the conception of it as so extended. If we concentrate our mind upon the diseased condition of the patient we are thinking of him as a separate personality, and are not fixing our mind upon that conception of him as pure spirit which will afford us effectual entry to his springs of being. We must therefore withdraw our thought from the contemplation of symptoms, and indeed from his corporeal personality altogether, and must think of him as a purely spiritual individuality, and as such entirely free from subjection to any conditions, and consequently as voluntarily externalizing the conditions most expressive of the vitality and intelligence which pure spirit is. Thinking of him thus, we then make mental affirmation that he shall build up outwardly the correspondence of that perfect vitality which he knows himself to be inwardly; and this suggestion being impressed by the healer's conscious thought, while the patient's conscious thought is at the same time impressing the fact that he is receiving the active thought of the healer, the result is that the patient's sub-conscious mind becomes thoroughly imbued with the recognition of its own life-giving power, and according to the recognized law of subjective mentality proceeds to work out this suggestion into external manifestation, and thus health is substituted for sickness.

It must be understood that the purpose of the process here described is to strengthen the subject's individuality, not to dominate it. To use it for domination is *inversion,* bringing its appropriate penalty to the operator.

In this description I have contemplated the case where the patient is consciously co-operating with the healer, and it is in order to obtain this co-operation that the mental healer usually makes a point of instructing the patient in the broad principles of Mental Science, if he is not already acquainted with them. But this is not always advisable or possible. Sometimes the statement of principles opposed to existing prejudices arouses opposition, and any active antagonism on the patient's part must tend to intensify the barrier of conscious personality which it is the healer's first object to remove. In these cases nothing is so effective as *absent treatment.* If the student has grasped all that has been said on the subject of spirit and matter, he will see that in mental treatment time and space count for nothing, because the whole action takes place on a plane where these conditions do not obtain; and it is therefore quite immaterial whether the patient be in the immediate presence of the healer or in a distant country. Under these circumstances it is found by experience that one of the most effectual modes of mental healing is by treatment during sleep, because then the patient's whole system is naturally in a state of relaxation which prevents him offering any conscious opposition to the treatment. And by the same rule the healer also is able to treat even more effectively during his own sleep than while waking. Before going to sleep he firmly impresses on his subjective mind that it is to convey curative suggestion to the subjective mind of the patient, and then, by the general principles of the relation between subjective and objective mind this suggestion is carried out during all the hours that the conscious individuality is wrapped in repose. This method is applicable to young children to whom the principles of the science cannot be explained; and also to persons at a distance: and indeed the only advantage gained by the personal meeting of the patient and healer is in the instruction that can be orally given, or when the patient is at that early stage of knowledge where the healer's visible presence conveys the suggestion that something is then being done which could not be done in his absence; otherwise the presence or absence of the patient are matters perfectly indifferent. The student must always recollect that the sub-conscious mind does not have to work *through* the intellect or conscious mind to produce its curative effects. It is part of the all-pervading creative force of Nature, while the intellect is not creative but distributive.

From mental healing it is but a step to telepathy, clairvoyance and other kindred manifestations of transcendental power which are from time to time exhibited by the subjective entity and which follow laws as accurate as those which govern what we are accustomed to consider our more normal faculties; but these subjects do not properly fall within the scope of a book whose purpose is to lay down the broad principles which underlie *all* spiritual phenomena. Until these are clearly understood the student cannot profitably attempt the detailed study of the more interior powers; for to do so without a firm foundation of knowledge and some experience in its practical application would only be to expose himself to unknown dangers, and would be contrary to the scientific principle that the advance into the unknown can only be made from the standpoint of the known, otherwise we only come into a confused region of guess-work without any clearly defined principles for our guidance.

XII

# THE WILL

THE WILL IS of such primary importance that the student should be on his guard against any mistake as to the position which it holds in the mental economy. Many writers and teachers insist on will-power as though that were the creative faculty. No doubt intense will-power can evolve certain external results, but like all other methods of compulsion it lacks the permanency of natural growth. The appearances, forms, and conditions produced by mere intensity of will-power will only hang together so long as the compelling force continues; but let it be exhausted or withdrawn, and the elements thus forced into unnatural combination will at once fly back to their proper affinities; the form created by compulsion never had the germ of vitality *in itself* and is therefore dissipated as soon as the external energy which supported it is withdrawn. The mistake is in attributing the creative power to the will, or perhaps I should say in attributing the creative power to ourselves at all. The truth is that man never creates anything. His function is, not to create, but to combine and distribute that which is already in being, and what we call our creations are new combinations of already existing material, whether mental or corporeal. This is amply demonstrated in the physical sciences. No one speaks of creating energy, but only of transforming one form of energy into another; and if we realize this as a universal principle, we shall see that on the mental plane as well as on the physical we never create energy but only provide the conditions by which the energy already existing in one mode can exhibit itself in another: therefore what, relatively to man, we call his creative power, is that receptive attitude of expectancy which, so to say, makes a mould into which the plastic and as yet undifferentiated substance can flow and take the desired form. The will has much the same place in our mental machinery that the tool-holder has in a power-lathe: it is not the power, but it keeps the mental faculties in that position relatively to the power which enables it to do the desired work. If, using the word in its widest sense, we may say that the imagination is the creative function, we may call the will the centralizing principle. Its function is to keep the imagination centred in the right direction. We are aiming at consciously controlling our mental powers instead of letting them hurry us hither and thither in a purposeless manner, and we must therefore understand the relation of these powers to each other for the production of external results. First the whole train of causation is started by some emotion which gives rise to a desire; next the judgment determines whether we shall externalize this desire or not; then the desire having been approved by the judgment, the will comes forward and directs the imagination to form the necessary spiritual prototype; and the imagination thus centred on a particular object creates the spiritual nucleus, which in its turn acts as a centre round which the forces of attraction begin to work, and continue to operate until, by the law of growth, the concrete result becomes perceptible to our external senses.

The business of the will, then, is to retain the various faculties of our mind in that position where they are really doing the work we wish, and this position may be generalized into the three following attitudes: either we wish to act upon something, or be acted on by it, or to maintain a neutral position; in other words we either intend to project a force, or receive a force, or keep a position of inactivity relatively to some particular object. Now the judgment determines which of these three positions we shall take up, the consciously active, the consciously receptive, or the consciously neutral; and then the function of the will is simply to maintain the position we have determined upon; and if we maintain any given mental attitude we may reckon with all certainty on the law of attraction drawing us to those correspondences which exteriorly symbolize the attitude in question. This is very different from the semi-animal screwing-up of the nervous forces which, with some people, stands for will-power. It implies no strain on the nervous system and is consequently not followed by any sense of exhaustion. The will-power, when transferred from the region of the lower mentality to the spiritual plane, becomes simply a calm and peaceful determination to retain a certain mental attitude in spite of all temptations to the contrary, knowing that by doing so the desired result will certainly appear.

The training of the will and its transference from the lower to the higher plane of our nature are among the first objects of Mental Science. The man is summed up in his will. Whatever he does by his own will is his own act; whatever he does without the consent of his will is not his own act but that of the power by which his will was coerced; but we must recognize that, on the mental plane, no other individuality can obtain control over our will unless we first allow it to do so; and it is for this reason that all legitimate use of Mental Science is towards the strengthening of the will, whether in ourselves or others, and bringing it under the control of an enlightened reason. When the will realizes its power to deal with first cause it is no longer necessary for the operator to state to himself *in extenso* all the philosophy of its action every time he wishes to use it, but, knowing that the trained will is a tremendous spiritual force acting on the plane of first cause, he simply expresses his desire with the intention of operating on that plane, and knows that the desire thus expressed will in due time externalize itself as concrete fact. He now sees that the point which really demands his earnest attention is not whether he possesses the power of externalizing any results he chooses, but of learning to choose wisely what results to produce. For let us not suppose that even the highest powers will take us out of the law of cause and effect. We can never set any cause in motion without calling forth those effects which it already contains in embryo and which will again become causes in their turn, thus producing a series which must continue to flow on until it is cut short by bringing into operation a cause of an opposite character to the one which originated it. Thus we shall find the field for the exercise of our intelligence continually expanding with the expansion of our powers; for, granted a good intention, we shall always wish to contemplate the results of our action as far as our intelligence will permit. We may not be able to see very far, but there is one safe general principle to be gained from what has already been said about causes and conditions, which is that the whole sequence always partakes of the same character as the initial cause: if that character is negative, that is, destitute of any desire to externalize kindness, cheerfulness, strength, beauty or some other sort of good, this negative quality will make itself felt all down the line; but if the opposite affirmative character is in the original motive, then it will reproduce its kind in forms of love, joy, strength and beauty with unerring precision. Before setting out, therefore, to produce new conditions by the exercise of our thought-power we should weigh carefully what further results they are likely to lead to; and here, again, we shall find an ample field for the training of our will, in learning to acquire that self-control which will enable us to postpone an inferior present satisfaction to a greater prospective good.

These considerations naturally lead us to the subject of concentration. I have just now pointed out that all duly controlled mental action consists in holding the mind in one of three attitudes; but there is a fourth mental condition, which is that of letting our mental functions run on without our will directing them to any definite purpose. It is on this word *purpose* that we must fix our whole attention; and instead of dissipating our energies, we must follow an intelligent method of concentration. The word means being gathered up at a centre, and the centre of anything is that point in which all its forces are equally balanced. To concentrate therefore means first to bring our minds into a condition of equilibrium which will enable us to consciously direct the flow of spirit to a definitely recognized purpose, and then carefully to guard our thoughts from inducing a flow in the opposite direction. We must always bear in mind that we are dealing with a wonderful *potential* energy which is not yet differentiated into any particular mode, and that by the action of our mind we can differentiate it into any specific mode of activity that we will; and by keeping our thought fixed on the fact that the inflow of this energy *is* taking place and that by our mental attitude we *are* determining its direction, we shall gradually realize a corresponding externalization. Proper concentration, therefore, does not consist of strenuous effort which exhausts the nervous system and defeats its own object by suggesting the consciousness of an adverse force to be fought against, and thus creating the adverse circumstances we dread; but in shutting out all thoughts of a kind that would disperse the spiritual nucleus we are forming and dwelling cheerfully on the knowledge that, because the law is certain in its action, our desire is certain of accomplishment. The other great principle to be remembered is that concentration is for the purpose of determining the *quality* we are going to give to the previously undifferentiated energy rather than to arrange the *specific circumstances* of its manifestation. *That* is the work of the creative energy itself, which will build up its own forms of expression quite naturally if we allow it, thus saving us a great deal of needless anxiety. What we really want is expansion in a certain direction, whether of health, wealth, or what not: and so long as we get this, what does it matter whether it reaches us through some channel which we thought we could reckon upon or through some other whose existence we had not suspected. It is the fact that we are concentrating energy of a particular kind for a particular purpose that we should fix our minds upon, and not look upon any specific details as essential to the accomplishment of our object.

These are the two golden rules regarding concentration; but we must not suppose that because we have to be on our guard against idle drifting there is to be no such thing as repose; on the contrary it is during periods of repose that we accumulate strength for action; but repose does not mean a state of purposelessness. As pure spirit the subjective mind never rests: it is only the objective mind in its connection with the physical body that needs rest; and though there are no doubt times when the greatest possible rest is to be obtained by stopping the action of our conscious thought altogether, the more generally advisable method is by changing the direction of the thought and, instead of centering it upon something we intend to *do,* letting it dwell quietly upon what we *are.* This direction of thought might, of course, develop into the deepest philosophical speculation, but it is not necessary that we should be always either consciously projecting our forces to produce some external effect or working out the details of some metaphysical problem; but we may simply realize ourselves as part of the universal livingness and thus gain a quiet centralization, which, though maintained by a conscious act of the volition, is the very essence of rest. From this standpoint we see that all is Life and all is Good, and that Nature, from her clearly visible surface to her most arcane depths, is one vast storehouse of life and good entirely devoted to our individual use. We have the key to all her treasures, and we can now apply our knowledge of the law of being without entering into all those details which are only needed for purposes of study, and doing so we find it results in our having acquired the consciousness of our *oneness with the whole.* This is the great secret: and when we have once fathomed it we can enjoy our possession of the whole, or of any part of it, because by our recognition we have made it, and can increasingly make it, our own. Whatever most appeals to us at any particular time or place is that mode of the universal living spirit with which at that moment we are most in touch, and realizing this, we shall draw from it streams of vital energy which will make the very sensation of livingness a joy and will radiate from us as a sphere of vibration that can deflect all injurious suggestion on whatever plane. We may not have literary, artistic, or scientific skill to present to others the results of our communings with Nature, but the joy of this sympathetic indrawing will nevertheless produce a corresponding outflow manifesting itself in the happier look and kindlier mien of him who thus realizes his oneness with every aspect of the whole. He realizes—and this is the great point in that attitude of mind which is not directed to any specific external object—that, for himself, he is, and always must be, the centre of all this galaxy of Life, and thus he contemplates himself as seated at the centre of infinitude, not an infinitude of blank space, but pulsating with living being, in all of which he knows that the true essence is nothing but good. This is the very opposite to a selfish self-centredness: it is the centre where we find that we both receive from all and flow out to all. Apart from this principle of circulation there is no true life, and if we contemplate our central position only as affording us greater advantages for in-taking, we have missed the whole point of our studies by missing the real nature of the Life-principle, which is action and re-action. If we would have life enter into us, we ourselves must enter into life—enter into the spirit of it, just as we must enter into the spirit of a book or a game to enjoy it. There can be no action at a centre only. There must be a perpetual flowing out towards the circumference, and thence back again to the centre to maintain a vital activity; otherwise collapse must ensue either from anæmia or congestion. But if we realize the reciprocal nature of the vital pulsation, and that the outflowing consists in the habit of mind which gives itself to the good it sees in others, rather than in any specific actions, then we shall find that the cultivation of this disposition will provide innumerable avenues for the universal livingness to flow through us, whether as giving or receiving, which we had never before suspected: and this action and re-action will so build up our own vitality that each day will find us more thoroughly alive than any that had preceded it. This, then, is the attitude of repose in which we may enjoy all the beauties of science, literature and art or may peacefully commune with the spirit of nature without the aid of any third mind to act as its interpreter, which is still a purposeful attitude although not directed to a specific object: we have not allowed the will to relax its control, but have merely altered its direction; so that for action and repose alike we find that our strength lies in our recognition of the unity of the spirit and of ourselves as individual concentrations of it.

## XIII

# IN TOUCH WITH SUB-CONSCIOUS MIND

THE PRECEDING PAGES have made the student in some measure aware of the immense importance of our dealings with the sub-conscious mind. Our relation to it, whether on the scale of the individual or the universal, is the key to all that we are or ever can be. In its unrecognized working it is the spring of all that we can call the automatic action of mind and body, and on the universal scale it is the silent power of evolution gradually working onwards to that "divine event, to which the whole creation moves"; and by our conscious recognition of it we make it, relatively to ourselves, all that we believe it to be. The closer our *rapport* with it becomes, the more what we have hitherto considered automatic action, whether in our bodies or our circumstances, will pass under our control, until at last we shall control our whole individual world. Since, then, this is the stupendous issue involved, the question how we are to put ourselves practically in touch with the sub-conscious mind is a very important one. Now the clue which gives us the right direction is to be found in the *impersonal* quality of sub-conscious mind of which I have spoken. Not impersonal as lacking the *elements* of personality; nor even, in the case of individual subjective mind, as lacking the sense of individuality; but impersonal in the sense of not recognizing the particular external relations which appear to the objective mind to constitute its personality, and having a realization of itself quite independent of them. If, then, we would come in touch with it we must meet it on its own ground. It can see things only from the deductive standpoint, and therefore cannot take note of the inductive standpoint from which we construct the idea of our external personality; and accordingly if we would put ourselves in touch with it, we cannot do so by bringing it down to the level of the external and non-essential but only by rising to its own level on the plane of the interior and essential. How can this be done? Let two well-known writers answer. Rudyard Kipling tells us in his story of "Kim" how the boy used at times to lose his sense of personality by repeating to himself the question, *Who* is Kim? Gradually his personality would seem to fade and he would experience a feeling of passing into a grander and a wider life, in which the boy Kim was unknown, while his own conscious individuality remained, only exalted and expanded to an inconceivable extent; and in Tennyson's life by his son we are told that at times the poet had a similar experience. We come into touch with the absolute exactly in proportion as we withdraw ourselves from the relative: they vary inversely to each other.

For the purpose, then, of getting into touch with our sub-conscious mind we must endeavour to think of ourselves as pure being, as that entity which interiorly supports the outward manifestation, and doing so we shall realize that the essential quality of pure being must be good. It is in itself *pure Life,* and as such cannot desire anything detrimental to pure Life under whatever form manifested. Consequently the purer our intentions the more readily we shall place ourself *en rapport* with our subjective entity; and *a fortiori* the same applies to that Greater Sub-conscious Mind of which our individual subjective mind is a particular manifestation. In actual practice the process consists in first forming a clear conception in the objective mind of the idea we wish to convey to the subjective mind: then, when this has been firmly grasped, endeavour to lose sight of all other facts connected with the external personality except the one in question, and then mentally address the subjective mind as though it were an independent entity and impress upon it what you want it to do or to believe. Everyone must formulate his own way of working, but one method, which is both simple and effective, is to say to the subjective mind, "This is what I want you to do; you will now step into my place and do it, bringing all your powers and intelligence to bear, and considering yourself to be none other than myself." Having done this return to the realization of your own objective personality and leave the subjective mind to perform its task in full confidence that, by the law of its nature, it will do so if not hindered by a repetition of contrary messages from the objective mind. This is not a mere fancy but a truth daily proved by the experience of increasing numbers. The facts have not been fabricated to fit the theory, but the theory has been built up by careful observation of the facts; and since it has been shown both by theory and practice that such is the law of the relation between subjective and objective mind, we find ourselves face to face with a very momentous question. Is there any reason why the laws which hold good of the individual subjective mind should not hold good of the Universal Mind also? and the answer is that there is not. As has been already shown the Universal Mind must, by its very universality, be purely subjective, and what is the law of a part must also be the law of the whole: the qualities of fire are the same whether the centres of combustion be great or small, and therefore we may well conclude these lectures by considering what will be the result if we apply what we have learnt regarding the individual subjective mind to the Universal Mind.

We have learnt that the three great facts regarding subjective mind are its creative power, its amenableness to suggestion, and its inability to work by any other than the deductive method. This last is an exceedingly important point, for it implies that the action of the subjective mind is in no way limited by precedent. The inductive method works on principles inferred from an already existing pattern, and therefore at the best only produces the old thing in a new shape. But the deductive method works according to the essence or spirit of the principle, and does not depend on any previous concrete manifestation for its apprehension of it; and this latter method of working must necessarily be that of the all-originating Mind, for since there could be no prior existing pattern from which it could learn the principles of construction, the want of a pattern would have prevented its creating anything had its method been inductive instead of deductive. Thus by the necessity of the case the Universal Mind must act deductively, that is, according to the law which has been found true of individual subjective mind. It is thus not bound by any precedent, which means that its creative power is absolutely unlimited; and since it is essentially subjective mind, and not objective mind, it is entirely amenable to suggestion. Now it is an unavoidable inference from the identity of the law governing subjective mind, whether in the individual or the universal, that just as we can by suggestion impress a certain character of personality upon the individual subjective mind, so we can, and do, upon the Universal Mind; and it is for this reason that I have drawn attention to the inherent personal *quality* of pure spirit when contemplated in its most interior plane. It becomes, therefore, the most important of all considerations with what character we invest the Universal Mind; for since our relation to it is *purely subjective* it will infallibly bear *to us* exactly that character which we impress upon it; in other words it will be to us exactly what we believe it to be. This is simply a logical inference from the fact that, as subjective mind, our primary relation to it can only be on the subjective plane, and indirectly our objective relations must also spring from the same source. This is the meaning of that remarkable passage twice repeated in the Bible, "With the pure thou wilt show thyself pure, and with the froward thou wilt show thyself froward" (Ps. xviii., 26, and II. Sam. xxii., 27), for the context makes it clear that these words are addressed to the Divine Being. The spiritual kingdom is *within* us, and as we realize it *there* so it becomes to us a reality. It is the unvarying law of the subjective life that "as a man thinketh in his heart so is he," that is to say, his inward subjective states are the only true reality, and what we call external realities are only their objective correspondences. If we thoroughly realize the truth that the Universal Mind must be to us exactly according to our conception of it, and that this relation is not merely imaginary but by the law of subjective mind must be to us an actual fact and the foundation of all other facts, then it is impossible to over-estimate the importance of the conception of the Universal Mind which we adopt. To the uninstructed there is little or no choice: they form a conception in accordance with the tradition they have received from others, and until they have learnt to think for themselves, they have to abide by the results of that tradition: for natural laws admit of no exceptions, and however faulty the traditional idea may be, its acceptance will involve a corresponding reaction upon the Universal Mind, which will in turn be reflected into the conscious mind and external life of the individual. But those who understand the law of the subject will have no one but themselves to blame if they do not derive all possible benefits from it. The greatest Teacher of Mental Science the world has ever seen has laid down sufficiently plain rules for our guidance. With a knowledge of the subject whose depth can be appreciated only by those who have themselves some practical acquaintance with it, He bids His unlearned audiences, those common people who heard Him gladly, picture to themselves the Universal Mind as a benign Father, tenderly compassionate of all and sending the common bounties of Nature alike on the evil and the good; but He also pictured It as exercising a special and peculiar care over those who recognize Its willingness to do so:—"the very hairs of your head are all numbered," and "ye are of more value than many sparrows." Prayer was to be made to the unseen Being, not with doubt or fear, but with the absolute assurance of a certain answer, and no limit was to be set to its power or willingness to work for us. But to those who did not thus realize it, the Great Mind is necessarily the adversary who casts them into prison until they have paid the uttermost farthing; and thus in all cases the Master impressed upon his hearers the exact correspondence of the attitude of this unseen Power towards *them* with their own attitude towards *it.* Such teaching was not a narrow anthropomorphism but the adaptation to the intellectual capacity of the unlettered multitude of the very deepest truths of what we now call Mental Science. And the basis of it all is the cryptic personality of spirit hidden throughout the infinite of Nature under every form of manifestation. As unalloyed Life and Intelligence it *can* be no other than good, it can entertain no intention of evil, and thus all intentional evil must put us in opposition to it, and so deprive us of the consciousness of its guidance and strengthening and thus leave us to grope our own way and fight our own battle single-handed against the universe, odds which at last will surely prove too great for us. But remember that the opposition can never be on the part of the Universal Mind, for in itself it is sub-conscious mind; and to suppose any active opposition taken on its own initiative would be contrary to all we have learnt as to the nature of sub-conscious mind whether in the individual or the universal; the position of the Universal Mind towards us is always the reflection of our own attitude. Therefore although the Bible is full of threatening against those who persist in conscious opposition to the Divine Law of Good, it is on the other hand full of promises of immediate and full forgiveness to all who change their attitude and desire to co-operate with the Law of Good so far as they know it. The laws of Nature do not act vindictively; and through all theological formularies and traditional interpretations let us realize that what we are dealing with is the supreme law of our own being; and it is on the basis of this natural law that we find such declarations as that in Ezek. xviii., 22, which tells that if we forsake our evil ways our past transgressions shall never again be mentioned to us. We are dealing with the great principles of our subjective being, and our misuse of them in the past can never make them change their inherent law of action. If our method of using them in the past has brought us sorrow, fear and trouble, we have only to fall back on the law that if we reverse the cause the effects will be reversed also; and so what we have to do is simply to reverse our mental attitude and then endeavour to act up to the new one. The sincere endeavour to act up to our new mental attitude is essential, for we cannot really think in one way and act in another; but our repeated failures to fully act as we would wish must not discourage us. It is the sincere intention that is the essential thing, and this will in time release us from the bondage of habits which at present seem almost insuperable.

The initial step, then, consists in determining to picture the Universal Mind as the ideal of all we could wish it to be both to ourselves and to others, together with the endeavour to reproduce this ideal, however imperfectly, in our own life; and this step having been taken, we can then cheerfully look upon it as our ever-present Friend, providing all good, guarding from all danger, and guiding us with all counsel. Gradually as the habit of thus regarding the Universal Mind grows upon us, we shall find that in accordance with the laws we have been considering, it will become more and more *personal* to us, and in response to our desire its inherent intelligence will make itself more and more clearly perceptible within as a power of perceiving truth far beyond any statement of it that we could formulate by merely intellectual investigation. Similarly if we think of it as a great power devoted to supplying all our needs, we shall impress this character also upon it, and by the law of subjective mind it will proceed to enact the part of that special providence which we have credited it with being; and if, beyond the general care of our concerns, we would draw to ourselves some particular benefit, the same rule holds good of impressing our desire upon the Universal Subjective Mind. And if we realize that above and beyond all this we want something still greater and more enduring, the building-up of character and unfolding of our powers so that we may expand into fuller and yet fuller measures of joyous and joy-giving Life, still the same rule holds good: convey to the Universal Mind the suggestion of the desire, and by the law of relation between subjective and objective mind this too will be fulfilled. And thus the deepest problems of philosophy bring us back to the old statement of the Law:—Ask and ye shall receive, seek and ye shall find, knock and it shall be opened unto you. This is the summing-up of the natural law of the relation between us and the Divine Mind. It is thus no vain boast that Mental Science can enable us to make our lives what we will. We must start from where we are now, and by rightly estimating our relation to the Divine Universal Mind we can gradually grow into any conditions we desire, provided we first make ourselves in habitual mental attitude the person who corresponds to those conditions: for we can never get over the law of correspondence, and the externalization will always be in accord with the internal principle that gives rise to it. And to this law there is no limit. What it can do for us to-day it can do to-morrow, and through all that procession of to-morrows that loses itself in the dim vistas of eternity. Belief in limitation is the one and only thing that causes limitation, because we thus impress limitation upon the creative principle; and in proportion as we lay that belief aside our boundaries will expand, and increasing life and more abundant blessing will be ours.

But we must not ignore our responsibilities. Trained thought is far more powerful than untrained, and therefore the more deeply we penetrate into Mental Science the more carefully we must guard against all thoughts and words expressive of even the most modified form of ill-will. Gossip, tale-bearing, sneering laughter, are not in accord with the principles of Mental Science; and similarly even our smallest thoughts of good carry with them a seed of good which will assuredly bear fruit in due time. This is not mere "goodie, goodie," but an important lesson in Mental Science, for our subjective mind takes its colour from our settled mental habits, and an occasional affirmation or denial will not be sufficient to change it; and we must therefore cultivate that tone which we wish to see reproduced in our conditions whether of body, mind, or circumstance.

In these lectures my purpose has been, not so much to give specific rules of practice as to lay down the broad general principles of Mental Science which will enable the student to form rules for himself. In every walk in life, book knowledge is only a means to an end. Books can only direct us where to look and what to look for, but we must do the finding *for ourselves;* therefore, if you have really grasped the principles of the science, you will frame rules of your own which will give you better results than any attempt to follow somebody else's method, which was successful in their hands precisely because it was theirs. Never fear to be yourself. If Mental Science does not teach you to be yourself it teaches you nothing. Yourself, more yourself, and yet more yourself is what you want; only with the knowledge that the true self includes the inner and higher self which is always in immediate touch with the Great Divine Mind.

As Walt Whitman says:—"You are not all included between your hat and your boots."

The growing popularity of the Edinburgh Lectures on Mental Science has led me to add to the present edition three more sections on Body, Soul, and Spirit, which it is hoped will prove useful by rendering the principles of the inter-action of these three factors somewhat clearer.

XIV

# THE BODY

SOME STUDENTS FIND IT difficult to realize that mental action can produce any real effect upon material substance; but if this is not possible there is no such thing as Mental Science, the purpose of which is to produce improved conditions both of body and environment, so that the ultimate manifestation aimed at is always one of demonstration upon the plane of the visible and concrete. Therefore to afford conviction of an actual connection between the visible and the invisible, between the inner and the outer, is one of the most important points in the course of our studies.

That such a connection must exist is proved by metaphysical argument in answer to the question, "How did anything ever come into existence at all?" And the whole creation, ourselves included, stands as evidence to this great truth. But to many minds merely abstract argument is not completely convincing, or at any rate it becomes more convincing if it is supported by something of a more concrete nature; and for such readers I would give a few hints as to the correspondence between the physical and the mental. The subject covers a very wide area, and the limited space at my disposal will only allow me to touch on a few suggestive points, still these may be sufficient to show that the abstract argument has some corresponding facts at the back of it.

One of the most convincing proofs I have seen is that afforded by the "biometre," a little instrument invented by an eminent French scientist, the late Dr. Hippolyte Baraduc, which shows the action of what he calls the "vital current." His theory is that this force, whatever its actual nature may be, is universally present, and operates as a current of physical vitality perpetually, flowing with more or less energy through every physical organism, and which can, at any rate to some extent, be controlled by the power of the human will. The theory in all its minutiæ is exceedingly elaborate, and has been described in detail in Dr. Baraduc's published works. In a conversation I had with him about a year ago, he told me he was writing another book which would throw further light on the subject, but a few months later he passed over before it was presented to the world. The fact, however, which I wish to put before the reader, is the ocular demonstration of the connection between mind and matter, which an experiment with the biometre affords.

The instrument consists of a bell glass, from the inside of which is suspended a copper needle by a fine silken thread. The glass stands on a wooden support, below which is a coil of copper wire, which, however, is not connected with any battery or other apparatus, and merely serves to condense the current. Below the needle, inside the glass, there is a circular card divided into degrees to mark the action of the needle. Two of these instruments are placed side by side, but in no way connected, and the experimenter then holds out the fingers of both hands to within about an inch of the glasses. According to the theory, the current enters at the left hand, circulates through the body, and passes out at the right hand, that is to say, there is an indrawing at the left and a giving-out at the right, thus agreeing with Reichenbach's experiments on the polarity of the human body.

I must confess that, although I had read Dr. Baraduc's book, "Les Vibrations Humaines," I approached the instrument in a very sceptical frame of mind; but I was soon convinced of my error. At first, holding a mental attitude of entire relaxation, I found that the left-hand needle was attracted through twenty degrees, while the right-hand needle, the one affected by the out-going current, was repelled through ten degrees. After allowing the instrument to return to its normal equilibrium I again approached it with the purpose of seeing whether a change of mental attitude would in the least modify the flow of current. This time I assumed the strongest mental attitude I could with the intention of sending out a flow through the right hand, and the result as compared with the previous one was remarkable. The left-hand needle was now attracted only through ten degrees, while the right-hand one was deflected through something over thirty, thus clearly indicating the influence of the mental faculties in modifying the action of the current. I may mention that the experiment was made in the presence of two medical men who noted the movement of the needles.

I will not here stop to discuss the question of what the actual constitution of this current of vital energy may be—it is sufficient for our present purpose that it is there, and the experiment I have described brings us face to face with the fact of a correspondence between our own mental attitude and the invisible forces of nature. Even if we say that this current is some form of electricity, and that the variation of its action is determined by changes in the polarization of the atoms of the body, then this change of polarity is the result of mental action; so that the quickening or retarding of the cosmic current is equally the result of the mental attitude whether we suppose our mental force to act directly upon the current itself or indirectly by inducing changes in the molecular structure of the body. Whichever hypothesis we adopt the conclusion is the same, namely, that the mind has power to open or close the door to invisible forces in such a way that the result of the mental action becomes apparent on the material plane.

Now, investigation shows that the physical body is a mechanism specially adapted for the transmutation of the inner or mental power into modes of external activity. We know from medical science that the whole body is traversed by a network of nerves which serve as the channels of communication between the indwelling spiritual ego, which we call mind, and the functions of the external organism. This nervous system is dual. One system, known as the Sympathetic, is the channel for all those activities which are not consciously directed by our volition, such as the operation of the digestive organs, the repair of the daily wear and tear of the tissues, and the like. The other system, known as the Voluntary or Cerebro-spinal system, is the channel through which we receive conscious perception from the physical senses and exercise control over the movements of the body. This system has its centre in the brain, while the other has its centre in a ganglionic mass at the back of the stomach known as the solar plexus, and sometimes spoken of as the abdominal brain. The cerebro-spinal system is the channel of our volitional or conscious mental action, and the sympathetic system is the channel of that mental action which unconsciously supports the vital functions of the body. Thus the cerebro-spinal system is the organ of conscious mind and the sympathetic is that of sub-conscious mind.

But the interaction of conscious and subconscious mind requires a similar interaction between the corresponding systems of nerves, and one conspicuous connection by which this is provided is the "vagus" nerve. This nerve passes out of the cerebral region as a portion of the voluntary system, and through it we control the vocal organs; then it passes onwards to the thorax sending out branches to the heart and lungs; and finally, passing through the diaphragm, it loses the outer coating which distinguishes the nerves of the voluntary system and becomes identified with those of the sympathetic system, so forming a connecting link between the two and making the man physically a single entity.

Similarly different areas of the brain indicate their connection with the objective and subjective activities of the mind respectively, and speaking in a general way we may assign the frontal portion of the brain to the former and the posterior portion to the latter, while the intermediate portion partakes of the character of both.

The intuitional faculty has its correspondence in this upper area of the brain situated between the frontal and posterior portions, and physiologically speaking, it is here that intuitive ideas find entrance. These at first are more or less unformed and generalized in character, but are nevertheless perceived by the conscious mind, otherwise we should not be aware of them at all. Then the effort of nature is to bring these ideas into more definite and usable shape, so the conscious mind lays hold of them and induces a corresponding vibratory current in the voluntary system of nerves, and this in turn induces a similar current in the involuntary system, thus handing the idea over to the subjective mind. The vibratory current which had first descended from the apex of the brain to the frontal brain and thus through the voluntary system to the solar plexus is now reversed and ascends from the solar plexus through the sympathetic system to the posterior brain, this return current indicating the action of the subjective mind.

If we were to remove the surface portion of the apex of the brain we should find immediately below it the shining belt of brain substance called the "corpus callosum." This is the point of union between the subjective and objective, and as the current returns from the solar plexus to this point it is restored to the objective portion of the brain in a fresh form which it has acquired by the silent alchemy of the subjective mind. Thus the conception which was at first only vaguely recognized is restored to the objective mind in a definite and workable form, and then the objective mind, acting through the frontal brain—the area of comparison and analysis—proceeds to work upon a clearly perceived idea and to bring out the potentialities that are latent in it.

It must of course be borne in mind that I am here speaking of the mental ego in that mode of its existence with which we are most familiar, that is as clothed in flesh, though there may be much to say as to other modes of its activity. But for our daily life we have to consider ourselves as we are in that aspect of life, and from this point of view the physiological correspondence of the body to the action of the mind is an important item; and therefore, although we must always remember that the origin of ideas is purely mental, we must not forget that on the physical plane every mental action implies a corresponding molecular action in the brain and in the two-fold nervous system.

If, as the old Elizabethan poet says, "the soul is form, and doth the body make," then it is clear that the physical organism must be a mechanical arrangement as specially adapted for the use of the soul's powers as a steam-engine is for the power of steam; and it is the recognition of this reciprocity between the two that is the basis of all spiritual or mental healing, and therefore the study of this mechanical adaptation is an important branch of Mental Science. Only we must not forget that it is the effect and not the cause.

At the same time it is important to remember that such a thing as reversal of the relation between cause and effect is possible, just as the same apparatus may be made to generate mechanical power by the application of electricity, or to generate electricity by the application of mechanical power. And the importance of this principle consists in this. There is always a tendency for actions which were at first voluntary to become automatic, that is, to pass from the region of conscious mind into that of subconscious mind, and to acquire a permanent domicile there. Professor Elmer Gates, of Washington, has demonstrated this physiologically in his studies of brain formation. He tells us that every thought produces a slight molecular change in the substance of the brain, and the repetition of the same sort of thought causes a repetition of the same molecular action until at last a veritable channel is formed in the brain substance, which can only be eradicated by a reverse process of thought. In this way "grooves of thought" are very literal things, and when once established the vibrations of the cosmic currents flow automatically through them and thus react upon the mind by a process the reverse of that by which our voluntary and intentional indrawing from the invisible is affected. In this way are formed what we call "habits," and hence the importance of controlling our thinking and guarding it against undesirable ideas.

But on the other hand this reactionary process may be used to confirm good and life-giving modes of thought, so that by a knowledge of its laws we may enlist even the physical body itself in the building up of that perfectly whole personality, the attainment of which is the aim and object of our studies.

## XV

# THE SOUL

HAVING NOW OBTAINED a glimpse of the adaptation of the physical organism to the action of the mind we must next realize that the mind itself is an organism which is in like manner adapted to the action of a still higher power, only here the adaptation is one of mental faculty. As with other invisible forces all we can know of the mind is by observing what it does, but with this difference, that since we ourselves *are* this mind, our observation is an interior observation of states of consciousness. In this way we recognize certain faculties of our mind, the working order of which I have considered before; but the point to which I would now draw attention is that these faculties always work under the influence of something which stimulates them, and this stimulus may come either from without through the external senses, or from within by the consciousness of something not perceptible on the physical plane. Now the recognition of these interior sources of stimulus to our mental faculties, is an important branch of Mental Science, because the mental action thus set up works just as accurately through the physical correspondences as those which start from the recognition of external facts, and therefore the control and right direction of these inner perceptions is a matter of the first moment.

The faculties most immediately concerned are the intuition and the imagination, but it is at first difficult to see how the intuition, which is entirely spontaneous, can be brought under the control of the will. Of course, the spontaneousness of the intuition cannot in any way be interfered with, for if it ceased to act spontaneously it would cease to be the intuition. Its province is, as it were, to capture ideas from the infinite and present them to the mind to be dealt with at its discretion. In our mental constitution the intuition is the point of origination and, therefore, for it to cease to act spontaneously would be for it to cease to act at all. But the experience of a long succession of observers shows that the intuition can be trained so as to acquire increased sensitiveness in some particular direction, and the choice of the *general direction* is determined by the will of the individual.

It will be found that the intuition works most readily in respect to those subjects which most habitually occupy our thought; and according to the physiological correspondences which we have been considering this might be accounted for on the physical plane by the formation of brain-channels specially adapted for the induction in the molecular system of vibrations corresponding to the particular class of ideas in question. But of course we must remember that the ideas themselves are not caused by the molecular changes, but on the contrary are the cause of them; and it is in this translation of thought action into physical action that we are brought face to face with the eternal mystery of the descent of spirit into matter; and that though we may trace matter through successive degrees of refinement till it becomes what, in comparison with those denser modes that are most familiar, we might call a spiritual substance, yet at the end of it it is not the intelligent thinking principle itself. The criterion is in the word "vibrations." However delicately etheric the substance its movement commences by the vibration of its particles, and a vibration is a wave having a certain length, amplitude, and periodicity, that is to say, something which can exist only in terms of space and time; and as soon as we are dealing with anything capable of the conception of measurement we may be quite certain that we are not dealing with Spirit but only with one of its vehicles. Therefore although we may push our analysis of matter further and ever further back—and on this line there is a great deal of knowledge to be gained—we shall find that the point at which spiritual power or thought-force is translated into etheric or atomic vibration will always elude us. Therefore we must not attribute the origination of ideas to molecular displacement in the brain, though, by the reaction of the physical upon the mental which I have spoken of above, the formation of thought-channels in the grey matter of the brain may tend to facilitate the reception of certain ideas. Some people are actually conscious of the action of the upper portion of the brain during the influx of an intuition, the sensation being that of a sort of expansion in that brain area, which might be compared to the opening of a valve or door; but all attempts to induce the inflow of intuitive ideas by the physiological expedient of trying to open this valve by the exercise of the will should be discouraged as likely to prove injurious to the brain. I believe some Oriental systems advocate this method, but we may well trust the mind to regulate the action of its physical channels in a manner suitable to its own requirements, instead of trying to manipulate the mind by the unnatural forcing of its mechanical instrument. In all our studies on these lines we must remember that development is always by perfectly natural growth and is not brought about by unduly straining any portion of the system.

The fact, however, remains that the intuition works most freely in that direction in which we most habitually concentrate our thought; and in practice it will be found that the best way to cultivate the intuition in any particular direction is to meditate upon the *abstract principles* of that particular class of subjects rather than only to consider particular cases. Perhaps the reason is that particular cases have to do with specific phenomena, that is with the law working under certain limiting conditions, whereas the *principles* of the law are not limited by local conditions, and so habitual meditation on *them* sets our intuition free to range in an infinitude where the conception of antecedent conditions does not limit it. Anyway, whatever may be the theoretical explanation, you will find that the clear grasp of abstract principles in any direction has a wonderfully quickening effect upon the intuition in that particular direction.

The importance of recognizing our power of thus giving direction to the intuition cannot be exaggerated, for if the mind is attuned to sympathy with the highest phases of spirit this power opens the door to limitless possibilities of knowledge. In its highest workings intuition becomes inspiration, and certain great records of fundamental truths and supreme mysteries which have come down to us from thousands of generations bequeathed by deep thinkers of old can only be accounted for on the supposition that their earnest thought on the Originating Spirit, coupled with a reverent worship of It, opened the door, through their intuitive faculty, to the most sublime inspirations regarding the supreme truths of the universe both with respect to the evolution of the cosmos and to the evolution of the individual. Among such records explanatory of the supreme mysteries three stand out preeminent, all bearing witness to the same ONE Truth, and each throwing light upon the other; and these three are the Bible, the Great Pyramid, and the Pack of Cards—a curious combination some will think, but I hope in another volume of this series to be able to justify my present statement. I allude to these three records here because the unity of principle which they exhibit, notwithstanding their wide divergence of method, affords a standing proof that the direction taken by the intuition is largely determined by the will of the individual opening the mind in that particular direction.

Very closely allied to the intuition is the faculty of imagination. This does not mean mere fancies, which we dismiss without further consideration, but our power of forming mental images upon which we dwell. These, as I have said in the earlier part of this book, form a nucleus which, on its own plane, calls into action the universal Law of Attraction, thus giving rise to the principle of Growth. The relation of the intuition to the imagination is that the intuition grasps an idea from the Great Universal Mind, in which all things subsist *as potentials,* and presents it to the imagination in its essence rather than in a definite form, and then our image-building faculty gives it a clear and definite form which it presents before the mental vision, and which we then vivify by letting our thought dwell upon it, thus infusing our own personality into it, and so providing that personal element through which the specific action of the universal law relatively to the particular individual always takes place.* Whether our thought shall be allowed thus to dwell upon a particular mental image depends on our own will, and our exercise of our will depends on our belief in our power to use it so as to disperse or consolidate a given mental image; and finally our belief in our power to do this depends on our recognition of our relation to God, Who is the source of all power; for it is an invariable truth that our life will take its whole form, tone, and color from our conception of God, whether that conception be positive or negative, and the sequence by which it does so is that now given.

In this way, then, our intuition is related to our imagination, and this relation has its physiological correspondence in the circulus of molecular vibrations I have described above, which, having its commencement in the

* See my "Doré Lectures."

higher or "ideal" portion of the brain flows through the voluntary nervous system, the physical channel of objective mind, returning through the sympathetic system, the physical channel of subjective mind, thus completing the circuit and being then restored to the frontal brain, where it is consciously modelled into clear-cut forms suited to a specific purpose.

In all this the power of the will as regulating the action both of the intuition and the imagination must never be lost sight of, for without such a central controlling power we should lose all sense of individuality; and hence the ultimate aim of the evolutionary process is to evolve individual wills actuated by such beneficence and enlightenment as shall make them fitting vehicles for the outflowing of the Supreme Spirit, which has hitherto created cosmically, and can now carry on the creative process to its highest stages only through conscious union with the individual; for this is the only possible solution of the great problem, How can the Universal Mind act in all its fulness upon the plane of the individual and particular?

This is the ultimate of evolution, and the successful evolution of the individual depends on his recognizing this ultimate and working towards it; and therefore this should be the great end of our studies. There is a correspondence in the constitution of the body to the faculties of the soul, and there is a similar correspondence in the faculties of the soul to the power of the All-originating Spirit; and as in all other adaptations of specific vehicles so also here, we can never correctly understand the nature of the vehicle and use it rightly until we realize the nature of the power for the working of which it is specially adapted. Let us, then, in conclusion briefly consider the nature of that power.

## XVI

# THE SPIRIT

WHAT MUST THE Supreme All-originating Spirit be in itself? That is the question before us. Let us start with one fact regarding it about which we cannot have any possible doubt—it is *creative.* If it were not creative nothing could come into existence; therefore we know that its purpose, or Law of Tendency, must be to bring individual lives into existence and to surround them with a suitable environment. Now a power which has this for its inherent nature must be a kindly power. The Spirit of Life seeking expression in individual lives can have no other intention towards them than "that they might have life, and that they might have it more abundantly." To suppose the opposite would be a contradiction in terms. It would be to suppose the Eternal Principle of Life acting against itself, expressing itself as the reverse of what it is, in which case it would not be expressing itself but expressing its opposite; so that it is impossible to conceive of the Spirit of Life acting otherwise than to the increase of life. This is as yet only imperfectly apparent by reason of our imperfect apprehension of the position, and our consequent want of conscious unity with the ONE Eternal Life. As our consciousness of unity becomes more perfect so will the life-givingness of the Spirit become more apparent. But in the realm of principles the purely Affirmative and Life-giving nature of the All-originating Spirit is an unavoidable conclusion.

Now by what name can we call such an inherent desire to add to the fulness of any individual life—that is, to make it stronger, brighter, and happier? If this is not Love, then I do not know what else it is; and so we are philosophically led to the conclusion that Love is the prime moving power of the Creating Spirit.

But expression is impossible without Form. What Form, then, should Love give to the vehicles of its expression? By the hypothesis of the case it could not find self-expression in forms that were hateful or repugnant to it—therefore the only logical correlative of Love is Beauty. Beauty is not yet universally manifested for the same reason that Life is not, namely, lack of recognition of its Principle; but, that the principle of Beauty is inherent in the Eternal Mind is demonstrated by all that is beautiful in the world in which we live.

These considerations show us that the inherent nature of the Spirit must consist in the eternal interaction of Love and Beauty as the Active and Passive polarity of Being. Then this is the Power for the working of which our soul faculties are specially adapted. And when this purpose of the adaptation is recognized we begin to get some insight into the way in which our intuition, imagination, and will should be exercized. By training our thought to habitually dwell upon this dual-unity of the Originating Forces of Love and Beauty the intuition is rendered more and more sensitive to ideas emanating from this supreme source, and the imagining faculty is trained in the formation of images corresponding to such ideas; while on the physical side the molecular structure of the brain and body becomes more and more perfectly adjusted to the generating of vibratory currents tending to the outward manifestation of the Originating Principle. Thus the whole man is brought into unison with himself and with the Supreme Source of Life, so that, in the words of St. Paul, he is being day by day renewed after the image of Him that created him.

Our more immediately personal recognition of the All-originating Love and Beauty will thus flow out as peace of mind, health of body, discretion in the management of our affairs, and power in the carrying out of our undertakings; and as we advance to a wider conception of the working of the Spirit of Love and Beauty in its infinite possibilities, so our intuition will find a wider scope and our field of activity will expand along with it—in a word we shall discover that our individuality is growing, and that we are becoming more truly ourselves than we ever were before.

The question of the specific lines on which the individual may be most perfectly trained into such recognition of his true relation to the All-embracing Spirit of Life is therefore of supreme importance, but it is also of such magnitude that even to briefly sketch its broad outlines would require a volume to itself, and I will therefore not attempt to enter upon it here, my present purpose being only to offer some hints of the principles underlying that wonderful three-fold unity of Body, Soul, and Spirit which we all know ourselves to be.

We are as yet only at the commencement of the path which leads to the realization of this unity in the full development of all its powers, but others have trodden the way before us, from whose experiences we may learn; and not least among these was the illustrious founder of the Most Christian Fraternity of the Rosicrucians. This master-mind, setting out in his youth with the intention of going to Jerusalem, changed the order of his journey and first sojourned for three years in the symbolical city of Damcar, in the mystical country of Arabia, then for about a year in the mystical country of Egypt, and then for two years in the mystical country of Fez. Then, having during these six years learned all that was to be acquired in those countries, he returned to his native land of Germany, where, on the basis of the knowledge he had thus gained, he founded the Fraternity R. C., for whose instruction he wrote the mystical books M. and T. Then, when he realized that his work in its present stage was accomplished, he of his own free will laid aside the physical body, not, it is recorded, by decay, or disease, or ordinary death, but by the express direction of the Spirit of Life, summing up all his knowledge in the words,

"Jesus mihi omnia."

And now his followers await the coming of "the Artist Elias," who shall bring the Magnum Opus to its completion.

"Let him that readeth understand."

# The Doré Lectures on Mental Science

1909

# CONTENTS

## FOREWORD

THE ADDRESSES CONTAINED in this volume were delivered by me at the Doré Gallery, Bond Street, London, on the Sundays of the first three months of the present year, and are now published at the kind request of many of my hearers, hence their title of "The Doré Lectures." A number of separate discourses on a variety of subjects necessarily labours under the disadvantage of want of continuity, and also under that of a liability to the frequent repetition of similar ideas and expressions, and the reader will, I trust, pardon these defects as inherent in the circumstances of the work. At the same time it will be found that, although not specially so designed, there is a certain progressive development of thought through the dozen lectures which compose this volume, the reason for which is that they all aim at expressing the same fundamental idea, namely that, though the laws of the universe can never be broken, they can be made to work under special conditions which will produce results that could not be produced under the conditions spontaneously provided by nature. This is a simple scientific principle and it shows us the place which is occupied by the personal factor, that, namely, of an intelligence which sees beyond the present limited manifestation of the Law into its real essence, and which thus constitutes the instrumentality by which the infinite possibilities of the Law can be evoked into forms of power, usefulness, and beauty.

The more perfect, therefore, the working of the personal factor, the greater will be the results developed from the Universal Law; and hence our lines of study should be two-fold—on the one hand the theoretical study of the action of Universal Law, and on the other the practical fitting of ourselves to make use of it; and if the present volume should assist any reader in this two-fold quest, it will have answered its purpose.

The different subjects have necessarily been treated very briefly, and the addresses can only be considered as suggestions for lines of thought which the reader will be able to work out for himself, and he must therefore not expect that careful elaboration of detail which I would gladly have bestowed had I been writing on one of these subjects exclusively. This little book must be taken only for what it is, the record of somewhat fragmentary talks with a very indulgent audience, to whom I gratefully dedicate the volume.

T.T.
*June 5, 1909.*

I

# ENTERING INTO THE SPIRIT OF IT

We all know the meaning of this phrase in our everyday life. The Spirit is that which gives life and movement to anything, in fact it is that which causes it to exist at all. The thought of the author, the impression of the painter, the feeling of the musician, is that without which their works could never have come into being, and so it is only as we enter into the *idea* which gives rise to the work, that we can derive all the enjoyment and benefit from it which it is able to bestow. If we cannot enter into the Spirit of it, the book, the picture, the music, are meaningless to us: to appreciate them we must share the mental attitude of their creator. This is a universal principle; if we do not enter into the Spirit of a thing, it is dead so far as we are concerned; but if we do enter into it we reproduce in ourselves the same quality of life which called that thing into existence.

Now if this is a general principle, why can we not carry it to a higher range of things? Why not to the highest point of all? May we not enter into the originating Spirit of Life itself, and so reproduce it in ourselves as a perennial spring of livingness? This, surely, is a question worthy of our careful consideration.

The spirit of a thing is that which is the source of its inherent movement, and therefore the question before us is, what is the nature of the primal moving power, which is at the back of the endless array of life which we see around us, our own life included? Science gives us ample ground for saying that it is not material, for science has now, at least theoretically, reduced all material things to a primary ether, universally distributed, whose innumerable particles are in absolute equilibrium; whence it follows on mathematical grounds alone that the initial movement which began to concentrate the world and all material substances out of the particles of the dispersed ether, could not have originated in the particles themselves. Thus by a necessary deduction from the conclusions of physical science, we are compelled to realize the presence of some immaterial power capable of separating off certain specific areas for the display of cosmic activity, and then building up a material universe with all its inhabitants by an orderly sequence of evolution, in which each stage lays the foundation for the development of the stage, which is to follow—in a word we find ourselves brought face to face with a power which exhibits on a stupendous scale, the faculties of selection and adaptation of means to ends, and thus distributes energy and life in accordance with a recognizable scheme of cosmic progression. It is therefore not only Life, but also Intelligence, and Life guided by Intelligence becomes Volition. It is this primary originating power which we mean when we speak of "The Spirit," and it is into this Spirit of the whole universe that we must enter if we would reproduce it as a spring of Original Life in ourselves.

Now in the case of the productions of artistic genius we know that we must enter into the movement of the creative mind of the artist, before we can realize the principle which gives rise to his work. We must learn to partake of the feeling, to find expression for which is the motive of his creative activity. May we not apply the same principle to the Greater Creative Mind with which we are seeking to deal? There is something in the work of the artist which is akin to that of original creation. His work, literary, musical, or graphic is original creation on a miniature scale, and in this it differs from that of the engineer, which is constructive, or that of the scientist which is analytical; for the artist in a sense creates something out of nothing, and therefore starts from the stand-point of simple feeling, and not from that of a pre-existing necessity. This, by the hypothesis of the case, is true also of the Parent Mind, for at the stage where the initial movement of creation takes place, there are no existing conditions to compel action in one direction more than another. Consequently the direction taken by the creative impulse is not dictated by outward circumstances, and the primary movement must therefore be entirely due to the action of the Original Mind upon itself; it is the reaching out of this Mind for realization of all that it feels itself to be.

The creative process thus in the first instance is purely a matter of feeling—exactly what we speak of as "motif" in a work of art.

Now it is this original feeling that we need to enter into, because it is the *fons et origo* of the whole chain of causation which subsequently follows. What then can this original feeling of the Spirit be? Since the Spirit is Life-in-itself, its feeling can only be for the fuller expression of Life—any other sort of feeling would be self-destructive and is therefore inconceivable. Then the full expression of Life implies Happiness, and Happiness implies Harmony, and Harmony implies Order, and Order implies Proportion, and Proportion implies Beauty; so that in recognizing the inherent tendency of the Spirit towards the production of Life, we can recognise a similar inherent tendency to the production of these other qualities also; and since the desire to bestow the greater fulness of joyous life can only be described as Love, we can sum up the whole of the feeling which is the original moving impulse in the Spirit as Love and Beauty—the Spirit finding expression through forms of beauty in centres of life, in harmonious reciprocal relation to itself. This is a generalized statement of the broad principle by which Spirit expands from the innermost to the outermost, in accordance with a Law of tendency inherent in itself.

It sees itself, as it were, reflected in various centres of life and energy, each with its appropriate form; but in the first instance these reflections can have no existence except within the originating Mind. They have their first beginning as mental images, so that in addition to the powers of Intelligence and Selection, we must also realise that of Imagination as belonging to the Divine Mind; and we must picture these powers as working from the initial motive of Love and Beauty.

Now this is the Spirit that we need to enter into, and the method of doing so is a perfectly logical one. It is the same method by which all scientific advance is made. It consists in first observing how a certain law works under the conditions spontaneously provided by nature, next in carefully considering what principle this spontaneous working indicates, and lastly deducing from this how the same principle would act under specially selected conditions, not spontaneously provided by nature.

The progress of shipbuilding affords a good example of what I mean. Formerly wood was employed instead of iron, because wood floats in water and iron sinks; yet now the navies of the world are built of iron; careful thought showed the law of floatation to be that anything could float which, bulk for bulk, is lighter than the mass of liquid displaced by it; and so we now make iron float by the very same law by which it sinks, because by the introduction of the *personal* factor, we provide conditions which do not occur spontaneously—according to the esoteric maxim that "Nature unaided fails." Now we want to apply the same process of specializing a generic Law to the first of all Laws, that of the generic life-giving tendency of Spirit itself. Without the element of *individual personality* the Spirit can only work cosmically by a *generic* Law; but this law admits of far higher specialization, and this specialization can only be attained through the introduction of the personal factor. But to introduce this factor the individual must be fully aware of the *principle* which underlies the spontaneous or cosmic action of the law. Where, then, will he find this principle of Life? Certainly not by contemplating Death. In order to get a principle to work in the way we require it to, we must observe its action when it is working spontaneously in this particular direction. We must ask why it goes in the right direction as far as it does—and having learnt this we shall then be able to make it go further. The law of floatation was not discovered by contemplating the sinking of things, but by contemplating the floating of things which floated naturally, and then intelligently asking why they did so.

The knowledge of a principle is to be gained by the study of its affirmative action; when we understand *that* we are in a position to correct the negative conditions which tend to prevent that action.

Now Death is the absence of Life, and disease is the absence of health, so to enter into the Spirit of Life we require to contemplate it, where it is to be found, and not where it is not—we are met with the old question, "Why seek ye the living among the dead?" This is why we start our studies by considering the cosmic creation, for it is there that we find the Life Spirit working through untold ages, not merely as deathless energy, but with a perpetual advance into higher degrees of Life. If we could only so enter into the Spirit as to make it personally *in ourselves* what it evidently is in *itself,* the *magnum opus* would be accomplished. This means realizing our life as drawn direct from the Originating Spirit; and if we now understand that the Thought or Imagination of the Spirit is the great reality of Being, and that all material facts are only correspondences, then it logically follows that what we have to do is to maintain our individual place in the Thought of the Parent Mind.

We have seen that the action of the Originating Mind must needs be *generic,* that is according to types which include multitudes of individuals. This type is the reflection of the Creative Mind at the level of that particular *genius;* and at the human level it is Man, not as associated with particular circumstances, but as existing in the absolute ideal.

In proportion then as we learn to dissociate our conception of ourselves from particular circumstances, and to rest upon our *absolute* nature, as reflections of the Divine ideal, we, in our turn, reflect back into the Divine Imagination its original conception of itself as expressed in generic or typical Man, and so by a natural law of cause and effect, the individual who realizes this mental attitude enters permanently into the Spirit of Life, and it becomes a perennial fountain of Life springing up spontaneously within him.

He then finds himself to be as the Bible says, "the image and likeness of God." He has reached the level at which he affords a new starting point for the creative process, and the Spirit, finding a personal centre in him, begins its work *de novo,* having thus solved the great problem of how to enable the Universal to act directly upon the plane of the Particular.

It is in this sense, as affording the requisite centre for a new departure of the creative Spirit, that man is said to be a "microcosm," or universe in miniature; and this is also what is meant by the esoteric doctrine of the Octave, of which I may be able to speak more fully on some other occasion.

If the principles here stated are carefully considered, they will be found to throw light on much that would otherwise be obscure, and they will also afford the key to the succeeding essays.

The reader is therefore asked to think them out carefully for himself, and to note their connection with the subject of the next article.

## II

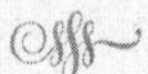

# INDIVIDUALITY

INDIVIDUALITY IS THE NECESSARY complement of the Universal Spirit, which was the subject of our consideration last Sunday. The whole problem of life consists in finding the true relation of the individual to the Universal Originating Spirit; and the first step towards ascertaining this is to realize what the Universal Spirit must be in itself. We have already done this to some extent, and the conclusions we have arrived at are:—

That the essence of the Spirit is Life, Love, and Beauty.

That its Motive, or primary moving impulse, is to express the Life, Love and Beauty which it feels itself to be.

That the Universal cannot act on the plane of the Particular except by becoming the particular, that is by expression through the individual.

If these three axioms are clearly grasped, we have got a solid foundation from which to start our consideration of the subject for to-day.

The first question that naturally presents itself is, If these things be so, why does not every individual express the life, love, and beauty of the Universal Spirit? The answer to this question is to be found in the Law of Consciousness. We cannot be conscious of anything except by realizing a certain relation between it and ourselves. It must affect us in some way, otherwise we are not conscious of its existence; and according to the way in which it affects us we recognize ourselves as standing related to it. It is this self-recognition on our own part carried out to the sum total of all our relations, whether spiritual, intellectual, or physical, that constitutes our realization of life. On this principle, then, for the *realization* of its own Livingness, the production of centres of life, through its relation to which this conscious realization can be attained, becomes a necessity for the Originating Mind. Then it follows that this realization can only be complete where the individual has perfect liberty to withhold it; for otherwise no true realization could have taken place. For instance, let us consider the working of Love. Love must be spontaneous, or it has no existence at all. We cannot imagine such a thing as mechanically induced love. But anything which is formed so as to automatically produce an effect without any volition of its own, is nothing but a piece of mechanism. Hence if the Originating Mind is to realize the reality of Love, it can only be by relation to some being which has the power to withhold love. The same applies to the realization of all the other modes of livingness; so that it is only in proportion, as the individual life is an independent centre of action, with the option of acting either positively or negatively, that any real life has been produced at all. The further the created thing is from being a merely mechanical arrangement, the higher is the grade of creation. The solar system is a perfect work of mechanical creation, but to constitute centres which can reciprocate the highest nature of the Divine Mind, requires not a mechanism, however perfect, but a mental centre which is, in itself, an independent source of action. Hence by the requirements of the case man should be capable of placing himself either in a positive or a negative relation to the Parent Mind, from which he originates; otherwise he would be nothing more than a clockwork figure.

In this necessity of the case, then, we find the reason why the life, love, and beauty of the Spirit are not visibly reproduced in every human being. They *are* reproduced in the world of nature, so far as a mechanical and automatic action can represent them, but their perfect reproduction can only take place on the basis of a liberty akin to that of the Originating Spirit itself, which therefore implies the liberty of negation as well as of affirmation.

Why, then, does the individual make a negative choice? Because he does not understand the law of his own individuality, and believes it to be a law of limitation, instead of a Law of Liberty. He does not expect to find the starting point of the Creative Process reproduced within himself, and so he looks to the mechanical side of things for the basis of his reasoning about life. Consequently his reasoning lands him in the conclusion that life is limited, because he has assumed limitation in his premises, and so logically cannot escape from it in his conclusion. Then he thinks that this is the law and so ridicules the idea of transcending it. He points to the sequence of cause and effect, by which death, disease, and disaster, hold their sway over the individual, and says that sequence is law. And he is perfectly right so far as he goes—it is *a* law; but not *the* Law. When we have only reached this stage of comprehension, we have yet to learn that a higher law can include a lower one so completely as entirely to swallow it up.

The fallacy involved in this negative argument, is the assumption that the law of limitation is essential in all grades of being. It is the fallacy of the old shipbuilders as to the impossibility of building iron ships. What is required is to get at the *principle* which is at the back of the Law in its affirmative working, and specialize it under higher conditions than are spontaneously presented by nature, and this can only be done by the introduction of the personal element, that is to say an individual intelligence capable of comprehending the principle. The question, then, is what is the principle by which we came into being? and this is only a personal application of the general question, How did anything come into being? Now, as I pointed out in the preceding article, the ultimate deduction from physical science is that the originating movement takes place in the Universal Mind, and is analogous to that of our own imagination; and as we have just seen, the perfect ideal can only be that of a being capable of reciprocating *all* the qualities of the Originating Mind. Consequently man, in his inmost nature, is the product of the Divine Mind imaging forth an image of itself on the plane of the relative as the complementary to its own sphere of the absolute.

If we will therefore go to the *inmost* principle in ourselves, which philosophy and Scripture alike declare to be made in the image and likeness of God, instead of to the outer vehicles which it externalizes as instruments through which to function on the various planes of being, we shall find that we have reached a principle in ourselves which stands in *loco dei* towards all our vehicles and also towards our environment. It is above them all, and creates them, however unaware we may be of the fact, and relatively to them it occupies the place of first cause. The recognition of this is the discovery of our own relation to the whole world of the relative. On the other hand this must not lead us into the mistake of supposing that there is nothing higher, for, as we have already seen, this inmost principle or *ego* is itself the effect of an antecedent cause, for it proceeds from the imaging process in the Divine Mind.

We thus find ourselves holding an intermediate position between true First Cause, on the one hand, and the world of secondary causes on the other, and in order to understand the nature of this position, we must fall back on the axiom that the Universal can only work on the plane of the Particular through the individual. Then we see that the function of the individual is to *differentiate* the undistributed flow of the Universal into suitable directions for starting different trains of secondary causation.

Man's place in the cosmic order is that of a distributor of the Divine power, subject, however, to the inherent Law of the power which he distributes. We see one instance of this in ordinary science, in the fact that we never create force; all we can do is to distribute it. The very word Man means distributor or measurer, as in common with all words derived from the Sanskrit root MN., it implies the idea of measurement, just as in the words moon, month, mens, mind, and "man," the Indian weight of 80 lbs.; and it is for this reason that man is spoken of in Scripture as a "steward," or dispenser of the Divine gifts. As our minds become open to the full meaning of this position, the immense possibilities and also the responsibility contained in it will become apparent.

It means that the individual is the creative centre of his own world. Our past experience affords no evidence against this, but on the contrary, is evidence for it. Our true nature is always present, only we have hitherto taken the lower and mechanical side of things for our starting point, and so have created limitation instead of expansion. And even with the knowledge of the Creative Law which we have now attained, we shall continue to do this, if we seek our starting point in the things which are below us and not in the only thing which is above us, namely the Divine Mind, because it is only there that we can find illimitable Creative Power. Life is *being,* it is the experience of states of consciousness, and there is an unfailing correspondence between these inner states and our outward conditions. Now we see from the Original Creation that the state of consciousness must be the cause, and the corresponding conditions the effect, because at the starting of the creation no conditions existed, and the working of the Creative Mind upon itself can only have been a state of consciousness. This, then, is clearly the Creative Order—from states to conditions. But we invert this order, and seek to create from conditions to states. We say, If I had such and such conditions they would produce the state of feeling which I desire; and in so saying we run the risk of making a mistake as to the correspondence, for it may turn out that the particular conditions which we fixed on are not such as would produce the desired state. Or, again, though they might produce it in a certain degree, other conditions might produce it in a still greater degree, while at the same time opening the way to the attainment of still higher states and still better conditions. Therefore our wisest plan is to follow the pattern of the Parent Mind and make mental self-recognition our starting point, knowing that by the inherent Law of Spirit the corelated conditions will come by a natural process of growth. Then the great self-recognition is that of our relation to the Supreme Mind. That is the generating centre and we are distributing centres; just as electricity is generated at the central station and delivered in different forms of power by reason of passing through appropriate centres of distribution, so that in one place it lights a room, in another conveys a message, and in a third drives a tram car. In like manner the power of the Universal Mind takes particular forms through the particular mind of the individual. It does not interfere with the lines of his individuality, but works along them, thus making him, not less, but more himself. It is thus, not a compelling power, but an expanding and illuminating one; so that the more the individual recognizes the reciprocal action between it and himself, the more full of life he must become.

Then also we need not be troubled about future conditions because we know that the All-originating Power is working through us and for us, and that according to the Law proved by the whole existing creation, it produces alt the conditions required for the expression of the Life, Love and Beauty which it is, so that we can fully trust it to open the way as we go along. The Great Teacher's words, "Take no thought for the morrow"—and note that the correct translation is "Take no anxious thought"—are the practical application of the soundest philosophy. This does not, of course, mean that we are not to exert ourselves. We must do our share in the work, and not expect God to do *for* us what He can only do *through* us. We are to use our common sense and natural faculties in working upon the conditions now present. We must make use of them, *as far as they go,* but we must not try and go further than the present things require; we must not try to force things, but allow them to grow naturally, knowing that they are doing so under the guidance of the All-Creating Wisdom.

Following this method we shall grow more and more into the habit of looking to mental attitude as the Key to our progress in Life, knowing that everything else must come out of that; and we shall further discover that our mental attitude is eventually determined by the way in which we regard the Divine Mind. Then the final result will be that we shall see the Divine Mind to be nothing else than Life, Love and Beauty—Beauty being identical with Wisdom or the perfect adjustment of parts to whole—and we shall see ourselves to be distributing centres of these primary energies and so in our turn subordinate centres of creative power. And as we advance in this knowledge we shall find that we transcend one law of limitation after another by finding the higher law, of which the lower is but a partial expression, until we shall see clearly before us, as our ultimate goal, nothing less than the Perfect Law of Liberty—not liberty without Law which is anarchy, but Liberty according to Law. In this way we shall find that the Apostle spoke the literal truth, when he said, that we shall become like Him when we see Him *as He is,* because the whole process by which our individuality is produced is one of reflection of the image existing in the Divine Mind. When we thus learn the Law of our own being we shall be able to specialize it in ways of which we have hitherto but little conception, but as in the case of all natural laws the specialization cannot take place until the fundamental principle of the generic law has been fully realized. For these reasons the student should endeavour to realize more and more perfectly, both in theory and practice, the law of the relation between the Universal and the Individual Minds. It is that of *reciprocal* action. If this fact of reciprocity is grasped, it will be found to explain both why the individual falls short of expressing the fulness of Life, which the Spirit is, and why he can attain to the fulness of that expression; just as the same law explains why iron sinks in water, and how it can be made to float. It is the individualizing of the Universal Spirit, by recognizing its reciprocity to ourselves, that is the secret of the perpetuation and growth of our own individuality.

## III

# THE NEW THOUGHT AND THE NEW ORDER

IN THE TWO PRECEDING LECTURES I have endeavoured to reach some conception of what the All-originating Spirit is in itself, and of the relation of the individual to it. So far as we can form any conception of these things at all we see that they are universal principles applicable to all nature, and, at the human level, applicable to all men: they are general laws the recognition of which is an essential preliminary to any further advance, because progress is made, not by setting aside the inherent law of things, which is impossible, but by specializing it through presenting conditions which will enable the same principle to act in a less limited manner. Having therefore got a general idea of these two ultimates, the universal and the individual, and of their relation to one another, let us now consider the process of specialization. In what does the specialization of a natural law consist? It consists in making that law or principle produce an effect which it could not produce under the simply generic conditions spontaneously provided by nature.

This selection of suitable conditions is the work of Intelligence, it is a process of consciously arranging things in a new order, so as to produce a new result. The principle is never new, for principles are eternal and universal; but the knowledge that the same principle will produce new results when working under new conditions is the key to the unfoldment of infinite possibilities. What we have therefore to consider is the working of Intelligence in providing specific conditions for the operation of universal principles, so as to bring about new results which will transcend our past experiences. The process does not consist in the introduction of new elements, but in making new combinations of elements which are always present; just as our ancestors had no conception of carriages that could go without horses, and yet by a suitable combination of elements which were always in existence, such vehicles are common objects in our streets today. How, then, is the power of Intelligence to be brought to bear upon the generic law of the relation between the Individual and the Universal so as to specialize it into the production of greater results than those which we have hitherto obtained?

All the practical attainments of science, which place the civilized world of to-day in advance of the times of King Alfred or Charlemagne, have been gained by a uniform method, and that a very simple one. It is by always enquiring what is the affirmative factor in any existing combination, and asking ourselves why, in that particular combination, it does not act beyond certain limits. What makes the thing a success, so far as it goes, and what prevents it going further? Then, by carefully considering the nature of the affirmative factor, we see what sort of conditions to provide to enable it to express itself more fully. This is the scientific method; it has proved itself true in respect of material things, and there is no reason why it should not be equally reliable in respect of spiritual things also.

Taking this as our method, we ask, What is the affirmative factor in the whole creation, and in ourselves as included in the creation, and, as we found in the first lecture, this factor is Spirit—that invisible power which concentrates the primordial ether into forms, and endows those forms with various modes of motion, from the simply mechanical motion of the planet up to the volitional motion in man. And, since this is so, the primary affirmative factor can only be the Feeling and the Thought of the Universal Spirit.* Now, by the hypothesis of the case, the Universal Spirit must be the Pure Essence of Life, and therefore its feeling and thought can only be towards the continually increasing expression of the livingness which it is; and accordingly the specialization, of which we are in search, must be along the line of affording it a centre from which it may more perfectly realize

* See my "Edinburgh Lectures on Mental Science."

this feeling and express this thought: in other words the way to specialize the generic principle of Spirit is by providing new mental conditions in consonance with its own original nature.

The scientific method of enquiry therefore brings us to the conclusion that the required conditions for translating the racial or generic operation of the Spirit into a specialized individual operation is a new way of *thinking*—a mode of thought concurring with, and not in opposition to, the essential forward movement of the Creative Spirit itself. This implies an entire reversal of our old conceptions. Hitherto we have taken forms and conditions as the starting point of our thought and inferred that *they* are the causes of mental states; now we have learnt that the true order of the creative process is exactly the reverse, and that thought and feeling are the causes, and forms and conditions the effects. When we have learnt this lesson we have grasped the foundation principle on which individual specialization of the generic law of the creative process becomes a practical possibility.

New Thought, then, is not the name of a particular sect, but is the essential factor by which our own future development is to be carried on; and its essence consists in seeing the relation of things in a New Order. Hitherto we have inverted the true order of cause and effect; now, by carefully considering the real nature of the Principle of Causation in itself—*causa causans* as distinguished from *causa causata*—we return to the true order and adopt a new method of thinking in accordance with it.

In themselves this order and this method of thinking are not new. They are older than the foundation of the world, for they are those of the Creative Spirit itself; and all through the ages this teaching has been handed down under various forms, the true meaning of which has been perceived only by a few in each generation. But as the light breaks in upon any individual it is a new light to him, and so to each one in succession it becomes the New Thought. And when anyone reaches it, he finds himself in a New Order. He continues indeed to be included in the universal order of the cosmos, but in a perfectly different way to what he had previously supposed; for, from his new standpoint, he finds that he is included, not so much as a part of the general effect, but as a part of the general cause; and when he perceives this he then sees that the method of his further advance must be by letting the General Cause flow more and more freely into his own specific centre, and he therefore seeks to provide thought conditions which will enable him to do so.

Then, still employing the scientific method of following up the affirmative factor, he realizes that this universal causative power, by whatever name he may call it, manifests as Supreme Intelligence in the adaptation of means to ends. It does so in the mechanism of the planet, in the production of supply for the support of physical life, and in the maintenance of the race as a whole. True, the investigator is met at every turn with individual failure; but his answer to this is that there is no cosmic failure, and that the apparent individual failure is itself a part of the cosmic process, and will diminish in proportion as the individual attains to the recognition of the Moving Principle of that process, and provides the necessary conditions to enable it to take a new starting point in his own individuality. Now, one of these conditions is to recognize it as Intelligence, and to remember that when working through our own mentality it in no way changes its essential nature, just as electricity loses none of its essential qualities in passing through the special apparatus which enables it to manifest as light.

When we see this, our line of thought will run something as follows:—"My mind is a centre of Divine operation. The Divine operation is always for expansion and fuller expression, and this means the production of something beyond what has gone before, something entirely new, not included in past experience, though proceeding out of it by an orderly sequence of growth. Therefore, since the Divine cannot change its inherent nature, it must operate in the same manner in me; consequently in my own special world, of which I am the centre, it will move forward to produce new conditions, always in advance of any that have gone before." This is a legitimate line of argument, from the premises established in the recognition of the relation between the individual and the Universal Mind; and it results in our looking to the Divine Mind, not only as creative, but also as directive—that is as determining the actual forms which the conditions for its manifestation will take in our own particular world, as well as supplying the energy for their production. We miss the point of the relation between the individual and the universal, if we do not see that the Originating Spirit is a *forming* power. It is the forming power throughout nature, and if we would specialize it we must learn to trust its formative quality when operating from its new starting point in ourselves.

But the question naturally arises, If this is so, what part is taken by the individual? Our part is to provide a concrete centre round which the Divine energies can play. In the generic order of being we exercise upon it a force of attraction in accordance with the innate pattern of our particular individuality; and as we begin to realize the Law of this relation, we, in our turn, are attracted towards the Divine along the lines of least resistance, that is on those lines which are most natural to our special bent of mind. In this way we throw out certain aspirations with the result that we intensify our attraction of the Divine forces in a certain specific manner, and they then begin to act both through us and around us in accordance with our aspirations. This is the rationale of the reciprocal action between the Universal Mind and the individual mind, and this shows us that our desires should not be directed so much to the acquisition of particular *things* as to the reproduction in ourselves of particular phases of the Spirit's activity; and this, being in its very nature creative, is bound to externalize as corresponding things and circumstances. Then, when these external facts appear in the circle of our objective life, we must work upon them from the objective stand-point. This is where many fall short of completed work. They realize the subjective or creative process, but do not see that it must be followed by an objective or constructive process, and consequently they are unpractical dreamers and never reach the stage of completed work. The creative process brings the materials and conditions for the work to our hands; then we must make use of them with diligence and common-sense—God will provide the food, but He will not cook the dinner.

This, then, is the part taken by the individual, and it is thus that he becomes a distributing centre of the Divine energy, neither on the one hand trying to lead it like a blind force, nor on the other being himself under a blind unreasoning impulsion from it. He receives guidance because he seeks guidance; and he both seeks and receives according to a Law which he is able to recognize; so that he no more sacrifices his liberty or dwarfs his powers, than does an engineer who submits to the generic laws of electricity, in order to apply them to some specific purpose. The more intimate his knowledge of this Law of Reciprocity becomes, the more he finds that it leads on to Liberty, on the same principle by which we find in physical science that nature obeys us precisely in the same degree to which we first obey nature. As the esoteric maxim has it, "What is a truth on one plane is a truth on all." But the key to this enfranchisement of body, mind, and circumstances is in that new thought which becomes creative of new conditions, because it realizes the true order of the creative process. Therefore it is that, if we would bring a new order of Life, Light, and Liberty into our lives we must commence by bringing a new order into our thought, and find in ourselves the starting point of a new creative series, not by the force of personal will, but by union with the Divine Spirit, which in the expression of its inherent Love and Beauty, makes all things new.

IV

# THE LIFE OF THE SPIRIT

THE THREE PRECEDING LECTURES have touched upon certain fundamental truths in a definite order—first the nature of the Originating Spirit itself, next the generic relation of the individual to this All-embracing Spirit, and lastly the way to specialize this relation so as to obtain greater results from it than spontaneously arise by its merely generic action, and we have found that this can only be done through a new order of thought. This sequence is logical because it implies a Power, an Individual who understands the Power, and a Method of applying the power deduced from understanding its nature. These are general principles without realizing which it is impossible to proceed further, but assuming that the reader has grasped their significance, we may now go on to consider their application in greater detail.

Now this application must be a personal one, for it is only through the individual that the higher specialization of the power can take place, but at the same time this must not lead us to suppose that the individual, himself, brings the creative force into being. To suppose this is inversion; and we cannot impress upon ourselves too deeply that the relation of the individual to the Divine Spirit is that of a distributor, and not that of the original creator. If this is steadily borne in mind the way will become clear, otherwise we shall be led into confusion.

What, then, is the Power which we are to distribute? It is the Originating Spirit itself. We are sure that it is this because the new order of thought always begins at the beginning of any series which it contemplates bringing into manifestation, and it is based upon the fact that the origin of everything is Spirit. It is in this that its creative power resides; hence the person who is in the true new order of thought assumes as an axiomatic fact that what he has to distribute, or differentiate into manifestation is nothing else than the Originating Spirit. This being the case, it is evident that the *purpose* of the distribution must be the more perfect expression of the Originating Spirit as that which it is in itself, and what it is in itself is emphatically Life. What is seeking for expression, then, is the perfect Livingness of the Spirit; and this expression is to be found, through ourselves, by means of our renewed mode of thought. Let us see, then, how our new order of thought, with regard to the Principle of Life, is likely to operate. In our old order of thought we have always associated Life with the physical body—life has been for us the supreme physical fact. Now, however, we know that Life is much more than this; but, as the greater includes the less, it includes physical life as one mode of its manifestation. The true order does not require us to deny the reality of physical life or to call it an illusion; on the contrary it sees in physical life the completion of a great creative series, but it assigns it the proper place in that series, which is what the old mode of thought did not.

When we realize the truth about the Creative Process, we see that the originating life is not physical: its livingness consists in thought and feeling. By this inner movement it throws out vehicles through which to function, and these become living forms because of the inner principle which is sustaining them; so that the Life with which we are primarily concerned in the new order is the life of thought and feeling in ourselves as the vehicle, or distributing medium, of the Life of the Spirit.

Then, if we have grasped the idea of the Spirit as the great *forming* Power, as stated in the last lecture, we shall seek in it the fountain-head of Form as well as of Power: and as a logical deduction from this we shall look to it to give form to our thoughts and feelings. If the principle is once recognised the sequence is obvious. The form taken by our outward conditions, whether of body or circumstance, depends on the form taken by our thoughts and feelings, and our thoughts and feelings will take form from that source from which we allow them to receive suggestion. Accordingly if we allow them to accept their fundamental suggestions from the relative and limited, they will assume a corresponding form and transmit them to our external environment, thus repeating the old order of limitation in a ceaselessly recurring round. Now our object is to get out of this circle of limitation, and the only way to do so is to get our thoughts and feelings moulded into new forms continually advancing to greater and greater perfection. To meet this requirement, therefore, there must be a forming power greater than that of our own unaided conceptions, and this is to be found in our realization of the Spirit as the Supreme Beauty, or Wisdom, moulding our thoughts and feelings into shapes harmoniously adjusted to the fullest expression, in and through us, of the Livingness which Spirit is in itself.

Now this is nothing more than transferring to the innermost plane of origination, a principle with which all readers who are "in the thought" may be presumed to be quite familiar—the principle of Receptiveness. We all know what is meant by a receptive mental attitude when applied to healing or telepathy; and does it not logically follow that the same principle may be applied to the receiving of life itself from the Supreme Source? What is wanted, therefore, is to place ourselves in a receptive mental attitude towards the Universal Spirit with the intention of receiving its forming influence into our mental substance. It is always the presence of a definite intention that distinguishes the intelligent receptive attitude of mind from a merely sponge-like absorbancy, which sucks in any and every influence that may happen to be floating round: for we must not shut our eyes to the fact that there are various influences in the mental atmosphere by which we are surrounded, and some of them of the most undesirable kind. Clear and definite intention is therefore as necessary in our receptive attitude as in our active and creative one; and if our intention is to have our own thoughts and feelings moulded into such forms as to express those of the Spirit, then we establish that relation to the Spirit which, by the conditions of the case, must necessarily lead us to the conception of new ideals vitalised by a power which will enable us to bring them into concrete manifestation. It is in this way that we become differentiating centres of the Divine Thought giving it expression in form in the world of space and time, and thus is solved the great problem of enabling the Universal to act upon the plane of the particular without being hampered by those limitations which the merely generic law of manifestation imposes upon it. It is just here that subconscious mind performs the function of a "bridge" between the finite and the infinite as noted in my "Edinburgh Lectures on Mental Science," and it is for this reason that a recognition of its susceptibility to impression is so important.

By establishing, then, a personal relation to the life of the Spirit, the sphere of the individual becomes enlarged. The reason is that he allows a greater intelligence than his own to take the initiative; and since he knows that this Intelligence is also the very Principle of Life itself, he cannot have any fear that it will act in any way to the diminution of his individual life, for that would be to stultify its own operation—it would be self-destructive action which is a contradiction in terms to the conception of Creative Spirit. Knowing, then, that by its inherent nature this Intelligence can only work to the expansion of the individual life, we can rest upon it with the utmost confidence and trust it to take an initiative which will lead to far greater results than any we could forecast from the stand-point of our own knowledge. So long as we insist on dictating the particular form which the action of the Spirit is to take, we limit it, and so close against ourselves avenues of expansion which might otherwise have been open to us; and if we ask ourselves why we do this we shall find that in the last resort it is because we do not believe in the Spirit as a *forming* power. We have, indeed, advanced to the conception of it as executive power, which will work to a prescribed pattern, but we have yet to grasp the conception of it as versed in the art of design, and capable of elaborating schemes of construction, which will not only be complete in themselves, but also in perfect harmony with one another. When we advance to the conception of the Spirit as containing in itself the ideal of Form as well as of Power, we shall cease from the effort of trying to force things into a particular shape, whether on the inner or the outer plane, and shall be content to trust the inherent harmoniousness or Beauty of the Spirit to produce combinations far in advance of anything that we could have conceived ourselves. This does not mean that we shall reduce ourselves to a condition of apathy, in which all desire, expectation and enthusiasm have been quenched, for these are the mainspring of our mental machinery; but on the contrary their action will be quickened by the knowledge that there is working at the back of them a Formative Principle so infallible that it cannot miss its mark; so that however good and beautiful the existing forms may be, we may always rest in the happy expectation of something still better to come. And it will come by a natural law of growth, because the Spirit is in itself the Principle of Increase. They will grow out of present conditions for the simple reason that if you are to reach some further point it can only be by starting from where you are now. Therefore it is written, "Despise not the day of small things." There is only one proviso attached to this forward movement of the Spirit in the world of our own surroundings, and that is that we shall co-operate with it; and this co-operation consists in making the best use of existing conditions in cheerful reliance on the Spirit of Increase to express itself through us, and for us, because we are in harmony with it. This mental attitude will be found of immense value in setting us free from worry and anxiety, and as a consequence our work will be done in a much more efficient manner. We shall do the present work *for its own sake,* knowing that herein is the principle of unfoldment; and doing it simply for its own sake we shall bring to bear upon it a power of concentration which cannot fail of good results—and this quite naturally and without any toilsome effort. We shall then find that the secret of co-operation is to have faith in ourselves because we first have faith in God; and we shall discover that this Divine self-confidence is something very different from a boastful egotism which assumes a personal superiority over others. It is simply the assurance of a man who knows that he is working in accordance with a law of nature. He does not claim as a personal achievement what the Law does *for* him: but on the other hand he does not trouble himself about outcries against his presumptuous audacity raised by persons who are ignorant of the Law which he is employing. He is therefore neither boastful nor timorous, but simply works on in cheerful expectancy because he knows that his reliance is upon a Law which cannot be broken.

In this way, then, we must realize the Life of the Spirit as being also the Law of the Spirit. The two are identical, and cannot deny themselves. Our recognition of them gives them a new starting point through our own mentality, but they still continue to be the same in their nature, and unless limited or inverted by our mental affirmation of limited or inverted conditions, they are bound to work out into fuller and continually fuller expression of the Life, Love, and Beauty which the Spirit is in itself. Our path, therefore, is plain; it is simply to contemplate the Life, Love, and Beauty of the Originating Spirit and affirm that we are already giving expression to it in our thoughts and in our actions however insignificant they may at present appear. This path may be very narrow and humble in its beginning, but it ever grows wider and mounts higher, for it is the continually expanding expression of the Life of the Spirit which is infinite and knows no limits.

# V

## ALPHA AND OMEGA

ALPHA AND OMEGA, the First and the Last. What does this mean? It means the entire series of causation from the first originating movement to the final and completed result. We may take this on any scale from the creation of a cosmos to the creation of a lady's robe. Everything has its origin in an idea, a thought; and it has its completion in the manifestation of that thought in form. Many intermediate stages are necessary, but the Alpha and Omega of the series are the thought and the thing. This shows us that in essence the thing already existed in the thought. Omega is already potential in Alpha, just as in the Pythagorean system all numbers are said to proceed from unity and to be resolvable back again into it. Now it is this general principle of the already existence of the thing in the thought that we have to lay hold of, and as we find it true in an architect's design of the house that is to be, so we find it true in the great work of the Architect of the Universe. When we see this we have realized a general principle, which we find at work everywhere. That is the meaning of a *general* principle: it can be applied to any sort of subject; and the use of studying general principles is to give them particular application to anything we may have to deal with. Now what we have to deal with most of all is ourselves, and so we come to the consideration of Alpha and Omega in the human being. In the vision of St. John, the speaker of the words, "I am

Alpha and Omega, the First and the Last," is described as "Like unto a son of man"—that is, however transcendent the appearance in the vision, it is essentially human, and thus suggests to us the presence of the universal principle at the human level. But the figure in the apocalyptic vision is not that of man as we ordinarily know him. It is that of Omega as it subsists enshrined in Alpha: it is the ideal of humanity as it subsists in the Divine Mind which was manifested in objective form to the eyes of the seer, and therefore presented the Alpha and Omega of that idea in all the majesty of Divine glory.

But if we grasp the truth that the thing is already existent in the thought, do we not see that this transcendent Omega must be already existent in the Divine ideal of every one of us? If on the plane of the absolute time is not, then does it not follow that this glorified humanity is a present fact in the Divine Mind? And if this is so, then this fact is eternally true regarding every human being. But if it is true that the thing exists in the thought, it is equally true that the thought finds form in the thing; and since things exist under the relative conditions of time and space, they are necessarily subject to a law of Growth, so that while the subsistence of the thing in the thought is perfect *ab initio,* the expression of the thought in the thing is a matter of gradual development. This is a point which we must never lose sight of in our studies; and we must never lose sight of the perfection of the thing in the thought because we do not yet see the perfection of the thought in the thing. Therefore we must remember that man, as we know him now, has by no means reached the ultimate of his evolution. We are only yet in the making, but we have now reached a point where we can facilitate the evolutionary process by conscious co-operation with the Creative Spirit. Our share in this work commences with the recognition of the Divine ideal of man, and thus finding the pattern by which we are to be guided. For since the person to be created after this pattern is ourself, it follows that, by whatever processes the Divine ideal transforms itself into concrete reality, the place where those processes are to work must be within ourselves; in other words, the creative action of the Spirit takes place through the laws of our own mentality. If it is a true maxim that the thing must take form in the thought before the thought can take form in the thing, then it is plain that the Divine Ideal can only be externalized in our objective life in proportion as it is first formed in our thought; and it takes form in our thought only to the extent to which we apprehend its existence in the Divine Mind. By the nature of the relation between the individual mind and the Universal Mind it is strictly a case of reflection; and in proportion as the mirror of our own mind blurs or clearly reflects the image of the Divine ideal, so will it give rise to a correspondingly feeble or vigorous reproduction of it in our external life.

This being the rationale of the matter, why should we limit our conception of the Divine ideal of ourselves? Why should we say, "I am too mean a creature ever to reflect so glorious an image"—or "God never intended such a limitless ideal to be reproduced in human beings." In saying such things we expose our ignorance of the whole Law of the Creative Process. We shut our eyes to the fact that the Omega of completion already subsists in the Alpha of conception, and that the Alpha of conception would be nothing but a lying illusion if it was not capable of expression in the Omega of completion. The creative process in us is that we become the individual reflection of what we realize God to be relatively to ourselves, and therefore if we realize the Divine Spirit as the *infinite potential* of all that can constitute a perfected human being, this conception must, by the Law of the Creative Process, gradually build up a corresponding image in our mind, which in turn will act upon our external conditions.

This, by the laws of mind, is the nature of the process and it shows us what St. Paul means when he speaks of Christ being formed in us (Gal. iv. 19) and what in another place he calls being renewed in knowledge after the image of Him that created us (Col. iii. 10). It is a thoroughly logical sequence of cause and effect, and what we require is to see more clearly the Law of this sequence and use it intelligently—that is why St. Paul says it is being "renewed in knowledge": it is a New Knowledge, the recognition of principles which we had not previously apprehended. Now the fact which, in our past experience, we have not grasped is that the human mind forms a new point of departure for the work of the Creative Spirit; and in proportion as we see this more and more clearly, the more we shall find ourselves entering into a new order of life in which we become less and less subject to the old limitations. This is not a reward arbitrarily bestowed upon us for holding dogmatically to certain mere verbal statements, but it is the natural result of understanding the supreme law of our own being. On its own plane it is as purely scientific as the law of chemical re-action; only here we are not dealing with the interaction of secondary causes but with the Self-originating action of Spirit. Hence a new force has to be taken into account which does not occur in physical science, the power of Feeling. Thought creates form, but it is feeling that gives vitality to thought. Thought without feeling may be constructive as in some great engineering work, but it can never be creative as in the work of the artist or musician; and that which originates within itself a new order of causation is, so far as all pre-existing forms are concerned, a creation *ex nihilo,* and is therefore Thought expressive of Feeling. It is this indissoluble union of Thought and Feeling that distinguishes creative thought from merely analytical thought and places it in a different category; and therefore if we are to afford a new starting-point for carrying on the work of creation it must be by assimilating the feeling of the Originating Spirit as part and parcel of its thought—it is that entering into the Mind of the Spirit of which I spoke in the first address.

Now the images in the Mind of the Spirit must necessarily be *generic.* The reason for this is that by its very nature the Principle of Life must be prolific, that is, tending to Multiplicity, and therefore the original Thought-image must be fundamental to whole races, and not exclusive to particular individuals. Consequently the images in the Mind of the Spirit must be absolute types of the true essentials of the perfect development of the race, just what Plato meant by archetypal ideas. This is the perfect subsistence of the thing in the thought. Therefore it is that our evolution as centres of *creative* activity, the exponents of new laws, and through them of new conditions, depends on our realizing in the Divine Mind the archetype of mental perfection, at once as thought and feeling. But when we find all this in the Divine Mind, do we not meet with an infinite and glorious Personality? There is nothing lacking of all that we can understand by Personality, excepting outward form; and since the very essence of telepathy is that it dispenses with the physical presence, we find ourselves in a position of interior communion with a Personality at once Divine and Human. This is that Personality of the Spirit which St. John saw in the apocalyptic vision, and which by the very conditions of the case is the Alpha and Omega of Humanity.

But, as I have said, it is simply *generic* in itself, and it becomes active and specific only by a purely personal relation to the individual. But once more we must realize that nothing can take place except according to Law, and therefore this specific relation is nothing arbitrary, but arises out of the generic Law applied under specific conditions. And since what makes a law generic is precisely the fact that it does not supply the specific conditions, it follows that the conditions for the specialising of the Law must be provided by the individual. Then it is that his recognition of the originating creative movement, as arising from combined Thought and Feeling, becomes a practical working asset. He realizes that there is a Heart and Mind of the Spirit reciprocal to his own heart and mind, that he is not dealing with a filmy abstraction, nor yet with a mere mathematical sequence, but with something that is pulsating with a Life as warm and vivid and full of interest as his own—nay, more so, for it is the Infinite of all that he himself is. And his recognition goes even further than this, for since this specialization can only take place through the individual himself, it logically follows that the Life, which he thus specializes, become *his own* life. *Quoad* the individual it does not know itself apart from him. But this self-recognition through the individual cannot in any way change the inherent nature of the Creative Spirit, and therefore to the extent to which the individual perceives its identification with himself, he places himself under its guidance, and so he becomes one of those who are "led by the Spirit." Thus he begins to find the Alpha and Omega of the Divine ideal reproduced in himself—in a very small degree at present, but containing the principle of perpetual growth into an infinite expansion of which we can as yet form no conception.

St. John sums up the whole of this position in his memorable words:—"Beloved now are we the Sons of God, and it doth not yet appear what we *shall* be; but we know that when He shall appear (*i.e.,* become clear to us) we shall be like Him; for (*i.e.,* the reason of all this) we shall see Him as He is" (I. John iii. 2).

VI

## THE CREATIVE POWER OF THOUGHT

ONE OF THE great axioms in the new order of ideas, of which I have spoken, is that our Thought possesses creative power, and since the whole superstructure depends on this foundation, it is well to examine it carefully. Now the starting point is to see that Thought, or purely mental action, is the only possible source from which the existing creation could ever have come into manifestation at all, and it is on this account that in the preceding addresses I have laid stress on the origin of the cosmos. It is therefore not necessary to go over this ground again, and we will start this morning's enquiry on the assumption that every manifestation is in essence the expression of a Divine Thought. This being so, our own mind is the expression of a Divine Thought. The Divine Thought has produced something which itself is capable of thinking; but the question is whether its thinking has the same creative quality as that of the Parent Mind.

Now by the very hypothesis of the case the whole Creative Process consists in the continual pressing forward of the Universal Spirit for expression through the individual and particular, and Spirit in its different modes is therefore the Life and Substance of the universe. Hence it follows that if there is to be an expression of thinking power it can only be by expressing the same thinking power which subsists latent in the Originating Spirit. If it were less than this it would only be some sort of mechanism and would not be thinking power, so that to be thinking power at all it must be identical in kind with that of the Originating Spirit. It is for this reason that man is said to be created in the image and likeness of God; and if we realize that it is impossible for him to be otherwise, we shall find a firm foundation from which to draw many important deductions.

But if our thought possesses this creative power, why are we hampered by adverse conditions? The answer is, because hitherto we have used our power invertedly. We have taken the starting point of our thought from external facts and consequently created a repetition of facts of a similar nature, and so long as we do this we must needs go on perpetuating the old circle of limitation. And, owing to the sensitiveness of the subconscious mind to suggestion—(See Edinburgh Lectures, chapter V.)—we are subject to a very powerful negative influence from those who are unacquainted with affirmative principles, and thus race-beliefs and the thought-currents of our more immediate environment tend to consolidate our own inverted thinking. It is therefore not surprising that the creative power of our thought, thus used in a wrong direction, has produced the limitations of which we complain. The remedy, then, is by reversing our method of thinking, and instead of taking external facts as our starting point, taking the inherent nature of mental power as our starting point. We have already gained two great steps in this direction, first by seeing that the whole manifested cosmos could have had its origin nowhere but in mental power, and secondly by realizing that our own mental power must be the same in kind with that of the Originating Mind.

Now we can go a step further and see how this power in ourselves can be perpetuated and intensified. By the nature of the creative process your mind is itself a thought of the Parent Mind; so, as long as this thought of the Universal Mind subsists, *you* will subsist, for you *are* it. But so long as you think this thought it continues to subsist, and necessarily remains present in the Divine Mind, thus fulfilling the logical conditions required for the perpetuation of the individual life. A poor analogy of the process may be found in a self-influencing dynamo where the magnetism generates the current and the current intensifies the magnetism with the result of producing a still stronger current until the limit of saturation is reached; only in the substantive infinitude of the Universal Mind and the potential infinitude of the Individual Mind there is no limit of saturation. Or we may compare the interaction of the two minds to two mirrors, a great and a small one, opposite each other, with the word "Life" engraved on the large one. Then, by the law of reflection, the word "Life" will also appear on the image of the smaller mirror reflected in the greater. Of course these are only very imperfect analogies; but if you can once grasp the idea of your own individuality as a thought in the Divine Mind which is able to perpetuate itself by thinking of itself as the thought which it is, you have got at the root of the whole matter, and by the same process you will not only perpetuate your life but will also expand it.

When we realize this on the one hand, and on the other that all external conditions, including the body, are produced by thought, we find ourselves standing between two infinites, the infinite of Mind and the infinite of Substance—from both of which we can draw what we will, and mould specific conditions out of the Universal Substance by the Creative Power which we draw in from the Universal Mind. But we must recollect that this is not by the force of personal will upon the substance, which is an error that will land us in all sorts of inversion, but by realizing our mind as a channel through which the Universal Mind operates upon substances in a particular way, according to the mode of thought which we are seeking to embody. If, then, our thought is habitually concentrated upon principles rather than on particular things, realizing that principles are nothing else than the Divine Mind in operation, we shall find that they will necessarily germinate to produce their own expression in corresponding facts, thus verifying the words of the Great Teacher, "Seek ye first the Kingdom of God and His righteousness and all these things shall be added unto you."

But we must never lose sight of the reason for the creative power of our thought, that it is because our mind is itself a thought of the Divine Mind, and that consequently our increase in livingness and creative power must be in exact proportion to our perception of our relation to the Parent Mind. In such considerations as these is to be found the philosophical basis of the Bible doctrine of "Sonship," with its culmination in the conception of the Christ. These are not mere fancies but the expression of strictly scientific principles, in their application to the deepest problems of the individual life; and their basis is that each one's world, whether in or out of the flesh, must necessarily be created by his own consciousness, and, in its turn, his mode of consciousness will necessarily take its colour from his conception of his relation to the Divine Mind—to the exclusion of light and colour, if he realizes no Divine Mind, and to their building up into forms of beauty in proportion as he realizes his identity of being with that All-Originating Spirit which is Light, Love, and Beauty in itself. Thus the great creative work of Thought in each of us is to make us consciously "sons and daughters of the Almighty," realizing that by our divine origin we can never be really separated from the Parent Mind which is continually seeking expression through us, and that any apparent separation is due to our own misconception of the true nature of the inherent relation between the Universal and the Individual. This is the lesson which the Great Teacher has so luminously put before us in the parable of the Prodigal Son.

VII

# THE GREAT AFFIRMATIVE

THE GREAT AFFIRMATIVE appears in two modes, the cosmic and the individual. In its essence it is the same in both, but in each it works from a different standpoint. It is always the principle of Being—that which *is,* as distinguished from that which is not; but to grasp the true significance of this saying we must understand what is meant by "that which is not." It is something more than mere non-existence, for obviously we should not trouble ourselves about what is non-existent. It is that which both is and is not at the same time, and the thing that answers to this description is "Conditions." The little affirmative is that which affirms particular conditions as all that it can grasp, while the great affirmative grasps a wider conception, the conception of that which gives rise to conditions. Cosmically it is that power of Spirit which sends forth the whole creation as its expression of itself, and it is for this reason that I have drawn attention in the preceding lectures to the idea of the creation *ex nihilo* of the whole visible universe. As Eastern and Western Scriptures alike tell us it is the breathing-forth of Original Spirit; and if you have followed what I have said regarding the reproduction of this Spirit in the individual—that by the very nature of the creative process the human mind must be of the same quality with the Divine Mind—then we find that a second mode of the Originating

Spirit becomes possible, namely that of operation through the individual mind. But whether acting cosmically or personally it is always the same Spirit and therefore cannot lose its inherent character which is that of the Power which creates *ex nihilo.* It is the direct contradiction of the maxim "ex nihilo nihil fit"—nothing can be made out of nothing; and it is the recognition of the presence in ourselves of this power, which can make something out of nothing, that is the key to our further progress. As the logical outcome of the cosmic creative process, the evolutionary work reaches a point where the Originating Power creates an image of itself; and thus affords a fresh point of departure from which it can work specifically, just as in the cosmic process it works generically. From this new standpoint it does not in any way contradict the laws of the cosmic order, but proceeds to specialize them, and thus to bring out results through the individual which could not be otherwise attained.

Now the Spirit does this by the same method as in the Original Creation, namely by creating *ex nihilo;* for otherwise it would be bound by the limitations necessarily inherent in the cosmic *form* of things, and so no fresh creative starting point would have been attained. This is why the Bible lays such stress on the principle of Monogenesis, or creation from a single power instead of from a pair or syzygy; and it is on this account that we are told that this One-ness of God is the foundation of all the commandments, and that the "Son of God" is declared to be "monogenes" or one-begotten, for that is the correct translation of the Greek word. The immense importance of this principle of creation from a single power will become apparent as we realize more fully the results proceeding from the assumption of the opposite principle, or the dualism of the creative power; but as the discussion of this great subject would require a volume to itself, I must, at present, content myself with saying that this insistence of the Bible upon the singleness of the Creative Power is based upon a knowledge which goes to the very root of esoteric principles, and is therefore not to be set aside in favour of dualistic systems, though superficially the latter may appear more consonant to reason.

If, then, it is possible to put the Great Affirmation into words it is that God is ONE and that this ONE finds centre in ourselves; and if the full meaning of this statement is realized, the logical result will be found to be a new creation both in and from ourselves. We shall realize in ourselves the working of a new principle whose distinguishing feature is its simplicity. It is ONE-ness and is not troubled about any second. Hence what it contemplates is not how its action will be modified by that of some second principle, something which will compel it to work in a particular manner and so limit it; but what it contemplates is its own Unity. Then it perceives that its Unity consists in a greater and a lesser movement, just as the rotation of the earth on its axis does not interfere with its rotation round the sun but are both motions of the same unit, and are definitely related to each other. In like manner we find that the Spirit is moving simultaneously in the macrocosm of the universe and in the microcosm of the individual, and the two movements harmonize because they are that of the same Spirit, and the latter is included in the former and pre-supposes it. The Great Affirmation, therefore, is the perception that the "I AM" is ONE, always harmonious with itself, and including all things in this harmony for the simple reason that there is no second creative power; and when the individual realizes that this always-single power is the root of his own being, and therefore has centre in himself and finds expression through him, he learns to trust its singleness and the consequent harmony of its action *in* him with what it is doing *around* him. Then he sees that the affirmation "I and my Father are ONE" is a necessary deduction from a correct apprehension of the fundamental principles of being; and then, on the principle that the less must be included in the greater, he desires that harmonious unity of action be maintained by the adaptation of his own particular movement to the larger movement of the Spirit working as the Creative Principle through the great whole. In this way we become centres through which the creative forces find specialization by the development of that personal factor on which the specific application of general laws must always depend. A specific sort of individuality is formed, capable of being the link between the great Spiritual Power of the universal and the manifestation of the relative in time and space because it consciously partakes of both; and because the individual of this class recognizes the singleness of the Spirit as the starting point of all things, he endeavours to withdraw his mind from all arguments derived from external conditions, whether past or present, and to fix it upon the forward movement of the Spirit which he knows to be always identical both in the universe and in himself. He ceases the attempt to dictate to the Spirit, because he does not see in it a mere blind force, but reveres it as the Supreme Intelligence: and on the other hand he does not grovel before it in doubt and fear, because he knows it is one with himself and is realizing itself through him, and therefore cannot have any purpose antagonistic to his own individual welfare. Realizing this he deliberately places his thoughts under the guidance of the Divine Spirit, knowing that his outward acts and conditions must thereby be brought into harmony with the great forward movement of the Spirit, not only at the stage he has now reached, but at all future stages. He does not at all deny the power of his own thought as the creative agent in his own personal world,—on the contrary it is precisely on the knowledge of this fact that his perception of the true adjustment between the principles of Life is based; but for this very reason he is the more solicitous to be led by that Wisdom which can see what he cannot see, so that his personal control over the conditions of his own life may be employed to its continual increase and development.

In this way our affirmation of the "I am" ceases to be the petulant assertion of our limited personality and becomes the affirmation that the Great I AM affirms its own I AM-ness both in us and through us, and thus our use of the words becomes in very truth the Great Affirmative, or that which is the root of all being as distinguished from that which has no being in itself but is merely externalized by being as the vehicle for its expression. We shall realize our true place as subordinate creative centres, perfectly independent of existing conditions because the creative process is that of monogenesis and requires no other factor than the Spirit for its exercise, but at the same time subordinate to the Divine Spirit in the greatness of its inherent forward movement because there is only ONE Spirit and it cannot from one centre antagonize what it is doing from another. Thus the Great Affirmation makes us children of the Great King, at once living in obedience to that Power which is above us, and exercising this same power over all that world of secondary causation which is below us.

Thus in our measure and station each one of us will receive the mission of the I AM.

VIII

# CHRIST THE FULFILLING OF THE LAW

*"Think not that I am come to destroy the law or the prophets: I am not come to destroy but to fulfil."* (MATT. V. 17.)

*"Christ is the end of the law for righteousness to everyone that believeth."* (ROM. X. 4.)

IF THESE WORDS are the utterance of a mere sectarian superstition they are worthless; but if they are the statement of a great principle, then it is worth our while to enquire what that principle is. The fulfilling of anything is the bringing into complete realization of all that it potentially contains, and so the filling of any law to its fulness means bringing out all the possibilities which are hidden in it. This is precisely the method which has brought forth all the advances of material civilization. The laws of nature are the same now that they were in the days of our rugged Anglo-Saxon ancestors, but they brought out only an infinitesimal fraction of the possibilities which those laws contain: now we have brought out a good deal more, but we have by no means exhausted them, and so we continue to advance, not by contradicting natural laws, but by more fully realizing their capacity. Why should we not, then, apply the same method to ourselves and see whether there are no potentialities hidden away in the law of our own being which we have not as yet by any means brought to their fulfilment? We talk of a good time coming and of the ameliorating of the race; but do we reflect that the race is composed of individuals and that therefore real advance is to be made only by individual improvement, and not by Act of Parliament? and if so, then the individual with whom to begin is ourself.

The complete manifestation of the Law of Individuality is the end or purpose of the Bible teaching concerning Christ. It is a teaching based upon Law, spiritual and mental, fully recognizing that no effect can be produced except by the operation of an adequate cause; and Christ is set before us both as explaining the causes and exhibiting the full measure of the effects. All this is according to Law; and the importance of its being according to Law is that Law is universal, and the potentialities of the Law are therefore inherent in everyone—there is no special law for anybody, but anybody can specialize the law by using it with a fuller understanding of how much can be got out of it; and the purpose of the Scripture teaching regarding Christ is to help us to do this.

The preceding lectures have led us step by step to see that the Originating Spirit, which first brought the world into existence, is also the root of our own individuality, and is therefore always ready, by its inherent nature, to continue the creative process from this individual stand-point as soon as the necessary conditions are provided, and these conditions are thought-conditions. Then by realizing the relation of Christ to the Originating Mind, the Parent Spirit or "Father," we receive a *standard* of thought which is bound to act creatively bringing out all the potentialities of our hidden being. Now the relation of Christ to the "Father" is that of the Archetypal Idea in the All-creating Mind of which I have previously spoken, and so we arrive at the conception of the Christ-idea as a universal principle, and as being an idea therefore capable of reproduction in the individual Mind, thus explaining St. Paul's meaning when he speaks of Christ being formed in us. It is here that the principle of monogenesis comes in, that principle which I have endeavoured to describe in the earlier part of the present series as originating the whole manifested creation by an internal action of the Spirit upon itself; and it is the entire absence of control by any second power that renders the realization in external actuality of a purely mental ideal possible. For this reason systematic spiritual study commences with the contemplation of the existing cosmos, and we then transfer the conception of the monogenetic power of the Spirit from the cosmos to the individual and realize that the same Spirit is able to do the same thing in ourselves. This is the New Thought which in time will fulfil itself in the New Order, and we thus provide new thought-conditions which enable the Spirit to carry on its creative work from a new stand-point, that of our own individuality. This attainment by the Spirit of a new starting-point is what is meant by the esoteric doctrine of the Octave. The Octave is the starting-point of a new series reduplicating the starting-point of the previous series at a different level, just as does the octave note in music. We find this principle constantly referred to in Scripture—the completion of a prior series in the number Seven, and the starting of a new series by the number Eight, which takes the same place in the second series that the number One did in the first. The second series comes out of the first by natural growth and could not come into existence without it, hence the First or Originating number of the second series is the Eighth if we regard the second series as the prolongation of the first. Seven is the numerical correspondence of complete manifestation because it is the combination of three and four, which respectively represent the complete working of the spiritual and material factors—involution and evolution—and thus together constitute the finished whole. Students of the Tarot will here realize the process by which the Yod of Yod becomes the Yod of He. It is for this reason that the primary or cosmic creation terminates in the rest of the Seventh Day, for it can proceed no further until a fresh starting-point is found. But when this fresh starting-point is found in Man realizing his relation to the "Father," we start a new series and strike the Creative Octave and therefore the Resurrection takes place, not on the Sabbath or Seventh Day, but on the Eighth day which then becomes the First day of the new creative week. The *principle* of the Resurrection is the realization by man of his individualization of the Spirit and his recognition of the fact that, since the Spirit is always the same Spirit, it becomes the Alpha of a new creation from his own centre of being.

Now all this is necessarily an interior process taking place on the mental plane; but if we realize that the creative process is always primarily one of involution, or formation in the spiritual world, we shall grasp something of the meaning of Christ as "The Son of God"—the concentration of the Universal Spirit into a Personality on the spiritual plane correlatively to the individuality of each one who affords the necessary thought-conditions. To all who apprehend it there is then discovered in the Universal Spirit the presence of a Divine Individuality reciprocal to that of the individual man, the recognition of which is the practical solution of all metaphysical problems regarding the emanation of the individual soul from the Universal Spirit and the relations arising therefrom; for it takes these matters out of the region of intellectual speculation, which is never creative but only analytical, and transfers it to the region of feeling and spiritual sensation which is the abode of the creative forces. This personal recognition of the Divine then affords us a new basis of Affirmation, and we need no longer trouble to go further back in order to analyze it, because we know experimentally that it is there; so now we find the starting-point of the new creation ready-made for us according to the archetypal pattern in the Divine Mind itself and therefore perfectly correctly formed. When once this truth is clearly apprehended, whether we reach it by an intellectual process or by simple intuition, we can make it our starting-point and claim to have our thought permeated by the creative power of the Spirit on this basis.

But vast as is the conception thus reached we must remember that it is still a starting-point. It, indeed, transcends our previous range of ideas and so presents a culmination of the cosmic creative series which passes beyond that series and thus brings us to number Eight or the Octave; but on this very account it is the number One of a new creative series which is personal to the individual.

Then, because the Spirit is always the same, we may look for a repetition of the creative process at a higher level, and, as we all know, that process consists first of the involution of Spirit into Substance, and consequently of the subsequent evolution of Substance into forms continually increasing in fitness as vehicles for Spirit: so now we may look for a repetition of this universal process from its new starting-point in the individual mind and expect a corresponding externalization in accordance with our familiar axiom that thoughts are things.

Now it is as such an external manifestation of the Divine ideal that the Christ of the Gospels is set before us. I do not wish to dogmatize, but I will only say that the more clearly we realize the nature of the creative process on the spiritual side the more the current objections to the Gospel narrative lose their force; and it appears to me that to deny that narrative as a point-blank impossibility is to make a similar affirmation with regard to the power of the Spirit in ourselves. You cannot affirm a principle and deny it in the same breath; and if we affirm the externalizing power of the Spirit in our own case, I do not see how we can logically lay down a limit for its action and say that under highly specialized conditions it could not produce highly specialized effects. It is for this reason that St. John puts the question of Christ manifest in the flesh as the criterion of the whole matter (I. John iv., 2). If the Spirit can create at all then you cannot logically limit the extent or method of its working; and since the basis of our expectation of individual expansion is the limitless creative power of the Spirit, to reject the Christ of the Gospels as an impossibility is to cut away the ground from under our own feet. It is one thing to say "I do not understand why the Spirit should have worked in that way"—that is merely an honest statement of our present stage of knowledge, or we may even go the length of saying that we do not feel convinced that it did work in that way—that is a true confession of our intellectual difficulty—but certainly those who are professedly relying on the power of the Spirit to produce external results cannot say that it does not possess that power, or possesses it only in a limited degree: the position is logically self-destructive. What we should do therefore, is to suspend judgment and follow the light as far as we can see it, and by-and-by it will become clearer to us. There are, it appears to me, occult heights in the doctrine of Christ designed by the Supreme Wisdom to counteract corresponding occult depths in the Mystery of Darkness. I do not think it is at all necessary, or even possible, for us to scale these heights or fathom those depths, with our present infantile intelligence, but if we realize how completely the law of our being receives its fulfilment in Christ as far as we know that law, may we not well conceive that there are yet deeper phases of that law the existence of which we can only faintly surmise by intuition? Occasionally just the fringe of the veil is lifted for some of us, but that momentary glance is enough to show us that there are powers and mysteries beyond our present conception. But even there Law reigns supreme, and therefore taking Christ as our basis and starting-point, we start with the Law already fulfilled, whether in those things which are familiar to us or in those realms which are beyond our thought, and so we need have no fear of evil. Our starting-point is that of a divinely ordained security from which we may quietly grow into that higher evolution which is the fulfilment of the law of our own being.

IX

# THE STORY OF EDEN

THE WHOLE BIBLE and the whole history of the world, past, present and future, are contained in embryo in the story of Eden, for they are nothing else than the continuous unfolding of certain great principles which are there allegorically stated. That this is by no means a new notion is shown by the following quotation from Origen:—"Who is there so foolish and without common-sense as to believe that God planted trees in the Garden of Eden like a husbandman; and planted therein the tree of life perceptible to the eyes and to the senses, which gave life to the eater; and another tree which gave to the eater a knowledge of good and evil? I believe that everybody must regard these as figures under which a recondite sense is concealed." Let us, then, follow up the suggestion of this early Father of the Church, and enquire what may be the "recondite sense" concealed under this figure of the two trees. On the face of the story there are two roots, one of Life and the other of Death, two fundamental principles bringing about diametrically opposite results. The distinctive mark of the latter is that it is the knowledge of good and evil, that is to say, the recognition of two antagonistic principles, and so requiring a knowledge of the relations between them to enable us to continually make the needful adjustments to keep ourselves going. Now, in appearance this is exceedingly specious. It looks so entirely reasonable that we do not see its ultimate destructiveness; and so we are told that Eve ate the fruit because she "saw that the tree was pleasant to the eyes." But careful consideration will show us in what the destructive nature of this principle consists. It is based on the fallacy that good is limited by evil, and that you cannot receive any good except through eliminating the corresponding evil by realizing it and beating it back. In this view life becomes a continual combat against every imaginable form of evil, and after we have racked our brains to devise precautions against all possible evil happenings, there remains the chance, and much more than the chance, that we have by no means exhausted the category of negative possibilities, and that others may arise which no amount of foresight on our part could have imagined. The more we see into this position the more intolerable it becomes, because from this stand-point we can never attain any certain basis of action, and the forces of possible evil multiply as we contemplate them. To set forth to out-wit all evil by our own knowledge of its nature is to attempt a task the hopelessness of which becomes apparent when we see it in its true light.

The mistake is in supposing that Life can be generated in ourselves by an intellectual process; but, as we have seen in the preceding lectures, Life is the primary movement of the Spirit, whether in the cosmos or in the individual. In its proper order intellectual knowledge is exceedingly important and useful, but its place in the order of the whole is not that of the Originator. It is not Life in itself, but is a function of life; it is an effect and not the cause. The reason why this is so is because intellectual study is always the study of the various laws which arise from the different *relations* of things to one another; and it therefore presupposes that these things together with their laws are already in existence. Consequently it does not start from the truly creative stand-point, that of creating something entirely new, creation *ex nihilo* as distinguished from *construction,* or the laying-together of existing materials, which is what the word literally means. To recognize evil as a force to be reckoned with is therefore to give up the creative stand-point altogether. It is to quit the plane of First Cause and descend into the realm of secondary causation and lose ourselves amid the confusion of a multiplicity of relative causes and effects without grasping any unifying principle behind them.

Now the only thing that can release us from the inextricable confusion of an infinite multiplicity is the realization of an underlying unity, and at the back of all things we find the presence of one Great Affirmative principle without which nothing could have existence. This, then, is the Root of Life; and if we credit it with being able, not only to supply the power, but also the form for its manifestation we shall see that we need not go beyond this *single* Power for the production of anything. It is Spirit producing Substance out of its own essence, and the Substance taking Form in accordance with the movement of the Spirit. What we have to realize is, not only that this is the way in which the cosmos is brought into existence, but also that, because the Spirit finds a new centre in ourselves, the same process is repeated in our own mentality, and therefore we are continually creating *ex nihilo* whether we know it or not. Consequently, if we look upon evil as a force to be reckoned with, and therefore requiring to be studied, we are in effect creating it; while on the other hand if we realize that there is only *one* force to be considered, and that absolutely good, we are by the law of the creative process bringing that good into manifestation. No doubt for this affirmative use of our creative power it is necessary that we start from the basic conception of a *single* originating power which is absolutely good and life-giving; but if there were a self-originating power which was destructive then no creation could ever have come into existence at all, for the positive and negative self-originating powers would cancel each other and the result would be zero. The fact, therefore, of our own existence is a sufficient proof of the singleness and goodness of the Originating Power, and from this starting-point there is no second power to be taken into consideration, and consequently we do not have to study the evil that may arise out of existing or future circumstances, but require to keep our minds fixed only upon the good which we intend to create. There is a very simple reason for this. It is that every new creation necessarily carries its own law with it and by that law produces new conditions of its own. A balloon affords a familiar illustration of my meaning. The balloon with its freight weighs several hundredweight, yet the introduction of a new factor, the gas, brings with it a law of its own which entirely alters the conditions, and the force of gravity is so completely overcome that the whole mass rises into the air. The Law itself is never altered, but we have previously known it only under limiting conditions. These conditions, however, are no part of the Law itself; and a clearer realization of the Law shows us that it contains in itself the power of transcending them. The law which every new creation carries with it is therefore not a contradiction of the old law but its specialization into a higher mode of action.

Now the ultimate Law is that of production *ex nihilo* by the movement of the Spirit within itself, and all subordinate laws are merely the measurements of the relations which spontaneously arise between different things when they are brought into manifestation, and therefore, if an entirely new thing is created it must necessarily establish entirely new relations and so produce entirely new laws. This is the reason why, if we take the action of pure unmanifested Spirit as our starting-point, we may confidently trust it to produce manifestations of law which, though perfectly new from the stand-point of our past experience, are quite as natural in their own way as any that have gone before. It is on this account that in these addresses I lay so much stress on the fact that Spirit creates *ex nihilo,* that is, out of no pre-existing forms, but simply by its own movement within itself. If, then, this idea is clearly grasped, it logically follows from it that the Root of Life is not to be found in the comparison of good and evil, but in the simple affirmation of the Spirit as the All-creating power of Good. And since, as we have already seen, this same all-creating Spirit finds a centre and fresh starting-point of operation in our own minds, we can trust it to follow the Law of its own being there as much as in the creation of the cosmos.

Only we must not forget that it is working through our own minds. It thinks through our mind, and our mind must be made a suitable channel for this mode of its operation by conforming itself to the broad generic lines of the Spirit's thinking. The reason for this is one which I have sought to impress throughout these lectures, namely, that the specialization of a law is never the denial of it, but on the contrary the fuller recognition of its basic principles; and if this is the case in ordinary physical science it must be equally so when we come to specialize the great Law of Life itself. The Spirit can never change its essential nature as the essence of Life, Love, and Beauty; and if we adopt these characteristics, which constitute the Law of the Spirit, as the basis of our own thinking, and reject all that is contrary to them, then we afford the broad generic conditions for the specialized thinking of the Spirit through our own minds: and the thinking of the Spirit is that *involution,* or passing of spirit into form, which is the whole being of the creative process.

The mind which is all the time being thus formed is our own. It is not a case of control by an external individuality, but the fuller expression of the Universal through an organized mentality which has all along been a less perfect expression of the Universal; and therefore the process is one of growth. We are not losing our individuality, but are coming into fuller possession of ourselves by the conscious recognition of our personal share in the great work of creation. We begin in some slight measure to understand what the Bible means when it speaks of our being "partakers of the Divine nature" (II. Peter i. 4) and we realize the significance of the "unity of the Spirit" (Ephesians iv. 3). Doubtless this will imply changes in our old mode of thinking; but these changes are not forced upon us, they are brought about naturally by the new stand-point from which we now see things. Almost imperceptibly to ourselves we grow into a New Order of Thought which proceeds, not from a knowledge of good and evil, but from the Principle of Life itself. That is what makes the difference between our old thought and our new thought. Our old thought was based upon a comparison of limited facts: our new thought is based upon a comprehension of principles. The difference is like that between the mathematics of the infant, who cannot count beyond the number of apples or marbles put before him, and that of the senior wrangler who is not dependent upon visible objects for his calculations, but plunges boldly into the unknown because he knows that he is working by indubitable principles. In like manner when we realize the infallible Principle of the Creative Law we no longer find we need to see everything cut and dried beforehand, for if so, we could never get beyond the range of our old experiences; but we can move steadily forward because we know the certainty of the creative principle by which we are working, or rather, which is working through us, and that our life, in all its minutest details, is its harmonious expression. Thus the Spirit thinks through our thought only its thought is greater than ours. It is the paradox of the less containing the greater. Our thought will not be objectless or unintelligible to ourselves. It will be quite clear as far as it goes. We shall know exactly what we want to do and why we want to do it, and so will act in a reasonable and intelligent manner. But what we do not know is the greater thought that is all the time giving rise to our smaller thought, and which will open out from it as our lesser thought progresses into form. Then we gradually see the greater thought which prompted our smaller one and we find ourselves working along its lines, guided by the invisible hand of the Creative Spirit into continually increasing degrees of livingness to which we need assign no limits, for it is the expansion of the Infinite within ourselves.

This, as it appears to me, is the hidden meaning of the two trees in Eden, the Garden of the Soul. It is the distinction between a knowledge which is merely that of comparisons between different sorts of conditions, and a knowledge which is that of the Life which gives rise to and therefore controls conditions. Only we must remember that the control of conditions is not to be attained by violent self-assertion which is only recognizing them as substantive entities to be battled with, but by conscious unity with that All-creating Spirit which works silently, but surely, on its own lines of Life, Love, and Beauty.

"Not by might, nor by power, but by My Spirit, saith the Lord of Hosts."

X

# THE WORSHIP OF ISHI

IN HOSEA II. 16 we find this remarkable statement:—"And it shall be at that day, saith the Lord, that thou shalt call Me Ishi, and shalt no more call Me Baali"; and with this we may couple the statement in Isaiah lxii. 4:—"Thou shalt be called Hephzibah, and thy land Beulah; for the Lord delighteth in thee, and thy land shall be married."

In both these passages we find a change of name; and since a name stands for something which corresponds to it, and in truth only amounts to a succinct description, the fact indicated in these texts is a change of condition answering to the change of name.

Now the change from Baali to Ishi indicates an important alteration in the relation between the Divine Being and the worshipper; but since the Divine Being cannot change, the altered relation must result from a change in the stand-point of the worshipper: and this can only come from a new mode of looking at the Divine, that is, from a new order of thought regarding it. Baali means Lord, and Ishi means husband, and so the change in relation is that of a female slave who is liberated and married to her former master. We could not have a more perfect analogy. Relatively to the Universal Spirit the individual soul is esoterically feminine, as I have pointed out in "Bible Mystery and Bible Meaning," because its function is that of the receptive and formative. This is necessarily inherent in the nature of the creative process. But the individual's development as the specializing medium of the Universal Spirit will depend entirely upon his own conception of his relation to it. So long as he only regards it as an arbitrary power, a sort of slave owner, he will find himself in the position of a slave driven by an inscrutable force, he knows not whither or for what purpose. He may worship such a God, but his worship is only the worship of fear and ignorance, and there is no personal interest in the matter except to escape some dreaded punishment. Such a worshipper would gladly escape from his divinity, and his worship, when analyzed, will be found to be little else than disguised hatred. This is the natural result of a worship based upon *unexplained* traditions instead of intelligible principles, and is the very opposite of that worship in Spirit and in truth which Jesus speaks of as the true worship.

But when the light begins to break in upon us, all this becomes changed. We see that a system of terrorism cannot give expression to the Divine Spirit, and we realize the truth of St. Paul's words, "He hath not given us the spirit of fear, but of power, and of love, and of a sound mind." As the true nature of the relation between the individual mind and the Universal Mind becomes clearer, we find it to be one of mutual action and re-action, a perfect reciprocity which cannot be better symbolized than by the relation between an affectionate husband and wife. Everything is done from love and nothing from compulsion, there is perfect confidence on both sides, and both are equally indispensable to each other. It is simply the carrying out of the fundamental maxim that the Universal cannot act on the plane of the Particular except through the Particular; only this philosophical axiom develops into a warm living intercourse.

Now this is the position of the soul which is indicated by the name Hephzibah. In common with all other words derived from the Semitic root "hafz" it implies the idea of guarding, just as in the East a *hafiz* is one who guards the letter of the Koran by having the whole book by heart, and in many similar expressions. Hephzibah may therefore be translated as "a guarded one," thus recalling the New Testament description of those who are "guarded into salvation." It is precisely this conception of being guarded by a superior power that distinguishes the worship of Ishi from that of Baali. A special relation has been established between the Divine Spirit and the individual soul, one of absolute confidence and personal intercourse. This does not require any departure from the general law of the universe, but is due to that specializing of the law through the presentation of special conditions personal to the individual, of which I have spoken before. But all the time there has been no change in the Universal Spirit, the only change has been in the mental attitude of the individual—he has come into a new thought, a clearer perception of God. He has faced the questions, What is God? Where is God? How does God work? and he has found the answer in the apostolic statement that God is "over all, through all, and in all," and he realises that "God" is the root of his (the individual's) own being, ever present *in* him, ever working *through* him, and universally present around him.

This realization of the true relation between the Originating Spirit and the individual mind is what is esoterically spoken of as the Mystical Marriage in which the two have ceased to be separate and have become one. As a matter of fact they always were one, but since we can apprehend things only from the stand-point of our own consciousness, it is our recognition of the fact that makes it a practical reality for ourselves. But an intelligent recognition will never make a confusion of the two parts of which the whole consists, and will never lead the individual to suppose that he is handling a blind force or that a blind force is handling him. He will neither dethrone God, nor lose himself by absorption in deity, but he will recognize the reciprocity of the Divine and the human as the natural and logical outcome of the essential conditions of the creative process.

And what is the Whole which is thus created? It is our conscious *personality;* and therefore whatever we draw from the Universal Spirit acquires in us the quality of personality. It is that process of differentiation of the universal into the particular of which I have so often spoken, which, by a rude analogy, we may compare to the differentiation of the universal electric fluid into specific sorts of power by its passage through suitable apparatus. It is for this reason that relatively to ourselves the Universal Spirit must necessarily assume a personal aspect, and that the aspect which it will assume will be in exact correspondence with our own conception of it. This is in accordance with mental and spiritual laws inherent in our own being, and it is on this account that the Bible seeks to build up our conception of God on such lines as will set us free from all fear of evil, and thus leave us at liberty to use the creative power of our thought affirmatively from the stand-point of a calm and untroubled mind. This stand-point can only be reached by passing beyond the range of the happenings of the moment, and this can only be done by the discovery of our immediate relation to the undifferentiated source of all good. I lay stress on these words "immediate" and "undifferentiated" because in them is contained the secret of the whole position. If we could not draw immediately from the Universal Spirit our receiving would be subject to the limitations of the channel through which it reached us; and if the force which we receive were not undifferentiated in itself it could not take appropriate form in our own minds and become to each of us just what we require it to be. It is this power of the human soul to differentiate limitlessly from the Infinite that we are apt to overlook, but as we come to realize that the soul is itself a reflection and image of the Infinite Spirit—and a clear recognition of the cosmic creative process shows that it cannot be anything else—we find that it must possess this power, and that in fact it is our possession of this power which is the whole *raison d'etre* of the creative process: if the human soul did not possess an unlimited power of differentiation from the Infinite, then the Infinite would not be reflected in it, and consequently the Infinite Spirit would find no outlet for its *conscious* recognition of itself as the Life, Love, and Beauty which it is. We can never too deeply ponder the old esoteric definition of Spirit as "the Power which knows itself": the secret of all things, past, present, and future is contained in these few words. The self-recognition or self-contemplation of Spirit is the primary movement out of which all creation proceeds, and the attainment in the individual of a fresh centre for self-recognition is what the Spirit *gains* in the process—this *gain* accruing to the Spirit is what is referred to in the parables where the lord is represented as receiving increase from his servants.

When the individual perceives this relation between himself and Infinite Spirit, he finds that he has been raised from a position of slavery to one of reciprocity. The Spirit cannot do without him any more than he can do without the Spirit: the two are as necessary to each other as the two poles of an electric battery. The Spirit is the unlimited essence of Love, Wisdom, and Power, all three in one undifferentiated and waiting to be differentiated by *appropriation,* that is, by the individual *claiming* to be the channel of their differentiation. It only requires the claim to be made with the recognition that by the Law of Being it is bound to be answered, and the right feeling, the right seeing, and the right working for the particular matter we have in hand will flow in quite naturally. Our old enemies, doubt and fear, may seek to bring us back under bondage to Baali, but our new stand-point for the recognition of the All-originating Spirit as being absolutely unified with ourselves must always be kept resolutely in mind; for, short of this, we are not working on the creative level—we are creating, indeed, for we can never divest ourselves of our creative power, but we are creating in the image of the old limiting and destructive conditions, and this is merely perpetuating the cosmic Law of Averages, which is just what the individual has to rise superior to. The creative level is where new laws begin to manifest themselves in a new order of conditions, something transcending our past experiences and thus bringing about a real advance; for it is no advance only to go on in the same old round even if we kept at it for centuries: it is the steady go-ahead nature of the Spirit that has made the world of to-day an improvement upon the world of the pterodactyl and the icthiosaurus, and we must look for the same forward movement of the Spirit from its new starting-point in ourselves.

Now it is this special, personal, and individual relation of the Spirit to ourselves which is typified by the names Ishi and Hephzibah. From this stand-point we may say that as the individual wakes up to the oneness with the Spirit, the Spirit wakes up to the same thing. It becomes conscious of itself through the consciousness of the individual, and thus is solved the paradox of individual self-recognition by the Universal Spirit, without which no *new*-creative power could be exercised and all things would continue to proceed in the old merely cosmic order. It is of course true that in the merely generic order the Spirit must be present in every form of Life, as the Master pointed out when He said that not a sparrow falls to the ground without "the Father." But as the sparrows He alluded to had been shot and were on sale at a price which shows that this was the fate of a good many of them, we see here precisely that stage of manifestation where the Spirit has not woke up to individual self-recognition, and remains at the lower level of self-recognition, that of the generic or race-spirit. The Master's comment, "Ye are of more value than many sparrows" points out this difference: in us the generic creation has reached the level which affords the conditions for the waking up of the Spirit to self-recognition in the Individual.

And we must bear in mind that all this is perfectly natural. There is no posing or straining after effect about it. If *you* have to pump up the Life, who is going to put the Life into you to pump it? Therefore it is spontaneous or nothing. That is why the Bible speaks of it as the free gift of God. It cannot be anything else. You cannot originate the originating force; it must originate you: but what you can do is to distribute it. Therefore immediately you experience any sense of friction be sure there is something wrong somewhere; and since God can never change, you may be sure that the friction is being caused by some error in your own thinking—you are limiting the Spirit in some way: set to work to find out what it is. It is always *limiting* the Spirit that does this. You are tying it down to conditions somewhere, saying it is bound by reason of some existing forms. The remedy is to go back to the original starting-point of the Cosmic Creation and ask, Where were the pre-existing forms that dictated to the Spirit then? Then because the Spirit never changes it is *still the same,* and is just as independent of existing conditions now as it was in the beginning; and so we must pass over all existing conditions, however apparently adverse, and go straight to the Spirit as the originator of new forms and new conditions. This is real New Thought, for it does not trouble about the old things, but is going straight ahead from where we are now. When we do this, just trusting the Spirit, and not laying down the particular details of its action—just telling it what we want without dictating *how* we are to get it—we shall find that things will open out more and more clearly day by day both on the inner and the outer plane. Remember that the Spirit is alive and working here and now, for if ever the Spirit is to get from the past into the future it must be by passing through the present; therefore what you have to do is to acquire the habit of living direct from the Spirit here and now. You will soon find that this is a matter of personal intercourse, perfectly natural and not requiring any abnormal conditions for its production. You just treat the Spirit as you would any other kind-hearted sensible person, remembering that it is always there—"closer than hands and feet," as Tennyson says—and you will gradually begin to appreciate its reciprocity as a very practical fact indeed.

This is the relation of Hephzibah to Ishi, and is that worship in Spirit and in truth which needs neither the temple in Jerusalem nor yet in Samaria for its acceptance, for the whole world is the temple of the Spirit and you yourself its sanctuary. Bear this in mind, and remember that nothing is too great or too small, too interior or too external, for the Spirit's recognition and operation, for the Spirit is itself both the Life and the Substance of all things and it is also Self-recognition from the stand-point of your own individuality; and therefore, because the Self-recognition of Spirit is the Life of the creative process, you will, by simply trusting the Spirit to work according to its own nature, pass more and more completely into that New Order which proceeds from the thought of Him who says, "Behold I make all things new."

# XI

# THE SHEPHERD AND THE STONE

THE METAPHOR OF the Shepherd and the Sheep is of constant occurrence throughout the Bible and naturally suggests the idea of the guiding, guarding, and feeding both of the individual sheep and of the whole flock and it is not difficult to see the spiritual correspondence of these things in a general sort of way. But we find that the Bible combines the metaphor of the Shepherd with another metaphor, that of "the Stone," and at first sight the two seem rather incongruous.

"From thence is the Shepherd the Stone of Israel," says the Old Testament (Genesis xlix. 24), and Jesus calls himself both "The Good Shepherd" and "The Stone which the builders rejected." The Shepherd and the Stone are thus identified and we must therefore seek the interpretation in some conception which combines the two. A shepherd suggests Personal care for the welfare of the sheep, and an intelligence greater than theirs. A stone suggests the idea of Building, and consequently of measurement, adaptation of parts to whole, and progressive construction according to plan. Combining these two conceptions we get the idea of the building of an edifice whose stones are persons, each taking their more or less conscious part in the construction—thus a building, not constructed from without, but self-forming by a principle of growth from within under the guidance of a Supreme Wisdom permeating the whole and conducting it stage by stage to ultimate completeness. This points to a Divine Order in human affairs with which we may more or less consciously co-operate: both to our personal advantage and also to the furtherance of the great scheme of human evolution as a whole; the ultimate purpose being to establish in *all* men that principle of "The Octave" to which I have already alluded; and in proportion as some adumbration of this principle is realized by individuals and by groups of individuals they specialize the law of race-development, even though they may not be aware of the fact, and so come under a *specialized* working of the fundamental Law, which thus differentiates them from other individuals and nationalities, as by a peculiar guidance, producing higher developments which the merely generic operation of the Law could not.

Now if we keep steadily in mind that, though the purpose, or Law of Tendency, or the Originating Spirit must always be universal in its nature, it must necessarily be individual in its operation, we shall see that this universal purpose can only be accomplished through the instrumentality of specific means. This results from the fundamental proposition that the Universal can only work on the plane of the Particular by becoming the individual and particular; and when we grasp the conception that the merely generic operation of the Creative Law has now brought the human race as far as it can, that is to say it has completely evolved the merely natural *genus homo,* it follows that if any further development is to take place it can only be by the co-operation of the individual himself. Now it is the spread of this individual co-operation that the forward movement of the Spirit is leading us to, and it is the gradual extension of this universal principle that is alluded to in the prophecy of Daniel regarding the Stone cut out without hands that spreads until it fills the whole earth (Daniel ii. 34 and 44). According to the interpretation given by Daniel, this Stone is the emblem of a spiritual Kingdom, and the identity of the Stone and the Shepherd indicates that the Kingdom of the Stone must be also the Kingdom of the Shepherd; and the Master, who identified himself with both the Stone and the Shepherd, emphatically declared that this Kingdom was, in its essence, an interior Kingdom—"the Kingdom of Heaven is within you." We must look for its foundation therefore, in a spiritual principle or mental law inherent in the constitution of all men but waiting to be brought into fuller development by more accurate compliance with its essential requirements; which is precisely the method by which science has evoked powers from the laws of nature which were undreamt of in former ages; and in like manner the recognition of our true relation to the Universal Spirit, which is the source of all individual being, must lead to an advance both for the race and for the individual such as we can at present scarcely form the faintest idea of, but which we dimly apprehend through the intuition and speak of as the New Order. The approach of this New Order is everywhere making itself vaguely felt; it is, as the French say, in the air, and the very vagueness and mystery attending it is causing a feeling of unrest as to what form it may assume. But to the student of Spiritual Law this should not be the case. He knows that the Form is always the expression of the Spirit, and therefore, since he is in touch with the forward movement of the Spirit, he knows that he himself will always be harmoniously included in any form of development which the Great Forward Movement may take. This is the practical and personal benefit arising from the realization of the Principle which is symbolized under the two-fold metaphor of the Shepherd and the Stone and in all those new developments which are perhaps even now within measurable distance, we can rest on the knowledge that we are under the care of a kind Shepherd, and under the formation of a wise Master Builder.

But the principle of the Shepherd and the Stone is not something hitherto unheard of which is only to come into existence in the future. If there were no manifestations of this principle in the past, we might question whether there were any such principle at all; but a careful study of the subject will show us that it has been at work all through the ages, sometimes in modes more immediately bearing the aspect of the Shepherd, and sometimes in modes more immediately bearing the aspect of the Stone, though the one always implies the other, for they are the same thing seen from different points of view. The subject is one of immense interest, but covering such a wide range of study that all I can do here is to point out that such a field of investigation exists and is worth exploration; and the exploration brings its reward with it, not only by putting us in possession of the key to the history of the past, but by showing us that it is the key to the history of the future also, and furthermore by making evident on a large scale the working of the same principle of Spiritual Law by cooperation with which we may facilitate the process of our own individual evolution. It thus adds a vivid interest to life, giving us something worth looking forward to and introducing us to a personal future which is not limited by the proverbial threescore years and ten.

Now, we have seen that the first stage in the Creative Process is always that of Feeling—a reaching-out by the Spirit in a particular direction, and therefore we may look for something of the same kind in the development of the great principle which we are now considering. And we find this first vague movement of this great principle in the intuitions of a particular race which appears from time immemorial to have combined the two characteristics of nomad wandering with their flocks and herds and the symbolization of their religious beliefs in monuments of stone. The monuments themselves have taken different forms in different countries and ages, but the identity of their symbolism becomes clear under careful investigation. Together with this symbolism we always find the nomad character of the builders and that they are invested with an aura of mystery and romance such as we find nowhere else, though we always find it surrounding these builders, even in countries so far apart as India and Ireland. Then, as we pass beyond the merely monumental stage, we find threads of historical evidence connecting the different branches of this race, increasing in their complexity and strengthening in their cumulative force as we go on, until at last we are brought to the history of the age in which we live; and finally most remarkable affinities of language put the finishing touch to the mass of proofs which can be gathered along all these different lines. In this magic circle countries so remote from one another as Ireland and Greece, Egypt and India, Palestine and Persia, are brought into close contiguity—a similar tradition, and even a similar nomenclature, unite the mysterious builders of the Great Pyramid with the equally mysterious builders of the Round Towers of Ireland—and the Great Pyramid itself, perhaps antedating the call of Abraham, re-appears as the official seal of the United States; while tradition traces the crowning-stone in Westminster Abbey back to the time of Solomon's temple and even earlier. For the most part the erewhile wanderers are now settled in their destined homes, but the Anglo-Saxon race—the People of the Corner-Stone—are still the pioneers among the nations, and there is something esoteric in the old joke that when the North Pole is reached a Scotchman will be found there. And not least in the chain of evidence is the link afforded by a tribe who are wanderers still, the Gipsies with their duplicate of the Pyramid in the pack of cards—a volume which has been called "The Devil's Picture Book" by those who know it only in its misuse and inversion, but which when interpreted in the light of the knowledge we are now gaining, affords a signal instance of that divine policy by which as St. Paul says, God employs the foolish things of this world to confute the wise; while a truer apprehension of the Gipsies themselves indicates their unmistakable connection with that race who through all its wanderings has ever been the guardian of the Stone.

In these few paragraphs I have only been able to point out very briefly the broad lines of enquiry into a subject of national importance to the British and American peoples, and which interests us personally, not only as members of these nations, but as affording proof on the largest scale of the same specialization of universal laws which each of us has to effect individually for ourself. But whether the process be individual or national it is always the same, and is the translation to the very highest plane—that of the All-originating Life itself—of the old maxim that "Nature will obey us exactly in proportion as we first obey Nature"; it is the old parable of the lord who, finding his servants girt and awaiting him, then girds himself and serves them (Luke xii. 35 to 37). The nation or the individual who thus realizes the true principle of the Shepherd and the Stone, comes under a special Divine guidance and protection, not by a favouritism incompatible with the conception of universal Law, but by the very operation of the Law itself. They have come into touch with its higher possibilities, and to recur to an analogy which I have already employed, they learn to make their iron float by the very same law by which it sinks; and so they become the flock of the Great Shepherd and the building of the Great Architect, and each one, however insignificant his or her sphere may appear, becomes a sharer in the great work, and by a logical consequence begins to grow on new lines of development for the simple reason that a new principle necessarily produces new modes of manifestation. If the reader will think over these things he will see that the promises contained in the Bible, whether national or personal, are nothing else than statements of the universal law of Cause and Effect applied to the inmost principles of our being, and that therefore it is not mere rhapsody, but the figurative expression of a great truth when the Psalmist says "The Lord is my Shepherd," and "Thou art my God and the Rock of my salvation."

## XII

# SALVATION IS OF THE JEWS

WHAT DOES THIS SAYING of the Master's mean? Certainly not a mere arrogant assumption in favour of His own nationality—such an idea is negatived, not only by the universality of all His other teaching, but also by the very instruction in which these words occur, for He declared that the Jewish temple was equally with the Samaritan of no account in the matter. He said that the true worship was purely spiritual and entirely independent of places and ceremonies, while at the same time He emphasized the Jewish expectation of a Messiah, so that in this teaching we are met by the paradox of a universal principle combined with what at first sight appears like a tribal tradition quite incompatible with any recognition of the universal reign of law. How to reconcile these apparent opposites, therefore, seems to be the problem which He here sets before us. Its solution is to be found in that principle which I have endeavoured to elucidate throughout these lectures, the specializing of universal law. Opinions may differ as to whether the Bible narrative of the birth of Christ is to be taken literally or symbolically, but as to the spiritual principle involved there can, I think, be no difference of opinion. It is that of the specialization by the individual of the generic relation of the soul to the Infinite Spirit from which it proceeds. The relation itself is universal and results from the very nature of the creative process, but the law of the universal relation admits of particular specialization exactly in the same way as all other natural laws—it is simply applying to the supreme Law of Life the same method by which we have learnt to make iron float, that is to say by a fuller recognition of what the Law is in itself. Whatever other meanings we may apply to the name Messiah, it undoubtedly stands for the absolutely perfect manifestation in the individual of all the infinite possibilities of the Principle of Life.

Now it was because this grand ideal is the basis on which the Hebrew nationality was founded that Jesus made this statement. This foundation had been lamentably misconceived by the Jewish people; but nevertheless, however imperfectly, they still held by it, and from them this ideal has spread throughout the Christian world. Here also it continues to be lamentably misconceived, nevertheless it is still retained, and only needs to be recognized in its true light as a universal principle, instead of an unintelligible dogma, to become the salvation of the world. Hence, as affording the medium through which this supreme ideal has been preserved and spread, it is true that "Salvation is of the Jews."

Their fundamental idea was right but their apprehension of it was wrong—that is why the Master at the same time sweeps away the national worship of the temple and preserves the national idea of the Messiah; and this is equally true of the Christian world at the present day. If salvation is anything real it must have its cause in some law, and if there is a law it must be founded upon some universal principle: therefore it is this principle which we must seek if we would understand this teaching of the Master's.

Now whether we take the Bible story of the birth of Christ literally or symbolically, it teaches one great lesson. It teaches that the All-originating Spirit is the true Parent of the individual both in soul and body. This is nothing else than realizing from the stand-point of the individual what we cannot help realizing in regard to the original creation of the cosmos—it is the realization that the All-originating Spirit is at once the Life and the Substance in each individual here and now, just as it must have been in the origin of all things. Human parentage counts for nothing—it is only the channel through which Universal Spirit has acted for the concentration of an individual centre; but the ultimate cause of that centre, both in life and substance, continues at every moment to be the One same Originating Spirit.

This recognition cuts away the root of all the power of the negative, and so in principle it delivers us from all evil, for the root of evil is the denial of the power of the Spirit to produce good. When we realize that the Spirit is finding its own individualization in us in its two-fold essence as Life and Substance, then we see that it must be both able and willing to create for us all good. The only limit is that which we ourselves impose by denying its operation, and when we realize the inherent creativeness of Spirit we find that there is no reason why we should stop short at any point and say that it can go no further. Our error is in looking on the life of the body as separate from the life of the Spirit, and this error is met by the consideration that, in its ultimate nature, Substance must emanate from Spirit and is nothing else than the record of Spirit's conception of itself as finding expression in space and time. And when this becomes clear it follows that Substance need not be taken into calculation at all. The material form stands in the same relation to Spirit that the image projected on the screen stands to the slide in the lantern. If we wish to change the exhibited subject we do not manipulate the reflection on the screen, but we alter the slide; and in like manner, when we come to realize the true nature of the creative process, we learn that the exterior things are to be changed by a change of the interior spiritual attitude. Our spiritual attitude will always be determined by our conception of our relation to God or Infinite Spirit; and so when we begin to see that this relation is one of absolute reciprocity—that it is the self-recognition of Infinite Spirit from our own centre of consciousness—then we find that the whole Secret of Life consists in simple reliance upon the All-creating Spirit as consciously identifying itself with us. It has, so to say, awakened to a new mode of self-recognition peculiar to ourselves, in which we individually form the centre of its creative energy. To realize this is to specialize the Principle of Life. The logic of it is simple. We have found that the originating movement of Spirit from which all creation proceeds can only be Self-contemplation. Then, since the Original Spirit cannot change its nature its self-contemplation through our own minds must be as creative in, for, and through us as it ever was in the beginning; and consequently we find the original creative process repeated in ourselves and directed by the conscious thought of our own minds.

In all this there is no place for the consideration of outward conditions, whether of body or circumstances; for they are only effects and not the cause; and therefore when we reach this stand-point we cease to take them into our calculations. Instead we employ the method of self-contemplation, knowing that this is the creative method, and so we contemplate ourselves as allied to the infinite Love and Wisdom of the Divine Spirit which will take form through our conscious thought, and so act creatively as a Special Providence entirely devoted to guarding, guiding, providing for, and illuminating us. The whole thing is perfectly natural when seen from a clear recognition of what the creative working of Spirit must be in itself; and when it is realized in this perfectly natural manner all strain and effort to compel its action ceases—we are at one with the All-creating Power which has now found a new centre in ourselves from which to continue its creative work to more perfect manifestation than could be attained through the unspecialized generic conditions of the merely cosmic order.

Now this is what Messiah stands for, and therefore it is written that "to them gave He power to become sons of God, even to as many as believe on His Name." This "belief" is the recognition of a universal principle and personal reliance upon it as a law which cannot be broken; for it is the Law of the whole creative process specialized in our own individuality. Then, too, however great may be the mystery, the removal and cleansing away of all sin follows as an essential part of this realization of new life; and it is in this sense that we may read all that the Bible tells us on this aspect of the subject. The *principle* of it is Love; for when we are reunited to the Parent Spirit in mutual confidence and love, what room is there on either side for any remembrance of our past failures?

This, then, is what Messiah stands for to the individual; but if we can conceive a nation based upon such a recognition of its special relation to the Directing Power of the Universe, such a people must of necessity become the leader of the nations, and those who oppose it must fail by a self-destructive principle inherent in the very nature of the position they take up. The leadership resulting from such a national self-recognition, will not be based upon conquest and compulsion, but will come naturally. Other nations will enquire the reason for the phenomenal success and prosperity of the favoured people, and finding this reason in a universal Law, they will begin to apply the same law in the same manner, and thus the same results will spread from country to country until at last the whole earth will be full of the glory of the Lord. And such a nation, and rather company of nations, exists. To trace its present development from its ancient beginnings is far beyond the scope of this volume, and still more to speculate upon its further growth; but to my readers on both sides of the Atlantic I may say that this people is the Anglo-Saxon race throughout the world. I write these lines upon the historic Hill of Tara; this will convey a hint to many of my readers. At some future time I may enlarge upon this subject; but at present my aim is merely to suggest some lines of thought arising from the Master's saying that "Salvation is of the Jews."

# The Creative Process in the Individual

1910, expanded 1915

THE AUTHOR HERE EXPLAINS SCIENTIFICALLY THE SEquence of creative action, from the first beginnings of life through the development of the race to the need of the present day—the perfect realization of the divine right of creation. The knowledge of oneself—made in the likeness of the great creative Power and necessarily sharing in that power to create what is good—will open up a wonderful vista of possibilities to all who follow unerringly the law of their own being. If we knowingly and willingly co-operate with this law, our outlook upon life broadens to great interests and to certainty in our own efforts toward accomplishing whatever end we desire—a wonderful promise to the faithful student.

# CONTENTS

*I say no man has ever yet been half devout enough,*
*None has ever yet adored or worship'd half enough,*
*None has begun to think how divine he himself is,*
*and how certain the future is.*
*I say that the real and permanent grandeur*
*of these States must be their religion,*
*Otherwise there is no real and permanent grandeur.*

—WALT WHITMAN

## FOREWORD

IN THE PRESENT volume I have endeavored to set before the reader the conception of a sequence of creative action commencing with the formation of the globe and culminating in a vista of infinite possibilities attainable by every one who follows up the right line for their unfoldment.

I have endeavored to show that, starting with certain incontrovertible scientific facts, all these things logically follow, and that therefore, however far these speculations may carry us beyond our past experience, they nowhere break the thread of an intelligible connection of cause and effect.

I do not, however, offer the suggestions here put forward in any other light than that of purely speculative reasoning; nevertheless, no advance in any direction can be made except by speculative reasoning going back to the first principles of things which we do know and thence deducing the conditions under which the same principles might be carried further and made to produce results hitherto unknown. It is to this method of thought that we owe all the advantages of civilization from matches and post-offices to motor-cars and aeroplanes, and we may therefore be encouraged to hope such speculations as the present may not be without their ultimate value. Relying on the maxim that Principle is not bound by Precedent we should not limit our expectations of the future; and if our speculations lead us to the conclusion that we have reached a point where we are not only able, but also *required,* by the law of our own being, to take a more active part in our personal evolution than heretofore, this discovery will afford us a new outlook upon life and widen our horizon with fresh interests and brightening hopes.

If the thoughts here suggested should help any reader to clear some mental obstacles from his path the writer will feel that he has not written to no purpose. Only each reader must think out these suggestions for himself.

No writer or lecturer can convey an idea *into* the minds of his audience. He can only put it before them, and what they will make of it depends entirely upon themselves—assimilation is a process which no one can carry out for us.

To the kindness of my readers on both sides of the Atlantic, and in Australia and New Zealand, I commend this little volume, not, indeed, without a deep sense of its many shortcomings, but at the same time encouraged by the generous indulgence extended to my previous books.

T.T.
*June, 1910.*

I

# THE STARTING-POINT

IT IS AN old saying that "Order is Heaven's First Law," and like many other old sayings it contains a much deeper philosophy than appears immediately on the surface. Getting things into a better order is the great secret of progress, and we are now able to fly through the air, not because the laws of Nature have altered, but because we have learnt to arrange things in the right order to produce this result—the things themselves had existed from the beginning of the world, but what was wanting was the introduction of a Personal Factor which, by an intelligent perception of the possibilities contained in the laws of Nature, should be able to bring into working reality ideas which previous generations would have laughed at as the absurd fancies of an unbalanced mind. The lesson to be learnt from the practical aviation of the present day is that of the triumph of principle over precedent, of the working out of an *idea* to its logical conclusions in spite of the accumulated testimony of all past experience to the contrary; and with such a notable example before us can we say that it is futile to enquire whether by the same method we may not unlock still more important secrets and gain some knowledge of the unseen causes which are at the back of external and visible conditions, and then by bringing these unseen causes into a better order make practical working realities of possibilities which at present seem but fantastic dreams? It is at least worth while taking a preliminary canter over the course, and this is all that this little volume professes to attempt; yet this may be sufficient to show the lay of the ground.

Now the first thing in any investigation is to have some idea of what you are looking for—to have at least some notion of the general direction in which to go—just as you would not go up a tree to find fish though you would for birds' eggs. Well, the general direction in which we all want to go is that of getting more out of Life than we have ever got out of it—we want to be more alive in ourselves and to get all sorts of improved conditions in our environment. However happily any of us may be circumstanced we can all conceive something still better, or at any rate we should like to make our present good permanent; and since we shall find as our studies advance that the prospect of increasing possibilities keeps opening out more and more widely before us, we may say that what we are in search of is the secret of getting more out of Life in a continually progressive degree. This means that what we are looking for is something personal, and that it is to be obtained by producing conditions which do not yet exist; in other words it is nothing less than the exercise of a certain creative power in the sphere of our own particular world. So, then, what we want is to introduce our own Personal Factor into the realm of unseen causes. This is a big thing, and if it is possible at all it must be by some sequence of cause and effect, and this sequence it is our object to discover. The law of Cause and Effect is one we can never get away from, but by carefully following it up we may find that it will lead us further than we had anticipated.

Now, the first thing to observe is that if *we* can succeed in finding out such a sequence of cause and effect as the one we are in search of, somebody else may find out the same creative secret also; and then, by the hypothesis of the case, we should both be armed with an infallible power, and if we wanted to employ this power against each other we should be landed in the "impasse" of a conflict between two powers each of which was irresistible. Consequently it follows that the first principle of this power must be Harmony. It cannot be antagonizing itself from different centers—in other words its operation in a simultaneous order at every point is the first necessity of its being. What we are in search of, then, is a sequence of cause and effect so universal in its nature as to include harmoniously all possible variations of individual expression. This primary necessity of the Law for which we are seeking should be carefully borne in mind, for it is obvious that any sequence which transgresses this primary essential must be contrary to the very nature of the Law itself, and consequently cannot be conducting us to the exercise of true creative power.

What we are seeking, therefore, is to discover how to arrange things in such an order as to set in motion a train of causation that will harmonize our own conditions without antagonizing the exercise of a like power by others. This therefore means that all individual exercise of this power is the particular application of a universal power which itself operates creatively on its own account independently of these individual applications; and the harmony between the various individual applications is brought about by all the individuals bringing their own particular action into line with this independent creative action of the original power. It is in fact another application of Euclid's axiom that things which are equal to the same thing are equal to one another; so that though I may not know for what purpose some one may be using this creative power in Pekin, I do know that if he and I both realize its true nature we cannot by any possibility be working in opposition to one another. For these reasons, having now some general idea of what it is we are in search of, we may commence our investigation by considering this common factor which must be at the back of all individual exercise of creative power, that is to say, the Generic working of the Universal Creative Principle.

That such a Universal Creative Principle is at work we at once realize from the existence of the world around us with all its inhabitants, and the inter-relation of all parts of the cosmic system shows its underlying Unity—thus the animal kingdom depends on the vegetable, the vegetable kingdom on the mineral, the mineral or globe of the earth on its relation to the rest of the solar system, and possibly our solar system is related by a similar law to the distribution of other suns with their attendant planets throughout space. Our first glance therefore shows us that the All-originating Power must be in essence Unity and in manifestation Multiplicity, and that it manifests as Life and Beauty through the unerring adaptation of means to ends—that is so far as its cosmic manifestation of ends goes: what we want to do is to carry this manifestation still further by operation from an individual standpoint. To do this is precisely our place in the Order of Creation, but we must defer the question why we hold this place till later on.

One of the earliest discoveries we all make is the existence of Matter. The bruised shins of our childhood convince us of its solidity, so now comes the question, Why does Matter exist? The answer is that if the form were not expressed in solid substance, things would be perpetually flowing into each other so that no identity could be maintained for a single moment. To this it might be replied that a condition of matter is conceivable in which, though in itself a plastic substance, in a fluent state, it might yet by the operation of will be held in any particular forms desired. The idea of such a condition of matter is no doubt conceivable, and when the fluent matter was thus held in particular forms you would have concrete matter just as we know it now, only with this difference, that it would return to its fluent state as soon as the supporting will was withdrawn. Now, as we shall see later on, this is precisely what matter really is, only the will which holds it together in concrete form is not individual but cosmic.

In itself the Essence of Matter is precisely the fluent substance we have imagined, and as we shall see later on the knowledge of this fact, when realized in its proper order, is the basis of the legitimate control of mind over matter. But a world in which every individual possessed the power of concreting or fluxing matter at his own sweet will irrespective of any universal coordinating principle is altogether inconceivable—the conflict of wills would prevent such a world remaining in existence. On the other hand if we conceive of a number of individuals each possessing this power and all employing it on the lines of a common cosmic unity, then the result would be precisely the same stable condition of matter with which we are familiar—this would be a necessity of fact for the masses who did not possess this power, and a necessity of principle for the few who did. So under these circumstances the same stable conditions of Nature would prevail as at present, varied only when the initiated ones perceived that the order of evolution would be furthered, and not hindered, by calling into action the higher laws. Such occasions would be of rare occurrence, and then the departure from the ordinary law would be regarded by the multitude as a miracle. Also we may be quite sure that no one who had attained this knowledge in the legitimate order would ever perform a "miracle" for his own personal aggrandizement or for the purpose of merely astonishing the beholders—to do so would be contrary to the first principle of the higher teaching which is that of profound reverence for the Unity of the All-originating Principle. The conception, therefore, of such a power over matter being possessed by certain individuals is in no way opposed to our ordinary recognition of concrete matter, and so we need not at present trouble ourselves to consider these exceptions.

Another theory is that matter has no existence at all but is merely an illusion projected by our own minds. If so, then how is it that we all project identically similar images? On the supposition that each mind is independently projecting its own conception of matter a lady who goes to be fitted might be seen by her dressmaker as a cow. Generations of people have seen the Great Pyramid on the same spot; but on the supposition that each individual is projecting his own material world in entire independence of all other individuals there is no reason why any two persons should ever see the same thing in the same place. On the supposition of such an independent action by each separate mind, without any common factor binding them all to one particular mode of recognition, no intercourse between individuals would be possible—then, without the consciousness of relation to other individuals the consciousness of our own individuality would be lost, and so we should cease to have any conscious existence at all. If on the other hand we grant that there is, above the individual minds, a great Cosmic Mind which imposes upon them the necessity of all seeing the same image of Matter, then that image is not a projection of the individual minds but of the Cosmic Mind; and since the individual minds are themselves similar projections of the Cosmic Mind, matter is for them just as much a reality as their own existence. I doubt not that material substance is thus projected by the all-embracing Divine Mind; but so also are our own minds projected by it, and therefore the relation between them and matter is a real relation and not a merely fictitious one.

I particularly wish the student to be clear on this point, that where two factors are projected from a common source their relation to each other becomes an absolute fact in respect of the factors themselves, notwithstanding, that the power of changing that relation by substituting a different projection must necessarily always continue to reside in the originating source. To take a simple arithmetical example—by my power of mental projection working through my eyes and fingers I write 4 × 2. Here I have established a certain numerical relation which can only produce eight as its result. Again, I have power to change the factors and write 4 × 3, in which case 12 is the only possible result, and so on. Working in this way calculation becomes possible. But if every time I wrote 4 that figure possessed an independent power of setting down a different number by which to multiply itself, what would be the result? The first 4 I wrote might set down 3 as its multiplier, and the next might set down 7, and so on. Or if I want to make a box of a certain size and cut lengths of plank accordingly, if each length could capriciously change its width at a moment's notice, how could I ever make the box? I myself may change the shape and size of my box by establishing new relations between the bits of wood, but for the pieces of wood themselves the proportions determined by my mind must remain fixed quantities, otherwise no construction could take place.

This is a very rough analogy, but it may be sufficient to show that for a cosmos to exist at all it is absolutely necessary that there should be a Cosmic Mind binding all individual minds to certain *generic* unities of action, and so producing all things as realities and nothing as illusion. The importance of this conclusion will become more apparent as we advance in our studies.

We have now got at some reason why concrete material form is a necessity of the Creative Process. Without it the perfect Self-recognition of Spirit from the Individual standpoint, which we shall presently find is the means by which the Creative Process is to be carried forward, would be impossible; and therefore, so far from matter being an illusion, it is the necessary channel for the self-differentiation of Spirit and its Expression in multitudinous life and beauty. Matter is thus the necessary Polar Opposite to Spirit, and when we thus recognize it in its right order we shall find that there is no antagonism between the two, but that together they constitute one harmonious whole.

## II

# THE SELF-CONTEMPLATION OF SPIRIT

If we ask how the cosmos came into existence we shall find that ultimately we can only attribute it to the Self-Contemplation of Spirit. Let us start with the facts now known to modern physical science. All material things, including our own bodies, are composed of combinations of different chemical elements such as carbon, oxygen, nitrogen, &c. Chemistry recognizes in all about seventy of these elements each with its peculiar affinities; but the more advanced physical science of the present day finds that they are all composed of one and the same ultimate substance to which the name of Ether has been given, and that the difference between an atom of iron and an atom of oxygen results only from the difference in the number of etheric particles of which each is composed and the rate of their motion within the sphere of the atom, thus curiously coming back to the dictum of Pythagoras that the universe has its origin in Number and Motion. We may therefore say that our entire solar system together with every sort of material substance which it contains is made up of nothing but this one primary substance in various degrees of condensation.

Now the next step is to realize that this ether is everywhere. This is shown by the undulatory theory of light. Light is not a substance but is the effect produced on the eye by the impinging of the ripples of the ether upon the retina. These waves are excessively minute, ranging in length from

1-39,000th of an inch at the red end of the spectrum to 1-57,000th at the violet end. Next remember that these waves are not composed of advancing particles of the medium but pass onwards by the push which each particle in the line of motion gives to the particle next to it, and then you will see that if there were a break of one fifty-thousandth part of an inch in the connecting ether between our eye and any source of light we could not receive light from that source, for there would be nothing to continue the wave-motion across the gap. Consequently as soon as we see light from any source however distant, we know that there must be a continuous body of ether between us and it. Now astronomy shows us that we receive light from heavenly bodies so distant that, though it travels with the incredible speed of 186,000 miles per second, it takes more than two thousand years to reach us from some of them; and as such stars are in all quarters of the heavens we can only come to the conclusion that the primary substance or ether must be universally present.

This means that the raw material for the formation of solar systems is universally distributed throughout space; yet though we find that millions of suns stud the heavens, we also find vast interstellar spaces which show no sign of cosmic activity. Then something has been at work to start cosmic activity in certain areas while passing over others in which the raw material is equally available. What is this something? At first we might be inclined to attribute the development of cosmic energy to the etheric particles themselves, but a little consideration will show us that this is mathematically impossible in a medium which is equally distributed throughout space, for all its particles are in equilibrium and so no one particle possesses *per se* a greater power of originating motion than any other. Consequently the initial movement must be started by something which, though it works on and through the particles of the primary substance, is not those particles themselves. It is this "Something" which we mean when we speak of "Spirit."

Then since Spirit starts the condensation of the primary substance into concrete aggregation, and also does this in certain areas to the exclusion of others, we cannot avoid attributing to Spirit the power of Selection and of taking an Initiative on its own account.

Here, then, we find the *initial* Polarity of Universal Spirit and Universal Substance, each being the complementary of the other, and out of this relation all subsequent evolution proceeds. Being complementary means that each supplies what is wanting in the other, and that the two together thus make complete wholeness. Now this is just the case here. Spirit supplies Selection and Motion. Substance supplies something from which selection can be made and to which Motion can be imparted; so that it is a *sine qua non* for the Expression of Spirit.

Then comes the question, How did the Universal Substance get there? It cannot have made itself, for its only quality is inertia, therefore it must have come from some source having power to project it by some mode of action not of a material nature. Now the only mode of action not of a material nature is Thought, and therefore to Thought we must look for the origin of Substance. This places us at a point antecedent to the existence even of primary substance, and consequently the initial action must be that of the Originating Mind upon Itself, in other words, Self-contemplation.

At this primordial stage neither Time nor Space can be recognized, for both imply measurement of successive intervals, and in the primary movement of Mind upon itself the only consciousness must be that of Present Absolute Being, because no external points exist from which to measure extension either in time or space. Hence we must eliminate the ideas of time and space from our conception of Spirit's *initial* Self-contemplation.

This being so, Spirit's primary contemplation of itself as simply Being necessarily makes its presence universal and eternal, and consequently, paradoxical as it may seem, its independence of Time and Space makes it present throughout all Time and Space. It is the old esoteric maxim that the point expands to infinitude and that infinitude is concentrated in the point. We start, then, with Spirit contemplating itself simply as Being. But to realize your being you must have consciousness, and consciousness can only come by the recognition of your relation to something else. The something else may be an external fact or a mental image; but even in the latter case to conceive the image at all you must mentally stand back from it and look at it—something like the man who was run in by the police at Gravesend for walking behind himself to see how his new coat fitted. It stands thus: if you are not conscious of something you are conscious of nothing, and if you are conscious of nothing, then you are unconscious, so that to be conscious at all you must have something to be conscious of.

This may seem like an extract from "Paddy's Philosophy," but it makes it clear that consciousness can only be attained by the recognition of something which is not the recognizing *ego* itself—in other words consciousness is the realization of some particular sort of *relation* between the cognizing subject and the cognized object; but I want to get away from academical terms into the speech of human beings, so let us take the illustration of a broom and its handle—the two together make a broom; that is one sort of relation; but take the same stick and put a rake-iron at the end of it and you have an altogether different implement. The stick remains the same, but the difference of what is put at the end of it makes the whole thing a broom or a rake. Now the thinking and feeling power is the stick, and the conception which it forms is the thing at the end of the stick, so that the quality of its consciousness will be determined by the ideas which it projects; but to be conscious at all it must project ideas of some sort.

Now of one thing we may be quite sure, that the Spirit of Life must *feel alive.* Then to feel alive it must be conscious, and to be conscious it must have something to be conscious of; therefore the contemplation of itself as standing related to something which is not its own originating self *in propria persona* is a necessity of the case; and consequently the Self-contemplation of Spirit can only proceed by its viewing itself as related to something standing out from itself, just as we must stand at a proper distance to see a picture—in fact the very word "existence" means "standing out." Thus things are called into existence or "outstandingness" by a power which itself does not stand out, and whose presence is therefore indicated by the word "subsistence."

The next thing is that since in the beginning there is nothing except Spirit, its primary feeling of aliveness must be that of being alive *all over;* and to establish such a consciousness of its own universal livingness there must be the recognition of a corresponding *relation* equally extensive in character; and the only possible correspondence to fulfil this condition is therefore that of a universally distributed and plastic medium whose particles are all in perfect equilibrium, which is exactly the description of the Primary Substance or ether. We are thus philosophically led to the conclusion that Universal Substance must be projected by Universal Spirit as a necessary consequence of Spirit's own inherent feeling of Aliveness; and in this way we find that the great Primary Polarity of Being becomes established.

From this point onward we shall find the principle of Polarity in universal activity. It is that relation between opposites without which no external Motion would be possible, because there would be nowhere to move from, and nowhere to move to; and without which external Form would be impossible because there would be nothing to limit the diffusion of substance and bring it into shape. Polarity, or the interaction of Active and Passive, is therefore the basis of all *Evolution.*

This is a great fundamental truth when we get it in its right order; but all through the ages it has been a prolific source of error by getting it in its wrong order. And the wrong order consists in making Polarity the originating point of the Creative Process. What this misconception leads to we shall see later on; but since it is very widely accepted under various guises even at the present day it is well to be on our guard against it. Therefore I wish the student to see clearly that there is something which comes before that Polarity which gives rise to Evolution, and that this something is the original movement of Spirit *within itself,* of which we can best get an idea by calling it Self-contemplation.

Now this may seem an extremely abstract conception and one with which we have no practical concern. I fancy I can hear the reader saying "The Lord only knows how the world started, and it is His business and not mine," which would be perfectly true if this originating faculty were confined to the Cosmic Mind. But it is not, and the same action takes place in our own minds also, only with the difference that it is ultimately subject to that principle of Cosmic Unity of which I have already spoken. But, subject to that unifying principle, this same power of origination is in ourselves also, and our personal advance in evolution depends on our right use of it; and our use of it depends on our recognition that we ourselves give rise to the particular polarities which express themselves in our whole world of consciousness, whether within or without. For these reasons it is very important to realize that Evolution is not the same as Creation. It is the unfolding of potentialities *in*volved in things already created, but not the calling into existence of what does not yet exist—*that* is Creation.

The order, therefore, which I wish the student to observe is, first the Self-contemplation of Spirit producing Polarity, and next Polarity producing Manifestation in Form—and also to realize that it is in this order his own mind operates as a subordinate center of creative energy. When the true place of Polarity is thus recognized, we shall find in it the explanation of all those relations of things which give rise to the whole world of phenomena; from which we may draw the practical inference that if we want to change the manifestation we must change the polarity, and to change the polarity we must get back to the Self-contemplation of Spirit. But in its proper place as the root-principle of all *secondary* causation, Polarity is one of those fundamental facts of which we must never lose sight. The term "Polarity" is adopted from electrical science. In the electric battery it is the connecting together of the opposite poles of zinc and copper that causes a current to flow from one to the other and so provides the energy that rings the bell. If the connection is broken there is no action. When you press the button you make the connection. The same process is repeated in respect of every sort of polarity throughout the universe. Circulation depends on polarity, and circulation is the *manifestation* of Life, which we may therefore say depends on the principle of polarity. In relation to ourselves we are concerned with two great polarities, the polarity of Soul and Body and the polarity of Soul and Spirit; and it is in order that he may more clearly realize their working that I want the student to have some preliminary idea of Polarity as a general principle.

The conception of the Creative Order may therefore be generalized as follows. The Spirit wants to enjoy the reality of its own Life—not merely to vegetate, but to enjoy living—and therefore by Self-contemplation it projects a polar opposite, or complementary, calculated to give rise to the particular sort of *relation* out of which the enjoyment of a certain mode of self-consciousness will necessarily spring. Let this sentence be well pondered over until the full extent of its significance is grasped, for it is the key to the whole matter. Very well, then: Spirit wants to Enjoy Life, and so, by thinking of itself as *having* the enjoyment which it wishes, it produces the conditions which, by their reaction upon itself, give rise to the reality of the sort of enjoyment contemplated. In more scientific language an opposite polarity is induced, giving rise to a current which stimulates a particular mode of sensation, which sensation in turn becomes a fresh starting-point for still further action; and in this way each successive stage becomes the stepping-stone to a still higher degree of sensation—that is, to a Fuller Enjoyment of Life.

Such a conception as this presents us with a Progressive Series to which it is impossible to assign any limit. That the progression must be limitless is clear from the fact that there is never any change in the method. At each successive stage the Creating Power is the Self-consciousness of the Spirit, as realized at that stage, still reaching forward for yet further Enjoyment of Life, and so always keeping on repeating the *one* Creative Process at an ever-rising level; and since these are the sole working conditions, the progress is one which logically admits of no finality. And this is where the importance of realizing the Singleness of the Originating Power comes in, for with a Duality each member would limit the other; in fact, Duality as the Originating Power is inconceivable, for, once more to quote "Paddy's Philosophy," "finality would be reached before anything was begun."

This Creative Process, therefore, can only be conceived of as limitless, while at the same time strictly progressive, that is, proceeding stage by stage, each stage being necessary as a preparation for the one that is to follow. Let us then briefly sketch the stages by which things in our world have got as far as they have. The interest of the enquiry lies in the fact that if we can once get at the principle which is producing these results, we may discover some way of giving it personal application.

On the hypothesis of the Self-contemplation of Spirit being the originating power, we have found that a primary ether, or universal substance, is the necessary correspondence to Spirit's simple awareness of its own being. But though awareness of being is the necessary foundation for any further possibilities it is, so to say, not much to talk about. The foundation fact, of course, is to know that I Am; but immediately on this consciousness there follows the desire for Activity—I want to enjoy my I Am-ness by doing something with it. Translating these words into a state of consciousness in the Cosmic Mind they become a Law of Tendency leading to *localized* activity, and, looking only at our own world, this would mean the condensation of the universal etheric substance into the primary nebula which later on becomes our solar system, this being the correspondence to the Self-contemplation of Spirit as passing into specific activity instead of remaining absorbed in simple awareness of Being. Then this self-recognition would lead to the conception of still more specific activity having its appropriate polar opposite, or material correspondence, in the condensation of the nebula into a solar system.

Now at this stage Spirit's conception of itself is that of Activity, and consequently the material correspondence is Motion, as distinguished from the simple diffused ether which is the correspondence of mere awareness of Being. But what sort of motion? Is the material movement evolved at this stage bound to take any particular form? A little consideration will show us that it is. At this initial stage, the first awakening, so to say, of Spirit into activity, its consciousness can only be that of activity *absolute;* that is, not as related to any other mode of activity because as yet there is none, but only as related to an all-embracing Being; so that the only possible conception of

Activity at this stage is that of *Self-sustained* activity, not depending on any preceding mode of activity because there is none. The law of reciprocity therefore demands a similar self-sustained motion in the material correspondence, and mathematical considerations show that the only sort of motion which can sustain a self-supporting body moving *in vacuo* is a rotary motion bringing the body itself into a spherical form. Now this is exactly what we find at both extremes of the material world. At the big end the spheres of the planets rotating on their axes and revolving round the sun; and at the little end the spheres of the atoms consisting of particles which, modern science tells us, in like manner rotate round a common center at distances which are astronomical as compared with their own mass. Thus the two ultimate units of physical manifestation, the atom and the planet, both follow the same law of self-sustained motion which we have found that, on *a priori* grounds, they ought in order to express the primary activity of Spirit. And we may note in passing that this rotary, or *absolute,* motion is the combination of the only two possible *relative* modes of motion, namely, motion from a point and motion to it, that is to say centrifugal and centripetal motion; so that in rotary, or absolute, motion we find that both the polarities of motion are included, thus repeating on the purely mechanical side the primordial principle of the Unity including the Duality in itself.

But the Spirit wants something more than mechanical motion, something more alive than the preliminary Rota, and so the first step toward individualized consciousness meets us in plant life. Then on the principle that each successive stage affords the platform for a further outlook, plant life is followed by animal life, and this by the Human order in which the liberty of selecting its own conditions is immensely extended. In this way the Spirit's expression of itself has now reached the point where its polar complementary, or Reciprocal, manifests as Intellectual Man—thus constituting the Fourth great stage of Spirit's Self-recognition. But the Creative Process cannot stop here, for, as we have seen, its root in the Self-contemplation of Spirit renders it of necessity an Infinite Progression. So it is no use asking what is its ultimate, for it has no ultimate—its word is "Excelsior"—ever Life and "Life more Abundant." Therefore the question is not as to finality where there is none, but as to the next step in the progression. Four kingdoms we know: what is to be the Fifth? All along the line the progress has been in one direction, namely, toward the development of more perfect Individuality, and therefore on the principle of continuity we may reasonably infer that the next stage will take us still further in the same direction. We want something more perfect than we have yet reached, but our ideas as to what it should be are very various, not to say discordant, for one person's idea of better is another person's idea of worse. Therefore what we want to get at is some broad generalization of principle which will be in advance of our past experiences. This means that we must look for this principle in something that we have not yet experienced, and the only place where we can possibly find principles which have not yet manifested themselves is *in gremio Dei*—that is, in the innermost of the Originating Spirit, or as St. John calls it, "in the bosom of the Father." So we are logically brought to personal participation in the Divine Ideal as the only principle by which the advance into the next stage can possibly be made. Therefore we arrive at the question, What is the Divine Ideal like?

## III

# THE DIVINE IDEAL

WHAT IS THE Divine Ideal? At first it might appear hopeless to attempt to answer such a question, but by adhering to a definite principle we shall find that it will open out, and lead us on, and show us things which we could not otherwise have seen—this is the nature of principle, and is what distinguishes it from mere rules which are only the application of principle under some particular set of conditions. We found two principles as essential in our conception of the Originating Spirit, namely its power of Selection and its power of Initiative; and we found a third principle as its only possible Motive, namely the Desire of the LIVING for ever increasing Enjoyment of Life. Now with these three principles as the very essence of the All-originating Spirit to guide us, we shall, I think, be able to form some conception of that Divine Ideal which gives rise to the Fifth Stage of Manifestation of Spirit, upon which we should now be preparing to enter.

We have seen that the Spirit's Enjoyment of Life is necessarily a *reciprocal*—it must have a corresponding fact in manifestation to answer to it; otherwise by the inherent law of mind no consciousness, and consequently no enjoyment, could accrue; and therefore by the law of continuous progression the required Reciprocal should manifest as a being awakening to the consciousness of the principle by which he himself comes into existence.

Such an awakening cannot proceed from a comparison of one set of existing conditions with another, but only from the recognition of a Power which is independent of all conditions, that is to say, the absolute Self-dependence of the Spirit. A being thus awakened would be the proper correspondence of the Spirit's Enjoyment of Life at a stage not only above mechanical motion or physical vitality, but even above intellectual perception of existing phenomena, that is to say at the stage where the Spirit's Enjoyment consists in recognizing itself as the Source of all things. The position in the Absolute would be, so to speak, the awakening of Spirit to the recognition of its own Artistic Ability. I use the word "Artistic" as more nearly expressing an almost unstatable idea than any other I can think of, for the work of the artist approaches more closely to creation *ex nihilo* than any other form of human activity. The work of the artist is the expression of the self that the artist is, while that of the scientist is the comparison of facts which exist independently of his own personality. It is true that the realm of Art is not without its methods of analysis, but the analysis is that of the artist's own feeling and of the causes which give rise to it. These are found to contain in themselves certain principles which are fundamental to all Art, but these principles are the laws of the creative action of mind rather than those of the limitations of matter. Now if we may transfer this familiar analogy to our conception of the working of the All-Originating Mind we may picture it as the Great Artist giving visible expression to His feeling by a process which, though subject to no restriction from antecedent conditions, yet works by a Law which is inseparable from the Feeling itself—in fact the Law *is* the Feeling, and the Feeling *is* the Law, the Law of Perfect Creativeness.

Some such Self-contemplation as this is the only way in which we can conceive the next, or Fifth, stage of Spirit's Self-recognition as taking place. Having got as far as it has in the four previous stages, that is to the production of intellectual man as its correspondence, the next step in advance must be on the lines I have indicated—unless, indeed, there were a sudden and arbitrary breaking of the Law of Continuity, a supposition which the whole Creative Process up to now forbids us to entertain. Therefore we may picture the Fifth stage of the Self-contemplation of Spirit as its awakening to the recognition of its own Artistic Ability, its own absolute freedom of action and creative power—just as in studio parlance we say that an artist becomes "free of his palette." But by the always present Law of Reciprocity, through which alone self-consciousness can be attained, this Self-recognition of Spirit in the Absolute implies a corresponding objective fact in the world of the Relative; that is to say, the coming into manifestation of a being capable of realizing the Free Creative Artistry of the Spirit, and of recognizing the same principle in himself, while at the same time realizing also the *relation* between the Universal Manifesting Principle and its Individual Manifestation.

Such, it appears to me, must be the conception of the Divine Ideal embodied in the Fifth Stage of the progress of manifestation. But I would draw particular attention to the concluding words of the last paragraph, for if we miss the *relation* between the Universal Manifesting Principle and its Individual Manifestation, we have failed to realize the Principle altogether, whether in the Universal or in the Individual—it is just their interaction that makes each become what it does become—and in this further becoming consists the progression. This relation proceeds from the principle I pointed out in the opening chapter which makes it necessary for the Universal Spirit to be always harmonious with itself; and if this Unity is not recognized by the individual he cannot hold that position of Reciprocity to the Originating Spirit which will enable it to recognize itself as in the Enjoyment of Life at the higher level we are now contemplating—rather the feeling conveyed would be that of something antagonistic, producing the reverse of enjoyment, thus philosophically bringing out the point of the Scriptural injunction, "Grieve not the Spirit." Also the reaction upon the individual must necessarily give rise to a corresponding state of in-harmony, though he may not be able to define his feeling of unrest or to account for it. But on the other hand if the grand harmony of the Originating Spirit within itself is duly regarded, then the individual mind affords a fresh center from which the Spirit contemplates itself in what I have ventured to call its Artistic Originality—a boundless potential of Creativeness, yet always regulated by its own inherent Law of Unity.

And this Law of the Spirit's Original Unity is a very simple one. It is the Spirit's necessary and basic conception of itself. A lie is a statement that something is, which is not. Then, since the Spirit's statement or conception of anything necessarily makes that thing exist, it is logically impossible for it to conceive a lie. Therefore the Spirit is Truth. Similarly disease and death are the negative of Life, and therefore the Spirit, as the Principle of Life, cannot embody disease or death in its Self-contemplation. In like manner also, since it is free to produce what it will, the Spirit cannot desire the presence of repugnant forms, and so one of its inherent Laws must be Beauty. In this threefold Law of Truth, Life, and Beauty, we find the whole underlying nature of the Spirit, and no action on the part of the individual can be at variance with the Originating Unity which does not contravert these fundamental principles.

This it will be seen leaves the individual absolutely unfettered except in the direction of breaking up the fundamental harmony on which he himself, as included in the general creation, is dependent. This certainly cannot be called limitation, and we are all free to follow the lines of our own individuality in every other direction; so that, although the recognition of our relation to the Originating Spirit safeguards us from injuring ourselves or others, it in no way restricts our liberty of action or narrows our field of development. Am I, then, trying to base my action upon a fundamental desire for the opening out of Truth, for the increasing of Livingness, and for the creating of Beauty? Have I got this as an ever present Law of Tendency at the back of my thought? If so, then this law will occupy precisely the same place in My Microcosm, or personal world, that it does in the Macrocosm, or great world, as a power which is in itself formless, but which by reason of its presence necessarily impresses its character upon all that the creative energy forms. On this basis the creative energy of the Universal Mind may be safely trusted to work through the specializing influence of our own thought* and we may adopt the maxim "trust your desires" because we know that they are the movement of the Universal in ourselves, and that being based upon our fundamental recognition of the Life, Love, and Beauty which the Spirit is, their unfoldments must carry these initial qualities with them all down the line, and thus, in however small a degree, becomes a portion of the working of the Spirit in its inherent creativeness.

This perpetual Creativeness of the Spirit is what we must never lose sight of, and that is why I want the student to grasp clearly the idea of the Spirit's Self-contemplation as the only possible root of the Creative Process. Not only at the first creation of the world, but at all times the plane of the

---

* See my Doré Lectures, 1909.

innermost is that of Pure Spirit,* and therefore at this, the originating point, there is nothing else for Spirit to contemplate excepting itself; then this Self-contemplation produces corresponding manifestation, and since Self-contemplation or recognition of its own existence must necessarily go on continually, the corresponding creativeness must always be at work. If this fundamental idea be clearly grasped we shall see that incessant and progressive creativeness is the very essence and being of Spirit. This is what is meant by the Affirmativeness of the Spirit. It cannot *per se* act negatively, that is to say uncreatively, for by the very nature of its Self-recognition such a negative action would be impossible. Of course if *we* act negatively then, since the Spirit is always acting affirmatively, we are moving in the opposite direction to it; and consequently so long as we regard our own negative action as being affirmative, the Spirit's action must appear to us negative, and thus it is that all the negative conditions of the world have their root in negative or inverted thought but the more we bring our thought into harmony with the Life, Love, and Beauty which the Spirit is, the less these inverted conditions will obtain, until at last they will be eliminated altogether. To accomplish this is our great object; for though the progress may be slow it will be steady if we proceed on a definite principle; and to lay hold of the true principle is the purpose of our studies. And the principle to lay hold of is the Ceaseless Creativeness of Spirit. This is what we mean when we speak of it as The Spirit of the Affirmative, and I would ask my readers to impress this term upon their minds. Once grant that the All-originating Spirit is thus the Spirit of the Pure Affirmative, and we shall find that this will lead us logically to results of the highest value.

If, then, we keep this Perpetual and Progressive Creativeness of the Spirit continually in mind we may rely upon its working as surely in ourselves as in that great cosmic forward movement which we speak of as Evolution. It is the same power of Evolution working within ourselves, only with this difference, that in proportion as we come to realize its nature we find ourselves able to facilitate its progress by offering more and more favorable conditions for its working. We do not add to the force of the Power, for we are products of it and so cannot generate what generates *us;* but by providing suitable conditions we can more and more highly specialize it.

* See my Edinburgh Lectures on Mental Science.

This is the method of all the advance that has ever been made. We never create any force (*e.g.* electricity) but we provide special conditions under which the force manifests *itself* in a variety of useful and beautiful ways, unsuspected possibilities which lay hidden in the power until brought to light by the cooperation of the Personal Factor.

Now it is precisely the introduction* of this Personal Factor that concerns us, because to all eternity we can only recognize things from our own center of consciousness, whether in this world or in any other; therefore the practical question is how to specialize in our own case the *generic* Originating Life which, when we give it a name, we call "the Spirit." The method of doing this is perfectly logical when we once see that the principle involved is that of the Self-recognition of Spirit. We have traced the *modus operandi* of the Creative Process sufficiently far to see that the existence of the cosmos is the result of the Spirit's seeing itself *in* the cosmos, and if this be the law of the whole it must also be the law of the part. But there is this difference, that so long as the normal average relation of particles is maintained the whole continues to subsist, no matter what position any particular particle may go into, just as a fountain continues to exist no matter whether any particular drop of water is down in the basin or at the top of the jet. This is the *generic* action which keeps the race going as a whole. But the question is, What is going to become of ourselves? Then because the law of the whole is also the law of the part we may at once say that what is wanted is for the Spirit *to see itself in us*—in other words, to find in us the Reciprocal which, as we have seen, is necessary to its Enjoyment of a certain Quality of Consciousness. Now, the fundamental consciousness of the Spirit must be that of Self-sustaining Life, and for the full enjoyment of this consciousness there must be a corresponding *individual* consciousness reciprocating it; and on the part of the individual such a consciousness can only arise from the recognition that his own life is identical with that of the Spirit—not something sent forth to wander away by itself, but something included in and forming part of the Greater Life. Then by the very conditions of the case, such a contemplation on the part of the individual is nothing else than the Spirit contemplating itself from the standpoint of the individual consciousness, and thus fulfilling the Law of the Creative Process under such

* See my Doré Lectures, 1909.

specialized conditions as must logically result in the perpetuation of the individual life. It is the Law of the Cosmic Creative Process transferred to the individual.

This, it seems to me, is the Divine Ideal: that of an Individuality which recognizes its Source, and recognizes also the method by which it springs from that Source, and which is therefore able to open up in itself a channel by which that Source can flow in uninterruptedly; with the result that from the moment of this recognition the individual lives directly from the Originating Life, as being himself *a special direct creation,* and not merely as being a member of a generic race. The individual, who has reached this stage of recognition thus finds a principle of enduring life *within himself;* so then the next question is in what way this principle is likely to manifest itself.

IV

# THE MANIFESTATION OF THE LIFE PRINCIPLE

WE MUST BEAR in mind that what we have now reached is a principle, or universal potential, only we have located it in the individual. But a principle, as such, is not manifestation. Manifestation is the growth proceeding *from* the principle, that is to say, some Form in which the principle becomes active. At the same time we must recollect that, though *a* form is necessary for manifestation, *the* form is not essential, for the same principle may manifest through various forms, just as electricity may work either through a lamp or a tram-car without in any way changing its inherent nature. In this way we are brought to the conclusion that the Life-principle must always provide itself with a body in which to function, though it does not follow that this body must always be of the same chemical constitution as the one we now possess. We might well imagine some distant planet where the chemical combinations with which we are familiar on earth did not obtain; but if the essential life-principle of any individual were transported thither, then by the Law of the Creative Process it would proceed to clothe itself with a material body drawn from the atmosphere and substance of that planet; and the personality thus produced would be quite at home there, for all his surroundings would be perfectly natural to him, however different the laws of Nature might be there from what we know here.

In such a conception as this we find the importance of the two leading principles to which I have drawn attention—first, the power of the Spirit to create *ex nihilo,* and secondly, the individual's recognition of the basic principle of Unity giving permanence and solidity to the frame of Nature. By the former the self-recognizing life-principle could produce any sort of body it chose; and by the latter it would be led to project one in harmony with the natural order of the particular planet, thus making all the facts of that order solid realities to the individual, and himself a solid and natural being to the other inhabitants of that world. But this would not do away with the individual's knowledge of how he got there; and so, supposing him to have realized his identity with the Universal Life-Principle sufficiently to consciously control the projection of his own body, he could at will disintegrate the body which accorded with the conditions of one planet and constitute one which accorded just as harmoniously with those of another, and could thus function on any number of planets as a perfectly natural being on each of them. He would in all respects resemble the other inhabitants with one all-important exception, that since he had attained to unity with his Creative Principle he would not be tied by the laws of matter as they were.

Any one who should attain to such a power could only do so by his realization of the all-embracing Unity of the Spirit as being the Foundation of all things; and this being the basis of his own extended powers he would be the last to controvert his own basic principle by employing his powers in such a way as to disturb the natural course of evolution in the world where he was. He might use them to help forward the evolution of others in that world, but certainly never to disturb it, for he would always act on the maxim that "Order is Heaven's First Law."

Our object, however, is not to transfer ourselves to other planets but to get the best out of this one; but we shall not get the best out of this one until we realize that the power which will enable us to do so is so absolutely universal and fundamental that its application in this world is precisely the same as in any other, and that is why I have stated it as a general proposition applicable to all worlds.

The principle being thus universal there is no reason why we should postpone its application till we find ourselves in another world, and the best place and time to begin are Here and Now. The starting point is not in time or locality, but in the mode of Thought; and if we realize that this

Point of Origination is Spirit's power to produce something out of nothing, and that it does this in accordance with the natural order of substance of the particular world in which it is working, then the spiritual ego in ourselves, as proceeding direct from the Universal Spirit, should be able first, to so harmoniously combine the working of spiritual and physical laws in its own body as to keep it in perfect health, secondly to carry this process further and renew the body, thus eradicating the effects of old age, and thirdly to carry the process still further and perpetuate this renewed body as long as the individual might desire.

If the student shows this to one of his average acquaintances who has never given any thought to these things, his friend will undoubtedly exclaim "Tommy rot!" even if he does not use a stronger expletive. He will at once appeal to the past experience of all mankind, his argument being that what has not been in the past cannot be in the future; yet he does not apply the same argument to aeronautics and is quite oblivious of the fact that the Sacred Volume which he reverences contains promises of these very things. The really earnest student must never forget the maxim that "Principle is not bound by Precedent"—if it were we should still be primitive savages.

To use the Creative Process we must Affirm the Creative Power, that is to say, we must go back to the Beginning of the series and start with Pure Spirit, only remembering that this starting-point is now to be found *in ourselves,* for this is what distinguishes the individual Creative Process from the cosmic one. This is where the importance of realizing only ONE Originating Power instead of two interacting powers comes in, for it means that we do not derive our power from any existing polarity, but that we are going to establish polarities which will start secondary causation on the lines which we thus determine. This also is where the importance comes in of recognizing that the only possible originating movement of spirit must be Self-contemplation, for this shows us that we do not have to contemplate existing conditions but the Divine Ideal, and that this contemplation of the Divine Ideal of Man is the Self-contemplation of the Spirit from the standpoint of Human Individuality.

Then the question arises, if these principles, are true, why are we not demonstrating them? Well, when our fundamental principle is obviously correct and yet we do not get the proper results, the only inference is that somewhere or other we have introduced something antagonistic to the fundamental principle, something not inherent in the principle itself and which therefore owes its presence to some action of our own. Now the error consists in the belief that the Creative Power is limited by the material in which it works. If this be assumed, then you have to calculate the resistances offered by the material; and since by the terms of the Creative Process these resistances do not really exist, you have no basis of calculation at all—in fact you have no means of knowing where you are, and everything is in confusion. This is why it is so important to remember that the Creative Process is the action of a Single Power, and that the interaction of two opposite polarities comes in at a later stage, and is not creative, but only distributive—that is to say, it localizes the Energy already proceeding from the Single Power. This is a fundamental truth which should never be lost sight of. So long, however, as we fail to see this truth we necessarily limit the Creative Power by the material it works in, and in practise we do this by referring to past experience as the only standard of judgment. We are measuring the Fifth Kingdom by the standard of the Fourth, as though we should say that an intellectual man, a being of the Fourth Kingdom, was to be limited by the conditions which obtain in the First or Mineral Kingdom—to use Scriptural language we are seeking the Living among the dead.

And moreover at the present time a new order of experience is beginning to open out to us, for well authenticated instances of the cure of disease by the invisible power of the Spirit are steadily increasing in number. The facts are now too patent to be denied—what we want is a better knowledge of the power which accounts for them. And if this beginning is now with us, by what reason can we limit it? The difference between the healing of disease and the renewal of the entire organism and the perpetuation of life is only a difference of degree and not of kind; so that the actual experience of increasing numbers shows the working of a principle to which we can logically set no limits.

If we get the steps of the Creative Process clearly into our minds we shall see why we have hitherto had such small results.

Spirit creates by Self-contemplation;
Therefore, What it contemplates itself
  as being, that it becomes.
You are individualized Spirit;
Therefore, What you contemplate as

the Law of your being becomes the
Law of your being.

Hence, contemplate a Law of Death arising out of the Forces of the Material reacting against the Power of the Spirit and overcoming it, and you impress this mode of self-recognition upon Spirit in yourself. Of course you cannot alter its inherent nature, but you cause it to work under negative conditions and thus make it produce negative results so far as you yourself are concerned.

But reverse the process, and contemplate a Law of Life as inherent in the very Being of the Spirit, and therefore as inherent in spirit in yourself; and contemplate the forces of the Material as practically non-existent in the Creative Process, because they are products of it and not causes—look at things in this way and you will impress a corresponding conception upon the Spirit which, by the Law of Reciprocity, thus enters into Self-contemplation on *these* lines from the standpoint of your own individuality; and then by the nature of the Creative Process a corresponding externalization is bound to take place. Thus our initial question, How did anything come into existence at all, brings us to the recognition of a Law of Life which we may each specialize for ourselves; and in the degree to which we specialize it we shall find the Creative Principle at work within us building up a healthier and happier personality in mind, body, and circumstances.

Only we must learn to distinguish the vehicles of Spirit from Spirit itself, for the distinction has very important bearings. What distinguishes the vehicles from the Spirit is the Law of Growth. The Spirit is the Formless principle of Life, and the vehicle is a Form in which this principle functions. Now the vehicle is a projection by the Spirit of substance coordinate with the natural order of the plane on which the vehicle functions, and therefore requires to be built up conformably to that order. This building up is what we speak of as Growth; and since the principle which causes the growth is the individualized Spirit, the rate at which the growth will go on will depend on the amount of vitalizing energy the Spirit puts into it, and the amount of vitalizing energy will depend on the degree in which the individualized Spirit appreciates its own livingness, and finally the degree of this appreciation will depend on the quality of the individual's perception of the Great All-originating Spirit as reflecting itself in him and thus making his contemplation of It nothing else than the Creative Self-contemplation of the Spirit proceeding from an individual and personal center.

We must therefore not omit the Law of Growth in the vehicle from our conception of the working of the Spirit. As a matter of fact the vehicle has nothing to say in the matter for it is simply a projection from the Spirit; but for this very reason its formation will be slow or rapid in exact proportion to the individual spirit's vitalizing conception. We could imagine a degree of vitalizing conception that would produce the corresponding form instantaneously, but at present we must allow for the weakness of our spiritual power—not as thinking it by any means incapable of accomplishing its object, but as being far slower in operation now than we hope to see it in the future—and so we must not allow ourselves to be discouraged, but must hold our thought knowing that it is doing its creative work, and that the corresponding growth is slowly but surely taking place—thus following the Divine precept that men ought always to pray and not to faint. Gradually as we gain experience on these new lines our confidence in the power of the Spirit will increase, and we shall be less inclined to argue from the negative side of things, and thus the hindrances to the inflow of the Originating Spirit will be more and more removed, and greater and greater results will be obtained.

If we would have our minds clear on this subject of Manifestation we should remember its threefold nature:—First the General Life-Principle, secondly the Localization of this principle in the Individual, and thirdly the Growth of the Vehicle as it is projected by the individualized spirit with more or less energy. It is a sequence of progressive condensation from the Undifferentiated Universal Spirit to the ultimate and outermost vehicle—a truth enshrined in the esoteric maxim that "Matter is Spirit at its lowest level."

The forms thus produced are in true accord with the general order of Nature on the particular plane where they occur, and are therefore perfectly different from forms temporarily consolidated out of material drawn from other living organisms. These latter phantasmal bodies are held together only by an act of concentrated volition, and can therefore only be maintained for a short time and with effort; while the body which the individualized spirit, or ego, builds for itself is produced by a perfectly natural process and does not require any effort to sustain it, since it is kept in touch with the whole system of the planet by the continuous and effortless action of the individual's sub-conscious mind.

This is where the action of sub-conscious mind as the builder of the body comes in. Sub-conscious mind acts in accordance with the aggregate of suggestion impressed upon it by the conscious mind, and if this suggestion is that of perfect harmony with the physical laws of the planet then a corresponding building by the sub-conscious mind will take place, a process which, so far from implying any effort, consists rather in a restful sense of unity with Nature.*

And if to this sense of union with the Soul of Nature, that Universal Sub-conscious Mind which holds in the cosmos the same place that the sub-conscious mind does in ourselves—if to this there be superadded a sense of union with the All-creating Spirit from which the Soul of Nature flows, then through the medium of the individual's sub-conscious mind such specialized effects can be produced in his body as to transcend our past experiences without in any way violating the order of the universe. The Old Law was the manifestation of the Principle of Life working under constricted conditions: the New Law is the manifestation of the same Principle working under expanding conditions. Thus it is that though God never changes we are said to "increase with the increase of God."

---

* For the relation between conscious and sub-conscious mind see my "Edinburgh Lectures on Mental Science."

V

# THE PERSONAL FACTOR

I HAVE ALREADY POINTED OUT that the presence of a single all-embracing Cosmic Mind is an absolute necessity for the existence of any creation whatever, for the reason that if each individual mind were an entirely separate center of perception, not linked to all other minds by a common ground of underlying mentality independent of all individual action, then no two persons would see the same thing at the same time, in fact no two individuals would be conscious of living in the same world. If this were the case there would be no common standard to which to refer our sensations; and, indeed, coming into existence with no consciousness of environment except such as we could form by our own unaided thought, and having by the hypothesis no standard by which to form our thoughts, we could not form the conception of any environment at all, and consequently could have no recognition of our own existence. The confusion of thought involved even in the attempt to state such a condition shows it to be perfectly inconceivable, for the simple reason that it is self-contradictory and self-destructive. On this account it is clear that our own existence and that of the world around us necessarily implies the presence of a Universal Mind acting on certain *fixed lines of its own* which establish the basis for the working of all individual minds. This paramount action of the Universal

Mind thus sets an unchangeable standard by which all individual mental action must eventually be measured, and therefore our first concern is to ascertain what this standard is and to make it the basis of our own action.

But if the independent existence of a common standard of reference is necessary for our self-recognition simply as inhabitants of the world we live in, then *a fortiori* a common standard of reference is necessary for our recognition of the unique place we hold in the Creative Order, which is that of introducing the Personal Factor without which the possibilities contained in the great Cosmic Laws would remain undeveloped, and the Self-contemplation of Spirit could never reach those infinite unfoldments of which it is logically capable.

The evolution of the Personal Factor is therefore the point with which we are most concerned. As a matter of fact, whatever theories we may hold to the contrary, we do all realize the same cosmic environment in the same way; that is to say, our minds all act according to certain generic laws which underlie all our individual diversities of thought and feeling. This is so because we are made that way and cannot help it. But with the Personal Factor the case is different. A standard is no less necessary, but we are not so made as to conform to it automatically. The very conception of automatic conformity to a *personal* standard is self-contradictory, for it does away with the very thing that constitutes personality, namely freedom of volition, the use of the powers of Initiative and Selection. For this reason conformity to the Standard of Personality must be a matter of choice, which amounts to the same thing as saying that it rests with each individual to form his own conception of a standard of Personality; but which liberty, however, carries with it the inevitable result that we shall bring into manifestation the *conditions* corresponding to the sort of personality we accept as our normal standard.

I would draw attention to the words "Normal Standard." What we shall eventually attain is, not what we merely wish, but what we regard as normal. The reason is that since we subconsciously know ourselves to be based upon the inherent Law of the Universal Mind we feel, whether we can reason it out or not, that we cannot force the All-producing Mind to work contrary to its own inherent qualities, and therefore we intuitively recognize that we cannot transcend the sort of personality which is normal according to the Law of Universal Mind. This thought is always at the back of our mind and we cannot get away from it for the simple reason that it is inherent in our mental constitution, because our mind is itself a product of the Creative Process; and to suppose ourselves transcending the possibilities contained in the Originating Mind would involve the absurdity of supposing that we can get the greater out of the less.

Nevertheless there are some who try to do so, and their position is as follows. They say in effect, I want to transcend the standard of humanity as I see it around me. But this is the normal standard according to the Law of the Universe, therefore I have to get above the Law of the Universe. Consequently I cannot draw the necessary power from that Law, and so there is nowhere else to get it except from myself. Thus the aspirant is thrown back upon his own individual will as the ultimate power, with the result that the onus lies on him of concentrating a force sufficient to overcome the Law of the Universe. There is thus continually present to him a suggestion of struggle against a tremendous opposing force, and as a consequence he is continually subjecting himself to a strain which grows more and more intense as he realizes the magnitude of the force against which he is contending. Then as he begins to realize the inequality of the struggle he seeks for extraneous aid, and so he falls back on various expedients, all of which have this in common that they ultimately amount to invoking the assistance of other individualities, not seeing that this involves the same fallacy which has brought him to his present straits, the fallacy, namely, of supposing that any individuality can develop a power greater than that of the source from which itself proceeds. The fallacy is a radical one; and therefore all efforts based upon it are foredoomed to ultimate failure, whether they take the form of reliance on personal force of will, or magical rites, or austerity practised against the body, or attempts by abnormal concentration to absorb the individual in the universal, or the invocation of spirits, or any other method—the same fallacy is involved in them all, that the less is larger than the greater.

Now the point to be noted is that the idea of transcending the present conditions of humanity does not necessarily imply the idea of transcending the normal law of humanity. The mistake we have hitherto made has been in fixing the Standard of Personality too low and in taking our past experiences as measuring the ultimate possibilities of the race. Our liberty consists in our ability to form our own conception of the Normal Standard of Personality, only subject to the conditions arising out of the inherent

Law of the underlying Universal Mind; and so the whole thing resolves itself into the question, What are those fundamental conditions? The Law is that we cannot transcend the Normal; therefore comes the question, What is the Normal?

I have endeavored to answer this question in the chapter on the Divine Ideal, but since this is the crucial point of the whole subject we may devote a little further attention to it. The Normal Standard of Personality must necessarily be the reproduction in Individuality of what the Universal Mind is in itself, because, by the nature of the Creative Process, this standard results from Spirit's Self-contemplation at the stage where its recognition is turned toward its own power of Initiative and Selection. At this stage Spirit's Self-recognition has passed beyond that of Self-expression through a mere Law of Averages into the recognition of what I have ventured to call its Artistic Ability; and as we have seen that Self-recognition at any stage can only be attained by the realization of a *relation* stimulating that particular sort of consciousness, it follows that for the purpose of this further advance expression through individuals of a corresponding type is a necessity. Then by the Law of Reciprocity such beings must possess powers similar to those contemplated in itself by the Originating Spirit, in other words they must be in their own sphere the image and likeness of the Spirit as it sees itself.

Now we have seen that the Creating Spirit necessarily possesses the powers of Initiative and Selection. These we may call its *active* properties—the summing up of what it *does.* But what any power does depends on what it *is,* for the simple reason that it cannot give out what it does not contain; therefore at the back of the initiative and selective power of the Spirit we must find what the Spirit *is,* namely, what are its *substantive* properties. To begin with it must be Life. Then because it is Life it must be Love, because as the undifferentiated Principle of Life it cannot do otherwise than tend to the fuller development of life in each individual, and the pure motive of giving greater enjoyment of life is Love. Then because it is Life guided by Love it must also be Light, that is to say, the primary all-inclusive perception of boundless manifestations yet to be. Then from this proceeds Power, because there is no opposing force at the level of Pure Spirit; and therefore Life urged forward by Love or the desire for recognition, and by Light or the pure perception of the Law of Infinite Possibility, must necessarily produce Power, for the simple reason that under these conditions it could not stop short of action, for that would be the denial of the Life, Love, and Light which it is. Then because the Spirit is Life, Love, Light, and Power, it is also Peace, again for a very simple reason, that being the Spirit of the Whole it cannot set one part in antagonism against another, for that would be to destroy the wholeness. Next the Spirit must be Beauty, because on the same principle of Wholeness it must duly proportion every part to every other part, and the due proportioning of all parts is beauty. And lastly the Spirit must be Joy, because, working on these lines, it cannot do otherwise than find pleasure in the Self-expression which its works afford it, and in the contemplation of the limitlessness of the Creative Process by which each realized stage of evolution, however excellent, is still the stepping-stone to something yet more excellent, and so on in everlasting progression.

For these reasons we may sum up the Substantive Being of the All-originating Spirit as Life, Love, Light, Power, Peace, Beauty, and Joy; and its Active Power as that of Initiative and Selection. These, therefore, constitute the basic laws of the underlying universal mentality which sets the Standard of Normal Personality—a standard which, when seen in this light, transcends the utmost scope of our thought, for it is nothing else than the Spirit of the Infinite Affirmative conceived in Human Personality. This standard is therefore that of the Universal Spirit itself reproduced in Human Individuality by the same Law of Reciprocity which we have found to be the fundamental law of the Creative Process—only now we are tracing the action of this Law in the Fifth Kingdom instead of in the Fourth.

This Standard, then, we may call the Universal Principle of Humanity, and having now traced the successive steps by which it is reached from the first cosmic movement of the Spirit in the formation of the primary nebula, we need not go over the old ground again, and may henceforward take this Divine Principle of Humanity as our Normal Standard and make it the starting point for our further evolution. But how are we to do this? Simply by using the one method of Creative Process, that is, the Self-contemplation of Spirit. We now know ourselves to be Reciprocals of the Divine Spirit, centers in which It finds a fresh standpoint for Self-contemplation; and so the way to rise to the heights of this Great Pattern is by contemplating it as the Normal Standard of our own Personality.

And be it noted that the Pattern thus set before us is Universal. It is the embodiment of all the great principles of the Affirmative, and so in no way interferes with our own particular individuality—*that* is something built up upon this foundation, something additional affording the differentiating medium through which this unifying Principle finds variety of expression, therefore we need be under no apprehension lest by resting upon this Pattern we should become less ourselves. On the contrary the recognition of it sets us at liberty to become more fully ourselves because we know that we are basing our development, not upon the strength of our own unaided will, nor yet upon any sort of extraneous help, but upon the Universal Law itself, manifesting through us in the proper sequence of the Creative Order; so that we are still dealing with Universal principles, only the principle by which we are now working is the Universal Principle of Personality.

I wish the student to get this idea very clearly because this is really the crux of the passage from the Fourth Kingdom into the Fifth. The great problem of the future of evolution is the introduction of the Personal Factor. The reason why this is so is very simple when we see it. To take a thought from my own "Doré Lectures" we may put it in this way. In former days no one thought of building ships of iron because iron does not float; yet now ships are seldom built of anything else, though the relative specific gravities of iron and water remain unchanged. What has changed is the Personal Factor. It has expanded to a more intelligent perception of the law of flotation, and we now see that wood floats and iron sinks, both of them by the same principle working under opposite conditions, the law, namely, that anything will float which bulk for bulk is lighter than the volume of water displaced by it, so that by including in our calculations the displacement of the vessel as well as the specific gravity of the material, we now make iron float by the very same law by which it sinks. This example shows that the function of the Personal Factor is to analyze the manifestations of Law which are spontaneously afforded by Nature and to discover the Universal Affirmative Principle which lies hidden within them, and then by the exercise of our powers of Initiative and Selection to provide such specialized conditions as will enable the Universal Principle to work in perfectly new ways transcending anything in our past experience. This is how all progress has been achieved up to the present; and is the way in which all progress must be achieved in the future, only for the purpose of evolution, or growth from within, we must transfer the method to the spiritual plane.

The function, then, of the Personal Factor in the Creative Order is to provide specialized conditions by the use of the powers of Selection and Initiative, a truth indicated by the maxim "Nature unaided fails"; but the difficulty is that if enhanced powers were attained by the whole population of the world without any common basis for their use, their promiscuous exercise could only result in chaotic confusion and the destruction of the entire race. To introduce the creative power of the Individual and at the same time avoid converting it into a devastating flood is the great problem of the transition from the Fourth Kingdom into the Fifth. For this purpose it becomes necessary to have a Standard of the Personal Factor independent of any individual conceptions, just as we found that in order for us to attain self-consciousness at all it was a necessity that there should be a Universal Mind as the *generic* basis of all individual mentality; only in regard to the generic build of mind the conformity is necessarily automatic, while in regard to the specializing process the fact that the essence of that process is Selection and Initiative renders it impossible for the conformity to the Standard of Personality to be automatic—the very nature of the thing makes it a matter of individual choice.

Now a Standard of Personality independent of individual conceptions must be the *essence* of Personality as distinguished from individual idiosyncrasies, and can therefore be nothing else than the Creative Life, Love, Beauty, etc., viewed as a Divine Individuality, by identifying ourselves with which we eliminate all possibility of conflict with other personalities based on the same fundamental recognition; and the very universality of this Standard allows free play to all our particular idiosyncrasies while at the same time preventing them from antagonizing the fundamental principles to which we have found that the Self-contemplation of the Originating Spirit must necessarily give rise. In this way we attain a Standard of Measurement for our own powers. If we recognize no such Standard our development of spiritual powers, our discovery of the immense possibilities hidden in the inner laws of Nature and of our own being, can only become a scourge to ourselves and others, and it is for this reason that these secrets are so jealously guarded by those who know them, and that over the entrance to the temple are written the words "Eskato Bebeloi"—"Hence ye Profane."

But if we recognize and accept this Standard of Measurement then we need never fear our discovery of hidden powers either in ourselves or in Nature, for on this basis it becomes impossible for us to misuse them.

Therefore it is that all systematic teaching on these subjects begins with instruction regarding the Creative Order of the Cosmos, and then proceeds to exhibit the same Order as reproduced on the plane of Personality and so affording a fresh starting-point for the Creative Process by the introduction of Individual Initiative and Selection. This is the doctrine of the Macrocosm and the Microcosm; and the transition from the generic working of the Creative Spirit in the Cosmos to its specific working in the Individual is what is meant by the doctrine of the Octave.

VI

# THE STANDARD OF PERSONALITY

WE HAVE NOW got some general idea as to the place of the personal factor in the Creative Order, and so the next question is, How does this affect ourselves? The answer is that if we have grasped the fundamental fact that the moving power in the Creative Process is the self-contemplation of Spirit, and if we also see that, because we are miniature reproductions of the Original Spirit, our contemplation of It becomes Its contemplation of Itself from the standpoint of our own individuality—if we have grasped these fundamental conceptions, then it follows that our process for developing power is to contemplate the Originating Spirit as the source of the power we want to develop. And here we must guard against a mistake which people often make when looking to the Spirit as the source of power. We are apt to regard it as sometimes giving and sometimes withholding power, and consequently are never sure which way it will act. But by so doing we make Spirit contemplate itself as having no definite action at all, as a plus and minus which mutually cancel each other, and therefore by the Law of the Creative Process no result is to be expected. The mistake consists in regarding the power as something separate from the Spirit; whereas by the analysis of the Creative Process which we have now made we see that the Spirit itself *is* the power, because the power comes into existence only through Spirit's self-contemplation. Then the logical inference from this is that by contemplating the Spirit *as* the power, and *vice versa* by contemplating the power *as* the Spirit, a similar power is being generated in ourselves.

Again an important conclusion follows from this, which is that to generate any *particular sort* of power we should contemplate it in the abstract rather than as applied to the particular set of circumstances we have in hand. The circumstances indicate the sort of power we want but they do not help us to generate it; rather they impress us with a sense of something contrary to the power, something which has to be overcome by it, and therefore we should endeavor to dwell on the power *in itself,* and so come into touch with it in its limitless infinitude.

It is here that we begin to find the benefit of a Divine Standard of Human Individuality. That also is an Infinite Principle, and by identifying ourselves with it we bring to bear upon the abstract conception of infinite Impersonal Power a corresponding conception of Infinite Personality, so that we thus import the Personal Factor which is able *to use* the Power without imposing any strain upon ourselves. We know that by the very nature of the Creative Process we are one with the Originating Spirit and therefore one with all the principles of its Being, and consequently one with its Infinite Personality, and therefore our contemplation of it as the Power which we want gives us the power to use that Power.

This is the Self-contemplation of Spirit employed from the individual standpoint for the generating of power. Then comes the application of the power thus generated. But there is only one Creative Process, that of the Self-contemplation of Spirit, and therefore the way to use this process for the application of the power is to contemplate ourselves as surrounded by the conditions which we want to produce. This does not mean that we are to lay down a hard and fast pattern of the conditions and strenuously endeavor to compel the Power to conform its working to every detail of our mental picture—to do so would be to hinder its working and to exhaust ourselves. What we are to dwell upon is the idea of an Infinite Power producing the happiness we desire, and because this Power is also the Forming Power of the universe trusting it to give that form to the conditions which will most perfectly react upon us to produce the particular state of consciousness desired.

Thus neither on the side of in-drawing nor of out-giving is there any constraining of the Power, while in both cases there is an initiative and selective action on the part of the individual—for the generating of power he takes, the initiative of invoking it by contemplation, and he makes selection of the sort of power to invoke; while on the giving-out side he makes selection of the purpose for which the Power is to be employed, and takes the initiative by his thought of directing the Power to that purpose. He thus fulfils the fundamental requirements of the Creative Process by exercising Spirit's inherent faculties of initiative and selection by means of its inherent method, namely by Self-contemplation. The whole action is identical in kind with that which produces the cosmos, and it is now repeated in miniature for the particular world of the individual; only we must remember that this miniature reproduction of the Creative Process is based upon the great fundamental principles inherent in the Universal Mind, and cannot be dissociated from them without involving a conception of the individual which will ultimately be found self-destructive because it cuts away the foundation on which his individuality rests.

It will therefore be seen that any individuality based upon the fundamental Standard of Personality thus involved in the Universal Mind has reached the basic principle of union with the Originating Spirit itself, and we are therefore correct in saying that union is attained through, or by means of, this Standard Personality. This is a great truth which in all ages has been set forth under a variety of symbolic statements; often misunderstood, and still continuing to be so, though owing to the inherent vitality of the idea itself even a partial apprehension of it produces a corresponding measure of good results. This falling short has been occasioned by the failure to recognize an Eternal Principle at the back of the particular statements—in a word the failure to see what they were talking about. All *principles* are eternal in themselves, and this is what distinguishes them from their particular manifestations as laws determined by temporary and local conditions.

If then, we would reach the root of the matter we must penetrate through all verbal statements to an Eternal Principle which is as active now as ever in the past, and which is as available to ourselves as to any who have gone before us. Therefore it is that when we discern an Eternal and Universal Principle of Human Personality as necessarily involved in the Essential Being of the Originating Universal Spirit—*Filius in gremio Patris*—we have discovered the true Normal Standard of Personality. Then because this standard is nothing else than the principle of Personality expanded to infinitude, there is no limit to the expansion which we ourselves may attain by the operation in us of this principle; and so we are never placed in a position of antagonism to the true law of our being, but on the contrary the larger and more fundamental our conception of personal development the greater will be the fulfilment which we give to the Law. The Normal Standard of Personality is found to be itself the Law of the Creative Process working at the personal level; and it cannot be subject to limitation for the simple reason that the process being that of the Self-contemplation of Spirit, no limits can possibly be assigned to this contemplation.

We need, therefore, never be afraid of forming too high an idea of human possibilities provided always that we take this standard as the foundation on which to build up the edifice of our personality. And we see that this standard is no arbitrary one but simply the Expression in Personality of the ONE all-embracing Spirit of the Affirmative; and therefore the only limitation implied by conformity to it is that of being prevented from running on lines the opposite of those of the Creative Process, that is to say, from calling into action causes of disintegration and destruction. In the truly Constructive Order, therefore, the Divine Standard of Personality is as really the basis of the development of specific personality as the Universal Mind is the necessary basis of generic mentality; and just as without this generic ultimate of Mind we should none of us see the same world at the same time, and in fact have no consciousness of existence, so apart from this Divine Standard of Personality it is equally impossible for us to specialize the generic law of our being so as to develop all the glorious possibilities that are latent in it.

Only we must never forget the difference between these two statements of the Universal Law—the one is cosmic and generic, common to the whole race, whether they know it or not, a Standard to which we all conform automatically by the mere fact of being human beings; while the other is a personal and individual Standard, automatic conformity to which is impossible because that would imply the loss of those powers of Initiative and Selection which are the very essence of Personality; so that this Standard necessarily implies a personal selection of it in preference to other conceptions of an antagonistic nature.

VII

# RACE THOUGHT AND NEW THOUGHT

THE STEADY FOLLOWING UP of the successive stages of the Creative Process has led us to the recognition of an Individuality in the All-creating Spirit itself, but an Individuality which is by its very nature Universal, and so cannot be departed from without violating the essential principles on which the further expansion of our own individuality depends. At the same time it is strictly *individual,* for it is the Spirit of Individuality, and is thus to be distinguished from that merely *generic* race-personality which makes us human beings at all. Race-personality is of course the necessary *basis* for the development of this Individuality; but if we do not see that it is only the preliminary to further evolution, any other conception of our personality as members of the race will prevent our advance toward our proper position in the Creative Order, which is that of introducing the Personal Factor by the exercise of our individual power of initiative and selection.

It is on this account that Race-thought, simply as such, is opposed to the attempt of the individual to pass into a higher order of life. It limits him by strong currents of negative suggestion based on the fallacy that the perpetuation of the race requires the death of the individual*; and it is only when the individual sees that this is not true, and that his race-nature constitutes the ground out of which his new Individuality is to be formed, that he becomes able to oppose the negative power of race-thought. He does this by destroying it with its own weapon, that is, by finding in the race-nature itself the very material to be used by the Spirit for building-up the New Man. This is a discovery on the spiritual plane equivalent to the discovery on the physical plane that we can make iron float by the same law by which it sinks. It is the discovery that what we call the mortal part of us is capable of being brought under a higher application of the Universal Law of Life, which will transmute it into an immortal principle. When we see what we call the mortal part of us in this light we can employ the very principle on which the negative race-thought is founded as a weapon for the destruction of that thought in our own minds.

The basis of the negative race-thought is the idea that physical death is an essential part of the Normal Standard of Personality, and that the body is composed of so much neutral material with which death can do what it likes. But it is precisely this neutrality of matter that makes it just as amenable to the Law of Life as to the Law of Death—it is simply neutral and not an originating power on either side; so then when we realize that our Normal Standard of Personality is not subject to death, but is the Eternal Essence and Being of Life itself, then we see that this neutrality of matter—its inability to make selection or take initiative on its own account—is just what makes it the plastic medium for the expression of Spirit in ourselves.

In this way the generic or race mind in the individual becomes the instrument through which the specializing power of the Spirit works toward the building up of a personality based upon the truly Normal Standard of Individuality which we have found to be inherent in the All-originating Spirit itself: and since the whole question is that of the introduction of the factor of personal individuality into the creative order of causation, this cannot be done by depriving the individual of what makes him a person instead of a thing, namely, the power of conscious initiative and selection.

For this reason the transition from the Fourth Kingdom into the Fifth

* See "Self-Synthesis" by Dr. Cornwall Round.

cannot be forced upon the race either by a Divine fiat or by the generic action of cosmic law, for it is a *specializing* of the cosmic law which can only be effected by *personal* initiative and selection, just as iron can only be made to float under certain specialized conditions; and consequently the passage from the Fourth into the Fifth Kingdom is a strictly individual process which can only be brought about by a personal perception of what the normal standard of the New Individuality really is. This can only be done by the active laying aside of the old race-standard and the conscious adoption of the new one. The student will do well to consider this carefully, for it explains why the race cannot receive the further evolution simply as a race; and also it shows that our further evolution is not into a state of less activity but of greater, not into being less alive but more alive, not into being less ourselves but more ourselves; thus being just the opposite of those systems which present the goal of existence as re-absorption into the undifferentiated Divine essence. On the contrary our further evolution is into greater degrees of conscious activity than we have ever yet known, because it implies our development of greater powers as the consequence of our clearer perception of our true relation to the All-originating Spirit. It is the recognition that we may, and should, measure ourselves by this New Standard instead of by the old race-standard that constitutes the real New Thought. The New Thought which gives New Life to the individual will never be realized so long as we think that it is merely the name of a particular sect, or that it is to be found in the mechanical observance of a set of rules laid down for us by some particular teacher. It is a New Fact in the experience of the individual, the *reason* for which is indeed made clear to him through intellectual perception of the real nature of the Creative Process, but which can become an actual experience only by habitual personal intercourse with that Divine Spirit which is the Life, Love and Beauty that are at the back of the Creative Process and find expression through it.

From this intercourse new thoughts will continually flow in, all of them bearing that vivifying element which is inherent in their source, and the individual will then proceed to work out these new ideas with the knowledge that they have their origin in the selection and initiative power of the All-creating Spirit itself, and in this way by combined meditation and action he will find himself advancing into increasing light, liberty and usefulness. The advance may be almost imperceptible from one day to another, but it will be perceptible at longer intervals, and the one who is thus moving forward with the Spirit of God will on looking back at any time always find that he is getting more livingness out of life than he was a year previously. And this without strenuous effort, for he is not having to manufacture the power from his own resources but only to *receive* it—and as for *using* it, that is only the exercise of the power itself. So following on these lines you will find that Rest and Power are identical; and so you get the real New Thought which grows in Newness every day.

## VIII

# THE DÉNOUEMENT OF THE CREATIVE PROCESS

THEN COMES THE QUESTION, What should logically be the dénouement of the progression we have been considering? Let us briefly recapitulate the steps of the series. Universal Spirit by Self-contemplation evolves Universal Substance. From this it produces cosmic creation as the expression of itself as functioning in Space and Time. Then from this initial movement it proceeds to more highly specialized modes of Self-contemplation in a continually ascending scale, for the simple reason that self-contemplation admits of no limits and therefore each stage of self-recognition cannot be other than the starting-point for a still more advanced mode of self-contemplation, and so on *ad infinitum.* Thus there is a continuous progress toward more and more highly specialized forms of life, implying greater liberty and wider scope for enjoyment as the capacity of the individual life corresponds to a higher degree of the contemplation of Spirit; and in this way evolution proceeds till it reaches a level where it becomes impossible to go any further except by the exercise of conscious selection and initiative on the part of the individual, while at the same time conforming to the universal principles of which evolution is the expression.

Now ask yourself in what way individual selection and initiative would be likely to act as expressing the Originating Spirit itself? Given the knowledge on the part of the individual that he is able by his power of initiative and selection to draw directly upon the All-originating Spirit of Life, what motive could he have for not doing so? Therefore, granted such a perfect recognition, we should find the individual holding precisely the same place in regard to his own individual world that the All-originating Spirit does to the cosmos; subject only to the same Law of Love, Beauty, &c, which we found to be necessarily inherent in the Creative Spirit—a similarity which would entirely prevent the individual from exercising his otherwise limitless powers in any sort of antagonism to the Spirit of the Great Whole.

At the same time the individual would be quite aware that he was not the Universal Spirit *in propria persona,* but that he was affording expression to it through his individuality. Now Expression is impossible except through Form, and therefore form of some sort is a necessity of individuality. It is just here, then, that we find the importance of that principle of Harmony with Environment of which I spoke earlier, the principle in accordance with which a person who had obtained complete control of matter, if he wished to transport himself to some other planet, would appear there in perfect conformity with all the laws of matter that obtained in that world; though, of course, not subject to any limitation of the Life Principle in himself. He would exhibit the laws of matter as rendered perfect by the Law of Originating Life. But if any one now living on this earth were thus perfectly to realize the Law of Life he would be in precisely the same position *here* as our imaginary visitor to another planet—in other words the dénouement of the Law of Life is not the putting off of the body, but its inclusion as part of the conscious life of the Spirit.

This does not imply any difference in the molecular structure of the body from that of other men, for by the principle of Harmony of which I have just spoken, it would be formed in strict accordance with the laws of matter on the particular planet; though it would not be subject to the limitations resulting from the average man's non-recognition of the power of the Spirit. The man who had thus fully entered into the Fifth Kingdom would recognize that, in its relation to the denser modes of matter his body was of a similar dense mode. That would be its relation to external environment as seen by others. But since the man now knew *himself* as not belonging to these denser modes of manifestation, but as an individualization of Primary Spirit, he would see that relatively to himself all matter was Primary Substance, and that from this point of view any condensations of that substance into atoms, molecules, tissues, and the like counted for nothing—for him the body would be simply Primary Substance entirely responsive to his will. Yet his reverence for the Law of Harmony would prevent any disposition to play psychic pranks with it, and he would use his power over the body only to meet actual requirements.

In this way, then, we are led to the conclusion that eternal life in an immortal physical body is the logical dénouement of our evolution; and if we reflect that, by the conditions of the case, the owners of such bodies could at will either transport themselves to other worlds or put off the physical body altogether and remain in the purely subjective life while still retaining the power to reclothe themselves in flesh whenever they chose, we shall see that this dénouement of evolution answers all possible questions as to the increase of the race, the final destruction of the planet, and the like.

This, then, is the ultimate which we should keep in view; but the fact remains that, though there may be hidden ones who have thus attained, the bulk of mankind have not, and that the common lot of humanity is to go through the change which we call death. In broad philosophical terms death may be described as the withdrawal of the life into the subjective consciousness to the total exclusion of the objective consciousness. Then by the general law of the relation between subjective and objective mind, the subjective mind severed from its corresponding objective mentality has no means of acquiring fresh impressions *on its own account,* and therefore can only ring the changes on those impressions which it has brought with it from its past life. But these may be of very various sorts, ranging from the lowest to the highest, from those most opposed to that ultimate destiny of man which we have just been considering, to those which recognize his possibilities in a very large measure, needing little more to bring about the full fruition of perfected life. But however various may be their experiences, all who have passed through death must have this in common that they have lost their physical instrument of objective perception and so have their mode of consciousness determined entirely by the dominant mode of suggestion which they have brought over with them from the objective side of life.* Of course if the objective mentality were also brought over this would give the individual the same power of initiative and selection that he possesses while in the body, and, as we shall see later on, there are excep-

* For the relation between subjective and objective mind see my "Edinburgh Lectures on Mental Science."

tional persons with whom this is the case; but for the great majority the physical brain is a necessity for the working of the objective mentality, and so when they are deprived of this instrument their life becomes purely subjective and is a sort of dream-life, only with a vast difference between two classes of dreamers—those who dream as they must and those who dream as they will. The former are those who have enslaved themselves in various ways to their lower mentality—some by bringing with them the memory of crimes unpardoned, some by bringing with them the idea of a merely animal life, others less degraded, but still in bondage to limited thought, bringing with them only the suggestion of a frivolous worldly life—in this way, by the natural operation of the Law of Suggestion, these different classes, either through remorse, or unsatisfied desires, or sheer incapacity to grasp higher principles, all remain earth-bound, suffering in exact correspondence with the nature of the suggestion they have brought along with them. The unchangeable Law is that the suggestion becomes the life; and this is equally true of suggestions of a happier sort. Those who have brought over with them the great truth that conditions are the creations of thought, and who have accustomed themselves while in objective life to dwell on good and beautiful ideas, are still able, by reason of being imbued with this suggestion, to mold the conditions of their consciousness in the subjective world in accordance with the sort of ideas which have become a second nature to them. Within the limits of these ideas the dominant suggestion to these entities is that of a Law which confers Liberty, so by using this Law of the constructive power of thought they can determine the conditions of their own consciousness; and thus instead of being compelled to suffer the nightmare dreams of the other class, they can mold their dream according to their will. We cannot conceive of such a life as theirs in the unseen as otherwise than happy, nevertheless its range is limited by the range of the conceptions they have brought with them. These may be exceedingly beautiful and thoroughly true and logical *as far as they go;* but they do not go the whole way, otherwise these spirits would not be in the category which we are considering but would belong to that still higher class who fully realize the ultimate possibilities which the Law of the Expression of Spirit provides.

The otherwise happy subjective life of these more enlightened souls has this radical defect that they have failed to bring over with them that power of original selection and initiative without which further progress is impossible. I wish the student to grasp this point very clearly, for it is of the utmost importance. Of course the basis of our further evolution is conformity to the harmonious nature of the Originating Spirit; but upon this foundation we each have to build up the superstructure of our own individuality, and every step of advance depends on our personal development of power to take that step. This is what is meant by taking an initiative. It is making a New Departure, not merely recombining the old things into fresh groupings still subject to the old laws, but introducing an entirely new element which will bring its own New Law along with it.

Now if this is the true meaning of "initiative" then that is just the power which these otherwise happy souls do not possess. For by the very conditions of the case they are living only in their subjective consciousness, and consequently are living by the law of subjective mind; and one of the chief characteristics of subjective mind is its incapacity to reason inductively, and therefore its inability to make the selection and take the initiative necessary to inaugurate a New Departure. The well established facts of mental law show conclusively that subjective mind argues only deductively. It argues quite correctly from any given premises, but it cannot take the initiative in selecting the premises—that is the province of inductive reasoning which is essentially the function of the objective mind. But by the law of Auto-suggestion this discarnate individual has brought over his premises with him, which premises are the sum-total of his inductions made during objective life, the conception of things which he held at the time he passed over, for this constituted his idea of Truth. Now he cannot add to these inductions, for he has parted with his instrument for inductive reasoning, and therefore his deductive reasoning in the purely subjective state which he has now entered is necessarily limited to the consequences which may be deducted from the premises which he has brought along with him.

In the case of the highly-developed individualities we are now considering the premises thus brought over are of a very far-reaching and beautiful character, and consequently the range of their subjective life is correspondingly wide and beautiful; but, nevertheless, it is subject to the radical defect that it is debarred from further progress for the simple reason that the individual has not brought over with him the mental faculty which can impress his subjective entity with the requisite forward movement for making a new departure into a New Order. And moreover, the higher the subjective development with which the individual passed over the more likely he will be to realize this defect. If during earth-life he had gained sufficient knowledge of these things he will carry with him the knowledge that his discarnate existence is purely subjective; and therefore he will realize that, however he may be able to order the pictures of his dream, yet it is still but a dream, and in common with all other dreams lacks the basis of solidity from which to take *really creative action.*

He knows also that the condition of other discarnate individualities is similar to his own, and that consequently each one must necessarily live in a world apart—a world of his own creation, because none of them possess the objective mentality by which to direct their subjective currents so as to make them penetrate into the sphere of another subjective entity, which is the *modus operandi* of telepathy. Thus he is conscious of his own inability to hold intercourse with other personalities; for though he may for his own pleasure create the semblance of them in his dream-life, yet he knows that these are creations of his own mind, and that while he appears to be conversing with a friend amid the most lovely surroundings the friend himself may be having experiences of a very different description. I am, of course, speaking now of persons who have passed over in a very high state of development and with a very considerable, though still imperfect, knowledge of the Law of their own being. Probably the majority take their dream-life for an external reality; and, in any case, all who have passed over without carrying their objective mentality along with them must be shut up in their individual subjective spheres and cease to function as centers of creative power so long as they do not emerge from that state.

But the highly advanced individuals of whom I am now speaking have passed over with a true knowledge of the Law of the relation between subjective and objective mind and have therefore brought with them a *subjective* knowledge of this truth; and therefore, however otherwise in a certain sense happy, they must still be conscious of a fundamental limitation which prevents their further advance. And this consciousness can produce only one result, an ever-growing longing for the removal of this limitation—and this represents the intense desire of the Spirit, as individualized in these souls, to attain to the conditions under which it can freely exercise its creative power. Sub-consciously this is the desire of *all* souls, for it is that continual pressing forward of the Spirit for manifestation out of which the whole Creative Process arises; and so it is that the great cry perpetually ascends to God from all as yet undelivered souls, whether in or out of the body, for the deliverance which they knowingly or unknowingly desire.

All this comes out of the well-ascertained facts of the law of relation between subjective and objective mind. Then comes the question, Is there no way of getting out of this law? The answer is that we can never get away from universal principles—*but we can specialize them.* We may take it as an axiom that any law which appears to limit us contains in itself the principle by which that limitation can be overcome, just as in the case of the flotation of iron. In this axiom, then, we shall find the clue which will bring us out of the labyrinth. The same law which places various degrees of limitation upon the souls that have passed into the invisible can be so applied as to set them free. We have seen that everything turns on the obligation of our subjective part to act within the limits of the suggestion which has been most deeply impressed upon it. Then why not impress upon it the suggestion that in passing over to the other side it has brought its objective mentality along with it?

If such a suggestion were effectively impressed upon our subjective mind, then by the fundamental law of our nature our subjective mind would act in strict accordance with this suggestion, with the result that the objective mind would no longer be separated from it, and that we should carry with us into the unseen our *whole* mentality, both subjective and objective, and so be able to exercise our inductive powers of selection and initiative as well there as here.

Why not? The answer is that we cannot accept any suggestion unless we believe it to be true, and to believe it to be true we must feel that we have a solid foundation for our belief. If, then, we can find a sufficient foundation for adequately impressing this suggestion upon ourselves, then the principles of mental law assure us that we shall carry our objective faculty of initiative and selection into the unseen. Therefore our quest is to find this Foundation. Then, since we cannot accept as true what we believe to be contrary to the ultimate law of the universe, if we are to find such a foundation at all it must be within that Law; and it is for this reason that I have laid so much stress upon the Normal Standard of Human Individuality. When we are convinced that this ideal completeness is quite normal, and is a spiritual fact, not dependent upon the body, but able to control the body, then we have got the solid basis on which to carry our objective personality along with us into the unseen, and the well-established laws of our mental constitution justify the belief that we can do so.

From these considerations it is obvious that those who thus pass over in possession of their complete mentality must be in a very different position from those who pass into a condition of merely subjective life, for they have brought their powers of selection and initiative with them, and can therefore employ their experiences in the unseen as a starting-point for still further development. So, then, the question arises, What lines will this further development be likely to follow?

We are now considering the case of persons who have reached a very high degree of development; who have succeeded in so completely uniting the subjective and objective portions of their spiritual being into a perfect whole that they can never again be severed; and who are therefore able to function with their whole consciousness on the spiritual plane. Such persons will doubtless be well aware that they have attained this degree of development by the Law of the Creative Process working in terms of their own individuality, and so they would naturally always refer to the original Cosmic Creation as the demonstration of the principle which they have to specialize for their own further evolution. Then they would find that the principle involved is that of the manifestation of Spirit in Form; and they would further see that this manifestation is not an illusion but a reality, for the simple reason that both mind and matter are equally projections from the Great Originating Spirit. Both alike are thoughts of the Divine Mind, and it is impossible to conceive any greater reality than the Divine Thought, or to get at any more substantial source of reality than that. Even if we were to picture the Divine Mind as laughing at its productions as being mere illusions *relatively to itself* (which I certainly do not), still the relation between the individual mind and material existence would be a reality for the individual, on the simple mathematical ground that like signs multiplied together invariably produce a positive result, even though the signs themselves be negative; so that, for us, at every stage of our existence substance must always be as much a reality as mind. Therefore the manifestation of Spirit in Form is the eternal principle of the Creative Process whether in the evolution of a world-system or in that of an individual.

But when we realize that by the nature of the Creative Process substance must be an eternal verity we must not suppose that this is true also of *particular forms* or of *particular modes* of matter. Substance is a necessity for the expression of Spirit, but it does not follow that Spirit is tied down to any particular mode of expression. If you fold a piece of paper into the form of a dart it will fly through the air by the law of the form which you have given it. Again, if you take the same bit of paper and fold it into the shape of a boat it will float on water by the law of the new form that you have given it. The thing formed will act in accordance with the form given it, and the same paper can be folded into different forms; but if there were no paper you could put it into any shape at all. The dart and the boat are both real so long as you retain the paper in either of those shapes; but this does not alter the fact that you can change the shapes, though your power to do so depends on the existence of the paper. This is a rough analogy of the relation between ultimate substance and particular forms, and shows us that neither substance nor shape is an illusion; both are essential to the manifestation of Spirit, only by the nature of the Creative Process the Spirit has power to determine what shape substance shall take at any particular time.

Accordingly we find the great Law that, as Spirit is the Alpha of the Creative Process, so solid material Form is its Omega; in other words the Creative Series is incomplete until solid material form is reached. Anything short of this is a condition of incompleteness, and therefore the enlightened souls who have passed over in possession of both sides of their mentality will realize that their condition, however beatific, is still one of incompleteness; and that what is wanted for completion is expression through a material body. This, then, is the direction in which such souls would use their powers of initiative and selection as being the true line of evolution—in a word they would realize that the principle of Creative Progression, when it reaches the level of fully developed mental man, necessarily implies the Resurrection of the Body, and that anything short of this would be retrogression and not progress.

At the same time persons who had passed over with this knowledge would never suppose that Resurrection meant merely the resuscitation of the old body under the old conditions; for they would see that the same inherent law which makes expression in concrete substance the ultimate of the creative series also makes this ultimate form depend on the originating movement of the spirit which produces it, and therefore that, although *some* concrete form is essential for complete manifestation, and is a substantial reality so long as it is maintained, yet the maintaining of the particular form is entirely dependent on the action of the spirit of which the form is the external clothing. This resurrection body would therefore be no mere illusory spirit-shape, yet it would not be subject to the limitations of matter as we now know it: it would be physical matter still, but entirely subject to the will of the indwelling spirit, which would not regard the denser atomic relations of the body but only its absolute and essential nature as Primary Substance. I want the student to grasp the idea that the same thing may be very different when looked at, so to say, from opposite ends of the stick. What is solid molecular matter when viewed from the outside is plastic primary substance when viewed from the inside. The relations of this new body to any stimulus proceeding from outside would be those of the external laws of Nature; but its relation to the spiritual ego working from within would be that of a plastic substance to be molded at will. The employment of such power would, however, at all times be based upon the reverent worship of the All-creating Spirit; and it would therefore never be exercised otherwise than in accordance with the harmonious progress of the Creative Process. Proceeding on these lines the spirit in the individual would stand in precisely the same relation to his body that the All-originating Spirit does to the cosmos.

This, then, is the sort of body which the instructed would contemplate as that in which he was to attain resurrection. He would regard it, not as an illusion, but as a great reality; while at the same time he would not need to trouble himself about its particular form, for he would know that it would be the perfect expression of his own conception of himself. He would know this because it is in accordance with the fundamental principle that external creation has its root in the Self-contemplation of Spirit.

Those passing over with this knowledge would obviously be in a very different position from those who passed over with only a subjective consciousness. They would bring with them powers of selection and initiative by which they could continue to impress fresh and expanding conceptions upon their subjective mind, and so cause it to carry on its work as the seed-ground of the whole individuality, instead of being shut up in itself as a mere circulus for the repetition of previously received ideas; and so in their recognition of the *principle* of physical resurrection they would have a clear and definite line of auto-suggestion. And because this suggestion is derived from the undeniable facts of the whole cosmic creation, it is one which both subjective and objective mind can accept as an established fact, and so the suggestion becomes effective. This suggestion, then, becomes the self-contemplation of the individual spirit; and because it is in strict conformity with the generic principle of the Original Creative Activity, of which the individual mind is itself a product, this becomes also the Self-contemplation of the Originating Spirit as seeing itself reflected in the individual spirit; so that, by the basic law of the Creative Process, this suggestion is bound sooner or later to work out into its corresponding fact, namely, the production of a material body free from the power of death and from all those limitations which we now associate with our physical organism.

This, then, is the hope of those who pass over in recognition of the great truth. But how about those who have passed over without that recognition? We have seen that their purely subjective condition precludes them from taking any initiative on their own account, for that requires the presence of objective mind. Their subjective mind, however, still retains its essential nature; that is, it is still susceptible to suggestion, and still possesses its inherent creativeness in working out any suggestion that is sufficiently deeply implanted in it. Here, then, opens up a vast field of activity for that other class who have passed over in possession of both sides of their mentality. By means of their powers of initiative and selection they can on the principle of telepathy cause their own subjective mind to penetrate the subjective spheres of those who do not possess those powers, and they can thus endeavor to impress upon them the great truth of the physical ultimate of the Creative Process—the truth that any series which stops short of that ultimate is incomplete, and, if insisted upon as being ultimate, must become self-destructive because in opposition to the inherent working of the Universal Creative Spirit. Then, as the perception of the true nature of the Creative Process dawned upon any subjective entity, it would by reason of accepting this suggestion begin to develop an objective mentality, and so would gradually attain to the same status as those who had passed over in full possession of all their mental powers.

But the more the objective mentality became developed in these discarnate personalities the more the need of a corresponding physical instrument would assert itself, both from their intellectual perception of the original cosmic process, and also from the inherent energy of the Spirit as centered in the ultimate ego of the individual. Not to seek material manifestation would be the contrary of all we have traced out regarding the nature of the Creative Process; and hence the law of tendency resulting from the conscious union of subjective and objective mind in the individual must necessarily be toward the production of a physical form. Only we must recollect, as I have already pointed out, that this concentration of these minds would be upon a principle and not upon a particular bodily shape. The particular form they would be content to leave to the inherent self-expressiveness of the Universal Spirit working through the particular ego, with the result that their expectation would be fixed upon a *general principle* of physical Resurrection which would provide a form suited to be the material instrument of the highest ideal of man as a spiritual and mental being. Then, since the subjective mind is the automatic builder of the body, the result of the individual's acceptance of the Resurrection principle must be that this mental conception will eventually work out as a corresponding fact. Whether on this planet or on some other, matters not, for, as we have already seen, the physical body evolved by a soul that is conscious of its unity with the Universal Spirit is bound to be in conformity with the physical laws of *any* planet, though from the standpoint of the conscious ego not limited by them.

In this way we may conceive that those who have passed over in possession of both sides of their spiritual nature would find a glorious field of usefulness in the unseen in helping to emancipate those who had passed over in possession of their subjective side only. But from our present analysis it will be seen that this can only be effected on the basis of a recognition of the principle of the Resurrection of the Body. Apart from the recognition of this principle the only possible conception which the discarnate individual could form of himself would be that of a purely subjective being; and this carries with it all the limitations of a subjective life unbalanced by an objective one; and so long as the principle of physical resurrection is denied, so long the life must continue to be merely subjective and consequently unprogressive.*

But it may be asked why those who have realized this great principle sufficiently to carry their objective mentality into the unseen state are liable to the change which we call death. The answer is that though they have re-

* This view, it may be remarked, is not necessarily incompatible with the conception of reincarnation, on which theory the final resurrection or transmutation of the body would terminate the series of successive lives and deaths, thus bringing the individual out of the circle of generation, which is the circle of Karma. I may, perhaps, have the opportunity of considering this subject on some future occasion.

alized *the general principle* they have not yet divested themselves of certain conceptions by which they limit it, and consequently by the law of subjective mind they carry those limitations into the working of the Resurrection principle itself.

They are limited by the race-belief that physical death is under all conditions a necessary law of Nature, or by the theological belief that death is the will of God; so then the question is whether these beliefs are well founded. Of course appeal is made to universal experience, but it does not follow that the universal experience of the past is bound to be the universal experience of the future—the universal experience of the past was that no man had ever flown across the English Channel, yet now it has been done. What we have to do, therefore, is not to bother about past experience, but to examine the inherent nature of the Law of Life and see whether it does not contain possibilities of further development. And the first step in this direction is to see whether what we have hitherto considered limitations of the law are really integral parts of the law itself. The very statement of this question shows the correct answer; for how can a force acting in one direction be an integral part of a force acting in the opposite direction? How can the force which pulls a thing down be an integral part of the force which builds it up? To suppose, therefore, that the limitations of the law are an integral portion of the law itself is a *reductio ad absurdum.*

For these reasons the argument from the past experience of the race counts for nothing; and when we examine the theological argument we shall find that it is only the old argument from past experience in another dress. It is alleged that death is the will of God. How do we know that it is the will of God? Because the facts prove it so, is the ultimate answer of all religious systems with one exception; so here we are back again at the old race-experience as the criterion of truth. Therefore the theological argument is nothing but the materialistic argument disguised. It is in our more or less conscious acceptance of the materialistic argument, under any of its many disguises, that the limitation of life is to be found—not in the Law of Life itself; and if we are to bring into manifestation the infinite possibilities latent in that Law it can only be by looking steadily into the *principle* of the Law and resolutely denying everything that opposes it. The Principle of Life must of necessity be Affirmative, and affirmative throughout, without any negative anywhere—if we once realize this we shall be able to unmask the enemy and silence his guns.

Now to do this is precisely the one object of the Bible; and it does it in a thoroughly logical manner, always leading on to the ultimate result by successive links of cause and effect. People will tell you that the Bible is their authority for saying that Death is the will of God; but these are people who read it carelessly; and ultimately the only reason they can give you for their manner of interpreting the Bible is that the facts prove their interpretation to be correct; so that in the last resort you will always find you have got back to the old materialistic argument from past race-experience, which logically proves nothing. These are good well-meaning people with a limited idea which they read into the Bible, and so limit its promises by making physical death an essential preliminary to Resurrection. They grasp, of course, the great central idea that Perfected Man possesses a joyous immortal Life permeating spirit, soul and body; but they relegate it to some dim and distant future, entirely disconnected from the present law of our being, not seeing that if we are to have eternal life it must necessarily be involved in some principle which is eternal, and therefore existing, at any rate latently, at the present moment. Hence, though their fundamental principle is true, they are all the time mentally limiting it, with the result that they themselves create the conditions they impose upon it, and consequently the principle will work (as principles always do) in accordance with the conditions provided for its action.

Unless, therefore, this limiting belief is entirely eradicated, the individual, though realizing the fundamental principle of Life, is bound to pass out of physical existence; but on the other hand, since he does take the recognition of this fundamental principle with him, it is bound to bear fruit sooner or later in a joyous Resurrection, while the intermediate state can only be a peaceful anticipation of that supreme event. This is the answer to the question why those who have realized the great principle sufficiently to carry their objective mentality into the unseen world are still liable to physical death; and in the last analysis it will be found to resolve itself into the remains of race-belief based upon past experience. These are they who pass over in sure and certain hope of a glorious Resurrection—sure and certain because founded upon the very Being of God Himself, that inherent Life of the All-creating Divine Spirit which is the perpetual interaction of the Eternal Love and Beauty. They have grasped the Life-giving Truth, only they have postponed its operation, because they have the fixed idea that its present fruition is an absolute impossibility.

But if we ask the reason for this idea it always comes back to the old materialistic argument from the experience of past conditions, while the whole nature of advance is in the opening up of new conditions. And in this advance the Bible is the pioneer book. Its whole purport is to tell us most emphatically that death is *not* the will of God. In the story of Eden God is represented as warning man of the poisonous nature of the forbidden fruit, which is incompatible with the idea of death as an essential feature of man's nature. Then from the point where man has taken the poison all the rest of the Bible is devoted to telling us how to get rid of it. Christ, it tells us, was manifested to bring Life and Immortality to light—to abolish death—to destroy the works of the devil, that is the death-dealing power, for "he that hath the power of death is the devil." It is impossible to reconcile this life-giving conception of the Bible with the idea that death at any stage or in any degree is the desire of God. Let us, therefore, start with the recognition that this negative force, whether in its minor degrees as disease or in its culmination as death, is that which it is the will of God to abolish. This also is logical; for if God be the Universal Spirit of Life finding manifestation in individual lives, how can the desire of this Spirit be to act in opposition to its own manifestation? Therefore Scripture and common-sense alike assure us that the will of God toward us is Life and not death.*

We may therefore start on our quest for Life with the happy certainty that God is on our side. But people will meet us with the objection that though God wills Life to us, He does not will it just yet, but only in some dim far-off future. How do we know this? Certainly not from the Bible. In the Bible Jesus speaks of two classes of persons who believe on Him as the Manifestation or Individualisation of the Spirit of Life. He speaks of those who, having passed through death, still believe on Him, and says that these *shall* live—a future event. And at the same time He speaks of those who are living and believe on Him, and says that they shall never die—thus contemplating the entire elimination of the contingency of death (John xi. 25).

Again St. Paul expresses his wish not to be unclothed but to be clothed upon, which he certainly would not have done had he considered the latter alternative a nonsensical fancy. And in another place he expressly states that we shall not all die, but that some shall be transmuted into the Resurrection body without passing through physical death. And if we turn to the Old

* See my "Bible Mystery and Bible Meaning."

Testament we find two instances in which this is said to have actually occurred, those of Enoch and Elijah. And we may note in passing that the Bible draws our attention to certain facts about these two personages which are important as striking at the root of the notion that austerities of some sort are necessary for the great attainment. Of Enoch we are expressly told that he was the father of a large family, and of Elijah that he was a man of like nature with ourselves—thus showing us what is wanted is not a shutting of ourselves off from ordinary human life but such a clear realization of the Universal Principle, of which our personal life is the more or less conscious manifestation, that our commonest actions will be hallowed by the Divine Presence; and so the grand dénouement will be only the natural result of our daily habit of walking with God. From the stand-point of the Bible, therefore, the attainment of physical regeneration without passing through death is not an impossibility, nor is it necessarily relegated to some far off future. Whatever any one else may say to the contrary, the Bible contemplates such a dénouement of human evolution as a present possibility.

Then if we argue from the philosophical stand-point we arrive at precisely the same result. Past experience proves nothing, and we must therefore make a fresh start by going back to the Original Creative action of the Spirit of Life itself. Then, if we take this as our starting point, remembering that at the stage of this *original* movement there can be no intervention by a second power, because there is none, why should we mentally impose any restriction upon the action of the Creative Power? Certainly not by its own Law of Tendency, for that must always be toward fuller self-expression; and since this can only take place through the individual, the desire of the Spirit must always be toward the increasing of the individual life. Nor yet from anything in the created substance, for that would either be to suppose the Spirit creating something in limitation of its own Self-expression, or else to suppose that the limiting substance was created by some other power working against the Spirit; and as this would mean a Duality of powers we should not have reached the Originating Power at all, and so we might put Spirit and Substance equally out of court as both being merely modes of secondary causation. But if we see that the Universal Substance must be created by emanation from the Universal Spirit, then we see that no limitation of Spirit by substance is possible. We may therefore feel assured that no limitation proceeds either from the will of the Spirit or from the nature of Substance.

Where, then, does limitation come from? Limiting conditions are created by the same power which creates everything else, namely, the Self-contemplation of Spirit. This is why it is so important to realize that the individual mind forms a center from which the self-contemplating action of Spirit is specialized in terms of the individual's own mode of thinking, and therefore so long as the individual contemplates negative conditions as being *of the essence* of his own personality, he is in effect employing the Creative Power of the Self-contemplation of Spirit invertedly, destructively instead of constructively. The Law of the Self-contemplation of Spirit as the Creative Power is as true in the microcosm as in the macrocosm, and so the individual's contemplation of himself as subject to the law of sin and death keeps him subject to that law, while the opposite self-contemplation, the contemplation of himself as rejoicing in the Life of the Spirit, the Perfect Law of Liberty, must necessarily produce the opposite results.

Why, then, should not regeneration be accomplished here and now? I can see no reason against it, either Scriptural or philosophical, except our own difficulty in getting rid of the race-traditions which are so deeply embedded in our subjective minds. To get rid of these we require a firm basis on which to receive the opposite suggestion. We need to be convinced that our ideal of a regenerated self is in accord with the Normal Standard of Humanity and is within the scope of the laws of the universe. Now to make clear to us the *infinitude* of the truly Normal Standard of Humanity is the whole purpose of the Bible; and the Manifestation of this Standard is set before us in the Central Personality of the Scriptures who is at once the Son of God and the Son of Man—the Great Exception, if you will, to man as we know him now, but the Exception which proves the Rule. In proportion as we begin to realize this we begin to introduce into our own life the action of that Personal Factor on which all further development depends; and when our recognition is complete we shall find that we also are children of God.

# IX

## CONCLUSION

WE ARE NOW in a position to see the place occupied by the individual in the Creative Order. We have found that the originating and maintaining force of the whole Creative Process is the Self-contemplation of the Spirit, and that this necessarily produces a Reciprocal corresponding to the idea embodied in the contemplation, and thus manifesting that idea in a correlative Form. We have found that in this way the externalization of the idea progresses from the condensation of the primary nebula to the production of human beings as a race, and that at this point the simple *generic* reproduction of the idea terminates. This means that up to, and including, *genus homo,* the individual, whether plant, animal, or man, is what it is simply by reason of race conditions and not by exercise of deliberate choice. Then we have seen that the next step in advance must necessarily be by the individual becoming aware that he has power to mold the conditions of his own consciousness and environment by the creative power of his thought; thus not only enabling him to take a conscious part in his own further evolution but precluding him from evolving any further except by the right exercise of this power; and we have found that the crux of the passage from the Fourth to the Fifth Kingdom is to get people so to understand the nature of their creative power as not to use it destructively. Now what we require to see is that the Creative Process has always only one way of working, and that is by Reciprocity or Reflection, or, as we might say, by the law of Action and Re-action, the re-action being always equivalent and correspondent to the action which generated it. If this Law of Reciprocity be grasped then we see how the progress of the Creative Process must at length result in producing a being who himself possesses the power of independent spiritual initiative and is thus able to carry on the creative work from the stand-point of his own individuality.

Now the great crux is first to get people to see that they possess this power at all, and then to get them to use it in the right direction. When our eyes begin to open to the truth that we do possess this power the temptation is to ignore the fact that our power of initiative is itself a product of the similar power subsisting in the All-originating Spirit. If this origin of our own creative faculty is left out of sight we shall fail to recognize the Livingness of the Greater Life within which we live. We shall never get nearer to it than what we may call its *generic* level, the stage at which the Creative Power is careful of the type or race but is careless of the individual; and so at this level we shall never pass into the Fifth Kingdom which is the Kingdom of Individuality—we have missed the whole point of the transition to the more advanced mode of being, in which the individual consciously functions as a creative center, because we have no conception of a Universal Power that works at any higher level than the generic, and consequently to reach a specific personal exercise of creative power we should have to conceive of ourselves as transcending the Universal Law. But if we realize that our own power of creative initiative has its origin in the similar faculty of the All-Originating Mind then we see that the way to maintain the Life-giving energy in ourselves is to use our power of spiritual initiative so as to impress upon the Spirit the conception of ourselves as standing related to It in a specific, individual, and personal way that takes us out of the mere category of *genus homo* and gives us a specific spiritual individuality of our own. Thus our mental action produces a corresponding re-action in the mind of the Spirit, which in its turn reproduces itself as a special manifestation of the Life of the Spirit in us; and so long as this circulation between the individual spirit and the Great Spirit is kept up, the individual life will be maintained, and will also strengthen as the circulation continues, for the reason that the Spirit, as the Original Creative Power, is a Multiplying Force, and the current sent into it is returned multiplied, just as in telegraphy the feeble current received from a distance at the end of a long line operates to start a powerful battery in the receiving office, which so multiplies the force as to give out a clear message, which but for the multiplication of the original movement could not have been done. Something like this we may picture the multiplying tendency of the Originating Mind, and consequently the longer the circulation between it and the individual mind goes on the stronger the latter becomes; and this process growing habitual becomes at last automatic, thus producing an endless flow of Life continually expanding in intelligence, love, power and joy.

But we must note carefully that all this can only proceed from the individual's recognition that his own powers are a derivative from the All-originating Spirit, and that they can continue to be used constructively only so long as they are employed in harmony with the inherent Forward Movement of the Spirit. Therefore to insure this eternally flowing stream of Life from the Universal Spirit into the individual there must be *no inversion* in the individual's presentation of himself to the Originating Power: for through the very same Law by which we seek Life—the Life namely, of reciprocal action and re-action—every inversion we bring with us in presenting ourselves to the Spirit is bound to be faithfully reproduced in a corresponding re-action, thus adulterating the stream of Pure Life, and rendering it less life-giving in proportion to the extent to which we invert the action of the Life-principle; so that in extreme cases the stream flowing through and from the individual may be rendered absolutely poisonous and deadly, and the more so the greater his recognition of his own personal power to employ spiritual forces.

The existence of these negative possibilities in the spiritual world should never be overlooked, and therefore the essential condition for receiving the Perfect Fulness of Life is that we should present ourselves before the Eternal Spirit free from every trace of inversion. To do this means to present ourselves in the likeness of the Divine Ideal; and in this self-presentation the initiative, so far as the individual is consciously concerned, must necessarily be taken by himself. He is to project into the Eternal Mind the conception of himself as identical with its Eternal Ideal; and if he can do this, then by the Law of the Creative Process a return current will flow from the Eternal Mind reproducing this image in the individual with a continually growing power. Then the question is, How are we to do this?

The answer is that to take the initiative for inducing this flow of Life individually it is a *sine qua non* that the conditions enabling us to do so should first be presented to us universally. This is in accordance with the general principle that we can never create a force but can only specialize it. Only here the power we are wanting to specialize is the very Power of Specialization itself; and therefore, paradoxical as it may seem, what we require to have shown us is the Universality of Specialization.

Now this is what the Bible puts before us in its central figure. Taking the Bible statements simply and literally they show us this unique Personality as the Principle of Humanity, alike in its spiritual origin and its material manifestation, carried to the logical extreme of specialization; while at the same time, as the embodiment of the original polarity of Spirit and Substance, this Personality, however unique, is absolutely universal; so that the Bible sets Jesus Christ before us as the answer to the philosophic problem of how to specialize the universal, while at the same time preserving its universality.

If, then, we fix our thought upon this unique Personality as the embodiment of *universal* principles, it follows that those principles must exist in ourselves also, and that His actual specialization of them is the earnest of our potential specialization of them. Then if we fix our thought on this potential in ourselves as being identical with its manifestation in Him, we can logically claim our identity with Him, so that what He has done we have done, what He is, we are, and thus recognizing ourselves in Him we present *this* image of ourselves to the Eternal Mind, with the result that we bring with us no inversion, and so import no negative current into our stream of Life.

Thus it is that we reach "the Father" through "the Son," and that He is able to keep us from falling and to present us faultless before the presence of the Divine glory with exceeding joy (Jude 24). The Gospel of "the Word made flesh" is not the meaningless cant of some petty sect nor yet the cunning device of priestcraft, though it has been distorted in both these directions; but it can give a reason for itself, and is founded upon the deepest laws of the threefold constitution of man, embracing the *whole* man, body, soul and spirit. It is not opposed to Science but is the culmination of all science whether physical or mental. It is philosophical and logical throughout if you start the Creative Process where alone it can start, in the Self-contemplation of the Spirit. The more carefully we examine into the claims of the Gospel of Christ the more we shall find all the current objections to it melt away and disclose their own superficialness. We shall find that Christ is indeed the Mediator between God and Man, not by the arbitrary fiat of a capricious Deity, but by a logical law of sequence which solves the problem of making extremes meet, so that the Son of Man is also the Son of God; and when we see the reason why this is so we thereby receive power to become ourselves sons of God, which is the dénouement of the Creative Process in the Individual.

These closing lines are not the place to enter upon so great a subject, but I hope to follow it up in another volume and to show in detail the logic of the Bible teaching, what it saves us from and what it leads us to; to show while giving due weight to the value of other systems how it differs from them and transcends them; to glance, perhaps, for a moment at the indications of the future and to touch upon some of the dangers of the present and the way to escape from them. Nor would I pass over in silence another and important aspect of the Gospel contained in Christ's commission to His followers to heal the sick. This also follows logically from the Law of the Creative Process if we trace carefully the sequence of connections from the indwelling Ego to the outermost of its vehicles; while the effect of the recognition of these great truths upon the individuality that has for a time put off its robe of flesh, opens out a subject of paramount interest. Thus it is that on every plane Christ is the Fulfilling of the Law, and that "Salvation" is not a silly shiboleth but the logical and vital process of our advance into the unfoldment of the next stage of the limitless capacities of our being. Of these things I hope to write in another volume, should it be permitted to me, and in the meanwhile I would commend the present abstract statement of principles to the reader's attention in the hope that it may throw some light on the fundamental nature of these momentous questions. The great thing to bear in mind is that if a thing is true at all there must be a reason why it is true, and when we come to see this reason we know the truth at first hand for ourselves and not from some one else's report—then it becomes really our own and we begin to learn how to use it. This is the secret of the individual's progress in any art, science, or business, and the same method will serve equally well in our search after Life itself, and as we thus follow up the great quest we shall find that on every plane the Way, the Truth, and the Life are ONE.

> "A little philosophy inclineth a man's mind to atheism, but depth in philosophy bringeth men's minds about to religion."
>
> — BACON. ESSAY XVI.

# X

## THE DIVINE OFFERING

I TAKE THE PRESENT opportunity of a new edition to add a few pages on certain points which appear to me of vital importance, and the connection of which with the preceding chapters will, I hope, become evident as the reader proceeds. Assuming the existence in each individual of a creative power of thought which, in relation to himself, reflects the same power existing in the Universal Mind, our right employment of this power becomes a matter of extreme moment to ourselves. Its inverted use necessarily holds us fast in the bondage from which we are seeking to escape, and equally necessarily its right use brings us into Liberty; and therefore if any Divine revelation exists at all its purpose must be to lead us away from the inverted use of our creative faculty and into such a higher specializing of it as will produce the desired result. Now the purpose of the Bible is to do this, and it seeks to effect this work by a dual operation. It places before us that Divine Ideal of which I have already spoken, and at the same time bases this ideal upon the recognition of a Divine Sacrifice. These two conceptions are so intimately interwoven in Scripture that they cannot be separated, but at the present day there is a growing tendency to attempt to make this separation and to discard the conception of a Divine Sacrifice as unphilosophical, that is as having no nexus of cause and effect. What I want, therefore, to point out in these additional pages is that there is such a nexus, and that so far from being without a sequence of cause and effect it has its root in the innermost principles of our own being. It is not contrary to Law but proceeds from the very nature of the Law itself.

The current objection to the Bible teaching on this subject is that no such sacrifice could have been required by God, either because the Originating Energy can have no consciousness of Personality and is only a blind force, or because, if "God is Love," He could not demand such a sacrifice. On the former hypothesis we are of course away from the Bible teaching altogether and have nothing to do with it; but, as I have said elsewhere, the fact of our own consciousness of personality can only be accounted for by the existence, however hidden, of a corresponding quality in the Originating Spirit. Therefore I will confine my remarks to the question how Love, as the originating impulse of all creation, can demand such a sacrifice. And to my mind the answer is that God does not demand it. It is Man who demands it. It is the instinctive craving of the human soul for *certainty* that requires a demonstration so convincing as to leave no room for doubt of our perfectly happy relation to the Supreme Spirit, and consequently to all that flows from it, whether on the side of the visible or of the invisible. When we grasp the fact that such a standpoint of certainty is the necessary foundation for the building up in ourselves of the Divine Ideal then it becomes clear that to afford us this firm basis is the greatest work that the Spirit, in its relation to human personality, could do.

We are often told that the offering of sacrifices had its origin in primitive man's conception of his gods as beings which required to be propitiated so as to induce them to do good or abstain from doing harm; and very likely this was the case. The truth at the back of this conception is the feeling that there is a higher power upon which man is dependent; and the error is in supposing that this power is limited by an individuality which can be enriched by selling its good offices, or which blackmails you by threats. In either case it wants to get something out of you, and from this it follows that its own power of supplying its own wants must be limited, otherwise it would not require to be kept in good temper by gifts. In very undeveloped minds such a conception results in the idea of numerous gods, each having, so to say, his own particular line of business; and the furthest advance this mode of thought is capable of is the reduction of these various deities to two antagonistic powers of Good and of Evil. But the result in either case is the same, so long as we start with the hypothesis that the Good will do us more good and the Evil do us less harm by reason of our sacrifices, for then it logically follows that the more valuable your sacrifices and the oftener they are presented the better chance you have of good luck. Doubtless some such conception as this was held by the mass of the Hebrew people under the sacrificial system of the Levitical Law, and perhaps this was one reason why they were so prone to fall into idolatry—for in this view their fundamental notion was practically identical in its nature with that of the heathen around them. Of course this was not the fundamental idea embodied in the Levitical system itself. The root of that system was the symbolizing of a supreme ideal of reconciliation hereafter to be manifested in action. Now a symbol is not the thing symbolized. The purpose of a symbol is twofold, to put us upon enquiry as to the reality which it indicates, and to bring that reality to our minds by suggestion when we look at the symbol; but if it does not do this, and we rest only in the symbol, nothing will come of it, and we are left just where we were. That the symbolic nature of the Levitical sacrifice was clearly perceived by the deeper thinkers among the Hebrews is attested by many passages in the Bible—"Sacrifice and burnt offering thou wouldest not" (Psalms xl: 6, and li: 16) and other similar utterances; and the distinction between these symbols and that which they symbolized is brought out in the Epistle to the Hebrews by the argument that if those sacrifices had afforded a sufficient standpoint for the effectual realization of cleansing then the worshiper would not need to have repeated them because he would have no more consciousness of sin (Hebrews x: 2).

This brings us to the essential point of the whole matter. What we want is the certainty that there is no longer any separation between us and the Divine Spirit by reason of sin, either as overt acts of wrong doing or as error of principle; and the whole purpose of the Bible is to lead us to this assurance. Now such an assurance cannot be based on any sort of sacrifices that require repetition, for then we could never know whether we had given enough either in quality or quantity. It must be a once-for-all business or it is no use at all; and so the Bible makes the once-for-allness of the offering the essential point of its teaching. "He that has been bathed does not need to be bathed again" (John xiii: 10). "There is now no condemnation to them which are in Christ Jesus" (Romans viii: 1).

Various intellectual difficulties, however, hinder many people from seeing the working of the law of cause and effect in this presentment. One is the question, How can moral guilt be transferred from one person to another? What is called the "forensic" argument (i.e., the court of law argument) that Christ undertook to suffer in our stead as our *surety* is undoubtedly open to this objection. Suretyship must by its very nature be confined to civil obligations and cannot be extended to criminal liability, and so the "forensic" argument may be set aside as very much a legal fiction. But if we realize the Bible teaching that Christ is the Son of God, that is, the Divine Principle of Humanity out of which we originated and subsisting in us all, however unconsciously to ourselves, then we see that sinners as well as saints are included in this Principle; and consequently that the Self-offering of Christ must actually include the self-offering of every human being in the acknowledgment (however unknown to his *objective* mentality) of his sin. If we can grasp this somewhat abstract point of view it follows that in the Person of Christ every human being, past, present, and to come, was self-offered for the condemnation of his sin—a *self*-condemnation and a *self*-offering, and hence a cleansing, for the simple reason that if you can get a man to realize his past error, really see his mistake, he won't do it again; and it is the perpetuation of sin and error that has to be got rid of—to do this universally would be to regain Paradise. Seen therefore in this light there is no question of transference of moral guilt, and I take it this is St. Paul's meaning when he speaks of our being partakers in Christ's death.

Then there is the objection, How can past sins be done away with? If we accept the philosophical conclusion that Time has no substantive existence then all that remains is states of consciousness. As I have said in the earlier part of this book, the Self-Contemplation of Spirit is the cause of all our perception of existence and environment; and consequently if the Self-Contemplation of the Spirit from any center of individualization is that of entire harmony and the absence of anything that would cause any consciousness of separation, then past sins cease to have any part in this self-recognition, and consequently cease to have any place in the world of existence. The foundation of the whole creative process is the calling into Light out of Darkness—"that which makes manifest is light"—and consequently the converse action is that of sending out of Light into Darkness, that is, into Not-being. Now this is exactly what the Spirit says in the Bible—"I, even I, am He that blotteth out thy transgressions" (Isaiah xliii:

25). Blotting out is the sending out of manifestation into the darkness of non-manifestation, out of Being into Not-being; and in this way the past error ceases to have any existence and so ceases to have any further effect upon us. It is "blotted out," and from this new standpoint has never been at all; so that to continue to contemplate it is to give a false sense of existence to that which in effect has no existence. It is that Affirmation of Negation which is the root of all evil. It is the inversion of our God-given creative power of thought, calling into existence that which in the Perfect Life of the Spirit never had or could have any existence, and therefore it creates the sense of inharmony, opposition, and separation. Of course this is only relatively to ourselves, for we cannot create eternal principles. They are the Being of God; and as I have already shown these great Principles of the Affirmative may be summed up in the two words Love and Beauty—Love in essence and Beauty in manifestation; but since we can only live from the standpoint of our own consciousness we can make a false creation built upon the idea of opposites to the all-creating Love and Beauty, which false creation with all its accompaniments of limitation, sin, sorrow, sickness, and death, must necessarily be real to us until we perceive that these things were not created by God, the Spirit of the Affirmative, but by our own inversion of our true relation to the All-creating Being.

When, then, we view the matter in this light the Offering once for all of the Divine Sacrifice for the sin of the whole world is seen not to be a mere ecclesiastical dogma having no relation of cause and effect, but to be the highest application of the same principle of cause and effect by which the whole creation, ourselves included, has been brought into existence—the Self-Contemplation of Spirit producing corresponding manifestation, only now working on the level of Individual Personality.

As I have shown at the beginning of this book the cosmic manifestation of principles is not sufficient to bring out all that there is in them. To do this their action must be specialized by the introduction of the Personal Factor. They are represented by the Pillar Jachin, but it must be equilibrated by the Pillar Boaz, Law and Personality the two Pillars of the Universe; and in the One Offering we have the supreme combination of these two principles, the highest specialization of Law by the highest power of Personality. These are eternal principles, and therefore we are told that the Lamb was slain from the foundation of the world; and because "thoughts are things" this supreme manifestation of the creative interaction of Law and Personality was bound eventually to be manifested in concrete action in the world conditioned by time and space; and so it was that the supreme manifestation of the Love of God to meet the supreme need of Man took place. The history of the Jewish nation is the history of the working of the law of cause and effect, under the guidance of the Divine Wisdom, so as to provide the necessary conditions for the greatest event in the world's history; for if Christ was to appear it must be in *some* nation, in *some* place, and at *some* time: but to trace the steps by which, through an intelligible sequence of causes, these necessary conditions were provided belongs rather to an investigation of Bible history than to our present purpose, so I will not enter into these details here. But what I hope I have in some measure made clear is that there is a reason why Christ should be manifested, and should suffer, and rise again, and that so far from being a baseless superstition the Reconciling of the world to God through the One Offering once-for-all offered for the sin of the whole world, lays the immovable foundation upon which we may build securely for all the illimitable future.

## XI

# OURSELVES IN THE DIVINE OFFERING

IF WE HAVE grasped the principle I have endeavored to state in the last chapter we shall find that with this new standpoint a new life and a new world begin to open out to us. This is because we are now living from a new recognition of ourselves and of God. Eternal Truth, that which is the essential reality of Being, is *always* the same; it has never altered, for whatever is capable of passing away and giving place to something else is not eternal, and therefore the real essence of our being, as proceeding from God and subsisting in Him has always been the same. But this is the very fact which we have hitherto lost sight of; and since our perception of life is the measure of our individual consciousness of it, we have imposed upon ourselves a world of limitation, a world filled with the power of the negative, because we have viewed things from that standpoint. What takes place, therefore, when we realize the truth of our Redemption is not a change in our essential relation to the Parent Spirit, the Eternal Father, but an awakening to the perception of this eternal and absolutely perfect relation. We see that in reality it has never been otherwise for the simple reason that in the very nature of Being it *could* not be otherwise; and when we see this we see also that what has hitherto been wrong has not been the working of "the Father" but our conception of the existence of some other power, a power of negation, limitation, and destructiveness, the very opposite to all that the Creative Spirit, by the very fact of Its Creativeness, must be. That wonderful parable of the Prodigal Son shows us that he never ceased to be a son. It was not his Father who sent him away from home but his notion that he could do better "on his own," and we all know what came of it. But when he returned to the Father he found that from the Father's point of view he had never been otherwise than a son, and that all the trouble he had gone through was not "of the Father" but was the result of his own failure to realize what the Father and the Home really were.*

Now this is exactly the case with ourselves. When we wake up to the truth we find that, so far as the Father is concerned, we have always been in Him and in His home, for we are made in His image and likeness and are reflections of His own Being. He says to us "Son, thou art ever with me and all that I have is thine." The Self-Contemplation of Spirit is the Creative Power creating an environment corresponding to the mode of consciousness contemplated, and therefore in proportion as we contemplate ourselves as centers of individualization for the Divine Spirit we find ourselves surrounded by a new environment reflecting the harmonious conditions which preexist in the Thought of the Spirit.

This, then, is the sequence of Cause and Effect involved in the teaching of the Bible. Man is *in essence* a spiritual being, the reflection on the plane of individual personality of that which the All-Originating Spirit is in Itself, and is thus in that reciprocal relation to the Spirit which is Love. This is the first statement of his creation in Genesis—God saw all that He had made and behold it was very good, Man included. Then the Fall is the failure of the lower mentality to realize that God IS Love, in a word that Love is the only ultimate Motive Power it is possible to conceive, and that the creations of Love cannot be otherwise than good and beautiful. The lower mentality conceives an opposite quality of Evil and thus produces a motive power the opposite of Love, which is Fear; and so Fear is born into the world giving rise to the whole brood of evil, anger, hatred, envy, lies, violence, and the like, and on the external plane giving rise to discordant vibrations which are the root of physical ill. If we analyze our motives we shall find that they are always some mode either of Love or Fear; and fear has its root in the recognition of some power other than Perfect Love, which is God the ONE all-embracing Good. Fear has a creative force which invertedly mimics that

* See "Bible Mystery and Bible Meaning" by the present author.

of Love; but the difference between them is that Love is eternal and Fear is not. Love as the Original Creative Motive is the only logical conclusion we can come to as to why we ourselves or any other creation exists. Fear is illogical because to regard it as having any place in the Original Creative Motive involves a contradiction in terms.

By accepting the notion of a dual power, that of Good *and* Evil, the inverted creative working of Fear is introduced with all its attendant train of evil things. This is the eating of the deadly tree which occasions the Fall, and therefore the Redemption which requires to be accomplished is a redemption from Fear—not merely from this or that particular fear but from the very Root of Fear, which root is unbelief in the Love of God, the refusal to believe that Love alone is the Creating Power in all things, whether small beyond our recognition or great beyond our conception. Therefore to bring about this Redemption there must be such a manifestation of the Divine Love to Man as, when rightly apprehended, will leave no ground for fear; and when we see that the Sacrifice of the Cross was the Self-Offering of Love made in order to provide this manifestation, then we see that all the links in the chain of Cause and Effect are complete, and that Fear never had any place in the Creative Principle, whether as acting in the creation of a world or of a man. The root, therefore, of all the trouble of the world consists in the Affirmation of Negation, in using our creative power of thought invertedly, and thus giving substance to that which *as principle* has no existence. So long as this negative action of thought continues so long will it produce its natural effect; whether in the individual or in the mass. The experience is perfectly real while it lasts. Its unreality consists in the fact that there was never any real need for it; and the more we grasp the truth of the all-embracingness of the ONE Good, both as Cause and as Effect, on all planes, the more the experience of its opposite will cease to have any place in our lives.

This truly New Thought puts us in an entirely new relation to the whole of our environment, opening out possibilities hitherto undreamt of, and this by an orderly sequence of law which is naturally involved in our new mental attitude; but before considering the prospect thus offered it is well to be quite clear as to what this new mental attitude really is; for it is our adoption of this attitude that is the Key to the whole position. Put briefly it is ceasing to include the idea of limitations in our conception of the working of the All-Creating Spirit. Here are some specimens of the way in which we limit the creative working of the Spirit. We say, I am too old now to start this or that new sort of work. This is to deny the power of the Spirit to vivify our physical or mental faculties, which is illogical if we consider that it is the same Spirit that brought us into any existence at all. It is like saying that when a lamp is beginning to burn low the same person who first filled it with oil cannot replenish it and make it burn brightly again. Or we say, I cannot do so and so because I have not the means. When you were fourteen did you know where all the means were coming from which were going to support you till now when you are perhaps forty or fifty? So you should argue that the same power that has worked in the past can continue to work in the future. If you say the means came in the past quite naturally through ordinary channels, that is no objection; on the contrary the more reason for saying that suitable channels will open in the future. Do you expect God to put cash into your desk by a conjuring trick? Means come through recognizable channels, that is to say we recognize the channels by the fact of the stream flowing through them; and one of our most common mistakes is in thinking that we ourselves have to fix the particular channel beforehand. We say in effect that the Spirit cannot open other channels, and so we stop them up. Or we say, our past experience speaks to the contrary, thus assuming that our past experiences have included all possibilities and have exhausted the laws of the universe, an assumption which is negatived by every fresh discovery even in physical science. And so we go on limiting the power of the Spirit in a hundred different ways.

But careful consideration will show that, though the modes in which we limit it are as numerous as the circumstances with which we have to deal, the thing with which we limit it is always the same—it is by the introduction of our own personality. This may appear at first a direct contradiction of all that I have said about the necessity for the Personal Factor, but it is not. Here is a paradox.

To open out into manifestation the wonderful possibilities hidden in the Creative Power of the Universe we require to do two things—to see that we ourselves are necessary as centers for focussing that power, and at the same time to withdraw the thought of ourselves as contributing anything to its efficiency. It is not I that work but the Power; yet the Power needs me because it cannot specialize itself without me—in a word each is the complementary of the other: and the higher the degree of specialization is to be the more necessary is the intelligent and willing co-operation of the individual.

This is the Scriptural paradox that "the son can do nothing of himself," and yet we are told to be "fellow-workers with God." It ceases to be a paradox, however, when we realize the relation between the two factors concerned, God and Man. Our mistake is in not discriminating between their respective functions, and putting Man in the place of God. In our everyday life we do this by measuring the power of God by our past experiences and the deductions we draw from them; but there is another way of putting Man in the place of God, and that is by the misconception that the All-Originating Spirit is merely a cosmic force without intelligence, and that Man has to originate the intelligence without which no specific purpose can be conceived. This latter is the error of much of the present day philosophy and has to be specially guarded against. This was perceived by some of the medieval students of these things, and they accordingly distinguished between what they called Animus Dei and Anima Mundi, the Divine Spirit and the Soul of the Universe. Now the distinction is this, that the essential quality of Animus Dei is Personality—not A Person, but the very Principle of Personality itself—while the essential quality of Anima Mundi is Impersonality. Then right here comes in that importance of the Personal Factor of which I have already spoken. The powers latent in the Impersonal are brought out to their fullest development by the operation of the Personal. This of course does not consist in changing the nature of those powers, for that is impossible, but in making such combinations of them by Personal Selection as to produce results which could not otherwise be obtained. Thus, for example, Number is in itself impersonal and no one can alter the laws which are inherent in it; but what we can do is to select particular numbers and the sort of relation, such as subtraction, multiplication, etc., which we will establish between them; and then by the inherent Law of Number a certain result is bound to work out. Now our own essential quality is the consciousness of Personality; and as we grow into the recognition of the fact that the Impersonal is, as it were, crying out for the operation upon it of the Personal in order to bring its latent powers into working, we shall see how limitless is the field that thus opens before us.

The prospect is wonderful beyond our present conception, and full of increasing glory if we realize the true foundation on which it rests. But herein lies the danger. It consists in not realizing that the Infinite of the Impersonal *is* and also that the Infinite of the Personal *is.* Both are Infinite and so require differentiation through our own personality, but in their essential quality each is the exact balance of the other—not in contradiction to each other, but as complementary to one another, each supplying what the other needs for its full expression, so that the two together make a perfect whole. If, however, we see this relation and our own position as the connecting link between them, we shall see only ourselves as the Personal Factor; but the more we realize, both by theory and experience, the power of human personality brought into contact with the Impersonal Soul of Nature, and employed with a Knowledge of its power and a corresponding exercise of the will, the less we shall be inclined to regard ourselves as the supreme factor in the chain of cause and effect. Consideration of this argument points to the danger of much of the present day teaching regarding the exercise of Thought Power as a creative agency. The principle on which this teaching is based is sound and legitimate for it is inherent in the nature of things; but the error is in supposing that we ourselves are the ultimate source of Personality instead of merely the distributors and specializers of it. The logical result of such a mental attitude is that putting ourselves in the place of all that is worshiped as God which is spoken of in the second chapter of the Second Epistle to the Thessalonians and other parts of Scripture. By the very hypothesis of the case we then know no higher will than our own, and so are without any Unifying Principle to prevent the conflict of wills which must then arise—a conflict which must become more and more destructive the greater the power possessed by the contending parties, and which, if there were no counterbalancing power, must result in the ultimate destruction of the existing race of men.

But there is a counterbalancing power. It is the very same power used affirmatively instead of negatively. It is the power of the Personal with the Impersonal when used under the guidance of that Unifying Principle which the recognition of the ONE-ness of the Personal Quality in the Divine Spirit supplies. Those who are using the creative power of thought only from the standpoint of individual personality, have obviously less power than those who are using it from the standpoint of the Personality inherent in the Living Spirit which is the Source and Fountain of all energy and substance, and therefore in the end the victory must remain with these latter. And because the power by which they conquer is that of the Unifying

Personality itself their victory must result in the establishment of Peace and Happiness throughout the world, and is not a power of domination but of helpfulness and enlightenment. The choice is between these two mottoes:— "Each for himself and Devil take the hindmost," or "God for us all." In proportion, therefore, as we realize the immense forces dormant in the Impersonal Soul of Nature, only awaiting the introduction of the Personal Factor to wake them up into activity and direct them to specific purposes, the wider we shall find the scope of the powers within the reach of man; and the more clearly we perceive the Impersonalness of the very Principle of Personality itself, the clearer our own proper position as affording the Differentiating Medium between these two Infinitudes will become to us.

The Impersonalness of the Principle of Personality looks like a contradiction in terms, but it is not. I combine these two seemingly contradictory terms as the best way to convey to the reader the idea of the essential Quality of Personality not yet differentiated into individual centers of consciousness for the doing of particular work. Looked at in this way the Infinite of Personality must have Unity of Purpose for its foundation, for otherwise it would consist of conflicting personalities, in which case we have not yet reached the ONE all-originating cause. Or to put it in another way, an Infinite Personality divided against itself would be an Infinite Insanity, a creator of a cosmic Bedlam which, as a scientific fact, would be impossible of existence. Therefore the conception of an Infinite of Personality necessarily implies a perpetual Unity of Purpose; and for the same reason this Purpose can only be the fuller and fuller expression of an Infinite Unity of Consciousness; and Unity of Consciousness necessarily implies the entire absence of all that would impair it, and therefore its expression can only be as Universal Harmony. If, then, the individual realizes this true nature of the source from which his own consciousness of personality is derived his ideas and work will be based upon this foundation, with the result that as between ourselves peace and good will towards men must accompany this mode of thought, and as between us and the strictly Impersonal Soul of Nature our increasing knowledge in that direction would mean increasing power for carrying out our principle of peace and good will. As this perception of our relation to the Spirit of God and the Soul of Nature spreads from individual to individual so the Kingdom of God will grow, and its universal recognition would be the establishing of the Kingdom of Heaven on earth.

Perhaps the reader will ask why I say the Soul of Nature instead of saying the material universe. The reason is that in using our creative power of Thought we do not operate directly upon material elements—to do that is the work of construction from without and not of creation from within. The whole tendency of modern physical science is to reduce all matter in the final analysis to energy working in a primary ether. Whence this energy and this ether proceed is not the subject of physical analysis. That is a question which cannot be answered by means of the vacuum tube or the spectroscope. Physical science is doing its legitimate work in pushing further and further back the unanalyzable residuum of Nature, but, however far back, an ultimate unanalyzable residuum there must always be; and when physical science brings us to this point it hands us over to the guidance of psychological investigation just as in the *Divina Commedia* Virgil transfers Dante to the guidance of Beatrice for the study of the higher realms. Various rates of rapidity of motion in this primary ether, producing various numerical combinations of positively and negatively electrified particles, result in the formation of what we know as the different chemical elements, and thus explains the phenomena of their combining quantities, the law by which they join together to form new substances only in certain exact numerical ratios. From the first movement in the primary ether to solid substances, such as wood or iron or our own flesh, is thus a series of vibrations in a succession of mediums, each denser than the preceding one out of which it was concreted and from which it receives the vibratory impulse. This is in effect what physical science has to tell us. But to get further back we must look into the world of the invisible, and it is here that psychological study comes to our aid. We cannot, however, study the invisible side of Nature by working from the outside and so at this point of our studies we find the use of the time-honored teaching regarding the parallelism between the Macrocosm and the Microcosm. If the Microcosm is the reproduction in ourselves of the same principles as exist in the Macrocosm or universe in which we have our being, then by investigating ourselves we shall learn the nature of the corresponding invisible principles in our environment. Here, then, is the application of the dictum of the ancient philosophy, "Know Thyself." It means that the only place where we can study the principles of the invisible side of Nature is in ourselves; and when we know them there we can transfer them to the larger world around us.

In the concluding chapters of my "Edinburgh Lectures on Mental Science" I have outlined the way in which the soul or mind operates upon the physical instrument of its expression, and it resolves itself into this—that the mental action inaugurates a series of vibrations in the etheric body which, in their turn, induce corresponding grosser vibrations in the molecular substance until finally mechanical action is produced on the outside. Now transferring this idea to Nature as a whole we shall see that if our mental action is to affect it in any way it can only be by the response of something at the back of material substance analogous to mind in ourselves; and that there is such a "something" interior to the merely material side of Nature is proved by what we may call the Law of Tendency, not only in animals and plants, but even in inorganic substances, as shown for instance in Professor Bose's work on the Response of Metals. The universal presence of this Law of Tendency therefore indicates the working of some non-material and, so to say, semi-intelligent power in the material world, a power which works perfectly accurately on its own lines so far as it goes, that is to say in a generic manner, but which does not possess that Personal power of *individual selection* which is necessary to bring out the infinite possibilities hidden in it. This is what is meant by the Soul of Nature, and it is for this reason I employ that term instead of saying the material universe. Which term to employ all depends on the mode of action we are contemplating. If it is construction from without, then we are dealing with the purely material universe. If we are seeking to bring about results by the exercise of our mental power from within, then we are dealing with the Soul of Nature. It is that control of the lower degree of intelligence by the higher of which I have spoken in my Edinburgh Lectures.

If we realize what I have endeavored to make clear in the earlier portion of this book, that the whole creation is produced by the operation of the Divine Will upon the Soul of Nature, it will be evident that we can set no limits to the potencies hidden in the latter and capable of being brought out by the operation of the Personal Factor upon it; therefore, granted a sufficiently powerful concentration of will, whether by an individual or a group of individuals, we can well imagine the production of stupendous effects by this agency, and in this way I would explain the statements made in Scripture regarding the marvelous powers to be exercised by the Anti-Christ, whether personal or collective. They are psychic powers, the power of the Soul of Man over the Soul of Nature. But the Soul of Nature is quite impersonal and therefore the moral quality of this action depends entirely on the human operator. This is the point of the Master's teaching regarding the destruction of the fig tree, and it is on this account He adds the warning as to the necessity for clearing our heart of any injurious feeling against others whenever we attempt to make use of this power (Mark xi: 20–26).

According to His teaching, then, this power of controlling the Soul of Nature by the addition of our own Personal Factor, however little we may be able to recognize it as yet, actually exists; its employment depends on our perception of the inner principles common to both, and it is for this reason the ancient wisdom was summed up in the aphorism "Know thyself." No doubt it is a wonderful Knowledge, but on analysis it will be found to be perfectly natural. It is the Knowledge of the cryptic forces of Nature. Now it is remarkable that this ancient maxim inscribed over the portals of the Temple of Delphi is not to be found in the Bible. The Bible maxim is not "Know thyself" but "Know the Lord." The great subject of Knowledge is not ourself but "the Lord"; and herein is the great difference between the two teachings. The one is limited by human personality, the other is based on the Infinitude of the Divine Personality; and because of this it includes human personality with all its powers over the Soul of Nature. It is a case of the greater including the less; and so the whole teaching of Scripture is directed to bringing us into the recognition of that Divine Personality which is the Great Original in whose image and likeness we are made. In proportion as we grow into the recognition of *this* our own personality will explain, and the creative power of our thought will cease to work invertedly until at last it will work only on the same principles of Life, Love and Liberty as the Divine Mind, and so all evil will disappear from our world. We shall not, as some systems teach, be absorbed into Deity to the extinction of our individual consciousness, but on the contrary our individual consciousness will continually expand, which is what St. Paul means when he speaks of our "increasing with the increase of God"—the continual expanding of the Divine element within us. But this can only take place by our recognition of ourselves as *receivers* of this Divine element. It is receiving into ourselves of the Divine Personality, a result not to be reached through human reasoning. We reason from premises which we have assumed, and the conclusion is already involved in the premises and can never extend beyond them. But we can only select our premises from among things that we know by experience, whether mental or physical, and accordingly our reasoning is always merely a new placing of the old things. But the receiving of the

Divine Personality into ourselves is an entirely New Thing, and so cannot be reached by reasoning from old things. Hence if this Divine ultimate of the Creative Process is to be attained it must be by the Revelation of a New Thing which will afford a new starting-point for our thought, and this New Starting-point is given in the Promise of "the Seed of the Woman" with which the Bible opens. Thenceforward this Promise became the central germinating thought of those who based themselves upon it, thus constituting them a special race, until at last when the necessary conditions had matured the Promised Seed appeared in Him of whom it is written that He is the express image of God's Person (Heb. I: 3)—that is, the Expression of that Infinite Divine Personality of which I have spoken. "No man hath seen God at any time or can see Him," for the simple reason that Infinitude cannot be the subject of vision. To become visible there must be Individualization, and therefore when Philip said "Show us the Father," Jesus replied, "He that hath seen me hath seen the Father." The Word must become flesh before St. John could say, "That which was from the beginning, which we have heard, which we have seen with our eyes, which we have looked upon, and our hands have handled, of the Word of Life." This is the New Starting-point for the true New Thought—the New Adam of the New Race, each of whom is a new center for the working of the Divine Spirit. This is what Jesus meant when he said, "Except ye eat the flesh and drink the blood of the Son of Man ye have no life in you. My flesh is meat indeed, and my blood is drink indeed—" such a contemplation of the Divine Personality in Him as will cause a like receiving of the Divine Personality into individualization in ourselves—this is the great purpose of the Creative Process in the individual. It terminates the old series which began with birth after the flesh and inaugurates a New Series by birth after the Spirit, a New Life of infinite unfoldment with glorious possibilities beyond our highest conception.

But all this is logically based upon our recognition of the Personalness of God and of the relation of our individual personality to this Eternal and Infinite Personality, and the result of this is Worship—not an attempt to "butter up" the Almighty and get Him into good temper, but the reverent contemplation of what this Personality must be in Itself; and when we see it to be that Life, Love, Beauty, etc., of which I spoke at the beginning of this book we shall learn to love Him for what He IS, and our prayer will be "Give me more of Thyself." If we realize the great truth that the Kingdom of Heaven is *within* us, that it is the Kingdom of the innermost of our own being and of all creation, and if we realize that this innermost is the place of the Originating Power where Time and Space do not exist and therefore antecedent to all conditions, then we shall see the true meaning of Worship. It is the perception of the Innermost Spirit as eternally subsisting independently of all conditioned manifestation, so that in the true worship our consciousness is removed from the outer sphere of existence to the innermost center of unconditioned being. There we find the Eternal Being of God pure and simple, and we stand reverently in this Supreme Presence knowing that it is the Source of our own being, and wrapt in the contemplation of This, the conditioned is seen to flow out from It. Perceiving this the conditioned passes out of our consideration, for it is seen not to be the Eternal Reality—we have reached that level of consciousness where Time and Space remain no longer. Yet the reverence which the vision of this Supreme Center of all Being cannot fail to inspire is coupled with a sense of feeling quite at home with It. This is because as the Center of *all* Being it is the center of our own being also. It is one-with-ourselves. It is recognizing Itself from our own center of consciousness; so that here we have got back to that Self-contemplation of Spirit which is the first movement of the Creating Power, only now this Self-contemplation is the action of the All-Originating Spirit upon Itself from the center of our own consciousness. So this worship in the Temple of the Innermost is at once reverent adoration and familiar intercourse—not the familiarity that breeds contempt, but a familiarity producing Love, because as it increases we see more clearly the true Life of the Spirit as the continual interaction of Love and Beauty, and the Spirit's recognition of ourselves as an integral portion of Its own Life.

This is not an unpractical dreamy speculation but has a very practical bearing. Death will some day cease to be, for the simple reason that Life alone can be the enduring principle; but we have not yet reached this point in our evolution. Whether any in this generation will reach it I cannot say; but for the rank and file of us the death of the body seems to be by far the more probable event. Now what must this passing out of the body mean to us? It must mean that we find ourselves without the physical vehicle which is the instrument through which our consciousness comes in touch with the external world and all the interests of our present daily life. But the mere putting off of the body does not of itself change the mental attitude; and so if our mind is entirely centered upon these passing interests and external conditions the loss of the instrument by which we held touch with them must involve a consciousness of desire for the only sort of life we have known coupled with a consciousness of our inability to participate in it, which can only result in a consciousness of distress and confusion such as in our present state we cannot imagine.

On the other hand if we have in this world realized the true principle of the Worship of the Eternal Source from which all conditioned life flows out—an inner communing with the Great Reality—we have already passed beyond that consciousness of life which is limited by Time and Space; and so when we put off this mortal body we shall find ourselves upon familiar ground, and therefore not wandering in confusion but quite at home, dwelling in the same light of the Eternal in which we have been accustomed to dwell as an atmosphere enveloping the conditioned life of to-day. Then finding ourselves thus at home on a plane where Time and Space do not exist there will be no question with us of duration. The consciousness will be simply that of peaceful, happy being. That a return to more active personal operation will eventually take place is evidenced by the fact that the basis of all further evolution is the differentiating of the Undifferentiated Life of the Spirit into specific channels of work, through the intermediary of individual personality without which the infinite potentialities of the Creative Law cannot be brought to light. Therefore, however various our opinions as to its precise form, Resurrection as a principle is a necessity of the creative process. But such a return to more active life will not mean a return to limitations, but the opening of a new life in which we shall transcend them all, because we have passed beyond the misconception that Time and Space are of the Essence of Life. When the misconception regarding Time and Space is entirely eradicated all other limitations must disappear because they have their root in this primary one—they are only particular forms of the general proposition. Therefore though Form with its accompanying relations of Time and Space is necessary for manifestation, these things will be found not to have any force in themselves thus creating limitation, but to be the reflection of the mode of thought which projects them as the expression of itself.

Nor is there any inherent reason why this process should be delayed till some far-off future. There is no reason why we should not commence at once. No doubt our inherited and personally engendered modes of thought make this difficult, and by the nature of the process it will be only when *all* our thoughts are conformed to this principle that the complete victory will be won. But there must be a commencement to everything, and the more we habituate ourselves to live in that Center of the Innermost where conditions do not exist, the more we shall find ourselves gaining control over outward conditions, because the stream of conditioned life flows out from the Center of Unconditioned Life, and therefore this intrinsic principle of Worship has in it the promise both of the life that now is and of that which is to come. Only we must remember that the really availing worship is that of the Undifferentiated Source *because It is the Source,* and not as a backhanded way of diverting the stream into some petty channel of conditions, for that would only be to get back to the old circle of limitation from which we are seeking to escape.

But if we realize these things we have already laid hold of the Principle of Resurrection, and in point of principle we are already living the resurrection life. What progress we may make in it depends on our practical application of the principle; but simply as principle there is nothing in the principle itself to prevent its complete working at any moment. This is why Jesus did not refer resurrection to some remote point of time but said, "I am the resurrection and the life." No principle can carry in itself an opposite and limiting principle contradictory of its own nature, and this is as true of the Principle of Life as of any other principle. It is we who by our thought introduce an opposite and limiting principle and so hinder the working of the principle we are seeking to bring into operation; but so far as the Principle of Life itself is concerned there is *in it* no reason why it should not come into perfect manifestation here and now.

This, then, is the true purpose of worship. It is to bring us into conscious and loving intercourse with the Supreme Source of our own being, and seeing this we shall not neglect the outward forms of worship. From what we now know they should mean more to us than to others and not less; and in especial if we realize the manifestation of the Divine Personality in Jesus Christ and its reproduction in Man, we shall not neglect His last command to partake of that sacred memorial to His flesh and blood which He bequeathed to His followers with the words "This do in remembrance of Me."

This holy rite is no superstitious human invention. There are many theories about it, and I do not wish to combat any of them, for in the end they all seem to me to bring us to the same point, that being cleansed from sin by the Divine Love we are now no longer separate from God but become "partakers of the Divine Nature" (II Peter 1: 4). This partaking of the Divine Nature could not be more accurately represented than by our partaking of bread and wine as symbols of the Divine Substance and the Divine Life, thus made emblematic of the whole Creative Process from its beginning in the Divine Thought to its completion in the manifestation of that Thought as Perfected Man; and so it brings vividly before us the remembrance of the Personality of God taking form as the Son of Man. We are all familiar with the saying that thoughts become things; and if we affirm the creative power of our own thought as reproducing itself in outward form, how much more must we affirm the same of that Divine Thought which brings the whole universe into existence; so that in accordance with our own principles the Divine Idea of Man was logically bound to show itself in the world of time and space as the Son of God and the Son of man, not two differing natures but one complete whole, thus summing up the foundation principle of all creation in one Undivided Consciousness of Personality. Thus "the Word" or Divine Thought of Man "became flesh," and our partaking of the symbolic elements keeps in our remembrance the supreme truth that this same "Word" or Thought of God in like manner takes form in ourselves as we open our own thought to receive it. And further, if we realize that throughout the universe there is only ONE Originating Life, sending forth only ONE Original Substance as the vehicle for its expression, then it logically follows that *in essence* the bread is a portion of the eternal Substance of God, and the wine a portion of the eternal Life of God. For though the wine is of course also a part of the Universal Substance, we must remember that the Universal Substance is itself a manifestation of the Life of the All-Creating Spirit, and therefore this fluid form of the primary substance has been selected as representing the eternal flowing of the Life of the Spirit into all creation, culminating in its supreme expression in the consciousness of those who, in the recognition of these truths, seek to bring their heart into union with the Divine Spirit. From such considerations as these it will be seen how vast a field of thought is covered by Christ's words "Do this in remembrance of Me."

In conclusion, therefore, do not let yourselves be led astray by any philosophy that denies the Personality of God. In the end it will be found to be a foolish philosophy. No other starting-point of creation is conceivable than the Self-Contemplation of the Divine Spirit, and the logical sequence from this brings us to the ultimate result of the Creative Process in the statement that "if any man be in Christ he is a New creature," or as the margin has it "a new creation" (II Cor. v: 17). Such vain philosophies have only one logical result which is to put *yourself* in the place of God, and then what have you to lean upon in the hour of trial? It is like trying to climb up a ladder that is resting against nothing. Therefore, says the Apostle Paul, "Beware lest any man spoil you through philosophy and vain deceit, after the tradition of man, after the rudiments of the world, and not after Christ." (Col. II: 8.) The teaching of the Bible is sound philosophy, sound reasoning, and sound science because it starts with the sound premises that all Creation proceeds out of God, and that Man is made in the image and likeness of his Creator. It nowhere departs from the Law of Cause and Effect, and by the orderly sequence of this law it brings us at last to the New Creation both in ourselves and in our environment, so that we find the completion of the Creative Process in the declaration "the tabernacle of God is with men" (Rev. xxi: 3), and in the promise "This is the Covenant that I will make with them after those days (i.e., the days of our imperfect apprehension of these things) saith the Lord, I will dwell *in them,* and walk *in them,* and I will be their God, and they shall be my people, and I will put my laws into their hearts, and in their minds will I write them, and their sins and their iniquities will I remember no more" (Heb. x: 16. II Cor. vi: 16. Jeremiah xxxi: 33).

Truly does Bacon say, "A little philosophy inclineth a man's mind to atheism, but depth in philosophy bringeth men's minds about to religion."—Bacon, Essay, xvi.

# Bible Mystery and Bible Meaning

1913

# CONTENTS

# FOREWORD

THE FAVORABLE RECEPTION accorded to my *Edinburgh Lectures on Mental Science* has encouraged me to offer another book to my readers. The present volume is written from the standpoint that we possess latent powers which a better knowledge of the truth regarding ourselves will enable us to develop, and that the purpose of the Bible is to lead us into this knowledge in a perfectly natural manner, while guarding us against the dangers arising from misuse of it. That we should ever arrive at a point when we shall be no longer confronted by the element of mystery which is inherent in the *livingness* of Life is impossible; but this mystery is the Mystery of Light and not of darkness, and will continually unfold itself into more light in response to our earnest inquiry into its meaning; and I have therefore given this book a title indicative of the ever-presence of an august Mystery together with intelligible Law.

Although my presentment of the Bible is in many respects very different from the generally accepted one, it will be found in no way really at variance with the doctrines of Christianity; on the contrary, I hope that by helping, in however small a measure, to elucidate them, it will show the reasonableness of great truths which those who reject them as unreasonable discredit to their own incalculable loss.

This book was originally the outcome of a number of lectures given by me in London, Edinburgh, Glasgow, Birmingham and elsewhere, but the great interest shown in it by a continually increasing circle of readers has led me to extend the present volume by four additional chapters touching on certain topics holding a pre-eminent place in Bible study. There is one other subject to which I have only been able to advert casually in the concluding pages, but which is of peculiar importance at the present day, that of chronological prophecy. The march of events and the rapid developments in various fields of knowledge show such a marked correspondence with the prophetic measures of time given in the Bible that the serious student cannot but feel convinced that we are very rapidly approaching that climax which the Bible speaks of as the End of the Age. I would most earnestly ask my readers to give this subject their attention, for the time is at hand. Its wide extent makes it impossible for me to treat of it in this book, but if such be the Lord's will, I may make it the subject of another volume.

T. Troward.
*Ruan Minor, August, 1913.*

I

# THE CREATION

THE BIBLE IS the Book of the Emancipation of Man. The emancipation of man means his deliverance from sorrow and sickness, from poverty, struggle, and uncertainty, from ignorance and limitation, and finally from death itself. This may appear to be what the euphuistic colloquialism of the day would call "a tall order," but nevertheless it is impossible to read the Bible with a mind unwarped by antecedent conceptions derived from traditional interpretation without seeing that this is exactly what it promises, and that it professes to contain the secret whereby this happy condition of perfect liberty may be attained. Jesus says that if a man keeps his saying he shall never see death (John viii. 51): in the Book of Job we are told that if a man has with him "a messenger, an interpreter," he shall be delivered from going down to the pit, and shall return to the days of his youth (Job xxxiii. 24): the Psalms speak of our renewing our youth (Psalm ciii. 5): and yet again we are told in Job that by acquainting ourselves with God we shall be at peace, we shall lay up gold as dust and have plenty of silver, we shall decree a thing and it shall be established unto us (Job xxii. 21–23).

Now, what I propose is that we shall re-read the Bible on the supposition that Jesus and these other speakers really meant what they said. Of course, from the standpoint of the traditional interpretation this is a startling proposition. The traditional explanation assumes that it is impossible for these things to be literally true, and therefore it seeks some other meaning in the words, and so gives them a "spiritual" interpretation. But in the same manner we may spiritualize away an Act of Parliament, and it hardly seems the best way of getting at the meaning of a book to follow the example of the preacher who commenced his discourse with the words, "Beloved brethren, the text doth not mean what it saith." Let us, however, start with the supposition that these texts do mean what they say, and try to interpret the Bible on these lines: it will at least have the attraction of novelty, and I think if the reader gives his careful attention to the following pages, he will see that this method carries with it the conviction of reason.

If a thing is true at all there is a *way* in which it is true, and when the *way* is seen, we find that to be perfectly reasonable which, before we understood the way, appeared unreasonable: we all go by railroad now, yet they were esteemed level-headed practical men in their day who proposed to confine George Stephenson as a lunatic for saying that it was possible to travel at thirty miles an hour.

The first thing to notice is that there is a common element running through the texts I have quoted; they all contain the idea of acquiring certain information, and the promised results are all contingent on our getting this information, and using it. Jesus says it depends on our keeping his saying, that is, receiving the information which he had to give and acting upon it. Job says that it depends on rightly interpreting a certain message, and again that it depends on our making ourselves acquainted with something; and the context of the passage in the Psalms makes it clear that the deliverance from death and the renewal of youth there promised are to be attained through the "ways" which the Lord "made known unto Moses." In all these passages we find that these wonderful results come from the attainment of certain knowledge, and the Bible therefore appeals to our Reason. From this point of view we may speak of the Science of the Bible, and as we advance in our study we shall find that this is not a misuse of terms, for the Bible is eminently scientific, only its science is not primarily physical but mental.

The Bible contemplates Man as composed of "Spirit, soul, and body" (I. Thess. v. 23), or in other words as combining into a single unity a threefold nature, spiritual, psychic, and corporeal; and the knowledge which it proposes to give us is the knowledge of the true relation between these three factors. The Bible also contemplates the totality of all Being, manifested and unmanifested, as likewise constituting a threefold unity, which may be distributed under the terms "God," "Man," and "the Universe"; and it occupies itself with telling us of the interaction, both positive and negative, which goes on between these three. Furthermore, it bases this interaction upon two great psychological laws, namely, that of the creative power of Thought and that of the amenability of Thought to control by Suggestion; and it affirms that this Creative Power is as innately inherent in Man's Thought as in the Divine Thought.

But it also shows how through ignorance of these truths we unknowingly misuse our creative power, and so produce the evils we deplore; and it also realizes the extreme danger of recognizing our power before we have attained the moral qualities which will fit us to use it in accordance with those principles which keep the great totality of things in an abiding harmony, and to avoid this danger the Bible veils its ultimate meaning under symbols, allegories, and parables. But these are so framed as to reveal this ultimate meaning to those who will take the trouble to compare the various statements with one another, and who are sufficiently intelligent to draw the deductions which follow from thus putting two and two together; while those who cannot thus read between the lines are trained into the requisite obedience to the Universal Law by means of suggestions suited to the present extent of their capacity, and are thus gradually prepared for the fuller recognition of the Truth as they advance.

Seen in this light, the Bible is found not to be a mere collection of old-world fables or unintelligible dogmas, but a statement of great universal laws, all of which proceed simply and naturally from the initial truth that Creation is a process of Evolution. Grant the evolutionary theory, which every advance in modern science renders clearer, and all the rest follows, for the entire Bible is based upon the principle of Evolution. But the Bible is a statement of universal Law, of that which obtains in the realm of the invisible as well as that which obtains in the realm of the visible, and therefore it deals with facts of a transcendental nature as well as with those of the physical plane, and accordingly it contemplates an earlier process anterior to Evolution, the process, namely, of Involution, the passing of Spirit into Form as antecedent to the passing of Form into Consciousness. If we bear this in mind, it will throw light on many passages which must remain wrapped in impenetrable obscurity until we know something of the psychic principles to which they refer. The fact that the Bible always contemplates Evolution as necessarily preceded by Involution should never be lost sight of, and therefore much of the Bible requires to be read as referring to the involutionary process taking place upon the psychic plane. But Involution and Evolution are not opposed to one another, they are only the earlier and later stages of the same process, the perpetual urging onward of Spirit for Self-expression in infinite varieties of Form; and therefore the grand foundation on which the whole Bible system is built up is that the Spirit which is thus continually passing into manifestation is always the *same* Spirit, in other words it is only ONE.

These two fundamental truths, that under whatever varieties of Form the Spirit is only ONE, and that the creation of all *forms,* and consequently of the whole world of *conscious relations* is the result of Spirit's ONE mode of action, which is Thought, are the basis of all that the Bible has to teach us, and therefore from its first page to its last, we shall find these two ideas continually recurring in a variety of different connections, the ONE-ness of the Divine Spirit and the Creative Power of Man's Thought, which the Bible expresses in its two grand statements, that "God is ONE," and that Man is made "in the image and likeness of God." These are the two fundamental statements of the Bible, and all its other statements flow logically from them; and since the whole argument of Scripture is built up from these premises, the reader must not be surprised at the frequency with which our analysis of that argument will bring us back to these two initial propositions; so far from being a vain repetition, this continual reduction of the statements of the Bible to the premises with which is originally sets out, is the strongest proof that we have in them a sure and solid foundation on which to base our present life and our future expectations.

But there is yet another point of view from which the Bible appears to be the very opposite of a logically accurate system built up on the broad foundations of Natural Law. From this point of view it at first looks like the egotistical and arrogant tradition of a petty tribe, the narrow book of a narrow sect, instead of a statement of universal Truth; and yet this aspect of it is so prominent that it can by no means be ignored. It is impossible to read the Bible and shut our eyes to the fact that it tells us of God making a covenant with Abraham, and thenceforward separating his descendants by a divine interposition from the remainder of mankind, for this separation of a certain portion of the race as special objects of the Divine favour, forms an integral part of Scripture from the story of Cain and Abel to the description of "the camp of the saints and the beloved city" in the Book of Revelation. We cannot separate these two aspects of the Bible, for they are so interwoven with one another that if we attempt to do so, we shall end by having no Bible left, and we are therefore compelled to accept the Bible statement as a whole or reject it altogether, so that we are met by the paradox of a combination between an all-inclusive system of Natural Law and an exclusive selection which at first appears to flatly contradict the processes of Nature. Is it possible to reconcile the two?

The answer is that it is not only possible, but that this exclusive selection is the necessary consequence of the Universal Law of Evolution when working in the higher phases of individualism. It is not that those who do not come within the pale of this Selection suffer any diminution, but that those who do come within it receive thereby a special augmentation, and, as we shall see by and by, this takes place by a purely natural process resulting from the more intelligent employment of that knowledge which it is the purpose of the Bible to unfold to us. These two principles of the inclusive and the exclusive are intertwined in a double thread which runs all through Scripture, and this dual nature of its statements must always be borne in mind if we would apprehend its meaning. Asking the reader, therefore, to carefully go over these preliminary remarks as affording the clue to the *reason* of the Bible statements, I shall now turn to the first chapter of Genesis.

The opening announcement that "in the Beginning God created the heaven and the earth" contains the statement of the first of those two propositions which are the fundamental premises from which the whole Bible is evolved. From the Master's instruction to the woman of Samaria we know that "God" means "Spirit"; not "*a* Spirit," as in the Authorised Version, thus narrowing the Divine Being with the limitations of individuality, but as it stands in the original Greek, simply "Spirit"—that is, *all* Spirit, or Spirit in the Universal. Thus the opening words of the Bible may be read, "in the beginning Spirit"—which is a statement of the underlying Universal Unity.

Here let me draw attention to the two-fold meaning of the words "in the beginning." They may mean first in order of time, or first in order of causation, and the latter meaning is brought out by the Latin version, which commences with the words *"in principio"*—that is, "in principle." This distinction should be borne in mind, for in all subsequent stages of evolution the initial principle which gives rise to the individualised entity must still be in operation as the *fons et origo* of that particular manifestation just as much as in its first concentration; it is the root of the individuality, without which the individuality would cease to exist. It is the "beginning" of the individuality in order of causation, and this "beginning" is, therefore, a *continuous fact, always* present, and not to be conceived of as something which has been left behind and done with. The same principle was, of course, the "beginning" of the entity in point of time also, however far back in the ages we may suppose it to have first evolved into separate existence, so that whether we apply the idea to the cosmos or to the individual, the words "in the beginning" both carry us back to the primordial out-push from non-manifestation into manifestation, and also rivet our attention upon the same power as still at work as the causal principle both in ourselves and in everything else around us. In both these senses, then, the opening words of the Bible tell us that the "beginning" of everything is "God," or Spirit in the universal.

The next statement, that God created the heaven and the earth, brings us to the consideration of the Bible way of using words. The fact that the Bible deals with spiritual and psychic matters, makes it of necessity an esoteric book, and therefore, in common with all other esoteric literature, it makes a symbolic use of words for the purpose of succinctly expressing ideas which would otherwise require elaborate explanation, and also for the purpose of concealing its meaning from those who are not yet safely to be entrusted with it. But this need not discourage the earnest student, for by comparing one part of the Bible with another he will find that the Bible itself affords the clue to the translation of its own symbolical vocabulary. Here, as in so many other instances, the Master has given us the key to the right interpretation. He says that the Kingdom of Heaven is *within* us; in other words, that "Heaven" is the kingdom of the innermost and spiritual, and if so, then by necessary implication "Earth" must be the symbol of the opposite extreme, and must metaphorically mean the outermost and material. We are starting the history of the evolution of the world in which we live, that is to say, this Power which the Bible calls "God" is first presented to us in the opening words of Genesis at a stage immediately preceding the commencement of a stupendous work.

Now what are the conditions necessary for the doing of any work? Obviously there must be something that works and something that is worked upon; an active and a passive factor; an energy and a material on or in which that energy operates. This, then, is what is meant by the creation of Heaven and Earth; it is that operation of the eternally subsisting ONE upon Itself which produces its dual expression, as Energy and Substance. And here remark carefully that this does not mean a *separation,* for Energy can only be exhibited by reason of something which is energized, or, in other words, for Life to manifest at all there must be something that lives. This is an all-important truth, for our conception of ourselves as beings separate from the Divine Life is the root of all our troubles.

In its first verse, therefore, the Bible starts us with the conception of Energy or Life *inherent in substance,* and shows us that the two constitute a dual-unity which is the first manifestation of the Infinite Unmanifested ONE; and if the reader will think these things out for himself, he will see that these are primary intuitions the contrary of which it is impossible to conceive. He may, if he please, introduce a Demiurge as part of the machinery for the production of the world, but then he has to account for his Demiurge, which brings him back to the Undistributed ONE of which I speak, and its first manifestation as Energy-inherent-in-Substance; and if he is driven back to this position, then it becomes clear that his Demiurge is a totally unnecessary wheel in the train of evolutionary machinery, and the gratuitous introduction of a factor which does no work but what could equally be done without it, is contrary to anything we can observe in Nature or can conceive of a Self-evolving Power.

But we are particularly cautioned against the mistake of supposing that Substance is the same thing as Form, for we are told that the "earth was without form." This is important because it is just here that a very prolific source of error in metaphysical studies creeps in. We see Forms which, simply as masses, are devoid of an organized life corresponding to the particular form, and therefore we deny the inherency of Energy or Life in ultimate substance itself. As well deny the pungency of pepper because it is not in the particular pepper-pot we are accustomed to. No, that primordial state of Substance with which the opening verse of the Bible is concerned, is something very far removed from any conception we can have of Matter as formed into atoms or electrons. We are here only at the first stage of Involution, and the presence of material atoms is a stage, and by no means the earliest, in the process of Evolution.

We are next told that the Spirit of God moved upon the face of the waters. Here we have two factors, "Spirit" and "Water," and the initial movement is attributed to Spirit. This verse introduces us to that particular mode of manifestation of the Universal Substance which we may denominate the Psychic. This psychic mode of the Universal Substance may best be described as Cosmic Soul-Essence, not, indeed, universal in the strictest sense otherwise than as always included in the original Primordial Essence, but universal to the particular world-system under formation, and as yet undifferentiated into any individual forms. This is what the mediæval writers spoke of as "the Soul of the Universe," or *Anima Mundi,* as distinguished from the Divine Spirit or *Animus Dei,* and it is the universal psychic medium in which the nuclei of the forms hereafter to become consolidated on the plane of the concrete and material, take their inception in obedience to the movement of the Spirit, or Thought. This is the realm of *Potential* Forms, and is the connecting link between Spirit, or pure Thought, and Matter, or concrete Form, and as such plays a most important part in the constitution of the Cosmos and of Man. In our reading of the Bible as well as in our practical application of Mental Science, the existence of this intermediary between Spirit and Matter must never be lost sight of. We may call it the Distributive Medium in passing through which the hitherto undistributed Energy of Spirit receives differentiation of direction, and so ultimately produces differentiation of forms and relations on the outermost or visible plane. This is the Cosmic Element which is esoterically called "Water," and so long ago as the reign of Henry VIII., Dean Collet explains it thus in a letter to his friend Randulph.

Dean Collet was very far from being a visionary. He was one of the precursors of the Reformation in England, and among the first to establish the study of Greek at Oxford, and as the founder of St. Paul's School in London, he took a leading part in introducing the system of public school education, which is still in operation in this country. There is no mistaking Dean Collet for any other than a thoroughly level-headed and practical man, and his opinion as to the meaning of the word "Water" in this connection therefore carries great weight.

But we have the utterance of a yet higher authority on this subject, for the Master Himself concentrates His whole instruction to Nicodemus on the point that the New Birth results from the interaction of "Spirit" and "Water," especially emphasizing the fact that "the flesh" has no share in the operation. This distinction between "the flesh," or the outermost principle, and "Water" should be carefully noted. The emphasis laid by the Master on the nothingness of "the flesh," and the essentialness of "Water," must mark a distinction of the most important kind, and we shall find it very helpful in unravelling the meaning of many passages of the Bible to grasp this distinction at the outset. The action of "Spirit" upon "Water" is that of an active upon a passive principle, and the result of any sort of Work is to reconstruct the material worked upon into a form which it did not possess before. Now the new form to be produced, whatever it may be, is a *result,* and therefore is not to be enumerated among the causes of its own production. Hence it is a self-obvious truism that any act of creative power must take place at a more interior level than that of the form to be created, and accordingly, whether in the Old or the New Testament, the creative action is always contemplated as taking place between the Spirit and the Water, whether we are thinking of producing a new world or a new man. We must always go back to First Cause operating on Primary Substance.

We are told that the first product of the movement of Spirit upon Water was Light, thereby suggesting an analogy with the discoveries of modern science that light and heat are modes of motion; but the statement that the Sun was not created till the fourth day guards us against the mistake of supposing that what is here meant is the light visible to the physical eye. Rather it is that all-pervading Inner Light, of which I shall have more to say by and by, and which only becomes visible as the corresponding sense of inward vision begins to be developed; it is that psychic condition of the Universal Substance in which the auras of the *potentials* of all forms may be discovered, and where, consciously or unconsciously, the Spirit determines the forms of those things which are to be. Like all other knowledge, the knowledge of the Inner Light is capable of application at higher and at lower levels, and the premature recognition of its power at the lower levels, uncontrolled by the recognition of its higher phases, is one of the most dangerous acquisitions; but duly regulated by the higher knowledge, the lower is both safe and legitimate, for in its due order it also is part of the Universal Harmony.

The initial Light having thus been produced, the introduction of the firmament on the second day indicates the separation of the spiritual principles of the different members of the world-system from one another, and the third day sees the emanation of Earth from "the Water," or the production of the actual corporeal system of Nature—the commencement of the process of Evolution. Up to this point the action has been entirely upon the inner plane of "Water," that is to say, a process of Involution, and consistently with this it was impossible for the heavenly bodies to begin giving physical light until the fourth day, for until then no physical sun or planets could have existed. With the fourth day, however, the physical universe is differentiated into shape; and on the fifth day the *terrestrial* waters begin to take their share in the evolutionary process, by spontaneously producing fish and fowl: and here we may remark in passing how Genesis has forestalled modern science in the discovery that birds are anatomically more closely related to fishes than to land animals. The terrestrial earth (I call it so to distinguish it from symbolic "earth"), already on the third day impregnated with the vegetable principle, takes up the evolutionary work on the sixth day, producing all those other animal races which had not already originated in the waters, and thus the preparation of the world as an abode for Man is completed.

It would be difficult to give a more concise statement of Evolution. Originating Spirit subsists at first as simple Unity, then it differentiates itself into the active and passive principles spoken of as "Heaven" and "Earth," or "Spirit" and "Water." From these proceed Light and the separation into their respective spheres of the spiritual principles of the different planets, each carrying with it the potential of the self-reproducing power. Then we pass into the realm of realization, and the work that has been done on the interior planes is now reproduced in physical manifestation, thus marking a still further unfoldment; and finally, in the phrases "let the waters bring forth" and "let the earth bring forth," the land and water of our habitable globe are distinctly stated to be the sources from which all vegetable and animal forms have been evolved. Thus creation is described as the self-transforming action of the ONE unanalysable Spirit passing by successive transitions into all the varieties of manifestations that fill the universe.

And here we may notice a point which has puzzled commentators unacquainted with the principles on which the Bible is written; this is the expression "the evening and the morning were the first, second, etc., day."

Why, it is asked, does each day begin with the evening? and various attempts have been made to explain it in accordance with Jewish methods of reckoning time. But as soon as we see what the Bible statement of creation is, the reason at once becomes clear. The second verse of the Bible tells us that the starting-point was Darkness, and the coming forth of Light out of Darkness cannot be stated in any other order than the dawning of morning from night.

It is the dawning into manifestation out of non-manifestation, and this happens at each successive stage of the evolutionary process. We should notice, also, that nothing is said as to the remainder of each day. All that we hear of each day is as "the morning," thus indicating the grand truth that when once a Divine day opens it never again descends into the shades of night. It is always "morning."

The Spiritual Sun is always climbing higher and higher, but never passes the zenith or commences to decline, a truth which Swedenborg expresses by saying that the Spiritual Sun is always seen in the eastern heavens at an angle of forty-five degrees above the horizon. What a glorious and inspiring truth: when once God begins a work, that work will never cease, but will go on for ever expanding into more and more radiant forms of strength and beauty, because it is the expression of the Infinite, which is Itself Love, Wisdom, and Power. These days of creation are still in their prime, and for ever will be so, and the germs of the New Heavens and the New Earth which the Bible promises are already maturing in the heavens and earth that now are, waiting only, as St. Paul tells us, for the manifestation of the Sons of God to follow up the old principle of Evolution to still further expansion in the glory that shall be revealed.

As himself included in the great Whole, Man is no exception to the Universal Law of Evolution. It has often been remarked that the account of his creation is two-fold, the two statements being contained in the first and second chapters of Genesis respectively. But this is precisely in accordance with the method adopted regarding the rest of creation. First we are told of the creation in the realm of the invisible and psychic, that is to say, the process of Involution, and afterwards we are told of the creation on the plane of the concrete and material, that is to say, the process of Evolution; and since Involution is the cause and Evolution the effect, the Bible observes this order both in the account of the creation of the world and in that of the creation of Man. In regard to his physical structure, Man's body, we are told, is formed from the "earth," that is, by a combination of the same material elements as all other concrete forms, and thus in the physical Man, the evolutionary process attains its culmination in the production of a material vehicle capable of serving as the starting-point for a further advance, which has now to be made on the plane of the Intellectual and Spiritual.

The principal of Evolution is never departed from, but its further action now includes the intelligent co-operation of the evolving Individuality itself as a necessary factor in the work. The development of merely animal Man is the spontaneous operation of Nature, but the development of the mental Man can only result from his own recognition of the Law of the self-expression of Spirit as operating in himself. It is, therefore, for the setting forth of Man's power to *use* this Law that the Bible was written, and, accordingly, the great fact on which it seeks to rivet our attention in its first utterance regarding Man is that he is made in the image and likeness of God. A very little reflection will show us that this likeness cannot be in the outward form, for the Universal Spirit in which all things subsist cannot be limited by a shape. It is a Principle permeating all things as their innermost substance and vivifying energy, and of it the Bible tells us that "in the beginning" there was nothing else. Now the one and only conception we can have of this Universal Life-Principle is that of Creative Power producing infinitely varied expressions of itself by Thought, for we cannot ascribe any other initial mode of movement to Spirit but that of thought, although as taking place in the universal, this mode of Thought must necessarily be, relatively to the individual and particular, a sub-conscious activity. The likeness, therefore, between God and Man must be a mental likeness, and since the only fact which, up to this point, the Bible has told us regarding the Universal Mind is its Creative Power, the resemblance indicated can only consist in the reproduction of the same Creative Power in the Mind of Man. As we progress we shall find that the whole Bible turns on this one fundamental fact. The Creative Power is inherent in our Thought, and we can by no means divest ourselves of it, but because we are ignorant that we possess this power, or because we misapprehend the conditions for its beneficial employment, we need much instruction in the nature of our own as yet unrecognized possibilities, and it is the purpose of the Bible to give us this teaching.

A little consideration of the terms of the evolutionary process will show us that since there is no other source from which it can proceed, the Individual Mind, which is the essential entity that we call Man, can be no other than a concentration of the Universal Mind into individual consciousness. Man's Mind is, therefore, a miniature reproduction of the Divine Mind, just as fire has always the same igneous qualities whether the centre of combustion be large or small; and so it is on *this* fact that the Bible would fix our attention from first to last, knowing that if the interior realm of Causation be maintained in a harmonious order the external realm of Effects is certain to exhibit corresponding health, happiness, and beauty. And further, if the human mind is the exact image and likeness of the Divine, then its creative power must be equally unlimited. Its *mode* is different, being directed to the individual and particular, but its *quality* is the same; and this becomes evident if we reflect that it is not possible to set any limit to Thought, and that its only limitations are such as are set by the limited conceptions of the individual who thinks. And it is precisely here that the difficulty comes in. Our Thought must necessarily be limited by our conceptions. We cannot think of something which we cannot conceive, and, therefore, the more limited our conceptions the more limited will be our thought, and its creations will accordingly be limited in a corresponding degree. It is for this reason that the ultimate purpose of all true instruction is to lead us into that Divine Light where we shall see things beyond the range of any past experiences—things which have not entered into the heart of man to conceive, revealings of the Divine Spirit opening to us untold worlds of splendour, delight, and unending achievement; but in our earlier stages of development, where we are still surrounded by the mists of ignorance, this correspondence between the range of Thought's creations and the range of our conceptions brings about the catastrophe of "the Fall" which forms the subject of our next chapter.

II

# THE FALL

IN THE LAST CHAPTER we reached the conclusion that in the nature of things Thought must always be limited by the range of the intelligence which gives rise to it. The power of Thought as the creative agent is perfectly unlimited in itself, but its action is limited by the particular conception which it is sent forth to embody. If it is a wide conception based upon an enlarged perception of truth, the thought which dwells upon it will produce corresponding conditions. This is self-evident: it is simply the statement that an instrument will not do work to which the hand of the workman does not apply it; and if the student will only fix this very simple idea in his mind, he will find in it the key to the whole mystery of man's power of self-evolution. Let us make our first use of this key to unlock the mystery of the story of Eden.

It is hardly necessary to say that the story of Eden is an allegory: that is clearly shown by the nature of the two trees that grew in the centre of the garden, the Tree of the Knowledge of Good and Evil and the Tree of Life. This allegory is one repeated in many lands and ages, as in the classical fable of the Garden of the Hesperides and in the mediæval Romance of the Rose—always the idea is repeated of a garden in whose centre grows some life-giving fruit or flower which is the reward of him who discovers the secret by which the centre of the garden may be reached.

The meaning in all these stories is the same. The garden is the Garden of the Soul, and the Tree of Life is that innermost perception of Spirit of which the Master said that it would be a well of water springing up to everlasting life to all who realized it. It is the garden which elsewhere in Scripture is called "the garden of the Lord," and in accordance with the nature of the garden the plants which grow in it, and which man has to tend and cultivate, are thoughts and ideas; and the chief of them are his idea of Life and his idea of Knowledge, and these occupy the centre of the garden because all our other ideas must take their colour from them.

We must recollect that human life is a drama whose action takes place in three worlds, and therefore, in reading the Bible, we must always make sure which world we are at any moment reading about, the spiritual, the intellectual, or the physical. In the spiritual world, which is that of the supreme ideal, there exists nothing but the potential of the absolutely perfect: and it is on this account that in the opening chapter of the Bible we read that God saw that all his work was good, the Divine eye could find no flaw anywhere; and we should note carefully that this absolutely good creation included Man also. But as soon as we descend to the Intellectual world, which is the world of man's *conception* of things, it is quite different; and until man comes to realize the truly spiritual, and therefore perfectly good, essential nature of all things, there is room for any amount of *mis*-conception, resulting in a corresponding misdirection of man's creative instrument of Thought, which thus produces correspondingly misformed realities.

Now the perfect life of Adam and Eve in Eden is the picture of Man as he exists in the spiritual world. It is not the tradition of some bygone age, but a symbolical representation of what we all *are* in our *innermost* being, thus recalling the words of the Master recorded in the Gospel of the Egyptians. He was asked when the Kingdom of Heaven should come, and replied, "When that which is without shall be as that which is within"; in other words, when the perfection of the innermost spiritual essence shall be reproduced in the external part. In the story of Man's pristine life of innocence and joy in Paradise, we are reading on the level of the highest of the three worlds.

The story of "the Fall" brings us to the envelopment of this spiritual nature in the lower intellectual and material natures, through which alone it can obtain perfect individualization and Man become a reality instead of remaining only a Divine dream. In the allegory Man is warned by God that Death will be the consequence of eating the fruit of the tree of the Knowledge of Good and Evil. This is not the threat of a sentence to be passed by God, but a warning as to the nature of the fruit itself; but this warning is disregarded by Eve, and she shares the forbidden fruit with Adam, and they are both expelled from Eden and become subject to Death as the consequence.

Now, if Eden is the garden of the Soul, it is clear that Adam and Eve cannot be separate personages, but must be two principles in the human individuality which are so closely united as to be represented by a wedded pair. What, then, are these principles? St. Paul makes a very remarkable statement regarding Adam and Eve. He tells us that "Adam was not deceived, but the woman being deceived was in the transgression" (I Tim. ii. 14). We have, therefore, Bible warrant for saying that Adam was not deceived; but at the same time the story of the Fall clearly shows that he was expelled from Eden from partaking of the fruit at Eve's instigation.

To satisfy both statements, therefore, we require to find in Adam and Eve two principles, one of which is capable of being deceived, and is deceived, and falls in consequence of the deception; and the other of which is incapable of being deceived but yet is involved in the fall of the former. This is the problem which has to be worked out, and the names of Adam and Eve supply the solution. Eve, we are told, was so called because she was the mother of all living (Gen. iii. 20). Eve, then, is the Mother of Life, a subject to which I shall have to refer again by and by. Eve, both syllables being pronounced, is the same word which in some Oriental languages is written "Hawa," by which name she is called in the Koran, and signifies Breath, the principle which we are told in Genesis ii. 7, constitutes Man a living Soul. Adam is rendered in the margin of the Bible "earth," or "red earth," and according to another derivation the name may also be rendered as Not-breath; and thus in these two names we have the description of two principles, one of which is "Breath" and Life-conveying, while the other is "Not-breath" and is nothing but earth.

It requires no great skill to recognize in these the Soul and the Body. Then St. Paul's meaning becomes clear. Any work on physiology will tell you that the human body is made up of certain chemical materials, so much chalk, so much carbon, so much water, etc., etc. Obviously these substances cannot be deceived because they have no intelligence, and any deception that occurs must be accepted by the soul or intellectual principle, which is Eve, the mother of the individual life.

New-Thought readers will have no difficulty in following the meaning of the poet Spencer when he says—

> *"For of the soul the body form doth take,*
> *For soul is form and doth the body make;"*

and since the soul is "the builder of the body," the deception which causes wrong thinking on the part of the intellectual man reproduces itself in physical imperfection and in adverse external circumstances.

What, then, is the deception which causes the "Fall"? This is figured by the Serpent. The serpent is a very favourite emblem in all ancient esoteric literature and symbolism, and is sometimes used in a positive and sometimes in a negative sense. In either case it means life—not the Originating Life-Principle but the ultimate outcome of that Life-Principle in its most external form of manifestation. This, of course, is not bad in itself. Recognized in full realization of the fact that it comes from God, it is the completion of the Divine work by outward manifestation; and in this sense it becomes the serpent which Moses lifted up in the wilderness.

But without the recognition of it as the ultimate mode of the Divine Spirit (which is *all* that is), it becomes the deadly reptile, not lifted up, but crawling flat upon the ground: it is that ignorant conception of things which cannot see the spiritual element in them, and therefore attributes all their energy of action and re-action to *themselves,* not perceiving that they are the creations of a higher power.

Ignorant of the Divine Law of Creation, we do not look beyond secondary causes; and therefore because our own creative thought-power is ever externalizing conditions *representative of our conceptions,* we necessarily become more and more involved in the meshes of a net-work of circumstances from which we can find no way of escape. How these circumstances come about we cannot tell. We may call it blind chance, or iron destiny, or inscrutable Providence; but because we are ignorant of the true Law of Primary Causation, we never suspect the real fact, which is that the originating power of all this inharmony is ourself.

This is the great deception. We believe the serpent, or that conception of life which sees nothing beyond secondary causation, and consequently we accept the Knowledge of Evil as being equally necessary with the Knowledge of Good, and so we eat of the tree of the Knowledge of Good *and* of Evil. It is this dual aspect of knowledge that is deadly, but knowledge itself is nowhere condemned in Scripture; on the contrary, it is repeatedly stated to be the foundation of all progress. "Wisdom is a Tree of Life to them that lay hold upon her," says the Book of Proverbs; "Salvation is of the Jews because we *know* what we worship," says Jesus, and so on throughout the Bible.

But what *is* deadly to the soul of Man is the conception that Evil is a subject of Knowledge as well as Good; for this reason, that by thinking of Evil as a subject to be studied, we thereby attribute to it a substantive existence of its own, in other words, we look upon it as something having a self-originating power, which, as we advance in our studies, we shall find more and more clearly is not the case; and so by the Law of the creative working of Thought, we bring the Evil into existence: we have not yet penetrated the great secret of the difference between causes and conditions.*

But this knowledge of our thought-action is not reached in the earlier history of the race or of the individual, for the simple reason that all evolution takes place by Growth; and consequently the history of Adam and Eve *in realization,* that is the external life of humanity as distinguished from our simultaneous existence on the supreme plane of Spirit, commences with their expulsion from Eden and their conflict with a world of sorrows and difficulties.

If the reader realizes how this expulsion results from the soul accepting Evil as a subject of Knowledge, he will now be able to understand certain further facts. We are told that "the Lord God said, 'Behold the man is become as one of us to know good and evil'; and now lest he put forth his hand and take of the tree of life and eat and live for ever; the Lord God sent him forth from the Garden of Eden" (Gen. iii. 22). Looked at superficially, this seems like jealousy that Man should have attained the same knowledge as God, and fear lest he should take the further step that would make him altogether God's equal. But such a reading of the text is babyish, and indicates no conception of God as Universal All-originating Spirit, and we must therefore look for some deeper interpretation.

The First Commandment is the recognition of the Divine Unity, a fact

* See my Edinburgh Lectures on Mental Science.

on which Jesus laid special emphasis when he was asked which was the chief commandment of the Law; and the purpose is to guard us against the root-error from which all other forms of error spring. If the mathematical statement of Truth is that God is ONE, then the mathematical expression of error is that God is Zero, and as the latter position has sometimes been taken by teachers of reputation, it may be well to show the student where the fallacy lies. The conclusion that the mathematical expression for God is Zero is reached in this way: as soon as you can conceive of anything as *being,* you can also conceive of it as *not-being,* in other words, the conception of any positive implies also the conception of its corresponding negative; consequently the conception of the positive or of the negative by itself is only half the conception, and a whole conception implies the recognition of both.

Therefore, since God contains the all, He must contain the negative as well as the positive of all potentiality, and the equal balance of positive and negative is Zero. But the radical error of this argument is the assumption that it is possible for two principles to neutralize each other, one of which *is,* and the other of which *is not.* We find the principle of neutralization by means of equilibration throughout Nature, but the equilibration is always between two things each of which actually exists. Thus in chemistry we find an acid exactly equilibrating an alkali and producing a neutral substance which is neither acid nor alkali; but this is because the acid and the alkali both really exist, each of them is something that *is;* but what should we say to a chemical formula which required us to produce a neutral substance by equilibrating an acid which did exist by an alkali which did not? Yet this is precisely the sort of equilibration we are asked to accept by those who would make Zero the mathematical expression of All-originating Being. They say that a Universal Principle which *is* is exactly balanced by a Universal Principle which *is not;* they affirm that Nothing is the equivalent of Something.

This is mere juggling with words and figures, and wilfully shutting our eyes to the fact that the only quality of Nothing is Nothingness. Can anything be plainer than the old philosophic dictum, *"ex nihilo nihil fit"?* (nothing is made out of nothing). Disintegrating forces there are in Nature, but they do not proceed out of Nothing. They are the ONE positive power acting at lower levels; not the absence of the One Universal Energy, but that same Energy working with less complex concentration and specific purpose than when directed by those higher modes *of itself* which constitute individual intelligences.

*There is no such thing as a Negative Power,* in the sense of power which is not the ONE All-originating Power. All energy is *some* mode of manifestation of the ONE, and it is *always making* something, though in doing so it may unmake something else; and what we loosely speak of as negative forces are the operation of the cosmical Law of Transition from one Form to another. Above this there is a higher Law, to lead us to the realization of which is the whole object of the Bible, and that is the Law of Individual Selection. It does not do away with the Law of Transition, for without transition there could be no Evolution, and the glory of Eternal Life is in continuous Evolution; but it substitutes the Individual Law of *conscious* Life for the Impersonal Cosmic Law, and effects transition by *living* processes of assimilation and readjustment which more perfectly build up the individuality, instead of by a process of unbalanced disintegration which would destroy it. This is the Living Law of Liberty, which at every stage of its progress makes us, not less, but more and yet more *ourselves.*

It is for this reason that the Bible so strongly insists upon the mathematical statement that God is ONE, and in fact makes this the basis of all that it has to say. God is Life, Expression, Reality; and how can these things comport with Nothingness? All we can know of any invisible power is through the effects we see it produce. Of electricity and chemical attraction it may be truly said that "no man hath seen them or can see them"; yet we know them by their working, and we rightly argue that if they work they exist. The same argument applies to the Divine Spirit. It is that which *is* and not that which *is not;* and therefore I ask the student who would realize reality and not nothingness once for all to convince himself of the fallaciousness of the argument that the Divine Being is Not-being, or that Naught is the same thing as ONE.

If he starts his search for Reality by assuming what contradicts mathematics and common-sense, he can never expect to find Reality, for he has denied its existence at the very outset and carries that initial denial all the way along with him. But if he realizes that all relations, whether *relatively* positive or negative, must necessarily be relations between factors which actually exist, and that there can be no relation with nothing, then, because he has assumed Reality in his premises he will eventually find it in his conclusions, and will learn that the Great Reality is the ONE expressing itself as the MANY, and the MANY recognizing themselves in the ONE.

The more advanced student will have no difficulty in recognizing the particular schools of teaching to which these remarks apply; their mathematics are unassailable, but the assumptions on which they make their selection of terms in the first instance are totally inapplicable to the subject-matter to which they apply them, for that subject is *Life-in-itself.*

Now, the deception into which Eve falls is mathematically represented by saying that God = Zero, and thus attributing to Evil the same self-existence as to Good. There is no such thing as Absolute Evil; and what we recognize as Evil is the ONE Good Power working as Disintegrating Force, because we have not yet learnt to direct it in such a way that it shall perform the functions of transition to higher degrees of Life without any disintegration of our individuality either in person or circumstances. It is this disintegrating action that makes the ONE Power *appear* evil relatively to ourselves; and, so long as we conceive ourselves thus related to it, it does look as though it were Zero balancing in itself the two opposite forces of Life and Death, Good and Evil, and it is in this sense that "God" is said to know both.

But this is a conception very different to that of the all-productive ONE, and arises, not from the true nature of Being, but from our own confused Thought. But because the action of our Thought is always creative, the mere fact of our regarding Evil as an affirmative force in itself makes it so *relatively to ourselves;* and therefore no sooner do we fear evil than we begin to create the evil that we fear. To extinguish evil we must learn not to fear it, and that means to cease recognizing it as having any power of its own, and so our salvation comes from realizing that in truth there is nothing but the good.

But this knowledge can only be attained through long experience, which will at last bring Man to the place where he is able to deduce Truth from *a priori* principles, and to learn that his past experiences of evil have proceeded from his own inverted conceptions, and are not founded upon Truth but upon its opposite. If then it were possible for him to attain the knowledge which would enable him to live for ever before gaining this experience, the result would be an immortality of misery, and therefore the Law of Nature renders it impossible for him to reach the knowledge which would place immortality within his grasp, until he has gained that deep insight into the true working of causation which is necessary to make Eternal Life a prize worth having. For these reasons Man is represented as being expelled from Eden lest he should eat of the Tree of Life and live for ever.

Before quitting this subject we must glance briefly at the sentences pronounced upon the man, the woman, and the serpent. The serpent in this connection being the principle of error, which results in Death, can never come into any sort of reconciliation with the Divine Spirit, which is Truth and Life, and, therefore, the only possible pronouncement upon the serpent is a curse—that is, a sentence of destruction; and the Bible goes on to show the stages by which this destruction is ultimately worked out. The penalty to Adam, or the corporeal body, is that of having to earn his bread by the sweat of his brow—that is, by toilsome labor, which would not be necessary if the true law of the creative exercise of our Thought were understood. The woman passes under a painful physiological law, but at the same time final deliverance and restoration from the "Fall" is promised through her instrumentality: her seed shall crush the serpent's head, that is, shall utterly destroy that false principle which the serpent represents.

Since the Woman is the Soul, or Individual Mind, her progeny must be *thoughts* and *ideas*. New ideas are not brought forth easily, they are the result of painful experiences and of long mental labor, and thus the physiological analogy contained in the text exactly illustrates the birth of new ideas into the world. And as the evolution of the Soul proceeds toward higher and higher intelligence, there is a corresponding increase in the lifeward tendency of its ideas, and thus there is enmity between the seed of "the Woman" or the enlightened conception of the principles of Life, and the seed of "the Serpent" or the opposite and unenlightened conception.

This is the same warfare which we find in Revelations between "the Woman" and "the Dragon." But in the end the victory remains with "the Woman" and her "Seed." During the progress of the struggle the Serpent must bruise the heel of the Divine Seed—that is to say, must impede and retard the progress of Truth on the earth; but Truth must conquer at last and crush the Serpent's head so that it shall never rise up again for ever. The "Seed of the Woman," the Fruit of the spiritually enlightened Mind, which must at last achieve the final victory, is that supreme ideal which is the recognition of Man's Divine Sonship. It is the realization of the fact that he is, indeed, the image and likeness of God. This is the Truth the knowledge of which Jesus said would set us free, and each one who attains to this knowledge realizes that he is at once the Son of Man and the Son of God.

Thus the story of the Fall contains also the statement of the principle of the Rising-again. It is the history of the human race, because it is first the history of the individual soul, and to each one of us the ancient wisdom says, *"de te fabula narratur."* These opening chapters of Genesis are, therefore, an epitome of all that the Bible afterwards unfolds in fuller detail, and the whole may be summed up in the following terms:—

The great Truth concerning Man is that he is the image and likeness of God.

Man is at first ignorant of this Truth, and this ignorance is his Fall.

Man at last comes to the perfect knowledge of this Truth, and this knowledge is his Rising-again, and these principles will expand until they bring us to the full Expression of the Life that is in us in all the glories of the Heavenly Jerusalem.

III

# ISRAEL

THE SPACE AT my disposal will allow me only to touch upon a few of the most conspicuous points in that portion of the Bible narrative which takes us from the story of Eden to the Mission of Moses, for the reader will kindly bear in mind that I am not writing a commentary on the whole Bible, but only a brief introduction to its study.

The episode of Cain and Abel will be dealt with in the next chapter, and I will, therefore, pass on at once to the Deluge. As most of my readers probably know, this story is not confined to the Jewish and Christian Scriptures, but is met with in one form or another in all the most ancient traditions of the world, and this universal concensus of mankind leaves no doubt of the occurrence of some overwhelming cataclysm which has indelibly stamped itself upon the memory of all nations.

Whether science will ever succeed in working out the problem of its extent and of the physical conditions that gave rise to it, remains to be seen, but it does not appear unreasonable to associate it with the tradition handed down to us by Plato of the sinking of the great continent of Atlantis, which is said to have once occupied the area now covered by the Atlantic ocean. I am well aware that some geologists dispute the possibility of any radical changes having ever taken place in the distribution of the land and water surfaces of the globe, but there are at least equally good opinions on the other side, and if there is any fact in the world's history regarding which tradition is unanimous, it is the catastrophe of the Deluge.

And here I would draw attention to the fact that the Bible specially warns us against the opinion that no such catastrophe ever took place, and points out this opinion as one of the signs of the time of the end; speaking of it as determined ignorance, and telling us that a similar catastrophe, only by fire instead of water, will at some future period overwhelm the existing world (II. Peter iii.); and I would add that the possible conditions for such an event may not unreasonably be inferred from certain facts in the science of astronomy. It is not my present purpose, however, to enter into the scientific and historical aspects of the Deluge tradition, but to point out its significance in that *inner* meaning of the Bible which I wish the student to grasp.

In the story as handed down by all nations, the Deluge is attributed to the wickedness of mankind, and according to some very ancient traditions this wickedness took largely the form of sorcery, a word which may perhaps provoke a smile in the uninitiated reader, but which holds a conspicuous place in the list of those causes which in the book of Revelations are enumerated as leading to exclusion from the Heavenly City, and it will become sufficiently clear why it should do so when we learn what it really means. Coupling this tradition with the symbolical significance of "water," a deluge would indicate a total submergence in a psychic environment which had become too powerful to be held under control.

The psychic world is an integral part of the universe, and the psychic element is an integral part of man; and it is in this circulus that we find the plastic material which forms the nucleus for those attractions which eventually consolidate as external facts. The psychic realm is therefore the realm of tremendous potentialities, and the deeper our knowledge of its laws the greater we see to be the need for bringing these potentialities under a higher control.

Now the opening verses of Genesis have shown us that "water" without the movement of the Spirit is darkness and the abode of chaos. The movement of the Spirit is the only power that can control the turbulence of "the waters," and bring them into that harmonious action which will result in forms of Life, Beauty, and Peace; and in the world of Man's Mind this movement of the Spirit upon "the waters" takes place exactly in proportion as the individual recognizes the true nature of the Divine Spirit, and wills to reflect its image and likeness. Where this recognition takes place the psychic forces are brought under the control of a harmonizing power which, reflecting itself into them, can only produce that which is Good and Beautiful, on a small scale at first because of our infantine knowledge of the powers with which we are dealing, but continually growing with our growth until the whole psychic world opens out before us as a limitless realm filled with the Glory of God and the Love of Man and the shapes of beauty to which these give rise.

But if a man forces his way into that realm on no other basis than his individual strength of will, he does so without reckoning that his will is itself a product of the psychic plane, and only one among untold organized entities and unorganized forces which sooner or later will overpower him and hurry him to age-long destruction—"age-long," for I use the Bible word *aionios,* which, as the learned Farrar has shown in his *Eternal Hope,* does not mean absolutely endless; yet, if we reflect what may be included in this word, infinite periods perhaps of withdrawal and renewal of our whole planetary system, we may well stand aghast at such prodigious ruin.

But if such dangers are in it, may we not say that we will have nothing to do with the psychic realm? No, for by our nature we are always immersed in it: it is *within* us, and we are, and always must be, inhabitants of it, and we are always unconsciously using its forces and being re-acted upon by them. What we need, therefore, is, not to escape from what is an essential part of our nature, but to learn to vivify this otherwise dark realm with the warmth of Divine Love and the illumination of Divine Light.

But the Bible tells how very far the antediluvian world was from recognizing these Divine principles, for "the earth was filled with violence," and, except in the family of Noah, the true worship of God had ceased among men. And remark this word "violence" as the summing-up of human iniquity. Violence is the clashing of individual wills not harmonized by the recognition of any *unifying* principle. The ONE-ness of the Spirit from which all individualization proceeds is entirely lost sight of, and "each for himself" becomes the ruling principle—a principle which cannot but result in violence under whatever disguise it may be masked for a time.

The earth filled with violence was the outward correspondence of the inward mental state of the masses of mankind, and we may, therefore, well imagine what the nature of their operations in the symbolic world of "Water" must have been. This state of things had been growing for generations until at last the inevitable result arrived, and the moral deluge produced its correspondence in the physical world.

The uninstructed reader will doubtless smile at my reference to a psychic environment, but those who have obtained at least some glimpses beyond the threshold will see the force of my argument when I direct their attention to the signs of a recurrence of a similar state of things at the present day. Research in various directions is making clearer and clearer the reality of the psychic forces, and increasing numbers are beginning to get some measure of practical insight into them; and while I rejoice to say, we see that for the most part these opening powers are being employed under the direction of sincere religious feeling and with charitable intention, yet there are not wanting reports of opposite uses, and this in connection with specific localities where the inverted employment of these great powers is secretly practised according to methodized system.

I cannot too strongly warn the student against any connection with such societies, and their existence is a terrible comment upon the Master's description of the latter days, which, He expressly tells us, will reproduce the character of those which immediately preceded the flood. The sole safeguard is in recognizing the Divine Spirit as the only Source of Power, and in regarding every action, whether of thought, word, or deed, as being in its form and measure an act of Divine worship. This is what St. Paul means when he says "Pray without ceasing." What needs to be cultivated is the habitual mental attitude that leads us to see God in *all* things, and it is for this reason that the foundation of conscious spiritual Life is that First Commandment to the consideration of which we are approaching.

It was, therefore, in consequence of their entire denial of the Divine Spirit that the antediluvians raised up an adverse power which at last became too strong for them to control. And here let me once for all set the student right with regard to those passages of the Bible in which God is represented as making up His mind to inflict injury, as in the announcement of the impending Deluge. These expressions are figurative. They represent the entrance upon the scene of that Cosmic Law of Disintegration which necessarily comes into play as soon as the highest directing power of Intelligence is inhibited, and, therefore, as soon as a man wilfully thrusts from him the recognition of the Universal Spirit in its higher manifestations as the Guardian and the Guide, he, *ipso facto,* calls it into action in its lower manifestations as the Universal Cosmic Force.

The reason for this will appear more clearly from a careful study of the relations between the Personal and the Impersonal modes of Spirit, but the explanation of these relations would occupy too large a space to be entered upon here, and the reader must be referred to other works on the subject; in the present connection it is sufficient to say that we can never get rid of God, for we ourselves are manifestations of His Being, and if we will not have *Him* as the Good, we shall be compelled to accept *It* as the Evil. This is what the Master meant when He said in the parable that on the lord's return to his city, he ordered those who would not accept him to reign over them to be slain before him.

Noah and his three sons are rescued from the universal overthrow by means of the Ark. As I am concerned in the present book with the inner meaning of the Bible rather than with the historical facts, I must leave the reader to form his own conclusions regarding the literal measurements of that vessel; but I would take this opportunity of observing that where distinct numbers and measurements are given in the Bible, they are not introduced at haphazard. From the standpoint of ordinary arithmetic they may seem to be so, and the main argument of Bishop Colenso's great work on the Pentateuch is based on these apparent discrepancies. For instance, speaking of the sacrifices to be offered for women after child-birth, he points out that during the march through the desert these could, according to the text, only be offered by Aaron and his two sons, and that calculated on ordinary averages, the offering of these sacrifices would have occupied each of these three priests fourteen hours a day without one moment's rest or intermission (vol. i., 123). From the point of view of simple arithmetic this result is unavoidable; but I cannot endorse the Bishop's conclusion that the scribes who wrote the Pentateuch under the direction of Ezra introduced any numbers that occurred to them without considering how they would work out.

On the contrary, such investigation as I have been able to make into the subject, convinces me that the Bible numbers are calculated with the most rigid accuracy, and with the very deepest thought of the results to which they will work out, only this is done according to a certain symbolic system known as Sacred Numeration; and the very impracticability of the figures when tested by ordinary arithmetic is intended to put us upon enquiry for some deeper meaning below the surface. To explain the principles of Sacred Numeration would be beyond the scope of an elementary book like the present, and probably few readers would care to undertake the requisite amount of study; but we must not suppose that the numbers given in the Bible are without significance whenever ordinary methods of calculation fail to elucidate them. The whole meaning of Scripture is not upon the surface, and in the present connection we are expressly pointed to a symbolic signification in I. Peter, iii. 20–21; and the recurrence of the Ark as a sacred emblem in the great race-religions clearly indicates it as representing some universal principle.

The Zoroastrian legend of the flood throws some light upon the subject, for Yima, the Persian Noah, is bidden by Ahura Mazda, the Deity, to bring "the *seeds* of sheep, oxen, men and women, dogs and birds, and of every kind of tree and fruit, two of every kind, into the ark and to seal it up with a golden ring and make in it a door and a window." The significance of the Ark is that of a vehicle for the transmission of the life-principle of beings from an old to a new order of life, and all that is not included in the Ark perishes.

This is the generalized statement of relations which the Ark sets forth, and, like all other generalizations, it admits of a great many particular applications, ranging from those which are purely physiological to those which are in the highest degree spiritual, and the study of comparative religions will show us that the idea has been employed in all its most varied applications; yet, however varied, they all have this common feature that they signify something which conveys individual life safely through a period of transition from one order of manifestation to another.

The Ark, as the sacred vessel, plays a conspicuous part throughout Scripture, but in the present connection we shall best realize its meaning by considering it as the opposite principle to that from which it affords deliverance. If "Water" signifies the psychic principle, then the Ark signifies that which the psychic principle supports, and which has an opposite but correspondent nature, that is to say, the Body. The Ark is not independent of the Water but is constructed for the purpose of floating upon it and similarly the body is expressly adapted to man's psychic nature so as to make with it and the spiritual principle of Life, a Whole individuality.

Now, it is precisely in the recognition of this Wholeness that refuge from all psychic entanglements is to be found. We must always remember that the body equally with the soul is the instrument of the manifestation of the Spirit. It is the union of the three into a single Whole that constitutes the full reality of Life and it is this sacredness of the body that is typified by the sacredness of the Ark. The Ark of Noah was a solid construction, built on a pattern all the details of which were laid down to scale by the Divine Architect and thus exemplifies the accurate proportions of the human body; and in passing it may interest the reader to note that the proportions of the human body numerically represent the principal measurements of the solar system, and also form the basis of the proportions observed in such ecclesiastical architecture as is designed according to canonical rules, of which Westminster Abbey and Milan Cathedral are good examples.

I cannot, however, stop to digress into this very interesting subject, and for our present purpose it will be sufficient to say that the Ark with its living freight is typical of the fact that the full *realization* of Life is only attained in the Threefold Unity of body, soul and spirit, and not by their dissociation. It is the assertion of the solid, living, Reality of the work of the Spirit as distinguished from those imperfect manifestations which are the subterranean roots of the true manifestation, but are not the real solid thing itself. It is the protest of healthy reality, which includes the psychic element *in its proper order* as the intermediary between the purely spiritual and the purely material, as against the rejection of the corporeal element and total absorption in the psychic, a condition which prevents the Spirit from attaining to self-expression as a synthesis, which alone is the completion of its evolutionary work.

For this reason undue absorption in the psychic sphere is contrary to the Spirit; and however we may apply to it the word "spiritual" in the sense of not being corporeal, if the psychic element is not taken in its proper connection with the two others, it is as far from being "spiritual" in the true sense of the word as the material element itself. The true reality is in the harmonious interaction of the Three-in-ONE. God's world is a world of Truth in which evanescent shapes do not take the place of Reality, and for these reasons the Bible everywhere insists on nothing short of the fulness of perfect realization, and the Ark is one of the figures under which it does so.

This realization of the Triple-Unity of Man is the first step towards our final enfranchisement; but in the very act of escaping from the danger of the Deluge we are exposed to a danger of the opposite kind, that of regarding the corporeal side of life as everything, and this is typified by the building of the Tower of Babel. This tower, note carefully, was built of brick, that is of a substance which is nothing but clay, the same "red earth" out of which Adam is formed, and it is therefore the very opposite to the Heavenly Jerusalem which is built of gold and precious stones. Now, a building naturally signifies a habitation, and the building of the Tower of Babel to escape the waters of a flood is that reaction against the psychic element which denies spiritual things altogether, and makes of the body and its physical environment the one and only dwelling-place of man. It is the same error as before of trying to erect the edifice of Wholeness on the foundation merely of a part, only now the part selected is the corporeal instead of the psychic. Arithmetically it is the attempt to make out that one-third is the same as ONE. The natural consequences soon follow in the confusion of tongues. Language is the expression of Thought, and if our ideas of reality include nothing more than the infinitude of secondary causes which appear in the material world, there is no central Unit around which they can be grouped, and consequently, instead of any certain knowledge, we have only a multitude of conflicting opinions based upon the ever-changing aspects of the world of appearances. *Quot homines tot sententiae,* and so the builders are dispersed in confusion, for theirs is not "the city that hath foundations whose builder and maker is God."

From this point in the Bible story a stretch of many ages brings us to the times of the Patriarchs, Abraham, Isaac, and Jacob. We are here in the transition stage from allegory to history, and St. Paul points out this intermingling of the two elements when he tells us that Hagar and Sarah represent the two covenants, and the earthly and heavenly Jerusalems. And here I would impress upon the student the dual character of scriptural personages and events. Because a personage or event is typical it does not follow that it is not also historical; on the contrary, certain personages, systems, and events, become typical, that is, specially emphasize certain principles, for the very reason that they give them concrete expression. As Johnson says of the Swedish monarch—

*"He left the name at which the world grew pale,*
*To point a moral or adorn a tale."*

In other words, historical realities become the very summing-up and visible form of abstract principles, and therefore we are justified by the Bible itself in finding in its personages types of principles as well as historical characters.

I will not, however, here open the question whether the three Patriarchs were actual personages, or, as some critics tell us, were merely the legendary ancestors of certain groups of wandering tribes, the Beni-Ibrahim, the Beni-Ishák, and the Beni-Yakub, which subsequently coalesced into the Hebrew nation. However interesting, the discussion of the historical facts would be remote from my present object, which is to throw some light upon the *inner* meaning of the Bible, and for this purpose we may be content to take the simple narrative of the text, for, whether actual or legendary, the only way in which Abraham, Isaac and Jacob can affect us at the present day is as characters in a history the significance of which will become clear if we read between the lines.

But from this latter point of view the biblical statement of the national origin of Israel carries enfolded within it the hidden statement of those great principles which it is the purpose of the Bible to reveal. And here let me draw attention to the method adopted in Scripture. There are certain great universal principles which permeate all planes of being from the highest to the lowest. They are not many in number, and the relations between them are not difficult of comprehension when clearly stated, but we find difficulty in recognizing the identity of the same principles when we meet with them, so to say, at different levels, as for example on the physical and the psychic planes respectively, and consequently we are apt to imagine them much more numerous and complicated than they really are.

Now, the purpose of the Bible is to convey instruction in the nature and use of these principles to those in whose hands this knowledge would be safe and useful, while concealing it from others, and in a manner appropriate to this object it continually repeats the same few all-embracing principles over and over and over again. This repetition is firstly unavoidable because the principles themselves are few in number, next it is necessary as a process of hammering-in and fixing it in our minds, and lastly it is not a bare repetition, but there is a progressive expansion of the statement so as to conduct us step by step to a further comprehension of its meaning. Now, this is done in a variety of ways and one of frequent occurrence is through the use of Names.

Sacred Nomenclature is as large a study as Sacred Numeration and indeed the two so shade off into one another that they may be regarded as forming a single study, and I will therefore no more attempt in the present book to elucidate the one system than the other, for they require a volume to themselves; but this need not prevent us considering occasional instances of both and the names of the Patriarchs are too important to be passed over without notice. The frequency with which God is called in Scripture the God of Abraham, of Isaac and of Jacob, shows that something more must be referred to than the mere fact that the ancestors of the Jews worshipped Him, and the consideration of some of the prominent points in the history of these allegorical personages will throw a light on the subject which will be very helpful in our further investigations.

If we realize the truth of St, Paul's statement that the real object of the Bible is to convey the history—of the spiritual Israel under the figure of Israel after the flesh, we shall see that the descent of Israel from the three Patriarchs must be a spiritual descent, and we may therefore expect to find in the Patriarchs themselves an adumbration of the principles which give rise to the spiritual Israel. Now, we should particularly notice that the name "Israel" was bestowed on Jacob, the third Patriarch, on the occasion when he wrestled with the angel at the ford Jabbok, and he obtained this name as the result of his successful wrestling. We are told that Jacob recognized that it was the Divine Being, the Nameless ONE, with whom he wrestled, and this at once gives us the key to the allegory; for we know from the Master's instruction to the woman of Samaria that God is Universal Spirit, and though the Universal is that which gives rise to all manifestations of the particular, yet it is logically and mathematically impossible for the Universal *as such* to assume individual personality.

Under the figure, therefore, of wrestling with "a man," we perceive that what Jacob wrestled with was the great problem of his own relation to the Universal Spirit under its two-fold aspect of Universal Energy and Universal Intelligence, allegorically represented as a powerful man; and he held on and wrestled till he gained the blessing, and the New Name in which the nature of that blessing was summed up. The conditions are significant. He was alone. Father of a large family as he was, none of his dear ones could help him in the struggle.

We must each solve the problem of our relation to the Infinite Mind for ourselves; and not our nearest and dearest can wrestle for us. And the struggle takes place in the darkness. It is when we begin to find that the light we thought we possessed is not the true light, when we find that its illuminating power is gone, that we rise nerved with an energy we never knew before, and commence in earnest the struggle for the Light, determined never to let go until we win the victory. And so we wrestle till the day begins to break, but even then we must not quit our hold; we must not be content until we have received the New Name which marks our possession of that principle of Light and Life which will for ever expand into brighter day and fuller livingness. "To him that overcometh will I give . . . a New Name" (Rev. ii. 17).

But Jacob carries with him the mark of the struggle throughout his earthly career. The angel touched the hollow of his thigh, and thenceforward he was lame. The meaning is simple enough to those who have had some experience of the wrestling. They can never again walk in earthly things with the same step as before. They have seen the Truth, and they can never again unsee it; their whole *standpoint* has been altered and is no longer understood by those around them; to those who have not wrestled with the angel, they appear to walk lamely.

What, then, was the New Name that was thus gained by the resolute wrestler? His original name of Jacob was changed to Israel. The definition given of Israel in the seventy-third Psalm is "such as are of a clean heart," and Jesus expressed the same idea when he said of Nathanael, "Behold an Israelite indeed in whom is no guile"; for the emphasis laid upon the word "Israelite" at once suggests some inner meaning, since Nathanael's nationality was no more remarkable under the circumstances than that of an Englishman in Piccadilly.

The great fact about the spiritual Israel is therefore cleanness of heart and absence of guile, in other words, perfect sincerity, which again implies singleness of purpose in the right direction. It is precisely that quality which our Buddhist friends call "one-pointedness," and on which, under various similitudes, the Master laid so much stress. This, then, is the distinctive characteristic which attaches to the name of Israel, for it is this *concentration* of effort that is the prime factor in gaining the victory which leads to the acquisition of the name. This is fundamental, and without it nothing can be accomplished; it indicates the sort of mental character which we must aim at, but it is not the meaning of the Name itself.

The name of Israel is composed of three syllables, each of which carries a great meaning. The first syllable "Is" is primarily the sound of the indrawing of the breath, and hence acquires the significance of the Life-principle in general, and more particularly of individual Life. This recognition of the individualization of the Life-principle formed the basis of the Assyrian worship. The syllable "Is" was also rendered "As," "Ish," and "Ash," and gave rise to the worship of the Life-principle under the plural name "Ashur," which thus represented the male and female elements, the former being worshipped as Ashr, or Asr, and the latter as Ashré, Ashira, Astarte, Iastara or Ishtar, and lunar goddess of Babylon, and the same idea of femininity is found in the Egyptian "Isis." Hence the general conception conveyed by the syllable "Is" is that of a feminine spiritual principle manifesting itself in individuality, that is to say the "Soul" or formative element, and it is thus indicative of all that we mean when we speak of the psychic side of nature. How completely the Assyrians identified themselves with the cultus of this principle is shown by the name of their country, which is derived from "Ashur."

The second syllable, "Ra," is the name of the great Egyptian sun-god, and is thus the complementary of everything that is signified by "Is." It is primarily indicative of physical life rather than psychic life, and in general represents the Universal Life-giving power as distinguished from its manifestation in particular individuality. Ra symbolizes the Sun, while Is is symbolized by the Moon, and represents the masculine element as emphatically as Is represents the feminine.

The third syllable, "El," has the significance of Universal Being. It is "THE," i.e., The nameless Principle which includes in itself both the masculine and feminine elements, both the physical and the psychic, and is greater than them and gives rise to them. It is another form of the word Al, Alé, or Ala, which means "High," and is indicative of the Supreme Principle *before it passes into any differentiated mode.* It is *pure* Spirit in the *universal.*

Now, if Man is to attain liberty, it can only be by the realization of these Three Modes of Being—the physical, the psychic, and the spiritual, or as the Bible expresses it, Body, Soul, and Spirit. He must know what these three are in himself and must also recognize the Source from which they spring, and he must at least have some moderately definite idea of their genesis into individuality. Therefore the man "instructed unto the kingdom of heaven" combines a threefold recognition of himself and of God which is accurately represented by the combination of the three syllables Is, Ra and El. Unless these three are joined into a single unity, a single word, the recognition is incomplete and the full knowledge of truth has not been attained. “Ra” by itself implies only the knowledge of the physical world, and results in Materialism. “Is” by itself realizes only the psychic world, and results in Sorcery. “El” by itself corresponds only with a vague apprehension of some over-ruling power, capricious and devoid of the element of Law, and thus results in Idolatry.

It is only in the combination of all three elements that the true Reality is to be found, whether we study it in its physical, psychic, or spiritual aspect. We may for particular purposes give special prominence to one aspect over the two others, but this is for a time only, and even while we do so we realize that the particular mode of Life-power with which we are dealing derives its efficiency only from the fact of its being permeated by the other two. We cannot too firmly impress upon our minds that, though there are *three modes,* there is only ONE LIFE; and in all our studies, and in their practical application, we must never forget the great truth that the Living power which we use is a Synthesis, and that whenever we make an analysis we theoretically destroy the synthesis. The only purpose of making an analysis is to learn how to build up the synthesis; and it is for this reason that the Bible equally condemns the opposite extremes of materialism and sorcery. It tells us that “dogs and sorcerers” are excluded from the heavenly city, and when we understand what is meant by these terms it becomes self-evident that it cannot be otherwise.

It is for this reason, also, that we find the Israelites so often warned both against the Babylonian and the Egyptian idolatries; not because there was no great underlying truth in the worship of those nations, but because it was a worship that excluded the idea of WHOLENESS. “Wilt thou be made whole?” is the Divine invitation to us all; and the Egyptian and Assyrian worships were eminently calculated to lead their votaries away from this Wholeness in opposite directions.

But that both the Assyrian and the Egyptian worship had a solid basis of truth is a fact to which the Bible itself bears this remarkable testimony:—“In that day shall Israel be the third with Egypt and Assyria, even a blessing in the midst of the land; whom the Lord of Hosts shall bless, saying, Blessed be Egypt my people, and Assyria the work of my hands, and Israel mine inheritance” (Isaiah xix. 24). The Israelite worship was as essentially that of the principle represented by “El” as those of Egypt and Assyria were of the two others, and it needed the balancing of those two extremes by the recognition of their relation to the central, or spiritual, principle to constitute the realization of the true Divine Sonship of Man in which no element of his threefold being—body, soul or spirit—is alien from unity with "the Father."

This, then, was the significance of the New Name given to Jacob. He had wrestled with the Divine until the light had begun to dawn upon him, and he thus acquired the right to a name which should correctly describe what he had now become. Formerly he had been Jacob, *i.e.,* Yakub, a name derived from the root "Yak" or "One." This signifies the third stage of apprehension of the Divine problem which immediately precedes the final discovery of the great secret of the Trinity-in-Unity of Being. We realize the ONE-ness of the Universal Divine Principle, though we have not yet realized its Three-fold nature both in ourselves and in the Universal.

But there are two other stages before this, the first of which is represented by Abraham and the second by Isaac. It should be noted that the two syllables "Ra" and "Is" reappear in these names, the former indicative, as we have seen, of the masculine element of Spirit, and the latter of the feminine, while Jacob, or simple unity, is indicative of the neuter.

If we look through the history of Abraham we find the masculine element especially predominant in it. He is the *father* of the nations that are to spring from him, he receives the covenant of circumcision, he is a warrior, and goes forth to victorious battle, and the change of his name from Abram to Abraham is the substitution of a masculine for a neuter element.

In Isaac's history the feminine element is equally predominant. His name is connected with the laughter of his mother (Genesis xviii.), and his marriage with Rebekah is the pivot round which all the events of his life center; and again, his acquiescence in his own sacrifice marks the predominance of the passive element in his character. To him there comes no change of name; he is neither leader, warrior, nor spiritual wrestler, but the calm, contemplative man who "went out to meditate in the field at eventide"; he is typical of the purely receptive attitude of mind, and therefore the syllable "Is" is as indicative of his nature as the masculine syllable "Ra" is of his father's, or the neutral and purely mathematical conception indicated by the syllable "Yak" is of his son's.

This affords a good instance of the way in which the deepest truths are often concealed in Bible names, and it should lead us to see that the value of the record does not turn on its literal accuracy at every point, but on its correct representation of the great principles to the knowledge of which it seeks to lead us.

It is of little moment to us at the present date how much of the book of Genesis is legendary and how much historical, and we can afford to view calmly such little inaccuracies on the face of the document as when we are told, in Exodus vi. 3, that God was not known to Abraham by the name Jehovah, and in Genesis xxii. 14, that Abraham called the place where he was delivered from sacrificing Isaac "Jehovah-jireh." There are two typical schools of Biblical interpretation, one of which is historically represented by St. Augustine, and the other by St. Jerome. Augustine, who was not an Orientalist and had not studied the original Hebrew, took his stand upon the textual accuracy of the Bible, and urged that if once any inaccuracy were admitted to exist in it, we could never be certain of anything in the whole book. Jerome, who had made an accurate study of the original Hebrew, admitted the existence of inaccuracies in the text from the operation of the same natural causes which affect other ancient literature, such as errors of copyists, variations of oral tradition, and even possible adaptation to the requirements of something which the transcriber believed to be an essential doctrine.

These two representative men were not separated by an interval of centuries, but were contemporaries, and actually in communication with each other, and we may therefore see from how early a date Christendom has been divided into blind reverence for the letter and intelligent inquiry into the history of its documents. St. Jerome was the father of the Higher Criticism, and with such a respectable authority to back us, we need not be afraid to attribute any such casual errors as the one now in question to those natural causes which render all ancient documents liable to variation, and the point to which I would draw attention is that merely superficial contradictions which can be reasonably accounted for on purely natural grounds, in no way affect the general inspiration of the Bible.

And by "inspiration" I mean an inner illumination on the part of the writers leading them to the immediate perception of Truth, which illumination is itself a fact in the regular order of Nature, the reason of which I hope to make clear in a subsequent volume. The books of the Pentateuch, as we possess them, were written by Ezra and his scribes after the return from the Babylonian captivity—those writers whom the Jews call "the men of the

Great Synagogue," and whose writings were separated from the time of Moses by exactly the same interval that separates Tennyson's *Idylls of the King* from the date of the actual King Arthur.

This alone leaves a sufficiently wide margin for errors to creep into such earlier documents as these writers may have availed themselves of; and we must next reflect that another interval of several centuries separated them from the copies conveyed to Egypt in the second century before Christ for Ptolemy Soter's Greek translation, commonly known as the Septuagint. The "Temple Standard" Pentateuch, preserved at Jerusalem at the time of Jesus, can hardly have been the original document written by Ezra, but even supposing it to have been so, what became of it at the destruction of Jerusalem? Tradition says it was sent by Josephus to the Emperor of Rome, and written, as it is said to have been, on bulls' hides, we may well imagine that it perished by damp or other agencies, neglected as a barbarous relic in a city whose energies were concentrated on maintaining its position as arbitress of the world by conquest and diplomacy; at any rate the document was never heard of again, and the oldest Jewish versions of the Pentateuch now extant are not older than the tenth century. Under these circumstances we need not be surprised if variations have found their way into the text, nor need we trouble ourselves much about them if we reflect that the real place where Truth exists is in Nature, and not in books, and that the book is merely a record of what others have learnt without book; and, moreover, owing to the deep reverence with which both Jewish and Christian Scriptures have been preserved, we may say that any errors or contradictions discovered in the text no more affect the body of the Truth contained in the Bible as a whole than the dust on the outside of an orange affects the value of the fruit. It is this *inner* Truth that we are seeking, and if we at all realize the Master's statement that the Kingdom is *within,* superficial discrepancies will not present any difficulties to us.

We see, then, in the typical history of the three Patriarchs the announcement of the three great principles into which all forms of manifestation may be analyzed—the Masculine, Positive, or generating principle; the Feminine, Receptive, or formative principle; and the Neuter or Mathematical principle, which, by determining the proportional relations between the other two, gives rise to the principle of variety and multiplicity. Their successive statement in the symbolical history indicates the need for the preparatory study of each in detail if we would arrive at the True Light; and it is precisely the discovery that this separate study is by itself *insufficient* that brings us to the point where we have to wrestle in the darkness with the Divine Angel until the day dawns; we must unite the three principles into a single Unity, and thus learn to form the name "Israel"; and in so doing we discover that it has now become *our own* name, for we find that the kingdom of heaven—the realm of eternal principles—is *within* us, and that, therefore, whatever we discover there is that which we ourselves are. Our wrestling ceases: the Divine Wrestler has put his name upon us, and the day is beginning to dawn; but as yet it is only the earliest hour of daybreak; it is the true sunlight, but it is still low on the horizon, and we must not make the mistake of supposing that this early morning hour is the same as the mid-day glory—in other words, we must not suppose that because we have once and for ever finished wrestling with an unknown antagonist in darkness therefore we have nothing more to do.

Life is a perpetual *doing,* though, thank God, not a perpetual wrestling. Our doing is the measure of our living, although the plane on which our doing is carried on may not be immediately patent to all observers; and it is exactly in proportion as we expand our doing that we expand our livingness. No one can grow for us, and it all depends upon ourselves how rapidly and how strongly we shall grow.

IV

# THE MISSION OF MOSES

HAVING NOW GATHERED UP in the briefest possible fashion the general gist of the history of the Patriarchs, we must pass on to the Mission of Moses. And here let me again impress upon the reader that the Bible repeats its few grand principles over and over again, only with greater detail as it proceeds, so that we shall find precisely the same principles involved in the history of the march of Israel into Canaan as in that of the three Patriarchs. It is the same statement as is contained in the story of Eden and in the tradition of the Flood, and we shall find it repeated throughout the Bible under other varieties of form which admit of more and more specific application of these principles to individual cases. I mention this to explain why we may sometimes appear to go over old ground: there is only ONE Truth, and more detailed acquaintance with it will not change its fundamentals.

We have seen that the Bible teaching regarding Man starts with two great facts: first, that he is the image of God reproducing in individuality the same Universal Mind which is the Origin of all things, and thus reproducing also its creative process of Thought; and, secondly, that he is ignorant of this truth, and so brings upon himself all sorts of trouble and limitation; and it is the purpose of the Bible to lead us step by step out of this ignorance into this knowledge—step by step, for it is a process of growth, first in the individual, then in the race, and this growth depends on certain clear and ascertainable Laws inherent in the constitution of Man. Now the peculiarity of inherent Law is that it always acts uniformly, making no exception in favor of anyone, and it does this as well positively as negatively.

Our ignorance of any Law of Nature will never exempt us from its operation, and this is as true of ignorant obedience as of ignorant disobedience: the natural reward of ignorant obedience is no less certain than the natural punishment of ignorant disobedience; and it is on this principle that the great leaders of the race have always worked. They themselves knew the Law; but to impart the understanding of the Law to people in general was not the work of a day, nor of a generation, nor of many generations—in fact it is a work which is still only in its infancy—and, therefore, if people were to be saved from the consequences of disobedience to the Law it could only be by some method of training which would lead them into ignorant obedience to it. But this was not to be done by making any false statement of the Law, for Truth can never come out of falsehood; it must be done by presenting the Truth under such figures as would indicate the real relations of things, though not explaining how these relations arise, because to undeveloped minds such an explanation would be worse than useless. Hence came the whole system of the Mosaic Law.

On one occasion, when the Master was asked which was the greatest commandment of the Law, He replied by quoting the fourth verse of the sixth chapter of Deuteronomy, "Hear, O Israel; the Lord our God is one Lord," or, as the Revised Version has it in Mark xii. 29, "the Lord is ONE." This, He says, is the first of all the commandments; and we may therefore expect to find in this statement of the Divine Unity the foundation on which everything else rests. Nor need we look far to find the reason of it, for we have already seen in the opening words of Genesis that *in principio*—that is, as the originating principle in all things—there *can* be nothing else but God or Spirit. That is a conclusion which becomes unavoidable if we simply follow up the chain of cause and effect until we reach a Universal First Cause. We may call it by what name we choose: that will make no difference so long as we realize what *must* be its inherent nature and what *must* be our necessary relation to it.

Whatever name we give it, it is always the ONE self-existent and self-transforming Power of which everything is some mode of manifestation, simply because there is no other source from which anything could come. This ultimate deduction of reason is the recognition of the Unity of God, and could not be more clearly stated than in the words which Isaiah puts into the mouth of the Divine Being, repeating the phrase in two consecutive sentences as though to lay additional stress upon it:—"There is none beside Me." "I am God and there is none else" (Isaiah xlv. 21, 22). That is to say, "God," or, as we have learnt from the instructions to the woman of Samaria, Universal Spirit, is all that is.

This is the great Truth on which the mission of Moses was founded, and therefore that mission starts with the announcement of the Divine Name at the Burning Bush. "Moses said unto God, Behold when I come unto the children of Israel and shall say unto them, The God of your fathers hath sent me unto you; and they shall say unto me, What is His name? what shall I say unto them? And God said unto Moses, I AM THAT I AM; and He said, Thus shalt thou say unto the children of Israel, I AM hath sent me unto you." So the name after which Moses inquired turned out to be no name, but the first person singular of the present tense of the verb TO BE, in its indicative mood. It is the announcement of BEING in the Absolute, in that first originating plane of Pure Spirit where, because the Material does not yet exist, there can be no extension in space, and consequently no sequence in time, and where, therefore, the only possible mode of being is the consciousness of Self-existence without limitation either of space or time, the realization of the "universal Here and the everlasting Now," the concentration of the All into the Point and the expansion of the Point into the All.*

But though this may have been a new announcement to the masses of the Hebrew people, it could have been no new announcement to Moses, for we are told in the Acts that Moses was learned in all the wisdom of the Egyptians, a circumstance which is fully accounted for by his education at the court of Pharaoh, where he would be as a matter of course initiated into the deepest mysteries of the Egyptian religion. He must therefore have been familiar from boyhood with the words, "I AM that I AM," which as the inscription "Nuk pu Nuk" appeared upon the walls of every temple; and having received the highest instruction in the land, brought up as the

* For further elucidation the reader is referred to my *Edinburgh Lectures on Mental Science.*

son of Pharaoh's daughter, he must have been well aware of their significance. But this instruction had hitherto been confined to those who had been initiated into the great mysteries of Osiris.

In whatever way we may interpret the story of Moses meeting with the Divine Being at the burning bush, one thing is evident, it indicates the point in his career when it became plain to him that the only possible way for the Liberation of mankind was through the universal recognition of that Truth which till now had been the exclusive secret of the sanctuaries. What, then, was the great central Truth which was thus announced in this proclamation of the Divine Name? It has two sides to it. First, that Pure Spirit is the ultimate essence of all that is, and as a consequence the All-presence, the All-knowledge, the All-livingness, and the All-lovingness of "God." Then as the corollary of the proposition that "Spirit is all that is," there must be the converse proposition that "all that is is Spirit"; and since Man is included in the "all" we are again brought back to the original description of him as the image and likeness of God.

But in those days people had to be educated up to these two great truths, and they have not advanced very far in this education yet; so from the time when Moses' eyes were opened to see in these truths, not a secret to be guarded for his private benefit, but the power which was to expand to the renovation of the world, he realized that it was his mission to set men free by educating them gradually into the true knowledge of the Divine Name. Then he conceived a great scheme. Modern research has shown us that the knowledge of this great fundamental truth was not confined to Egypt, but formed the ultimate centre of all the religions of antiquity; it was that secret in which the supreme initiation of all the highest mysteries culminated. It could not be otherwise, for it was the only ultimate conclusion to which generations of clear-headed thinkers could come. But these were sages, priests, philosophers, men of education and leisure; and this final deduction was beyond the reach of the toiling multitudes, whose whole energies had to be devoted to the earning of their daily bread.

Still it was impossible for these thinkers who *had* arrived at the great knowledge to pass over the multitudes without allowing them at least a few crumbs from their table. The true recognition of the "Self" must always carry with it the purpose of helping others to acquire it also; but it does not necessarily imply the immediate perception of the best means of doing so, and hence throughout antiquity we find an inner religion, the Supreme

Mysteries, for the initiated few; and an outer religion, for the most part idolatrous, for the people. The people were not to be left without any religion, but they were given a religion which was deemed suited to their gross apprehension of things, and in the hands of lower orders of priests, themselves little, if at all, better instructed than the worshippers, these conceptions often became very gross indeed. Nevertheless, in their first intention the "idols" were not without meaning.

The cultured Greeks laughed at the Egyptian temples as places where, in the midst of a magnificent edifice, when the sacred curtain of the innermost sanctuary was withdrawn, there was revealed an onion or a cat. Yet here was surely enough to prompt an intelligent person to enquiry. Why did the innermost sanctuary contain no Apollo Belvedere or other marvel unique and worthy to be enshrined, but only one of those wretched animals which disturbed the rest of the Greek traveller newly arrived in Egypt, by nocturnal caterwaulings which must have been a marked feature in cities where pussy held undisputed sway? Or why was the odoriferous onion that lay by tons for sale in the markets here set up upon a pedestal as an object of reverence? Surely there must be some deep significance in elevating such common objects to the central place of mystery. Yes, because in these commonest of common things there appeared the Great Central Mystery of LIFE more than in the sculptured marble of Phidias or Praxiteles.

Thus the Egyptian religion signified, to all who had the "nous" to penetrate it, the All-presence of the Eternal Living Spirit as the ONE true object of worship, to be found, not only in temples, but in streets and fields, in all places alike. It signified this to those who had the intelligence to lift the veil, and this meant, perhaps, one in ten thousand of the population; and as soon as he had penetrated the real meaning his lips were sealed, for he was admitted to the Mysteries. For the rest, the priests had such trivial superficial explanations as those which ages later they sought to palm off upon Herodotus; it was no part of their business to lift the veil of Isis.

And so Moses saw the generations toiling on and on in an ignorance which could not but have disastrous consequences sooner or later. Under the paternal rule of a truly illuminated priesthood, such a relation between the inner and the outer religion might be employed to maintain a condition of peaceful well-being for the masses during their intellectual infancy; but he saw that this state of things could not go on indefinitely. With a general advance in intelligence must come a general disposition to question the outward forms of religion, while yet this general advance fell very far short of that fuller development which in solitary instances led the individual to grasp the meaning of the inner Truth. Then, when to any nation comes the ridicule of all it has hitherto held sacred, because it has never learnt the Eternal Truth itself, but has placed its faith in forms and ceremonies and traditions, which, useful in their day and generation, should have been unfolded to meet growing intelligence—when this condition of the national mind supervenes, woe to that nation, for it is left without God and without hope, and by the inevitable Law of Nature on the plane of MIND, it cannot but bring upon itself dire calamity. From the standpoint of the governed, this benign, paternal government could not go on for ever, and equally so from that of the rulers. What guarantee was there of a perpetual succession of priests illuminated not only in head but also in heart? Egypt was old when Moses was a youth, and the signs of decadence were not wanting; for the cruel oppression of the Israelites, whom four centuries of naturalization should have placed on equality with their fellow-subjects, was the very reverse of all that was truest in the inner teaching of the Egyptian temples. It was the index of practical atheism. The Science of the temples continued, but it had reached the bifurcation of the Way, and it had taken the Left-hand Path.

And if this was the case in Egypt, which led the van of civilization, what was to be expected from the rest of the world? What was the outlook into the future with an intellectual development expanding only on the material side, without any knowledge of those spiritual truths in which lies the real livingness of Life? Surely nothing but the ultimate destruction of mankind in internecine strife, led up to by long ages of that awful spiritual condition in which the outward polish of materialized intellectuality only serves to place additional resources at the disposal of the unmitigated savage within.

The system then in vogue had once been a valuable system, perhaps the only one possible, but Egypt was no longer young, and the day of that system had palpably gone by. What was to be done? That great central Truth which the old system had handed down from hoary antiquity must be made the common appanage of mankind. "Nuk-pu-Nuk" must no longer be the mysterious legend of the temples, but it must become the household word of every family throughout the world. This is the work of generation upon generation, very far from being accomplished yet; and the only way to inaugurate it was by a new departure in which the great announcement that had hitherto been reserved as the last and final teaching must become the first and initial teaching; the supreme secret of the Mysteries must be made the starting-point of the child's education; and, therefore, the mission to Israel must open with the declaration of the I AM as the all-embracing ONE.

A sentence consists of a subject, copula, and predicate, but in the announcement of the Divine Name made to Moses, there is no predicate. The reason is that to predicate anything of a subject implies some special aspect of it, and thus by implication *limits* it, however extensive the predicate may be; and it is impossible to apply this mode of statement to the Universal Living Spirit. There can be nothing *outside* it. Itself is the Substance and the Life of all that is or ever can be: that is an ultimate conception from which it is impossible to get away.

Therefore, the only predicate corresponding to the Universal Subject must be the enumeration of the innumerable—the statement of all that is contained in infinite possibility—and, consequently, the place of the predicate must be left apparently unfilled, because it is that fulness which includes *all.* The only possible statement of the Divine is that of Present Subjective Being, the universal "I" and the ever-present "AM." Therefore I AM is the Name of God; and the First of all the Commandments is the announcement of the Divine Being as the Infinite ONE.

I have discussed the subject of the Unity of Spirit in my *Edinburgh Lectures on Mental Science,* but I may repeat here the truth that, mathematically, the Infinite *must* be Unity. We cannot think of two Infinites, for as soon as duality appears, each member of it is limited by the other, else there would be no duality: therefore we cannot multiply the Infinite. Similarly, we cannot divide it, for division again implies multiplicity or Numbers, and though these may be conceived of as existing relatively to each other *within* the Infinite, the very relation between them establishes limits where one begins and the other ends, and thus we are no longer dealing with the Infinite.

Of course all this is self-evident to the mathematician, who at once sees the absurdity of attempting to multiply or divide infinity; but the non-mathematical reader should endeavor to realize the full meaning of the word "Infinite" as that which, being without limits, necessarily occupies all space, and, therefore, includes all that is. The announcement that God is ONE is, therefore, the mathematical statement of the Universal Presence of Spirit, and the phrase "I AM" is the grammatical statement of the same thing. And because the Universal Spirit is the Universal Life Itself, "over all, through all, and in all," there is yet a third statement of it, which is its Living statement, the reproduction of it in the man himself; and these three statements are one, and cannot be separated. Each implies the two others, like the three sides of an equilateral triangle, and, therefore, the First of all the Commandments is that we shall recognize THE ONE. As numerically all other numbers are developed from unity, so all the possibilities of ever expanding Life are developed from the all-including UNIT of Being, and, therefore, in this Commandment we find the root of our future growth to all eternity. This is why both Moses and Jesus assign to it the supreme place.

And here let me point out the intimate relation between the teaching of Jesus and the teaching of Moses. They are the two great figures of the Bible. As the Old Testament centres round the one, so the New Testament centres round the other. Each appeals to the other. Moses says, "Of thy brethren, shall the Lord thy God raise up a prophet *like unto me*"—the prophet that was to come should duplicate Moses—and when that prophet came, he said, "If they hear not Moses and the prophets, neither will they be persuaded though one rose from the dead." Each is the complement of the other. We shall never understand Jesus until we understand Moses, and we shall never understand Moses until we understand Jesus.

Yet this is not a paradox, for to grasp the meaning of either we must find the key to their utterances in our own hearts, and on our own lips in the words "I AM"; that is, we must go back to that Divine Universal Law of Being which is written within us, and of which both Moses and Jesus were the inspired exponents.

The mission of Moses, then, was to build up a nationality which should be independent both of time and country, and which should derive its solidarity from its recognition of the principle of THE ONE. Its national being must be based upon its expanding realization of the great central Truth, and to the guarding and developing of that Truth this nation must be consecrated; and in the enslaved but not subdued children of the desert—the children of Israel—Moses found ready to hand the material which he needed. For these erewhile wanderers had brought with them a simple monotheistic creed, a belief in the God of Abraham, Isaac, and Jacob, which, vaguely though it might be, already touched the threshold of the sacred mystery, and four hundred years of residence in Egypt had not extinguished, however it may have obscured, the great tradition. Here, then,

Moses found the nucleus for the nationality he designed to found, and so he led forth the people in that great symbolic march through the wilderness whose story is told in the Exodus.

To the details of that history we may turn more intelligently after we have gained a clearer idea of what the great work really was which Moses inaugurated on the night of the first Passover. Perhaps some of my readers may be surprised to learn that it is still going on, and that they are called upon to take a personal part in continuing the work of Moses, which has now so expanded as to reach themselves.

But all this is contained in the commission which Moses first announced to those he was to deliver, and grows naturally out of its unfoldment. The people he was to lead into liberty were "the people of God," and since "God" is the I AM, they were "THE PEOPLE OF THE I AM." This was the true Name of this nation, which was to be founded upon an Eternal Ideal instead of on the historical conditions of time and the geographical conditions of place; and this *essential* name of the New Nation has been as accurately translated into its equivalent of "Israel" as we shall later see that the *essential* Name of God has been translated by the word "Jehovah." "The People of God" led forth by Moses were proclaimed by the very terms of his commission to be "The People of the I AM."

Now, the history of this people is dignified by a succession of Prophets such as no other nation lays claim to; yet the great Prophet who first consolidated their scattered tribes into a compact community, in prophesying of the future of the people he had founded, passes over all these and, looking down the long centuries, points only to one other Prophet "like unto me." We constantly miss those little indications of Scripture on which the fuller understanding of it so greatly depends; and just as we miss the point when we are told that Man is created in the likeness of God, so we miss the point when we are told that this other Prophet, Jesus, is a Prophet of the same type as Moses.

The whole line of intervening prophets were not of that type. They had their own special work, but it was not a work like that of Moses. Isaiah, Jeremiah, Ezekiel, and the rest sink out of sight, and the only Prophet whom Moses sees in the future is brought into his field of vision by His likeness to himself. Any child in a Sunday-school, if asked what it knew about Moses, would answer that he brought the children of Israel out of Egypt. No one would question that this was the distinctive fact regarding him, and therefore if we are to find a Prophet of the same type as Moses, we should expect to find in Him the founder of a New Nationality of the same order as that founded by Moses: that is to say, a nationality subsisting independently of time and place and cohering by reason of its recognition of an Eternal Ideal.

To make Jesus a Prophet like unto Moses, he must in some way repeat the Exodus and re-establish "the people of the I AM." Now, turning to the teaching of Jesus, we find that this is exactly what He did. There was nothing on which he laid greater stress than the I AM. "Except ye believe that I AM ye shall perish in your sins," was the emphatic summary of His whole teaching. And here read carefully. Distinguish between what Jesus said and what the translators of our English Bible say that he said, for it makes all the difference. Our English version runs, "If ye believe not that I am *He* ye shall die in your sins" (John viii. 24), thus by the introduction of a single word assuming all sorts of theological doctrines having their origin in Persian and Neo-platonic speculations, the discussion of which would require a volume to itself. Not false doctrines, but great truths are presented in such infantine notions as to convey the most limiting conception of ideals whose vitality consists in their transcending all limitations.

Thus both as theologians and grammarians the translators of the Authorized Version felt the want of a predicate to complete the words I AM, and so they added the word *"he"*; but faithful according to their light, they were careful to draw attention to the fact that there was no "he" in the original, and therefore that word is printed in italics to show that it was supplied by the translators; and the Revised Version carefully notes this fact in the margin.

In the parallel case of the announcement to Moses at the burning bush, the translators did not attempt to introduce any predicate; they felt what I have pointed out, that no predicate could be sufficiently extensive to define Infinite Being; but here, supposing that Jesus was speaking of Himself personally they thought it necessary to introduce a word which should limit His statement accordingly. Now the only comment to be made on this passage of the English Bible is to note carefully that it is exactly what Jesus *never said.* In this connection He made no personal application of the verb "to be." What he said was, "Except ye believe that I AM, ye shall die in your sins" (R. V.). Now, if the criterion by which we are to recognize Him as the Prophet predicted by Moses, is His reproduction of the doings of Moses, then we cannot be wrong in supposing that His use of the I AM was as complete a *generalization* as was employed by Moses.

On the same principle on which theologians or grammarians would particularize the words to the individuality of Jesus, they might particularize them to Moses also. But going back to that generalized statement of Man which is the very first intimation the Bible gives of him, we find that if I AM is the generalized statement of "God," it must also be the generalized statement of "Man," for man is the image and likeness of God. Whatever is true of one is true of the other, only conversely, and, as it were, by reflection, so that whatever is universal in God becomes individual in man.

If, then, Jesus was to duplicate the work of Moses, it could only be by taking as the foundation of his teaching the same statement of *essential* Being that Moses took as the foundation of his; and therefore we must look for a generic, and not for specific, application of the I AM in his teaching also. And as soon as we do this the veil is lifted and a power streams forth from all his instructions which shows us that it was no mere figure of speech when He said that the water which He should give would become in each one who drank of it a well of water springing up into everlasting life. He came, not to proclaim Himself, but Man; not to tell us of His Own Divinity separating Him from the race and making Him the Great Exception, but to tell us of *our* Divinity and to show in Himself the Great Example of the I AM reaching its full personal expression in Man.

This Prophet is raised up "of our brethren," He is one of ourselves, and therefore He said, "The disciple when he is perfected shall be *as his Master.*" It is the Universal I AM reproducing itself in the individuality of Man that Jesus would have us believe in. He is preaching nothing but the same old Truth with which the Bible begins, that Man is the image and likeness of God. He says in effect, Make this recognition the centre of your life, and you have tapped the source of everlasting life; but refuse to believe it, and you will die in your sins. Why? As a Divine vengeance upon you for daring to question a theological formulary to which some narrow-minded ecclesiastic applies the words of the Vincentian canon, "Quod semper, quod ubique, quod ab omnibus," when his formulary has never even been heard of outside such limits as both historically and geographically give the lie direct to his assertion of "always," "everywhere," and "by all men"? Certainly not. Truth has a surer foundation than forms of words; it is deep down in the foundations of Being; and it is the failure to realize this Truth of Being *in ourselves* that is the refusal to believe in the I AM which must necessarily cause us to perish in our sins. It is not a theological vengeance, but the Law of Nature. Let us enquire, then, what this Law is.

It is the great Law that, to live at all, we must primarily live in ourselves. No one can live for us. We can never get away from being the centre of our own world; or, in scientific language, our life is essentially subjective. There could be no objective life without a subjective entity to receive the perceptions which the objective faculties convey to it; and since the receiving entity is ourself, the only life possible to us is that of living in our own perceptions. Whatever we believe, does, for us, in very fact exist. Our beliefs may be erroneous from the standpoint of a happier belief, but this does not alter the fact that for ourselves our beliefs are our realities, and these realities must continue until some ground is found for a change of belief.

And in turn the subjective entity re-acts upon the objective life, for if there is one fact which the advance of modern psychological science is making more clear than another it is that the subjective entity is "the builder of the body." And this is precisely what, on the information we have already gleaned from the Bible, it ought to be; for we have seen that the statement that Man is the image of God can only be interpreted as a statement of his having in himself the same creative process of Thought to which alone it is possible to attribute the origin of anything. He is the image of God because he is the individualization of the Universal Mind at that stage of self-evolution in which the individual attains the capacity for reasoning from the seen to the unseen, and thus penetrating behind the veil of outward appearances; so that, because of the reproduction of the Divine creative faculty in himself, the man's mental states or modes of thought are bound to externalize themselves in his body and his circumstances.

This, then, is the Law of Man's Being. I do not stop to discuss it in detail, as, writing for New Thought readers, I assume at least an elementary knowledge of these things on their part; and accordingly this being the Law we see that the more closely our conception of ourselves approximates to a *broad generalization* of the factors which go to make human personality, rather than that narrow conception which limits our notion of ourselves to certain particular relations that have gathered around us, the more fully we shall externalize *this* idea of ourselves; and because this idea is a *generalization* independent of any particular circumstance, it must necessarily externalize as a corresponding independence of circumstances, in other words, it must result in a control over conditions, whether of body or environment, proportioned to the completeness of our generalization.

The more perfect the generalization the more perfect the corresponding control over conditions, and therefore to attain the most complete control, which means the most perfect Liberty, we need to conceive of ourselves as embodying the idea of the most perfect generalization. But complete generalization is only another expression for infinitude, and therefore we have again reached the point where it becomes impossible to attach any predicate to the verb "to Be," and so the only statement which contains the whole Law of Man's Being is identical with the only statement which contains the whole Law of God's Being, and consequently I AM is as much the correct formula for Man as for God.

But if we do not believe this and make it the centre of our life, we must perish in our sins. The Bible defines "sin" as "the transgression of the Law," and Jesus' warning is that by transgressing the Law of our own Being we shall die. It would carry me beyond the general lines of this book to discuss the question of what is here meant by "Death"; but that it is not the everlasting damnation of the Western creeds is obvious from the single statement of the Bible, that the Master employed the interval between His death and resurrection in teaching those souls who had passed out of physical life in the catastrophe of the Deluge, persons who most assuredly had perished on account of their transgression of the Law. For further study of this subject I would refer the reader to the works of two orthodox divines, Farrar's *Eternal Hope,* and Plumptree's *Spirits in Prison.*

The transgression of which Jesus speaks is the transgression of the Law of the I AM in ourselves, the non-recognition of the fact that we are the image and likeness of God. This is the old original sin of Eve. It is the belief in Evil as a substantive self-originating power. We believe ourselves under the control of all sorts of evils having their climax in Death; but whence does the evil get its power? Not from God, for no diminution of Life can come from the Fountain of Life. And if not from God, then from where else? God is the ONLY BEING—that is the teaching of the First Commandment—and therefore whatever is is some mode of God: and if this be so, then however evil may have *relative* existence, it can have no *substantive* existence of its own. It is not a Living Originating Power. God, the Good, alone is *that;* and it is for this reason that in the doctrine of THE ONE and in the statement of the I AM, is the foundation of eternal *individual* Life and Liberty.

So then the transgression is in supposing that there is, or can be, any Living Originating Power outside the I AM. Let us once see that this is impossible, and it follows that evil has no more dominion over us and we are free. But so long as we limit the I AM in ourselves to the narrow boundaries of the relative and conditioned, and do not realize that, personified in ourselves, it must by its very nature still be as unfettered as when acting in the first creation of the universe, we shall never pass beyond the Law of Death which we thus impose upon ourselves.

In this way, then, Jesus proved himself to be the Prophet of whom Moses had spoken. He made the recognition of the I AM the sole foundation of his work; in other words, He placed before men the same radical and ultimate conception of Being that Moses had done. But with a difference. Moses elaborated this conception from the standpoint of the Universal: Jesus elaborated it from that of the Individual. The work of Moses must necessarily precede that of Jesus, for if the Universal Mind is not in some measure apprehended first, the individual mind cannot be apprehended as its image and reflection.

But it takes the teaching both of Moses and Jesus to make the complete teaching, for each is the complement to the other, and it is for this reason that Jesus said he came not to destroy the Law but to fulfil. Jesus took up the work where Moses left it off, and expanded Moses' initial conception of a people founded on the recognition of the unity of God into its proper outcome of the conception of a people founded on the recognition of the unity of Man as the expression of the Unity of God.

How can we doubt that this latter conception also was in the mind of Moses? Had it not been he would not have spoken of the Prophet like unto himself that should come hereafter. But he saw the ages during which his great idea must germinate within the limits of a single nationality before it could expand to humanity at large; and therefore before Jesus could gather into one the "People of the I AM" from every nation under heaven, it was necessary that one exclusive nation should be the official custodians of the great secret, and mature it till the time was ripe for the formation of that great international nationality which is only now beginning to show forth its earliest blossoms.

## V

# THE MISSION OF JESUS

HITHERTO, OUR INTERPRETATION of the Bible has worked along the line of great Universal Laws naturally inherent in the constitution of Man and thus applicable to all men alike; but now we must turn to that other line of an Exclusive Selection to which I referred in the opening chapter. This is not an arbitrary selection, for that would contradict the very conception of unchangeable Universal Law on which the whole Bible is founded, but it is a process of "natural selection" arising out of the Law itself, and results, not from any change in the Law, but from the attainment of an exalted realization of what the Law really is.

The first suggestion of this process of separation is contained in the promise that the deliverance of the race should come through "the Seed of the Woman," for in contradistinction to this "Seed" there is the seed of the Serpent; "I will put enmity between thy seed and her seed." Again we see the process of selection coming out in the preference given to the offering of Abel over that of Cain, and again the selection is repeated in the intimation that Seth took the place of Abel, while it is to be remarked that the New Testament genealogy traces the ancestry of Jesus to Seth; so that the line of Seth is clearly indicated as carrying on the selection originally made in favor of Abel. In this line we find Noah, who, with his family, was alone excepted from the universal overthrow of the Deluge; and many centuries later we find one man, Abraham, selected by means of a special covenant to be the progenitor of a chosen race from which in process of time the Messiah, the Promised Seed of the Woman, was to be born.

Now, was there in these things any arbitrary selection? After due consideration, we shall find that there was not, and that they arose out of the perfectly natural operation of mental laws working on the higher levels of Individualism, and the indications of this operation are given in the story of Cain and Abel. Abel was a keeper of sheep and Cain was a tiller of the earth, and if the reader will bear in mind what I have said regarding the symbolic character of Bible personages and the metaphorical use of words, the meaning of the story will become clear.

There is a great difference between animal and vegetable life: the one is cold and devoid of any apparent element of volition, the other is full of warmth and adumbrates the quality of Will; so that as symbols the animal represents the emotional qualities in Man, while the vegetable, following a mere law of sequence without the exercise of individual choice, more fitly represents the purely logical processes of reasoning. Now, we all know that the first spring of action in any chain of cause and effect which we set going starts with some emotion, some manner of *feeling* and not with a mere argument. Argument, a reasoning process, may cause us to change the standpoint of our feeling and to conceive that as desirable, which at first we did not consider so, but at the end it is the recognition of a desire which is the one and only spring of action. It is, therefore, the feelings and desires that give the true key to our life, and not mere logical statements; and so if the feelings and desires are going in the right direction we may be very sure that the logic will not be wrong in its conclusions, even though it may be blundering in its method: take care of the heart, and the head will take care of itself.

This, then, is the meaning of the story of Cain and Abel. If we realize that the Universal Mind, as the all-pervading undistributed Creative Power must be subjective mind, we shall see that it can only respond in accordance with the Law of subjective mind; that is to say, its relation to the individual mind must always be in exact correspondence to what the individual mind conceives of it. This is unequivocally stated in a passage which is twice repeated in Scripture: "With the pure Thou wilt show Thyself pure, and with the froward Thou wilt show Thyself froward" (Psalm xviii. 26, and II. Sam. xxii. 27), where the context makes it clear that these words are addressed to the Divine Being. If, therefore, we grasp this Law of Correspondence, we shall see that the only conception of the Divine Mind which will really vivify our souls with living and life-giving power is to realize it, not merely as a tremendous force to be mapped out intellectually according to its successive stages of sequence—though it is this also—but above all things as the Universal Heart with which our own must beat in sympathetic vibration if we would attain the true development of that power, the possession of which constitutes "the glorious liberty of the sons of God."

In all our operations we must always remember that the Creative Power is a process of *feeling* and not of reasoning. Reasoning analyzes and dissects; feeling evolves and builds up. The relation between them is that reasoning explains *how* it is that feeling has this power, and the more plainly we see *why* it should be so the more completely we are delivered from those negative feelings which act destructively by the same law by which affirmative feelings work constructively.

The first requisite, therefore, for drawing to ourselves that creative action of the Universal Spirit, which alone can set us free from the bondage of Limitation, is to call up its response on the side of feeling; and unless this be done first, no amount of argument, mere intellectuality, can have the desired effect, and this is what is symbolically represented in the statement that God accepted Abel's offering and rejected Cain's. It is the veiled statement of the truth that the action of the intellect alone, however powerful, is not sufficient to move the Creative Power. This does not in the least mean that the intellectual process is hurtful in itself or unacceptable before God, but it must come in its proper order as joining with feeling instead of taking its place. When a mere cold ratiocination is substituted for hearty warmth of volition, then Abel is symbolically slain by Cain.

But the allegory goes further. It tells us that the particular animal which Abel offered in sacrifice was the sheep, and from this point onward we find the metaphor of the shepherd and the sheep recurring throughout Scripture, and the reason is that the relation between the Shepherd and the Sheep is peculiarly one of Guidance and Protection. Now, this brings us to the point which we may call the "Severance of the Way." When we realize the Unity of the I AM, the identity, that is, of the Self-recognizing Principle in the Universal and in the Individual, we may form three conceptions of it: one according to which the Universal I AM is reduced to a mere unconscious force, which the individual mind can manipulate without any sort of responsibility; another, the converse of this, in which Volition remains entirely on the side of the Universal Mind, and the individual becomes a mere automaton; and the third, in which each phase of Mind is the reciprocal of the other, and consequently the inceptive action may commence on either side.

Now, it is this *reciprocal* action that the Bible all along puts before us as the true Way. From the centre of his own smaller circle of perception the individual is free to make any selection that he will, and if he acts from a clear recognition of the true relations of things, the first use he will make of this power will be to guard himself against any possible misuse of it by recognizing that his own circle revolves within the greater circle of that Whole of which he is an infinitesimal part; and, therefore, he will always seek to conform his individual action to the movement of the Universal Spirit.

His sense of the *Wholeness* of that Universal Life which finds Individual centre in himself, and his consciousness of his identity with it, will lead him to see that there must be, above his own individual view of things derived from a merely partial knowledge, a higher and more far-seeing Wisdom which, because it is the Life-in-itself, cannot be in any way adverse to him; and he will, therefore, seek to maintain such a mental attitude as will draw towards himself the response of the Universal Mind as a Power of unfailing Guidance, Provision and Protection. But to do this means the curbing of that self-will which is guided only by the narrow perception of expediency derived from past experiences; in other words, it requires us to act from trust in the Universal Mind, thus investing it with a Personal character, rather than from calculations based on our own objective view, which is necessarily limited to secondary causes; in a word, we must learn to walk by faith and not by sight.

Now the institution of Sacrifice is the most effective way for impressing this mental attitude. Viewed merely superficially, it implies the desire of the worshipper to submit himself to the Divine Guidance by reconciliation through a propitiatory offering, and thus the required mental attitude is maintained. If we see that the blood of bulls and goats and the ashes of an heifer can have no power in themselves to effect reconciliation, and yet cannot see any more intelligible reason, then, if we will to accept the principle of sacrifice in the light of a mere mystery, we hereby still submit our individual will to the conception of a Higher Guidance, and so in this view also the desired mental attitude is maintained.

And at last when we reach the point where we see that the Universal Mind, which is also the Universal LAW, cannot have a retrospective vindictive character any more than any of the Laws of Nature which emanate from it, we see that the true sacrifice is the willingness to give up smaller personal aims for the purpose of bringing into concrete manifestation those great principles of universal harmony which are the foundations of the Kingdom of God; and when we reach this point we see the philosophical reasons why the maintenance of this attitude of the individual towards the Universal Mind is the one and only basis on which the individuality can expand, or, indeed, continue to exist at all.

It is in correspondence with these three stages that the Bible first puts before us the patriarchal and Levitical sacrifices, next explains these as symbols of the Great Sacrifice of the Suffering Messiah, and finally tells us that God does not require the death of any victim, and that the true offering is that of the heart and will; and so the Psalms sum up the whole matter by saying, "Sacrifice and burnt-offering thou wouldest not," and instead of these, "Lo, I come to do Thy will, O my God; yea, Thy law is within my heart."

But the idea of Sacrifice has the idea of Covenant for its correlative. If the acceptance of the principle of Sacrifice brings the worshipper into a peculiarly close relation to the Divine Mind, it equally brings the Divine Mind into a peculiarly close relation to the worshipper; and since the Divine Mind is the Life-in-itself, the very Essence-of-Being which is the *root* of all conscious individuality, this identification of the Divine with the Individual results in his continual expansion, or, to use the Master's words, in his having Life and having it more abundantly; and, consequently, his powers steadily increase, and he is led by the most unlooked-for sequences of cause and effect into continually improving conditions which enable him to do more and more effectual work, so as to make him a centre of power, not only to himself, but to all with whom he comes in contact.

This continual progress is the result of the natural Law of the relation between himself and the Universal Mind when he does not invert its action, and because it works with the same unchangeableness as all other Natural Laws, it constitutes an Everlasting Covenant which can no more be broken than those astronomical laws which keep the planets in their orbits, the smallest infraction of which would destroy the entire cosmic system; and it is for this reason that we find in the Bible such frequent allusions to the Laws of Nature as typical of the certainty of the relation between God and his people, "Gather My saints (separated ones) together unto Me; those that have made a covenant with me by sacrifice" (Psalm 1.5); the two principles of Sacrifice and Covenant rightly understood will always be found to go hand in hand.

The idea of Guidance and Protection which is thus set forth, recurs, throughout the Bible under the emblem of the Shepherd and the Sheep, and it is in a peculiar manner appropriated to "the People of the I AM"; "From thence is the Shepherd the Stone of Israel" (Gen. xlix. 24); "Give ear, O Shepherd of Israel, Thou that leadest Joseph like a flock" (Psalm lxxx. 1); "The Lord is My Shepherd I shall not want" (Psalm xxiii. 1); "I am the Good Shepherd," and similarly in many other passages. If then this conception of the Shepherd and the Sheep represents the mental attitude of "Israel," we may reasonably expect it to be precisely opposite to all that is symbolically meant by "Egypt." If "Israel" takes for its Stone of Foundation the principle of Guidance by the Supreme Power, then "Egypt" must base itself on the contrary principle of making its own choice without any guidance, that is to say, determined self-will, and hence we find it written that "every Shepherd is an abomination to the Egyptians" (Gen. xlvi. 34).

Now, it is a very remarkable thing that tradition points to the Great Pyramid as having been erected by a "Shepherd" power which dominated Egypt, not by force of arms, but by a mysterious influence, which, although they detested it, the Egyptians found it impossible to resist. These "Shepherds" built the Great Pyramid, and then, having accomplished their work, returned to the land from whence they came. So says the tradition. The Pyramid remains to this day, and the researches of modern science show us that it is a monumental statement of all the great measures of the cosmic system wrought out with an accuracy which can only be accounted for by more than human knowledge.

And where should we find this knowledge except in the Universal Mind, of which the cosmic system is the visible manifestation? If, as it appears to me, that mind is primarily subconscious, then by the general law of relation between subjective and objective mind it could reproduce its inherent knowledge of all cosmic facts in any individual mind that had systematically trained itself into sympathy with the Universal Mind in that particular direction. But such training is impossible unless the individual mind first recognizes the Universal Mind as an Intelligence capable of giving the highest instruction, and to which, therefore, the individual mind is bound to look for guidance.

We must carefully avoid the mistake of supposing that *sub*-consciousness means *un*consciousness. That idea is clearly negatived by the fact of hypnotism. Whatever unconsciousness there may be is on the part of the objective mind, which is unconscious of the action of the subjective mind, but a careful study of the subject shows that subjective mind, so far from knowing less than the objective mind, knows infinitely more; and if this be true of the individual subjective mind, how much more must it be true of the Universal Subjective Mind, of which all individual consciousness is a particular mode of manifestation?

For these reasons, the only people who could build such a monument as a Great Pyramid must be those who realized the principles of Divine Guidance or the Power which is set forth under the emblem of the Shepherd and the Sheep, and, therefore, we can see how it is that tradition associates the building of the Pyramid with a Shepherd Power.

Nor is this all. Having first demonstrated its trustworthiness by the refined accuracy of its astronomical and geodetic measurements, the Pyramid challenges our attention with a series of time measurements, all of which were prophetic at the date of its erection, and some of which have already become historic, while the period of others is now rapidly running out. The central point of these time-measurements is the date of the birth of Christ, and if we think of Him in His character of "the Good Shepherd" we have yet another testimony to the supreme importance which Scripture attaches to the relation between the Shepherd and the Sheep. For the Great Pyramid is a Bible in stone, and there can be no doubt that it is this marvel of the ages which is referred to in the nineteenth chapter of Isaiah, where it says—"In that day there shall be an altar to the Lord in the midst of the land of Egypt." And so we find that the central fact to which the Great Pyramid leads up is the coming of "the Good Shepherd"; and Jesus explains the reason for this title in the fact that "the Good Shepherd giveth His life for the Sheep"; that is what distinguishes Him from the hireling who is not a true shepherd; so that here we find ourselves back again at the idea of Sacrifice, only now it is not the Sheep that are sacrificed but the Shepherd.

Could anything be plainer? The sacrifice is not an offering of blood to a sanguinary Deity, but it is the Chief Shepherd sacrificing Himself *to the necessities of the case.*

And what are the necessities of the case? The student of Mental Science should see here the grandest application of the Law of Suggestion in a supreme act of self-devotion logically proceeding from the knowledge of the fundamental truths regarding Subjective and Objective Mind. Jesus stands before us as the Grand Master of Mental Science. It is written that "He knew what was in man," and in His mission we have the practical fruits of that knowledge. The Great Sacrifice is also the Great Suggestion. If we realize that the Creative Power of our Thought is the root from which all our experiences, whether subjective or objective, arise, we shall see that everything depends on the nature of the suggestions which give color to our Thought. If from our consciousness of guilt they are suggestions of retribution, then in accordance with the predominating tone of our Thought we shall externalize the evil that we fear; and if we carry this terrible suggestion with us through the gate of death into that other life which is purely subjective, then assuredly it will work itself out in our realizations, and so we must continue to suffer until we believe that we have paid the uttermost farthing. This is not a judicial sentence, but the inexorable working of Natural Law. But if we can find a counter-suggestion of such paramount magnitude as to obliterate all sense of liability to punishment, then by the same Law our fears are removed, and, whether in the body or out of the body, we rejoice in the sense of pardon and reconciliation to our Father which is in heaven.

Now we can well imagine that one who has attained the supreme knowledge of all Laws, and, as a consequence, has developed the powers which that knowledge must necessarily carry with it, would find in the conveying of such an incalculably valuable suggestion to the race an object worthy of his exalted capacities. For such a one ordinary ambitions would have no meaning, he has already left them far behind; but if he elect to devote himself to this great work he must count the cost, for nothing short of delivering himself to death can accomplish it. The Master said, "Greater love hath no man than this that a man lay down his life for his friends," and if the Law of Suggestion was to be employed in such a way as to appeal to the whole race, it could only be by so deeply impressing them with the realization of the Divine Love that all fear should be for ever cast out; therefore, the suggestion must be that of a Love which nothing can exceed, and so it must consist in him who undertakes the mission giving himself to Voluntary Death.

For herein is the difference between the crucifixion of Jesus and those thousands of other crucifixions which disgraced the annals of Rome; it was entirely voluntary. This also places it above all other acts of heroism. Many have died for the sake of others, but to them death was a necessity, and their devotion consisted in accepting it when and how they did. But with Jesus the case was entirely different. He was beyond the necessity of death, and no man could take His life from Him; He Himself had power to lay it down and to take it up again (John x. 17), but He was under no compulsion to do so; therefore, His yielding Himself to a death of excruciating agony was the master-stroke of Love and the supreme practical application of Mental Science.

When He said "It is finished," He had accomplished a work which is aptly represented by The Cubical Stone, which is The Figure of the New Jerusalem, of which it is written that "the length, and the breadth, and the height thereof are equal"; for turn it which way you will it still always serves its great purpose of impressing the suggestion of superlative Love which can be trusted to the uttermost. Even the crude conception of the Father's "justice" being satisfied by the sacrifice of "the Son," however faulty both as Law and as Theology, in no way misses the mark from the metaphysical standpoint of Suggestion; and those who have not yet got beyond this stage in their conception of the Divine Being, receive the assurance of the Divine Love towards themselves as completely as those who are able to grasp most clearly the sequence of cause and effect really involved; and for these latter it resolves itself into the simple argument *a fortiori* that if the Universal Spirit could thus inspire one to die for us who was already beyond the necessity of death, then It cannot be less loving in the bulk than it has shown Itself in the sample. It is an axiom that the Universal cannot act on the plane of the Particular except by becoming individualized upon that plane, and therefore we may argue that so far as it was possible for the Universal Spirit to give Itself to death for us It did so in the person of Jesus Christ; and so we may say that to all intents and purposes God died for us upon the Cross to prove to us the Love of God.

Let us, then, no longer doubt the fact of this Love, but realizing it to the full let us make the Cross of Christ, not the mysterious end of an unintelligent religion, but the beginning of a bright, practical, and glorious New Life, taking for our starting-point the apostolic words, "there is now no condemnation to them that are in Christ Jesus." We have now *consciously* left all condemnation behind us, and we set forward on our New Life with the self-obvious maxim that "if God be for us, who can be against us?" We may meet with opposition, but there is with us a Power and an Intelligence which no opposition can overcome, and so we become "more than conquerors through Him that loved us" (Rom. viii. 37).

This is the nature of the Great Suggestion wrought out by Jesus; so that here again we find that the acceptance of the Great Sacrifice gives rise to the consciousness of a peculiarly close and endearing relation between the Individual and the Universal Mind, which may well be described as an Everlasting Covenant because it is founded, not on any favoritism on the part of God, neither on any deeds of merit on the part of Man, but on the accurate working of Universal Law when realized in the higher manifestations of Individualism; and so it is truly written, "by His *Knowledge* shall My righteous servant justify many." Thus it is that Jesus completes the work of Moses in building up into a peculiar people, a chosen generation, "the People of the I AM" (I. Peter ii. 9).

It was this conception of themselves as a chosen nation, separate from all others, and united to God by a special covenant based upon sacrifice, that did in effect operate to produce the reality of this ideal in the people of Israel. Here again we see the Law of Suggestion at work. All their institutions, whether religious or political, were based upon the assumption of a covenant with Abraham for ever ratified to his descendants, and centering round the promised Messiah; and so, whether looking at the past, the present, or the future, an Israelite was perpetually met by the most powerful suggestion of his peculiar position in the Divine favor.

If we recognize in Abraham one whose deep realization of the truth concerning the promised "Seed" had specially placed him in touch with the Universal Mind in that particular direction, we may naturally suppose a special illumination on this subject which would lead him to impress this idea upon his son Isaac as the foundation-fact of his life; and so from generation to generation the supreme realization to all his descendants would be that of their covenant relation to God. And besides the impression conveyed by personal teaching, the law of heredity would cause each member of this race to be born with a pre-natal subjective consciousness of this great Suggestion, which would carry its effect into the building up of his life, quite independently of any objectively conscious knowledge of the subject. This involves intricate psychological problems which I cannot stop to discuss here, but all New Thought readers are sufficiently acquainted with the potency of "race-beliefs" to realize how powerful a factor this subjective transmission of a hereditary suggestion would be in forming "the People of the I AM."

And there is yet another aspect of this subject which is of peculiar interest to the British and American nations, into which, however, I shall not enter in this book; but it will be sufficient for me to say that when a suggestion has once been implanted by the Divine Mind, as the Bible tells us that God did to Abraham in the most emphatic manner, taking oath by His own Being because He could swear by none greater (Heb. vi. 13), that suggestion is bound to grow to the most magnificent fulfillment: "My word that goeth forth out of My mouth shall not return unto Me void, but shall accomplish that which I please, and it shall prosper in the thing whereunto I sent it" (Isaiah lv. 11).

For the reasons which I have now endeavored to explain, the principle of "the Shepherd" is "the Stone of Israel"; it is that great ideal by which the nationality of the "People of the I AM" coheres, and it is, therefore, at once the Foundation Stone and the Crowning Stone of the whole edifice. To those who cannot realize the great universal truths which are summed up in the two-fold ideal of Sacrifice and Covenant, it must always be the Stone of stumbling and the Rock of offence; but to "the People of the I AM," whether individually or collectively, it must for ever be "the Stone of Israel," and "the Rock of our Salvation." To lay in Zion this Chief Corner Stone was the mission of Jesus Christ.

VI

# THE BUILDING OF THE TEMPLE

IN OUR STUDY of the Bible, we must always remember that what it is seeking to teach us is the knowledge of the grand universal principles which are at the root of all modes of living activity, whether in that world of environment which we commonly speak of as Nature, or in those human relations which we call the World of Man, or in those innermost springs of being which we speak of as the Divine World. The Bible is throughout dealing with those three factors, which I have spoken of in the commencement of this book as "God," "Man," and "the Universe," and is explaining the Law of Evolution by which "God" or Universal Undifferentiated Spirit continually passes into more and more perfect forms of self-expression culminating in Perfected Man.

However deep the mysteries we may encounter, there is nothing unnatural anywhere. Everything has its place in the due order of the Great Whole. A mistaken conception of this Order may lead us to invert it, and by so doing we provide those negative conditions whose presence calls forth the Power of the Negative with all its disastrous consequences; but even this inverted action is perfectly natural, for it is all according to recognizable Law whether on the side of calculation or of feeling.

These Laws of the universe whether within or around us, are always the same, and the only question is whether through our ignorance we shall use them in that inverted sense which sums them all up in the Law of Death, or in that true and harmonious order which sums them up in the Law of Life. These are the things which under a variety of figures the Bible presents to us, and it is for us by reverent, yet intelligent, inquiry to penetrate the successive veils which hide them from the eyes of those who will not take the trouble to investigate for themselves. It is this Grand Order of the Universe that is symbolized by Solomon's Temple.

We have seen that it was the mission of Moses to mould into definite form the material which ages of unnoticed growth had prepared, to consolidate into national being "the People of the I AM," and to lead them out of Egypt. This work, with which the truly national history of Israel commenced, had its completion in the reign of Solomon, when all enemies had been extirpated from the Promised Land, and the state founded by Moses out of wandering tribes had culminated in a powerful monarchy, ruled over by a king whose name has ever since become both in East and West the synonym for the supreme attainment of wisdom, power, and glory.

If the purpose of Moses had been only that of a national law-giver and the founder of a political state, a Lycurgus or a Rollo, it would have found its perfect attainment in the reign of Solomon; but Moses had a far grander end in view, and looking down the long vista of the ages he saw, not Solomon, but the Carpenter, who said "a greater than Solomon is here"; and the way for the Carpenter could only be prepared by that long period of decadence which set in with the first days of Solomon's successor. "The People of the I AM" are concealed among all nations, and must be brought forth by the Prophet, who should realize the work of Moses, not only in a national, but also in a universal significance.

These are the three typical figures of Hebrew history, the beginning, the middle, and the end—Moses, Solomon, Jesus—and the three are distinguished by one common characteristic; they are all Builders of the Temple. Moses erected the tabernacle, that portable temple which accompanied the Israelites in their journeyings. Solomon reproduced it in an edifice of wood and stone fixed firmly upon its rocky foundation. Jesus said, "Destroy this temple, and in three days I will raise it up again; but He spake of the temple of His body."

Thus they stand before us the Three Great Builders, each building with a perfect knowledge according to a Divine pattern; and if the Divine is that in which there is no variableness nor shadow of turning, how can we suppose that the pattern was other than one and the same? We may, therefore, expect to find in the work of the Three Builders the same *principles* however differently expressed; for they each in different ways proclaimed the same all-embracing truth that God, Man, and the Universe, however varied may be the multiplicity of outward forms, are ONE.

St. Paul gives us an important key to the interpretation of Scripture, when he tells us that its leading characters also represent great universal principles, and this is pre-eminently the case with Solomon. His name, in common with the names Salem and Jerusalem, is derived from a word signifying Wholeness (Sálim, the Whole), and therefore means the man who has realized "the Wholeness," or in other words the Universal Unity. This is the secret of his greatness.

He who has found the Unity of the Whole has obtained "the Key of Knowledge," and it is now in his power to enter intelligently upon the study of his own being and of the relations which arise out of it, and to help others as he himself advances into greater light. This is the man who is able to become a Builder.

But such a man cannot come of any parentage; he must be the "Son of David"; and it was to test their knowledge in this respect that the Master posed the carping scribes with the question as to how the Son of David could also be his Lord. As rulers in Israel they should have known these things, and instructed the people in them, but they would not come as Nicodemus to Him who could teach them, and so, like Hiram, the architect of Solomon's Temple, the Master was murdered by those who should have been His scholars and helpers.

The Builder of the Temple, then, must be "the Son of David"; and again we find that much of the significance of this saying is concealed in the names. David is the English form of the Oriental "Daud," which means "Beloved," and the Builder is therefore the Son of the Beloved. David is called in Scripture "the man after God's own heart," a description exactly answering to the name; and we, therefore, find that Solomon the Builder is the son of the man who has entered into that reciprocal relation with "God," or the Universal Spirit, which can only be described as Love.

To define what is primarily *feeling* is to attempt the impossible; but the essence of the feeling consists in the recognition of such a reciprocity of nature that each supplies what the other wants, and that neither is complete without the other. In the last analysis, the reason for this feeling is to be discovered in the relation of the Individual to the Universal Mind as each being the necessary correlative of the other, and it is the recognition of this truth that makes David the father of Solomon.

When this recognition by the individual mind of its own nature and of its relation to the Universal Mind takes place, it gives birth to a new being in the man; for he now finds, not that he has ceased to be the self he was before, but that that self includes a far greater self, which is none other than the reproduction of the Universal Self in his individual consciousness. Thenceforward he works more and more *of set purpose* by means of this greater self, the self within the self, as he grows into fuller understanding of the Law by which this greater self has become developed within him.

He learns that it is this greater self within the self that is the true Builder, because it is none other than the reproduction of the Infinite Creative Power of the Universe. He realizes that the working of this power must always be a continual building up. It is the Universal Life-Principle, and to suppose *that* to have any other action than continual expansion into more and more perfect forms of self-expression, would be to suppose it acting in contradiction of its own nature, which, whether on the colossal scale of a solar system or on the miniature one of a man, must be that of a self-inherent activity which is for ever building up.

When any one is thus intellectually enlightened, he has reached that stage of development which is signified by the name David: he is "beloved," that is to say, he is exercising a specific individual *attraction* towards the Spirit in its universal and undifferentiated mode.

We are here dealing with the Principle of Evolution in its highest phases, and if we keep this in mind, it becomes clear that the intellectual man, who perceives this, is himself the evoluting principle manifesting at that stage where it becomes an individuality capable of understanding its own identity with the Spiritual Force which, by self-evolution, produces all things. He thus realizes himself to be the Reciprocal of the Universal Mind, which is the Divine Spirit, and he sees that his reciprocity consists in Evolution having reached in him the point where that factor is developed, which cannot have a place in the Universal Mind *as such,* but without which the continuation of Evolution in its higher phases is impossible, the factor, namely, of *individual* will.

We lose the key to the whole teaching of the Bible if we lose sight of the truth that the Universal cannot, as such, initiate a course of action on the plane of the particular. It can do so only by becoming the individual, which is precisely the production of the intellectually enlightened man we are speaking about. The failure to see this very obvious Law is the root of all the theological discordances that have retarded the work of true religion to the present time, and, therefore, the sooner we see through the error the better.

Any one, who has advanced to the perception of this Law, necessarily becomes a centre of attraction to Undifferentiated Spirit in its highest modes, the modes of Intelligence and Feeling, as well as in its lower modes of Vital Energy. This results from the very nature of the evolutionary hypothesis. All creation commences with the primary movement of the Spirit, and since the Spirit is Life-in-itself, this movement must be for ever going on.

To take an analogy from chemistry, it is perpetually in the nascent state, that is, continually pressing forward to find the most suitable affinities with which to coalesce into self-expression. This is exactly what Jesus said to the woman of Samaria: "The Father (Universal Spirit) *seeketh* such to worship Him"; and it is because of this mutual attraction between the individual mind, that has come to the knowledge of its own true nature, and the Universal Mind, that the person who is thus enlightened is called "the Beloved"; he is beginning to understand what is meant by man being the image of God, and to grasp the significance of the old-world saying that "Spirit is the power that knows itself."

As this intellectual comprehension of the great truth matures, it gives rise to the recognition of an interior power which is something beyond the intellect, but yet not independent of it, something regarding which we can make intellectual statements that clear the way for its recognition, but which is itself a Living Power and not a mere statement about such a power.

It may seem a truism to say that no statement about a thing *is* the thing, yet we are apt to miss this in practice. The Master pointed this out very clearly when He said to the Jews, "Search the Scriptures, for in them ye *think* ye have everlasting life, and they are they which testify of Me." "You make a mistake," He said in effect, "by supposing that the reading of a book can in itself confer Life. What your Scriptures do is to make statements regarding that which I am. Realize what those statements mean, and then you will see in Me the Living Example of the Living Truth; and seeing this you will seek for the development of the same thing in yourselves—the disciple when he is perfected shall be as his Master."

The Building-Power is that innermost spiritual faculty which is the reproduction in the individual of the same Universal Building-Power by which the whole creation exists, and the purpose of intellectual statements regarding it is to remove mental obstacles and to induce the mental state, which will enable this supreme innermost power to work in accordance with conscious selection on the part of the individual. It is the same power which has brought the race up to where it is, and which has evolved the individual as part of the race.

All further evolution must result from the conscious employment of the Evolutionary Law by the intelligence of the individual himself. Now, it is this recognized innermost creative power that is signified by Solomon—it must be preceded by the purified and enlightened intellect—and therefore it is called the Son of David, and becomes the Builder of the Temple. For the Master's statement shows that, in its true significance, the Temple is that of Man's individuality; and if this is so with the individual, equally it must be so in the totality of manifested being, and thus it is also true that the whole universe is none other than the Temple of the Living God.

This great truth of the Divine Presence is what the instructed builders sought to symbolize in Solomon's Temple, whether that Presence be considered on the scale of the universe or of an individual man. If the Universal Divine Presence is a fact, then the Individual Divine Presence is a fact also, because the individual is included in the universal; it is the working of the general Law in a particular instance, and thus we are brought to one of the great statements of the ancient wisdom, that Man is the Microcosm, that is to say, the reproduction of all the principles which give rise to the manifestation of the universe, or the Macrocosm; and therefore, to serve its proper emblematical purpose, the Temple must represent both the Macrocosm and the Microcosm.

It would be far too elaborate a work, for the present volume, to enter in detail into the symbolical statements of both physical and supra-physical nature contained first in the Tabernacle and afterwards in the Temple: but as the Universal Mind inspired the builders of the Pyramid with the correct knowledge of the cosmic measures, so the Bible tells us that Moses was inspired to produce in the Tabernacle the symbolic representation of great universal truths; he was bidden to make all things accurately according to the pattern showed him in the Mount, and the same truths received a more permanent symbolization in Solomon's Temple.

An excellent example of this symbolism is afforded by the two pillars set up by Solomon at the entrance to the Temple: the one on the right hand called Jachin, and the one on the left called Boaz (I. Kings vii. 21). They seemed to have had no structural connection with the building, but merely to have stood at its entrance for the purpose of bearing these symbolic names. What, then, do they signify? The English J often stands for the Oriental Y, and the name Jachin is therefore Yakhin, which is an intensified form of the word Yak or ONE, thus signifying first the principle of Unity as the Foundation of all things, and then the Mathematical element throughout the universe, since all numbers are evolved from the ONE, and under certain methods of treatment will always resolve themselves again into it.

But the Mathematical element is the element of Measurement, Proportion, and Relation. It is not the Living Life, but only the recognition of the proportional adjustments which the Life gives rise to. To balance the Mathematical element we require the Vital element, and this element finds its most perfect expression in that wonderful complex of Thought, Feeling, and Volition which we call Personality. The pillar Jachin is therefore balanced by the pillar Boaz, a name connected with the root of the word "awáz" or Voice.

Speech is the distinguishing characteristic of Personality. To clothe a conception in adequate language is to give it definition, and thus make it clear to ourselves and to others. A distinct statement of our idea is the first step in the operation of consciously building it up into concrete existence, and therefore we find that, in all the great religions of the race, the Divine Creative Power is spoken of as "the Word."

Let us get away from all confused mysticism regarding this term. The formulated Word is the expression of a definite Purpose, and therefore it stands for the action of Intelligent Volition; and it is as showing the place which this factor holds in the evolutionary process that the pillar Boaz stands opposite the pillar Jachin as its necessary complement and equilibration. The union of the two signifies Intelligent Purpose working by means of Necessary Law, and the only way of entering into "the Temple," whether of the cosmos or of the individual, is by passing between these Two Pillars of the Universe, and realizing the combined action of Law and Volition.

This is the Narrow Way that leads us into the building not made with hands, within which all the mysteries shall be unfolded before us in a regular order and succession. He who climbs up some other way is a thief and a robber, and brings punishment upon himself as the natural effect of his own rashness, for knowing nothing of the *true* Order of the Inner Life, he plunges prematurely into the midst of things of whose real nature he is ignorant, and sooner or later learns to his cost the truth of the Scriptural warning, "whoso breaketh an hedge a serpent shall bite him" (Eccl. x. 7).

We may not enter the Temple save by passing between the pillars, and we cannot pass between them till we can tell their meaning. It is the purpose of the Bible to give us the Key to this Knowledge: it is not the only instruction it has to give, but it is its initial course, and when this has been mastered it will open out deeper things, the inner secrets of the sanctuary. But the first thing is to pass between Jachin and Boaz, and then the Divine Interpreter will meet us on the threshold and will unfold the mysteries of the Temple in their due order, so that as each one is opened to us in succession, we are prepared for its reception and thus need fear no danger, because at each step we always know what we are dealing with, and have attained the spiritual, intellectual, and physical development qualifying us to employ each new revelation in the right way.

For the opening of the inner mysteries is not for the gratification of mere idle curiosity; it is for the increasing of our Livingness, and the highest quality of Livingness is Life-givingness; and every measure of Life-givingness, be it only the giving of a cup of cold water, means *use* of the powers and knowledge which we possess. The Temple instruction is therefore intended to qualify us as *workers,* and the value to ourselves of what we receive within is seen in the measure of intelligence and love with which we transmute our Temple gold into the current coin of daily life.

The building-up process is that of Evolution, whether in the material world or in the human individuality or in the race as a whole, and the Bible presents the analogy to us very forcibly under the metaphor of "the Stone." Speaking of the rejection of His own teaching, the Master said, "What is this, then, that is written, the Stone which the builders rejected the same is become the head of the corner?" referring to the 118th Psalm (Luke xx. 17). A careful perusal of the Master's history as given in the Gospel, will show us very clearly what "the Stone" is; it is the material out of which the Temple of the Spirit is to be built up, which we now see is nothing else than Perfected Humanity.

Each individual is a temple himself, as St. Paul tells us, and at the same time a single stone in the construction of the Great Temple which is the regenerated race, that "People of the I AM," which was inaugurated when Moses first pitched the tabernacle in the wilderness. But the process must always be an individual one, for a nation is nothing but an aggregation of individuals, and therefore in considering the metaphor of "the Stone" as applied to the individual, we shall realize its wider application also.

Now the Master was executed on the charge of blasphemy for asserting the identity of His own nature with that of God. The subjection of the Jews to the Roman rule placed the power of life and death in the hands of a tribunal which could not take cognizance of such an offence—"Take ye Him and judge Him according to *your* law," said Pilate, when the charge of blasphemy was proffered before him—and in order to bring Him to execution it became necessary to substitute for the original charge of blasphemy one of high treason, so as to bring it within the jurisdiction of the court. "Whosoever maketh himself a king speaketh against Cæsar"—and so the inscription fastened to the cross was "Jesus of Nazareth, the King of the Jews." But the true reason why He was hunted to death was expressed by the scribes, who mocked the Sufferer with the words, "He trusted in God; let Him deliver Him now if He will have Him, for He said, 'I am the Son of God.'"

The teaching of Jesus was the inversion of all that was taught by the official priesthood. Their whole teaching rested on the hypothesis that God and Man are absolutely distinct *in nature,* thus directly contradicting the earliest statement of their own Scriptures regarding Man, that he is the image and likeness of God. As a consequence of this false assumption, they supposed that the whole Mosaic Law and Ritual was intended to pacify God and make Him favorable to the worshipper, and so in their minds the entire system tended only to emphasize the gulf that separated Man from God.

What was the *nexus* of cause and effect by which this system operated to produce the result of reconciling God to the worshipper was a question which they never attempted to face, for had they, after the example of their patriarch, determinedly wrestled with the problem of why their Law was what it was, that Law would have shone forth with a self-illuminating light which would have made clear to them that all the teaching of Moses and the Prophets and the Psalms was concerning that grand ideal of a Divine Humanity which it was the mission of Jesus to proclaim and exemplify.

But they would not face the question of the *reason* of these things. They had received a certain traditional interpretation of their Scriptures and their Ritual, and, as Jesus said, made the real commands of God void by their traditions. They were tied by "authorities," and this at second-hand. They did not inquire what Moses meant, but only followed on the lines of what somebody else said he meant; in other words, they would not think for themselves. They were content to say, "Our Law and Ritual are what they are because God has so ordered them"; but they would not go further and inquire why God ordered them so.

With them the whole question of revelation became the question whether *Moses* had or had not made such an announcement of the Divine will, and so their religion rested ultimately only on historical evidences. But they did not face the question, "How am I to know that the so-called prophet ever received any communication from the Divine at all?" In the last resort, there can be only one criterion by which to judge the truth of any claim to a Divine communication, which is that the message should present an intelligible sequence of cause and effect.

No man can prove that God has spoken to him; the only possible proof is the inherent truth of the message, making it appeal to our feelings and our reason with a power that carries conviction with it. The Spirit of Truth shall convince you, said the Master; and when this inner conviction of Truth is felt, it will invariably be found that, by thinking it out carefully, the reason of the feeling will manifest itself in an intelligible sequence of cause and effect. Short of realizing such a sequence, we have not realized the Truth. The only other proof is that of practical results, and to this test the Master tells us to bring the teaching that we hear, and the teaching He bid us judge by this standard was His own.

It is a principle that no great system can endure for ages, exercising a wide-spread and permanent influence over large masses of mankind without *any* element of Truth in it. There have been, and still are, great systems influencing mankind which contain many and serious errors, but what has given them their power is the Truth that is in them and not the error: and careful inquiry into the secret of their vitality will enable us to detect and remove the error.

Now, had the leaders of the Jews investigated their national system with intelligence and moral courage, they would have argued that its manifest vitality and elevating spiritual tone showed that it contained a great and living Truth. This Truth could not be in the mere external observances prescribed by its Law, for no *nexus* of cause and effect was traceable between the external observances and the promised results, and therefore the vitalizing Truth must be in some principle which supplied the connection that was apparently wanting. They would have argued that God could not have arbitrarily commanded a set of meaningless observances, and that therefore these observances must be the expression of some LAW inherent in the very nature of Man's being.

In a word, they would have realized that, to be true at all, a thing must be within the all-embracing Law of cause and effect, and that religion itself could be no exception to the rule—it must, in short, be *natural* because, if God be ONE, He cannot introduce anywhere an arbitrary and meaningless caprice subversive of the principle of Order throughout the universe. To suppose the introduction of anything by a mere act of Divine Volition, without a foundation in the sequence of the Universal Order, would be to deny the Unity of God, and thus to deny the Divine Being altogether.

Had the rulers of Israel, therefore, understood the meaning of the first two Commandments, they would have realized that their first duty, as instructors of the people, was to probe the whole Mosaic system until they reached the bed-rock of cause-and-effect on which it rested. But this is just what they did not do. Their reverence for names was greater than their reverence for Truth, and, assuming that Moses taught what he never did, they put to death the Teacher of whom Moses had prophesied as the One who should complete his work in building up "the People of the I AM."

Thus they rejected "the Stone of Israel," and in so doing they fought against God, that is, against the Law of Spirit in Self-evolution. For it was this Law, and this only, that the Carpenter of Nazareth taught. He came, not to destroy the teachings of Moses and of the Prophets, but to fulfill by showing what it was that, under various veils and coverings, had been handed down through the generations. It was His mission to complete the Building of the Temple by exhibiting Perfected Man as the apex of the Pyramid of Evolution.

Broad and strong and deep was laid the foundation of this Pyramid, in that first movement of the ONE which the Bible tells of in its opening words; and thenceforward the building has progressed through countless ages till Man, now sufficiently developed intellectually, requires only the final step of recognizing that the Universal Spirit reaches, in him, the reproduction of itself in individuality to take his proper place as the crown and completion of the whole evolutionary process. He has to realize that the opening statement of Scripture concerning himself is not a mere figure of speech, but a practical fact, and that he really is the image and likeness of the Universal Spirit.

This was the teaching of Jesus. When the Jews sought to stone Him for saying that God was His Father (John x. 34), He replied by quoting the 82d Psalm, "I said ye are gods," and laid stress on this as "Scripture that cannot be broken"; that is, as written in the very nature of things, that *signatura rerum* by which each thing has its proper place in the universal order. He replied in effect, "I am only saying of Myself what your own Law says of every one of you. I do not set Myself forth as an exception, but as the example of what the nature of every man truly is." The same mistake has been perpetuated to the present day; but gradually people are beginning to see what the great truth is which Jesus taught, and which Moses and the Prophets and the Psalms had proclaimed before Him.

Perfected Man is the apex of the Evolutionary Pyramid, and this by a necessary sequence. First comes the Mineral Kingdom, lying inert and motionless, without any sort of individual recognition. Then comes the Vegetable Kingdom, capable of assimilating its food, with individual life, but with only the most rudimentary intelligence, and rooted to one spot. Next comes the Animal Kingdom, where intelligence is manifestly on the increase, and the individual is no longer rooted to a single spot physically, yet is so intellectually, for its round of ideas is limited only to the supply of its bodily wants.

Then comes the fourth or Human Kingdom, where the individual is not rooted to one spot either physically or intellectually, for his thought can penetrate all space. But even he has not yet reached Liberty, for he is still the slave of "circumstances over which he has no control"—his thoughts are unlimited, but they remain mere dreams until he can attain the power of giving them realization. Unlimited power of conception is his, but to complete his evolution he must acquire a corresponding power of creation—with that he will arrive at Perfect Liberty.

Throughout the Four Kingdoms which have yet been developed, the progress from the lower to the higher is always towards greater liberty, and, therefore, in accordance with that principle of Continuity which Science recognizes as nowhere broken in Nature, Perfect Liberty must be the goal towards which the evolutionary process is tending.

One stage more is necessary to complete the Pyramid of Manifested Nature, the addition of a Fifth Kingdom, which shall complete the work for which the four lower Kingdoms are the preparation—the Kingdom in which Spirit shall be the ruling factor, and thus the Kingdom of Spirit which is the Kingdom of God.

These considerations bring out into a very clear light one meaning of Daniel's prophecy of "the Stone," cut out without hands, which grew until it filled the whole earth. It is the same "Stone" of which Jesus spoke, and is bound by the inevitable sequence of Evolution to become the Chief Corner-Stone; that is, the angular or five-pointed stone in which all four sides of the Pyramid find their completion. It is that headstone capping the whole, of which it is written that it shall be brought forth with shoutings of "Grace, grace unto it" (Zech. iv. 7).

The Fifth Kingdom, the Kingdom of spiritually developed Man, is that which is now slowly growing, as one individual after another awakes to the recognition of his own spiritual nature, seeing in it, not a mere vague religious sentiment, but an actual working principle to be consciously used in everything that concerns himself. This "Kingdom of God," or of Spirit, was compared by the Master to leaven hidden in meal, which spread by a silent process until the whole was leavened.

The establishment of this Fifth Kingdom is a natural process of growth, a great silent revolution which will gradually change the face of society by first changing its spirit; and for this reason the Master said, "The Kingdom of God cometh not with observation." Outward forms of government will perhaps always vary in different countries, but the recognition of Man as the true Temple must produce the same effects of "justice, mercy, and truth" in every land, so that war and crime, ignorance and want, sickness and fear, shall be known no more, and sorrow and sighing shall flee away (Isaiah xxxv. 10).

This is the meaning of the Building of the Temple, and in studying it we must remember that the sacred symbols apply, not only to Man, but also to his environment. The Tabernacle of Moses and the Temple of Solomon not only represent the Microcosm but also the Macrocosm. And this leads us to the threshold of a very deep mystery, the effect of the spiritual condition of the human race upon Nature as a whole, regarding which St. Paul tells us that the entire creation is waiting in anxious expectation for the revealing of the sons of God (Rom. viii.).

The Building of the Temple is thus a three-fold process, commencing with the individual man, spreading from the individual to the race, and from the race to the whole environment in which we live. This is the return to Eden, where there is nothing hurtful or destructive.

The expulsion from the spiritual "Garden of the Land" led man into a world that brought forth thorns and thistles, "and the earth was cursed for his sake"; that is to say, the mental attitude resulting from "the Fall" induced a corresponding condition in Nature; and by the same Law the mental attitude which is restoration from "the Fall," will produce a corresponding renovation of the material world, a state of things which is described with poetic imagery in the eleventh chapter of Isaiah.

This influence of the human race upon their surroundings, whether for good or for evil, is only the natural result of carrying out to its final consequences the initial proposition of the Bible that Man is the image of God. This is the affirmation of the inherently creative power of his Thought; and if this be true, then the collective Thought of the race must be the subtle power which determines the prevailing conditions of the natural world.

The uncertain mixed conditions among which we live very accurately represent our uncertain and mixed modes of Thought. We think from the standpoint of a mixture of good and evil, and have no certainty as to which is really the controlling power. Good, we say, works "within certain limits"; but who or what fixes those limits we cannot guess—in short, if we analyze the average belief of mankind as represented in Christian countries at the present day, it resolves itself into belief in a sort of rough-and-tumble between God and the Devil, in which sometimes one is uppermost and sometimes the other; and so we entirely lose the conception of a definite control by the Power of Good steadily acting in accordance with its own character, and not subject to the dictation of some Evil Power which prescribes "certain limits" for it.

This balance between good and evil is undoubtedly the present state of things, but it is the reflection of our own Thought, and the remedy for it is therefore that knowledge of the inner Law which shows us that we ourselves are producing the evils we deplore. It is for this reason that the Apostle warns us against emulations, wrath, and strife (Gal. v. 20). They all proceed from a denial of the Creative Power of our Thought; in other words, the denial that Man is the "image of God." They proceed from the hypothesis that good can exist only "within certain limits," and that, therefore, our work must not be directed towards the producing of more good, but to scrambling for a larger share of the limited quantity of good that has been doled out to the world by a bankrupt Deity.

Whether this scramble be between individuals in the commercial world, or between classes in social life, or between nations in the glorious game of murder with the best modern appliances, the underlying principle is always that of competition based on the idea that the gain of one can only accrue by another's loss; and, therefore, what prevents us to-day from "entering into rest" is the same cause that produced the same effect in the time of the Psalmist, "they could not enter in because of unbelief," and "they *limited* the Holy ONE of Israel."

So long as we persist in the belief that the truly originating causes of things are to be found anywhere but in our own mental attitude, we condemn ourselves to interminable toil and strife.

But if, instead of looking at *conditions,* we endeavored to realize First Cause as that which acts independently of all conditions, because the conditions flow from it and not *vice versa,* we should see that the whole teaching of the Bible is to lead us to understand that, because Man is the image of God, he can never divest his Thought of its inherent creative power; and for this reason it sets before us the limitless goodness of the Heavenly Father as the model which in our own use of this power we are to follow. "He maketh His sun to rise on the evil and on the good, and sendeth His rain on the just and on the unjust." In other words, the Universal First Cause is not concerned with pre-existing conditions, but continually radiates forth its creative energy, transmuting the evil into the good and the good into something still better; and since it is the prerogative of Man to use the same creative power from the standpoint of the individual, he must use it in the same manner, if he would produce effects of Life and not of Death.

He cannot divest his Thought of its creative power, but it rests with him to choose between Life and Death according to the way in which he employs it. As each one realizes that conditions are created from within and not from without, he begins to see the force of the Master's invitation: "Come unto Me all ye that labor and are heavy laden, and I will give you rest"; he sees that the only thing that has prevented him from entering into rest has been unbelief in the limitless goodness of God, and in his own limitless power of drawing from that inexhaustible storehouse; and when we thus realize the true nature of the Divine Law of Supply, we see that it depends, not on taking from others without giving a fair equivalent, but rather on giving good measure pressed down and shaken together.

The Creative Law is that the quality of the Thought, which starts any particular chain of cause and effect, continues through every link of the chain, and therefore, if the originating Thought be that of the absolute goodness-in-itself of the intended creation, irrespective of all circumstances, then this quality will be inherent not only in the thing immediately created, but also in the whole incalculable series of results flowing from it.

Therefore, to make our work *good for its own sake* is the surest way to make it return to us in a rich harvest, which it will do by a natural Law of Growth if we only allow it time to grow. By degrees, one after another finds this out for himself, and the eventual recognition of these truths by the mass of mankind must make "the desert rejoice and blossom as the rose" (Isaiah xxxv. 1). Let each one, therefore, take part joyfully in the Building of the Temple, in which shall be offered, for ever, the two-fold worship of Glory to God and Goodwill to Man.

VII

# THE SACRED NAME

A POINT THAT CAN hardly fail to strike the Bible student is the frequency with which we are directed to the *Name* of the Lord, as the source of strength and protection, instead of to God Himself, and the steady uniformity of this practice, both in the Old and New Testaments, clearly indicates the intention to put us upon some special line of inquiry with regard to the Sacred Name. Not only is this suggested by the frequency of the expression, but the Bible gives a very remarkable instance which shows that the Sacred Name must be considered as a formula containing a summary of all wisdom.

The Master tells us that the Queen of the South came to hear the wisdom of Solomon, and if we turn to I. Kings x. 1, we find that the fame of Solomon's wisdom, which induced the Queen of Sheba to come to prove him with hard questions, was "concerning the *Name* of the Lord." This accords with the immemorial tradition of the Jews, that the knowledge of the secret Name of God enables him who possesses it to perform the most stupendous miracles. This Hidden Name—the "Schem-hammaphoraseh"—was revealed, they say, to Moses and taught by him to Aaron and handed on by him to his successors; it was the secret enshrined in The Holy of Holies, and was scrupulously guarded by the successive High Priests; it is the supreme secret, and its knowledge is the supreme object of attainment; thus tradition and Scripture alike point to "The NAME" as the source of Light and Life, and Deliverance from all evil.

May we not therefore suppose that this must be the veiled statement of some great Truth? The purpose of a name is to call up, by a single word, the complete idea of the thing named, with all those qualities and relations that make it what it is, instead of having to describe all this in detail every time we want to suggest the conception of it. The correct name of a thing thus conveys the idea of its whole nature, and accordingly the correct Name of God should, in some manner, be a concise statement of the Divine Nature as the Source of all Life, Wisdom, Power, and Goodness, and the Origin of all manifested being.

For this reason the Bible puts before us "the Name of the Lord," not only as the object of supreme veneration, but also as the grand subject of study, by means of which we may command the Power that will provide us with all good and protect us from all ill. Let us, then, see what we can learn regarding this marvellous Name.

The Bible calls the Divine Being by a variety of Names, but when we have once got the general clue to the Sacred Name, we shall find that each of them implies all the others, since each suggests some particular aspect of THAT which is the all-embracing UNIT, the everlasting ONE, which cannot be divided, and any one aspect of which must therefore convey to the instructed mind the suggestion of all the others. We will therefore seek first this general clue which will throw light on more particular appellations.

I think most people will agree that the specially personal Name by which the Divine Being is called in the Bible is Jehovah. If any Name, throughout the entire range of Scriptures, seems to invest the Divine Being with a distinct individuality it is this one, and yet when we come to inquire into its meaning, we find that it is precisely the most emphatic statement of a universality, which is the very antithesis of all that we understand by the word "individual."

The clue to this discovery is contained in the statement that God revealed Himself to Moses by the Name Jehovah (Ex. vi. 3); for since the Bible contains no statement of any other revelation of the Divine Name to Moses, except that made at the burning bush, we are at once put upon the track of some connection between the Name Jehovah and the command received by Moses to tell the children of Israel that I AM had commissioned him to deliver them.

Now, the Name which in English is rendered "Jehovah," is composed of four Hebrew letters, Yod, Hé, Wau, Hé, thus spelling "Yevé," and this is the word which we have to analyze. And this brings us to the fact that the whole Hebrew alphabet is invested with a certain symbolical character, because, in the estimation of learned Jews, it exemplifies the great principle of Evolution, for they rightly consider that Evolution is nothing else than the working of the Divine Spirit through all worlds, whether visible or invisible.

It would require a long study to take the reader through the detailed examination of every letter, but the general idea may be stated as follows: The letter Yod is a minute mark of a definite shape, though little more than a point, and a careful inspection of the Hebrew alphabet shows that all the other letters are combinations of this initial form. It is thus the "generating point" from which all the other letters proceed, each letter being in some way or other a reproduction of the Yod; and, accordingly, it has not inaptly been regarded as a symbol of the all-originating First Principle.

If, therefore, a Name was to be devised which should represent the mystery of the Divine Being as at once the Unity, which includes all Multiplicity and the Multiplicity which is included in the Unity, the logical sequence of ideas required that the Hebrew form of such a word should commence with the letter Yod. The name of the letter is suggested by the sound of the in-drawing of the breath, and thus indicates self-containedness. The opposite conception is that of the sending forth of the breath, which is represented by the sound Hé, and this letter thus indicates that which is not self-contained, but which emanates from the Source of Life. Yod thus represents Essential Life, while Hé represents Derived Life.

The letter "Wau" or "Vau," taken alone, signifies "and," and thus conveys the idea of a "Link." This is followed by a repetition of the "Hé," so that the second portion of the Sacred Name conveys the idea of a plurality of derived lives connected together by some common link, and is, therefore, the symbol of the Unity passing into manifestation as the Multiplicity of all individual beings.

The whole Name thus constitutes a most perfect statement of the Divine Being, as that Universal Life, which, to use the apostolic words, is "over all, and through all, and in all"; so that once more we are brought back to what the Master said was the fundamental statement of all Truth, namely, that

God is THE ONE, thus indicating that Unity of Spirit from which all individualities proceed and in which they are all included.

But the second portion of the Divine Name is EVE (the Hebrew Hé corresponds with the English E), which we have found to be the *individualized* Life-principle or the Soul, and thus this portion of the Sacred Name not only denotes Multiplicity, but also indicates the fact that the derived life stands towards the Originating Life in the relation of the feminine to the masculine. If this *feminine* nature of the Soul relatively to the Universal Spirit be steadily kept in mind, it will be found to contain the key not only to many passages of Scripture, but also to many facts of Nature both in the inner and outer worlds. The words of Isaiah liv. 5, "Thy Maker is thine husband," are not a mere figure of speech, but a statement of the great fundamental law of human personality; and this relative femininity of the Soul, which in this passage is pronounced so unequivocally, will be found, on investigation, to be assumed as a general principle throughout Scripture.

We have already seen from the story of "the Fall," that Eve represents the soul as distinguished from the body; and just as the Bible opens with this assertion of the feminine nature of the Soul, so it closes with it, and a large portion of the magnificent symbolism of Revelation is occupied in depicting, under the form of two mystical "Women," the generalized history of the adulterous soul and of the faithful soul, which as "the Bride" joins with "the Spirit" in the universal invitation to all who will, to drink of the water of Life and live for ever.

It is, then, this mystery of the femininity of the soul as a general principle of Nature, and its necessary relation to the corresponding Masculine principle, that is the great truth enshrined in the Sacred Name Jehovah. The first letter of the name implies "self-containedness," the statement in the universal of all that we mean individually when we speak of ourselves as "I"; and the remaining portion is the form of a verb expressing continuous Being, and the whole Name therefore is the exact statement of "I AM" which was made to Moses at the burning bush.

The Name "Jehovah" is thus the concealed statement of the great doctrine of Evolution seen in its spiritual aspect. It is the statement that every form of manifestation is an unfolding of the ONE original principle, and that beside this original ONE reappearing under infinite variety of forms there *is* no other.

But further, this Name is a statement that the passing of the Unity into that infinite galaxy of Life which, though now sometimes sorrowing, is destined to become one glorious rose of myriad petals, each of which is a rejoicing creative being, can take place only through Duality. Is this a mystery? Yes, the greatest of mysteries, including all others, for it is that universal mystery of Attraction upon which all research, even in physical science, eventually abuts; and yet that Duality must be established before Unity can pass into all the powers and beauties of external manifestation, is a proposition so self-evident as to be almost absurd in its simplicity; indeed, the very simplicity of the great universal truths is a stumbling-block to many who, like Naaman, expect something sensational.

Now, this very simple proposition is, that in order to do any kind of work there must not only be something that works, but also something that is worked upon; in other words, there must be both an active and a passive factor. The scope of this book will not allow me to discuss the process by which the Duality is evolved from the Unity, though physical science supplies us with very clear analogies. But in general terms, the Universal Passive is evolved by the Universal Active as its necessary complement, and provides all those conditions which are required to enable the Active Principle to manifest itself in the varied forms that constitute the successive stages of Evolution; and the interaction of these two reciprocal principles throughout Nature is as clearly indicated by the Sacred Name as the principle of Unity itself.

And the Threefold nature of all defined being at once follows from the recognition of these two interacting principles, for whatever is produced by their interaction can be neither a simple reproduction of the Active principle alone, nor of the Passive alone, but must be an intermingling of the two, combining in itself the nature of both, and thus possessing an independent nature of its own, which is not exactly that of either of the originating principles.

Other and very important deductions again follow from this one, but they cannot be adequately entered upon in an introductory book like the present; still, enough has now been said to show that the Name "Jehovah" contains in itself the statement of the Three Fundamental Principles of the Universe, the Unity, the Duality, and the Trinity; and by their inclusion in a single word affirms that no contradiction exists between them, but that they are all necessary phases of the Universal Truth which is only ONE.

Much search has been made by many for what the Cabalists call "the Lost Word," that "Word of Power," the possession of which makes all things possible to him who discovers it. Great students in by-gone days devoted their lives to this search, such as Reuchlin in Germany, and Pico Della Mirandola in Italy, and, so far as the outside world judges, without any result; while later centuries discredited their studies by comparison with the practical nature of the Baconian philosophy, not wotting that Bacon himself was a leader in the school to which these men belonged.

But now the tide is beginning to turn, and improved methods of scientific research are approaching, from the physical side, that One Great Centre in which all lines of truth eventually converge; and so the fast-spreading recognition of Man's spiritual nature is leading once more to the search for "the Word of Power." And rightly did the old Hebrew builders and their followers in the fifteenth, sixteenth, and seventeenth centuries connect this "Lost Word" with the Sacred Name; but whether because they purposely surrounded it with mystery, or because the simplicity of the truth proved a stumbling block to them, their open writings only indicate a search through endless mazes, while the clue to the labyrinth lay in the Word itself.

Are we any nearer its discovery now? The answer is at once Yes and No. The "Lost Word" was as close to those old thinkers as it is to us, but to those whose eyes and ears are sealed by prejudice, it will always remain as far off as though it belonged to another planet. The Bible, however, is most explicit upon this subject, and as in the children's game the hidden thimble is concealed from the seekers by its very conspicuousness, so the concealment of the "Lost Word" lies in its absolute simplicity.

Nothing so common-place could possibly be it, and yet the Scripture plainly tells us that its intimate familiarity is the token by which we shall know it. We need not say "Who shall go up for us to heaven and bring it unto us, that we may hear it and do it? Neither is it beyond the sea that thou shouldest say, Who shall go over the sea for us and bring it unto us, that we may hear it and do it? But the Word is very nigh unto thee, in thy mouth and in thy heart, that thou mayest do it" (Deut. xxx. 12). Realize that the only "Word of Power" is the Divine Name, and the mystery at once flashes into light.

The "Lost Word" which we have been seeking to discover with pain, and cost, and infinite study, has been all the time in our heart and in our mouth—it is nothing else than that familiar expression which we use so many times a day—I AM. This is the Divine Name revealed to Moses at the burning bush, and it is the Word that is enshrined in the Name Jehovah; and if we believe that the Bible means what it says, when it tells us that Man is the image and likeness of God, then we shall see that the same statement of Being, which in the universal applies to God, must in the individual and particular apply to Man also.

This "Word" is always in our hearts, for the consciousness of our own individuality consists only in the recognition that I AM, and the assertion of our own being, as one of the necessities of ordinary speech is upon our lips continually. Thus the "Word of Power" is close at hand to every one, and it continues to be the "Lost Word" only because of our ignorance of all that is enfolded in it.

A comparison of the teaching of Moses and Jesus will show that they are two complementary statements of the one fundamental truth of the "I AM." Moses views this truth from the standpoint of *universal* being, and sees Man evolving from the Infinite Mind and subject to it as the Great Law-giver. Jesus views it from the standpoint of the *individual,* and sees Man comprehending the Infinite by limitless expansion of his own mind, and thus returning to the Universal Mind as a son coming back to his natural place in the house of his father.

Each is necessary to the correct understanding of the other, and thus Jesus came, not to abrogate the work of Moses but to complete it. The "I AM" is ever in the forefront of His teaching: "I AM the Way, the Truth, and the Life"—"I AM the Resurrection and the Life"—"Except ye believe I AM ye shall perish in your sins." These and similar sayings shine forth with marvellous radiance when once we see that He was not speaking of Himself personally, but of the Individualized Principle of Being in the generic sense which is applicable to all mankind.

What is wanted is our recognition of that innermost self which is pure spirit, and therefore not subject to any conditions whatever. All conditions arise from one combination or another of the two original conditions, Time and Space; and since these two primary conditions can have no place in essential being, and are only created by its Thought, the true recognition of the "I AM" is a recognition of the Self, which sees it as eternally subsisting in its own Being, sending forth all forms at its will and withdrawing them again at its pleasure.

To know this is to know Life-in-itself; and any knowledge short of this is only to know the appearance of Life, to recognize merely the activity of the vehicles through which it functions, while failing to recognize the motive power itself—it is recognizing only "EVE" without "YOD." The "Word of Power" which sets us free is the *whole* Divine Name, and not one part of it without the other. It is the separation of its two portions, the Masculine and the Feminine, that has caused the long and weary pilgrimage of mankind through the ages.

This separation of the two elements of the Divine Name is not true in the Heart of Being, but Man, by reasoning only from the testimony of the outward senses, forcibly puts asunder what God for ever joins together; and it is because the Bridegroom has thus been taken away that the children of the bridechamber have been starved upon meagre fare, coarse and hardly earned, when they ought to have feasted with continual joy.

But the Great Marriage of Heaven and Earth at last takes place, and all Nature joins in the song of exultation, a glorious epithalamium, whose cadences roll on through the ages, ever spreading into fresh harmonies as new themes evolve from that first grand wedding march which celebrates the eternal union of the Mystical Marriage.

When this union is realized by the individual as subsisting in himself, then the I AM becomes to him personally all that the Master said it would. He realizes that it is in him a deathless principle, and that though its mode of self-expression may alter, its essential Beingness, which is the I Myself consciousness in each of us, never can: and so this principle is found to be in us both Life and Resurrection. As Life it never ceases, and as Resurrection it is continually providing higher and higher forms for its expression of itself, which is *ourself.*

No matter what may be our particular theory of the specific *modus operandi* by which this renewal takes place, there can be no mistake about the principle; our physical theory of the Resurrection may be wrong, but the Law that Life will always provide a suitable form for its self-expression is unchangeable and universal, and must, therefore, be as true of the Life-principle manifesting itself as the individuality which I AM, as in all its other modes of manifestation.

When we thus realize the true nature of the I AM that I AM, that is, the Beingness that I Myself AM, we discover that the *whole* principle of Being is in ourselves, not "Eve" only, but "YOD" also; and this being the case, we no longer have to go with our pitcher to draw temporary draughts from a well outside, for now we discover that the exhaustless spring of Living Water is within ourselves.

Now, we can see why it is that except we believe in the I AM we must perish in our sins, for "sin is the transgression of the Law," and ignorant infraction of the Law will bring its penalty as certainly as wilful infraction. "Ignorantia legis neminem excusat" is a legal maxim which obtains throughout Nature, and the innocent child, who ignorantly applies a light to a barrel of gunpowder, will be as ruthlessly blown up as the anarchist who perishes in the perpetration of some hideous outrage; if, therefore, we ignorantly controvert the Law of our own Being we must suffer the inevitable consequences by our failure to rise into that Life of Liberty and Joy, which the full knowledge of the power of our I AMness must necessarily carry with it.

Let us remember that Perfect Liberty is our goal. The perfect Law is the Law of Liberty. The Tree of Life is the Tree of Liberty, and it is not a plant of spontaneous growth; but as the centre of the Mystical Garden it is its chief glory, and, therefore, deserves the most assiduous cultivation. But it yields its produce as it grows, and does not keep us waiting till it reaches maturity before giving us any reward for work; for if maturity means a point at which it will grow no more, then it will never reach maturity, for since the ground in which this Tree has its root is the Eternal Life-in-itself, there is nowhere in the universe any power to limit its growth, and so, under intelligent cultivation, it will go on expanding into increasing strength, beauty, and fruitfulness for ever.

This is the meaning of the Scriptural saying, "His reward is with him and his work before him." Ordinarily, we should suppose it would be the other way; but when we see that the possibilities of self-expansion are endless and depend on our intelligent study and work, and that at every step of the way we are bound to derive all present benefit from the degree of knowledge we are working up to, it becomes clear that the sacred text has kept the right order, and that always our reward is *with* us and our work *before* us; for the reward is the continually increasing joy and glory of perpetually unfolding Life.

All along the line our progress depends on working up to the knowledge we possess, for what we do not act up to we do not really believe; and the power which will overcome all difficulties is confidence in the Eternal

Life-in-ourself, which is the individualized expression of the ONE I AM that spoke to Moses at the burning bush.

For what is meant by the burning bush? Surely, as we see the refugee feeding Jethro's flock in the solitudes of the desert, and gazing on the Fire enveloping the bush without consuming it, we realize that here again we are turning over the pages, of a sacred picture-book, which first attracts the little child with its vivid scenes painted in glowing colors of a wonderful Eastern life in the dim far-back ages—that prompts him as he grows older to ask the meaning of the pictures—and at last reveals it to him in the discovery that they are pictures neither of the East nor of the West, not of this century nor of that, but of all time and of all place, and that he himself is the central figure in them all.

The Bible is the picture-book of the evolution of Man, and this particular picture of the "burning bush" is that of human individuality in its unity with the all-enveloping Fire of the Universal Spirit of Life. The "bush" represents "Wood," which, under its Greek name of *"hulé"* we recognize as the generic term for "Matter"; and the "burning bush" thus signifies the union of Spirit and Matter into a single whole, that perfectness of manifested Being in which the lower principles of the individual are recognized as forming the vehicle for the concentration of the All-originating Spirit. The "bush" still remains a bush, but it is a glorified bush sending forth a glorious *aura* of warmth and light, from the midst of which proceeds the creative voice of the I AM.

This is the great truth symbolized by the revelation to Moses as he fed his father-in-law's flock in the wilderness, and, as the same revelation comes to each one of us now, the words of that other Prophet of whom Moses spoke become clear to us, and we see that by realizing the true being of the I AM in ourselves, we grasp that principle which will put an end to our infraction of the Law, because it is the very Law itself for ever becoming personal with our own personality.

This, then, is the great truth which we learn from the Name "Jehovah." As the Name is infinite, so also will be the expansions of its meaning, but this book not being infinite, I have been able only to touch on the broad outlines of its vastness; still enough has been said to give the clue we were seeking, to elucidate the meaning of other forms of the Sacred Name.

Naturally, the reader will first think of that other Name, of which it is written that there is none other under heaven whereby we may be saved, which statement at once confronts us with the astonishing assertion that we are saved by a *Name.* "What's in a name?" asks Shakespeare—or Bacon (?) A good deal, we may suppose, when we meet with such a statement as this, or its Old Testament equivalent, "the Name of the Lord is a strong tower; the righteous runneth into it and is safe."

But we have already found that the Great Name of the Old Testament is something very different from a merely personal appellation, and the same is true of the Great Name of the New Testament also. It is, indeed, the Name of that Prophet of the I AM whom Moses predicted as completing the work which he had begun; but precisely because he is *the* Representative Man of all ages, his Name must represent all that constitutes Perfected Humanity.

And it is so with a Divine simplicity. It is the combination of the earthly name with the heavenly; Jesus, at that time a very common name among the Jews, and Christ, which is not a name but a description, "the Anointed One." Each name is the proper complement of the other, and together they indicate the sublime truth that the anointing of the Divine Spirit is the birthright of every human being, only awaiting our recognition of our true nature to show itself with power. The carpenter—the workman with his everyday name—is the Christ; and the lesson to be learned is that the ONE I AM is in every man, and that that forming of Christ in us, which St. Paul speaks of, is a personal development in accordance with recognizable laws inherent in every human being. If Christ is the Great Example, it must be as the Example of that which we have it in us to become, and not of something entirely foreign to our nature; and it is because of this community of nature that He is "the first-born among many brethren."

The space at my disposal will not allow me to enter here into the deeply important questions of the Nativity and the Resurrection. The Bible affirms them both, and they are the necessary and logical results of that specialized and selective line of Evolution of which I have spoken on page 257; but to show the sequence of cause and effect by which this is brought about, and its dependence upon the initial *Impersonal* nature of the Universal Mind is not to be done in a few pages.

If, however, I should meet with sufficient encouragement from the readers of the present volume, I hope to follow it up with another in which these topics will be discussed, and in the meanwhile we may learn from the generalization contained in the Great Name of the New Testament, that lesson of the Brotherhood of Humanity which the Master has impressed upon us in the words, "The King shall answer and say unto them, Verily I say unto you, inasmuch as ye have done it unto one of the least of these My brethren, ye have done it unto Me" (Matt. xxv. 40). The Name of Jesus Christ is, therefore, the proclamation of the inherent Divine nature of Man, with all its limitless possibilities, and is thus once more the statement of the Bible's initial proposition that Man is made in the image and likeness of God.

And these thoughts recall yet another of the Divine Names which teaches the same lesson, Immanuel, "God with us," or, as it might perhaps be better rendered, "God in us," "Immanent God," the finding of God *in ourselves,* which is in exact accordance with the Master's teaching that the Kingdom of Heaven is *within* us. This Name, which occurs in Isaiah vii. 14, speaks for itself, and should be compared with the description given in Isaiah ix. 6, 7, which is the old familiar Christmas text, "Unto us a child is born," etc. Now, whoever the "us" may be, the prophet clearly speaks of the Wonderful Child as being born to them, they are the parents and He is their Child; but in the description which follows we are told equally clearly that He is "the Everlasting Father"; and the teaching of Jesus leaves us in no doubt that "the Father" is the Divine All-creating Spirit, which is therefore "the Father" of the "us" who are the parents of the Child.

This lands us in a curious paradox. There can be no reasonable doubt that the word "us" is here spoken of human personalities, and that in the same breath the Divine Being who is spoken of as their Father is announced to them as their Child. We have therefore here a sequence of three generations, the Father of the parents, the "us" who are the parents, and the Child who is born to them; and since the Father of the parents and the Child of the parents is said to be the same Being, there is no avoiding the conclusion that the Wonderful Child is his own Grandfather, and *vice versa.*

This is one of those sacred puzzles of which many instances occur in the Bible, and whose meaning is clear enough when we know the answer, and the purpose of which is to lead us to look for an answer, which will put us in possession of the great truth which it is the purpose of all Scripture to teach us. The riddle propounded by Isaiah, "What is that which becomes its own grandson?" is substantially the same with which the Master posed the scribes when He asked them how David's son could at the same time be his Lord (Luke xx. 41); and the identity of the question is apparent from the fact that in the passage in Isaiah we are told that this Wonderful Child shall sit on the throne of David.

A further description of him occurs in Isaiah xi. 1, where we again find the same three stages—first Jesse, next the stem proceeding out of Jesse, and lastly the Rod or Branch growing out of the stem. Now Jesse is the father of David, and, therefore, "the Branch" is the same person regarding whom Isaiah and Jesus propounded their conundrums. Placing these four remarkable passages together, we get the following description of the Wonderful Child:

His name is Immanuel.
His father's name is David.
His grandfather's name is Jesse.
And He is His own grandfather and Lord over His father.

What is it that answers to this description? Again we find the solution of the enigma in the names. "Jesse" means "to be," or "he that is," which at once brings us back to all we have learned concerning the Universal I AM—the ONE Eternal Spirit which is "the Everlasting Father."

"David" means "the Beloved," or the man who realizes his true relation to the Infinite Spirit; and the description of Daniel as a man greatly beloved and who had set his heart to understand (Daniel x. 11), shows us that it is this set purpose of seeking to understand the nature of the Universal Spirit and the mode of our own relation to it, that raises the individual to the position of David or "the Beloved."

This is in strict agreement with the Master's teaching to the woman of Samaria, that the Eternal Spirit, which is "the Father," *seeks* those who will worship, not according to this or that traditionary form, but in spirit and in truth, having a real knowledge of what it is they worship and of the true nature of the mental act they perform—"we *know* what we worship" is the mark by which Jesus distinguishes the worship of the "Israelites indeed," the "People of the I AM," from that of the Samaritans, though fully recognizing the right intention of their worship of the "unknown God."

It was after his successful wrestling with the Divine Being, and in consequence of his determination not to let go until it had been fully revealed, that Jacob obtained the name of "Israel."

Then from the individual's illuminated recognition of the Truth of

Being—the discovery that he himself is the concentration of the Universal Spirit into particular personality—there necessarily arises the reproduction of the Universal Spirit in the Individual Mind. This is *re*-generation; that is to say, the second generating of the Divine UNIT as another Unity or manifestation of itself in the form of the Individual, in no way differing in nature from the original all-embracing Unit, but only in mode of expression, having now become individual personality with all the attributes of personality.

On the plane of the universal, the place of these more highly specialized attributes was held by a *generic* tendency towards life-givingness, increase, and beauty; and this generic tendency the reproduced Unit now follows up with the additional powers it has evolved by the attainment of self-recognizing individuality.

The new personality thus generated may be considered as the child of the individual soul which gives birth to it; and since there is only ONE Spirit anywhere and everywhere, it can be only another mode of the original ONE—consequently the "Son" who is thus born to David "the Beloved," is Himself "the Everlasting Father," and thus the answer to the sacred puzzle is that the man, who has really learned the inner meaning of the words "know thyself," discovers that the true I AM in himself is one with the Universal I AM, which is the root of all individualized being.

It is in the light of these sublime truths, that the Name of "the Son" is equally with that of "the Father" the Sacred Name, in the true knowledge of which salvation is alone to be found. For what do we mean by "Salvation?" "That we might be saved from the hand of all that hate us," is the answer; that is, from the power of everything that in any way militates against our enjoyment of the fullest life. That we might attain to continually increasing degrees of Life was the declared object of the Master's mission, and, therefore, salvation means the power to ask and receive that our joy may be full; and the only way this power can ever come to us is by the recognition of our own possibilities as being each of us the image and likeness of God.

Therefore it is written, "to them gave He power to become the Sons of God, even to them that believe in His Name"; and the word rendered "power" may also be rendered as "right," so that this passage assures us both of our power and right to take possession of our inheritance as sons and daughters of the Almighty. Now, mark well that this promise is not held forth as a reward for the acceptance of some theological speculation, which conveys no real meaning to us, and which by its very terms must be incapable of proof; but it is the natural and logical outcome of the initial proposition with which the Bible opens, that Spirit is the ONE and Only Source, Origin, and Substance of all things, a self-evident truth the contrary of which it is impossible to conceive.

What I here call "Spirit" you may, if you please, call "the Unknowable," or *x,* or denote it by a single stroke; the name or symbol we choose is quite immaterial, so long as we grasp the fact that the initial originating Power must of necessity reproduce itself all the way down the scale, no matter how different the forms under which it does so. In whatever way we may denote it, it is always the Great Expressor; and all that is, we ourselves included, is its Expression of itself; so that the whole teaching of Truth may be summed up in the words, "The Expressor and the Expressed are ONE."

Work out the problem in any way you will and you will never arrive at any other final result than this; and so we always come back to that fundamental axiom which Jesus announced as the supreme statement of the LAW. This is the great truth enshrined in every form of the Sacred Name; and therefore, it is that every form of the Great Name, when rightly understood, is found to be "the Word of Power."

But we must never forget that the opening description of Man, as made in the image and likeness of God, has added to it the words "male and female created He them"; and if we grasp the full significance of this statement, we shall see that the recognition of Truth is not complete unless we realize the place of the Passive or Feminine element in Being.

It is for this reason that in ancient times initiation could be entered upon either along the Doric or Ionic line, the former being more especially the initiation for males and the latter for females; but by whichever line it was commenced, a perfect initiation implied a return along the opposite line, in accordance with St. Paul's dictum that "neither is the man without the woman, neither the woman without the man, in the Lord" (I. Cor. xi. 2), and, therefore, there are not wanting in Scripture statements of the Sacred Name answering to this fact.

One of the most remarkable of these is found in Hosea, ii. 16: "And it shall be at that day, saith the Lord, that thou shalt call Me Ishi, and shalt call Me no more Baali." What is the meaning of this change of Name? Realize that a name has a *meaning,* and it becomes clear that some radical change must be intended. But this cannot be any change in the Divine Being, for from first to last the Scripture bears emphatic testimony to the unchangeableness of "God." "I am the Lord, I change not; therefore ye sons of Jacob are not consumed," says the Old Testament. "The Father of lights with whom there is no variableness, neither shadow of turning," says the New (Malachi, iii. 6, and James i. 17).

The change cannot, then, be in the nature of "God," and, therefore, cannot be a change in the Law by which that nature expresses itself; consequently, it can only be a change in the *conditions* under which that Law is working. Now, this is precisely the sort of change that is spoken of. "Baali" means Lord, the master of a servant, the proprietor of a slave. "Ishi," on the other hand, means "Husband," and the change of name, therefore, indicates a change in the condition of some feminine element towards its correlative masculine element.

This corresponding change is stated in Isaiah lxii. 4: "Thou shalt no more be termed Forsaken, neither shall thy land any more be termed Desolate; but thou shalt be called Hephzibah and thy land Beulah; for the Lord delighteth in thee, and thy land shall be married." The word "Hephzibah" is rendered in the margin "my delight," which is sufficiently significant, but its derivation is from the Semitic root *"hafz,"* which in all its combinations always carries the idea of protection or guarding; and the name Hephzibah may, therefore, be more accurately rendered "a guarded one," thus at once recalling the words in which the New Testament describes those "who by the power of God are *guarded* through faith unto salvation" (1 Peter i. 5, R.V.).

Now, the change indicated by these names is that of a female slave who is set free by her master and then married by him, and I think it would be impossible to hit upon a more accurate analogy for describing the emancipation of the soul from bondage, and its establishment in a relation of confidence and love towards the Divine Universal Mind.

We must never forget the feminine nature of the soul relatively to the Universal Mind. Their union produces the Wonderful Child who shall rule all things, and who is the Essential Male called in the Bible "the Son"; but the soul itself is, and always must be, feminine. Until she becomes illuminated, the soul can only conceive of God as a master whom she is bound to obey, and hence she strives to keep in His good graces by sacrifices, ceremonies, and observances of all sorts—he is "Baali" and must be propitiated. But when the liberating light breaks upon her, she discovers that the Universal Principle has hitherto held this relation to her because she had conceived of it only in this way, and had thus provided it only with such conditions as compelled it to exhibit itself in this form.

Now she learns that these conditions are not imposed by the Universal Principle itself, but that it must of necessity follow that line of expression which each particular individuality opens up for it; and when this is clearly perceived, with all the consequences that flow from it, the soul finds that she is no longer a slave but is in perfect Liberty, and that her relation to the Great Mind is that of a beloved wife, guarded, honored, and treated on terms of equality.

This is the truth illustrated, as St. Paul tells us, in the allegory of Sarah and Hagar. Hagar, the slave, is expelled, and Sarah, the Princess, takes her place. These two symbolical women, like the two "women" of Revelations, indicate two opposite conditions of the soul; and similarly their "sons," like the offspring of those two other "women," represent the respective powers which these two conditions of soul generate—the one living in the wilderness of secondary causes and becoming an archer, that is, relying upon the use of external means, not understanding the true nature of causation, and therefore dependent for his results upon just happening to make a good shot, and often making very bad ones—the other, like Isaac, the acknowledged heir of all the Father's possessions, assuming gradually more and more of his powers and responsibilities, until by the combined influence of natural growth and careful training, he at last attains that mature development which qualifies him to participate in the administration of the paternal authority.

The true relation of the individual soul to the Universal Principle could not be more perfectly depicted than by the names Ishi and Hephzibah. We have only to turn to any well-ordered family to see the force of the illustration. The respective spheres of the husband and wife as the heads of such a household are clearly defined. The husband provides the supplies and the wife distributes them, and each has that confidence in the other which renders any interference with one another's action quite unnecessary.

This is the precise analogue of the relation between the individual and the Universal Mind. The individual mind is not the creator of power, but the distributor of it; just as in physical science we realize that we do not create energy, but only change its form and direction. But exactly as the universal store of Nature from which we draw physical energy does not dictate to us in what form, in what quantities, or for what purpose we shall use it, so in like manner the Universal Principle does not dictate the specific conditions under which it is to be employed, but will manifest itself according to any conditions that we may provide for it by our own mental attitude; and therefore the only limitations to be laid upon our use of it are those arising from the Law of Love. Liberty without Love is Destruction, and Love without Liberty is Despair.

Just as in photography we need for the production of a perfect image the combined action of an accelerator and a restrainer, so to produce perfect images of the Divine strength, beauty, and gladness, we require a self-projecting force, which is the full liberty of Creative Power combined with a directing and restraining force which is the tenderness of wisdom and love; and so in the description of the Perfect Woman we read that in her mouth is the Law of Kindness. Hephzibah, the Perfect Woman, rules her household wisely in love, and so applies the raw material which she can draw from her husband's storehouse without stint that, by her diligence and understanding, she converts it into all those varied forms of use and beauty, which are indicated under the similitudes of domestic provision and merchandise in the thirty-first chapter of Proverbs.

We find, then, two aspects of the Sacred Name, one which presents it as the Universal I AM, the all-productive Power which is the root of all manifestation, and thus includes all individualities within itself, involving them in the circulus of its own movement; and the other indicative of the reciprocal relation between this Power and the individual soul. But there is yet a third aspect under which this Power may be viewed, and that is as *working through the individual* who has become conscious of his own relation to it, and of his consequent direction and instruction by it. In this sense the Old Testament enumerates its Names in the text I have already quoted, "His Name shall be called Wonderful, Counsellor, the Mighty God, the Everlasting Father, and the Prince of Peace" (Isaiah ix. 6). In the Book of Job this is called "the Interpreter" (xxxiii. 23), and in the New Testament this Name is called "The Word."

What may be the nature of the Divine self-consciousness in itself is a matter on which we can in no way profitably speculate—to do so is trying to analyze that which, as the starting-point of all else, must necessarily be incapable of analysis for the simple reason that there can be nothing before the First. But what we *can* realize is the mode in which we experience our own relation to the Originating Spirit, and this will be found to form a threefold recognition of it, corresponding with what I have said above. Our primary recognition of the Spirit is that of an all-embracing Universal Principle, a simple Unity; but gradually we shall come to find that our perception of this Unity contains enfolded in it a threefold relation to our personality which implies the existence of a corresponding threefold aspect in the Unity. We must always recollect that all we can know of God is our own consciousness of our relation to Him, and eventually we shall find that this relation is first, generic, as to the Creating Spirit; secondly, specific, as forming a particular *class* of individuals holding a special relation to the Spirit; and thirdly, individual, as differentiated units of this particular class. Thus by a Law of Reciprocity, we realize "the Father" or Parent Spirit, "the Son" or Divine Ideal of Human Personality, and "the Holy Spirit" as the operation of the Original Spirit upon the individual, resulting from the individual's recognition of his relation to the Father in a Divine Sonship. Seen in this light, the doctrine of the Trinity in Unity ceases to be either a contradiction in terms or the conception of a limiting anthropomorphism, but on the contrary it is found to be the statement of the highest experiences of the human soul.

With these preliminary remarks, I would lay particular stress upon the Name given to the Universal Principle in its Third aspect, that of manifestation through the individual mind. In this sense it is emphatically called "The Word," and a study of comparative religions shows that this conception of the Universal Mind, manifesting itself as Speech, has been reached by all the great race-religions in their deeper significances. The "Logos" of Greek philosophy, the "Vach" of the Sanskrit, are typical instances, and the reason is to be found, as in all statements of truth, in the nature of the thing itself.

The Biblical account of creation represents the work as completed by the appearing of Man; that is to say, the evolutionary process culminates in the Creative Principle expressing itself in a form differing from all lower ones in its capacity for reasoning. Now, reasoning implies the use of words either spoken or employed mentally, for whether we wish to make the stages of an argument plain to another or to ourselves, it can only be done by putting the sequence of cause and effect into *words.*

The first idea suggested by the principle of Speech is, therefore, that of individual intelligence, and next, as following from this, we get the idea of expressing individual will; then, as we begin to realize the reciprocal relation between the Universal Mind and the individual mind, which necessarily results from the latter being an evolution from the former, our conception of intelligence and volition becomes extended from the individual to the Universal, and we see that because these qualities exist in human personality, they must exist *in some more generalized mode* in that Universal Mind, of which the individual mind is a more specialized reproduction; and so we arrive at the result that the Speech-principle is the highest expression of the Divine Wisdom, Power, and Love, whose combined action produces what we call Creation.

In this sense, then, the Bible attributes the creation of the world to the Divine Word, and it therefore rightly says that "In the beginning was The Word, and The Word was with God, and The Word was God," and that without The Word "was not anything made that was made"; and from this commencement, the natural sequence of evolution brings us to the crowning result in the manifestation of The Word as Man, at first ignorant of his Divine origin, but nevertheless containing all the potentialities which the recognition of his true nature as the image of God will enable him to develop. And when at length this recognition comes to any one he arises and returns to "The Father," and in the discovery of his true relation to the Divine Mind, finds that he also is a child of the Almighty and can speak "the Word of Power."

He may have been the prodigal who has wasted his substance, or the respectable brother who thought that only limited supplies were doled out to him; but as soon as the truth dawns upon him he realizes the meaning of the words, "Son, thou art ever with Me, and all that I have is thine." In its Third aspect as "the Word," the Universal Principle becomes specialized. In its earlier modes it is the Life-principle working by a Law of Averages, and thus maintaining the race as a whole, but not providing special accommodation for the individual. And it is inconceivable that the Cosmic Power, *as such,* should ever pass beyond what we may call the administration of the world *in globo,* for to suppose it doing so would involve the self-contradiction of the Universal acting on the plane of the Particular without becoming the particular; and it precisely by *becoming* the particular, or by evolution into individual minds, that it carries on the work beyond the stage at which things are governed by a mere Law of Averages.

It is thus that we become "fellow-workers with God," and that "the

Father" is represented as inviting His sons to work in His vineyard. By recognition of his own true place in the scheme of evolution, Man learns that his function is to *carry on* the work which has been begun in the Universal, to still further applications in the Particular, thus affording the key to the Master's words, "My Father worketh *hitherto, and* I work"; and the instrument by which the instructed man does this is his knowledge of the Sacred Name in its Threefold significance.

The study of the Sacred Name is the study of the Livingness of Being and of the Law of Expression in all its phases, and no book or library of books is sufficient to cope with such a vast idea. All any writer can do is to point out the broad lines of the subject, and each reader must make his own personal application of it. But the Law remains for ever, that the sincere desire for Truth produces a corresponding unfoldment of Truth, and the supreme Truth is reached in that final recognition of the Divine Name, "God is Love."

## VIII

# THE DEVIL

IT IS IMPOSSIBLE to read the Bible and ignore the important part which it assigns to the Devil. The Devil first appears as the Serpent in the story of "the Fall," and figures throughout Scripture till the final scene in Revelations, where "the old Serpent, which is the Devil and Satan," is cast into the lake of fire. What, then, is meant by the Devil? We may start with the self-obvious proposition that "God" and the "Devil" must be the exact opposites of each other. Whatever God is, the Devil is not. Then, since God alone *is,* the Devil *is not.* Since God is Being, the Devil is Not-Being. And so we are met by the paradox that though the Bible says so much about the Devil, yet the Devil does not exist. It is precisely this fact of non-existence that makes up the Devil; it is that power which in appearance is, and in reality is not; in a word, it is the Power of the Negative.

We are put upon this track by the statement in II. Corinthians, i. 20, that in Christ, all the promises of God are Yea and Amen, that is, *essentially Affirmative;* in other words, that all our growth towards Perfected Humanity must be by recognition of the Positive and not by recognition of the Negative. The prime fact of Negation is its Nothingness; but owing to the impossibility of ever divesting our Thought of its Creative Power, our *conception* of the Negative as something having a substantive existence of its own becomes a very real power indeed, and it is this power that the Bible calls "the Devil and Satan," the same old serpent which we find beguiling Eve in the Book of Genesis. It is equally a mistake to say that there is an Evil Power or that there is not. Let us examine this paradox.

A little consideration will show us that it is impossible for there to be an Infinite and Universal Power of Evil, for unless the Infinite and Universal Power were *Creative* nothing could exist. If it be creative then it is the Life-principle working always for self-expression, and to suppose the undifferentiated principle of Life acting otherwise than life-givingly, would contradict the very idea of its livingness.

Whatever tends to expand and improve life is the Good, and therefore it is a primary intuition from which we cannot get away, that the Infinite, Originating, and Maintaining Power can only be Good. But to find this absolute and unchangeable "Good," we require to get to the very bed-rock of Being, to that as yet undifferentiated Life-in-itself inherent in, and forming one with, universal primordial Substance, of which I have spoken in a former chapter. This all-underlying Life is for ever expressing itself through Form; but the Form is not the Life, and it is from not seeing this that so much confusion arises.

The Universal Life-principle, simply as such, finds expression as much in one form as another, and is just as active in the scattered particles which once made a human body as it was in those particles when they cohered together in the living man; this is merely the well-recognized scientific truth of the Conservation of Energy.

On the other hand, we cannot help perceiving that there is something in the individual which exercises a greater power than the perpetual energy residing in the ultimate atoms; for, otherwise, what is it that maintains in our bodies for perhaps a century the unstable equilibrium of atomic forces which, when that something is withdrawn, cannot continue for twenty-four hours? Is this something another something than that which is at work as the perpetual energy within the atoms? No, for otherwise there would be two originating powers in the universe, and if our study of the Bible teaches us anything, it is that the Originating Power is only ONE; and we must therefore conceive of the Power we are examining as the same Power that resides in the ultimate atoms, only now working at a higher level. It has welded the atoms into a distinct organism, however lowly, and so to distinguish this mode of power from the mere atomic energies, we may call it the Integrating Power, or the Power which Builds-up.

Now, evolution is a continuous process of building-up, and what makes the world of to-day a different world from that of the ichthyosaurus and the pterodactyl, is the successive building up of more and more complex organisms, culminating at last in the production of Man as an organism, both physically and mentally capable of expressing the Life of the Supreme Intelligence by means of Individual Consciousness. Why, then, should not the Power, which is able to carry on the race as a perpetually improving expression of itself, do the same thing *in the individual?* That is the question with which we have to deal; in other words, Why need the individual die? Why should he not go on in a perpetual expansion?

This question may seem absurd in the light of past experience. Those who believe only in blind forces, answer that death is the law of Nature, and those who believe in the Divine Wisdom answer that it is the appointment of God. But, strange as it may seem, both these answers are wrong. That death should be the ultimate law of Nature contradicts the principle of continuity as exemplified in the Lifeward tendency of evolution; and that it is the will of God is most emphatically denied by the Bible, for that tells us that he that has the power of death is the Devil (Hebrews ii. 14). There is no beating about the bush; not God but the Devil sends death. There is no getting out of the plain words. Let us examine this statement.

We have seen that whatever God is, the Devil, must be the opposite, and, therefore if God is the Power that builds up, the Integrating Power, the Devil must be the power that pulls down, or the Disintegrating Power. Now, what is Disintegration? It is the breaking up of what was previously an "integer" or perfect Whole, the separation of its component parts. But what is it that causes the separation? It is still the Building-up Power, only the Law of Affinity by which it works is now acting from other centres, so as to build up other organisms.

The Universal Power is still at its building work, only it seems to have lost sight of its original motive in the organism which is falling to pieces, and to have taken up fresh motives in other directions. And this is precisely the state of the case; it is just the want of continuous motive that causes disintegration. The only possible motive of the All-originating Life-principle must be the expression of *Life,* and, therefore, we may almost picture it as continually seeking to embody itself in intelligences, which shall be able to grasp its motive and co-operate with it by keeping that motive constantly in mind.

Granted that this *individualization of motive* could take place, there appears no reason why it should not continue to work on indefinitely. A tree is an organized centre of life, but without the intelligence which would enable it to individualize the *motive* of the Universal Life-principle. It individualizes a certain measure of the Universal Vital Energy, but it does not individualize the Universal Intelligence, and, therefore, when the measure of energy which it has individualized is exhausted it dies; and the same thing happens with animals and men.

But as the particular intelligence advances in the recognition of itself as the individualization of the Universal Intelligence, it becomes more and more capable of seizing upon the *initial motive* of the Universal Mind and giving it permanence. And supposing this recognition to be complete, the logical result would be never-ceasing and perpetually-expanding individual life; thus bringing us back to those promises which I have quoted in the opening pages of this book, and reminding us of the Master's statement to the woman of Samaria that "the Father" is always "seeking" those who will worship Him in spirit and in truth; that is, those who can enter into the spirit of what "the Father" is aiming at.

But what happens, in the absence of a perfect recognition of the Universal Motive, is that sooner or later the machinery runs down, and the "motive" is transferred to other centres where the same process is repeated, and so Life and Death alternate with each other in a ceaseless round. The disintegrating process is the Universal Builder taking the materials for fresh constructions from a tenement without a tenant; that is, from an organism which has not reached the measure of intelligence necessary to perpetuate the Universal Motive in itself, or, as the Master put it in the parable of the ten virgins such as have not a supply of oil to keep their lamps burning.

This Negative disintegrating force is the Integrating Power working, so to say, at a lower level relatively to that at which it had been working in the organism that is being dissolved. It is not another power. Both the Bible and common-sense tell us that ultimately there can be only ONE power in the universe, which must, therefore, be the Building-power, so that there can be no such thing as a power which is negative *in itself;* but it shows itself negatively *in relation to the particular individual,* if through want of recognition he fails to provide the requisite conditions for it to work positively.

Work it always will, for its very being is ceaseless activity; but whether it will act positively or negatively towards any particular individual depends entirely on whether he provides positive or negative conditions for its manifestation, just as we may produce a positive or a negative current according to the electrical conditions which we supply.

We see, then, that what gives the Positive Power a negative action is the failure to intelligently recognize our own individualization of it. In the lower forms of life this failure is inevitable, because they are not provided with an organism capable of such a recognition. In Man the suitable organism is present, but he seeks knowledge only from past experiences which have necessarily been of the negative order, and does not, by the combined action of reason and faith, look into the Infinite for the unfoldment of limitless possibilities; and so he employs his intelligence to deny that which, if he affirmed it, would be in him the spring of perpetual renovation.

The Power of the Negative, therefore, has its root in our denial of the Affirmative; and so we die because we have not yet learned to understand the Principle of Life; we have yet to learn the great Law, that "the higher mode of intelligence controls the lower." In consequence of our ignorance we attribute an affirmative power to the Negative; that is to say, the power of taking an initiative on its own account, not seeing that it is a *condition* resulting from the absence of something more positive; and so the power of the Negative consists in affirming that to be true which is not true, and for this reason it is called in Scripture the father of lies, or that principle from which all false statements are generated.

The word "Devil" means "false accuser" or "false affirmer," and this name is, therefore, in itself sufficient to show us that what is meant is the creative principle of Affirmation used in the wrong direction, a truth which has been handed down to us from old times in the saying "Diabolus est Deus inversus." This is how it is that "the Devil" can be a vast impersonal power while at the same time having no existence, and so the paradox with which we started is solved. And now also it becomes clear why we are told that "the Devil" has the power of death. It is not held by a personal individual, but results quite naturally from that ignorant and inverted Thought which is "the Spirit that denies."

This is the exact opposite to "the Son of God," in whom all things are only "Yea and Amen." That is the Spirit of the Affirmative, and, therefore, the Spirit of Life; and so it is that the Son of God was manifested that

"He might destroy him that had the power of death, that is the Devil, and deliver them who, through fear of death, were all their life-time subject to bondage" (Hebrews ii. 14).

Again, we are told that the Devil is Satan. This name appears to be another form of "Saturn," and may also be connected with the root "sat" or "seven," Saturn being in the old symbolical astronomy the outermost or seventh planet. In that system the centre is occupied by Sol or the Sun, which represents the Life-giving principle, and Saturn represents the opposite extreme, or Matter at the point furthest removed from Pure Spirit.

Now, taken in due order, Matter or Concrete Form is as necessary as Spirit itself, for without it there could be no manifestation of Spirit, in other words, there could be no *ex*istence at all. Seen from this point of view, there is nothing evil in it, but on the contrary, it may be compared to the lamp which concentrates the light, and gives it a particular direction, and in this aspect Matter is called "Lucifer" or the Light-bearer. This is Matter taking its proper place in the order of the Kingdom of Heaven. But if "Lucifer" falls from heaven, becomes rebellious, and endeavors to usurp the place of "Sol," then it is the fallen Archangel and becomes "Satan," or that outermost planet which moves in an orbit whose remoteness from the warmth and light of the Sun renders all human life and joy impossible, a symbolism which we retain in our common speech when we say that a man has a saturnine aspect.

Thus "Satan" is the same old serpent that deceived Eve; it is the wrong belief that sets merely secondary causes, which are only *conditions,* in the place of First Cause or that originating power of Thought which makes enlightened Man the image of his Maker and the Son of God.*

But we must not make the mistake of supposing that because there is no Universal Devil in the same sense as there is Universal God, therefore there are no individual devils. The Bible frequently speaks of them, and one of the commissions given by the Master to His followers was to cast out devils.

The words used for *the* Devil are in the Greek, "Diabolos," and in the Hebrew, "Satan," both having the same general meaning of the Principle of Negation; but individual devils are called in the Hebrew, "sair," a hairy one,

* For the all-important distinction between Causes and Conditions, see chapter ix. of my *Edinburgh Lectures on Mental Science.*

and in the Greek, "daimon," a spirit or shade, and these terms indicate evil spirits having personal identity.

Now, without stopping to discuss the question whether there are orders of spiritual individualities which have never been human, let us confine our attention to the immense multitudes of disembodied human spirits which, under any hypothesis, must crowd the realms of the unseen. Can we suppose them all to be good? Certainly not, for we have no reason to suppose that mere severance from its physical instrument either changes the moral quality or expands the intelligence of the mind, and therefore, if there is such a thing as survival after death at all, we cannot conceive of the other world otherwise than as containing millions upon millions of spirits in various stages of ignorance and ill-will, and consequently ready to make the most unscrupulous use of their powers where opportunity offers.

The time is fast passing away when it will be possible to regard such a conception as fantastic, and taking our stand simply upon the well-ascertained ground of thought-transference and telepathy, we may well ask, if such powers as these can be exercised by the spiritual entity while still clothed in flesh, why should they not be equally, or even more powerfully, employed by spirits out of the flesh?

This opens an immense field of inquiry which we cannot stop to investigate; but setting aside all other classes of evidence on this subject, the experimentally ascertained facts of telepathy bring to light possibilities which would explain all that the Bible says regarding the malific influence of evil spirits. But the inference to be drawn from this is not that we should go in continual terror of obsession or other injury, but that we should realize that our position as "sons and daughters of the Almighty," places us beyond the reach of such malignant entities.

Our familiar principle, the Law of Attraction, is at work here also. Like attracts like; and if we would keep these undesirable entities at a distance, we can do so most effectually by centering our thoughts on those things which we *know* from their nature cannot invite evil influences. Let us follow the apostolic advice, and "whatsoever things are true, whatsoever things are honest, whatsoever things are just, whatsoever things are pure, whatsoever things are lovely, whatsoever things are of good report; if there be any virtue and if there be any praise, think on these things" (Philippians iv. 8).

Then, however far the Law of Attraction may extend from us into the other world, we may rest assured that it will only act to bring us in touch with that innumerable company of angels and spirits of just men made perfect, of whom we are told in the twelfth chapter of Hebrews, and who, because they are joined in the same worship of the ONE Divine Spirit as ourselves, can only act in accordance with the principles of harmony and love.

I will not attempt the analysis of so important a subject in the short space at my disposal, but I would caution all students against tampering with anything that savors of ceremonial magic. However little acknowledged in public, it is by no means unfrequently practised at the present day, and, if on no other grounds, it should be resolutely shunned as a powerful system of auto-suggestion capable of producing the most disastrous effects on those who employ it. No New Thought reader can be ignorant of the power of auto-suggestion, and I would therefore ask each one to think out for himself what the tendency of auto-suggestion conducted on such lines as these must be. "I speak as unto wise men, judge ye what I say."

The Bible is by no means silent on this subject, but I may sum up its teaching in a few lines. It assumes throughout, the possibility of intercourse between men and spirits, but with the exception of the Master's temptation, where I understand a symbolic representation of the general principle of evil, the Power of the Negative which we have already considered, it should be remarked that all its record is of appearances of good angels as ministering spirits to heirs of salvation.

Nor were these visitants sought after by those who received them, their appearance was always spontaneous; and the solitary instance which the Bible records of a spirit appearing whom it was sought to raise by incantation, is of the appearance of Samuel to Saul, announcing that his rebellion had culminated in this act of witchcraft, and this was followed by the suicide of Saul on the next day.

If, then, our study of the Bible has led us to the conclusion that it is the statement of the Law of the inevitable sequences of cause and effect, this uniform direction of its teachings must indicate the presence of certain sequences in this connection also, which follow definite laws, although we may not yet understand them. This knowledge will come to us by degrees with the natural expansion of our powers, and when it arrives in its proper order we shall be qualified to use it; and if we realize that there is a Universal Mind capable of guiding us at all, we may trust it not to keep back from us anything it is necessary we should know at each stage of our onward journey. Do we want knowledge? The Master has promised that the Spirit of Truth shall guide us into all truth. "Should not a people seek unto their God instead of unto them that have familiar spirits?" (Isaiah viii. 19). There is a *reason* at the back of all these things.

We thus see that the whole question of the power of evil turns on the two fundamental Laws which I spoke of in the opening pages of this book, as forming the basis of Bible teaching; the Law of Suggestion and the Law of the Creative Power of Thought. The conception of an abstract principle of evil, the Devil, receives its power from our own auto-suggestion of its existence; and the power of evil spirits results from a mental attitude which allows us to receive their suggestions.

Then, in both cases, the suggestion having been accepted, our own creative power of Thought does the rest, and so prepares the way for receiving still further suggestions of the same sort. Now, the antidote to all this is a right conception of God or the Universal Spirit of Life as the ONE and only *originating* Power. If we realize that relatively to us, this Power manifests itself through the medium of our own Thought, and that in so doing it in no way changes its inherent quality of Life-givingness; this recognition must constitute such a supremely powerful and all-embracing Suggestion as must necessarily eradicate all suggestions of a contrary description; and so our Thought being based on this Supreme Suggestion of Good, is certain to have a correspondingly life-giving character.

To recognize the essential One-ness of this Power is to recognize it as God, and to recognize its essential Life-givingness is to recognize it as Love, and so we shall realize in ourselves the truth that "God is Love." Then, "if God be for us who can be against us?" and so we realize the further truth that "perfect love casteth out fear," with the results that in our own world there can be no devil.

IX

# THE LAW OF LIBERTY

NOTHING IS MORE indicative of our ignorance regarding the purpose and meaning of the Bible, than the distinction which it is often sought to draw between the Law and the Gospel. We are told of different "dispensations," as though the Divine method of conducting the world changed after the fashion of political constitutions. If this were the case, we should never know under what system of administration we were living, for we could only be informed of these alterations by persons who were "in the know" with the Divine Power, and we should have nothing but their bare assertion to depend on, that they were "in the know."

This is the logical outcome of any system which is based upon the allegation of specific determinations by a Divine Autocrat. It cannot be otherwise, and therefore all such systems are destined sooner or later to fall to pieces, because their foundation of so-called "authority" crumbles away under the scrutiny of intelligent investigation. The Divine orderings can only be known by the Divine workings, and the intelligent study of the Divine working is the only criterion which the Bible, rightly understood, anywhere sets up for the recognition of Truth.

The whole of the Psalms are based entirely on this principle, and the Master claimed their testimony to His mission. He himself spoke of tradition as rendering void the true Law of God; and so far from claiming to introduce any new dispensation, he emphatically declared that his special business was to fulfil the Law, that is, to demonstrate it in all its completeness. If the Law taught by Moses is true, and the Gospel preached by Jesus is true, then they are both true together, and are simply statements of the same Truth from different standpoints; and the proofs of their truth will be found in their agreement with one another, and with the universal principles of Natural Law which we can learn by the study of ourselves and of our environment.

If the Old and New Testaments are right in saying that the foundation of all other knowledge is that God is ONE, then we may be certain that we are on a wrong track if we think that Divine truth can be different at one time to what it is at another. We realize the principle of "continuity" throughout physical nature, and if we see that the physical must originate in the spiritual, we cannot deny the extension of "continuity" throughout the entire system; and therefore, if the messages of the Old and New Testaments are both true, we may expect to find the same principle of "continuity" running through both. On investigation this will be found to be the case, and no truer definition can be given of the Gospel than that it is the Law worked out to its logical conclusions.

The Law which the Bible sets forth from first to last is the Law of Human Individuality. The Bible is the spiritual Natural History Book of Man. It begins with his creation by evolution from the kingdoms which had preceded him, and it terminates with his apotheosis—the line is long, but it is straight, and reaches its glorious destination by an orderly sequence of cause and effect. It is the statement of the evolution of the individual as the result of his recognition of the Law by which he came to be a human being at all.

When he sees that this happened neither by chance nor by arbitrary command, then, and not till then, will he wake up to the fact that he is what he is by reason of a Law inherent in himself—the action of which he can therefore carry on indefinitely, by correctly understanding and cheerfully following it.

His first general perception that there is such a Law at all is followed by the realization that it must be the Law of his own individuality, for he has only discovered the existence of the Law by recognizing himself as the Expression of it; and therefore he finds that before all else, the Law is that he shall be *himself.* But a Law which allows us to be entirely *ourselves* is Perfect

Liberty, and thus we get back to St. James' statement that the Perfect Law is the Law of Liberty.

Obviously it is not Liberty to allow ourselves to be depressed into such a mental attitude of submission to every form and degree of misery as coming to us "by the will of God," that we at last reach a condition of apathy in which one blow more or less makes very little difference. Such teaching is based on the Devil's beatitude—"Blessed are they that expect nothing for they shall not be disappointed"—but that is not the Gospel of Deliverance which Jesus preached in His first discourse in the synagogue of Nazareth. Jesus' teaching was not the deification of suffering, but the fulness of Joy; and He emphatically declared that all bondage, everything which keeps us from enjoying our life to the full, is the working of that Power of the Negative which the Bible calls the Devil. To give up hope and regard ourselves as the sport of an inexorable fate is not Liberty. It is not obedience to a higher power, but abject submission to a lower—the power of ignorance, unintelligence, and negation.

Perfect Liberty is the consciousness that we are not thus bound by any power of evil, but that, on the contrary, we are centers in which the Creative Spirit of the Universe finds particular expression. Then we are in harmony with its continual progressive movement towards still more perfect modes of expression, and therefore Its thought and our thought, Its action and our action, become identical, so that in expressing the Spirit we express ourselves. When we reach this unity of consciousness we cannot but find it to be perfect Liberty; for our own self-expression, being also that of the All-Creating Spirit as It manifests in our individuality, is no longer bound by antecedent conditions, but starts fresh from the standpoint of Original Creative Energy.

This is Liberty, according to Law, the law of the All-Creating Harmony, in which God's way and our way co-incide. The idea of Liberty, without a unifying Harmony as its basis, is inconceivable, for with every one *struggling* to get their own way *at somebody else's expense,* you create a pandemonium; and that is just why there is so much of that element in the world at the present time. But such an inverted idea of Liberty is based on the assumption that Man does not possess the power of controlling his conditions by his Thought; in other words, the flat denial of the initial statement of Scripture regarding him that he is made "in the image and likeness of God."

Once grant the creative power of our Thought and there is an end of *struggling* for our own way, and an end of gaining it *at some one else's expense;* for, since by the terms of the hypothesis we can create what we like, the simplest way of getting what we want is, not to snatch it from somebody else, but to make it for ourselves; and, since there is no limit to Thought there can be no need for straining, and for every one to have his own way in *this* manner would be to banish all strife, want, sickness, and sorrow from the earth.

Now, it is precisely on this assumption of the creative power of our Thought that the whole Bible rests. If not, what is the meaning of being saved by Faith? Faith is essentially Thought; and, therefore, every call to have Faith in God is a call to trust in the power of our own Thought about God. "According to your faith be it unto you," says the New Testament. "As a man thinketh in his heart so is he," says the Old Testament. The entire Book is nothing but one continuous statement of the Creative Power of Thought.

The whole Bible is a commentary on the text, "Man is the image and likeness of God." And it comments on this text sometimes by explaining why, by reason of the ONE-ness of the Spirit, this must necessarily be so; sometimes by incitements to emotional states calculated to call this power into activity; sometimes by precepts warning us against those emotions which would produce its inverse action; sometimes by the example of those who have successfully demonstrated this power, and conversely by examples of those who have perverted it; sometimes by statements of the terrible consequences that must inevitably follow such perversion; and sometimes by glorious promises of the illimitable possibilities residing in this wonderful power, if used in the right way; and thus it is that "all Scripture is profitable for doctrine, for reproof, for correction, for instruction in righteousness."

All this proceeds from the initial assumption with which the Bible starts regarding Man, that he is the reproduction in individuality of that which God is in universality. Start with this assumption, and the whole Bible works out logically. Deny it, and the Book becomes nothing but a mass of inconsistencies and contradictions. The value of the Bible as a storehouse of knowledge and a guide into Life, depends entirely on our attitude with regard to its fundamental proposition.

But this proposition contains in itself the Affirmation of our Liberty;

and the Gospel preached by Jesus amounts simply to this, that if any one realizes himself as the reproduction, in conscious individuality, of the same principles which the Law of the Old Testament bids us recognize in the Divine Mind, he will thereby enter upon an unlimited inheritance of Life and Liberty. But to do this we must realize the Divine image in ourselves *on all lines.*

We cannot enter upon a full life of Joy and Liberty by trying to realize the Divine image along one line only. If we seek to reproduce the Creative Power without its correlatives of Wisdom and Love, we shall do so only to our own injury; for there is one thing which is impossible alike to God and Man, and that is to plant a seed of one sort and make it yield fruit of another. We can never get beyond the Law that the effect must be of the same nature as the cause. To abrogate this Law would be to destroy the very foundation of the Creative Power of Thought, for then we could never reckon upon what our Thought might produce; so that the very same Law which places creative power at our disposal, necessarily provides punishment for its misuse and reward for its right employment.

And this is equally the case along the two other lines. To seek development only on the line of Knowledge is to contemplate a store of wealth, while remaining ignorant of the one fact which gives it any value, that it is *our own;* and, in like manner, to cultivate only Love makes our great motive power evaporate in a weak sentimentality which accomplishes nothing, because it does not *know how* and does not *feel able.* So, here we see the force of the Master's words when he bids us aim at a perfection like that of our "Father" in heaven, a perfection based on the knowledge that all being is three-fold in essence and one in expression; and that, therefore, we can attain Liberty only by recognizing this universal Law in ourselves also, and that accordingly the Thought that sets us free must be a simultaneous movement along all three lines of our nature.

The Divine Mind may be represented by a large circle and the individual mind by a small one, but that is no reason why the smaller circle should not be as perfect for its own area as the larger; and, therefore, the initial statement of the Bible that Man is the image of God is the charter of Individual Liberty for each one, provided we realize that this likeness must extend to the whole three-fold unity that is ourself and not to a part only.

Our Liberty, therefore, consists in being ourselves in our *Wholeness,* and this means the conscious exercise of *all* our powers, whether of our visible or invisible personality. It means being ourselves, not trying to be somebody else.

The *principles* by which any one ever attains to self-expression, whether in the humblest or the most exalted degree, are always the same, for they are *universals* and apply to every one alike, and, therefore, we may advantageously study their working in the lives of others; but to suppose that the expression of these principles is bound to take the same form in us that it did in the individual who is the object of our hero-worship, is to deny the first principle of manifested being, which is Individuality.

If some one towers above the crowd it is because he has grown to that height, and I cannot permanently attain the same elevation by climbing on his shoulders, but only by growing to the same height myself. Therefore, the attempt to copy a particular individual, however beautiful his character, is bondage, and a relinquishing of our birthright of Selfhood.

What we have to do in studying those lives which we admire, is to discover the universal principles which those persons embodied in their way, and then set to work to embody them in *ours.* To do this is to realize the Universal I AM manifesting itself in every Individuality; and when we see this, we find that the statement of the Law of Individual Liberty is the declaration that was made to Moses at the burning bush, and is the truth which Jesus proclaimed when He said that it was the recognition of the I AM that would set us free from the Law of bondage and death.

In speaking of the I AM as the Principle of Life, neither Jesus nor Moses used the words personally, and Jesus especially avoids any such misconstruction by saying "If I bear witness of Myself My witness is not true"; in other words, He came to set forth, not Himself personally, but those great principles common to all mankind, of which He exemplified the full development.

When a little child is first told that God made the world, it accepts the statement without doubting, but immediately and logically follows it up with the question, then who made God? And the unsophisticated mother very often gives the correct answer, God made himself. There is the whole secret, and when we come down—or rather when we rise—to the level of these souls whose pure intuitions have not been warped by arguments drawn only from the outside of things, we see that the principle of continual self-creation into all varieties of individuality, affords the true clue to all that we are and to all that is around us; and when we see this, the teaching regarding the I AM in ourselves becomes clear, logical, and simple.

Then we understand that the Law of our *Whole* Being—that which is Cause as well as Effect—is the reproduction in Individuality of the same power which makes the worlds; and when this is understood in its Wholeness, we see that this principle cannot, as manifested in us, be in opposition to its manifestation of itself in other forms. The Whole must be homogeneous—that which is homogeneous cannot act in opposition to itself—and consequently this homogeneous principle, which underlies all individuality, and is the I AM in each, can never act contrary to the true Law of Life; therefore, to know ourselves as the concentration of this principle into a focus of self-recognition, is to be at one with the Life-Principle which is all that is in all worlds and under all forms.

It is this recognition of our own Individuality as being a reproduction of the Universal Principle in the *whole* personality that constitutes belief in "the Son," or the principle of spiritual sonship, which brings us out of the bondage of ignorance and impotence into the liberty of knowledge and power.

But the reader, who is still within the trammels of the traditional exegesis, will probably say, if this be so, what is meant by such texts as that contained in the fifty-third chapter of Isaiah, "He was wounded for our transgressions," etc.? and the answer is that the personality here spoken of it still the same Typical Man—the Divine Son—who is described by Isaiah as "the Wonderful Child," only seen from another point of view. This is the description of him in his prenatal stage, that is, before his manifestation as the Son whose Name is Wonderful, Counsellor, etc.

And this brings us to the consideration of a very recondite subject, the question whether "Spirit" ever does pass into unconsciousness. Whether from the physiological or the psychological side, there is important evidence tending to the conclusion that "Spirit" is never in a condition of unconsciousness; and if this is the case with that concentration of *pure* Spirit which is the individualized I AM in each of us, how can we conceive its suffering from those transgressions of the Law of our own being, which result in all the misery, pain, and death that the world has witnessed.

If the Spirit in us is the very Impersonation of the Law of Life, what woundings, what bruisings it must suffer in the course of educating the lower principles into self-recognition and spontaneous compliance with the true Law of the Individuality in its Wholeness?

Then we see that it is only by the infinite persistence of the Spirit, in its struggle towards perfecting the vehicles of its self-expression, that the Individuality in all its completeness can ever be brought to maturity, and the crown set to the work of Evolution which commenced far back in the dim unfathomable past; we realize St. Paul's meaning in saying that the Spirit groans with unutterable groanings, for it is that principle which St. John tells us cannot sin (I. John iii. 9, and v. 18), that is, cannot act contrary to the true Law of Being; and thus a peculiar emphasis is set on the injunctions, "Grieve not the Spirit," "Quench not the Spirit," for the individualized Spirit is the intensely Living Centre of ourselves—the I AM that I Myself AM in every one of us.

The question of the ultimate consciousness of the individuality under the outward semblance of unconsciousness, as in trance, or under the conditions induced by hypnotism, or anæsthetics, involves problems of a scientific character which I hope to have an opportunity of discussing on another occasion; but even supposing there is no such latent consciousness of suffering as I have suggested, we may well transfer the whole description of the fifty-third chapter of Isaiah to the conscious sufferings of the outer man. That, at any rate, is a "man of sorrows and acquainted with grief," and the reason of these sufferings is the want of Wholeness; they are the result of trying to live only in one portion of our nature—and that the lower—instead of in the Whole, and, consequently, these sufferings will continue until we realize that even balance of all parts of our nature which alone constitutes true *individuality,* or that which is without division.

By the buffetting of experience, the lower personality is being continually driven to inquire more and more into the *reason* of its sufferings, and as it grows in intelligence, it sees that they always result from some wilful or ignorant infraction of the Law of Things-as-they-are, as distinguished from Things-as-they-look; and so by degrees the lower personality grows into union with the higher personality, which itself is the Law of Things-as-they-are become Personal, until at last the two are found to be ONE, and the Perfected Man stands forth Whole.

This is the process to which the writer of the Epistle to the Hebrews refers, when he says that "though he were a son, yet learned he obedience by the things which he suffered," thus indicating a course of education which can only apply to a personality whose evolution is not yet completed. But by these sufferings of the lower personality the salvation of the entire individuality is at length accomplished, for being thus led to study the Law of the Whole, the lower or simply intellectual mentality, at last discovers its relation to the Intuitive and Creative Principle, and realizes that nothing short of the harmonious union of the two makes a Complete Man. Until this recognition takes place, the real meaning of suffering is not understood.

To talk about "the Mystery of Pain" is like talking of the mystery of broken glass if we throw a stone at a window—it is of our own making. We attribute our sufferings to "the will of God," simply because we can think of nothing else to attribute them to, being ignorant alike of ourselves as centres of causation and of God as the Universal Life-Principle, which cannot will evil against any one.

So long as we are at this stage of intelligence, we esteem the lower personality (the only self we yet know) to be "stricken and smitten of God"—we put it all down to God's account—while all the time the cause of our wounding and bruising was, not the will of God, but our own transgressions and iniquities—transgression, the infraction of the Law of Causation, and iniquity, unequalness, or the want of even balance between all portions of our Individuality, without which the liberating recognition of our own I AM-ness can never take place.

This reading of this wonderful chapter takes it out of the region of merely speculative theology, and brings it into a region where we can understand its statements as links in a chain of cause and effect connecting the promised redemption with facts that we know, and starting from causes whose working is obvious to us.

This reading in no way detracts from the value of this passage as a prophecy of the great work of the Master, for it is a generic description applicable to each, in his degree, who in any way labors or suffers for the good of others; and the description is, therefore, supremely applicable to Jesus, in whom that perfect Individualization of the Divine of which we speak was fully accomplished.

The Law of Man's Individuality is, therefore, the Law of Liberty, and equally it is the Gospel of Peace; for when we truly understand the Law of our own individuality, we see that the same Law finds its expression in every one else, and, consequently, we shall reverence the Law in others exactly in proportion as we value it in ourselves. To do this is to follow the golden rule of doing to others what we would they should do unto us; and because we know that the Law of Liberty in ourselves must include the free use of our own creative power, there is no longer any inducement to infringe the rights of others, for we can satisfy all our desires by the exercise of our knowledge of the Law.

As this comes to be understood, co-operation will take the place of competition with the result of removing all ground of enmity, whether between individuals, classes, or nations; and thus the continual recognition of the Divine or "highest" principles in ourselves brings "peace on earth and good-will among men" naturally in its train, and it is for this reason that the Bible everywhere couples the reign of peace on earth with the Knowledge of God.

The whole object of the Bible is to teach us to be ourselves and yet more ourselves. It does not trouble itself with political or social questions, or even with those of religious organization, but it goes to the root of all, which is the Individual. First set people right individually, and they will naturally set themselves right collectively. It is only applying to mankind the old proverb, "take care of the pence and the pounds will take care of themselves"; and, therefore, the Bible deals only with the two extremes of the scale, the Universal Mind and the Individual Mind. Let the relation between these two be clearly understood, and all other relations will settle themselves on lines which, however varied in form, will always be characterized by individual Liberty working to the expression of perfect social harmony.

X

# THE TEACHING OF JESUS

IN THIS CHAPTER I shall endeavor to give a connected idea of the general scope and purpose of the Master's teachings, the point of which we, in great measure, miss by taking particular sayings separately, and so losing the force which pertains to them, by reason of the place they hold in His system as a whole. For, be it remembered, Jesus was teaching a definite system, not a creed, nor a ritual, nor a code of speculative ethics, but a system resulting from the threefold source of spiritual inspiration, intellectual reasoning, and experimental observation, which are the three modes in which the Universal Mind manifests itself as Conscious Reasoning Power or "the Word." And therefore this system combines the religious, philosophical, and scientific characters, because it is a statement of the action of universal principles at the level where they find expression through the human mind.

As we proceed, we shall find that the basis of this system is the same perception of the unity between the Expressor and the Expressed, which is also the basis of the teaching of Moses, and which is summed up in the significant phrase I AM. Jesus brings out the consequences of this Unity in their relation to the Individual, and therefore presupposes the teaching of Moses, regarding the Universal Unity, as the necessary foundation for its reflection in the individual.

The great point to be noted, in the teaching of Jesus, is His statement of the absolute liberty of the individual. That was the subject of His first discourse in the synagogue of Nazareth (Luke iv. 16); He continued His teaching with the statement, "the truth shall make you free"; and He finished it with the final declaration before Pilate, that He had come into the world to the end that He should bear witness to the Truth (John xviii. 37). Thus, to teach us the knowledge of Liberating Truth was the beginning, the middle, and the end of the great work which the Master set before Him.

Now, there are two facts about this teaching that deserve our special attention. The first is that the perfect liberty of the individual must be in accordance with the will of God; for on any other supposition Jesus would have been teaching rebellion against the Divine will; and, therefore, any system of religion which inculcates blind submission to adverse circumstances, as submission to the will of God, must do so at the cost of branding Jesus as a leader of rebellion against the Divine authority.

The other point is that this freedom is represented simply as the result of coming *to know the Truth.* If words mean anything, this means that Liberty in truth exists at the present moment, and that what keeps us from enjoying it is simply our ignorance of the fact. In other words, the Master's teaching is that the essential, and, therefore, ever-present Law of each individual human life is absolute Liberty—it is so in the very nature of Being, and it is only our ingrained belief to the contrary that keeps us in bondage to all sorts of limitation.

Of course, it is easy to explain away all that the Master said, by interpreting it in the light of our past experiences; but these experiences themselves constitute the very bondage from which He came to deliver us, and, therefore, to do this is to destroy His whole work. We do not require His teaching to go back to the belittling and narrowing influence of past experiences; we do that naturally enough so long as we remain ignorant of any other possibilities. It is just this being tied up that we want to get loose from, and He came to tell us that, when we know the Truth, we shall find we are not tied up at all. If we hold fast to the initial teaching of Genesis, that the Divine Principle makes things by *itself becoming* them, then it follows that when it becomes the individual man, it cannot have any other than its own natural movement in him; that is, a continual pushing forward into fuller and fuller expression of itself, which, therefore, becomes fuller and fuller life in the individual; and, consequently, anything that tends to limit the full expression of the individual life must be abhorrent to the Universal Mind expressing itself *in that individuality.*

Then comes the question as to the way in which this truth is to be realized, and the practical way inculcated by the Master is very simple; it is only that we are to take this truth for granted, that is all. We may be ready to exclaim that this is a large demand upon our faith, but after all it is the only way in which we ever do anything. We take all the operations of the Life-principle in our physical body for granted, and what is wanted is a similar confidence in the working of our spiritual faculties.

We trust our bodily powers because we assume their action as the natural Law of our being; and in just the same way we can only use our interior powers, by tacitly assuming them to be as natural to us as any others. We must bear in mind that from first to last the Master's teaching was never other than a *veiled* statement of Truth: He spoke "the word" to the people in parables, and "without a parable spake He not unto them" (Matt. iv. 34). It is indeed added "and when they were alone He expounded all things to His disciples"; but if we take the interpretation of the parable of the sower as a sample, we can see how very far these expositions were from being a full and detailed explanation.

The thickest and outermost veil is removed, but we are still very far from that plain speaking among "the full-grown" which St. Paul tells us was equally distant from his own writing to the Corinthians. I say this on the best authority, that of the Master Himself. We might have supposed that in that last discourse, which commences with the fourteenth chapter of St. John's Gospel, He had withdrawn the final veil from His teaching; but, no, we have His own words for it that even this is a veiled statement of the Truth. He tells His disciples that the time when He shall show them plainly of "the Father" is still future (John xiv. 25).

He left the final interpretation to be given by the only possible interpreter, the Spirit of Truth, as the real significance of His words should in time dawn upon each of His hearers, with an inner meaning that would be none other than the revelation of The Sacred Name. As this meaning dawns upon us we find that Jesus no longer speaks to us in proverbs, but that His parables tell us plainly of "the Father," and our only wonder is that we did not discern His true meaning long ago.

He is telling us of great universal principles which are reproduced everywhere and in everything with special reference to their reproduction on the plane of Personality. He is not telling us of rules which God has laid down in one way, and could, had He chosen, have laid down in another, but of universal Laws which are the very Being of God, and which are, therefore, inherent in the constitution of Man. Let us, then, examine some of His sayings in this light.

The thread on which the pearls of the Master's teaching are strung together, is that Perfect Liberty is the natural result of knowing the Truth. "When you find what the Truth really is, you will find it to be that you are perfectly free," is the centre from which all His other statements radiate; but the final discovery cannot be made *for* you, you must each make it *for yourself,* therefore, "he that hath ears to hear let *him* hear."

This is nowhere brought out more clearly than in the parable of the Prodigal Son. The fact of sonship had never altered for either of the two brothers, but in different ways they each missed the point of their position as sons. The one limited himself by separating off a particular *share* of the Father's goods for himself, which, just because of being a limited share and not the whole, was speedily exhausted, leaving him in misery and want.

The other brother equally limited himself by supposing that he had no power to draw from his Father's stores, but must wait till he in some way acquired a specific permission to do so, not realizing his inherent right, as his Father's son, to take whatever he wanted.

The one son took up a false idea of independence, thinking it consisted in separating himself and, to use an expressive vulgarism, in being entirely "on his own hook," while the other, in his recoil from this conception, went to the opposite extreme, and believed himself to have no independence at all.

The younger son's return, so far from extinguishing the instinct of Liberty, gratified it to the full, by placing him in a position of honor and command in his Father's house; and the elder son is rebuked with the simple words, "Why wait for me to give you what is yours already? All that I have *is* thine." It would be impossible to state the relation between the Individual Mind and the Universal Mind more clearly than in this parable, or the two classes of error which prevent us from understanding and utilizing this relation.

The younger brother is the man who, not realizing his own spiritual nature, lives on the resources of the lower personality, till their failure to meet his needs drives him to look for something which cannot thus be exhausted, and eventually he finds it in the recognition of his own spiritual being as his inalienable birthright, because he was made in the image and likeness of God, and could not by any possibility have been created otherwise.

Gradually, as he becomes more and more conscious of the full effects of this recognition, he finds that "the Father" advances to meet him, until at last they are folded in each other's arms, and he realizes the true meaning of the words, "I and my Father are ONE." Then he learns that Liberty is in union and not in separation, and realizing his identity with the Infinite he finds that all its inexhaustible stores are open to him.

This is not rhapsody but simple fact, which becomes clear if we see that the only possible action of the undifferentiated Life-Principle must be to always press forward into fuller and fuller expression of itself, in particular forms of life, *in strict accordance with the conditions which each form provides for its manifestation.* And when any one thoroughly grasps this principle of the differentiation through form of an entirely undistributed universal potential, then he will see that the mode of differentiation depends on the direction in which the specializing entity is reaching out.

If he further gets some insight into the boundless possibilities which must result from this, he will realize the necessity, before all things, of seeking to reproduce in individuality that Harmonious Order which is the foundation of the universal system.

And, since he cannot particularize the whole Infinite at a single stroke, which would be a mathematical impossibility, he utilizes its boundless stores by particularizing, from moment to moment, the specific desires, powers, and attractions, which at that moment he requires to employ.

And, since the Energy from which he draws is infinite in quantity and unspecialized in quality, there is no limit either of extent or kind to the purposes for which he may employ it. But he can only do this by abiding in "the Father's" house, and by conforming to the rule of the house which is the Law of Love.

This is the only restriction, if it can be called a restriction to avoid using our powers injuriously; and this restriction becomes self-obvious, when we consider that the very thing which puts us in possession of this limitless power of drawing from the Infinite is the recognition of our identity with the Universal One, and that any employment of our powers to the intentional injury of others is in itself a direct denial of that "unity of the Spirit which is the bond of peace."

The binding power (religio) of Universal Love is thus seen to be inherent in the very nature of the Liberty, which we attain by the Knowledge of the Truth; but except this there is no other restriction. Why? Because, by the very hypothesis of the case, we are employing First Cause when we consciously use our creative power with the knowledge that our Thought is the *individual* action of the same Spirit which, in its universal action, is both the Cause and the Being of every mode of manifestation; for the great fact which distinguishes First Cause from secondary causation is its entire independence of all *conditions,* because it is not the outcome of conditions but itself creates them—it produces its own conditions step by step as it goes along.*

If, therefore, the Law of Love be taken as the foundation, *any* line of action can be worked out successfully and profitably; but this does not alter the fact that a higher degree of intelligence will see a much wider field of action than a lower one, and, therefore, if our field of activity is to grow, it can only be as the result of the growth of our intelligence; and, consequently, the first use we should make of our power of drawing from the Infinite should be for steady growth in understanding.

Life is the capacity for action and enjoyment, and, therefore, any extension of the field for the exercise of our capacities is an increase of our own livingness and enjoyment, and so the continual companionship of the Spirit of Truth, leading us into continually expanding perception of the limitless possibilities that are open to ourselves and to the whole race, is the supreme Vivifying Influence; and thus we find that the Spirit of Truth is identical with the Spirit of Life.

It is this consciousness of companionship that is the Presence of the Father; and it is in returning to this Presence and dwelling in it that we get back to the Source of our own spiritual nature, and so find ourselves in possession of boundless possibilities without any fear of misusing them, because we do not seek to be possessors of the Divine Power without being possessors of the Divine Love and Wisdom also.

---

* For fuller explanation regarding our use of First Cause, see my *Edinburgh Lectures on Mental Science.*

And the elder brother is the man who has not thrown off the Divine guidance as the younger had done, but who has realized it only in the light of a restriction. Always his question is "Within what limits may I act?" and, consequently, starting with the idea of limitation, he finds limitation everywhere; and thus, though he does not go into a far country like his brother, he relegates himself to a position no better than that of a servant—his wages are measured by his work, his creeds, his orthodoxies, his limitations of all sorts and descriptions, which he imagines to be of Divine appointment, while all the time he has imported them himself.

But him also "the Father" meets with the gracious words, "Son, thou art *ever* with me, and all that I have *is* thine"; and, therefore, as soon as this elder brother becomes sufficiently enlightened to perceive that all the elements of restriction in his beliefs, save only the Law of Love, have no place in the ultimate reality of *Life,* he too re-enters the house, now no longer as a servant but as a son, and joins in the festival of everlasting joy.

We find the same lesson in the parable of the Talents. The use of the powers and opportunities we have, just where we are *now,* naturally opens up sequences by which still further opportunities, and, consequently, higher development of our powers become possible; and these higher developments in their turn open the way to yet further expansion, so that there is no limit to the process of growth other than what we set to it by denying or doubting the principle of growth in ourselves, which is what is meant by the servant burying his talent in the earth.

"The lord" is the Living Principle of Evolution which obtains equally on all planes, and nothing has been more fully established by science than the Law that as soon as progress stops retrogression begins, so that it is only by continual advance we can escape the penalty with which Professor Aytoun threatens us in his humorous verses, that we shall

*"Return to the monad from which we all sprang,*
*Which nobody can deny."*

But on the other hand, the employment of our faculties and opportunities, so far as we realize them, is, by the same Law, certain to produce its own reward. By being faithful over a few things we shall become rulers over many things, for God is not unmindful to forget your labor of love, and so day by day we shall enter more and more fully into the joy of our Lord.

The same idea is repeated in the parable of the man who contrived to get into the wedding feast without the wedding garment. The Divine Marriage is the attainment by the individual mind of conscious union with the Universal Mind or "the Spirit"; and the feast, as in the parable of the Prodigal Son, signifies the joy which results from the attainment of Perfect Liberty, which means power over all the resources of the universe, whether within us or around us.

Now, as I have already pointed out, the only way in which this power can be used safely and profitably is through that recognition of its Source, which makes it in all points subservient to the Law of Love, and this was precisely what the intruder did not realize. He is the type of the man who fails in exactly the opposite way to the servant who buries his Lord's talent in the earth. This man has cultivated his powers to the uttermost, and so is able to enter along with the other guests. He has attained that Knowledge of the Laws of the spiritual side of Nature (which gives him a place at that Table of the Lord, which is the storehouse of the Infinite; but he has missed the essential point of all his Knowledge, the recognition that the Law of Power is one with the Law of Love, and so, desiring to separate the Divine Power from the Divine Love, and to grasp the one while rejecting the other, he finds that the very Laws of which he has made himself master, by his knowledge, overwhelm him with their own tremendousness, and by their reflex action become the servants who bind him hand and foot, and cast him into the outer darkness. The Divine Power can never be separated with impunity from the Divine Love and Guidance.

The parable of the unjust steward is based upon the Law of the subjective nature of individual life. As in all the parables, "the lord" is the supreme Self-evolving Principle of the universe, which, relatively to us, is purely subjective, because it acts in and through ourselves. As such it follows the invariable Law of subjective mind, which is that of response to any suggestion that is impressed upon it with sufficient power.*

Consequently, "the lord" does not dispute the correctness of the accounts rendered by the steward, but, on the contrary, commends him for his wisdom in recognizing the true principle by which to escape the results of his past mal-administration of the estate.

---

* I have discussed this subject at greater length in my *Edinburgh Lectures on Mental Science.*

St. Paul tells us that he is truly approved "whom the Lord commendeth," and the commendation of the steward is unequivocally stated by Jesus, and, therefore, we must realize that we have here the statement of some principle which harmonizes with the Life-giving tendency of the Universal Spirit. And this principle is not far to seek. It is the acceptance by "the Lord" of less than the full amount due to Him.

It is the statement of Ezekiel xviii. 22, that if the wicked man forsake his way "he shall surely live and not die. All his transgressions that he hath committed shall not be mentioned unto him; in his righteousness that he hath done he shall live." It is what the Master speaks of as agreeing with the adversary while we are still in the way with him; in other words, it is the recognition that because the Laws of the universe are not vindictive but simply causal, therefore, the reversal of our former mis-employment of First Cause, which in our case is our Thought demonstrated in a particular line of action, must necessarily result in the reversal of all those evil consequences which would otherwise have flowed from our previous wrongdoing.

I have enlarged in a previous chapter on the operation of the Law of Suggestion with regard to the question of sacrifice; and when we either see that the Law of Sacrifice culminates in No Sacrifice, or reach the place where we realize that a Great and Sufficient Sacrifice has been offered up once for all, then we have that solid ground of suggestion which results in the summing-up of the whole Gospel in the simple words, "Don't do it again."

If we once realize the great truth stated in Psalm xviii. 26 and II. Samuel xxii. 27, that the Divine Universal Spirit always becomes to us exactly the correlative of our own principle of action, and that it does so naturally by the Law of Subjective Mind, then it must become clear that it can have no vindictive power in it, or, as the Bible expresses it, "Fury is not in Me" (Isaiah xxvii. 9).

But for the very same reason we cannot trifle with the Great Mind by trying to impress one character upon it by our thought, while we are impressing another upon ourselves by our actions. This is to show our ignorance of the nature of the Law with which we are dealing; for a little consideration will show us that we cannot impress two opposite suggestions at the same time. The man who tried to do so is described in the parable of the servant, who threw his fellow-servant into prison after his own debt had been cancelled. The previous pardon availed him nothing, and he was cast into prison till he should pay the uttermost farthing.

The meaning becomes evident when we see that what we are dealing with is the supreme Law of our own being. We do not really believe what we do not act up to; if, therefore, we cast our fellow-servant into prison, no amount of philosophical speculation in an opposite direction will set us at liberty. Why? Because our action demonstrates that our real belief is in limitation. Such compulsion can only proceed from the idea that we shall be the poorer, if we do not screw the money out of our fellow-servant, and this is to deny our own power of drawing from the Infinite in the most emphatic manner, and so to destroy the whole edifice of Liberty.

We cannot impress upon ourselves too strongly the impossibility of living by two contradictory principles at the same time. And the same argument holds good when we conceive that the debt is due to our injured feelings, our pride, and the like—the principle is always the same; it is that perfect Liberty places us above the reach of all such considerations, because by the very hypothesis of being absolute freedom, it can create far more rapidly than any of our fellow-servants can run up debts; and our attitude towards those who are thus running up scores should be to endeavor to lead them into that region of fulness where the relation of debtor and creditor cannot exist, because it becomes merged in the radiation of creative power.

But perhaps the most impressive of all the parables was that in which, on the night when He was betrayed, the Master expressed the great mystery of God and Man by symbolic action rather than by words, girding Himself with a towel and washing the disciples' feet. He assured Peter that though the meaning of this symbolic act was not apparent at the time, it should become clear later on.

A wonderful light is thrown on this dramatization of a great principle by comparing it with the Master's utterance in Luke xiii. 35–37. The idea of girding is very conspicuous in that parable. First, we are bidden to have our loins girded and our lights burning, like unto men that wait for their Lord. Then we are told that, if the servants are found thus prepared, when the Lord does come *the positions will be reversed,* and He will make *them* sit down and will gird Himself and serve *them.*

Now, what Jesus in this parable taught in words, He taught on the night of the Last Supper in acts. There is a strict parallel; in both cases the

Master, the Lord, girds Himself and serves those who had hitherto accounted themselves His servants. The emphatic reduplication of this parable shows that here we have something of the very highest importance presented to us; and, undoubtedly, it is the veiled statement of the supreme mystery of individual being. And this mystery is the raising to the highest spiritual levels of the old maxim that Nature will obey us in proportion as we first obey Nature. This is the ordinary rule of all science. The universal principles can never act contrary to themselves, whether on the spiritual or the physical level, and, therefore, unless we are prepared by study of the Law and obedience to it, we cannot make use of these principles at any level; but granted such preparation on our part, and the Law becomes our humble servant, obeying us in every particular on the one condition that we first obey it.

It is thus that modern science has made us masters of a world of power which, for all practical purposes, did not exist in the times of the Tudors; and, transferring this truth to the highest and innermost, to the very Principle of Life itself, the meaning becomes plain. Because the Life-Principle is not something separate from ourselves, but is the Supporter of our individuality, therefore, the more we understand and obey its great *generic* Law, the more fully shall we be able to make any *specific* applications of it that we like. But on one condition. We must be washed. "If I wash thee not thou hast no part with Me," were the words of the Master. He spoke as the conscious mouthpiece of the Universal Spirit, and this must, therefore, be taken as the personal utterance of the Spirit itself; and seen in this light the meaning becomes clear; we must first be cleansed by the Spirit.

And here we meet with another symbolical fact of the highest importance. This dramatization of the final truth of spiritual knowledge took place after the supper was ended. Now, as we all know, the supper was itself of supreme symbolical significance. It was the Jewish Passover and the Christian Commemoration, and tradition tells us it was also the symbolic act by which, throughout antiquity, the highest initiates signified their identical realization of Truth, however apparently separated by outward forms or nationality.

We find these mystical emblems of bread and wine presented to Abraham by Melchizedek, himself the type of the man who has realized the supreme truth of the birth which is "without father, without mother, without beginning of days or end of years"; and, therefore, if we would grasp the full meaning of the Master's action on that last night, we must understand the meaning of the symbolic meal of which He and His followers had just partaken. Briefly stated, it is the recognition by the participant of his unity with, and power of appropriating, the Divine in its twofold mode of Spirit and Substance.

Science and Religion are not two separate things. They both have the same object, to bring us nearer and nearer to the point where we shall find ourselves in touch with the ONE Universal Cause. Therefore, the two were never dissociated by the greatest thinkers of antiquity, and the inseparableness of energy and matter, which is now recognized by the most advanced science as the starting-point of all its speculations, is none other than the old, old doctrine of the identity of Spirit and ultimate Substance.

Now, it is this twofold nature of the Universal First Cause that is symbolized by bread and wine. The fluid and the solid, or Spirit and Substance, as the two universal supports of all manifested Forms—these are the universal principles which the two typical elements signify. But in order that the individual may be consciously benefited by them, he must recognize his own participation in them, and he denotes his Knowledge on this point by eating the bread and drinking the wine; and his intention in so doing is to signify his recognition of two great facts; one, that he lives by continually drawing from the Infinite Spirit in its twofold unity; and the other, that he not only does this automatically, but also has power to consciously differentiate the Universal Energy for any specific purpose that he will.

Now, this combination of dependence and control could not be more perfectly symbolized than by the acts of eating and drinking—we cannot do without food, but it is at our own discretion to select what and when we shall eat. And if we realize the true meaning of "the Christ," we shall see that it is that principle of Perfected Humanity which is the highest expression of the Universal Spirit-Substance; and taken in this sense, the bread and wine are fitting emblems of the flesh and blood, or Substance and Spirit, of "the Son of Man," the ideal Type of all Humanity.

And so it is that we cannot realize the Eternal Life except by consciously partaking of the innermost Life-Principle, with due recognition of its true nature—not meaning the mere observance of a ceremonial rite, however august in its associations, and however useful as a powerful suggestion; but meaning personal recognition of the Supreme Truth which that rite signifies.

This, then, was the meaning of the symbolic meal which had just concluded. It indicated the participant's recognition of his union with the Universal Spirit, as being the supreme fact on which his individual life was based, the ultimate of all Truth. Now, the word rendered "washed," in John xiii. 10, is more correctly given in the Revised Version as "bathed," a word which signifies total immersion. But no "bathing" had taken place on this occasion; to what, then, did Jesus allude when He spoke to His disciples as men who had been "bathed"? It is precisely that which, in Ephesians v. 26, is spoken of as "the washing of water by the word"; "water" being, as we have already seen, the Universal Substance, and "the word" the synonym for that Intelligence which is the very essence of Spirit. The meaning, then, is that by partaking of this symbolic meal they had signified their recognition of their own total immersion in the ONE Universal Divine Being, which is at once both Spirit and Substance; and since they could not conceive of It otherwise than as Most Holy, this recognition must thenceforward have a purifying influence upon the whole man.

This great recognition does not need to be repeated—seen once it is seen for ever; and, therefore, "he that is washed needeth not save to wash his feet, but is clean every whit." But though the principle is grasped—which, of course, is the substantial foundation of the new life—immediate perfection does not follow. Very far from it. And so we have to come day by day to the Spirit, for the washing away of those stains which we contract in our daily walk through life. "If we say that we have no sin, the truth is not in us; but if we confess our sin, He is faithful and just to forgive us our sin and to cleanse us from all unrighteousness."

It is this daily confession, not to man, but to the Divine Spirit Itself, which produces the daily cleansing, and thus Its first service to us is to wash our feet. If we thus receive the daily washing, we shall, day by day, put away from us that sense of separation from the Divine Universal Mind, which only the conscious retention of guilt in the heart can produce, after once we have been "bathed" by the recognition of our individual relation to It; and if our study of the Bible has taught us anything, it has taught us that the very Essence of Life is in its identity and unity throughout all forms of manifestation.

To allow ourselves, therefore, to remain conscious of separation from the Spirit of the Whole is to accept the idea of Disintegration, which is the very principle of death; and if we thus accept death at the fountain-head, it must necessarily spread through the whole stream of our individual existence and poison the waters. But it is inconceivable that any one who has once realized the Great Unity, should ever again willingly remain in conscious separation from it, and, therefore, immediate open-hearted approach to the Divine Spirit is the ever ready remedy as soon as any consciousness of separation makes itself felt.

And the symbol includes yet another meaning. If the bathing or total immersion signifies our unity with the Spirit of the Whole, then the washing of the feet must signify the same thing in a lesser degree, and the meaning implied is the ever-present attendance of the Infinite Undifferentiated Spirit ready to be differentiated by us to any daily service, no matter how lowly. Seen in this light, this acted parable is not a mere reminder of our imperfection, which, unless corrected by a sense of power, could only be a perpetual suggestion of weakness that would incapacitate us from doing anything; but it indicates our continual command over all the resources of the Infinite, for every object that all the endless succession of days can ever bring before us. We may draw from it what we like, when we like, and for what purpose we like; nothing can prevent us but ignorance or consciousness of separation.

The idea thus graphically set forth, was expanded throughout that marvellous discourse with which the Master's ministry in His mortal body terminated. As ever, His theme was the perfect Liberty of the individual resulting from recognition of our true relation to the Universal Mind. The ONE great I AM is the Vine, the lesser ones are the branches. We cannot bear fruit except we abide in the Vine; but abiding in it there is no limit to the developments we may attain.

The Spirit of Truth will guide us into *all* Truth, and the possession of all Truth must carry the possession of all Power along with it; and since the Spirit of Truth can be none other than the Spirit of Life, to be guided into all Truth must be to be guided into the Power of an endless life.

This does not need our removal from the world: "I pray not that Thou shouldest take them out of the world, but that Thou shouldest keep them from the evil." What is needed is ceasing to eat of that poisonous fruit, the tasting of which expelled Man from the Paradise he is designed to inhabit. The true recognition of the ONE leaves no place for any other; and if we follow the Master's direction not to estimate things by their superficial appearance, but by their central principle of being, then we shall find that nothing is evil in essence, and that the origin of evil is always in a wrong application of what is good in itself, thus bringing us back to the declaration of the first chapter of Genesis, that God saw all that He had created, "and behold it was very good."

If, then, we realize that our Liberty resides in the creative power of our Thought, we shall see the immense importance of recognizing the essence of things as distinguished from the misplaced order in which we often first become acquainted with them. If we let our Thought dwell on an inverted order we perpetuate that order; but if, going below the surface, we fix our Thought upon the essential nature of things, and see that it is logically impossible for anything to be *essentially* bad which is a specific expression of the Universal Good, then we shall in our Thought call all things good, and so help to bring about that golden age when the old inverted order shall have passed away, and a new world of joy and liberty shall take its place.

This, then, is briefly the line followed by the Master's teaching, and His miracles were simply the natural outcome of His perfect recognition of His own principles. Already the unfolding recognition of these principles is beginning to produce the same results at the present day, and the number of well-authenticated cures effected by mental means increases every year. And this is precisely in accordance with Jesus' own prediction. He enumerated the signs which should follow those who really believed what He really taught, and in so saying He was simply making a statement of cause and effect. He never set up His power as proof of a nature different from our own; on the contrary, He said that those who learned what He taught should eventually be able to do still greater miracles, and He summed up the whole position in the words, "the disciple when he is perfected shall be as his Master."

Again, He laid special stress on the perfect naturalness of all that He taught, by guarding us against the error of supposing that the intervention of any intermediary was required between us and "the Father." If we could assign such a position to any being it would be to Himself, but He emphatically disclaims it. "In that day ye shall ask in My name; *and I say not unto you that I will pray the Father for you,* for the Father Himself loveth you, because ye have loved Me and believed that I came forth from the Father" (John xvi. 26). If the student has realized what has been said in the chapter on "the Sacred Name," he will see that the opening words of this utterance can be nothing else than a statement of universal Truth; and that the love and belief in Himself, spoken of in the concluding clause, are the love of this Truth exhibited in its highest form as Man evolved to perfection, and belief in the power of the Spirit to produce such an evolution.

I do not say that there is nothing personal in the statement; on the contrary, it is eminently personal to "the Man Christ Jesus," but as the Type of Perfected Humanity—the first-fruit of the further evolution which is to complete the pyramid of manifested being upon earth by the introduction of the Fifth Kingdom, which is that of the Spirit.

When we realize what is accomplished in Him, we see what is potential in ourselves; and since we have now reached the point beyond which any further evolution can only result from our conscious cooperation with the evolutionary principle, all our future progress depends on the extent to which we do recognize the potentialities contained in our own individuality.

Therefore, to realize the manifestation of the Divine which Jesus stands for, and to love it, is the indispensable condition for attaining that access to "the Father" which means the full development in ourselves of all the powers of the Spirit.

The point which rivets our attention in this utterance of the Master's is the fact that we do not need the intervention of any third party to beseech "the Father" for us, because "the Father" Himself loves us. This statement, which we may well call the greatest of all the teachings of Jesus, setting us free, as it does, from the cramping influences of a limited and imperfect theology, He has bracketed together with the recognition of Himself; and therefore, if we would follow His teaching, we cannot separate these two things which He has joined; but if we realize in Him the embodiment of the Divine Ideal of Humanity, His meaning becomes clear—it is that our recognition of this ideal is itself the very thing that places us in immediate touch with "the Father."

By accepting the Divine Ideal as our own, we *provide the conditions* under which the Undifferentiated Universal Subconscious Mind becomes able to differentiate Itself into the particular and concrete expression of that Potential of Personality which is eternally inherent in It; and thus, in each one who realizes the Truth which the Master taught, the Universal Mind attains an individualization capable of consciously recognizing Itself.

To attain this is the great end of Evolution, and in thus gaining Its end the ONE becomes the MANY, and the MANY return into the ONE; not by an absorption depriving them of individual identity, which would be to stultify the entire operation of the Spirit in Evolution by simply ending where it had begun, but by impressing upon innumerable individualities the perfect and completed likeness of that Original in the *potential* image of which they were first created.

The entire Bible is the unfolding of its initial statement that Man is made in the image of God, and the teaching of Jesus is the proclamation and demonstration of this Truth in its complete development, the Individual rejoicing in perfect Life and Liberty because of his conscious ONE-ness with the Universal.

The teaching of Jesus, whether by word or deed, may, therefore, be summed up as follows. He says in effect to each of us: What you really are in essence is a concentration of the ONE Universal Life-Spirit into conscious Individuality—if you live from the recognition of this Truth as your starting-point, it makes you Free. You cannot do this so long as you imagine that you have one centre and the Infinite another—you can only do it by recognizing that the two centres coincide, and that That which, as being Infinite, is incapable of centralization in Itself, finds centre in you.

Think of these things until you see that it is impossible for them to be otherwise, and then step forward in perfect confidence, knowing that the universal principles must necessarily act with the same mathematical precision in yourself, that they do in the attractions of matter or in the vibrations of ether. His teaching is identical with the teaching of Moses, that there is only ONE Being anywhere, and that the various degrees of its manifested consciousness are to be measured by one standard—the recognition of the meaning of the words I AM.

I have endeavored to show that the Bible is neither a collection of traditions belonging only to a petty tribe, nor yet a statement of dogmas which can give no account of themselves beyond the protestation that they are mysteries which must be accepted by faith—which faith, when we come to analyze it, consists only in accepting the bare assertion of those very persons who, when we ask them for the explanation of the things they bid us believe, are unable to give any explanation beyond the word "MYSTERY."

The true element of Mystery we shall never get rid of, for it is inherent in the ultimate nature of all things; but it is an element that perpetually unfolds, inviting us at each step to still further inquiry by satisfactorily and intelligently answering every question that we put in really logical succession, and thus the Mystery continually opens out into Meaning and never pulls us up short with an anathema for our irreverence in daring to inquire into Divine secrets.

When the interrogated is driven to the fulmination of anathemas, it is very plain that he has reached the end of his tether. As Byron says in "Don Juan"—

> "*He knew not what to say, and so he swore*";

and therefore this mode of answering a question always indicates one of two things, ignorance of the subject or intentional concealment of facts, and on either alternative, any "authority" which thus only tells us to "shut up" thereby at once loses all claim to our regard. Every undiscovered fact in the great Universal Order is a Divine Secret until we find the key that unlocks it; but the Psalmist tells us that the secret of the Lord is with them that fear Him, and the Master says that there is nothing hidden that shall not be revealed.

To seek, therefore, to understand the great principles on which it is written, so far from being an act of presumption, is the most practical proof we can give of our reverence for the Sacred Volume; and if the foregoing pages have in any way helped the reader to see in the Bible a statement of the working of Laws, which are inherent in the nature of things and follow an intelligible sequence of cause and effect, my purpose in writing will be answered.

The limited space at my disposal has allowed me only to treat the whole subject in an introductory manner, and in particular I have not yet shown the method by which the ONE Universal Principle follows out an *exclusive* line of unfoldment, building up a "Chosen People" by a process of *natural selection* culminating in the Great Central Figure of the Gospels. It does this without in any way departing from its *universal* character, for it is that Power which cannot deny itself; but it does it as a consequence of this very universality, and upon the importance of this specialized action of the Universal Principle to the future development of the race, it is impossible to lay too much stress.

The Bible tells us that there is such a special selection, and if we have found truth in its more general statements, we may reasonably expect to find the same truth in its more specialized statements also.

XI

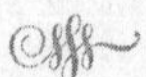

# THE FORGIVENESS OF SIN

In the preceding chapters I have dealt principally with the teaching of the Bible regarding the *reciprocity* of being between God and man, that ultimate spiritual nature of man which affords the *generic* basis in *all* men upon which the Spirit of God can work to produce the further *specific* development of the individual. But if we stop short at the recognition of this merely generic similarity we are liable to be led into an erroneous course of reasoning resulting in logical conclusions the very opposite of all that the Bible is seeking to teach us—in a word we shall be led into an atheism far deeper than that of the mere materialist in that it is on the spiritual plane, the inverted development of the supreme principle of our nature.

Such a dire result comes from a one-sided view of things, a knowledge of certain truths without the knowledge of their counterbalancing truths, and the counter-balancing truth which will preserve us from so great a calamity is contained in the Bible teaching regarding the forgiveness of sin.

Once grant that there is such a thing as the forgiveness of sin, and the root of all possible spiritual inversion is logically cut away, for then there must be One who is able and willing to forgive, and who is therefore the object of worship and is capable of entering into a specific, conscious, personal relation to us. It is therefore important to realize what the Bible teaching on this subject is.

The logic of it is sufficiently simple if we grant the premises on which it starts. It is that man, by his essential and true innermost nature, is a being fitted and intended to live in uninterrupted intercourse with the All-creating Spirit, thus continually receiving a ceaseless inflow of life from this infinite source. At the same time it is impossible for a being capable of thus partaking of the infinite life of the Originating Spirit to be a mere piece of mechanism, mechanically incapable of moving in more than one direction; for if he is to reproduce in his individuality that power of origination and initiative which must be the very essence of the Creative Spirit's recognition of itself he must possess a corresponding liberty of choice as to the way in which he will use his powers; and if he chooses wrongly the inevitable law of cause and effect must produce the natural consequences of his choice.

The nature of this wrong choice is told us in the allegorical story of "the Fall." It is mistaking the sequence of laws which necessarily proceeds from any creative act for the creative power itself; the error of looking upon secondary causes as the originating cause and not seeing that they are themselves effects of something antecedent which works through them to the production of the ultimate effect. This is the fundamental error, and the opposite truth consists in connecting the ultimate effect intended *directly* with the intention of the originating intelligence, and (from this point of view) excluding all consideration of the chain of intermediary causes which links these two extremes together.

The exact weighing and balancing and calculating of the action of secondary causes, or particular laws of *relation,* has its proper place—it is the necessary basis of our work when we are *constructing* anything *from without,* just as an architect could not build a safe house without carefully calculating the strains and thrusts to which his materials would be subjected; but when we are considering an act of *creation* we are dealing with an exactly opposite process, one that works *from within* by a *vital growth* which naturally assimilates to itself all that is necessary for its completion.

In the latter case we do not have to consider the mechanism through which the vital energy brings forth its ultimate fruition, for by the very fact of its being inherent energy working for manifestation in a certain direction it must necessarily produce all those relations, visible or invisible, which go to make the completed whole.

The fundamental error consists in ignoring this distinction between *direct creation* and external construction, in entirely losing sight of the former and consequently attempting to accomplish by knowledge of particular laws, which are applicable only to construction from without, what can only be accomplished by a direct creation which produces laws instead of being restricted by them.

The temptation, then, is to substitute our intellectual knowledge of the relations between various existing laws with which we are acquainted, for that Creative Power which is not subject to any antecedent conditions and can produce what it will, while conforming always to its own recognition of itself as perfectly harmonious Being.* This temptation is a very subtle one. It appeals to our intellect. It appeals to all that we can gather from secondary causes whether in the seen or the unseen, and to all the deductions we can make from those observations. To all appearances it is so entirely reasonable, only its reasoning is restricted to the circle of secondary causation and contemplates the great First Cause as a mere force whose action is limited by certain particular laws.

Looked at superficially it does appear as if this course of reasoning was correct. But in truth it does not take into account the *originating* power of the Creative Spirit, and is in reality a course of reasoning which is only applicable to construction from without and not to growth from within.

Now so long as we do not recognize a Power which can transcend all our past experiences we naturally look to a more extended knowledge of particular laws as the means by which we can attain to a power of control which will at last place us beyond subjection to any control—the general principle involved being that by our knowledge we can balance the positive and negative aspects of law against each other in any proportion we like and become masters of the situation by this method.

Is not this a correct description of much of the teaching we meet with at the present day? and does it not exactly agree with the words of the old allegory, "ye shall be as gods knowing good and evil"?

The ultimate desire of every human being is for more fulness of life—to thoroughly enjoy living—and the more we enjoy living the more we shall naturally desire to live and to enjoy living still more. In a word our true desire, under whatever disguises we may try to conceal it, is to "have life and to have it more abundantly." This desire is innate in us because of our

* See my "Creative Process in the Individual."

*generic* relation to the Spirit of Life, and therefore, so far from being condemned by Scripture, its fulfillment is placed before us as the one object of attainment, and the professed purpose of the Bible is to lead us to seek it in the right way instead of in the wrong one. To seek it in the right way is Righteousness or Rightness. To seek it in the wrong way is the Inversion of Rightness, and is what is meant by Sin.

Those grosser forms of sin, which we all recognize as such, are only the one original transgression of seeking from without what can only come by growth from within when assuming its crudest aspect, but the underlying principle is the same; and so the allegory of the Fall is typical of all sin, of that inverted conception of life which, because it is inverted, must necessarily lead us away from the Spiritual Source of Life instead of towards it. The story is, so to say, a sort of algebraical generalization of the factors concerned.

When this becomes clear to us we begin to see the necessity for the removal of sin. We see that hitherto we have been trying to live by an inverted conception of the principle of Life, whether this wrong conception has shown itself in crude and gross forms, or more subtly in the purely intellectual region.

In either case the result is the same, the consciousness that we have not free intercourse with the Spiritual Source of Life, and as this dawns upon us we instinctively feel the need of some other way than the one we have been hitherto pursuing. We find that what we want is not Knowledge but Love. And this is logical, for in the last analysis we shall find that Love is the only Creative Power.*

Then we perceive that what we require for the perpetuation and continual increase of our individual life is a mental attitude which renders us perpetually and increasingly receptive of the Creative Love, the consciousness of a personal and individual relation to it beyond, and in addition to, our merely generic relation as items in the cosmic whole.

Then something must be done to assure us of this specific relation, to assure us that neither our erroneous thoughts in the past, nor yet the erroneous action to which they have given rise, can separate us from this Love, either by making it turn away from us, or by a law of cause and effect proceeding from our wrong thoughts and acts themselves. And to give us such

---

* See "The Creative Process in the Individual."

a confidence we require to be assured that the initiative movement proceeds from the side of the Divine Spirit; for if we suppose that the initiative starts from *our* side then we can have no assurance that it has been accepted, or that the law of "Karma" is not dogging our steps.

It is this misconception of pacifying the Almighty by an initiative originating on *our* side that shows itself in penances, sacrifices, and various rites and ceremonies, at the end of which we do not know whether our operations have been successful, or whether through deficiency in quantity or quality they have failed of the desired result.

All such performances are vitiated by the inherent defect of making the first move towards reconciliation come from *our* side—it is nothing else than carrying into our highest spiritual yearnings the old error of trying to produce by working from without what can only be produced by growth from within—we are still substituting the constructive process for the creative.

Accordingly, the Bible tells us that the fundamental proposition that there is such a thing as forgiveness of sin is enunciated by God Himself; and so we find that the story of the Fall includes the promise of One by whom man shall be redeemed and released from sin, and brought into conscious realization of that reciprocal intercourse with the Source of Life which is the essence of his innermost being. Man is told to look to the Divine promise of forgiveness, and from this point onwards belief in this promise is set forth as the way by which sin and its consequences are effectually removed.

I sometimes meet with those who object to the teaching that there is forgiveness. To such I would say, Why do you object to this teaching? Of course, if you are entirely without sin you have no need of it for yourself, but then you are a very rare exception, and at the same time beastly selfish not to consider all the rest of us who are of the more ordinary sort. Or if you put it that everybody is without sin, then the newspapers of all countries flatly contradict you with their daily details of thefts, murders, swindles, and the like.

But perhaps you will say that sin must be punished. Why *must?* What is the object of punishment? Its purpose is to rub it well in, so that the offender may not do it again for fear of consequences. But supposing he has become convinced of the true nature of his offence so as to hate it for its own sake and to shrink from it with abhorrence, what then is to be gained by going on whacking him? The change in his own view of things has already accomplished all, and more than all, that any amount of whacking could do, and this is the teaching of the Bible. Its purpose is to see sin in its true light as severance from the Source of Life, and if this has been accomplished why should punishment be prolonged?

Again, the conception of a God who *will* not forgive sin when repented of is the conception of a monstrosity. It is the conception of the Spirit of Life determining to deal death, when by its very nature it must be seeking to express Life to the fullest extent that the expressing vehicle will admit of; and repentance is turning away from something that had previously hindered this fuller expression. Therefore such a conception is illogical, for it implies the Spirit of Life acting in opposition to itself. Also such a God ceases to be the object of worship, for there is nothing to be gained by worshipping Him. He can only be the object of our fear and hatred.

On the other hand the conception of a God who *cannot* forgive sin is the conception of no God at all. It is the conception of a mere Force, and you cannot enter into a personal relation with unintelligent forces—you can only study them scientifically and utilize them so far as your knowledge of their law admits; and this logically brings you back to your own knowledge and power as your only source of life, so that in this case also there is nothing to worship.

If, then, there is such a mental attitude as that of worship, the looking to an Infinite Source of life and joy and strength, it can only be based upon the recognition that this All-creating Spirit is able to forgive sin and desires to do so.

We may therefore say that the conception of itself as pardoning all who ask for pardon is necessarily an integral portion of the Spirit's self-recognition in its relation to the human race, and the inherentness of this idea is set forth in Scripture in such phrases as "the Lamb of God that taketh away the sin of the world," and "the Lamb slain from the foundation of the world," thus pointing to an aspect of the Spirit's self-contemplation exactly reciprocal to the need of all who desire to be set free from that inversion of their true nature which, while it continues, must necessarily prevent their unimpeded access to the Spirit of Life.

Then, since the Divine self-conception is bound to work out into realization, a supreme manifestation of this eternal principle is the legitimate outcome of all that we can conceive of the creative working of the Spirit when viewed from the particular standpoint of the existence of sin in the world, and so the appearing of One who should give complete expression in space and time to the Spirit's recognition of human needs by a supreme act of self-sacrificing Love reasonably forms the grand centre of the whole teaching of the Bible.

The Great Sacrifice is the self-offering of Love to meet the requirements of the soul of man. Our psychological constitution requires it, and it is adequately adapted to fit in with every aspect of our mental nature, whether in the least or the most advanced members of the race. It is the supreme manifestation of that Love which is the Original Creative Power, and the Bible presents it to us as such.

Hear Christ's own description of it: "Greater love hath no man than this, that a man lay down his life for his friends"—"God so loved the world that He sent His only begotten Son into the world, that whosoever believeth on Him should not perish but should have everlasting life."

All is attributed to Love on the one hand and Belief on the other—the Creating Spirit and the simple reception of it—thus meeting exactly those conditions which we found to constitute the conditions for vital growth from within as distinguished from mechanical construction from without, and therefore not depending on our knowledge but on our faith.

Nor is this conception of the forgivingness of the All-originating Love to be found in the New Testament only. If we turn to the Old Testament we find such statements as the following: "And the Lord descended in a cloud and stood with him (Moses) there, and proclaimed the Name of the Lord. And the Lord passed by and proclaimed, The Lord, the Lord God, merciful and gracious, long-suffering and abundant in goodness and truth, keeping mercy for thousands, forgiving iniquity, transgression, and sin" (Ex. xxxiv. 5–7). "I, even I, am he that blotteth out thy transgressions *for my own sake,* and will not remember thy sins" (Isaiah xliii. 25). "I have blotted out as a thick cloud thy transgressions, and as a cloud thy sins; return unto me, for I have redeemed thee" (Isaiah xliv. 22). "If the wicked will turn from all his sins that he hath committed, and keep my statutes, and do that which is lawful and right, he shall surely live, he shall not die. All his transgressions that he hath committed they shall not be mentioned unto him; in his righteousness that he hath done he shall live" (Ezek. xviii. 21–22).

No doubt on the other hand there are threatenings against sin; but the whole tenour of the Bible is clear, that these threatenings apply only so long as we continue to do evil. Both the promises and the threatenings are nothing else than the statement of that Law of Correspondence with which my readers are no doubt sufficiently familiar—the great creative law by which spiritual causes produce their analogues in the outer world, and which is identically the same law whether it works positively or negatively.

The phrase, "for my own sake," in Isaiah xliii. 25, should be noted, as it exactly bears out what I have said about the inherent quality of forgiveness as forming a necessary part of the Creating Spirit's conception of itself in its relation to the human race. This is the fundamental basis of the whole matter, and this truth has been dimly perceived by all the great religions of the world; in fact, it is just the perception of this truth that distinguishes a *religion* from a mere philosophy on the one hand and from magical rites on the other, and I think I cannot end this chapter more suitably than by a quotation which shows how, ages before Christianity was known to them, our rude Norse ancestors had at least some adumbration that the supreme offering must be that of the Divine Love to itself. The passage occurs in the Elder Edda, where O-din, the Supreme God, addresses himself while hanging in self-sacrifice in Vgdrasil the Cosmic Tree:

"*I knew that I hung*
*In the wind-rocked tree*
*Nine whole nights,*
*Wounded with a spear,*
*And to O-din offered,*
*Myself to myself,*
*On that tree*
*Of which no one knows*
*From what root it springs.*"

(From *Strange Survivals* by BARING GOULD.)

XII

# FORGIVENESS

## *Its Relation to Healing and to the State of the Departed in the Other World*

IF WE HAVE NOW grasped some conception of forgiveness as one of the essential qualities of the All-Creating Spirit it will throw some light on several occasions when Jesus accompanied His miracles of healing with the words, "Thy sins are forgiven."

There must have been some intimate connection between the forgiveness and the healing, and though the exact nature of this connection may be beyond our present perception, involving relations of cause and effect too deep for our imperfect powers of analysis, still we can see in a general way that it is in accordance with the teaching of the Bible on the subject.

The Bible is a book about man in his relation to God, and it therefore starts with certain fundamental statements regarding this relation. These are to the effect that death, and consequently disease and decrepitude, are not laws of man's innermost being. How *could* they be? How could the negative be the law of the positive? How could death be the law of Life? Therefore we are told that in the true order of things this is not the case.

The first thing we are told about man is that he is made in the image and likeness of God, the Spirit of Life; therefore capable of manifesting a similar equality of Life. But we must note the words "image" and "likeness." They do not impart identity but resemblance. An "image" implies an original to which it conforms, and so does a "likeness." These words remind us of the passage in which St. Paul speaks of our "Reflecting as a mirror the glory of the Lord," and being thus "transformed into the same image from glory to glory" (2 Cor. iii. 18 R.V.). It is this same idea as in the first chapter of Genesis only expanded so as to show the method by which the image and likeness are produced. It is by Reflection. Our mind is, as is were, a mirror reflecting that towards which it is turned. This is the nature of Mind.

We become like what we contemplate. We cannot avoid it, for we are made that way, and therefore everything depends on what we are in the habit of contemplating. Then if we realize that growth, or the manifestation of the spiritual principle, always proceeds from the innermost to the outermost, by a creative process from within as distinguished from a constructive process from without, we shall see that the working of the mind upon the body and the effect it will produce upon it depends entirely on what form the mind itself is taking; and what form it will take depends on what it is reflecting.

This is the key to the great enigma. In proportion as we reflect the Pure Spirit of Life we live; and in proportion as we reflect the Material, contemplating it as a power in itself instead of as the plastic vehicle of the Spirit, we bring ourselves under a law of limitation which culminates in death. It is the same law of Mind in both cases, only in the one case it is employed positively and in the other negatively.

Something like this seems to be St. Paul's idea when he says that the Law of the Spirit of Life makes him free from the law of sin and death (Rom. viii. 2). It is always this law of mental reflection that is at work within us producing its logical effects, positively or negatively, according to the image which it mirrors forth.

At the risk of appearing tedious I may dwell for a while on the word "image." It is the substantive corresponding to the verb "to image," that is to fashion an "image," or "thought-form" by our mental power of imagery.

Now, as I have endeavored to make clear in my book, *The Creative Process in the Individual*, the life and substance of all things must first subsist as images in the Divine Mind before they can come into manifestation in the world of time and space, much as in Plato's conception of archetypal ideas; therefore we may read the text in Genesis as indicating that Man exists primarily in the Divine conception of him. The real, true Man subsists eternally in the Divine Imagination as the necessary correlative to the Spirit's Self-recognition as all that constitutes Personality.

If the Universal Spirit is to realize in itself the consciousness of Will, the perception of Beauty, and the reciprocity of Love—all in fact that makes life intelligently living—it can do so only by projecting a mental image which will give rise to the corresponding consciousness; and so we may read the text as meaning that Man thus subsists in the Divine image, or creating thought of him. If the reader grasps this idea he will find it throws light upon many otherwise perplexing problems.

This, then, is the real nature of sin. Whatever shape it may take, its essence is always the same; it is turning our mental mirror the wrong way and so reflecting the limited and negative, that which is not Life-in-itself, and consequently forming ourselves into a corresponding image and likeness.

The story of the Fall typifies the essential quality of *all* sin. It is seeking the Living among the dead—trying to build up the skill and power of the worker out of the atoms of the material in which he works; just as though, when you wanted a carpenter, you went into his workshop and tried to make him out of the saw-dust.

Now if we grasp the great fundamental law that our mind, meaning by this our spiritual creative power, attracts conditions which correspond to its own conception of itself, and that its conception of itself must always be the exact reflection of its own dominant thought, then we can in some measure understand why Christ announced forgiveness of sin as the accompaniment of physical healing.

By sin, in the sense we have now seen, death and all lesser evils enter into the world—sin is the cause and they are the effect. Then if the cause is removed the effect must cease, the root of the plant has been cut away, and so the fruit must wither; it is a simple working of cause and effect.

It is true that Jesus is not recorded to have announced forgiveness in every case in which he bestowed healing, and no doubt he had as good reasons for not making the announcement in some cases as for making it in others.

I cannot pretend to analyze those reasons for that would imply a knowledge on my part equal to his own; but from what we do know of psychological laws and of the power of mind over body I might hazard the conjecture that in those cases where he pronounced forgiveness the sufferer apprehended that his sickness was in some way the consequence of his sins, and therefore it was necessary to his bodily healing that he should be assured of their pardon.

In other cases there may not have been such a conviction, and to speak of forgiveness would only withdraw the mind of the sufferer from that immediately receptive attitude which was necessary for the working of the spiritual power.

But who shall say that the principle of the removal of the root of suffering by the forgiveness of sin was not always present in the mind of the august Healer? Rather we may suppose that it always was.

On one occasion he very pointedly put this forward. The proof, he said, that the Son of Man has power on earth to forgive sins is this, I can say to this palsied man, "Arise and walk," and it is accomplished (Luke v. 20). This was what was in the mind of the Great Healer, and comparing it with the general teaching of Scripture on the subject we may reasonably suppose that he always worked from this basic principle, whether the exigencies of the particular case made it, or not, to impress the fact of forgiveness upon the person to be healed.

If we start with the assumption that sickness and death of the body result from imperfect realization of life by the soul, and that the extent and mode of the soul's realization of life is the result of the extent and mode of its realization of union with its Divine Source, then it follows that the logical root of healing must be in the removal of the sense of separation—the removal, that is, of that inverted conception of our relation to the Spirit of Life which is "sin," and the replacing of it by the right conception, in accordance with which we shall more and more fully reflect the true image of "the Father" or Parent Spirit.

When we see this we begin to apprehend more clearly the meaning of St. Paul's words, "There is now no condemnation to them that are in Christ Jesus, which walk not after the flesh but after the Spirit."

Again, there is another phase of this subject which we cannot afford to neglect. Although, as it appears to me, there are grounds for supposing that the *present* resurrection of the body, its transmutation while in the present life into a body of another order, like to the resurrection body of Christ, is not beyond the bounds of possibility, still this supreme victory of the Life-principle is not a thing of general realization; and so we are confronted by the question, What happens on the other side when we get there? I have treated this question at some length in my "Creative Process in the Individual," but I would here refer to it chiefly in connection with the subject of the forgiveness of sin.

Now if, as I apprehend, the condition of consciousness when we pass out of the body is in the majority of cases purely subjective, then from what we know of the laws of subjective mind we may infer that we live there in the consciousness of whatever was our dominant mode of thought during earth life.

We have brought this over with us on parting with our objective mentality, as it operates through its physical instrument the brain, and if this is the case, then the nature of our experiences in the other world will depend on the nature of the dominant thought with which we have left this one, the idea which was most deeply impressed upon our subjective mind.

If this be so, what a stupendous importance it gives to the question whether we do, or do not, believe in the forgiveness of sin. If we pass into the unseen with the fixed idea that no such thing is possible, then what can our subjective experience be but the bearing of a burden of which we can find no way to rid ourselves; for by the conditions of the case all those objective things with which we can now distract our attention will be beyond our reach.

When the loss of our objective mentality deprives us of the power of inaugurating fresh trains of ideas, which practically means new outlooks upon life, we shall find ourselves bound within the memories of our past life on earth, and since the outward conditions, which then colored our view of things, will no longer exist we shall see the motives and feelings which led to our actions in their true light, making us see what it was *in ourselves* rather than in our circumstances which led us to do as we did.

The mode of thought which gave the key to our past life will still be there, and no doubt the memory of particular facts also, for this is what has been most deeply impressed upon our subjective mind; and since by the conditions of the case the consciousness is entirely subjective these memories will appear to be the re-enacting of past things, only now seen in their true nature stripped of all the accessories which gave a false coloring to them.

Of course what the pain of such a compulsory re-enacting of the past life may amount to must depend on what the past life has been; but even in the most blameless life we can well suppose that there have been passages which we would rather not repeat when we saw the mental conditions in ourselves which gave rise to them—not necessarily crimes or grave moral delinquencies, but the shortcomings of the every day respectable life, the unkind words we thought so little of but which cut so deep, the selfishness which perhaps ran on for years, and which, because of that very self-centredness, we did not see dimming the happiness of those around us. These and the like things of even the most blameless life we should not like to be compelled to repeat when seen in their true light, and how much less the episodes of a life which has not been blameless.

That there should be such a re-enacting of past memories is what we might infer from our knowledge of the law of subjective mind, but there are not wanting certain facts of experience which go to support the *a priori* argument.

Many of my readers, I daresay, will smile at the mention of ghosts, but I can assure them there is a good deal of reality in ghosts, especially *to the ghosts themselves.* Remember that if there are such things as ghosts they were once people such as you and I are today, and the practical point is that the reader may be a ghost himself before very long; therefore one of my objects in the present chapter is to show how to avoid becoming a ghost.

I used to laugh at ghosts when I was a young man and thought it all bunkum, but an experience which I went through many years ago entirely changed my ideas on the subject, and indeed was the starting-point of my giving consideration to the laws of the unseen side of things—if it had not been for that ghost you would not be reading this book. However, I will not go into the details here, for the story has already been published both in French and English magazines.

Of course, I don't believe everything I hear, nor do I think that because a thing is in print it is necessarily true—heaven forbid, for then how could I read the daily papers?—but applying to each case the rules of evidence as strictly as though I were trying a man for his life I find a residuum of instances in which it is impossible to come to any other conclusion than that a haunting spirit has actually been seen.

We are often told that you never meet persons who have themselves seen a ghost but only those who know somebody else who has; in other words, you can never get at the actual witness to cross-examine him, but only at hearsay evidence. But I can contradict this entirely.

Since I began to investigate the subject seriously I am surprised at the number of persons of both sexes who have circumstantially related to me their personal experiences of this sort, and have stood the test of careful cross-examination in which I held a brief for the standpoint of "scientific doubt." Therefore, when I say a few words about ghosts I am talking on a subject that I have investigated.

In a large majority of cases it will be found that the spirit appears to be bound to a particular spot and to go on repeating certain actions, and the inference is that the subjective dreaming, so to say, of the departed is in these cases so intense as to create a thought-form of their conception of themselves sufficiently vivid to impress itself upon the etheric atmosphere of the locality and so become visible to those who are sufficiently sensitive.

Now, that this is not always the consequence of some great crime or other terrible happening is shown by a case in which the former owners of a house, husband and wife, after having long been habitually seen about the premises, were at last questioned by a lady who was sufficiently sensitive to communicate with them. They stated that the only thing that bound them to the house was their inordinate love of it during life. They had so centred their minds upon it that now they could not get away though they longed to do so; and, judging by their appearance and the confirmation of their identity subsequently obtained from some old documents, it would seem that they had been tied up like this for several generations.

This is an instance of having rather too much of a "pied-à-terre," and I don't think any of us would like it to become our own case; and *a fortiori* the same must hold good where the recollections of the departed are of a darker kind.

What, then, is the way out of the dilemma? It must be by some working of the law of cause and effect, and this working must take place somewhere within our own mind—we must in some way get a state of consciousness which will set us free from all troubling memories and keep before us, even in the unseen world, the prospect of happier developments.

Then the only mental attitude which can produce this effect is belief in forgiveness, the assurance that all the transgressions and shortcomings of the past have been blotted out for ever. If we attain this realization in this present life, if this assurance is our dominant idea, the idea upon which all our other ideas are based, then by all the laws of mind we are bound to carry this consciousness with us into the other world, and thus find ourselves free from all that would make our existence there unhappy.

Or even if we have not yet attained such a vivid assurance as to be able to say "I know," and can as yet only say "I hope," still the fact that we recognize that the *principle* of forgiveness exists will cause us to lay hold of it as our dominant idea in the subjective state and so place us in a position to gain clearer and clearer perception of the truth that there IS forgiveness, and that it is *for us.*

Perhaps the critical reader may here remark that I am attributing to the subjective mind the power of starting a new train of ideas, and so contradicting what I have just said about the departed being shut up within the circle of those ideas which they have brought over with them from this world. It looks as if I had made a slip, but I haven't; for if we have carried over with us, not perhaps the full assurance of actual pardon, but even the belief that forgiveness is possible, we have brought along with us a root idea whose very essence is that of making a new start.

It is the fundamental conception of a new order, and as such carries with it the conception of ourselves as entering upon new trains of thought and new fields of action—in a word the dominant idea of the subjective mind is that of having brought the objective mental faculties along with it. If this is the mode of self-consciousness then it becomes an actual fact, and the *whole* mentality is brought over in its entirety; so that those who are thus in the light are liberated from imprisonment within the circulus of past memories by the very same law which binds those fast who refuse to admit the liberating principle of forgiveness.

It is the same law of our mental constitution in both cases, only acting affirmatively in the one and negatively in the other, just as an iron ship floats by the identical law by which a solid lump of iron sinks.

Of course we may conceive of degrees in these things. We may well suppose that some may recognize the actual working of forgiveness in their own case less clearly than others; but whatever may be the degree of recognition of the personal fact the realization of the *principle* is the same for all; and this principle must assuredly bear fruit in due time in the complete deliverance of the soul from all that would otherwise hold it in bondage.

Far be it from me to say that the case of those who pass over convinced in their denial of the principle of forgiveness is forever hopeless; but by the nature of mental law they must remain bound until they see it. Moreover by their denial of this principle they must fail to bring over their objective mentality, and so they must remain shut up in the world of their subjective memories until some of those who have brought over their *whole* mentality are able to penetrate the spheres of their subjective mind and impress upon it a new conception, that of forgiveness, and so plant in them the seed for the new growth of their objective mental powers.

And perhaps we may even go so far as to suppose that the power of those who are thus in wholeness of mind to aid those who are not is not confined to such as have passed over; it may be the privilege also of those who are still in the body, for the action of mind upon mind is not a thing of physical substances. If so, then we can see a reason for prayers for the departed, to say nothing of the many instances in which ghosts are reported to have besought the intercession of the living for their liberation. There is, however, in certain quarters a lamentable inversion of this principle where prayers for the departed are turned into an article of traffic and a means of making money. I may have something to say about this in another book, and in the meanwhile I would only say, Beware of spurious imitations.

Of course this picture of the condition of souls in the other world does not profess to be drawn from actual knowledge, but it appears to me to be a reasonable deduction from all that we know of the laws of our mental constitution; and if the experiences of the departed logically result from the working of those laws, then what greater action of the Divine Love and Wisdom can we conceive than such an expression of itself as must utilize these laws affirmatively for our liberation instead of negatively for our bondage. The law of Cause and Effect cannot be broken, but it can be applied with intelligence and love instead of being left to work itself out negatively for want of guidance.

So it is, then, that the doctrine of the forgiveness of sins is the mainspring of the Bible—the promise of a Messiah in the Old Testament and the fulfillment of that promise in the New; and the realization, whether in or out of the body, that God is both able and desiring to forgive, freely and without any offering save that of His own providing, and requiring nothing in return except this—that "to whom much hath been forgiven, the same loveth much."

XIII

# THE DIVINE GIVING

In the last two chapters we have considered the principle of the forgiveness of sin, and having laid this foundation I would now direct attention to the working of the same principle in other directions. In its essence it is the Quality of Givingness—Free Giving, having Simple Accepting for its correlative, for the clear reason that you cannot put a man in possession of a gift if he will not take it. Now a little consideration will show us that Free Givingness is a necessity of the very being of the All-Originating Spirit. By the very fact that It is All-Originating we have nothing to give to It, nothing except that reciprocity of feeling which, as we have seen, is fundamental to the Divine ideal of Man, that ideal which has called the human race into existence.

If, then, we have nothing to *give* but our love and worship, why not take up the position of grateful and expectant *receivers?* It simplifies matters and relieves us of a great deal of worry, and moreover it is undoubtedly scriptural. The reason we don't do so is because we don't believe in the free givingness and consequently we cannot adopt a mental attitude of receiving, and so the Spirit cannot make the gift.

If we seek the reason why this is so we shall find it in our materialism, our inability to see beyond secondary causes. We get things through certain visible channels, and we mistake these for the source.

"The things I possess I got with my money, and my money I got by my work." Of course you did. God doesn't put dollar-bills or bank-notes into your cash-box by a conjuring trick. God makes things *generically* whether it be iron or brains, and then we have to use them. But the iron or the brains, or whatever else it may be, ultimately proceeds from the All-Creating Spirit; and the more clearly we see this the easier we shall find it to go direct to the Spirit for all we want.

Then we shall argue that, just as the Spirit can create the thing we desire, so it can also create *the way* by which that thing shall come to us, and so we shall not be bothered about the way. We shall work according to the sort of abilities God has bestowed upon us, and according to the opportunities provided; but we shall not try to force circumstances or to do something out of our line.

Then we shall find circumstances open out and our abilities increase, and this without putting any undue strain upon ourselves, but on the contrary with a great sense of restfulness.

And the secret is this. We are not bearing the burden ourselves. We are not trying to force things on the external plane by our objective powers, nor yet on the subjective plane by trying to compel the Spirit; therefore, though diligent in our calling, we are at rest. And the foundation of this rest is that we believe in a Divine Promise, and the Promise is in the nature of the Divine Being.

This is why the Bible lays so much stress upon the idea of Promise. Promise is the law of Creative Power simplified to the utmost simplicity. Faith in a Divine Promise is the strongest attitude of mental Affirmation. It is the affirmation of the *desire* of the Creative Spirit to create the gift, and of its power and willingness to do so, and therefore of the production also of all the means by which the gift is to be brought to us. Also it fixes no limits, and so does not restrict the mode of operation, and thus it conforms exactly to the principles of the original cosmic creation, so that the whole universe around us becomes a testimony to the stability of the foundation on which our hope is based. This reference to the cosmic creation as bearing witness to the ground of our faith is of constant recurrence in the Bible, and its purpose is to impress upon us that the Power to which we look is that Power which in the beginning made the heavens and the earth.

The reason why this is made the starting-point of faith is that we start with an undoubted fact—the universe exists. Then a little consideration will show us that it must have had its origin in the Thought of the Universal Spirit before its manifestation in time and space, so that here we start with another self-evident fact; and these two obvious and incontrovertible facts supply us with premises from which to reason, so that knowing our premises to be true we know that our conclusion must be true also, if we only reason correctly from the premises. This is the logic of it.

Then the reasoning proceeds as follows: In the beginning there were no antecedent conditions, and the whole creation came out of the desire of the Spirit for self-expression. By the nature of the case the conception of the existence of any antecedent conditions is impossible; and so we see that creation from within (as distinguished from construction from without), has the entire absence of pre-determining and limiting conditions as its distinguishing characteristic.

Then our thought, *inspired by the promise,* is, so to say, reflected back into the mind of the Universal Spirit in direct relation to ourselves, and thus becomes part and parcel of the self-realization of the Spirit in connection with ourselves personally, thus bringing about a working of the creative Law of Reciprocity from the standpoint of our own individuality; and because the activity thus called forth is that of the Original Creative Energy, the First Cause itself, it is as unhampered by antecedent conditions as was the original cosmic creation itself.

I have gone more fully into this subject in my "Creative Process in the Individual," but I hope I have now said sufficient to make the general principle clear, and to show that the Bible promises are nothing else than the statement of the *essential creativeness* of the All-Originating Spirit when operating in reciprocity with the individual mind. If we believe in the power of Affirmation, then trust in the Divine promise is the strongest affirmation we can make. And if we believe in the power of Denials, then such a simple trust is also the strongest denial we can make, for, being absolute confidence, it constitutes an emphatic denial of any power, whether in the visible or the invisible, to prevent the fulfillment of the promise.

It is for this reason that the Bible lays such stress on belief in the Divine promises as the way to receive the blessing. The Bible was written for the benefit of *any* reader, whether learned or unlearned, and takes into consideration the fact that the latter are by far the more numerous; therefore, it reduces the matter to its simplest elements:—Hear the Promise, Believe it, and Receive its fulfillment.

The fact that the statement of any truth has been reduced to its simplest terms does not imply that it cannot stand the test of investigation; all that it implies is that it has been put into the best shape for immediate use alike for those who are able, and for those who are unable, to investigate the underlying principle. We press the button and the electric bell rings, whether we are trained electricians or not; but the fact that the bell rings for those who know nothing about electricity does not hinder the investigator from learning why it rings. On the other hand the greatest electrician does not have to go through the whole theory of the working of the current when he rings at the door of your house, which would be inconvenient to say the least of it; and still less does he have to solve the ultimate problem of what electricity actually is in itself, for he knows no more about that than anybody else.

And so in the end he has to come back to the same simple faith in electricity as the man who does not know the difference between the positive and negative poles of a battery. His greater knowledge ought to *extend* his faith in electricity because he knows it can do much greater things than ringing a bell; and in like manner any clearer insight we may gain into the *modus operandi* of the Divine promises should increase our trust in them, while at the same time it leaves us just on the same level with the most ignorant as to what the Divine Spirit actually is in itself.

We all alike have to come back to the standpoint of a simple faith in the vitalizing working of the energizing power, whether God or electricity, therefore the Bible simplifies matters by bidding us take this ultimate position as our starting point, and not say "I am confident because I know the law," but "I am confident because I know in whom I have believed."

I think some such considerations as these must have been at the back of St. Paul's mind making him draw that distinction between Law and Faith which runs through all his Epistles. It is true he is, in the first instance, speaking of the ceremonial law of the Mosaic ritual, for he was addressing Jews for the most part; but if we reflect that reliance on that ceremonial was only one particular mode of relying upon knowledge of laws, we shall see that the principle is applicable to all laws, and moreover the original Greek word used by St. Paul implies law in general, thus giving a scope to his argument which makes it as applicable to ourselves as to Jews.

And the point is this: Laws are statements of the *relations* of certain things to certain other things under certain conditions. Given the same things and the same conditions, the same laws will come into play because the same relation has been established between the things; but this is exactly the sphere which excludes the idea of original creation.

It is the sphere of science, of analysis, of measurement; it is the proper domain of all merely constructive work; but that is just what original creation is not. Original creation is not troubled about antecedent conditions; it creates new conditions, and by doing so establishes new relations and therefore new laws; and since the declared purpose of the Bible is to bring us into a new order, in which all that is meant by "the Fall" shall be obliterated, this is nothing else than a New Creation, which, indeed, the Bible calls it.

Therefore our knowledge of particular laws, whether mental or material, is of no avail for this purpose, and we have to come back to the standpoint of simple faith.

I do not wish to say anything against the knowledge of particular laws, either mental or material, which is useful in its way; but what I do want to emphasize is that this knowledge is not the Creative Power. If we get hold of this distinction we shall see what is meant by the promises contained in the Bible. They are statements of the original creating power of the spirit as it works from the standpoint of a specific personal relation to the individual, which relation is brought about by the expectant attitude of the individual mind which renders it receptive to the anticipated creative action of the Spirit; and it is this mental attitude that the Bible calls Faith.

Seen in this light faith in the promise is not a mere unreasoning belief, neither is it in opposition to law; but on the contrary it is the most all-embracing conclusion to which reasoning can lead us, and the channel through which the Supreme Law of the universe, the Law of the creative activity of the All-Originating Spirit, operates to make new conditions for the individual. It is not trying to make yourself believe what you know is not true; but it is the exercise of the highest reason based upon the knowledge of the highest truth.

The Divine promise and the individual faith are thus the correlatives of each other, and together constitute a creative power to which we can assign no limits. When we begin to apprehend this connection of Cause and Effect we see the force of the statements made by the Divine Master: "All things are possible to him that believeth." "Have faith in God and nothing shall be impossible unto you," and the like.

If we attribute any authority whatever to His sayings we are justified by them in affirming that there is no limit to the power of faith, and that His declarations on this subject are not mere figures of speech, but statements of the special and individual working of the Creative Law of the universe.

Viewed in this light the Bible promises assume a practical aspect and a personal application, and we see what is meant by being Children of Promise. We are no longer under bondage to Law, that is to those laws of sequences which arise from the *relations* of existing things to one another, but have risen into what the Bible tells us is the Perfect Law, the Law of Liberty; and so according to the symbolism of the two representative mothers, Hagar and Sarah, we are now no longer children of the bond woman but of the free (Gal. iv. 31).

Only to be "heirs according to promise" we must be descendants of Abraham. I am not prepared to say that the majority of readers of this book are not so literally, though they may not be aware of the fact, but that is another branch of the subject with which I may deal in a subsequent volume.

But setting aside this historical question let us here consider the question of spiritual principles. On this point the teaching of the Bible is very plain. It is that they are children of Abraham who are of the faith of Abraham; they are his seed according to promise, that is they are living by the same principle which is set forth as forming the groundwork of Abraham's life—"Abraham believed God, and it was counted unto him for righteousness" (Rom. iv. 3).

Now what will be the fruit of such a root? It must necessarily produce two results in our inner life—Restfulness and Enthusiasm. At first sight these two might appear opposed to one another, but it is not so, for Enthusiasm is born of confidence and so also is Restfulness. Both are necessary for the work we have to do. Without Enthusiasm there can be no vigorous work; even if attempted it would only be done as task-work, something which we had to grind at compulsorily, and though I would not deny that a certain amount of good and useful work may be done from a mere sense of obligation still it will be of a very inferior quality to what is done spontaneously for love of the work itself.

Take the case of the poor artist who is the slave of the dealer and has to labor from morning to night to turn out scores of little pot-boilers by a more or less mechanical process. If he be a born artist the fact will assert itself in spite of the conditions, and even the pot-boilers will have some degree of merit. But put the same man in more favorable circumstances where he is no longer restricted by trade requirements, but is allowed to give full scope to his genius, then the artist in him rises up, he gives us his own vision of nature, and masterpieces come from his brush.

This is because he is now working from Enthusiasm and not from Compulsion. It is also because he is working with a sense of Restfulness; he is no longer obliged to turn out so many pot-boilers per week to meet the demands of the petty dealer but can take his own time and choose his own subject and treat it in his own way.

Then the business side of his work will be negotiated for him by the big dealer, the man who also is an artist in his own way and knows the difference between the productions of spontaneous feeling and mere mechanical dexterity, and who finds his own profit in helping the artist to maintain that freedom from anxiety and the sense of compulsion without which such high class works as the big dealer's business depends on cannot be produced.

Now this is a parable. God is the big dealer, and His best work through man is done for love and not by compulsion, and the more we realize this the better work we shall do. Am I irreverent in comparing God to some great picture-dealer of world-wide reputation and saying that He, too, gains His profits in the transaction? I think not; for Christ Himself tells us of the master who looked to receive a profit out of his servants' work, and I have only clothed the old parable in modern garb and colored it with a familiar coloring.

And we may carry the simile yet further. The great dealer knows how to place the masterpieces in which he deals, he is in touch with connoisseurs with whom the artist cannot come in contact; and if the artist had to attend to all this what would become of his creative vision?

How do you manage to paint such exquisite pictures, it was once asked of Carot, and he replied, "Je-rêve mon tableau, et plus tard je peindrai mon rêve." There spoke the true artist, "I dream my picture, and afterwards I paint my dream." The true artist dreams with his eyes open looking at nature, and it is because he thus sees the inner spirit of her beauty through its external veil of form that he can show others what they could not see, unaided, for themselves. This is his function, and the large-minded dealer enables him to perform it by taking the business side of the matter in hand in a generous spirit combined with a shrewd knowledge of the market, and so leaves the painter to his proper work by seeing his vision of nature and interpreting it by his individual method of interpretation.

So with the Divine Dealer. He knows the ropes, He has command of the market, and He will deal in a liberal spirit with all who place their work in His hands. Let us, then, do diligently, honestly, and cheerfully the work of today, not as serving a hard taskmaster, but in happy confidence, and day by day hand it over to the Loving Creating Spirit who will bring out connections we had never dreamt of, and open up fresh avenues for us where we saw no way. You are the artist, and God is your honest, appreciative, and powerful Dealer.

But what else is this except exchanging the burden of Law for the peaceful liberty of Faith in the Divine Goodness, the All-givingness of the Heavenly Father? To attain this is far better than puzzling our brains over abstruse questions of theology and metaphysics. The whole thing is summed up in this: if you take your own knowledge of law as the starting-point of the creative action in your personal life you have inverted the true order, and the logical result from your premises will be to bring the whole burden upon yourself like a thousand bricks; but if you take the All-givingness of the Creating Spirit as your starting-point then everything else will fall into a harmonious order, and all *you* will have to do is to receive and use what you receive, asking the Divine guidance to use it rightly.

You throw the burden on whichever side you regard as taking the initiative in your personal creative series. If *you* take it, you make God a mere impersonal force, and ultimately you have nothing to depend upon but your own unaided knowledge and power. If on the other hand you regard God as taking the initiative by an All-givingness peculiarly connected with yourself, then the action is reversed and you will find yourself backed-up by the Infinite Love, Wisdom, and Power.

Of course there is a reason for these things, and I have endeavored to suggest a few thoughts as to the reason; but the practical advice I give to each reader is: Stop arguing about it. Try it, my boy. Try it, my dear girl—for the promise is: "Let him take hold of my strength that he may be at peace with me, and he shall make peace with me" (Isaiah xxvii. 5).

## XIV

# THE SPIRIT OF ANTICHRIST

WHEN WE HAVE realized the essential nature of any principle we can form a pretty fair guess as to the general lines on which it will show itself in action, whether in individuals, or institutions, or nations, or events. The evolution of principles is the key to all history in the past, and similarly it is the key to all the history that is to come; therefore, if we grasp the significance of any principle, though we may not be able to prophesy particular events, we shall be able to form some general idea of the sort of developments its prevalence must give rise to.

Now all through the Bible we find the statement of two leading principles which are diametrically opposed to one another—the principle of Sonship or reliance upon God, and its opposite or the denial of God, and it is this latter that is called the spirit of Antichrist.

This spirit, or mode of thought, is described in the second chapter of the second epistle to the Thessalonians and the fourth chapter of the first epistle to Timothy; and its distinctive note is that it sets itself up in the temple of God, placing itself above all that is worshipped, and a similar description is given in Daniel xi. 36–39.

The widespread development of this inverted principle, the Bible tells us, is the key to the history of "the latter days," those times in which we now live, and the prophetic Scriptures are largely occupied with the struggle which must take place between these opposing principles. It is impossible for the two to amalgamate for they are in direct antagonism; and the Bible tells us that, though the struggle may be severe, the victory must at last remain with those who worship God.

And the reason for this becomes evident if we look at the fundamental nature of the principles themselves. One is the principle of the Affirmative and the other is the principle of the Negative. One is that which builds up, and the other is that which pulls down. One consents to the initiative being taken by that Spirit which has brought all creation into existence, and the other bids this Spirit take a back seat and denies that it has any power of initiative. This is the essence of the opposition between the two principles. Whatever the one affirms the other denies; and so, since no agreement is possible, the conflict between them must continue until one or the other gets the final victory.

Now if the spirit of Antichrist is what the Bible describes it, we cannot shut our eyes to the fact that it is now present among us. St. Paul tells us that it was already beginning to work in his day, only that at that time there was a hindrance to its fuller development, but he adds that when that hindrance should be removed the development of the spirit of Antichrist would be phenomenal.

Various commentators on this text have explained the hindrance alluded to by St. Paul to have been the existence of the Roman Empire, and no doubt this is true as far as it goes. In this passage (II. Thess. ii. 1–11) St. Paul reminds the Thessalonians of something he had *told* them on the subject, that is something he had communicated verbally, and not in writing, regarding the falling away which would take place before the resurrection. He says, "Remember ye not, when I was yet with you, I told you of these things? And now *ye know* what withholdeth that he might be revealed in his time."

The very earliest traditions tell us that what St. Paul had then verbally explained to the Thessalonians was that the Roman Empire as then existing must pass away before these further developments could take place; but he was careful not to put this in writing lest it should expose the Christians to additional persecution on the charge of being enemies to the state.

The tradition that this was what St. Paul had told the Thessalonians is by no means a vague one. We first find it mentioned by Irenæus the disciple of Polycarp, who was himself the disciple of St. John; so that we get it on the authority of one who had been instructed by a personal friend and acquaintance of the apostles, and we may therefore feel assured that in this tradition we have a correct statement of what St. Paul had said regarding the nature of the hindrance to which he alludes in this epistle.

The existence of the Roman Empire, then, was doubtless the outward and immediate cause of this hindrance to the coming of Antichrist; but we must remember that at the back of the external and visible circumstances which are instrumental in the history of the world there are mental and spiritual causes, and so the matter goes further and deeper than any existing political conditions. It is a question of *spiritual* principles, a question of *causes,* and so long as any given cause is at work its effects will continue to show themselves, though the particular *form* they will assume will vary with the conditions under which the manifestation takes place.

Therefore, we may look deeper than the political conditions of St. Paul's time to find the spiritual and causal nature of the hindrance to which he alludes. He tells us that at the time when he wrote the spirit of Antichrist was already working, but that its complete manifestation was delayed till a later period by reason of a certain impediment which would be removed in due time; and a comparison of his statement with that of St. Peter in the third chapter of the second epistle shows that the removal of this impediment and the full manifestation of the spirit of Antichrist were to be looked for in the time of the end.

Now Daniel says the very same thing (Dan. xii. 1–4), and he points out the marks by which the time of the end is to be recognized. They are two: "Many shall run to and fro, and knowledge shall be increased"; and if this is not an accurate description of things at the present time, well—I leave the reader to fill in the blank. We may say, then, that the time when the hindrance to the manifestation of Antichrist is to be removed is a time when knowledge has been increased; and if we reflect that the whole matter is one of spiritual powers, is it not reasonable to suppose that the hindrance which in St. Paul's time prevented the fuller development of the spiritual power of Antichrist was ignorance of the nature of spiritual power in general?

Now this knowledge is becoming more and more widely diffused, and consequently the danger of its inverted application is today far greater than in St. Paul's time; and therefore the more we realize what potentialities open before us the more it behooves us to be on our guard lest we regard them in such a way as to take the place of God in the temple of God.

It may, or may not, be that "the Man of Sin" exhibiting himself as God in the Temple of God is to be understood as an actual ceremony taking place in an actual building; though even this is not altogether inconceivable if we recollect that during the French Revolution a notorious actress was enthroned upon the high altar in the Cathedral of Notre Dame as the Goddess of Reason and received the public adoration of the official representatives of France. What has been may be again, and we know that history repeats itself; but I think we have to look for something much more personal and powerful than any theatrical exhibition of this kind.

If we search the Scriptures we shall find that the real Temple of God is Man. When Christ said, "Destroy this temple, and in three days I will raise it up, he spake of the temple of his body" (John ii. 19–21); and again St. Paul says, "Know ye not that ye are the temple of God?" (I Cor. iii. 16). Moreover, the promise is, "I will dwell in them, and walk in them; and I will be their God, and they shall be my people" (2 Cor. vi. 16), and so in many similar passages, a careful consideration of which leaves no doubt but that the true significance of "the temple" in Scripture is that of human individuality. The meaning then becomes clear. The temple which is profaned is that innermost sanctuary of our heart out of which come all the issues of our individual life—"as he thinketh in his heart so is he" (Prov. xxiii. 7); and if this be true then it is of the utmost importance who is enthroned there. Is it the All-originating Creative Spirit with its infinite love, wisdom, and power? or is it our personal knowledge and will? It must be one of the two—which is it?

The difference is immense, and it consists in this. If our personal knowledge, wisdom, and will-power are the highest things we know, then we are left exactly where we were and are making no advance. We may, indeed, accumulate a certain amount of knowledge of the hidden laws of physical and psychic forces not commonly known to our fellow-men, which knowledge must necessarily carry a corresponding power along with it; but this only places us in a position where we more urgently need a higher knowledge and a higher wisdom to guide us.

The greater the power you put into any one's hands the more mischief will result if through ignorance of its true uses he misapplies it. He may understand the mere mechanism, so to say, of this power perfectly, so that he will know how to make it work—it is not on the mechanical side that the mistake will occur; but the mistake will be in the *purpose* to which the power is applied, and if that be wrong, the greater the power the worse will be the results. You may teach a child to drive a motor-car, but unless you can at the same time invest him with powers of observation and caution and promptness of resource in emergency beyond his years his driving will end in a smash.

Now it is just this inspiration of wisdom beyond our natural acuteness, of foresight beyond our unaided vision, that we require for the really useful employment of any enhanced powers that may come to us as the result of our increasing knowledge; and this is not to be drawn from the knowledge of what we may call the merely mechanical working of the Law of Cause and Effect, whether on the side of the visible or of the invisible. *That* knowledge, taken by itself, is only the lower knowledge, learning, so to say, how to do the particular trick; but to make it of real value we need to know, not only *how* to do it, but *why* to do it; and since the only true *why* is the building up of a harmonious whole both in ourselves and in the race—a whole which, by an organic connection between the causes sown today and the results produced tomorrow, shall continually germinate into greater and greater fulness of joyous life—since the production of such a continuously growing and rejoicing wholeness is the only reasonable purpose to which our knowledge and our powers, whether great or small, can be applied, how are we to get such an out-look into the unending future and into our present relations in all their ultimate consequences by our own personal knowledge however extended?

We are sowing causes all the time with only a very limited outlook as to what they will produce; but if we are conscious that we have submitted our action to the guidance of the Supreme Wisdom and Love we know that we must be importing into it an adjustment to wholeness which will make it co-operative with the great purpose of the universe.

We cannot grasp that purpose in all its details and infinite extent, but we can see that it must be an unending growth into ever increasing manifestation of the Life, Love, and Beauty which the All-originating Spirit is in itself.

That Spirit is in itself Unity, and its Self-expression is through its manifestation in Multi-plicity; and the more clearly we see this the more clearly we shall see that the way to co-operate with it is by seeking to make our own thought the channel of *its* Thought. But to do this is to recognize the presence of a Divine Intelligence guiding our thought and a Divine Power working through our actions; and this recognition coupled with the desire that our thought *should* be thus guided and our actions thus vivified is the very essence of Worship. It is the very opposite to the mental attitude which sets itself up as needing no guidance and no help from a higher source, and which denies the working of any higher power; and so worship becomes the foundation principle of the life. This does not mean a specific ceremonial observance but the adoption of the *principle* of worship, which is the recognition of the true relation of the individual mind to the Parent Mind from which it springs.

If any one finds that a particular ceremonial conduces towards this end then that ceremonial is useful to him, but it does not follow that the same ceremonial is necessary for somebody else. It is just like water-color painting. One man requires to keep his paper dry through the whole progress of the work, while another paints entirely in the wet; yet if they are both artists each will record his vision in a way that will unfold to the spectator some secret of nature's beauty. Each must use the means which at his present stage he finds most conducive to the end, only let him remember that it is the end alone which really counts.

Therefore it is that the Great Teacher laid down only one rule for worship—that it should be "in spirit and in truth." The essence and not the form is what counts, because the whole thing is a question of mental attitude. It is that attitude of constant Receptiveness which is the only possible *conscious* correlative to the infinite Divine Givingness. To attain this is conscious union with the All-creating Spirit.

The logic of it may be briefly put thus: we want to come into touch with the Power which originates the universe; but we cannot do this and at the same time disqualify it by denying that it continues to be originative when it comes in touch with ourselves. Therefore to be really in touch with it as the *originating* Power we must let it lead *us* and not try to compel *it;* and to do this is to worship.

The mark of the opposite mental attitude is to take no heed of such a Guiding Power, and then the only alternative is to set one's self in its place. When we realize that spiritual causes are always at the back of external phenomena and the more we come to see that particular causes can be resolved into variations of an ultimate cause, the more our intent to rule that ultimate cause must result in self-deification.

But the bad logic comes in in not seeing that the real ultimate cause must be *entirely originative*—that this is just what makes it worth seeking—and trying to deprive it of this power by attempting to compel it instead of looking to it for leading.

It is just here that those who realize the nature of spiritual causation are in greater danger than the mere materialist. There really is an unseen Force which can be controlled in the manner they contemplate, and their mistake is in supposing that this Force is the ultimate Creating Power.

I daresay some readers will smile at this, and I am well aware that it is quite possible to build up an apparently logical argument to show that what I am now speaking of is a merely fanciful idea, but to these I will not now make any reply—the matter is one requiring careful development, and a partial and inadequate explanation would be worse than useless. I must therefore leave its discussion to some other occasion, and in the meanwhile ask my readers to assume the existence of this Force simply as a working hypothesis. In asking this I am not asking more than they are ready to concede in the case of physical science where it is necessary to assume the existence of purely speculative conditions of energy and matter if we would co-ordinate the observed phenomena of nature into an intelligible whole; and in like manner I would ask the critical reader to assume as a working hypothesis the existence of an Essence intermediate between the Originating Spirit and the world of external manifestation.

The existence of such an intermediary is a conclusion which has been arrived at by some of the deepest thinkers who have ever lived, and it has been called by various names in different countries and ages; but for the purpose of the present book I think I cannot do better than adopt the name given to it by the European writers of the fifteenth, sixteenth and seventeenth centuries. They called it "Anima Mundi," or the Soul of the World, as distinguished from "Animus Dei," or the Divine Spirit, and they were careful to discriminate between the two.

If you look in a Latin dictionary you will find that this word, which means life, mind, or soul, is given in a twofold form, masculine and feminine, Animus and Anima. Now it is in the dual nature thus indicated that the action of spiritual causation consists, and we cannot eliminate either of the two factors without involving a confusion of ideas which the recognition of their interaction would prevent us falling into.

When once we recognize the nature and function of Anima Mundi we shall find that, under a variety of symbols, it is referred to throughout the Bible, and indeed forms one of the principal subjects of its teaching; but to explain these Bible references in detail would require a book to itself. In general terms, however, we may say that Anima Mundi is "the Eternal Feminine," and the necessary correlative to Animus Dei, the true Originating Spirit. It is what the mediæval writers called "the Universal Medium," and is that principle which, as I pointed out in the opening chapter of this book, is esoterically called "Water."

It is not the Originating Principle itself, but it is that principle *through* which the Originating Principle operates. It is not originative but receptive, not the seed but the ground, formative of that with which it is impregnated, as is indicated by the old French expression for it "ventre saint gris," the "holy blue womb"—the innermost maturing place of Nature; and its power is that of *attracting the conditions* necessary for the full maturing of that seed with which it is impregnated, and thus bringing about the growth which ultimately culminates in completed manifestation.

Perhaps the idea may be best put into terms of modern Western thought by calling it the Subconscious Mind of the Universe; and if we regard it in this light we may apply to it all those laws of the interaction between conscious and subconscious mentality with which I conclude most of my readers are familiar.*

Now the two chief characteristics of subconscious mind are its amenability to suggestion and its power of working out into material conditions the logical consequences of the suggestion impressed upon it. It it not originative, but formative. It does not provide the seed but it causes it to grow; and the seed is the suggestion impressed upon it by the objective mind.

If, then, we credit the Universal Subjective Mind with these same qualities we find ourselves face to face with a stupendous power which by its nature affords a matrix for the germination of all the seeds of thought that are planted in it.

---

* On this subject I would refer the reader to my "Edinburgh Lectures on Mental Science."

Looking at the totality of Nature as we see it—the various types of life, vegetable, animal, and human, and the evolution of these types from earlier ones, we can only come to the conclusion that the Originating Mind, Animus Dei as distinguished from Anima Mundi, must in the first instance see things *generically,* the type rather than the individual, much as Plato puts it in his doctrine of archetypal ideas, and so the world, as we know it, is governed by a Law of Averages which maintains and advances the race whatever may become of the individual.

We may call this a generic or type creation as distinguished from the conception of a specific creation of particular individuals; but, as I have explained more fully in my book, "The Creative Process in the Individual," the culminating point of such a generic creation must be the production of individual minds which are capable of realizing the general principle at work, and therefore of giving it individual application.

Now it is the imperfect apprehension of this principle that causes its inversion. It is recognizing Anima Mundi without Animus Dei; and the more a man sees of the immense possibilities of his own thought and volition working upon Anima Mundi, while at the same time ignoring Animus Dei, the more likely he is to grow too big for his boots. He then logically has nothing to guide him but his own personal will, and with all the resources of Anima Mundi at his disposal there is no saying to what extremes he may not go. "L'appétit vient en mangeant," and the more power he gets the more he will want, and the more his desires are gratified the more he will become satiated and require fresh stimulus to his jaded appetites.

This is no fancy picture. History tells us of the Emperor Tiberius offering great rewards to any one who would discover a new pleasure, and Nero burning Rome for a sensation. Picture such men in possession of a knowledge of psychic laws which would place all the powers of Anima Mundi at their disposal, and then imagine, not one such, but hundreds or thousands combining in some common enterprise under the leadership of some preeminently gifted individual and recollect in this connection the accumulated power of massed mental action—and what must the result be? Surely just what the Bible tells us—the working of all sorts of prodigies which to the uninstructed multitude must appear to be nothing else than miracles.

The knowledge, then, of the enormous possibilities stored up in Anima Mundi, or the Soul of Nature, is the great instrument through which the power of Antichrist will work. It is, indeed, the acquisition of this power that will more and more confirm him in his idea of self-deification; and note that though for convenience I use the singular pronoun, I am speaking of a class, that is of all who do not offer to God the sincere worship of trust in the Divine Love, Wisdom, and Power. I use the name Antichrist as that of a class, and one which seems likely to be widespread before long, though this in no way excludes the possibility of some phenomenally powerful leader of this class attaining to a pre-eminence which will make him the typical manifestation of the principle of self-deification.

Antichrist, whether as class or as individual, has attained to the recognition of a great universal principle, which I have endeavored to set forth in this and other books, the principle of the introduction of "the Personal Factor" into the realm of unseen causes. He has laid hold of a great truth.

All progress beyond the merely generic working of the Law of Averages is to be made by the introduction of the Personal Factor; but the mistake which Antichrist makes is that he cannot see any personality but his own. He sees the Soul of Nature and the power of its responsiveness to the Personal elements in the mind of man, and he sees no further. Therefore, after his own fashion, he recognizes a spiritual power of mere *forces,* but he does not recognize beyond this the presence of "the God of gods" (Dan. xi. 36–38). Logically therefore he becomes to himself *the* Person. He rightly says that the Law of Cause and Effect is universal, and that the expansion of this law to the production of hitherto unknown effects depends upon the introduction of the personal factor; but he does not understand the reinforcement of the individual human personality by a Divine Personality, the recognition of which would bring in that principle of Worship, which from the standpoint of his imperfect assumption of premises he logically denies.

To this power based upon self-deification there is opposed the opposite power based upon the worship of God; and the fact to be noted is that they are both using the same instrument. Both work by the power of the personal factor acting upon the impersonal Soul of Nature. The Anima Mundi itself is simply neutral. It is responsive to impression and generative of the conditions corresponding to the seed sown in it, but being entirely impersonal it is without any sort of moral consciousness, and will therefore respond equally to the impress of good or of evil.

Therefore in estimating the final result Anima Mundi *may be entirely eliminated from our calculations.* To put it mathematically, if Anima Mundi be represented by the same quantity on either side of the equation, it may be struck out from both sides, and then the real calculation will involve only the remaining factors. In the case we are considering the only other factor is that of Personality, and consequently the ultimate question at issue is this—on which side is the greater force of Personality?

The answer to this question is to be found in the Cosmic Creation. We are part of that creation; our personality is part of it. Our personality proceeds by derivation from the All-originating Spirit, and therefore logically that Spirit must be the Infinite of Personality.

It is true we cannot analyze or fathom the profundities of that Spirit, and from this point of view we may speak of it as "the Unknowable"; and so we may not be able to define what the All-creating Spirit's consciousness of Personality may be to itself; but, unless we entirely deny our derivation from it, must it not be clear that it must contain the infinite potential of all that can ever constitute personality in ourselves? And if this be so, then the growth of our own personality must be proportioned to the extent to which this potential flows into us; and to adopt the receptive mental attitude towards our Creator which will allow of such an inflowing is to take that attitude of Worship which Antichrist denies. Therefore the greater power of Personality is on the side of the worshippers of God.

Then, if this be so, their control over the powers of the unseen is greater than that of Antichrist, but they do not seek to control those powers in the same way that he does. He knows no personality but his own, and so he seeks to gain this control by his own knowledge of particular laws and by his own force of will, and is thus limited by the capacities of his own personality, however extensive they may be. His method is to *consciously* control Anima Mundi for his own purposes by his own strength.

Those on the opposite side do not thus seek to subject Anima Mundi to their personal will. Many, perhaps the majority of them, do not even know that there is any such thing as Anima Mundi, and so they rely on a simple trust in "the Father." And those among them who do know it know also that the worshipper of God may entirely eliminate it from consideration, as I have already said, and so they also rely upon simple trust in "the Father"; the only difference being that knowing something of the nature of the medium through which the unseen powers are working on *both* sides, and that the ultimate question is only that of Personality, they should have a yet stronger faith than their less instructed brethren, though in kind it is still the *same* faith, that of the Son in the Father.

Whether, then, instructed in these matters or not, the worshippers of God will by their very faith and worship be exercising a constant influence upon Anima Mundi, attracting all those conditions which must tend to their final victory over the opposing force.

Their worship enshrines the All-creating Spirit in their hearts, and their thoughts of Him and desires towards Him go forth into the Soul of Nature impregnating it with the seed of the good, the beautiful, and the life-giving which must assuredly bring forth fruit in its own likeness in due time.

Their method may not produce the sensational effects which may, perhaps, be produced by their opponents when the development of psychic forces reaches its climax, but in the end all such temporary wonders will be swept away by the overflowing of power which must result when Anima Mundi becomes permeated by Animus Dei, not merely as now in the generic sense of the maintenance of the world, but also in the specific sense of the introduction of the Personal Factor in its complete Divine manifestation.

Thus it will be seen that in its grand delineations of the closing scenes of the present age, the Bible nowhere departs from the universal law of cause and effect. There is a reason for everything if we can only penetrate deep enough to find it; and the laws of causation with which we are gradually gaining a better acquaintance in the realm of our own mentality are the same laws which in their wider scope embrace nations and make history.

When we see this the why and wherefore of even that great climax of the present age which the Bible sets before us becomes intelligible. We may not be able to predict specific events but we can recognize the development of principles, and so we see more clearly the meaning of those inspired prophecies which would otherwise be enigmatical to us.

Then when we see that these prophecies are in no way isolated from the natural laws of the universe, but rather are based upon them, and are in fact the description of those very laws operating in their widest field of action on the human plane we shall feel the more confidence in those hints of *definite measures of time* which they afford us.

This is a very important part of their message, and though we may not be able to reckon the precise day or year we may yet come to a very close approximation of our present whereabouts in the chronological calendar, and there are many indications to show that we are very rapidly approaching that climax which the Bible calls the end of the age.

This, however, is far too large a question for me to open up in these concluding pages, and perhaps it may be my privilege to treat of it at some future time; but I have endeavored here to offer some suggestions of the general lines on which the Bible student may intelligently approach the subject, realizing the close connection that exists between the Bible teachings regarding the forgiveness of sin, the spirituality of worship, the development of personality, and the originative action of the All-creating Spirit. These are all parts of one great whole and cannot be dissociated. To dissociate them is to pull down the edifice of the Divine Temple; to realize their unity is to build it up—that true Temple of God which is the Individuality of Man made perfect by the indwelling of the Holy Spirit.

It shall come to pass that whosoever shall call
on the name of the lord shall be saved.
Him that cometh to me I will in no wise cast out.
MARANATHA

# The Law and the Word

1917

# CONTENTS

## FOREWORD

# THOMAS TROWARD: AN APPRECIATION

HOW IS ONE to know a friend? Certainly not by the duration of acquaintance. Neither can friendship be bought or sold by service rendered. Nor can it be coined into acts of gallantry or phrases of flattery. It has no part in the small change of courtesy. It is outside all these, containing them all and superior to them all.

To some is given the great privilege of a day set apart to mark the arrival of a total stranger panoplied with all the insignia of friendship. He comes unannounced. He bears no letter of introduction. No mutual friend can vouch for him. Suddenly and silently he steps unexpectedly out of the shadow of material concern and spiritual obscurity, into the radiance of intimate friendship, as a picture is projected upon a lighted screen. But unlike the phantom picture he is an instant reality that one's whole being immediately recognizes, and the radiance of fellowship that pervades his word, thought and action holds all the essence of long companionship.

Unfortunately there are too few of these bright messengers of God to be met with in life's pilgrimage, but that Judge Troward was one of them will never be doubted by the thousands who are now mourning his departure from among us. Those whose closest touch with him has been the reading of his books will mourn him as a friend only less than those who listened to him on the platform. For no books ever written more clearly expressed the author. The same simple lucidity and gentle humanity, the same effort to discard complicated non-essentials, mark both the man and his books.

Although the spirit of benign friendliness pervades his writings and illuminated his public life, yet much of his capacity for friendship was denied those who were not privileged to clasp hands with him and to sit beside him in familiar confidence. Only in the intimacy of the fireside did he wholly reveal his innate modesty and simplicity of character. Here alone, glamoured with his radiating friendship, was shown the wealth of his richly-stored mind equipped by nature and long training to deal logically with the most profound and abstruse questions of life. Here indeed was proof of his greatness, his unassuming superiority, his humanity, his keen sense of honour, his wit and humour, his generosity and all the characteristics of a rare gentleman, a kindly philosopher and a true friend.

To Judge Troward was given the logician's power to strip a subject bare of all superfluous and concealing verbiage, and to exhibit the gleaming jewels of truth and reality in splendid simplicity. This supreme quality, this ability to make the complex simple, the power to subordinate the non-essential, gave to his conversation, to his lectures, to his writings, and in no less degree to his personality, a direct and charming naïveté that at once challenged attention and compelled confidence and affection.

His sincerity was beyond question. However much one might differ from him in opinion, at least one never doubted his profound faith and complete devotion to truth. His guileless nature was beyond ungenerous suspicions and selfish ambitions. He walked calmly upon his way wrapped in the majesty of his great thoughts, oblivious to the vexations of the world's cynicism. Charity and reverence for the indwelling spirit marked all his human relations. Tolerance of the opinions of others, benevolence and tenderness dwelt in his every word and act. Yet his careful consideration of others did not paralyze the strength of his firm will or his power to strike hard blows at wrong and error. The search for truth, to which his life was devoted, was to him a holy quest. That he could and would lay a lance in defence of his opinions is evidenced in his writings, and has many times been demonstrated to the discomfiture of assailing critics. But his urbanity was a part of himself and never departed from him.

Not to destroy but to create was his part in the world. In developing his philosophy he built upon the foundation of his predecessors. No good and true stone to be found among the ruins of the past, but was carefully worked into his superstructure of modern thought, radiant with spirituality, to the building of which the enthusiasm of his life was devoted.

To one who has studied Judge Troward, and grasped the significance of his theory of the "Universal Sub-conscious Mind," and who also has attained to an appreciation of Henri Bergson's theory of a "Universal Livingness," superior to and outside the material Universe, there must appear a distinct correlation of ideas. That intricate and ponderously irrefutable argument that Bergson has so patiently built up by deep scientific research and unsurpassed profundity of thought and crystal-clear reason, that leads to the substantial conclusion that man has leapt the barrier of materiality only by the urge of some external pressure superior to himself, but which, by reason of infinite effort, he alone of all terrestrial beings has succeeded in utilizing in a superior manner and to his advantage: this well-rounded and exhaustively demonstrated argument in favour of a super-livingness in the universe, which finds its highest terrestrial expression in man, appears to be the scientific demonstration of Judge Troward's basic principle of the "Universal Sub-conscious Mind." This universal and infinite God-consciousness which Judge Troward postulates as man's sub-consciousness, and from which man was created and is maintained, and of which all physical, mental and spiritual manifestation is a form of expression, appears to be a corollary of Bergson's demonstrated "Universal Livingness." What Bergson has so brilliantly proven by patient and exhaustive processes of science, Judge Troward arrived at by intuition, and postulated as the basis of his argument, which he proceeded to develop by deductive reasoning.

The writer was struck by the apparent parallelism of these two distinctly dissimilar philosophies, and mentioned the discovery to Judge Troward who naturally expressed a wish to read Bergson, with whose writings he was wholly unacquainted. A loan of Bergson's "Creative Evolution" produced no comment for several weeks, when it was returned with the characteristic remark, "I've tried my best to get hold of him, but I don't know what he is talking about." I mention the remark as being characteristic only because it indicates his extreme modesty and disregard of exhaustive scientific research.

The Bergson method of scientific expression was unintelligible to his mind, trained to intuitive reasoning. The very elaborateness and microscopic detail that makes Bergson great is opposed to Judge Troward's method of simplicity. He cared not for complexities, and the intricate minutiæ of the process of creation, but was only concerned with its motive power—the spiritual principles upon which it was organized and upon which it proceeds.

Although the conservator of truth of every form and degree wherever found, Judge Troward was a ruthless destroyer of sham and pretence. To those submissive minds that placidly accept everything indiscriminately, and also those who prefer to follow along paths of well-beaten opinion, because the beaten path is popular, to all such he would perhaps appear to be an irreverent iconoclast seeking to uproot long accepted dogma and to overturn existing faiths. Such an opinion of Judge Troward's work could not prevail with any one who has studied his teachings.

His reverence for the fundamental truths of religious faith was profound, and every student of his writings will testify to the great constructive value of his work. He builded upon an ancient foundation a new and nobler structure of human destiny, solid in its simplicity and beautiful in its innate grandeur.

But to the wide circle of Judge Troward's friends he will best and most gloriously be remembered as a teacher. In his magic mind the unfathomable revealed its depths and the illimitable its boundaries; metaphysics took on the simplicity of the ponderable, and man himself occupied a new and more dignified place in the Cosmos. Not only did he perceive clearly, but he also possessed that quality of mind even more rare than deep and clear perception, that clarity of expression and exposition that can carry another and less-informed mind along with it, on the current of its understanding, to a logical and comprehended conclusion.

In his books, his lectures and his personality he was always ready to take the student by the hand, and in perfect simplicity and friendliness to walk and talk with him about the deeper mysteries of life—the life that includes death—and to shed the brilliant light of his wisdom upon the obscure and difficult problems that torment sincere but rebellious minds.

His artistic nature found expression in brush and canvas and his great love for the sea is reflected in many beautiful marine sketches. But if painting was his recreation, his work was the pursuit of Truth wherever to be found, and in whatever disguise.

His life has enriched and enlarged the lives of many, and all those who knew him will understand that in helping others he was accomplishing exactly what he most desired. Knowledge, to him, was worth only what it yielded in uplifting humanity to a higher spiritual appreciation, and to a deeper understanding of God's purpose and man's destiny.

*A man, indeed! He strove not for a place,*
*Nor rest, nor rule. He daily walked with God.*
*His willing feet with service swift were shod—*
*An eager soul to serve the human race,*
*Illume the mind, and fill the heart with grace—*
*Hope blooms afresh where'er those feet have trod.*

PAUL DERRICK

I

# SOME FACTS IN NATURE

If I were asked what, in my opinion, distinguishes the thought of the present day from that of a previous generation, I should feel inclined to say, it is the fact that people are beginning to realize that Thought is a power in itself, one of the great forces of the Universe, and ultimately the greatest of forces, directing all the others. This idea seems to be, as the French say, "in the air," and this very well expresses the state of the case—the idea is rapidly spreading through many countries and through all classes, but it is still very much "in the air." It is to a great extent as yet only in a gaseous condition, vague and nebulous, and so not leading to the practical results, both individual and collective, which might be expected of it, if it were consolidated into a more workable form. We are like some amateurs who want to paint finished pictures before they have studied the elements of Art, and when they see an artist do without difficulty what they vainly attempt, they look upon him as a being specially favoured by Providence, instead of putting it down to their own want of knowledge. The idea is true. Thought *is* the great power of the Universe. But to make it practically available we must know something of the principles by which it works—that it is not a mere vaporous indefinable influence floating around and subject to no known laws, but that on the contrary, it follows laws as uncompromising as those of mathematics, while at the same time allowing unlimited freedom to the individual.

Now the purpose of the following pages, is to suggest to the reader the lines on which to find his way out of this nebulous sort of thought into something more solid and reliable. I do not profess, like a certain Negro preacher, to "unscrew the inscrutable," for we can never reach a point where we shall not find the inscrutable still ahead of us; but if I can indicate the use of a screw-driver instead of a hatchet, and that the screws should be turned from left to right, instead of from right to left, it may enable us to unscrew some things which would otherwise remain screwed down tight. We are all beginners, and indeed the hopefulness of life is in realizing that there are such vistas of unending possibilities before us, that however far we may advance, we shall always be on the threshold of something greater. We must be like Peter Pan, the boy who never grew up—heaven defend me from ever feeling quite grown up, for then I should come to a standstill; so the reader must take what I have to say simply as the talk of one boy to another in the Great School, and not expect too much.

The first question then is, where to begin. Descartes commenced his book with the words "Cogito, ergo sum." "I think, therefore I am," and we cannot do better than follow his example. There are two things about which we cannot have any doubt—our own existence, and that of the world around us. But what is it in us that is aware of these two things, that hopes and fears and plans regarding them? Certainly not our flesh and bones. A man whose leg has been amputated is able to think just the same. Therefore it is obvious that there is something in us which receives impressions and forms ideas, that reasons upon facts and determines upon courses of action and carries them out, which is not the physical body. This is the real "I Myself." This is the Person we are really concerned with; and it is the betterment of this "I Myself" that makes it worth while to enquire what our Thought has to do in the matter.

Equally true it is on the other hand that the forces of Nature around us do not think. Steam, electricity, gravitation, and chemical affinity do not think. They follow certain fixed laws which we have no power to alter. Therefore we are confronted at the outset by a broad distinction between two modes of Motion—the Movement of Thought and the Movement of Cosmic Energy—the one based upon the exercise of Consciousness and Will, and the other based upon Mathematical Sequence. This is why that system of instruction known as Free Masonry starts by erecting the two symbolic pillars Jachin and Boaz—Jachin so called from the root "Yak" meaning "One," indicating the Mathematical element of Law; and Boaz, from the root "Awáz" meaning "Voice" indicating Personal element of Free Will. These names are taken from the description in I Kings vii, 21 and II Chron. iii, 17 of the building of Solomon's Temple, where these two pillars stood before the entrance, the meaning being that the Temple of Truth can only be entered by passing between them, that is, by giving each of these factors their due relation to the other, and by realizing that they are the two Pillars of the Universe, and that no real progress can be made except by finding the true balance between them. Law and Personality—these are the two great principles with which we have to deal, and the problem is to square the one with the other.

Let me start, then, by considering some well established facts in the physical world which show how the known Law acts under certain known conditions, and this will lead us on in an intelligible manner to see how the same Law is likely to work under as yet unknown conditions. If we had to deal with unknown laws as well as unknown conditions we should, indeed, be up a gum tree. Fancy a mathematician having to solve an equation, both sides of which were entirely made up of unknown quantities—where would he be? Happily this is not the case. The Law is ONE throughout, and the apparent variety of its working results from the infinite variety of the conditions under which it may work. Let us lay a foundation, then, by seeing how it works in what we call the common course of Nature. A few examples will suffice.

Hardly more than a generation ago it was supposed that the analysis of matter could not be carried further than its reduction to some seventy primary chemical elements, which in various combinations produced all material substances; but there was no explanation how all these different elements came into existence. Each appeared to be an original creation, and there was no accounting for them. But now-a-days, as the rustic physician says in Molière's play of the "Médecin Malgré Lui," "nous avons changé tout cela." Modern science has shown conclusively that every kind of chemical atom is composed of particles of one original substance which appears to pervade all space, and to which the name of Ether has been given. Some of these particles carry a positive charge of electricity and some a negative, and the chemical atom is formed by the grouping of a certain number of negatively charged particles round a centre composed of positive electricity around which they revolve; and it is the number of these particles and the rate of their motion that determines the nature of the atom, whether, for instance, it will be an atom of iron or an atom of hydrogen, and thus we are brought back to Plato's old aphorism that the Universe consists of Number and Motion.

The size of these etheric particles is small beyond anything but abstract mathematical conception. Sir Oliver Lodge is reported to have made the following comparison in a lecture delivered at Birmingham. "The chemical atom," he said, "is as small in comparison to a drop of water as a cricket-ball is compared to the globe of the earth; and yet this atom is as large in comparison to one of its constituent particles as Birmingham town-hall is to a pin's head." Again, it has been said that in proportion to the size of the particles the distance at which they revolve round the centre of the atom is as great as the distance from the earth to the sun. I must leave the realization of such infinite minuteness to the reader's imagination—it is beyond mine.

Modern science thus shows us all material substance, whether that of inanimate matter or that of our own bodies, as proceeding out of one primary etheric substance occupying all space and homogeneous, that is being of a uniform substance—and having no qualities to distinguish one part from another. Now this conclusion of science is important because it is precisely the fact that out of this homogeneous substance particles are produced which differ from the original substance in that they possess positive and negative energy and of these particles the atom is built up. So then comes the question: What started this differentiation?

The electronic theory which I have just mentioned takes us as far as a universal homogeneous ether as the source from which all matter is evolved, but it does not account for how motion originated in it; but perhaps another closely allied scientific theory will help us. Let us, then, turn to the question of Vibrations or Waves in Ether. In scientific language the length of a wave is the distance from the crest of one wave to that of the wave immediately following it. Now modern science recognizes a long series of waves in ether, commencing with the smallest yet known measuring 0.1 micron, or about $\frac{1}{254,000}$ of an inch, in length, measured by Professor Schumann in 1893, and extending to waves of many miles in length used in wireless telegraphy—for instance those employed between Clifden in Galway and

Glace Bay in Nova Scotia are estimated to have a length of nearly four miles. These infinitesimally small ultra-violet or actinic waves, as they are called, are the principal agents in photography, and the great waves of wireless telegraphy are able to carry a force across the Atlantic which can sensibly affect the apparatus on the other side; therefore we see that the ether of space affords a medium through which energy can be transmitted by means of vibrations.

But what starts the vibrations? Hertz announced his discovery of the electro-magnetic waves, now known by his name, in 1888; but, following up the labours of various other investigators, Lodge, Marconi and others finally developed their practical application after Hertz's death which occurred in 1894. To Hertz, however, belongs the honour of discovering how to generate these waves by means of sudden, sharply defined, electrical discharges. The principle may be illustrated by dropping a stone in smooth water. The sudden impact sets up a series of ripples all round the centre of disturbance, and the electrical impulse acts similarly in the ether. Indeed the fact that the waves flow in all directions from the central impulse is one of the difficulties of wireless telegraphy, because the message may be picked up in any direction by a receiver tuned to the same rate of vibration, and the interest for us consists in the hypothesis that thought-waves act in an analogous manner.

That vibrations are excited by sound is beautifully exemplified by the eidophone, an instrument invented, I believe, by Mrs. Watts-Hughes, and with which I have seen that lady experiment. Dry sand is scattered on a diaphragm on which the eidophone concentrates the vibrations from music played near it. The sand, as it were, dances in time to the music, and when the music stops is found to settle into definite forms, sometimes like a tree or a flower, or else some geometrical figure, but never a confused jumble. Perhaps in this we may find the origin of the legends regarding the creative power of Orpheus' lyre, and also the sacred dances of the ancients—who knows!

Perhaps some critical reader may object that sound travels by means of atmospheric and not etheric waves; but is he prepared to say that it cannot produce etheric waves also. The very recent discovery of transatlantic telephoning tends to show that etheric waves can be generated by sound, for on the 20th of October, 1915, words spoken in New York were immediately heard in Paris, and could therefore only have been transmitted through the ether, for sound travels through the atmosphere only at the rate of about 750 miles an hour, while the speed of impulses through ether can only be compared to that of light or 186,000 miles in a second. It is therefore a fair inference that etheric vibrations can be inaugurated by sound.

Perhaps the reader may feel inclined to say with the Irishman that all this is "as dry as ditch-water," but he will see before long that it has a good deal to do with ourselves. For the present what I want him to realize by a few examples is the mathematical accuracy of Law. The value of these examples lies in their illustration of the fact that the Law can always be trusted to lead us on to further knowledge. We see it working under known conditions, and relying on its unchangeableness, we can then logically infer what it will do under other hypothetical conditions, and in this way many important discoveries have been made. For instance it was in this way that Mendeléef, the Russian chemist, assumed the existence of three then unknown chemical elements, now called Scandium, Gallium and Germanium. There was a gap in the orderly sequence of the chemical elements, and relying on the old maxim—"Natura nihil facit per saltum"—Nature nowhere leaves a gap to jump over—he argued that if such elements did not exist they ought to, and so he calculated what these elements ought to be like, giving their atomic weight, chemical affinities, and the like; and when they were discovered many years later they were found to answer exactly to his description. He prophesied, not by guesswork, but by knowledge of the Law; and in much the same way radium was discovered by Professor and Madame Curie. In like manner Hertz was led to the discovery of the electro-magnetic waves. The celebrated mathematician Clerk-Maxwell had calculated all particulars of these waves twenty-five years before Hertz, on the basis of these calculations, worked out his discovery. Again, Neptune, the outermost known planet of our system was discovered by the astronomer Galle in consequence of calculations made by Leverrier. Certain variations in the movements of the planets were mathematically unaccountable except on the hypothesis that some more remote planet existed. Astronomers had faith in mathematics and the hypothetical planet was found to be a reality. Instances of this kind might be multiplied, but as the French say "à quoi bon?" I think these will be sufficient to convince the reader that the invariable sequence of Law is a factor to be relied upon, and that by studying its working under known conditions we may get at least some measure of light on conditions which are as yet unknown to us.

Let us now pass on to the human subject and consider a few examples of what is usually called the psychic side of our nature. Walt Whitman was quite right when he said that we are not all included between our hat and our boots; we shall find that our modes of consciousness and powers of action are not entirely restricted to our physical body. The importance of this line of enquiry lies in the fact that if we do possess extra-physical powers, these also form part of our personality and must be included in our estimate of our relation to our environment, and it is therefore worth our while to consider them.

Some very interesting experiments have been made by De Rochas, an eminent French scientist, which go to show that under certain magnetic conditions the sensation of physical touch can be experienced at some distance from the body. He found that under these conditions the person experimented on is insensible to the prick of a needle run into his skin, but if the prick is made about an inch-and-a-half away from the surface of the skin he feels it. Again at about three inches from this point he feels the prick of the needle, but is insensible to it in the space between these two points. Then there comes another interval in which no sensation is conveyed, but at about three inches still further away he again feels the sensation, and so on; so that he appears to be surrounded by successive zones of sensation, the first about an inch-and-a-half from the body, and the others at intervals of about three inches each. The number of these zones seems to vary in different cases, but in some there are as many as six or seven, thus giving a radius of sensation, extending to more than twenty inches beyond the body.

Now to explain this we must have recourse to what I have already said about waves. The heart and the lungs are the two centres of automatic rhythmic movement in the body, and each projects its own series of vibrations into the etheric envelope. Those projected by the lungs are estimated to be three times the length of those projected by the heart, while those projected by the heart are three times as rapid as those projected by the lungs. Consequently if the two sets of waves start together the crest of every third wave of the rapid series of short waves will coincide with the crest of one of the long waves of the slower series, while the intermediate short waves will coincide with the depression of one of the long waves. Now the effect of the crest of one wave overtaking that of another going in the same direction, is to raise the two together at that point into a single wave of greater amplitude or height than the original waves had by themselves; if the reader has the opportunity of studying the inflowing of waves on the seabeach he can verify this for himself. Consequently when the more rapid etheric waves overtake the slower ones they combine to form a larger wave, and it is at these points that the zones of sensation occur. If the reader will draw a diagram of two waved lines travelling along the same horizontal line and so proportioned that the crest of each of the large waves coincides with the crest of every third wave of the small ones, he will see what I mean: and if he then recollects that the fall in the larger waves neutralizes the rise in the smaller ones, and that because this double series starts from the interior of the body the surface of the body comes just at one of these neutralized points, he will see why sensation is neutralized there; and he will also see why the succeeding zones of sensation are double the distance from each other that the first one is from the surface of the body; it is simply because the surface of the body cuts the first long wave exactly in the middle, and therefore only half that wave occurs outside the body. This is the explanation given by De Rochas, and it affords another example of that principle of mathematical sequence of which I have spoken. It would appear that under normal conditions the double series of vibrations is spread all over the body, and so all parts are alike sensitive to touch.

I think, then, we may assume on the basis of De Rochas' experiments and others that there are such things as etheric vibrations proceeding from human personality, and in the next chapter I will give some examples showing that the psychic personality extends still further than these experiments, taken by themselves, would indicate—in fact that we possess an additional range of faculties far exceeding those which we ordinarily exercise through the physical body, and which must therefore be included in our conception of ourselves if we are to have an adequate idea of what we really are.

## II

# SOME PSYCHIC EXPERIENCES

THE PRECEDING CHAPTER has introduced the reader to the general subject of etheric vibration as one of the natural forces of the Universe, both as the foundation of all matter and as the medium for the transmission of energy to immense distances, and also as something continually emanating from human beings. In the present chapter I shall consider it more particularly in this last aspect, which, as included in our own personality, very immediately concerns ourselves. I will commence with an instance of the practical application of this fact. Some years ago I was lunching at the house of Lady—— in company of a well-known mental healer whom I will call Mr. Y. and a well-known London physician whom I will call Dr. W. Mr. Y. mentioned the case of a lady whose leg had been amputated above the knee some years previously to her coming under his care, yet she frequently felt pains in the (amputated) knee and lower part of the left leg and foot. Dr. W. said this was to be attributed to the nerves which convey to the brain the sensation of the extremities, much as a telegraph line might be tapped in the middle, and Mr. Y. agreed that this was perfectly true on the purely physical side. But he went on to say, that accidentally putting his hand where the amputated foot should have been he felt it there. Then it occurred to him that since there was no material foot to be touched, it must be through the medium of his own psychic body that the sensation of touch was conveyed to him, and accordingly he asked the lady to imagine that she was making various movements with the amputated limb, all of which he felt, and was able to tell her what each movement was, which she said he did correctly. Then, to carry the experiment further, he reversed the process and with his hand moved the invisible leg and foot in various ways, all of which the lady felt and described. He then determined to treat the invisible leg as though it were a real one, and joined up the circuit by taking her left foot in his right hand and her right foot (the amputated one) in his left, with the result that she immediately felt relief; and after successive treatments in this way was entirely cured.

A well authenticated case like this opens up a good many interesting questions regarding the Psychic Body, but the most important point appears to me to be that we are able to experience sensation by means of it. In this case, however, and those mentioned in the preceding chapter, the physical body was actually present, and if we stopped at this point, we might question whether its presence was not a *sine qua non* for the action of the etheric vibrations. I will therefore pass on to a class of examples which show that very curious phenomena can take place without the physical body being on the spot. There are numerous well verified cases of the kind to be found in the records of the Society for Psychical Research and in other books by trustworthy writers; but it may perhaps interest the present reader to hear one or two instances of my personal experience which, though they may not be so striking as some of those recorded by others, still point in the same direction.

My first introduction to Scotland was when I delivered the course of lectures in Edinburgh which led to the publication of my first book, the "Edinburgh Lectures on Mental Science." The following years I gave a second course of lectures in Edinburgh, but the friends who had kindly entertained me on the former occasion had in the meanwhile gone to live elsewhere. However, a certain Mr. S., whose acquaintance I had made on my previous visit, invited me to stay with him for a day or two while I could look round for other accommodation, though, as it turned out, I remained at his house during the whole month I was in Edinburgh. I had, however, never seen his house, which was on the opposite side of the town to where I had stayed before. I arrived there on a Tuesday, and Mr. S. and his family at once met me with the question:

"What were you thinking of at ten o'clock on Sunday evening?"

I could not immediately recall this, and also, wanted to know the reason of their question.

"We have something curious to tell you," they replied, "but first try to remember what you were thinking of at ten o'clock on Sunday evening—were you thinking about us?"

Then I recollected that about that time I was saying my usual prayers before going to bed and had asked that, if I could stay only a day or two with Mr. S., I should be directed to a suitable place for the remainder of the time.

"That explains it," they replied; and then they went on to tell me that at the hour in question Mr. S. and his son, a young man of about twenty, had entered their dining-room together and seen me standing leaning against the mantel-shelf. They were both hard-headed Scotchmen engaged in business in Edinburgh, and certainly not the sort of people to conjure up fanciful imaginings, nor is it likely that the same fancy should have occurred to both of them; and therefore I can only suppose that they actually saw what they said they did. Now I myself was in London at the time of this appearance in Edinburgh, of which I had no consciousness whatever; at the same time the fact of my being seen in Edinburgh exactly at the time when my thought, in prayer, was centred upon Mr. S.'s house (which I had not then seen) is a coincidence suggesting that in some way my Thought had made itself visible there in the image of my external personality.

In this case, as I have said, I was not conscious of my psychic visit to Edinburgh, but I will now relate a converse instance, which occurred in connection with my first visit there. At that time I had never been in Scotland, and so far as I knew was never likely to go there. I was wide awake, writing in my study at Norwood, where I then lived, when I suddenly found myself in a place totally unknown to me, where stood the ruins of an ancient abbey, part of which, however, was still roofed over and used as a place of worship. I felt much interested, and among other things I noted a Latin inscription on a tablet in one of the walls. There seemed to be an invisible guide showing me over the place, who then pointed out a long low house opposite the abbey, and said: "This is the house of the clergyman of the abbey"; and I was then taken inside the house and shown a number of antique-looking rooms. Then I came to myself, and found I was sitting at my writing-table in Norwood. I had, however, a clear recollection of the place I had seen, but no idea where it was, or indeed whether any such place really existed. I also remembered a portion of the Latin inscription, which I at once wrote down in a note-book, as my curiosity was aroused.

As I have said, I had no reason at that time to suppose I should ever go to Scotland, but some weeks later I was invited to lecture in Edinburgh. Another visitor in the house where I was a guest there, was the wife of the County Court Judge of Cumberland, and I showed her and our hostess the part of the Latin inscription I had retained, and suggested that perhaps it might exist somewhere in Edinburgh. However nothing answering to what I had seen was to be found, so we relegated the whole thing to the region of unaccountable fancies, and thought no more about it. The Judge's wife took her departure before me, and kindly invited me to spend a few days at their residence near Carlisle oh my return journey, which I did. One day she drove me out to see Lanercost Abbey, one of the show-places of the neighbourhood, and walking round the building I found in one of the walls the Latin inscription in question. I called Mrs.——, who was a little way off, and said: "Look at this inscription."

She at once replied: "Why! that is the very inscription we were all puzzling over in Edinburgh!"

It turned out to be an inscription in memory of the founder of the abbey, dating from somewhere in the eleven-hundreds. The whole place answered exactly to what I had seen, and the long low parsonage was there also.

"I should have liked you to see it inside," said Mrs.——, "but I have never met the vicar, though I know his mother-in-law, so we must give it up."

We were just entering our carriage when the garden-gate opened, and who should come out but the mother-in-law.

"Oh, Mrs.——," she said, addressing the Judge's wife, "I am here on a visit and you must come in and take tea." So we went in and were shown over the house, much as I had been in my vision, and some portions were so old that, among other rooms, we were shown the one occupied by King Edward I on his march against Scotland in the year 1296, when the Scottish regalia was captured, and the celebrated Crowning-Stone was brought to England and placed in Westminster Abbey, where it has ever since remained—a stone having an occult relation to the history of the British and American peoples of the highest interest to both, but as there is already an extensive literature on this subject I will not enter upon it here.

I will now relate another curious experience. We had only recently taken up our residence at Norwood, when one day I was seated in the dining-room, but suddenly found myself in the hall, and saw two ladies going up the stairs. They passed close to me, and turning round the landing at the top of the stairs passed out of sight in a perfectly natural manner. They looked as solid as any one I have ever seen in my life. One of them was a stout lady with a rather florid complexion, apparently between forty-five and fifty, wearing a silk blouse with thin purple and white stripes. Leaning on her arm was a slightly-built old lady with white ringlets, dressed all in black and wearing a lace mantilla. I noticed their appearance particularly. The next moment I found I was really sitting in the dining-room, and that the ladies I had seen were nothing but visionary figures. I wondered what it could mean, but as we had only recently taken the house, thought it better not to mention it to any of my family, for fear of causing them alarm. But a few days later I mentioned it to a Mrs. F. who I knew had had some experience in such matters, and she said: "You have seen either some one who has lived in the house or who is going to live there." Then the matter dropped.

About a month later my wife arranged by correspondence for a certain Miss B. to come as governess to our children. When she arrived there was no mistaking her identity. She was the stout lady I had seen, and the next morning she came down to breakfast dressed in the identical blouse with purple and white stripes. There was no mistaking her, but I was puzzled as to who the other figure could be whom I had seen along with her. I resolved, however, to say nothing about the matter until we became better acquainted, lest she should think that my mind was not quite balanced. I therefore held my peace for six months, at the end of which time I concluded that we knew enough of each other to allow one another credit for being fairly level-headed. Then I thought, now if I tell her what I saw she may perhaps be acted upon by suggestion and imagine a resemblance between the unknown figure and some acquaintance of hers, so I will not begin by telling her of the vision, but will first ask if she knows any one answering to the description, and give her the reason afterwards. I therefore took a suitable opportunity of asking her if she knew any such person, describing the figure to her as accurately as I could.

Her look of surprise grew as I went on, and when I had finished she explained with astonishment: "Why, Mr. Troward, where *could* you have seen my mother? She is an invalid, and I am certain you have never seen her, and yet you have described her most accurately."

Then I told her what I had seen. She asked what I thought was the explanation of the appearance, and the only explanation I could give was, that I supposed she was on the look-out for a post and paid us a preliminary visit to see whether ours would suit her, and that, being naturally interested in her welfare, her mother had accompanied her. Perhaps you will say: "What came of it?" Well, nothing "came of it," nor did anything "come" of my psychic visits to Edinburgh and Lanercost Abbey. Such occurrences seem to be simple facts in Nature which, though on some occasions connected with premonitions of more or less importance, are by no means necessarily so. They are the functioning of certain faculties which we all possess, but of the nature of which we as yet know very little.

It will be noticed that in the first of these three cases I myself was the person seen, though unaware of the fact. In the last I was the percipient, but the persons seen by me were unconscious of their visit; and in the second case I was conscious of my presence at a place which I had never heard of, and which I visited some time after. In two of these cases, therefore, the persons, making the psychic visit, were not aware of having done so, while in the third, a memory of what had been seen was retained. But all three cases have this in common, that the psychic visit was not the result of an act of conscious volition, and also, that the psychic action took place at a long distance from the physical body.

From these personal experiences, as well as from many well authenticated cases recorded by other writers, I should be inclined to infer that the psychic action is entirely independent of the physical body, and in support of this view I will cite yet another experience.

It was about the year 1875, when I was a young Assistant Commissioner in the Punjab, that I was ordered to the small up-country station of Akalpur,* and took possession of the Assistant Commissioner's bungalow there. On the night of our arrival in the bungalow, my wife and I had our charpoys—light Indian bedsteads—placed side by side in a certain room and went to bed. The last thing I remembered before falling asleep, was seeing my wife

* For various reasons I am not giving the actual names of places and persons in this story.

sitting up in bed, reading with a lamp on a small table beside her. Suddenly I was awakened by the sound of a shot, and starting up, found the room in darkness. I immediately lit a candle which was on a chair by my bedside, and found my wife still sitting up with the book on her knee, but the lamp had gone out.

"Take me away, take me into another room," she exclaimed.

"Why, what is the matter?" I said.

"Did you not see it?" she replied.

"See what?" I asked.

"Don't stop to ask any questions," she replied; "get me out of this room at once; I can't stop here another minute."

I saw she was very frightened, so I called up the servants, and had our beds removed to a room on the other side of the house, and then she told me what she had seen. She said: "I was sitting reading as you saw me, when looking round, I saw the figure of an Englishman standing close by my bedside, a fine-looking man with a large fair moustache and dressed in a grey suit. I was so surprised that I could not speak, and we remained looking at each other for about a minute. Then he bent over me and whispered: 'Don't be afraid,' and with that there was the sound of a shot, and everything was in darkness."

"My dear girl, you must have fallen asleep over your book and been dreaming," I said.

"No, I was wide awake," she insisted; "you were asleep, but I was awake all the time. But you heard the shot, did you not?"

"Yes," I replied, "that is what woke me—some one must have fired a shot outside."

"But why should any one be shooting in our garden at nearly midnight?" my wife objected.

It certain seemed strange, but it was the only explanation that suggested itself; so we had to agree to differ, she being convinced that she had seen a ghost, and that the shot had been inside the room, and I being equally convinced that she had been dreaming, and that the shot had been fired outside the house.

The next morning the owner of the bungalow, an old widow lady, Mrs. La Chaire, called to make kindly enquiries as to whether she could be of any service to us on our arrival. After thanking her, my wife said: "I expect you will laugh at me, but I cannot help telling you there is something strange about the bungalow"; and she then went on to narrate what she had seen.

Instead of laughing the old lady looked more and more serious as she went on, and when she had done asked to be shown exactly where the apparition had appeared. My wife took her to the spot, and on being shown it old Mrs. La Chaire exclaimed: "This is the most wonderful thing I have ever heard of. Eighteen years ago my bed was on the very spot where yours was last night, and I was lying in it too ill to move, when my husband, whom you have described most accurately, stood where you saw him and shot himself dead."

This statement of the widow convinced me that my wife had really seen what she said she had, and had not dreamed it; and this experience has led me to make further enquiries into the nature of happenings of this kind, with the result, that after carefully eliminating all cases which could be accounted for in any other manner, I have found myself compelled to admit a considerable number of instances of what are called "ghosts," on the word of persons whose veracity and soundness of judgment I should not doubt on any other subject. It is often said that you never meet any one who has himself seen a ghost, but only those who have heard of somebody else seeing one. This I can entirely contradict, for I have met with many trustworthy persons of both sexes, who have given me accounts of such appearances having been actually witnessed by themselves. In conclusion, I may mention that I was telling this story some twenty years later to a Colonel Fox, who had known the unfortunate man who committed suicide, and he said to me: "Do you know what were the last words he said to his wife?"

"No," I replied.

"The very same words he spoke to your wife," said Colonel Fox.

This is the story I refer to in my book "Bible Mystery and Bible Meaning" as that of "the Ghost that I did not see." I do not attempt to offer any explanation of it, but merely give the facts as they occurred, and the reader must form his own theory on the subject; but the reason I bring in this story in the present connection is, that in this instance there could be no question of the physical body contributing to the psychic phenomenon, since the person seen had been dead for nearly twenty years; and coupling this fact with the distance from the physical body at which the psychic action took place in the other cases I have mentioned, I think there is a very strong presumption that the psychic powers can, and do, act independently of the physical body; though of course it does not follow from this that they cannot also act in conjunction with it.

On the other hand, a comparison of the present case with those previously mentioned, fails to throw any light on the important question whether the deceased feels any consciousness of the action which the percipient sees, or whether what is seen is like a sort of photograph impressed upon the atmosphere of a particular locality, and visible only to certain persons, who are able to sense etheric wave-lengths which are outside the range of the single octave forming the solar spectrum. It throws no light on this question, because, in the case of my being seen by Mr. S. in Edinburgh and that of Miss B. and her mother being seen by me at Norwood, none of us were conscious of having been at those places; while in the case of my psychic visit to Lanercost Abbey, and other similar experiences I have had, I have been fully aware of seeing the places in question. The evidence tells both ways, and I can therefore only infer that there are two modes of psychic action, in one of which the person projecting that action, whether voluntarily or involuntarily, experiences corresponding sensations, and the other in which he does not; but I am unable to offer any criterion by which the observer can, with certainty, distinguish between the two.

It appears to me, that such instances as those I have mentioned, point to ranges of etheric action beyond those ordinarily recognized by physical science, but the principle seems to be the same, and it is for this reason that I have taken the modern scientific theory of etheric vibration as our starting-point. The universe is one great whole, and the laws of one part cannot contradict those of another; therefore the explanation of such queer happenings is not to be found by denying the well-ascertained laws of Nature on the physical plane, but by considering whether these laws do not extend further. It is on this account that I would lay stress on the Mathematical side of things, and have adduced instances where various discoveries have been made by following up the sequence indicated by the laws already known, and which have thus enabled us to fill up gaps in our knowledge, which would otherwise stop, or at least seriously hinder, our further progress. It is in this way that Jachin helps Boaz, and that the undeviating nature of Law, so far from limiting us, becomes our faithful ally if we will only allow it to do so.

I think, then, that the scientific idea of the ether, as a universal medium pervading all space, and permeating all substance, will help us to see that many things which are popularly called super-natural, are to be attributed to the action of known laws working under, as yet, unknown conditions, and therefore, when we are confronted with strange phenomena, a knowledge of the general principles involved, will show us in what direction to look for an explanation. Now applying this to the present subject, we may reasonably argue, that since all physical matter is scientifically proved to consist of the universal ether in various degrees of condensation, there may be other degrees of condensation, forming other modes of matter, which are beyond the scope of physical vision and of our laboratory apparatus. And similarly, we may argue, that just as various effects can be produced on the physical plane, by the action of etheric waves of various lengths, so other effects might be produced on these finer modes of matter, by etheric waves of other lengths. And in this connection we must not forget that a gap occurs between the "dark heat" groups and the Hertzian group, consisting of five octaves of waves, the lengths of which have been theoretically calculated, but whose action has not yet been discovered. Here we admittedly have a wide field for the working of known laws under as yet unknown conditions; and again, how can we say that there are not ranges of unknown waves, yet smaller than the minute ultra-violet ones, which commence the present known scale, or transcending those largest ones, which bear our messages across the Atlantic? Mathematically, there is no limit to the scale in either direction; and so, taking our stand on the demonstrated facts of science, we find, that the known laws of Nature point to their continuation in modes of matter and of force, of which we have as yet no conception. It is therefore not at all necessary to spurn the ground of established science to spread the wings of our fancy; rather it affords us the requisite basis from which to start, just as the aeronaut cannot rise without a solid surface from which to spring.

Now if we realize that the ether is an infinitely subtle fluid, pervading all space, we see that it must constitute a connecting link between all modes of substance, whether visible or invisible, in all worlds, and may therefore be called the Universal Medium; and following up our conception of the Continuity of Law, we may suppose that trains of waves, inconceivably smaller or greater than any known to modern science, are set up in this medium, in the same way as the electro-magnetic waves with which we are acquainted; that is, by an impulse which generates them from some particular point. In the region of finer forces we are now prospecting, this impulse might well be the Desire or Will of the spiritual entity which we ourselves are—that thinking, feeling, inmost essence of ourself, which is the "noumenon" of our individuality, and which, for the sake of brevity we call our "Ego," a Latin word which simply means "I myself." This idea of spiritual impulse is quite familiar to us in our every-day talk. We speak of an impulsive person, meaning one who acts on a sudden thought without giving due heed to consequences; so in our ordinary speech we look upon thought as the initial impulse, only we restrict this to the case of unregulated thought. But if unregulated thought acts as a centre of impulse, why should not regulated thought do the same? Therefore we may accept the idea of Thought as the initial impulse, which starts trains of waves in the Universal Medium, whether with or without due consideration, and having thus recognized its dynamic power, we must learn to make the impulsions we thus send forth intelligent, well defined, and directed to some useful purpose. The operator at some wireless station does not use his instruments to send out a lot of jumbled-up waves into the ether, but controls the impulsions into a definite and intelligible order, and we must do the same.

On some such lines as these, then, we may picture the desire of the Ego as starting a train of waves in the Universal Medium, which are reproduced in corresponding *form* on reaching their destination. As with the electromagnetic waves, they may spread all round, just as ripples do if we throw a stone into a pond; but they will only take form where there is a correspondence able to receive them. This is what in the language of electrical engineers is called "Syntony," which means being tuned to the same rate of vibration, and no doubt it is from some such cause, that we sometimes experience what seem inexplicable feelings of attraction or repulsion towards different persons. This also appears to furnish a key to thought-transference, hypnotism, and other allied phenomena.

If the reader questions whether thought is capable of generating impulses in the etheric medium I would refer him to the experiment mentioned in Chapter XIV of my "Edinburgh Lectures on Mental Science," where I describe how, when operating with Dr. Baraduc's biometer, I found that the needle revolved through a smaller or larger arc of the circle, in response to my mental intention of concentrating a smaller or larger degree of force upon it. Perhaps you will say that the difference in the movement of the needle depended on the quantity of magnetism that was flowing from me, to say nothing of other known forces, such as heat, light, electricity, etc.

Well, that is precisely the proposition I am putting forward. What caused the difference in the intensity of the magnetic flow was my intention of varying it, so that we come back to mental action as the centre of impulsion from which the etheric waves were generated. If, then, such a demonstration can be obtained on the plane of purely physical matter, why need we doubt that the same Law will work in the same way, in respect of those finer modes of substance, and wider ranges of etheric vibrations, which, starting from the basis of recognized physical science, the Law of Continuity would lead to by an orderly sequence, and which the occurrence of what, for want of a better name, we call occult phenomena require for their explanation?

Before passing on to the more practical generalizations to be drawn from the suggestions contained in this chapter, I may advert to an objection sometimes brought by the sceptical in this matter. They say: "How is it that apparitions are always seen in the dark?" and then they answer their own question by saying, it is because superstitious people are nervous in the dark and imagine all sorts of things. Then they laugh and think they have disposed of the whole subject. But it is not disposed of quite so easily, for not only are there many well attested cases of such appearances in broad daylight, but there are also scientific facts, showing that if we are right in explaining such happenings by etheric action, such action is more readily produced at night than in the presence of sunlight.

In the early part of 1902 Marconi made some experiments on board the American liner *Philadelphia,* which brought out the remarkable fact that, while it was possible to transmit signals to a distance of fifteen hundred miles during the night, they could not be transmitted further than seven hundred miles during the day. The same was found to be the case by Lieutenant Solari of the Italian Navy, at whose disposal the ship *Carlo Alberta* was placed by the King of Italy in 1902, for the purpose of making investigations into wireless telegraphy; and summing up the points which he considered to have been fully established by his experiments on board that ship, he mentions among them the fact, that sunlight has the effect of reducing the power of the electro-magnetic waves, and that consequently a greater force is required to produce a given result by day than by night. Here, then, is a reason why we might expect to see more supernatural appearances, as we call them, at night than in the day—they require a smaller amount of force to produce them. At the same time, it is found that the great magnetic waves which cover immense distances, work even more powerfully in the light than in the dark. May it not be that these things show, that there is more than a merely metaphorical use of words, when the Bible tells us of the power of Light to dissipate, and bring to naught, the powers of Darkness, while the Light itself is the Great Power, using the forces of the universe on the widest scale? Perhaps it is none other than the continuity of unchanging universal principles extending into the mysterious realms of the spiritual world.

III

# MAN'S PLACE IN THE CREATIVE ORDER

IN THE PRECEDING chapters we have found certain definite facts,—that all known matter is formed out of one primordial Universal Substance,—that the ether spreading throughout limitless space is a Universal Medium, through which it is possible to convey force by means of vibrations,—and that vibrations can be started by the power of Sound. These we have found to be well established facts of ordinary science, and taking them as our starting-point, we may now begin to speculate as to the possible workings of the known laws under unknown conditions.

One of the first things that naturally attract our attention is the question,—How did Life originate? On this point I may quote two leading men of science. Tyndall says: "I affirm that no shred of trustworthy experimental testimony exists, to prove that life in our day has ever appeared independently of antecedent life"; and Huxley says: "The doctrine of biogenesis, or life only from life, is victorious along the whole line at the present time." Such is the testimony of modern science to the old maxim "Omne vivum ex-vivo." "All life proceeds from antecedent life." Think it out for yourself and you will see that it could not possibly be otherwise.

Whatever may be our theory of the origin of life on the physical plane, whether we regard it as commencing in a vivified slime at the bottom of the sea, which we call protoplasm, or in any other way, the question of how life got there still remains unanswered. The protoplasm being material substance, must have its origin like all other material substances, in the undifferentiated etheric Universal Substance, no particle of which has any power of operating upon any other particle until some initial vibration starts the movement; so that, on any theory whatever, we are always brought back to the same question: What started the condensation of the ether into the beginnings of a world-system? So whether we consider the life which characterizes organized matter, or the energy which characterizes inorganic matter, we cannot avoid the conclusion, that both must have their source in some Original Power to which we can assign no antecedent. This is the conclusion which has been reached by all philosophic and religious systems that have really tried to get at the root of the matter, simply because it is impossible to form any other conception.

This Living Power is what we mean when we speak of the All-Originating Spirit. The existence of this Spirit is not a theological invention, but a logical and scientific ultimate, without predicating which, nothing else can be accounted for. The word "Spirit" comes from the Latin "spiro" "I breathe," and so means "The Breath," as in Job xxxiii, 4,—"The Spirit of God hath made me, and the breath of the Almighty hath given me life"; and again in Ps. xxxiii, 6—"By the word of the Lord were the heavens made, and all the host of them by the breath of his mouth."

In the opening chapter of Genesis, we are told that "the Spirit of God moved upon the face of the waters." The words rendered "the Spirit of God" are, in the original Hebrew "rouah Ælohim," which is literally "the Breathing of God"; and similarly, the ancient religious books of India, make the "Swára" or Great Breath the commencement of all life and energy. The word "rouah" in Genesis is remarkable. According to rabbinical teaching, each letter of the Hebrew alphabet has a certain symbolic significance, and when examined in this manner, the root from which this word is derived conveys the idea of Expansive Movement. It is the opposite of the word "hoshech," translated "darkness" in the same passage of our Bible, which is similarly derived from a root conveying the idea of Hardening and Compressing. It is the same idea that is personified in the Zendavesta, the sacred book of the ancient Persians, under the names of Ormuzd, the Spirit of Light; and Ahriman, the Spirit of Darkness; and similarly in the old Assyrian myth of the struggle between the Sun-God and Tiámat, the goddess of darkness.

This conception of conflict between two opposite principles, Light and Darkness, Compression and Expansion, will be found to underlie all the ancient religions of the world, and it is conspicuous throughout our own Scriptures. But it should be borne in mind that the oppositeness of their nature does not necessarily mean conflict. The two principles of Expansion and Contraction are not necessarily destructive; on the contrary they are necessary correlatives to one another. Expansion alone cannot produce form; cohesion must also be present. It is the regulated balance between them that results in Creation. In the old legend, if I remember rightly, the conflict is ended by Tiámat marrying her former opponent. They were never really enemies, but there was a misunderstanding between them, or rather there was a misunderstanding on the part of Tiámat so long as she did not perceive the true character of the Spirit of Light, and that their relation to one another was that of co-operation and not of opposition. Thus also St. John tells us that "the light shineth in darkness and the darkness comprehended it not" (John i, 5). It is this want of comprehension that is at the root of all the trouble.

The reader should note, however, that I am here speaking of that Primeval Substance, which necessarily has no light in itself, because there is as yet no vibration in it, for there can be no light without vibration. We must not make the mistake of supposing that Matter is evil in itself: it is our misconception of it that makes it the vehicle of evil; and we must distinguish between the darkness of Matter and moral darkness, though there is a spiritual correspondence between them. The true development of Man consists in the self-expansion of the Divine Spirit working through his mind, and thence upon his psychic and physical organisms, but this can only be by the individual's *willingness to receive* that Spirit. Where the hindrance to this working is only caused by ignorance of the true relation between ourselves and the Divine Spirit, and the desire for truth is present, the True Light will in due course disperse the darkness. But on the other hand, if the hindrance is caused by *unwillingness* to be led by the Divine Spirit, then the Light cannot be *forced* upon any one, and for this reason Jesus said: "This is the condemnation, that light is come into the World, and men loved darkness rather than light, because their deeds were evil. For every one that doeth evil hateth the light, neither cometh to the light, lest his deeds should be reproved. But he that doeth truth cometh to the light, that his deeds may be made manifest, that they are wrought in God" (John iii: 19–21). In physical science these things have an exact parallel in "Ohm's Law" regarding the resistance offered by the conductor to the flow of the electric current. The correspondence is very remarkable and will be found more fully explained in a later chapter. The Primary Darkness, both of Substance and of Mind, has to be taken into account, if we would form an intelligent conception of the twofold process of Involution and Evolution continually at work in ourselves, which, by their combined action, are able to lead to the limitless development both of the individual and of the race.

According to all teaching, then, both ancient and modern, all life and energy have their source in a Primary Life and Energy, of which we can only say that IT IS. We cannot conceive of any time when it was not, for, if there was a time when no such Primary Energizing Life existed, what was there to energize it? So we are landed in a *reductio ad absurdum* which leaves no alternative but to predicate the Eternal Existence of an All-Originating Living Spirit.

Let us stop for a moment to consider what we mean by "Eternal." When, do you suppose, twice two began to make four? And when, do you suppose, twice two will cease to make four? It is an eternal principle, quite independent of time or conditions. Similarly with the Originating Life. It is above time and above conditions—in a word it is *undifferentiated* and contains in itself the *potential* of infinite differentiation. This is what the Eternal Life is, and what we want for the expansion of our own life is a truer comprehension of it. We are like Tiámat, and must enter into intelligent and loving union with the Spirit of Light, in order to realize the infinite possibilities that lie before us. This is the ultimate meaning of the maxim "Omne vivum ex vivo."

We see, then, that the material universe, including our own bodies, has its origin in the undifferentiated Universal Substance, and that the first movement towards differentiation must be started by some initial impulse, analogous to those which start vibrations in the ether known to science; and that therefore this impulse must, in the first instance, proceed from some Living Power eternal in itself, and independent of time and conditions. Now all the ancient religions of the world concur, in attributing this initial impulse to the power of Sound; and we have seen, that as a matter of fact, sound has the power of starting vibrations, and that these vibrations have an exact correspondence with the quality of the sound, what we now call synchronous vibration.

At this point, however, we are met by another fact. Cosmic activity takes place only in certain definite areas. Solar systems do not jostle each other in space. In a word the Sound, which thus starts the initial impulse of creation, is guided by Intelligent Selection. Now sounds, directed by purposeful intention, amount to Words, whether the words of some spoken language or the tapping of the Morse code—it is the meaning at the back of the sound that gives it verbal significance. It is for this reason, that the concentration of creative energy in particular areas, has from time immemorial been attributed to "The Word." The old Sanskrit books call this selective concentrative power "Vach," which means "Voice," and is the root of the Latin word "Vox," having the same meaning. Philo, and the Neo-Platonists of Alexandria who follow him, call it "Logos," which means the same; and we are all familiar with the opening verses of St. John's Gospel and First Epistle in which he attributes Creation to "The Word."

Now we know, as a scientific fact, that solar systems have a definite beginning in the gyration of nebulous matter, circling through vast fields of interstellar space, as the great nebula in Andromeda does at the present day. Æons upon æons elapse, before the primary nebula consolidates into a solar system such as ours is now; but science shows, that from the time when the nebula first spreads its spiral across the heavens, the mathematical element of Law asserts itself, and it is by means of our recognition of the mathematical relations between the forces of attraction and repulsion, that we have been able to acquire any knowledge on the subject. I do not for an instant wish to suggest that the Spiritual Power has not continued to be in operation also, but a centre for the working of a Cosmic Law being once established, the Spiritual Power works through that Law and not in opposition to it. On the other hand, the selection of particular portions of space for the manifestation of cosmic activity, indicates the action of free volition, not determined by any law except the obvious consideration of allowing room for the future solar system to move in. Similarly also with regard to time. Spectroscopic analysis of the light from the stars, which are suns many of them much greater than our own, shows that they are of various ages—some quite young, some arrived at maturity, and some passing into old age. Their creation must therefore be assigned to different epochs, and we thus see the Originating Spirit exercising the powers of Selection and Volition as to the time when, as well as to the place where, a new world-system shall be inaugurated.

Now it is this power of inauguration that all the ancient systems of teaching attribute to the Divine Word. It is the passing of the undifferentiated into differentiation, of the unmanifested into manifestation, of the unlocalized into localization. It is the ushering in of what the Brahminical books call a "Manvantara" or world-period, and in like manner our Bible says that "In the beginning was the Word." The English word "word" is closely allied to the Latin word "verbum" which signifies both *word* and *verb.* Grammarians tell us that the verb "to be" is a verb-substantive, that is, it does not indicate any action passing from the subject to the object. Now this exactly describes the Spirit in its Eternity. We cannot conceive of It except as always BEING; but the distribution of world-systems both in time and space shows that it is not always cosmically active. In itself, apart from manifestation, it is Pure Beingness, if I may coin such a word; and it is for this reason that the Divine Name announced to Moses was "I AM." But the fact that Creation exists, shows that from this Substantive Pure Being there flows out a Verb Active, which reproduces in action, what the I AM is in essence. It is just the same with ourselves. We must first *be* before we can *do,* and we can *do* only to the extent to which we *are.* We cannot express powers which we do not possess; so that our doing necessarily coincides with the quality of our being. Therefore the Divine Verb reproduces the Divine Substantive by a natural sequence. It is *generated* by the Divine "I AM," and for this reason it is called "The Son of God." So we see that The Verb, The Word, and The Son of God, are all different expressions for the same Power.

Creative vibration in the Universal Substance can, therefore, only be conceived of, as being inaugurated by the "Word" which *localizes* the activity of the Spirit in particular centres. This idea, of the localization of the Spirit through the "Word," should be fully realized as the energizing principle on the scale of the Macrocosm or "Great World," because, as we shall find later on, the same principle acts in the same way on the scale of the Microcosm or "Small World," which is the individual man. This is why these things have a personal interest for us, otherwise they would not be worth troubling about. But a mistake to be avoided at this point, is that of supposing that the "Word" is something which dictates to the Spirit when and where to operate. The "Word" is the word of the Spirit itself, and not that of some higher authority, for the Spirit being First Cause there can be nothing anterior to dictate to it; there can be nothing before that which is

First. The "Word" which centralizes the activity of the Spirit, is therefore that of the Spirit itself. We have an analogy in our own case. If I go to New York the first movement in that direction is that of my Thought or Desire. It is true that in my present state of evolution I have to follow the usual methods of travel, but so far as my Thought is concerned, I have been there all the time. Indeed, such a case as the one I have mentioned, of my being seen in Edinburgh while I was physically in London, seems to point to the actual transference of some part of the personality to another locality, and similarly with my visit to Lanercost Abbey; and the reader must remember, that such phenomena are by no means uncommon—they are the natural action of some part of our personality, and must therefore follow some natural law, even though we may at present know very little of how it works.

We see, therefore, both from *a priori* reasoning, and from observed facts, that it is the Word, Thought, or Desire of the Spirit, that localizes its activity in some definite centre. The student should bear this in mind as a leading principle, for he will find that it is of general application, alike in the case of individuals, of groups of individuals, and of entire nations. It is the key to the relation between Law and Personality, the opening of the Grand Arcanum, the equilibrating of Jachin and Boaz, and it is therefore of immediate importance to ourselves.

We may take, then, as a starting-point for further enquiry, the maxim that Volition creates Centres of Spiritual Activity. But perhaps you will say: "If this be true, what word or words am I to employ?" This is a question which has puzzled a good many people before you. This "Word" which so many have been in search of, has been variously called "the Lost Word," "the Word of Power," "the Schemhammaphorasch or Secret Name of God," and so on. A quaint Jewish legend of the Middle Ages says that the "Hidden Name" was secretly inscribed in the innermost recesses of the Temple; but that, even if discovered, which was most unlikely, it could not be retained because, guarding it, were sculptured lions, which gave such a supernatural roar as the intruder was quitting the spot, that all memory of the "Hidden Name" was driven from his mind. Jesus, however, says the legend, knew this and dodged the lions. He transcribed the Name, and cutting open his thigh, hid the writing in the incision, which, by magical art, he at once closed up; then, after leaving the Temple, he took the writing out and so retained the knowledge of the Name. In this way the legend accounts for his power to work miracles.

Jesus, indeed, possessed the Word of Power, though not in the way told in the legend, and he repeatedly proclaimed it in his teaching:—"According to your Faith be it unto you"—"Verily, I say unto you, whosoever shall say to this mountain, 'Be thou taken up and cast into the sea'; and shall not doubt in his heart, but shall believe that what he saith shall come to pass, he shall have whatsoever he saith" (Mark xi, 23). And similarly in the Old Testament we are told that the Word is nigh to us, even in our hearts and in our mouth (Deut. xxx, 14). What keeps the Word of Power hidden, is our belief that nothing so simple could possibly be it.

At the same time, simple though it be, it has Law and Reason at the back of it, like everything else. The ancient Egyptians seem to have had clearer ideas on this subject than we have. "The name was to the Egyptians the *idea* of the thing, without which it could not exist, and the knowledge of which therefore gave power over that which answered to it." "The *idea* of the thing represented its *soul.*"* This is the same conception as the "archetypal ideas" of Plato, only carried further, so as to apply, not only to classes, but to each individual of the class, and, as we shall see later, there is a good deal of truth in it. Put broadly, the conception is this—every external fact must have a spiritual origin, an internal energizing principle, which causes it to exist in the particular form in which it does. The outward fact is called the Phenomenon, and the corresponding inward principle is called the Noumenon. The dictionary definition of these two words is as follows: "Phenomenon—the appearance which anything makes to our consciousness as distinguished from what it is in itself." "Noumenon—an unknown and unknowable substance or thing as it is in itself—the opposite to the Phenomenon or form through which it becomes known to the senses or the understanding" (Chambers' Twentieth Century Dictionary). Whether the dictionary be right in saying that the "noumena" of things are entirely unknowable, the reader must decide for himself; but the present book is an attempt to learn something about the "noumena" of things in general, and of ourselves in particular, and what I want to convey is, that the "noumenon" of anything is its essence, *in terms of the Universal Energy and the Universal Substance, in their relation to the particular Form in question.* Probably the Latin word "Nomen," a Name, is derived from this Greek word, and in this sense everything has its "hidden name"; and the region in which Thought-

* "Out of Egypt" by Miss Crouse. Gorham Press, Boston, U. S. A.

Power works, is this region of spiritual beginnings. It deals with "hidden names"—that inward essence which determines the outward form of things, persons, and circumstances alike; and it is in order to make this clearer, that I have commenced by sketching briefly the general principles of Substance and Energy as now recognized by modern science.

If I have made my meaning clear, you will see that what is wanted is not the knowledge of particular words, but an understanding of general principles. At the same time I would not assert that the reciting of certain forms of words, such as the Indian "mantras" or the word AUM, to which Oriental teachers attach a mystic significance, is entirely without power. But the power is not in the words *but in our belief in their power.* I will give an amusing instance of this. On several occasions I have been consulted by persons who supposed themselves to be under the influence of "malicious magnetism," emanating in some cases from known, and in others from unknown, sources; and the remedy I have prescribed has been this. Look the adverse power, mentally, full in the face, and then assuming an attitude of confidence say "Cock-a-doodle-doo." The enquirers have sometimes smiled at first, but in every case the result has been successful. Perhaps this is why Æsculapius is represented as accompanied by a cock. Possibly the ancient physicians were in the habit of employing the "Cock-a-doodle-doo" treatment; and I might recommend it to the faculty to-day as very effective in certain cases. Now I do not think the reader will attribute any particularly occult significance to "Cock-a-doodle-doo." The power is in the mental attitude. To "cock-a-doodle-doo" at any suggestion is to treat it with scorn and derision, and to assume the very opposite of that receptive attitude which enables a suggestion to affect us. That is the secret of this method of treatment, and the principle is the same in all cases.

It matters, then, very little what particular words we use. What does matter is the intention and faith with which we use them. But perhaps some reader will here take the role of cross-examining counsel, and say: "You have just said it is a case of synchronous vibration—then surely it is the actual sound of the particular syllables that counts—how do you square this with your present statement?" The answer is that the Law is always the same, but the mode of response to the Law is always according to the nature of the medium in which it is operating. On the plane of physical matter the vibrations are in tune with physical sounds, as in the experiments with the eidophone; and similarly, on the plane of ideas or "noumena," the response is in terms of that plane. The word which creates "noumena," or spiritual centres of action, must itself belong to the world of "noumena," so that it is not illogical to say that it is the intention and faith that counts, and not the external sound. In this is the secret of the Power of Thought. It is the reproduction, on the miniature scale of the individual, of the same mode of Power that makes the worlds. It is that Power of Personality, which, combined with the action of the Law, brings out results which the Law alone could never do—as the old maxim has it, "Nature unaided fails."

This brings us to another important question—is not the creative power of the Word limited by the immutability of the Law? If the Law cannot be altered in the least particular, how can the Word be free to do what it likes? The answer to this is contained in another maxim: "Every creation carries its own mathematics along with it." You cannot create anything without at the same time creating its relation to everything else, just as in painting a landscape, the contour you give to the trees will determine that of the sky. Therefore, whenever you create anything, you thereby start a train of causation, which will work out in strict accordance with the sort of thought that started it. The stream always has the quality of its source. Thought which is in line with the Unity of the Great Whole, will produce correspondingly harmonious results, and Thought which is disruptive of the great Principle of Unity, will produce correspondingly disputive results—hence all the trouble and confusion in the world. Our Thought is perfectly free, and we can use it either constructively or destructively as we choose; but the immutable Law of Sequence will not permit us to plant a thought of one kind, and make it bear fruit of another.

Then the question very naturally suggests itself: Why did not God create us so that we could not think negative or destructive thoughts? And the answer is: Because He could not. There are some things which even God cannot do. He cannot do anything that involves a contradiction in terms. Even God could not make twice two either more or less than four. Now I want the student to see clearly why making us incapable of wrong-thinking would involve a contradiction in terms, and would therefore be an impossibility. To see this we must realize what is our place in the Order of the Universe. The name "Man" itself indicates this. It comes from the Sanskrit root MN, which, in all its derivatives, conveys the idea of Measurement, as in the word Mind, through the Latin *mens,* the faculty which compares things and estimates them accordingly; Moon, the heavenly body whose phases afford the most obvious standard for the periodical measurement of time; Month, the period thus measured; "Man," the largest of the Indian weights; and so on. Man therefore means "The Measurer," and this very aptly describes our place in the order of evolution, for it indicates the relation between Personal Volition and Immutable Law.

If we grant the truth of the maxim "Nature unaided fails" the whole thing becomes clear, and the entire progress of applied science proves the truth of this maxim. To recur to an illustration I have employed in my previous books, the old ship-builders thought that ships were bound to be built of wood and not of iron, because wood floats in water and iron sinks; but now nearly all ships are made of iron. Yet the specific gravities of wood and iron have not altered, and a log of wood floats while a lump of iron sinks, just the same as they did in the days of Drake and Frobisher. The only difference is, that people thought out the *underlying principle* of the law of flotation, and reduced it to the generalized statement that anything will float, the weight of which is less than that of the mass displaced by it, whether it be an iron ship floating in water, or a balloon floating in air. So long as we restrict ourselves to the mere recollection of observed facts, we shall make no progress; but by carefully considering *why* any force acted in the way it did, under the particular conditions observed, we arrive at a generalization of principle, showing that the force in question is capable of hitherto unexpected applications if we provide the necessary conditions. This is the way in which all advances have been made on the material side, and on the principle of Continuity we may reasonably infer that the same applies to the spiritual side also.

We may generalize the whole position thus. When we first observe the working of the Law under the conditions spontaneously provided by Nature, it appears to limit us; but by seeking the *reason* of the action exhibited under these limited conditions, we discover the principle, and true nature, of the Law in question, and we then learn from the Law itself, what conditions to supply in order to give it more extended scope, and direct its energy to the accomplishment of definite purposes. The maxim we have to learn is that "Every Law *contains in itself* the principle of its own Expansion," which will set us free from the limitation which that Law at first appeared to impose upon us. The limitation was never in the Law, but in the conditions under which it was working, and our power of selection and volition enables us to provide new conditions, not spontaneously provided by Nature, and thus to *specialize* the Law, and disclose immense powers which had always been latent in it, but which would for ever remain hidden unless brought to light by the co-operation of the Personal Factor. The Law itself never changes, but we can *specialize* it by realizing the principle involved and providing the conditions thus indicated. This is our place in the Order of the Universe. We give definite direction to the action of the Law, and in this way our Personal Factor is always acting upon the law, whether we know it or not; and the Law, under the influence thus impressed upon it, is all the time re-acting upon us.

Now we cannot conceive any limit to Evolution. To suppose a point where it comes to an end is a contradiction in terms. It is to suppose that the Eternal Life Principle is used up, which is to deny its Eternity; and, as we have seen, unless we assume its Eternity, it is impossible to account either for our own existence or that of anything else. Therefore, to say that a point will ever be reached where it will be used up, is as absurd as saying that a point will be reached where the sequence of numbers will be used up. Evolution, the progress from lower to higher modes of manifestation of the underlying Principle of Life, is therefore eternal, but, in regard to the human race, this progress depends entirely on the extent to which we grasp the principles of the Law of our own Being, and so learn to specialize it in the right direction. Then if this be our place in the Universal Order, it becomes clear that we could not occupy this place unless we had a perfectly free hand to choose the conditions under which the Law is to operate; and therefore, in order to pass beyond the limits of the mineral, vegetable and animal kingdoms, and reach the status of being Persons, and not things, we must have a freedom of selection and volition, which makes it equally possible for us to select either rightly or wrongly; and the purpose of sound teaching is to make us see the eternal principles involved, and thus lead us to impress our Personality upon the Law, in the way that will bring out the infinite possibilities of good which the Law, rightly employed, contains. If it were possible to do this by an automatic Law, doubtless the Creative Wisdom would have made us so. This is why St. Paul says: "If there had been a law given which could have given life, verily righteousness should have been by the law" (Gal. iii, 21). Note the words "a law *given,*" that is to say, imposed by external command; but it could not be. The laws of the Universe are Cosmic. In themselves they are *impersonal,* and the infinite possibilities contained in them, can only be brought out by the co-operation of the Personal Factor. It is only as we grasp the true relation between Jachin and Boaz, that we can enter into the Temple either of our own Individuality, or of the boundless Universe in which we live. The reason, therefore, why God did not make us mechanically incapable of wrong thinking, is simply because the very idea involves a contradiction in terms, which negatives all possibility of Creation. The conception lands us in a *reductio ad absurdum.*

Therefore, we are free to use our powers of Personality as we will, only we must take the consequences. Now one error we are all very apt to fall into, is the mistaken use of the Will. Its proper function is to keep our other faculties in line with the Law, and thus enable us to specialize it; but many people seem to think that by force of will they can somehow manage to coerce the Law; in other words, that by force of will they can sow a seed of one kind and make it bear fruit of another. The Spirit of Life seeks to express itself in our individuality, through the three avenues of reason, feeling, and will; but as in the Masonic legend of the murder of Hiram Abif, the architect of Solomon's Temple, it is beaten back on the side of reasoning, by the plummet of a logic based on false premises; on the side of feeling, by the level of conventional ideas; and on the side of will, by the hammer of a shortsighted self-will, which gives the finishing blow; and it is not until the true perception of the Principle of Life is resurrected within us, that the Temple can be completed according to the true plan.

It should be remembered that the will is *not* the Creative Faculty in us. It is the faculty of Conception that is the creative agent, and the business of the Will is to keep that faculty in the right direction, which will be determined by an enlightened Reason. Conception creates ideas which are the seed, that, in due time, will produce fruit after its own kind. In a broad sense we may call it the Imaging Faculty, only we must not suppose that this necessarily implies the visualizing of mental images, which is only a subsidiary mode of using this faculty. An "immaculate conception" is therefore the only means by which the New Liberated Man can be born in each of us. The sequence is always the same. The Will holds the Conception together, and the idea thus formed gives direction to the working of the Law. But this direction may be either true or inverted; and the impersonal Law will work constructively or destructively, according to the conception which it embodies. In this way, then, will-power may be used to hold together an inverted conception—the conception that our personal force of will is sufficient to bear down all opposition. But this mental attitude ignores the fact, that the fundamental principle of creative power is the Wholeness of the Creation; and that, therefore, the idea of forcing compliance with our wishes, by the power of our individual will, is an inverted conception, which, though it may appear to succeed for a time, is bound to fail eventually, because it antagonizes the very power it is seeking to use. This inverted use of the Will is the basis of "Black Magic," a term some readers will perhaps smile at, but which is practised at the present day to a much greater extent than many of us have any idea of—not always, indeed, with a full consciousness of its nature, but in many ways which are the first steps on the Left-hand Path. Its mark is the determination to act by Self-will, rather than using our will to co-operate with that continuous forward movement of the Great Whole, which is the Will of God. This inverted will entirely misses the point regarding the part we are formed to play in the Creative Order, and so we miss the development of our own individuality, and retrograde instead of going forward.

But if we work *with* the Law instead of against it, we shall find that our word, that is to say our conception, will become more and more the Word of Power, because it specializes the general Law in some particular direction. The Law will serve us exactly to the extent to which we first observe the Law. It is the same in everything. If the electrician tries to go counter to the fundamental principle, that the electric current always flows from a higher to a lower potential, he will be able to do nothing with it; but let him observe this fundamental law and there is nothing that electricity will not do for him within the field of its own nature. In this sense, then, of specializing the general Law in a particular direction, we may lay down the maxim that "The Law flows from the Word, and not *vice versa.*"

When we use our Word in this way, not as expressing a self-will that seeks to crush all that does not submit to it, but as a portion, however small, of the Universal Cause, and therefore with the desire of acting in harmony with that Cause, then our word becomes a constructive, instead of a destructive power. Its influence may be very small at first, because there is still a great mass of doubt at the back of our mind, and every doubt is, in reality, a Negative Word warring against our Affirmative Word; but, by adhering to our principle, we shall gradually gain experience in these things, and the creative value of our word will grow accordingly.

## IV

# THE LAW OF WHOLENESS

IT MAY SEEM a truism to say that the whole is made up of its parts, but all the same we often lose sight of this in our outlook on life.

The reason we do so is because we are apt to take too narrow a view of the whole; and also because we do not sufficiently consider that it is not the mere arithmetical sum of the parts that makes the whole, but also the harmonious agreement of each part with all the other parts. The extent of the whole and the harmony of the parts is what we have to look out for, and also its objective; this is a universal rule, whatever the whole in question may be.

Take, for instance, the case of the artist. He must start by having a definite objective, what in studio phrase is called a "motif"; something that has given him a certain impression which he wants to convey to others, but which cannot be stated as an isolated fact without any surroundings. Then the surroundings must be painted so as to have a natural relation to the main motif; they must lead up to it, but at the same time they must not compete with it. There must be only one definite interest in the picture, and minor details must not be allowed to interfere with it. They are there only because of the main motif, to help to express it. Yet they are not to be treated in a slovenly manner. As much as is seen of them must be drawn with an accuracy that correctly suggests their individual character; but they must not be accentuated in such a way as to emphasize details to the detriment of the breadth of the picture. This is the artistic principle of unity, and the same principle applies to everything else.

What, then, is the "Motif" of Life? Surely it must be, to express its own Livingness. Then in the True Order all modes of life and energy must converge towards this end, and it is only our short-sightedness that prevents us from seeing this,—from seeing that the greater the harmony of the whole Life, the greater will be the inflow of that Life in each of the parts that are giving it expression. This is what we want to learn with regard to ourselves, whether as individuals, classes or nations. We have seen the cosmic workings of the Law of Wholeness in the discovery of the planet Neptune. Another planet was absolutely necessary to complete the unity of our solar system, and it was found that there is such a planet, and similarly in other branches of natural science. The Law of Unity is the basic law of Life, and it is our ignorant or wilful infraction of this Law that is the root of all our troubles.

If we take this Law of Unity as the basis of our Thought we shall be surprised to find how far it will carry us. Each part is a complete whole in itself. Each inconceivably minute particle revolves round the centre of the atom in its own orbit. On its own scale it is complete in itself, and by co-operation with thousands of others forms the atom. The atom again is a complete whole, but it must combine with other atoms to form a molecule, and so on. But if the atom be imperfect as an atom, how could it combine with other atoms?

Thus we see that however infinitesimal any part may be as compared with the whole, it must also be a complete whole on its own scalc, if thc greater whole is to be built up. On the same principle, our recognition that our personality is an infinitesimal fraction of an inconceivably greater Life, does not mean that it is at all insignificant in itself, or that our individuality becomes submerged in an indistinguishable mass; on the contrary, our own wholeness is an essential factor towards the building up of the greater whole; so that as long as we keep before us the building up of the Great Whole as the "main motif," we need never fear the expansion of our own individuality. The more we expand, the more effective units we shall become.

We must not, however, suppose that Unity means Uniformity. St. Paul puts this very clearly when he says, if the whole body be an eye, where would be the hearing, etc. (I Cor. xii, 14). How could you paint a picture without distinction of form, colour, or tone? Diversity in Unity is the necessity for any sort of expression, and if it be the case in our own bodies, as St. Paul points out, how much more so in the expressing of the Eternal Life through endless ages and limitless space! Once we grasp this idea of the unity and progressiveness of Life going on *ad infinitum,* what boundless vistas of possibility open before us. It would be enough to stagger the imagination were it not for our old friends, the Law and the Word. But these will always accompany us, and we may rely upon them in all worlds and under all conditions. This Law of Unity is what in natural science is known as the Law of Continuity, and the Ancient Wisdom has embodied it in the Hermetic axiom "Sicut superius, sicut inferius; sicut inferius, sicut superius"—As above, so below; as below, so above. It leads us on from stage to stage, unfolding as it goes; and to this unfolding there is no end, for it is the Eternal Life finding ever fuller expression, as it can find more and more suitable channels through which to express itself. It can no more come to an end than numbers can come to an end.

But it *must* find suitable channels. Let there be no mistake about this. Perhaps some one may say: Cannot it *make* suitable channels for any sort of expression that it needs? The answer is, that it can, and it does so up to a certain point. As we have seen, the Word, Thought, or Initial Impulse of the Ever-Living Spirit starts a centre of cosmic activity in which the mathematical element of Law at once asserts itself; thenceforward everything goes on according to certain broad principles of sequence. This is a Generic Creation, creation according to *genera* or classes, like the "archetypal ideas" of Plato. This creation is governed by a Law of Averages, and the legal maxim "De minimis non curat lex"—the Law cannot trouble about minorities—applies to it. This generic law keeps the class going, and slowly advancing, simply as a class, but it can take no notice of individuals as such. As Tennyson puts it in "In Memoriam," speaking of Nature:

*"So careful of the type she seems,*
*So careless of the single life."*

This mode of creation reaches its highest level, at any rate in our world, in Genus Homo, or the human race. We also, as a race, are under the Law of Averages. The race continues to exist, but from the moment of birth the individual life is liable to be cut short in a hundred different ways. In producing man, however, Generic Creation has produced a *type* having a mental and physical constitution capable of perceiving the underlying principle of *all* creation, that is, of seeing the relation between the Word and the Law. We cannot conceive creation by type going further than this. By the nature of this type every human being has the potential of a further evolution, which will set it free from bondage to an impersonal Law of Averages, by specializing it through the Power of the Word, that is, by bringing the Personal Factor to bear upon the Impersonal Factor, and so unfolding the possibilities which can be achieved by their united activities. We have the power of using the Word so as to specialize the action of the Law, not by altering the Law, which is impossible, but by realizing its principle, and enabling it to work under conditions which are not spontaneously provided by Nature, but are provided by our own selection. The *capacity* for this exists in all human beings, but the practical application of this capacity depends on our recognition of the principles involved; and it is for this reason that I commenced this book by citing instances of the combined working of Law and Personality in purely physical science. I wanted first to convince the reader from well ascertained facts, that the Law contains infinite possibilities, but that this can only be brought out through the operation of the mind of man.

It is here that we find the value of the maxim "Nature unaided fails." The more we consider this maxim and the principle of Unity and Continuity, the clearer it will become, that Limitation is no part of the Law itself, but results only from our own limited comprehension of it; and that St. James uses no meaningless phrase, but is stating a logical and scientific truth, when he speaks of "The perfect Law of Liberty" (Jas. i, 25). What we have to do is, to follow this up, not by petulant self-assertion, but by quietly considering the why and wherefore of the whole thing. In doing so we can fortify ourselves with another maxim, that "Principle is not limited by Precedent." When we spread the wings of thought and speculate as to future possibilities, our conventionally-minded friends may say we are talking bosh; but if you ask them why they say so, they can only reply that the past experience of the whole human race is against you. They do not speak like this in the matter of flying-machines or carriages that go without horses; they say these are scientific discoveries. But when it comes to the possibilities of our own souls, they at once set a limit to the expansion of ideas, and do not see that the scientific principle of discovery is not confined to laboratory experiments. Therefore, we must not let ourselves be discouraged by such arguments. If our friends doubt our sanity, let them doubt it. The sanity of such men as Galileo and George Stephenson was doubted by their contemporaries, so we are in good company. At the same time we must not neglect to look after our own sanity. We must know some intelligible reason for our conclusions, and realize that however unexpected, they are the logical carrying out of principles which we can recognize in the Creation around us. If we do this we need not fear to spread the wings of fancy, even though some may not be able to accompany us; only we must remember that we are using wings. Fancy, in the ordinary acceptation of the word, has really no wings; it is like a balloon that just floats wherever any passing current of air may drive it. The possession of wings implies power to direct our flight, and fancy must be converted into trained Imagination, just as the helpless balloon has been superseded by navigable aircraft. It must be "the scientific imagination"; and the "scientific imagination" carried into the world of spiritual causation becomes the Word of Power, and its Power is derived from the fact that it is always working according to Law. Then we may go on confidently, because we are following the same universal principles by which all creation has been evolved, only now we are specializing its action from the standpoint of our own individuality, according to the ancient teaching that Man, the Microcosm, repeats in himself all the laws of the Macrocosm, or great world, around him.

As we begin to see the truth of these things, we begin to transcend the simply generic stage. That first stage is necessary to provide a starting-point for the next. The first stage is that of Bondage to Law. It could not be otherwise for the simple reason that you must learn the law before you can use it. Then from the stage of Generic Creation we emerge into that of individual Creation, in which we attain liberty through Knowledge of the Law of our own Being; so that it is not a mere theological myth to talk of a New Creation, but it is the logical outcome of what we now are, if, to our recognition of the Power of the Law we add the recognition of the Power of the Word.

V

# THE SOUL OF THE SUBJECT

WE MAY NOW turn to speculate a little on some conceivable application of the general principle we have been considering. It seems to me that, as a result of the generic creation of which I have just spoken, there is in everything what, for want of a better name, I may call "The soul of the subject."

Creation being by type, everything must have a *generic* basis of being in the Cosmic Law, not peculiar to that individual thing, but peculiar to the class to which it belongs, an adaptation of the Cosmic Soul for the production of all things belonging to that particular order, in fact, what makes them what they are and not something else. Now just because this basis is generic and common to the whole genus that is built upon it, it is not specific, but it acquires *localization through Form;* the form being that of the class to which it belongs, thus producing the individual of that class, whether a cat or a cabbage. It is this underlying *generic* being of the thing, that I want the student to understand by "the soul of the subject." In fact we may call it the Noumenon or essential being of the class, as distinguished from the specific characteristics that differentiate the individual from others of the same class. It follows from this that this *generic* soul has no individuality of its own, and consequently is open to receive impressions from any source that can penetrate the sheath of outward form and specific characteristic that envelops it. At the same time it is a manifestation of Cosmic Law, and so cannot depart from its own class-nature, and therefore any influence that may be impressed upon it from some other source will always show itself *in terms of the sort of generic soul that is thus impressed;* for instance, it would be impossible so to impress a dog as to make it write a book; and we may therefore generalize the statement, and lay down the rule, that "Every *im*-press receives *ex*pression in terms of the medium through which it is expressed." This becomes almost a self-obvious truism when put into plain language like this; thus, if I paint a picture in oils, my impression is conveyed in terms of this medium, and if I paint one in water-colours my conception will be conveyed in terms of that medium, and the methods of handling will be perfectly different in the two pictures.

This applies all round; and if we keep this generalization in mind, it will render many things clear, especially in psychic matters, which would otherwise seem puzzling.

Now we ourselves are included in the general creation, and consequently we have in us a generic or *type basis* of personality, which is entirely impersonal. This is not a contradiction in terms, though it may look like one. We belong to the class Genus Homo, the distinctive quality of which is Personality, that is to say, the possession of certain faculties which constitute us persons, and not things or animals; but at the same time this merely generic personality is common to all mankind, and is not that which distinguishes one individual from another, and in this sense it is impersonal; so we may call it our Cosmic or Impersonal Personality.

Now it is upon this cosmic element, inherent in all things from mineral to man, that Thought-Power acts, because, being impersonal, it has no private purpose of its own with which to oppose the suggestion that is being impressed upon it. The only thing is, that according to the rule just laid down, the response will always be in terms of the cosmic element which we have thus set in motion. Therefore on the human plane it will always be in terms of Personality.

The whole thing comes to this, that we impart to this impersonal element the reflection of our own personality, and thereby create in it a certain personality of its own, which will express itself in terms of the inherent nature of the impersonal factor, which we have thus temporarily invested with a personal quality; we are continually doing this unconsciously, either for good or ill; but when we come to understand the law of it, we must try so to regulate the habitual current of our thoughts, that even when we are not using this power intentionally, they may only exercise a beneficial influence.

In our normal state this cosmic element in ourselves is so closely united with our more conscious powers of volition and reasoning, that they constitute a single unity; and this is how it should be, only, as we shall see later on, with a difference. But there are certain abnormal states which are worth considering, because they make clearer the existence in us of this impersonal self, which in academical language is called the subliminal consciousness. The work of the subliminal consciousness exhibits itself in various ways, such as clairvoyance, clair-audience, and conditions of trance; all of which either occur spontaneously, or are induced by experimental means, such as hypnotism; but the similarity of the phenomena in either case shows, that it is the same faculty that is in evidence.

In those hypnotic experiments in which the operator merely makes the subject do some external act, we get no further than the fact that the person's individual will has been temporarily put to sleep, and that of the hypnotist has taken its place; still even this shows a power of impressing upon the subliminal consciousness a personal quality of its own, but it does not enable it to exhibit its own powers. The object of such experiments is, to exhibit the powers of the hypnotist, not to investigate the powers of the subliminal personality, which is of more importance in the present connection. But where the hypnotist employs his power of command to tell the subliminal self of the patient to exercise its own powers, merely directing it as to the subject upon which it is to be exercised, very wonderful powers indeed are exhibited. Places unknown to the percipient are accurately described; correct accounts are given of what people are doing elsewhere; the contents of sealed letters are read; the symptoms of disease are diagnosed and suitable remedies sometimes prescribed; and so on. Distance appears to make no difference. In many cases time also does not count, and historical events of long ago, with the details of which the seer had no acquaintance, are accurately described in all their minutiæ, which have afterwards been corroborated by contemporary documents. Nor are cases wanting in which events still future have been correctly predicted, as, for example, in Cazotte's celebrated prediction of the French Revolution, and of the fate that awaited each member of a large dinner-party when it should occur—though this was a spontaneous case, and not under hypnotism, which perhaps gives it the greater value.

The same powers are shown in spontaneous cases also, of which my own experiences related in a previous chapter may serve as a small example; but as there are many books exclusively devoted to the subject I need not go into further details here. If the reader be curious for further information, I would recommend him to read Gregory's "Letters on Animal Magnetism." It was published some fifty years ago, and, for all I know, may be out of print, but if the reader can procure it, he will find that it is a book to be relied upon, the work of a Professor of Chemistry in the University of Edinburgh, who investigated the matter calmly with a thoroughly trained scientific mind. But what I want the reader to lay hold of is the fact, that whether the action occur spontaneously or be induced by experimental means, these powers actually exist in us, and therefore in reckoning up the faculties at our disposal they must not be omitted.

In our more usual condition however, these faculties are subordinate to those which put us in touch with the every-day world, and I cannot help thinking, that at our present stage this is the best place for them. In this place they have a special function to perform, which I will speak of in another chapter, and in the meanwhile for my own part I should prefer to leave their development to the ordinary course of Nature, neither stimulating them by hypnotic influence, or auto-suggestion, nor repressing them if they manifest themselves of their own accord. However, every one must follow his or her own discretion in this matter; the only thing is, do not deny the existence of these faculties in yourself because you may not consciously exercise them, for they hold a very important place in our complex personality.

All such evidence on the subject as has come my way, appears to me to point to the fact, that it is through this impersonal or cosmic portion of our mind that Thought-Power operates upon us, whether in the form of telepathy, or of healing treatment, or in any other way; and it is through this channel also that thought currents, not specially directed towards ourselves, nevertheless affect us, just as the first wireless telephone message sent on September 29, 1915, from the office of the American Telephone Company in New York, and directed to San Francisco, was simultaneously heard at

San Diego, at Darien in Panama, and even as far away as Pearl Island, Honolulu, in the Pacific Ocean.

We sometimes pick up messages which are not intended for us; so we must keep our receiver in perfect syntony of reciprocal vibration with the stations from which we require to receive messages, to the exclusion of others which would produce confusion.

But I have strayed a little from our present point, which is rather that of giving out influence than of receiving it. Through the instrumentality of this impersonal cosmic soul we can send out our Thought for the healing of disease, for the suggestion of good and happy ideas, and for many other beneficial purposes; though the extent of the result will of course be considerably influenced by the mental attitude of the recipient, which is therefore a factor to be reckoned with.

But this power of sending out a subtle influence, call it magnetism or what you will, is not confined to operations upon the human subject. Two ladies of my acquaintance experimented on two rose-trees, which, to all appearances, were both in equally good condition. They daily blessed one and cursed the other, with the result that at the end of a month the anathematized plant had withered up from the roots, while the other was in an abnormally nourishing condition. Nor are we entirely without scientific backing even in such a case as this; for Professor Bose tells us in his work on the "Response of Metals," that not only can they be poisoned by certain chemicals, so as to deprive them of their normal qualities, but that they can be mesmerized into a similar condition. Such facts as these therefore give considerable support to the theory of the existence in everything of a "soul of the subject," which responds after its own manner to the power of human thought.

In what manner, then, is this influence conveyed? It is here that our study of etheric waves comes to our assistance, by carrying the same principle further, and picturing the working of the known Law under unknown conditions. It will at least enable us to form a working hypothesis. I have stated that our actual commercial application of the etheric waves extends from the ultra-violet waves used in photography, and measuring only $\frac{1}{254{,}000}$ of an inch, to those measuring many miles employed in wireless telegraphy; but this practical application by no means exhausts the conceivable possibilities of etheric vibrations; for not only do we find a gap of five octaves of as yet unknown waves between the dark heat group and the Hertzian group, but mathematically there is no limit to the greatness or smallness of the waves, and the scale may be prolonged indefinitely in either direction. Nor is this to be wondered at; for if we consider that vibration is not a progress of individual particles from one place to another, but the alternate rising and falling of the substance at the same point, and that the ether is a homogeneous and universally present substance, it is obvious that there is nothing to limit the minuteness or the greatness of the intervals at which the rising and falling will occur. Therefore we have an unlimited field for our imagination to play about in. Then, if we further reflect that all forms are built up of denser or finer aggregations of ether, and that what determines the generic form of anything is its cosmic soul, or the generating principle of the *class* to which it belongs, it follows that this soul must have a corresponding form, however inconceivably fine may be the etheric condensation which thus differentiates it from other souls, and prevents it from all being mixed up together in an indistinguishable mass. If now, we combine these two facts, that the soul of anything must have a form, however fine, and that there is no limit either to the greatness or the minuteness of etheric vibrations, we can draw certain deductions from these premises.

It is an established fact of ordinary science that, however closely particles of any substance may seem to cohere, they are in reality separated by interstices through which etheric waves can penetrate.

The principle may be illustrated by the power of the X-rays to penetrate apparently solid bodies, such as iron. Then, if we combine with this the fact, that there is no limit to the minuteness of etheric waves, we see that however fine may be the particles constituting any form, it is always possible to have etheric waves still finer and thus able to penetrate that form and set up vibrations in it. It is our familiarity with the denser modes of matter that makes it difficult for us to grasp the idea of these finer activities; but there is nothing in what we know of the denser modes to contradict the conception; on the contrary, it is just by what we have learned of these denser modes that we reach the principles on which these further conceptions are founded. Looking at this, therefore, in the light of a mathematical proposition, there is absolutely no limit to the fineness of any form, or to its susceptibilities to etheric vibrations.

Finally, to this add the power of the Word to start trains of etheric vibration, and you get the following series: The Word starts the etheric waves;

these waves produce corresponding vibration in the soul of the subject; and the soul of the subject in turn communicates corresponding vibration to its body. We may thus explain the Creative Power of Thought on the basis of recognizable Law, and so we believe, because we know *why* we believe, not because somebody else has told us so. Doubt is still the creative action of Thought, only it is creating negatively; so it is helpful to feel that we have some reason for confidence in the Power of the Word. There are a great many "Thomases" among us, and as one of the number I shall be glad if I can help my "Brother Tommies" to get a grip of the why and wherefore of the things which appear at first sight so fantastic and improbable.

But the conception we are considering is not limited to concrete entities, whether persons or things. It applies to abstractions also, and it it for this reason that I have called it the "Soul of the Subject." We often speak of the "Soul of Music," or the "Soul of Poetry," and so on. Thus our ordinary talk stands on the threshold of a great mystery, which, however, is simple enough in practice. If you want to get a clearer view of any subject than you have at present, address yourself mentally to the abstract soul of that subject, and ask it to tell you about itself, and you will find that it will do so. I do not say that it will do this in any miraculous manner, but what you already know of the subject will range itself into a clearer order, and you will see connections that have not previously occurred to you. Then again, you will find that information of the class required will begin to flow towards you through quite ordinary channels, books, newspapers, or conversation, without your especially laying yourself out to hunt for it; and again, at other times, ideas will come into your mind, you do not know how, but illuminating the subject with a fresh light. I cannot explain how all this takes place. I can only say from personal experience that it happens. But of course we must not throw aside ordinary common-sense. We must sort out the information that comes to us, and compare it with our previous knowledge; in fact we must *work* at it: there is no premium for laziness. Nor must we expect to receive by a sudden afflatus a complete acquaintance with some subject of which we are entirely ignorant. I do not say that such a thing is altogether impossible, for I cannot venture to limit the possibilities of the Universe; but it is certainly not to be looked for in the ordinary course. I have sometimes been shown specimens of "inspirational painting" done by persons said to be entirely ignorant of art, and the ignorance is very apparent on the face of the work. I dare say an artist may be inspired in the production of a picture, but the technical training comes first, and the inspiration afterwards. The same I believe to be true of all other subjects, so that we come back to the maxim of the power always expressing itself in terms of the instrument through which it works. With this reservation, however, it appears to me, that every class of subject has a sort of soul of its own with which we can put ourselves *en rapport* by, so to say, mentally unifying our own personality—with its abstract principle.

We are told by some teachers, that we can in the same way even construct entities in the nature of our Thought, and possessing a personality of their own with which we have endowed them. Whether this be the case I cannot say—I do not know all the secrets of the invisible. But if our thoughts do not create personal entities able to hang "on their own hook," they create forces which come to much the same thing. They start waves in the Universal etheric medium, which, like the electro-magnetic waves of telegraphy, spread all round from the point of initial impulse, and are picked up whenever a centre happens to be attuned to a similar rate of vibration, and each new centre energizes these vibrations again with a fresh impulse of its own; so in this way thought-currents become very real things.

Such, then, is the power of our Word, whether spoken or only dwelt upon in Thought, to impress itself upon the impersonal element around us, whether in persons or things. We cannot divest it of the power, though we may intensify its action by deliberate use of it, with knowledge of the principle involved, and therefore, whether consciously or unconsciously, we are sending out the influence of our personality all the time.

Now the more we know of these things the greater becomes our responsibility, and I would therefore solemnly warn the reader against any attempt to use the powers now indicated to the injury of any other person, or for the purpose of depriving any one else of that liberty of action which he would wish to enjoy himself. Such use of our mental powers is in direct opposition to the Law of Unity which I have spoken of; and since that Law is the basic principle of the whole Universe, any opposition to it places us in antagonism with a force immeasurably greater than ourselves.

Our Thought always continues to be creative; but in destructive use it becomes creative for destructive forces, and, since it has its origin in our own personality, we are certain sooner or later to feel its effects, on the principle that every action always produces a corresponding reaction. As we have seen, the Law knows nothing of persons, but acts automatically in strict accord with the nature of the power which has set it in motion. Under negative conditions the great Law of the Universe becomes your adversary, and must continue to be so, until by your altered mode of Thought you put yourself in line with it.

But on the other hand, if our intention be to co-operate with the Great Law, we shall find that in it also exists a mysterious "Soul of the Subject," which will respond to us, however imperfectly we may understand its *modus operandi.* It is the intention that counts, not the theoretical knowledge. The knowledge will grow by experience and meditation, and its value is measured entirely by the intention that is at the back of it.

VI

## THE PROMISES

WE HAVE NOW, I hope, laid a sufficiently broad foundation of the relation between the Law and the Word. The Law cannot be changed, and the Word can. We have two factors, one variable, and the other invariable; so that from this combination any variety of resultants may be expected. The Law cannot be altered, but it can be specialized, just as iron can be made to float by the same law by which it sinks. Now let us try to figure out in our imagination an ideal of the sort of results we should want to bring out from these two factors.

In the first place I think we should like to be free from all worry and anxiety; for a life of continual worry is not worth living. And in the second we should like always to have something to look forward to and feel an interest in; for a life entirely devoid of all interest is also not worth living. But, granted that these two conditions be fulfilled, I think we should all be well pleased to go on living *ad infinitum.* Now can we conceive any combination of the Law and the Word which would produce such results? that is the question before us. The first step is to generalize our principle as widely as possible, for the wider the generalization, the larger becomes the scope for specialization. The invariable factor we already know. It is the Law, always creating in accordance with the Word that sets it in motion, whether constructive or destructive; so what we really have to consider is the sort of

Word (i.e. Thought or Desire) which will set the Law working in the right direction. It must be a Word of confidence in its own power; otherwise by the hypothesis of the case it would be giving contradictory directions to the Law, or to borrow a simile from what we have learnt about waves in ether, it would be sending out vibrations that would cancel one another and so produce no effect. Then it must be a Word that does not compromise itself by antagonizing the Law of unity, and so producing disruptive forces instead of constructive ones. And finally, we must be quite sure that it really is the right Word, and that we have been making no mistake about it. If these conditions be fulfilled the logical result will be entire freedom from anxiety. Similarly with regard to maintaining a continued interest in life. We must have a continued succession of ideals, whether great or small, that will carry us on with something always just ahead of us; and we must work the ideals out, and not let them evaporate in dreams. If these conditions be fulfilled we have before us a life of never-ending interest and activity, and therefore a life worth living. Where then are we to find the Word which will produce these conditions: perfect freedom from anxiety and continual, happy interest? I do not think it is to be found in any way but by identifying our own Word with the Word which brings all creation into existence, and keeps it always moving onward in that continuous forward movement which we call Evolution. We must come back to the old teaching, that the Macrocosm is reproduced in the Microcosm, with the further perception that this identity of principle can only be produced by identity of cause. Law cannot be other than eternal and self-demonstrating, just as $2 \times 2$ must eternally $= 4$; but it remains only an abstract conception until the Creative Word affords it a field of operation, just as twice two is four remains only a mathematical abstraction until there is something for you to count; and accordingly, as we have already seen, all our reasoning concerning the origin of Creation, whether based on metaphysical or scientific grounds, brings us to the conception of a Universal and Eternal Living Spirit localizing itself in particular areas of cosmic activity by the power of the Word. Then, if a similar Creative Power is to be reproduced in ourselves, it must be by the same method: the localizing of the same Spirit in ourselves by the power of the same "Word." Then our Word, or Thought, will no longer be that of separate personality, but that of the Eternal Spirit finding a fresh centre from which to specialize the working of the Law, and so produce still further results than that of the First or simply Cosmic and

Generic Creation, according to the two maxims that "Nature unaided fails," and that "Principle is not limited by Precedent."

I want to make this sequence clear to the student before proceeding further:

1. Localization of the Spirit in specific areas of Creative Activity.
2. Cosmic and Generic Creation, including ourselves as a race resulting from this, and providing both the material and the instruments for carrying the work further by *specializing the Original Creative Power* through individual Thought, just as in all cases of scientific discovery.
3. Then, since what is to be specialized through our individual Thought is the Word of the Originating Power itself, in order to do this we must think in terms of the Originating Word, on the general principle, that any power must always exhibit itself in terms of the instrument through which it works.

This, it appears to me, is a clear logical sequence, just as a tree cannot make itself into a box, unless there be first the idea of a box which does not exist in the tree itself, and also the tools with which to fashion the wood into a box; while on the other hand there could never be any box unless there be first a tree. Now it is just such a sequence as this that is set before us in the Bible, and I do not find it adequately set forth in any other teaching, either philosophical or religious, with which I am acquainted. Some of these systems contain a great deal of truth, and are therefore helpful as far as they go; but they do not go the whole way, and for the most part stop short at the first or simply Cosmic Creation; or, if they attempt to pass beyond this, it is on the line of making unaided power of the individual the sole means by which to do so, and thus in fact always keeping us at the merely generic level. Such a mode of Thought as this, fails to meet the requirements of our conception of a happy life as one entirely exempt from fear and anxiety. In like manner also it fails to meet the first requirements of the whole series, viz.: the Word should be certain of itself; and if it be not certain of itself we have no assurance that it may not eventually disappoint our hopes. In short, this mode of thought leaves us to bear the whole burden from which we want to escape. So it is not good enough; we must look for something better.

Now this something better I find in the *Promises* contained in the Bible, and it is this that to my mind distinguishes our own Scriptures from the sacred books of all other nations, and from all systems of philosophy. I do not at all ignore the current objections to the possibility of Divine Promises, but I think that on examination they will be found to be superficial and resulting from want of careful enquiry into the true nature of the Promises themselves. How is it possible for the Laws of the Universe to make exceptions? How can God act by individual favouritism unless it be either through sheer caprice, or by the individual managing to get round Him in some way, either by supplying some need which He cannot supply for Himself, in which case God is of limited power, or else by flattering Him, in which case He is the apotheosis of absurd vanity. The two are really the same question put in different ways—the question of individual exceptions to the general Law.

The answer is that there are no individual exceptions to the general Law; but there are very various degrees of realization of the Principle of the Law, and the more a man works with the Principle the more the Law will work for him; so that the finer his perception of the Principle becomes, the more he will appear to be an exception to the Law as commonly recognized.

Edison and Marconi are not capriciously favoured by the laws of Nature, but they know more about them than most of us.

Now it is just the same with the Bible Promises. They are Promises according to Law. They are based upon the widest generalization and hence lead to the highest specialization through the combined action of the Law and the Word—Jachin and Boaz, the Two Pillars of the Universe.

These Promises comprise all sorts of desirable things: health of body, peace of mind, earthly prosperity, prolongation of life, and, finally, even the conquest of death itself; but always on one condition: perfect "Confidence in the power of the All-Originating Spirit in response to our reliance on the Word." This is what the Bible calls Faith; and it is perfectly logical when we understand the principle of it, for every Thought of doubt is, in effect, the utterance of a Word which produces negative results by the very same law by which the Word of Faith produces positive ones. This is the only condition which the Bible imposes for the fulfilment of its Promises, and this is because it is inherent in the nature of the Law by which their fulfilment is to be brought about.

A few texts will suffice as examples of the Bible Promises, and no doubt most of my readers are familiar with many others; but it would be worth while to read the Bible through, marking all such texts, and classifying them according to the sort of promises they contain.

Read, for instance, Job xxii, 21, etc. This is a most remarkable passage containing among other things the promise of earthly wealth; or again Job v, 19, etc., where we find promises of protection in time of danger, power over material nature, and prolonged life. While in Job xxxiii, 23, etc., there is promise of return to youth, a promise which is repeated in Psalm ciii, 5. Again in Isaiah lxi, 20, etc., there is the promise of immensely extended physical life, death at the age of one hundred being counted so premature as to resemble that of an infant, and the normal standard of age being compared to a tree which lives for centuries; and the same passage also promises immediate answer to prayers. The Psalms are full of such promises, and they are scattered throughout the Bible.

Now there is an unfortunate tendency among people who read their Bible with reverence, to what they call "spiritualize" such passages as these, which means that they do not believe them. They say such things are impossible; and therefore they must have some other meaning, and accordingly they interpret the words metaphorically, as referring to something to be experienced in another life, but quite impossible in this one.

Of course there are spiritual equivalents to these things, and the teaching of the Bible is, that they are the outward correspondences of inward spiritual states; but to "spiritualize" them in the way I am speaking of, is nothing but unbelief in the power of God to work on the plane of Nature. How such readers square their opinion with the fact that God has created Nature, I do not know. Even in the animal world we find wonderful instances of longevity. If an elephant be not overworked before he is twenty, he is in full working power up to eighty, and will then be capable of light work for another twenty years, after which he may yet enjoy another twenty years of quiet old age as the reward of his labours, while crocodiles and tortoises have been known to live for centuries. If then such things be possible in the ordinary course of Nature in the animal world, why need we doubt the specializing power of the Word to produce far greater results in the case of man? It is because we will not accept the maxim, that "Principle is not limited by Precedent" in regard to ourselves, though we see it demonstrated by every new scientific discovery. We rely more on the past experience of the race, than on the Creative Power of God. We call Him Almighty, and then say that in His Book He promises things which He is not able to perform. But the fault is with ourselves. We limit "the Holy ONE of Israel," and as a consequence get only so much as by our mental attitude we are able to receive—again the old maxim that "Power can only work in terms of the instrument it works through." I do not say that it is at all easy for us to completely rid ourselves of negative race-thought ingrained into us from childhood, and subtly playing upon that generic impersonal self in us of which I have spoken, and which readily responds to those thought-currents to which we are habitually attuned. It is a matter of individual growth. But the promises themselves contain no inherent impossibility, and are logical deductions from the principles of the Creative Law.

If the power of the Spirit over things of the material plane be an impossibility, then by what power did Jesus perform his miracles? Either you must deny his miracles, or you must admit the power of the Spirit to work on the material plane—there is no way out of the dilemma. Perhaps you may say: "Oh, but He was God in person!" Well, all the promises affirm that it is God who does these things; so what it is possible for God to do at one time, it is equally possible for Him to do at all times. Or perhaps you hold other theological views, and will say that Jesus was an exception to the rest of the race; but, on the contrary, the whole Bible sets Him forth as the Example—an exception certainly to men as we now know them, but the Example of what we all have it in us to become—otherwise what use is He to us? But apart from all argument on the subject we have his own words, telling us that those who believe in Him, i.e., believe what He said about Himself—shall be able to do works as great as His own, and even greater (John xiv, 12). For these reasons it appears to me that on the authority of the Bible itself, and also on metaphysical and scientific grounds we are justified in taking such promises as those I have quoted in a perfectly literal sense.

Then there are promises of the power that will attend our utterance of the Word. "Thou shalt also decree a thing and it shall be established unto thee" (Job xxii, 28). "All things are possible unto you" (Mark ix, 23). "Whosoever . . . shall believe that what he sayeth cometh to pass, he shall have whatsoever he sayeth" (Mark xi, 23), and so on.

Other passages again promise peace of mind. "Thou wilt keep him in perfect peace whose mind is staid on Thee, because he trusteth in Thee" (Isaiah xxvi, 3). "Let him take hold of my strength that he may make peace with me" (Isaiah xxvii, 5). St. Paul speaks of "The God of Peace" in many passages, e.g., Rom. xv, 33; 2 Cor. xiii, 11; 1 Thess. v, 23, and Hebr. xiii, 20; and Jesus, in his final discourse recorded in the fourteenth, fifteenth and sixteenth chapters of St. John's Gospel, lays peculiar stress on the gift of Peace.

And lastly there are many passages which promise the overcoming of death itself; as for instance Job xix, 25–27; John viii, 51, and x, 28, and xi, 25 and 26; Hebr. ii, 14 and 15; 1 Cor. xv, 50–57; 2 Tim. i, 10; Rom. vi, 23 ("The gift of God is eternal life in Jesus Christ, our Lord").

"God commanded the blessing, even Life for evermore" (Ps. cxxxiii, 3).

Now I hope the reader will take the trouble to look up the texts to which I have referred, and not be lazy. I am sure he would do so if he were promised a ten pound note or a fifty dollar bill for his pains, and if these promises are not all bosh, there is something worth a good deal more to be got by studying them. Just run through the list: health, wealth, peace of mind, safety, creative power, and eternal life. You would be willing to pay a good premium to an Insurance Office that could guarantee you all these. Well, there is a Company that does this without paying any premium, and its name is "God and Co., Unlimited"; the only condition is that you yourself have to take the part of "Co.", and it is not a sleeping partnership, but a wide-awake one!

So I hope you will take the trouble to look up the texts; but at the same time you must remember that the reading of single texts is not sufficient. If you take any isolated phrase you choose, without reference to the rest of the Book, there is no nonsense you cannot make out of the Bible. You would not be allowed to do that sort of thing in a Court of Law. When a document is produced in evidence, the meaning of the words used in it is very carefully construed, not only in reference to the particular clause in which they occur, but also with reference to the intention of the document as a whole, and to the circumstances under which they were written. The same word may mean very different things in different connections; for instance I remember two reported cases in one of which the word "Spanish" meant a certain sort of leather, and in the other a kind of material used in brewing; and in like manner particular texts are to be interpreted in accordance with the gist of the Bible as a whole.

This is just the mistake the Jews made, of building up theories on particular texts, and which Jesus corrected when he said: "Search the Scriptures, for in them ye think ye have eternal life, and these are they which testify of me" (John v, 39), or, as the Revised Version puts it: "Ye search the Scriptures because ye think that in them ye have eternal life; and these are they which bear witness of me," which appears to be the better rendering. The words "ye think" is the key to the whole passage. He says in effect: "You fancy that eternal life is to be found in the book. It is not to be found in the book, but in what the book tells you about, and here I am as a living example of it." It is just the same with everything else. No book can do more than tell you about a thing; it cannot produce it. You may study the cookery book from morning till night, but that will not give you your dinner.

What Jesus meant was, that we should read the Scriptures in the same way we should read any other book of practical instruction. First think what it is all about; then look at the nature of the general principles involved, and then see what instruction the book gives you for their practical application. *Then go and do it.* And remember also a further difference between reading about a thing and doing it. A book is for everybody, and can therefore only give general instruction; but when you come to do the thing you will always find it works with some personal modifications,—not departures from the general principles you have read about, but specializations of them—and in this way you will learn much that is not to be got out of books, even the best.

I remember many years ago, when I was much younger, asking one of our leading water-colour artists,* how he would recommend me to study landscape painting, and he said: "Practise continually from Nature, and you will learn more than any one can teach you; that is how I have learnt, myself." On the subject, then in question, he said just what Jesus did: "Here I am as a practical example of what I tell you." And another thing is, that the more you think principles out for yourself and try to observe them in practice, the clearer the meaning of your book will become to you. I have a few excellent books on painting, but I had no idea how excellent they were when I first got them; practical experience has taught me to find much more in them than I did at first, for now I understand better what they are talking about. Well, that is the way to read the Bible, neither despising it as worthless tradition, nor treating the mere letter of it with superstitious veneration; both extremes are to be equally avoided. In fact the Bible tells

* R. W. Allen.

us so itself: "The letter killeth, but the Spirit giveth life" (2 Cor. iii, 6); this, of course, does not mean that the letter can be tampered with, any more than a judge can alter the wording of a document put in evidence; it must be interpreted in the general sense of the document as a whole; and when the letter is thus vivified by the Spirit, it will be found fully to express it. But we require to enter into the Spirit of it first.

Now it appears to me, that taken in this way, the Bible is an exceedingly practical book, and that is why I want the reader to get at some general principles which he will find, *mutatis mutandis,* equally applicable all round, whether to electricity, or to life, and whatever may be the subject-matter, it will always be found to resolve itself into a question of the relation between Law and Personality. If now we read the Bible Promises in the light of the general principles we have considered in the earlier pages, we shall find that they are all Promises according to Law. They are statements of the results to be obtained by a truer realization of the principles of Law and Personality than we have hitherto apprehended.

We must always bear in mind that the Law is set in motion by the Word. The Word does not *make* the Law, but gives it something to work upon, so that without the Word there could be no manifestation of the Law, a truth embodied in the maxim, that "Every Creation carries its own mathematics along with it." If the reader remembers what I have said in the chapter of "The Soul of the Subject," he will see that the principle involved, is that of the susceptibility of the Impersonal to suggestions from the Personal. This follows of course from the very Conception of Impersonality; it is that which has no power of selection and volition, and which is therefore without any power of taking an initiative on its own account.

In a previous chapter I have pointed out that the only possible conception of the inauguration of a world-system, resolves itself into the recognition of one original and universal Substantive Life, out of which proceeds a corresponding Verb, or active energy, reproducing in action what the Substantive is in essence. On the other hand there must be something for this active principle to work in; and since there can be nothing anterior to the Universal Life or Energy, both these factors must be potentially contained in it. If, then, we represent this Eternal Substantive Life by a circle with a dot in the centre, we may represent these two principles as emerging from it by placing two circles at equal distance below it, one on either side, and placing the sign + in one, and the sign – in the other. This is how students of these subjects usually map out the relation of the *prima principia,* or first abstract principles. The sign + indicates the Active principle, and the sign – the Passive principle. If the reader will draw a little diagram as described, it will help to make what follows clearer.

Necessarily the initiative must be taken by the Active principle; and the taking of initiative implies selection and volition, that is to say, the essential qualities of personality; and Passivity implies the converse of all this, and therefore is Impersonality. The two principles in no way conflict with one another, but are polar opposites, like the positive and negative plates of a battery, or the two ends of a magnet. They are complementary to one another, and neither can work without the other. A little consideration will show that this is not a mere fancy, but a self-obvious generalization, the contrary to which it is impossible to conceive. It is simply the case of the box which cannot come into existence without the activity of the carpenter and the passivity of the wood.

From such considerations as this the deep thinkers of old times posited the generating of a world-system by the inter-action of what they named Animus Dei, the Active principle, and Anima Mundi, or Soul of the Universe, the Passive principle—the one Personal, and the other Impersonal; and by the hypothesis of the case the only mode of activity possible to Anima Mundi is response to Animus Dei. But the same impersonal passivity must also make Anima Mundi receptive likewise to lesser and more individualized modes of Personality, and it becomes, so to say, fecundated by the ideas thus impressed upon it. In every case "the word is the seed." We may picture this planting of an idea or "word" in the Cosmic soul as acting very much like the initial impulse that starts a train of waves in ether, and these thought-waves are reproduced in corresponding forms; or, to recur to the simile of seed, the cosmic soul acts like the soil and gives it nourishment. Looking at it in this way the old exponents of these things regarded the Active principle as Masculine, and the Passive as Feminine, the one generating and the other nutritive, corresponding to the words *rouah* and *hoshech,* the expansion and compression principles in the Hebrew text of the opening verses of Genesis.

If then we posit this impersonal Soul of the Universe as the living principle dwelling in the substance of the etheric Universal Medium it will account for a good many things. If it be asked why we should assume the presence of a living principle in the Universal Substance the answer is in the maxim "Quod ex Vivo Vivum," what proceeds from Life is living. Then as we see by our diagram, Anima Mundi equally with Animus Dei proceeds from the original Substantive of Life, and therefore, on the principle of the above maxim, that like produces like, Anima Mundi must also be a living thing whose vehicle is the Universal Substance.

We may picture then, the response of the indwelling Soul of the Universal Medium to our Thought, as starting corresponding vibrations in the Substance of the Medium, just as our own thought, acting through the vibratory system of our nerves, causes our body to make the movement we intend. But perhaps you will say: How can this be, seeing that by the hypothesis the Soul of the Universe is Impersonal, and therefore unintelligent? Well, it is just this fact of having no thought of its own, that enables us to impress our thought upon it and cause it, so to say, to "take on" an intelligence relatively to the subject of our thought, much in the same way that the impersonal soul in the human subject "takes on" or reflects the thought of the hypnotist, and not infrequently develops it to a far greater extent than the original thought of the operator expressed. Such a hypothesis—and I think some such hypothesis is needed to account for any creation at all—throws light on the *modus operandi* of the Bible Promises. We plant the Word of the Promise in the womb of Anima Mundi, and if we do not uproot it by using the same power adversely, it is bound to come to fruition in due course, by the same Law by which the world-systems are formed; and if we are to believe that the Word of the Promise is not our own word, but the Word of God, then our Thought of it is imbued with a corresponding power as we hand it over to Anima Mundi. Thus the Promises fulfil themselves automatically, in accordance with the principles of the relations between Law and Personality, and they do so, *not in our own power,* but by the Power of the Word of God.

This, then, gives us at least an intelligible working hypothesis of the rationale of the Bible Promises. The measurement of their fulfilment is exactly proportional to our belief in them, not from any unintelligible cause, and still less from any unreasoning feat of a capricious Deity, but by the working of an intelligible Law. If any of my readers happens to be an electrician, he will find an exact parallel in what is known as Ohm's Law. Such readers will be familiar with the formula C = ER, but for the benefit of those to whom this formula may be unintelligible, I will give a few words of explanation. C means the current of electricity which is to be delivered for any work that is to be done. E stands for the Electro-motive force which generates the current; and R is the Resistance offered to the current by the conductor, such as the wires through which it flows. If there be no resistance, the full amount of current generated would be delivered. But without any conductor no current could be delivered, and therefore there must be *some* resistance, and so the full power of the Electro-motive force can never be delivered by the Current. The amount that will be delivered is the original power of the Electro-motive force divided by the Resistance. The Resistance therefore acts as a restricting force, limiting the extent to which the power of the original Electro-motive force shall be delivered at the point where the work is to be done, but at the same time no delivery at that point could be effected without it; so the Resistance also has a necessary part to play in the working of the circuit. Now if we want to translate the formula C = ER into terms of spiritual force we may put it thus: E stands for the limitless Potential of the Eternal Spirit; C stands for the current flowing from it; and R stands for the localizing quality of our thought. We cannot entirely dispense with this localizing quality, for our whole purpose is to transmute the *unlimited,* undifferentiated power, which subsists in the Eternal Substantive of Spirit, into a particular differentiated mode of action, which therefore implies a corresponding centralization. This is the proper function of our thought. It is this compressing power which, as I said above, the Hebrew renders by the word *"hoshech"* in the opening verses of Genesis, and which is the necessary complementary to the converse expanding power or *"rouah."* It takes the co-operation of the two to produce any results.

Restricted, then, to its proper function our R or condensing quality is an essential factor in the work. But if it be allowed to take the form of doubt or unbelief, then it renders the flow of the current from the Spirit ineffective to the extent to which the doubt is entertained; and if doubt be allowed to degenerate into total unbelief and denial of the Power of the Spirit, we thereby cancel the originating force altogether. To put it in terms of the electrical formula, we make R greater than E, in which case no current can flow. We thus find that the words "According to your faith be it unto you" are actually the statement of a Mathematical Law, having nothing vague about them. This may be a somewhat original application of Ohm's Law, but the parallel is so exact, that I cannot help thinking it will appeal to some of my readers who may be conversant with Electrical Science. For those who are not, a simpler simile may be, that you cannot deliver a more powerful stream of water than the bore of the pipe through which it flows will admit of; or, to employ a legal truism, delivery on the part of the donor must be met by acceptance on the part of the donee before a deed of gift can become operative; or, in still simpler language, "you may take a horse to the water but you can't make him drink."

We see, then, that there is a Law of Faith, and that Faith is not a denial of the universal reign of Law, but the perception of its widest generalization, and therefore giving scope to its highest specialization. The opposition between Faith and Law, of which St. Paul so often speaks, is the opposition between this broad view of the ultimate Principle of the Creative Law and that narrower view of restriction by particular laws, which prevents us from grasping the Law of Faith; but that he does not deny the *Principle* of Law, that is the relation between C and E, is clear from his own statement in Rom. viii, where he says: "The Law of the Spirit of Life in Christ Jesus sets me free from the law of Sin and Death"; in other words: the Law of the Good sets us free from the Law of Evil; and for the same reason St. James says, that the perfect law is the law of Liberty (Jas. i, 25).

Of course if we suppose that faith is something contrary to the law of the Universe we at once import into our thought the negative quality which entirely vitiates our action. We rightly perceive that the laws of the Universe can never be altered, and if our notion of Faith be, that it is an attempt to work in contradiction to these laws, the best definition we can give it is that given by the little girl in the Sunday school, who said that "Faith is trying to make yourself believe what you know is not true." The reason for such a misconception is, that it entirely omits one of the factors in the calculation. It considers only the Law, and gives no place to the Word in the scheme of things. Yet we do not carry this misconception into the sciences of chemistry and electricity. We take the immutability of the Law as the basis of these sciences, but we do not expect the immutable Law to produce a photographic apparatus, or an electric train, without the intervention of a reasoning and selective power which specializes the fundamental general Law into particular uses. We do not look to the Law for those powers of reasoning and selection, through which we make it work in all the highly complex ways of our ordinary commercial applications of it—we know better than that. We look to Personality for this. In our every-day pursuits we always act on the maxim that "Nature unaided fails," and that the infinite possibilities stored up in the Law, can only be brought to light by a power of reasoning and selection working through the Law. This co-operation of the Personal with the Impersonal is the Law *of* the Law; and since the Law is unchangeable, this Law *of* the Law must also be unchangeable, and must therefore apply on all planes, and through all time—the Law, that without co-operation of the Law and the Word nothing can be brought into existence, from a solar system to a pin; while on the other hand there is no limit to what can be got out of the Law by the operation of the Word.

If the student will look at the Bible Promises in the light of the general principles, he will find that they are perfectly logical, whether from the metaphysical or from the scientific standpoint, and that their working is only from the same Law through which all scientific developments are made. If this be apprehended it will be clear that the Word of Faith is not "trying to make ourselves believe what we know is not true," but, as St. Paul puts it, it is "giving substance to things not yet seen" (Heb. xi, 1, R. V.).

VII

# DEATH AND IMMORTALITY

I THINK MOST OF my readers will agree with me, that the greatest of all the promises is that of the overcoming of death, for, as the greater includes the less, the power which can do *that* can do anything else. We think that there are only two things that are certain in this world—death and taxes, and no doubt, under the ordinary past conditions, this is quite true; but the question is: are they really inherent in the essential nature of things; or are they not the outcome of our past limited, and often inverted modes of Thought? The teaching of the Bible is that they are the latter. On the subject of taxes the Master says: "Render unto Cæsar the things that are Cæsar's" (Matth. xxii, 21), but on another occasion he said that the children of the King were not liable to taxation (Matth. xvii, 26). However we may leave the "taxes" alone for the present, with the remark that their resemblance to death consists in both being, under present conditions, regarded as compulsory. Under other conditions, however, we can well imagine "taxes" disappearing in a unity of thought which would merge them in cooperation and voluntary contribution; and it appears to me quite possible for death to disappear in like manner.

In whatever way we may interpret the story of Eden, whether literally, or if, like some of the Fathers of the church such as Origen, we take it as an allegory, the result is the same—that Death is not in the essence of man's creation, but supervened as the consequence of an inverted mode of thinking. The Creative Spirit thought one way, and Eve thought another; and since the Thought of the Creating Spirit is the origin of Life, this difference of opinion naturally resulted in death. Then, from this starting-point, all the rest of the Bible is devoted to getting rid of this difference of opinion between us and the Spirit of Life, and showing us that the Spirit's opinion is truer than ours, and so leading us to adopt it as our own. The whole thing turns on the obvious proposition, that if you invert the cause you also invert the effect. It is the principle that division is the inversion of multiplication, so that if $2 \times 2 = 4$ then you cannot escape from the consequence that $\frac{4}{2} = 2$. The question then is, which of the two opinions is the more reasonable—that death is essentially inherent in the nature of things, or that it is not?

Probably ninety-nine out of a hundred readers will say, the whole experience of mankind from the earliest ages proves that Death is the unchangeable Law of the Universe, and there have been no exceptions. I am not quite sure that I should altogether agree with them on this last point; but putting that aside, let us consider whether it really is the essential Law of the Universe. To say that this is proved by the past experience of the race, is what logicians call a *petitio principii*—it is assuming the whole point at issue. It is the same argument which our grandfathers would have used against aerial navigation—no one had ever travelled in the air, and that proved that no one ever could. My father, who was a junior officer in India when the first railway was run in England, used to tell a story of one of his senior officers, who, on being asked what he thought of the rapidity of the new mode of travelling, said he thought it was "all a damned lie," which opinion appeared to him to settle the whole question. But I hope that none of my readers will hold the same opinion regarding the overcoming of death, even though they might express it in more polite language. At any rate it may be worth while to examine the theoretical possibility of the idea.

To begin with, it involves a self-contradiction to say that the energy of any force can stop the working of that force. If a force stops working, it is for one of two reasons, either that the supply of it is exhausted, or that it is overcome by an opposite and neutralizing force. But we have seen that the Originating Cause of all things can only be an inexhaustible Power of Life, and therefore the hypothesis of it becoming exhausted is eliminated; and similarly, since all the forces of the Universe proceed from this Source, it is impossible for any of them to have a nature diametrically opposite to that of the source from which they flow. So the alternative must be eliminated also. Accordingly, the outflow, undifferentiated, of Life and Energy from the Eternal Substantive of Spirit, is never stopped *by its own current* in any of its differentiated streams; it is impossible for a current to be stopped by its own flow, whether it be a current of electricity, steam, water, or anything else. What then does stop the flow of any sort of current? It is the Resistance or *inertia* of the channel through which it flows; so that we come back to the formula of Ohm's Law, $C = \frac{E}{R}$ as a general proposition applicable to any conceivable sort of energy.

The neutralizing power then, is not that of the flowing of any sort of energy, but the rigidity, or inertia of the medium through which the energy has to make its way; thus bringing us back to *rouah* and *hoshech,* the expansive and compressive principles of the opening verses of Genesis. It is the broad scientific generalization of the opposition between Ertia, or Energy, and Inertia, or Absence of Energy; and since, for the reasons just given, Ertia cannot go against itself, the only thing that can stop it is Inertia.

Now the components of the human body are simply various chemical elements—so much carbon, so much hydrogen, etc., as any textbook on the subject will tell you; and although, of course, every sort of substance is the abode of ceaseless *atomic* energy, we all recognize that merely atomic energy is not that of the powers of thought, will, and perception, which make us organized mentalities instead of a mere aggregation of the various substances exposed to view in a biological museum, as constituting the human body—you might take all these substances in their proper proportions, and shake them up together, but you would not make an intelligent man of them. We are therefore safe in saying that the physiological body represents the principle of inertia in us, while the something that thinks in us represents the principle of ertia.

The balance of power between the Life Principle in us and the Death Principle, is then, necessarily, a question of the balance between these two, the spirit and the flesh, or ertia and inertia.

Why then does the balance preponderate to the life-side for a certain length of time, and then go over to the opposite side?

Now this brings us to the distinction which the old writers drew, between the "Vital Soul" of any living thing and the Spirit. Their conception of the "Vital Soul" was very much the same as I have set forth in the chapter on "The Soul of the Subject." It is the individual's particular share of the Cosmic Soul or Anima Mundi, whether it be an individual tree, or an individual person; and the ordinary maximum length of time, during which the Vital Soul will be able to overcome the inertia of its physical vehicle, depends upon the particular class to which the individual belongs. What the ordinary maximum is in regard to any species is a matter of experience, and it is in this way that we have fixed the usual limit of human life at threescore years and ten.

Now it is here that we shall begin to profit by some knowledge about the invisible part of ourselves. The actual molecules of our body, as I have just said, are only so much dead matter. This inert material is pulled about in various directions by strings which we call muscles, according to the movements we wish our bodies to make, and these muscles are set in motion by the vibrations of the nerves.* But what is it that occasions these vibrations of the nerves? Here we begin to pass beyond the limits of official Science, though not beyond the limits of recognizable Law. We have to recognize the existence of an etheric body acting as an intermediary between intention, desire, or (in the case of human beings) thought of the soul and the physical vibrations of the nerves. This is why, in an earlier chapter, I have drawn attention to our power of sending out etheric vibrations beyond the limits of the physical body, as in the case of De Rocha's experiments. Such experiments show that there is in us something not composed of dense matter, which is able to convey vibrations to dense matter; and it is this something which we speak of as the etheric body.

But if we wish to trace the links by which our thought operates upon the physical body, we find ourselves compelled to postulate yet another intermediary, what I have spoken of as the "Vital Soul"—a vehicle which does not *consciously think,* but in which what we may call race-consciousness becomes centred in the individual. This race-consciousness is none other than the ever-present "will-to-live" which is the basis of physical evolution—that automatically acting principle—which causes plants to turn towards the sun, animals to seek their proper food, and both animals and men to try instantly to escape from immediate danger. It is what we call instinct which does not reason. I may give a laughable experience of my own to illustrate the fact that conscious reason is not the method of this faculty. Once when

* See Chapters on "Body, Soul, and Spirit" in my "Edinburgh Lectures on Mental Science."

on leave from India I was walking along a street in London in the heat of a summer's day and suddenly noticed just at my feet a long dark thing apparently wriggling across the white glare of the pavement. "Snake!" I exclaimed, and jumped aside for all I was worth, and the next moment was laughing at myself for not recollecting that cobras were not common objects in the London streets. But it looked just like one, and of course turned out to be nothing but a piece of rag. Well, instinct did its duty even if it did make a fool of me; but there is certainly no conscious reasoning in the matter, only the automatic action of inherent Law—"Self-preservation is the first law of Nature."

This Vital Soul, then, is the seat of all those instincts which go towards the preservation of the individual's physical body, and towards the propagation of the race; and it is on this account that our theosophical friends call it the "Desire Body" or, to use the Indian term "Kama rupa." It acts with conscious intention, but not with conscious *reasoning.* It is thus distinguished on the one hand from the etheric body, which is a mere vehicle for finer vibrations than can take place in the denser matter of the physical body, but which has *no intention;* and on the other from the *mind* which acts by conscious reasoning, and it thus forms an intermediary between the two.

The importance of recognizing the place of this higher intermediary in the ascending scale of living principle is, that for all practical purposes the animal world does not rise higher than this in the scale. It is true that in particular instances we find the first dawning of the mental faculty in an animal, but it is only very faint; so this does not affect the broad general principle. The point to be noted is that up to this stage human beings are built on the same lines as animals, and what distinguishes us, is the addition in ourselves of a higher factor,—that of the reasoning mind exercising the power of conscious thought.

Now it is the direction of this thought that influences the three lower factors. The sequence, going upwards, is as follows:—movement is communicated to the physical body by the etheric body; and movement is communicated to the etheric body by the Vital Soul; then, in proportion as the purely instinctive action of the Vital Soul is controlled by the conscious thought, so its action upon the two lowest principles is modified.

Here, then, is the crucial point. In what direction is the conscious thought going to modify the action of the three principles that are below it?

If it takes the soul of mere racial desire and the physical body as its standard of thought, then it naturally follows that it cannot raise it any higher. It has descended to *their* level and so cannot pour any stream of life into it, on the simple principle that no current can ever flow from a lower to a higher level, whether the difference in level be that of actual elevation, as in the case of water, or difference in potential, as in the case of electricity. On the other hand if the conscious mind recognizes that itself proceeds from some higher source, it looks to receive life from that source, and its thought is modified accordingly, and in turn re-acts correspondingly upon the lower principles.

If this is clear to the student, he will now see how it is that by limiting our conception of life to the current ideas entertained by the race, we impress these ideas on our three lower principles. It is true that these three principles are not capable of reasoning themselves, but the highest of them, the Vital Soul, has its action modified by the reasoning principle above it, and so communicates to the two lowest principles corresponding waves of vibration. And in this connection we must remember the distinction between the two systems of nerves; the voluntary system connected with the brain and forming the medium of all voluntary action, and the involuntary, or sympathetic system connected with the solar plexus and controlling all the automatic actions of the body, and thus being the agent of that continual renewal of the physical organism which is always going on, and keeps in existence for a life time a body which begins to disintegrate immediately the soul has left it.* Now it is through this inner Builder of the Body that our Thought re-acts upon our physical organism. The response is purely automatic, for the simple reason that there is no original thinking power in the three lower principles; the action is that of the Law as directed by Thought or Word.

In this way then, it appears to me, the Personal in us acts upon the Impersonal in us; and if we assume, as I think we may, that this action takes place by means of etheric waves, we have, on general scientific principles, a clue to what we read in the Bible about the transmutation of the body. The theory of the constitution of the atom shows us that its nature is determined by the number of its particles and their rate of revolution, and that a change in the rate of revolution results in the throwing off of some of the particles.

---

* See "Edinburgh Lectures."

Then the number of particles being altered, there results a change in the distribution of the positive and negative charges within the sphere of the atom, since they must always exactly balance one another; and this change in the distribution of the positive and negative charges must instantly result in a corresponding change in the geometrical configuration of particles constituting the atom.

That the particles automatically arrange themselves into groups of different geometrical forms within the sphere of the atom, has been demonstrated both mathematically and experimentally by Professor J. J. Thompson,* these geometrical forms resulting of course from the balance of attraction and repulsion between the positive and negative charges of the particles.

That the transmutation of one substance into another is not a mere dream of the mediæval alchemists is now already shown by Modern Science. Under suitable conditions an atom of Radium breaks down into atoms of another sort known as Radium Emanations, and these again break down into yet another sort of atoms to which the name of Radium Emanations X has been given, while Radium Emanation also gives rise to the atom of Helium (N. K. 124). Thorium also behaves in the same manner, transmuting into atoms called Thorium X, which again change into atoms of another sort to which the name of Thorium Emanations has been given and these in turn transmute into atoms of yet another kind, known as Thorium Emanations X. The same is the case also with Uranium which, however, so far as is yet known, undergoes only one transmutation into what is known as Uranium X.

The transmutation of one sort of atom into another is therefore not a mere visionary fancy, but an established fact; and although our laboratory experiments in this direction may not as yet have gone very far, they have gone far enough to show that a Law of Transmutation does exist in Nature. Then, since the difference between one sort of atom and another results from the difference and arrangement of their particles, and the difference in the number and arrangement of the particles results from the difference in the speed of their rotation, and this again results from the difference in the energy or rate of vibration of the particles, we come back to different rates of etheric vibrations as the commencement of the whole series of changes; and as is proved by the facts of wireless telephoning, different

* "New Knowledge."

rates of etheric vibrations can be set in motion by the varying sounds of the human voice, even on the physical plane. May it not be then, that by the same law, vibrations of other wave-lengths, yet unknown to science, will be set in motion by the unspoken word of our thought?

The substance known as Polonium, even by its near approach to an electric bell, causes it to ring, and if etheric waves can thus be started by an inanimate substance, why should we suppose that our thought has less power, especially when metaphysically we cannot avoid the conclusion that the whole creation must have its origin in the Divine Thought?

From such considerations as these, I think we may reasonably infer that if the mind be illuminated by a range of thought coming from a higher mind, there is no limit to the power which may thus be exercised over the material world, and that therefore St. Paul's statement regarding the transmutation of the present physical body, is one which should be included in the circle of our ideas, as being within the scope of the Laws of the Universe when their action is specialized by the power of the Word (1 Cor. xv); and similarly with regard to other statements to the same effect contained in the Bible. What is wanted is the realization of a greater Word than that which we form from the current experience of the race. The race has formed its Word on the basis of the lower principles of our being, and if we are to advance beyond this, the Law of the subject clearly indicates that it can only be by adopting a more fundamental Word, or Idea, than that which we have hitherto thought to include the entire range of possibilities. The Law of our further Evolution demands a Word not formed from past experiences, but based upon the eternal principle of the All-Originating Life itself. And this is in strict accord with scientific method. If we had always allowed ourselves to be ruled by past experiences we should still be primitive savages; and it is only by the gradual perception of underlying principles, that we have attained the degree of civilization we have reached to-day; so what the Bible puts before us is simply the application to the life in ourselves of the maxim that "Principle is not limited by Precedent."

Now the Bible Promises serve to put us on the track of this Principle: they suggest lines of enquiry. And the enquiry leads to the conclusion that the two ultimate factors are the Law and the Word. What we have missed hitherto is the conception of the limitless possibilities of the Law, and the limitless power of the Word. On one occasion the Master said to the Jews "Ye know not the Scriptures neither the power of God" (Matth. xxii, 29) and the same is the case with ourselves. The true "Scripture" is the "scriptura rerum" or the Law indelibly written in the nature of things, and the written Scriptures are true only because they contain the statement of the Principle of the Law. Therefore until we see the Principle of the Law we "know not the Scriptures." On the other hand, until we see the Principle of the operation of the Word through the Law, we do not know "the Power of God"; and it is only as we come to perceive the interaction of the Law and the Word that we see the beginning of the way that leads to Life and Liberty.

But although it is evident from the text just quoted, as well as from other intimations in his Epistles, that St. Paul fully grasped the principle of the transmutation of the body, he himself tells us that he has not yet realized it in practice. He says he has not yet "attained to the resurrection from the dead," but is still pressing on towards its attainment (Ph. iii, 12). And it is to be remarked that he is not here speaking of a general "resurrection *of* the dead," but, as the word *exanastasis* in the original Greek indicates, of a special resurrection from among the dead; this indicates an *individual* achievement, not merely something common to the whole race. From this and other passages it is evident that by "the dead" it means those whose conception of Life is limited to the four lower principles, thus unifying the mind with the three principles which are below it; and the same idea is expressed in a variety of ways all through the Bible. This therefore shows that he is quite aware that knowledge of a principle does not enable us then and there to attain the completeness of the application, and if this be the case with St. Paul, we cannot be surprised to find it the same with ourselves. But on the other hand knowledge of the principle is the first step towards getting it to work.

Well, St. Paul is dead and buried, and so I suppose will most of us be in a few years; so the question confronts us, what becomes of us then?

As Milton puts it in "Il Penseroso" we want

*"to unsphere*
*The spirit of Plato and unfold*
*What worlds or what vast regions hold*
*The immortal mind that hath forsook*
*Her mansion in the fleshly nook."*

Yes, this is a question of deep personal interest to us; but as I cannot speak from experience, I will restrict myself to seeing whether we can form any sort of general hypothesis on the basis of the principles we have recognized. What then is likely to survive? The physical body is of course disintegrated by the chemistry of Nature. The etheric body probably continues to retain its form longer, because it is a condensation of etheric particles wrought together by the etheric waves sent out by the Vital Soul, and is therefore not subject to the laws of chemical affinity. The Vital Soul, being the race-principle of life in the individual,—that principle which automatically seeks to preserve the individual from disintegration,—probably survives longer still, until, ceasing to receive any reflex vibrations from the body, it grows gradually weaker in its sense of individual guardianship, and so is eventually absorbed into the group-soul or generic essence of the class to which it belongs. This is probably what happens in the case of animals for want of any higher vivifying principle, and would be the same with us were it not for the fact of having such a higher principle. In our case I should imagine that the influx of etheric waves, received from the thought action of the mind, would have the effect of continuing to impress the Vital Soul with a sense of individuality, in terms of its own plane, which would prevent it from being absorbed into the group-soul so long as the vital current from the mind continued to reach it. But eventually that current would cease to reach it, and in some cases, because the individual mind that governed it would gradually realize that its connection with the physical plane had ceased, and in others, because through a higher illumination the mind had, of its own volition, turned its thought in another direction. In either case, on the ceasing of the influx of that vitalizing current, the Vital Soul of the human being would likewise be absorbed into the Cosmic Soul, or Anima Mundi.

How long the processes of the disintegration of the etheric body, and absorption of the vital soul may take, is a question on which I can offer no opinion beyond saying that certain psychic phenomena suggest that in some cases they may take a long period of time. But for the reasons I have now given, it appears to me that the permanently surviving factor is the thinking mind which is our real self, and is positively our centre of consciousness after the physical body has been put off.

By the facts of the case its consciousness is no longer affected by vibrations received from the physical body; and therefore, to the extent to which our idea of life has been centred in that body, we shall feel its loss. If our motto has been "Let us eat and drink, for to-morrow we die" we shall feel very dead indeed—a living death, a consciousness of being cut off from all that constituted our enjoyment of life—a thirst for the satisfaction of our customary ideas, which we have no power to quench; and, in proportion as our habitual mode of thought is raised above that lowest level, so will our sense of loss be less. Then, by the same Law, if our habitual mode of thought is turned towards pure, beautiful, and helpful ideals, we shall feel no loss at all, for we shall carry our own ideals with us, and, I hope, see them more clearly by reason of their disentanglement from mundane considerations. In what precise way we may then be able to work out our ideals I will not now stop to discuss. What we want first is a reasonable theory, based upon the principle of that universal Law which is only varied in its actions by the conditions under which it works; so, instead of speculating as to precise details, we may generalize the question of how we can work out the good ideals which we carry over with us, and put it this way:—Our ideas are embodied in thoughts; thoughts start trains of etheric waves, which waves induce reciprocal action whenever they meet with a receiver capable of vibrating synchronously with them, and so eventually the thought becomes a fact, and our helpful and beautiful ideal becomes a work of power, whether in this world or in any other.

Now it is to the forming of such ideals that the Bible, from first to last is trying to lead us. From first to last it is working upon one uniform principle, that the Thought is the Word, that the Word sets in motion the Law, and that when the Law is set in motion it acts with mathematical precision. The Bible is a handbook of instruction for the use of our Creative Power of Thought, and this is the sequence which it follows—one definite method, so fundamental in its nature, that it applies equally to the making of a packing-case or the making of a solar system.

Now we have formed a generalized conception, based on this universal method, of the sort of consciousness we are likely to have when we pass out of the physical body. Then our thought naturally passes on to the question what will happen after this?

It is here that some theory of the reconstitution of the physical body appears to me to hold a most important place in the order of our evolution. Let us try to trace it out on the general lines of the Creative Power of

Thought indicated above, the keynote to which is that the Law is specialized by the Word, and cannot of itself bring out the infinite possibilities contained in it without such specializing, just as in all scientific development of ordinary life. The clue to the whole question is, that our place in the Universal Order is to develop the infinite resources of the Original Life and Substance into actual facts. "Nature unaided fails." The Personal Factor must co-operate with the Impersonal, alike for setting up an electric bell, or for the furtherance of cosmic evolution; and the reason it is so is, because it could not possibly be otherwise.

If now we start by recognizing this as our necessary place in the Progressive Order of the Universe, I think it will help us to form a reasonable theory as to the reconstruction of the body. First of all, why have we any physical body at all? As a matter of fact we have one, and no amount of transcendental philosophizing will alter the fact, and so we may conclude that there is some reason for it. We have seen the truth of the maxim "Omne vivum ex vivo," and therefore that all particular forms of life are differentiations of the one Basic Life. This means a localizing of the Life-Principle in individual centres. The formation of a centre implies condensation; for where there is no condensation the Energy, whether electricity or Life, is simply *dispersed* and *achieving no purpose.* Therefore distinctness from the undifferentiated Original Life is a necessity of the case. Consequently the higher the degree of Consciousness of Individuality, the greater must be the Consciousness of *Distinctness of Personality.*

We say of a "wobbly" sort of person: "That fellow is no use, you can't depend on him." We say of a person whose ideas, intentions, and methods are subject to continual variations under all sorts of outside influences, whether of opinions or circumstances, that he has "no backbone," meaning that he is in want of individuality. He has no real thought of his own, and so has no Word of Power by which to co-operate with the Law; therefore, to the extent to which this is the case with any of us, we are of no use in furthering the unfoldment of Evolution, whether in ourselves or anywhere else.

Now we talk a lot about Evolution or the *un*folding, but we seem often not to realize that there must be something to unfold; and that therefore *In*-volution, or the concentration of the Life-principle, must be a condition precedent to its *E*-volution. This process of Involution must therefore be a process of gradually increasing concentration of the Life-principle, by association with denser and denser modes of the Universal Substance. Then, on the principle of Vibration, the less dense the substance in which the Life is immersed, the more it must be subject to being stirred by vibratory currents other than those produced by the conscious action of the Ego, or inherent Life, of the individuality that is being formed.

But *"the Sum of the Vibrations in anything determines the mode, power, and direction of its action";* therefore, the less the Ego be concentrated through association with a dense vehicle, the more "wobbly" it must be, and consequently the less able to take any effective part in the further work of Creation. But in proportion as the Ego builds up an *Individual Will,* the more it gets out of the "wobbly" state—or, to refer once more to the idea of etheric waves—it becomes able to select what vibrations it will receive, and what vibrations it will send out.

The involution of the Ego into the physical body, such as we at present know it, is thereforce a necessity of the case, if any effective Individuality is to be brought into existence, and the work of Creation carried on instead of being cut short, not for want of material, but for want of workmen capable of using the tools of the builders' craft—the Law as "Strength" and the Word as "Beauty."

The Descending Arc of the Circle of Being is therefore that of the Involution of Spirit into denser and denser modes of Substance,—a process called in technical language by the Greek name "Eleusin," and the process continues until a point is reached where Spirit and Substance are in equal balance, which is where we are now. Then comes the tug of war. Which of the two is to predominate? They are the Expansive and Constrictive primal elements, the "rouah" and "hoshech" of the Hebrew Genesis.

If the Constrictive element be allowed to go further than giving necessary form to the Expansive element, it imprisons the latter. The condensation becomes too dense for the Ego to receive or send forth vibrations according to its free will, and so the Individuality becomes lost. If the condensation process be not carried far enough, no Individuality can be built up, and if it be carried too far, no Individuality can emerge; so in both cases we get the same result that there is no one to speak the Word of Power without which "Nature unaided fails."

Thus we are now exactly at the bottom of the Circle of Being. We have completed the Descending Arc and reached the point where the realization of the Distinctness of Conscious Individuality enables us to choose our own line, whether that of progressing through the stages of the Ascending Arc of Being, or of falling out from the living Circle of Progression, at least for a period, into what is sometimes mystically spoken of as "the Moon," or (in descending order) the "Eighth Sphere," and which is called in Scripture "The Outer Darkness,"—the rigidity which stops the action of Life.

Therefore it is with regard to this stage of our career that the Bible lays so much stress on the conflict between the Spirit and the Flesh—it is a fact in the course of our evolution, and the purpose of the Bible is to teach us how to move forward along the Ascending Arc of the Circle of Being, so as to build up individualities which will be able to use the tools of Intelligence and Will in the great work of Evolution, both Personal and Cosmic.

Now what is shown diagrammatically as the Ascending Arc of the Circle of Life is the Return from its lowest point, or the *Full Consciousness of Personal Distinctness,* gained through *the Material Body,* back to its highest point or the Originating Life itself. This is the truth embodied in the parable of the Prodigal Son. It is a Cosmic truth, and this return journey is technically called by the Greek name "Anaktorion." It is the Rising-again, that is from matter to Spirit, and is the Resurrection Principle.

But what is accomplished by the journey of the Ego round the Circle of Life?

*A New Centre* of Intelligence and volition is established; from this the Creative Word of Power can be spoken—a *Complete Man* has been brought into existence, who can take a *free and intelligent* part in the further work of Creation, by his understanding of the interaction between the Law and the Word. The "Volume of the Sacred Law" lies open before us, and the Vibratory Power of the Word to give effect to it is the "Blazing Star" that illuminates its contents, and so we become fellow-workers with the Great Architect of the Universe.

For these reasons it appears to me that our self-recognition in a physical body is a necessary step in our growth. But why should the reconstruction of a physical body be either necessary or desirable? The answer is as follows:

Obviously self-recognition is the necessary basis for all use of those powers of selection and volition by which the Impersonal Law is to be specialized so as to bring to light its limitless potentialities; and self-recognition means the recognition of our personal Distinctness from our environment.

Therefore it must always mean the possessing of a body as a vehicle, by means of which to act upon that environment, and to receive the corresponding reaction from it. In other words it must always be a body constituted in terms of the plane upon which we are functioning. But it does not follow that we should always be tied down to one plane.

On the contrary, the very conception of the power of the Word to specialize the action of the Law, implies the power of functioning on any plane we choose; but always subject to the Law, that if we want to act on any particular plane in *propria persona,* and not merely by influencing some other agent, we can only do so by assuming a body in terms of the nature of that plane. Therefore, if we want to act on the physical plane, we must put on a physical body. But when we have fully grasped the Power of the Word we cannot be tied to a body. We shall no longer regard it as composed of so many chemical elements, but we shall see beyond them into the real primary etheric substance of which they are composed, and so by our volition shall be able to put the physical body on or off at pleasure,—that at least is a quite logical deduction from what we have learnt in the preceding pages.

Seen in this light the "Resurrection Body" is not the old body resuscitated, but a new body, just as real and tangible as the old one, only not subject to any of its disabilities,—no longer a limitation, but the ever ready instrument for any work we may desire to do upon the physical plane.

But perhaps you will say, "Why should we want to have anything more to do with the physical plane? surely we have had enough of it already!" Yes; in its old sense of limitation; but not in the new sense of a world of glorious possibilities, a new field for our creative activities; not the least of which is the helping of those who are still in those lower stages which we have already passed through.

I think if we realize the position of the Fully Risen Man, we shall see that he is not likely to turn his back upon the Earth as a rotten, old thing. Therefore a new physical body is a necessary part of his equipment.

If, then, we take it as a general principle, that for self-recognition upon any plane a body in terms of that plane is a necessity, this will throw some light on the Bible narrative of our Lord's appearances after his Resurrection. It is noteworthy that he himself lays stress on the body as an integral part of the individuality. When the disciples thought they had seen an apparition he said: "Handle me and see that it is I *myself,* and *not* a spirit, for a spirit hath not flesh and bones as ye see I have" (Luke xxiv, 39). This very clearly states that the spirit without a corresponding body is not the complete "I myself"; yet from the same narrative we gather that the solid body in which he appeared is able to pass through closed doors, and to be disintegrated and re-integrated at will. Now on the electronic theory of the constitution of matter which I have spoken of in the earlier part of this book, there is nothing impossible in this; on the contrary it is only the known Law of synchronous vibration carried into those further ranges of wavelengths which, though not yet produced by laboratory experiment, are unavoidably recognized by the mathematicians.

In this way then the Resurrection of the Body appears to me to be the legitimate termination of our present stage of existence. What further developments may follow, who shall say? for we must remember that the end of one series is always the commencement of another—that is the doctrine of the Octave. But this is far enough to look forward in all conscience. As to *when* the completion of our present stage of evolution will be attained, it is impossible even to hazard a guess; but that the *individual* attainment of such a Resurrection is not dependent on any particular date in the world's history, is clearly the teaching of Scripture. When Martha said to Jesus that she knew her brother would rise again "at the last day," he ignored the question of "the last day," and said "I am the Resurrection and the Life" (St. John xi, 25); and similarly St. Paul puts it forward as a thing to be attained (Ph. iii, 15). It is not a resurrection *of* the dead but *from among* the dead that St. Paul is aiming at—not an "anastasis ton nekron," but an "anastasis *ek* ton nekron."

Doubtless there are other passages of Scripture which speak of a general resurrection, which to some will be a resurrection to condemnation (St. John v, 29), a resurrection to shame and everlasting contempt (Dan. xii, 2). This is a subject upon which I will not attempt to enter—I have a great many things to learn, and this is one of them; but if the Bible statements regarding resurrection are to be taken as a whole, these passages cannot be passed over without notice. On the other hand the Bible statements regarding *individual* resurrection are there also, and the general principle on which they are based becomes clear when we see the fundamental relation between the Law and the Word. Only we must remember that the Word that can thus set in motion the Law of Life, and make it triumph over the Law of Death, cannot be spoken by the limited personality which only knows itself as John Smith or Mary Jones. We must attain a larger personality than that, before we can speak the Word. And this larger personality is not just John Smith or Mary Jones magnified; that is the mistake we are all so apt to fall into. Mere magnification will not do it. A square will continue to be a square however large you make it; it will never become a circle. But on the other hand, there is such a thing as stating the area of a circle in the form of a square; and when we learn to regard our square as not existing on its own account, but as an expression of the circle in another form, our attention will be directed to the circle first, as the generating figure, and *then* to the square as a particular mode of expressing the same area. If we look at it in this way we shall never mistake the square for the circle, but we shall see that as the circle grows, the corresponding square will grow with it. It is this dependence of the square on the circle that makes all the difference, and makes it a living, growing square. For the true circle represents Infinitude. It is not bounded by a limiting circumference as in the merely symbolic geometrical figure, but is rather represented by the impulse which generates an ever widening circle of electro-magnetic waves; and when we realize this, our square becomes a living thing. The "Word" that we speak with this recognition is no longer ours, but His who sent us—the expression, on the plane of individuality, of the Thought that sent us into existence and so it is the "Word of Life." This is the true Resurrection of the Individual.

VIII

# TRANSFERRING THE BURDEN

THE MORE WE GROW into a clear perception of what is really meant by "Squaring the Circle," the freer we shall find ourselves from the burden of anxiety. We shall rise to a larger generalization of the Law of Cause and Effect. We shall learn in all things to reach out to First Cause as operating through the channels of secondary causation,—"causa causas" as producing, and therefore controlling "causa causata"—and so we cease to worry about secondary causes. On the plane of the lower personality we see certain facts, and argue that they are bound to produce certain results, which would be quite true if we really saw *all* the facts; or, again, allowing that in any particular case we actually did see all the facts as they now exist, we can either deny the operation of First Cause, or recognize its infinite capacity for creating new facts. Therefore, whatever may be the nature of our anxiety, we should endeavour to dispel it by the consideration that there may be already existing other facts we do not know of, which will produce a different result from the one we fear, and that in any case there is a power which can produce new facts in answer to our appeal to it.

But I can imagine some one saying to us, "You bumptious little midget, do you think First Cause is going to trouble Itself about you and your petty concerns? Do you not know that First Cause works by universal Law, and makes no exceptions?" Well, I would not have written this book if I did not suppose that First Cause works by universal Law, and it is just because It does so that I believe It *will* work for me and my concerns. The Law makes no exceptions, but it can be specialized through the power of the Word. Then our sceptic says, "What, do you think *your* word can do that?" To which I reply, "It is not my word because I am not using it in my lower personality, as John Smith or Mary Jones, but in that higher personality which recognizes only one all-embracing Personality and itself as included in that."

Which comes first, the Law or the Word?

The distribution of the solar systems in space, the localization of the Spirit in specific areas of cosmic activity, proclaims the starting of all manifestation through the "Word." Then the operation of Law follows with mathematical precision, just as when we write 2 × 2 we cannot avoid getting 4 as the result—only there is no reason why we should not write 2 × 3 and so get 6 instead of 4. Let it be borne in mind that the Law flows from the Word, and not *vice versa,* and you have got the clue to the enigma of Life.

How far we shall be able to make practical use of this clue depends, of course, on our acceptance of its principle.

The Directing Power of the Word is *inherent* in the Word, and we cannot alter it. *It is the Law* OF *the Law,* and so, like any other law, it cannot be broken, but its action can be inverted. We cannot deprive the Word of its efficacy, but our denial of it as the Word of Expansion is equivalent to an affirmation of it as the Word of Contraction, and so the Law acts towards us as a Limitation. But the fault is not in the Law, but in the way we use the Word. Now if the reader grasps this, he will see that the less we trouble ourselves about what appear to us to be the visible and calculable causes of things, the freer we must become from the burden of anxiety; and as we advance step by step to a clearer recognition of the true order of Cause and Effect, so all intermediate causes will fade from our view. Only the two extremes of the sequence of Cause and Effect will remain in sight. First Cause, moving as the Word, starting a sequence, and the desired result terminating it, as the Word taking Form in Fact. The intermediate links in the chain will be there, but they will be seen as effects, not causes. The wider the generalization we thus make, the less we shall need to trouble about particulars, knowing that they will form themselves by the natural action of the Law; and the widest generalization is therefore, to state not what we want to *have,* but what we want to *be.* The only reason we ever want to *have* anything, is because we think it will help us to be something—

something more than we are now; so that the "having" is only a link in the chain of secondary causes, and may therefore be left out of consideration, for it will come of itself through the natural workings of the Law, set in operation by the Word as First Cause. This principle is set forth in the statement of the Divine Name given to Moses (Ex. iii, 13–14). The Name is simply "I AM"—it is Being, not having—the having follows as a natural consequence of the Being; and if it be true that we are made in the likeness and image of God, that is to say on the same Principle, then what is the Law of the Divine nature must be the Law of ours also—and as we awake to this we become "partakers of the Divine Nature" (2 Pet. i, 4).

What we really want, therefore, is to *be* something—something more than we are now; and this is quite right. It is our consciousness of the continually generative impulse of the Eternal Living Spirit, which is the *fons et origo* (fountain and source) of all differentiated life working within us for ever more and more perfect individual expression of all that is in Itself. If the reader remembers what I said at the beginning of this book about the Verb Substantive of Being, he will see that each of us is in truth a "Word (verbum) of God." Let not the orthodox reader be shocked at this—I am only saying what the Bible does. Look up the following passages: "I will write upon him the name of my God and my own new name" (Rev. xiii, 12). "I saw, and behold a lamb standing on the Mount Zion (note, the word Zion means the principle of Life), and with him a hundred and forty and four thousand, having his name and the name of his Father written on their foreheads" (Rev. xiv, 1). "His name shall be on their foreheads" (Rev. xxii, 4). Read particularly the whole passage Rev. xix, 11–16, where we are expressly told that the name in question is "the Word of God"; and that this name is the one put upon those who follow their Leader, is shown by the same description being given of the followers as of the Leader. They all ride upon "white horses," and the "horse" is the symbol of the intellect. Also in the case of the Leader, the peculiarity of his Name is that "no one knows it but himself," and in Rev. ii, 17, exactly the same thing is said of the "New Name" to be given "to him that overcometh." Again, in Isaiah lxii, 2, "Thou shalt be called by a new name, which the mouth of the Lord shall name"; and again in Num. vi, 27, "They shall put my name upon the children of Israel."

Then as the meaning of that Name "the Word of God." In Ps. cxix, 160: "Thy word is true from the beginning," and Jesus said: "Thy Word is Truth" (John xvii, 17).

This also corresponds with the description in Rev. xix, 11–16 where another name for "the Word of God" is "Faithful and True"; and the same metaphor of the Truth *"riding into action"* is contained in Ps. xlv, 3, 4. "Gird thy sword upon thy thigh, O most mighty, with thy glory and thy majesty; and in thy majesty ride prosperously because of Truth." The same symbol of "riding" also occurs in Ps. lxviii: "Extol him that rideth upon the heavens," "Sing praises to him that rideth upon the heaven of heavens which were of old (i.e., *ab initio*); lo, he doth send out his Voice and that a mighty Voice"—and the word "Voice" is the Hebrew Word "Kōl," meaning "Sound" or "Word"—so that here again we have the idea of "The Word" riding into action. Once more—"Thou hast magnified thy Word above all thy Name" (Ps. cxxxviii, 2), thus repeating the idea of the Word as the Name.

In other passages we have the idea of the Word as a Weapon. "The Sword of the Spirit which is the Word of God" (Eph. vi, 17), which answers to the description in Revelations of the Sword proceeding out of the mouth of the Word; and we have the same metaphor of the Word riding into action in Habakkuk iii, 8 and 9. "Thou didst ride upon thine horses and thy chariots of salvation. Thy bow was made quite naked . . . even thy Word"; and similarly those that oppose the Word are "killed with the sword of him that sat upon the horse, which sword proceeded out of his mouth."

In other passages we have the Word put before us as a Defence. "His Truth shall be thy shield and buckler" (Ps. xci, 4); and again "The Name of the Lord is a strong tower; the righteous runneth into it and is safe" (Prov. xviii, 10); and we have already seen that this Name is "The Word of God"; and similarly in Ps. cxxiv, 8: "Our help is in the name of the Lord, who made heaven and earth."

Lastly, we get "the Word" as the final deliverance from all ill; "Into thy hand I commit my spirit: thou hast redeemed me, O Lord God of Truth" (Ps. xxxi, 5).

And the reason of all this is because "His Truth endureth to all generations" (Ps. c, 5); it is everlasting, Changeless Principle. "By the Word of the Lord were the heavens made; and all the host of them by the breath of his mouth" (Ps. xxxiii, 6), as is also said of the Word in the opening of St. John's Gospel and First Epistle.

Now a careful comparison of these and similar passages will make it clear that the sequence presented to us is as follows: The "Word" is the passing of the Verb Substantive of Being into Action. It is always the same in Principle, on whatever scale, and therefore applies to ourselves also, so that each one of us is a "Word of God." We are this by the very essence of our being, and that is why the first thing we are told about Man is, that he is made in the image and likeness of God. But how far any of us will become a really effective "Word," depends upon our acceptance of the New Name which is ready to be bestowed upon each one. "To as many as *receive* him, to them gives he power to become Sons of God, even to them that believe on his Name" (John 1–12). We get the New Name by realizing the Truth, which Truth is that we ourselves are included in THE NAME, and that name is called "The Word of God."

The meaning of which becomes clear if we remember that the spiritual name of anything is its "Noumenon" or essential being, which is manifested through its "Phenomenon" or outward reproduction in Form; so that the true order is first our "Name" or essential Being, then our "Word" or active manifestation of this essential Being, then the "Truth" or the unchangeable Law of Being passing into Manifestation—and these three are ONE. Then when we see that this is true of ourselves, not because of some arbitrary favouritism making us exceptions to the human race, but because it is the working on the plane of Human Individuality of the same Power and the same Law by which the world has come into existence, we can see that we have here a Principle which we can trust to work as infallibly as the principle of Mathematics; and that therefore the desire to become something more than we now are is nothing else than the Eternal Spirit of Life seeking ever fuller expression.

The correction which our mode of thinking needs therefore is to start with Being, not with Having, and we may then trust the Having to come along in its right order; and if we can get into this new manner of thinking, what a world of worry it will save us! If we realize that the Law flows from the Word, and not vice versa, then the Law of attraction must work in this manner, and will bring to us all those conditions through which we shall be able to express the more expanded Being towards which we are directing our Word; and as a consequence, we shall have no need to trouble about forcing particular conditions into existence—they will grow spontaneously out of the seed we have planted. All we have to do now, or at any time, is to take the conditions that are ready to hand and use them on the lines of the sort of "being" towards which we are directing our Thought—use them just as far as they go at the time, without trying to press them further—and we shall find by experience that out of the present conditions thus used to-day, more favourable conditions will grow in a perfectly natural manner to-morrow, and so on, day by day, until, when later on we look back, we shall be surprised to find ourselves expressing all, and more than all, the sort of *"being"* we had thought of. Then, from this new stand-point of our being, we shall continue to go on in the same way, and so on *ad infinitum,* so that our life will become one endless progress, ever widening as we go on. And this will be found a very quiet and peaceful way, free from worry and anxiety, and wonderfully effective. It may lead you to some position of authority or celebrity; but as such things belong to the category of "Having" and not of "Being" they were not what you aimed at, and are only by-products of what you have become in yourself. They are conditions, and like all other conditions should be made use of for the development of still more expanded "being"; that is to say, you will go on working on the more extended scale which such a position makes possible to you. But the one thing you would not try to do with it would be to "boss the show." The moment you do this you are no longer using the Word of the larger Personality, and have descended to your old level of the smaller personality, just John Smith or Mary Jones, ignorant of yourselves as being anything greater. It is true your Word still directs the operation of the Law towards yourself—it always does this—but your word has become inverted, and so calls into operation the Law of Contraction instead of the Law of Expansion. A higher position means a wider field for usefulness—that is all; and to the extent to which you fit yourself for it, it will come to you. So, if you content yourself with always speaking in your Thought the Creative Word of "Being" from day to day, you will find it the Way of Peace and the Secret of a Happy Life—by no means monotonous, for all sorts of unexpected interests will be continually opening out to you, giving you scope for all the activities of which your present degree of "being" renders you capable. You will always find plenty to do, and find pleasure in doing it, so you need never be afraid of feeling dull.

But perhaps you will say:

"How am I to know that I am not speaking my own Word instead of that of the Creative Spirit?"

Well, the word of the smaller personality is always based on the idea of possessing, and the Word of the Spirit is always based on the idea of Becoming—that is the criterion. And also, if we base our speaking of the Word on the Promises of Spirit, we may be sure that we are on the right track.

We may be sure of it, because when we come to analyze these promises we shall find that they are all statements of the Creative Law of Being, and the nature of this Law is obvious from the facts of the Visible Creation.

These things are not true because they are written in the Bible, but the Bible is true because these things are written in it. The more we examine the Bible Promises, the more they will impress themselves upon us as being Promises according to Law; and since the Law can never be broken, we can feel quite secure of it, subject to the one condition that we do not stop the Law from working to the fulfilment of the Promise, by our own inverted use of the Word. But if we take the *Word of the Promise* and make it our own Word, then we know that we are speaking the right Word, which will so specialize the action of the Law, as to produce the fulfilment of the Promise. Apart from the Word there is no Foundation. In all other systems we have either Law without Will, or Will without Law.

Then we know that we are not speaking of ourselves, but are speaking the Word of the Power that sent us into the World. The Law alone cannot fulfil the Promises. It is in itself Cosmic and Impersonal, and, as every scientific discovery amply demonstrates, it needs the co-operation of the Personal Factor to bring out its latent possibilities; so that the Word is as necessary as the Law for the fulfilment of the Promises; but if the Word which we speak is that of the Creating Spirit, we may reckon it as being just as certain in its operation as the Law, and the two together form an infallible Power.

But there is one thing we must not forget, and this is the Law of Growth. If the Law which we plant is the seed, then we must allow time for it to grow; we must leave it alone and go about our business as usual, and the seed we have sown will spring and grow up of itself, we know not how, a truth which we have been told by the Master himself (Mark iv, 26, 29).

We must not be like children who plant a seed one day, and dig it up the next to see whether it is growing. Our part is to plant the seed, not to make it grow,—the Creative Law of Life will do that. It is for this reason that the Bible gives us such injunctions as "Study to be quiet" (1 Thess. iv, 11). "He that believeth shall not make haste" (Is. xxviii, 16). "In quietness and in confidence shall be your strength" (Is. xxx, 15). To make ourselves anxious as to whether the Word we have planted will fructify is just to dig it up again, and then of course it will not grow.

The fundamental maxim, then, which we must always keep in mind is that "Every creation carries its own Mathematics along with it," and that therefore "The Law flows from the Word," and not *vice versa;* and consequently *"The Word is the Foundation of every creative series,"* whether that series be great or small, cosmic or individual, constructive or destructive. Every series commences with Intention; and remember the exact meaning of the Word. It is from the two Latin words "in," towards, and "tendere," to stretch, and it therefore means a "reaching out in a certain direction." This "reaching out in a certain direction" is the Conception of ourself as arrived at the destination towards which our Thought tends, and is therefore *the conceiving of an idea,* and our formulated idea is stated, if only mentally, in Words—and the termination of the series is the realization of the idea in actual fact. Therefore it is equally true of every series, whether it be the creation of a lady's blouse or the creation of a world, that "in the Beginning is the Word"—the Word is *the Point of Origination.*

Then, since the Word is the Point of Origination, what is our conception of the best thing we can originate with it? There is a great variety of opinion as to what is desirable; and it is only natural and right that it should be so, for otherwise we should be without any individuality, which means that we should have no real life in us—in fact such a world is unthinkable; it would be a world that had ceased to move, it would be a dead world. So it is the varied conception of "the Good" that makes the world go on. Uniformity means reducing things to one dead level. But on the other hand there must be Unity—unity of action resulting from unity of purpose, otherwise the world logically terminates in internecine strife. If then the world is to go on, it can only be by means of Unity expressing itself in Variety, and therefore the question is: What is the *unifying Desire* which underlies all the varieties of expression? It is a very simple one—it is just to ENJOY LIVING. Our ideas of an enjoyable life may be very various, but that is what we all really want; so what we want to get at is: What is the basis of an enjoyable life?

I have no hesitation in saying that the secret of enjoying life is *to take an interest in it.* The opposite of Livingness is Deadness, that is, inertia and stagnation. Dying of "ennui" is a very real thing indeed, and if we would not die of this malady we must have an interest in life that will always keep going on.

Now for anything to interest us we must enter into the spirit of it. If we do not enter into the spirit of a game it does not interest us; if we do not enter into the spirit of a book, it does not interest us, we are bored to death with it; and so on with everything. So from our own experience we may lay down the maxim that "To enjoy anything we must enter into the spirit of it," and if this be so, then, to enjoy the "Living Quality of Life" we must enter into the Spirit of Life itself. I say the "Living Quality of Life" so as to dissociate it from all ideas of particular conditions; because what we are trying to get at is the fundamental principle of Life which creates conditions, and not the reflex of sensations, whether physical or mental, which any particular set of conditions may induce in us for the time being. In this way we come back to the initial proposition with which we started—that the origin of everything is only to be found in a Universal Ever-Living Spirit, and that our own life proceeds from this Spirit in accordance with the maxim "Omne vivum ex vivo." Thus we are logically brought to the conclusion that the ultimate Desire of all Humanity is to consciously enter into the Spirit of Life as it is *in itself,* antecedently to all conditions. This is the widest of all generalizations, and so opens the door to the highest of all specializations; for it is a scientific fact, that the more widely we can generalize the principle of any Law, the more highly we can specialize its working. It is only as our conception of it is limited that any Law limits us.

A principle *per se* is always undifferentiated, and capable of any sort of differentiation into particular modes of expression that are not in opposition to the principle itself; and it is true of the Principle of Life as of all others. There is therefore no limit to its expression except that which inverts it,—that is to say, anything which tends towards Death; and, accordingly, what we have to avoid is the negative mode of Thought, which starts an inverted action of the Law, logically resulting in destructiveness instead of constructiveness. But the mistake we make from not seeing the basic principle of the whole thing, is that of looking to the conditions to form the Life, instead of looking to the Life to form the conditions; and therefore what we require is a *Standard of Measurement* for our Thought, by which we shall be able to form *The Perfect Word* which will set in motion the Law of Cause and Effect in such a manner as to fulfil that *Basic Desire of Life* which is common to all Humanity. The Perfect Word must therefore fulfil two

Conditions—it must have the essential Quality of the Undifferentiated Eternal Life, and it must have the essential Quality of "Genus Homo." It must say with Horace "Homo sum; nihil humani mihi alienum puto" (I am Man; I regard nothing human as alien to myself). When we think it out carefully, there is no escaping the conclusion that this must be the essential Quality of the Perfect Word we are in search of. It is the final logical inference from all that we have learnt regarding the interaction between Law and Personality, that the Perfect Word must combine in itself the Quality of each—it must be at once both Human and Divine.

Of course all my readers know where the description of such a Word is to be found; but what I want them to realize is the way in which we have now reached a similar description of the Perfect Word. We have not accepted it unquestioningly as the teaching of a scholastic theology, but have arrived at it by a course of careful reasoning from the facts of physical Nature and from our experience of our own mental powers. This way of getting at it makes it really our own. We know what we mean by it, and it is no longer a mere traditional form of words. It is the same with everything else; nothing becomes our own by being just told about it.

For instance, if I show an artist a picture, and he tells me that a boat in it is half a mile away from the spectators, I may accept this on his authority, because I suppose he knows all about it. But if next day a friend shows me a picture of a bit of coast with a fishing-boat in the distance, and asks me how far off that boat is, I am utterly stumped because I do not know how the artist was able to judge the distance. But if I understand the principle, I give my friend a very fair approximation of the distance of the boat. I work it out like this. I say:—the immediate foreground of the picture shows an amount of detail which could not be seen more than twenty yards away, and the average size of such details in nature shows that the bottom edge of the picture must measure about ten yards across. Then from experience I know that the average length of craft of the particular rigging in the picture is, say, about eighty feet, and I then measure that this length goes sixteen and a half times across the picture on the level where the boat is situated, and so I know that a line across the picture at this level measures $80 \times 16\frac{1}{2} = 1320$ ft. = 440 yards. Then I make the calculation: 10 yds. : 440 yds. :: 20 yds.: the distance required to be ascertained $\frac{440 \times 20}{10} = 880$ yds. 1760 yds. = 1 mile and $\frac{1760}{2} = 880$ yds. Therefore I know that the boat in the picture is represented as being about half a mile from the spectator. I really know the distance and do not merely guess it, and I know *how* I know it. I know it simply from the geometrical principle that with a given angle at the apex of a triangle the length of a perpendicular dropped from the apex to the base of the triangle will always bear the same ratio to the length of the base, whatever the size of the triangle may be. In this way I know the distance of the boat in the picture by combining mathematics and my own observation of facts—once again to co-operation of Law and Personality. Now a familiar instance like this shows the difference between being told a thing and really knowing it, and it is by an analogous method that we have now arrived at the conclusion that the Perfect Word is a combination of the Human and the Divine. We have definite reasons for seeing this as the ultimate fact of human development—the power to give expression to the Perfect Word—, and that this follows naturally from the fact of our own existence and that of some originating source from which we derive it.

But perhaps the reader will say: How can a Word take form as a Person? Well, words which do not eventually take form as facts only evaporate into thin air, and we cannot conceive the Divine Ideals of Man doing this. Therefore the expression of the Perfect Word on the plane of Humanity must take substance in the Form of Humanity. It is not the manifestation of any limited personality with all his or her idiosyncrasies, but the manifestation of the basic principle of Humanity itself common to us all.

To quote Dryden's words—but in a very different sense to that intended in "Absalom and Achitophel,"—such a one must be "Not one, but all Mankind's epitome." The manifestation must be the Perfect Expression of that fundamental Life which is the Root Desire in us all, and which is therefore called "The Desire of all nations."

Here then we have reached (Haggai ii, 7) the foundation fact of Human Personality. It is the Eternal "Will-to-live," as Schopenhauer calls it, which works subconsciously in all creation; therefore it is the root from which all creation springs. In the atom it becomes atomic energy, in the plant it becomes vegetable life, in the animal it becomes animal life, and in man it becomes personal life, and therefore, if a Perfect Standard of the Eternal Life is to be set before us, it must be in terms of Human Personality.

But some one will say: Why should we need such a Standard? The answer is that since the working of the Law towards each of us is determined by our mode of Thought, we require to be guarded against an inverted use of the Word. "Ignorantia Legis nemini excusat" (ignorance of the Law does not excuse you from its operation), is a scientific, as well as a forensic maxim, for the Law of Cause and Effect can never be altered. Our ignorance of the laws of electricity will not prevent us from being electrocuted if we get into the circuit of some powerful voltage.

Therefore, because the Law is *Impersonal* and knows no exceptions, and will bring us either Life or Death according to the direction which we give it by our Word, it is of the first importance for us to have a Standard by which to measure the Word expressed through our own Personality. This is why St. Paul speaks of our growing to "the measure of the stature of the fulness of Christ," (Eph. iv, 13) and why we find the symbol of "Measurement" so frequently employed in the Bible.

Therefore, if a great scale of measurement for our Word is to be exhibited, it can only be by its presentation in human form.

Then if the purpose be to establish such a standard of measurement, the scale must be expressed in units of the same denomination as that of our own nature—you cannot divide miles by ampères—and it is because the scale of our potential being is laid out in the same denomination as that of the Spirit of Life itself that we can avail ourselves of the standard of "the Word made Flesh."

When this is clearly seen it removes those intellectual difficulties which so many feel with regard to the doctrine of the Atonement. If we want to avail ourselves of the Bible Promises on the basis of the Bible teaching, we cannot throw the teaching overboard. As I have said before, if a doctrine is to be rightly interpreted, it must be interpreted as a whole, and in one form or another the doctrine of the Atonement is the pivot point of the whole Bible. To omit it is like trying to play "Hamlet" with Hamlet left out, and you may put your Bible out on the rubbish-heap. How, then, does the Atonement come in?

Here are the usual intellectual difficulties. To whom is the sacrifice offered? To God or to the Devil? If it be to the Devil, then the Devil is a greater power than God. If it be to God, then how can a God who demands a sacrifice of blood be Love? And in either case how can guilt be transferred from one person to the other?

Now as a matter of fact none of these questions arise. They are beside the real point at issue, which is: How can we so combine the Personal action of the Word with the Impersonal action of the Law, as to make the Law become to us the Law of Life instead of the Law of Death (Rom. viii, 2)?

Let us recur to the principles which we have worked out. The Law flows from the Word and not *vice versa*—it acts for good or ill according to the Quality of the Word which calls it into action. Therefore to get the Law of Life we must speak the Word of Life. Then, on the principle of "Omne vivum ex vivo," the Word of Fundamental Basic Life, which is not subject to conditions because it is antecedent to all conditions, can only be spoken through consciousness of participating in the Eternal Life which is the "fons et origo" of all particular being. Therefore, to be able to speak this Word we must have a foundation of assurance that we are in no way separated from the Eternal Life, and since this foundation is required for all men, it must be broad enough to accommodate all grades of perceptions.

Theologically the separation from the Eternal Life is said to be caused by "Sin." But what do we mean by "Sin"?

We can only judge of what a thing *is* by what it *does;* and so, if "Sin" is that which prevents the inflowing of the Eternal Life, which we know is the root of our individual being, then it must be the transgression of the inherent Law of our own Being. The truth is that we live simultaneously in two worlds, the visible and the invisible, just as trees draw their life from the earth beneath and from the air and light above, and the transgression consists in limiting ourselves only to the lower world, and thereby cutting ourselves off from the essential part of our own life, that which *really lives.*

We do not realize the true function of the three lower principles of our nature, viz.: Vital Spirit, etheric body, and outward form; the function of which is to give concentration to the current of spiritual life flowing from the Eternal Spirit, and thus enable the undifferentiated Life to differentiate itself into Individual Consciousness, which will be able to specialize the action of the Law into higher manifestations than it can produce without the co-operation of Personality.

On the analogy of Ohm's Law our error is making our *"R"* so rigid that it ceases to be a conductor, and so no current is delivered and no work done. This is the true nature of sin, and it is this opposition of our *R* to E. M. F. or Eternal Motive Force that has to be removed. We have to realize the true function of our R, as the channel through which the E. M. F. is enabled to carry on its work. When we awake to the fact that our true place in the Order of the Universe is to be fellow-workers with God in carrying on the work of Creation, then we see that hitherto we have entirely missed the purpose of our calling, and have misused the Divine image in which we were created; and therefore we want an assurance that our past errors will not stand in the way of our future advance into continually fuller participation in the Divine Creative Work, which, in virtue of our true nature should be our rightful inheritance.

That our future destiny is to actually take an individual part, however small, in guiding the great work of Evolution, may not be evident to us in the earlier stages of our awakening; but what is clear as a matter of feeling, but not yet intellectually, is, that in some way or other we have been cutting ourselves off from the Great Source of Light, and that what we therefore want, is to be re-united to it. What is wanted, then, is something which will give us a firm ground of assurance that we *are* re-united to it, and that that something must be of such a nature as never to lose anything of its efficiency at any stage of our progress—it must cover the whole ground.

Now, if we think deeply upon this question, we shall gradually come to see that this expansive quality is to be found in the doctrine of the Atonement. It meets all the needs of our spiritual nature in a way that no other theory does, and responds to every stage of our progress. There is only one thing that will prevent it working, and that is, saying that we have no need of it. That is why St. John said, that if we say we have no sin, we deceive ourselves, and the truth is not in us (1 John i, 8). But the more we come into the light of Truth, and realize that sin is everything that is not in accordance with the Law of our own essential being as related to the Eternal Life, the more we shall see, not only that we have transgressed the Law in the past, but also that even now we are very far from completely fulfiling it; and the more light we get the more clearly we shall see this to be the case. Therefore, whatever may be the stage of our mental development, the assurance which we all need for the basis of our new life is that of the removal of sin—the sins of the past, and the daily errors of the present. We may form various theories, each to our own satisfaction, as to *how* this takes place. For instance we may argue that, since "the Word" is the undifferentiated potential of Humanity, every human soul is included in the Self-offering of Christ, and that in Him we ourselves suffered on the Cross. Or we may say that our confession that such an offering is needed amounts to our participation in it. Or we may say with St. Paul that, as in Adam all are sinners, so in Christ all are made free from sin (1 Cor. xv, 22). That is, taking Adam and Christ as the representatives of two orders of men. Or we may fall back on the statement "Sacrifice and burnt offerings Thou wouldst not" (Ps. xl, 6), and on Jesus' own explanation of his death, that He offered himself in testimony to the Truth—that is, that the Eternal Life will no more exercise a retrospective vengeance upon us for our past misunderstanding of It, than would electricity or any other force. We may explain the *modus operandi* of the great offering in any of these ways, for the Scripture presents it in all of them—but the great thing is to accept it; for by the nature of our mental constitution, such an acceptance, whether with or without an intellectual explanation, affords the assurance which we stand in need of; and building upon the Foundation we can safely rear the edifice of our future development.

Also it affords us a continual safeguard in all the further stages of our evolution. As our psychic consciousness increases, we become more and more responsive to psychic stimulus whether that stimulus proceed from a good or evil influence; and therefore the recognition of our Redemption in Christ surrounds us with a protecting barrier, through which no evil spirit or malign influence can pass; so that, resting upon this Truth, we need never be in fear of any such invasion, but shall at all times be clothed with the whole armour of God (Eph. vi, 11).

From whatever point of view we regard it, we therefore find in the One Offering once made for the sin of the whole world, a stand-point such as is provided by no other teaching, whether religious or philosophical; and we shall see on examination that it is not an arbitrary decree for which we can give no account, but that it is based on the psychological constitution of man—a provision so perfectly adapted to our requirements at every stage of our evolution, that we can only attribute it to the Divine Wisdom acting through One, who by Perfect Love, thus willingly offered himself, in order to provide the Foundation of complete assurance for all who recognize their need of it.

On this basis, then, of reunion with the Eternal Source of Life, all the Promises of the Bible are found to be according to Law—that is, according to the inherent Law of our Being; so that, in the laying of this Foundation, we find the supreme manifestation of the interaction between the Law and the Word, which, when its significance is apprehended, opens out vistas of limitless possibilities to the individual and to the race.

But the race, as a whole, is yet very far from apprehending this, and for the most part has no perception of spiritual causation. Where some dim perception of spiritual causation is beginning to emerge, it is very frequently inverted, because people only apprehend it as giving them an additional power of exercising compulsion over their fellow-men, and thus depriving them of that individuality which it is the one purpose of Evolution to develop. This is because people do not look beyond the three lower principles of life, those principles which animals have in common with man; and consequently the higher principle of mind, which distinguishes man, is brought down to the lower level, so that the man is distinguished from the beast only by the possession of intellectual faculties, which by their perversion make him not merely a beast, but a devil of a beast. Therefore the recognition of psychic powers, when not safeguarded by the higher principles of Truth, plunges man even deeper into darkness than does a simple materialism; and so the two go hand in hand on the downward path. There is abundant evidence that this is increasingly the case at the present day; and therefore it is that the Bible Promises culminate in the Promise of the return of Him who offered himself in order to lay the foundation of Peace. As I have said before, we must either take the Bible as a whole, or reject it entirely. We cannot pick and choose what pleases us, and refuse what does not. No legal document could be treated in this way; and in like manner the Bible is one great whole, or else it is just—"skittles."

Therefore, if that Divine "Word" was manifested to save the world from destruction, by opening the way for the *individual* through recognition of his true relation to God, then it is only a reasonable carrying out of the same thought that, when the bulk of mankind fail to realize the beneficent use of these powers, and persist in using them invertedly, the same Being should again appear to save the race from utter self-destruction, but not by the same method, for that would be impossible.

The individual method is that of individual self-recognition in the light of Truth; but that cannot be *forced* upon any one. The headlong downward career of the race as a whole cannot therefore be stopped *vi et armis,* and this can only be done by first letting it have a bitter experience of what intellect, depraved to the service of the Beast in Man, leads to, and then forcibly restraining those who persist in this madness. Therefore a Second Coming of the Divine Man is a logical sequence to the first, and equally logical, this Second Coming must be as One who will rule the nations with irresistible power; so that men, reflecting upon the evils of the past, and enquiring into their cause, may be led to see that cause in the inverted action of the Law of their own being, and may therefore learn so to renew their thoughts in accordance with the Divine Thought as to bring them into the glorious liberty of the Sons of God.

This, then, is the Promise we have to look forward to at the present day, and though it might not be wise to speculate as to the precise time and manner of its fulfilment, there can be no doubt as to the nature of the general principles involved; and I trust the reader has at least learned from this book that principles unfold themselves with unfailing accuracy, though it depends on our Word, or mental attitude, in what way their unfoldment will affect us personally.

For such reasons as these, it appears to me, that the current objections to the doctrine of Atonement are entirely beside the mark. They miss the whole point of the thing. Punishment for Sin? Of course there is punishment for sin so long as it is persisted in. It is the natural working of the Law of Cause and Effect. Forgiveness of sin? Of course there is forgiveness of sin as soon as, through knowledge, we make a right use of the Law of our own Being. It could not be otherwise. It is the natural working of the Law of Cause and Effect.

"This is the covenant that I will make with them after those days, saith the Lord, I will put my laws into their hearts, and in their minds will I write them; and their sins and iniquities will I remember no more" (Heb. x, 16); and similarly in Jer. xxxi, 32, from which the writer of the Epistles to the Hebrews quotes this. "Now the Lord is the Spirit" (2 Cor. iii, 17, R. V.), i.e., the Originating Spirit of life, and therefore "my laws" means the inherent Law of the Originating Principle of Being, so that here we have a plain statement that the realization of the True Law of our Being *ipso facto* results in the cancelling of all our past errors. When once we see the principle of it the whole sequence becomes perfectly plain.

There is nothing arbitrary in all this. It results naturally from a New mode of Thought producing a New order of Consciousness; and it is written that "if any man be in Christ he is a new creature" or, as it says in the margin, "a new creation" (2 Cor. v, 17), and on the principle that "every Creation carries its own mathematics with it," every such man has passed from the Law of Death into the Law of Life. The full fruition may not yet be visible—we must allow for the Law of Growth—but the Principle is in him and has become the central, generating point of his consciousness, and is therefore bound, sooner or later, to develop into perfect manifestation by the Law of its own nature. If the Principle be accepted it will work all the same, whether we accept it by simple trust in the written Word, or whether we analyze the grounds of our trust; just as an electric bell will ring when you press the button, whether you are an electrical engineer or not. But there will be this difference, that if you *are* an electrical engineer you will see the principle implied in the ringing of the bell, and you will find in it the promise of infinite possibilities which it is open to you to develop; and in like manner, the more clearly you see the relation which necessarily exists between yourself and the All-Originating Living Spirit, the more clear it will become to you, that this relation opens up an endless vista of boundless potentialities which can never be exhausted. This is the true nature of the Bible Promises; they were not made by some external Deity about whose ideas we can never have any certainty, but by the Indwelling God, who is at once the Life, the Law, and the Substance of all things, and therefore they are Promises according to Law, containing in themselves the principle of their own fulfilment.

But, as I trust the reader is now convinced, the Law can fulfil the Promise which is latent in it only by the co-operation of the Word, that is, the Personal Factor which provides the necessary conditions for the Law to work under; and therefore, if the Promise is to be fulfilled, we must meet the All-originating Life, the "Premium mobile," not only on the Plane of Law, but on the Plane of Personality also. This becomes evident if we consider that this Originating Life must be *entirely undifferentiated* in Itself; for otherwise it could not be the origin of all differentiated modes of Life and Energy. As long as we find differentiation, on however wide a scale, we have not arrived at First Cause. There will still be something further back, out of which the differentiations have proceeded; and it is this "Something" which is at the back of "Everything" that we are in search of. Therefore the Originating Spirit must be *absolutely undifferentiated,* and consequently the Personal Factor in ourselves must be the differentiation into individuality of a Quality eternally subsisting in the All-Originating Undifferentiated Spirit.

Then, since our individual differentiation of this Quality must depend on the mode of our recognition of it, it follows that a Standard of Measurement is needed, and the Standard is presented to us in the form of the

Personality around whom the whole Bible centres, and who, as the Standard of the Divine Infinitude differentiating Himself into units of individual personality, can only be described as at once The Son of God and The Son of Man. If we see that the Eternal Life, by reason of its non-differentiation in itself, must needs become to each of us *exactly what we take it to be,* then it follows that in order to realize it on our own plane of Personality we must see it *through the medium of Personality,* and it is therefore not a theological figment, but the Supreme Psychological Truth that no man can come to "the Father"—that is, to the Parent Spirit—except through the Son (John xiv, 6).

When we see the reason at the back of it, the Bible becomes a New Book to us, and we learn that the interpretation of it is not to be found in learned commentaries, but in ourselves. Then we find that it is indeed The Book of Promises, not vague and uncertain, but logical and scientific, teaching us how to combine the instrumentality of the Law with the freedom of the Word; so that through the Perfect Word, manifested as the Perfect Man, we reach the Perfect Law, and find that THE PERFECT LAW IS THE LAW OF LIBERTY.

# The Hidden Power

1921

# PUBLISHER'S NOTE

THE MATERIAL COMPRISED in this volume has been selected from unpublished manuscripts and magazine articles by Judge Troward, and "The Hidden Power" is, it is believed, the last book which will be published under his name. Only an insignificant portion of his work has been deemed unworthy of permanent preservation. Whenever possible, dates have been affixed to these papers. Those published in 1902 appeared originally in "EXPRESSION: A Journal of Mind and Thought," in London, and to some of these have been added notes made later by the author.

The Publishers wish to acknowledge their indebtedness to Mr. Daniel M. Murphy of New York for his services in the selection and arrangement of the material.

# CONTENTS

I

# THE HIDDEN POWER

TO REALISE FULLY how much of our present daily life consists in symbols is to find the answer to the old, old question, What is Truth? and in the degree in which we begin to recognise this we begin to approach Truth. The realisation of Truth consists in the ability to translate symbols, whether natural or conventional, into their equivalents; and the root of all the errors of mankind consists in the inability to do this, and in maintaining that the symbol has nothing behind it. The great duty incumbent on all who have attained to this knowledge is to impress upon their fellow men that there is an *inner side* to things, and that until this *inner* side is known, the things themselves are not known.

There is an inner and an outer side to everything; and the quality of the superficial mind which causes it to fail in the attainment of Truth is its willingness to rest content with the outside only. So long as this is the case it is impossible for a man to grasp the import of his own relation to the universal, and it is this relation which constitutes all that is signified by the word "Truth." So long as a man fixes his attention only on the superficial it is impossible for him to make any progress in knowledge. He is denying that principle of "Growth" which is the root of all life, whether spiritual, intellectual, or material, for he does not stop to reflect that all which he sees as the outer side of things can result only from some germinal principle hidden deep in the centre of their being.

Expansion from the centre by growth according to a necessary order of sequence, this is the Law of Life of which the whole universe is the outcome, alike in the one great solidarity of cosmic being, as in the separate individualities of its minutest organisms. This great principle is the key to the whole riddle of Life, upon whatever plane we contemplate it; and without this key the door from the outer to the inner side of things can never be opened. It is therefore the duty of all to whom this door has, at least in some measure, been opened, to endeavour to acquaint others with the fact that there is an inner side to things, and that life becomes truer and fuller in proportion as we penetrate to it and make our estimates of all things according to what becomes visible from this interior point of view.

In the widest sense everything is a symbol of that which constitutes its inner being, and all Nature is a gallery of arcana revealing great truths to those who can decipher them. But there is a more precise sense in which our current life is based upon symbols in regard to the most important subjects that can occupy our thoughts: the symbols by which we strive to represent the nature and being of God, and the manner in which the life of man is related to the Divine life. The whole character of a man's life results from what he really believes on this subject: not his formal statement of belief in a particular creed, but what he realises as the stage which his mind has actually attained in regard to it.

Has a man's mind only reached the point at which he thinks it is impossible to know anything about God, or to make any use of the knowledge if he had it? Then his whole interior world is in the condition of confusion, which must necessarily exist where no spirit of order has yet begun to move upon the chaos, in which are, indeed, the elements of being, but all disordered and neutralising one another. Has he advanced a step further, and realised that there is a ruling and an ordering power, but beyond this is ignorant of its nature? Then the unknown stands to him for the terrific, and, amid a tumult of fears and distresses that deprive him of all strength to advance, he spends his life in the endeavour to propitiate this power as something naturally adverse to him, instead of knowing that it is the very centre of his own life and being.

And so on through every degree, from the lowest depths of ignorance to the greatest heights of intelligence, a man's life must always be the exact reflection of that particular stage which he has reached in the perception of the divine nature and of his own relation to it; and as we approach the full perception of Truth, so the life-principle within us expands, the old bonds and limitations which had no existence in reality fall off from us, and we enter into regions of light, liberty, and power, of which we had previously no conception. It is impossible, therefore, to overestimate the importance of being able to realise the symbol *for* a symbol, and being able to penetrate to the inner substance which it represents. Life itself is to be realised only by the conscious experience of its livingness in ourselves, and it is the endeavour to translate these experiences into terms which shall suggest a corresponding idea to others that gives rise to all symbolism.

The nearer those we address have approached to the actual experience, the more transparent the symbol becomes; and the further they are from such experience the thicker is the veil; and our whole progress consists in the fuller and fuller translation of the symbols into clearer and clearer statements of that for which they stand. But the first step, without which all succeeding ones must remain impossible, is to convince people that symbols *are* symbols, and not the very Truth itself. And the difficulty consists in this, that if the symbolism is in any degree adequate, it must, in some measure, represent the form of Truth, just as the modelling of a drapery suggests the form of the figure beneath. They have a certain consciousness that somehow they are in the presence of Truth; and this leads people to resent any removal of those folds of drapery which have hitherto conveyed this idea to their minds.

There is sufficient indication of the inner Truth in the outward form to afford an excuse for the timorous, and those who have not sufficient mental energy to think for themselves, to cry out that finality has already been attained, and that any further search into the matter must end in the destruction of Truth. But in raising such an outcry they betray their ignorance of the very nature of Truth, which is that it can never be destroyed: the very fact that Truth is Truth makes this impossible. And again they exhibit their ignorance of the first principle of Life—namely, the Law of Growth, which throughout the universe perpetually pushes forward into more and more vivid forms of expression, having expansion everywhere and finality nowhere.

Such ignorant objections need not, therefore, alarm us; and we should endeavour to show those who make them that what they fear is the only natural order of the Divine Life, which is "over all, and through all, and in all." But we must do this gently, and not by forcibly thrusting upon them the object of their terror, and so repelling them from all study of the subject. We should endeavour gradually to lead them to see that there is something interior to what they have hitherto held to be ultimate Truth, and to realise that the sensation of emptiness and dissatisfaction, which from time to time will persist in making itself felt in their hearts, is nothing else than the pressing forward of the spirit within to declare that inner side of things which alone can satisfactorily account for what we observe on the exterior, and without the knowledge of which we can never perceive the true nature of our inheritance in the Universal Life which is the Life Everlasting.

## II

What, then, is this central principle which is at the root of all things? It is Life. But not life as we recognise it in particular forms of manifestation; it is something more interior and concentrated than that. It is that "unity of the spirit" which *is* unity, simply because it has not yet passed into diversity. Perhaps this is not an easy idea to grasp, but it is the root of all scientific conception of spirit; for without it there is no common principle to which we can refer the innumerable forms of manifestation that spirit assumes.

It is the conception of Life as the sum-total of all its undistributed powers, being as yet none of these in particular, but all of them in potentiality. This is, no doubt, a highly abstract idea, but it is essentially that of the centre from which growth takes place by expansion in every direction. This is that last residuum which defies all our powers of analysis. This is truly "the unknowable," not in the sense of the unthinkable but of the unanalysable. It is the subject of perception, not of knowledge, if by knowledge we mean that faculty which estimates the *relations* between things, because here we have passed beyond any questions of relations, and are face to face with the absolute.

This innermost of all is absolute Spirit. It is Life as yet not differentiated into any specific mode; it is the universal Life which pervades all things and is at the heart of all appearances.

To come into the knowledge of this is to come into the secret of power, and to enter into the secret place of Living Spirit. Is it illogical first to call this the unknowable, and then to speak of coming into the knowledge of it? Perhaps so; but no less a writer than St. Paul has set the example; for does he not speak of the final result of all searchings into the heights and depths and lengths and breadths of the inner side of things as being, to attain the knowledge of that Love which passeth knowledge. If he is thus boldly illogical in phrase, though not in fact, may we not also speak of knowing "the unknowable"? We may, for this knowledge is the root of all other knowledge.

The presence of this undifferentiated universal life-power is the final axiomatic fact to which all our analysis must ultimately conduct us. On whatever plane we make our analysis it must always abut upon pure essence, pure energy, pure being; that which knows itself and recognises itself, but which cannot dissect itself because it is not built up of parts, but is ultimately integral: it is pure Unity. But analysis which does not lead to synthesis is merely destructive: it is the child wantonly pulling the flower to pieces and throwing away the fragments; not the botanist, also pulling the flower to pieces, but building up in his mind from those carefully studied fragments a vast synthesis of the constructive power of Nature, embracing the laws of the formation of all flower-forms. The value of analysis is to lead us to the original starting-point of that which we analyse, and so to teach us the laws by which its final form springs from this centre.

Knowing the law of its construction, we turn our analysis into a synthesis, and we thus gain a power of building up which must always be beyond the reach of those who regard "the unknowable" as one with "not-being."

*This* idea of the unknowable is the root of all materialism; and yet no scientific man, however materialistic his proclivities, treats the unanalysable residuum thus when he meets it in the experiments of his laboratory. On the contrary, he makes this final unanalysable fact the basis of his synthesis. He finds that in the last resort it is energy of some kind, whether as heat or as motion; but he does not throw up his scientific pursuits because he cannot analyse it further. He adopts the precisely opposite course, and realises that the conservation of energy, its indestructibility, and the impossibility of adding to or detracting from the sum-total of energy in the world, is the one solid and unchanging fact on which alone the edifice of physical science can be built up. He bases all his knowledge upon his knowledge of "the unknowable." And rightly so, for if he could analyse this energy into yet further factors, then the same problem of "the unknowable" would meet him still. All our progress consists in continually pushing the unknowable, in the sense of the unanalysable residuum, a step further back; but that there should be no ultimate unanalysable residuum anywhere is an inconceivable idea.

In thus realising the undifferentiated unity of Living Spirit as the central fact of any system, whether the system of the entire universe or of a single organism, we are therefore following a strictly scientific method. We pursue our analysis until it necessarily leads us to this final fact, and then we accept this fact as the basis of our synthesis. The Science of Spirit is thus not one whit less scientific than the Science of Matter; and, moreover, it starts from the same initial fact, the fact of a living energy which defies definition or explanation, wherever we find it; but it differs from the science of matter in that it contemplates this energy under an aspect of responsive intelligence which does not fall within the scope of physical science, as such. The Science of Spirit and the Science of Matter are not opposed. They are complementaries, and neither is fully comprehensible without some knowledge of the other; and, being really but two portions of one whole, they insensibly shade off into each other in a border-land where no arbitrary line can be drawn between them. Science studied in a truly scientific spirit, following out its own deductions unflinchingly to their legitimate conclusions, will always reveal the twofold aspect of things, the inner and the outer; and it is only a truncated and maimed science that refuses to recognise both.

The study of the material world is not Materialism, if it be allowed to progress to its legitimate issue. Materialism is that limited view of the universe which will not admit the existence of anything but mechanical effects of mechanical causes, and a system which recognises no higher power than the physical forces of nature must logically result in having no higher ultimate appeal than to physical force or to fraud as its alternative. I speak, of course, of the tendency of the system, not of the morality of individuals, who are often very far in advance of the systems they profess. But as we would avoid the propagation of a mode of thought whose effects history shows only too plainly, whether in the Italy of the Borgias, or the France of the First Revolution, or the Commune of the Franco-Prussian War, we should set ourselves to study that inner and spiritual aspect of things which is the basis of a system whose logical results are truth and love instead of perfidy and violence.

Some of us, doubtless, have often wondered why the Heavenly Jerusalem is described in the Book of Revelations as a cube; "the length and the breadth and the height of it are equal." This is because the cube is the figure of perfect stability, and thus represents Truth, which can never be overthrown. Turn it on what side you will, it still remains the perfect cube, always standing upright; you cannot upset it. This figure, then, represents the manifestation in concrete solidity of that central life-giving energy, which is not itself any one plane but generates all planes, the planes of the above and of the below and of all four sides. But it is at the same time a city, a place of habitation; and this is because that which is "the within" is Living Spirit, which has its dwelling there.

As one plane of the cube implies all the other planes and also "the within," so any plane of manifestation implies the others and also that "within" which generates them all. Now, if we would make any progress in the spiritual side of science—and *every* department of science has its spiritual side—we must always keep our minds fixed upon this "innermost within" which contains the potential of all outward manifestation, the "fourth dimension" which generates the cube; and our common forms of speech show how intuitively we do this. We speak of the spirit in which an act is done, of entering into the spirit of a game, of the spirit of the time, and so on. Everywhere our intuition points out the spirit as the true essence of things; and it is only when we commence arguing about them from without, instead of from within, that our true perception of their nature is lost.

The scientific study of spirit consists in following up intelligently and according to definite method the same principle that now only flashes upon us at intervals fitfully and vaguely. When we once realise that this universal and unlimited power of spirit is at the root of all things and of ourselves also, then we have obtained the key to the whole position; and, however far we may carry our studies in spiritual science, we shall nowhere find anything else but particular developments of this one universal principle. "The Kingdom of Heaven is *within* you."

## III

I have laid stress on the fact that the "innermost within" of all things is living Spirit, and that the Science of Spirit is distinguished from the Science of Matter in that it contemplates Energy under an aspect of responsive intelligence which does not fall within the scope of physical science, as such.

These are the two great points to lay hold of if we would retain a clear idea of Spiritual Science, and not be misled by arguments drawn from the physical side of Science only—the livingness of the originating principle which is at the heart of all things, and its intelligent and responsive nature. Its livingness is patent to our observation, at any rate from the point where we recognise it in the vegetable kingdom; but its intelligence and responsiveness are not, perhaps, at once so obvious. Nevertheless, a little thought will soon lead us to recognise this also.

No one can deny that there is an intelligent order throughout all nature, for it requires the highest intelligence of our most highly-trained minds to follow the steps of this universal intelligence which is always in advance of them. The more deeply we investigate the world we live in, the more clear it must become to us that all our science is the translation into words or numerical symbols of that order which already exists. If the clear statement of this existing order is the highest that the human intellect can reach, this surely argues a corresponding intelligence in the power which gives rise to this great sequence of order and interrelation, so as to constitute one harmonious whole. Now, unless we fall back on the idea of a workman working upon material external to himself—in which case we have to explain the phenomenon of the workman—the only conception we can form of this power is that it is the Living Spirit inherent in the heart of every atom, giving it outward form and definition, and becoming in it those intrinsic polarities which constitute its characteristic nature.

There is no random work here. Every attraction and repulsion acts with its proper force collecting the atoms into molecules, the molecules into tissues, the tissues into organs, and the organs into individuals. At each stage of the progress we get the sum of the intelligent forces which operate in the constituent parts, *plus* a higher degree of intelligence which we may regard as the collective intelligence superior to that of the mere sum-total of the parts, something which belongs to the individual *as a whole,* and not to the parts as such. These are facts which can be amply proved from physical science; and they also supply a great law in spiritual science, which is that in any collective body the intelligence of the whole is superior to that of the sum of the parts.

Spirit is at the root of all things, and thoughtful observation shows that its operation is guided by unfailing intelligence which adapts means to ends, and harmonises the entire universe of manifested being in those wonderful ways which physical science renders clearer every day; and this intelligence must be in the generating spirit itself, because there is no other source from which it could proceed. On these grounds, therefore, we may distinctly affirm that Spirit is intelligent, and that whatever it does is done by the intelligent adaptation of means to ends.

But Spirit is also responsive. And here we have to fall back upon the law above stated, that the mere sum of the intelligence of Spirit in lower degrees of manifestation is not equal to the intelligence of the complex *whole,* as a whole. This is a radical law which we cannot impress upon our minds too deeply. The degree of spiritual intelligence is marked by the wholeness of the organism through which it finds expression; and therefore the more highly organised being has a degree of spirit which is superior to, and consequently capable of exercising control over, all lower or less fully-integrated degrees of spirit; and this being so, we can now begin to see why the spirit that is the "innermost within" of all things is responsive as well as intelligent.

Being intelligent, it *knows,* and spirit being ultimately all there is, that which it knows is itself. Hence it is that power which recognises itself; and accordingly the lower powers of it recognise its higher powers, and by the law of attraction they are bound to respond to the higher degrees of themselves. On this general principle, therefore, spirit, under whatever exterior revealed, is necessarily intelligent and responsive. But intelligence and responsiveness imply personality; and we may therefore now advance a step further and argue that *all* spirit contains the elements of personality, even though, in any particular instance, it may not yet be expressed as that individual personality which we find in ourselves.

In short, spirit is always personal in its nature, even when it has not yet attained to that degree of synthesis which is sufficient to render it personal in manifestation. In ourselves the synthesis has proceeded far enough to reach that degree, and therefore we recognise ourselves as the manifestation of personality. The human kingdom is the kingdom of the manifestation of that personality, which is of the essence of spiritual substance on every plane. Or, to put the whole argument in a simpler form, we may say that our own personality must necessarily have had its origin in that which is personal, on the principle that you cannot get more out of a bag than it contains.

In ourselves, therefore, we find that more perfect synthesis of the spirit into manifested personality which is wanting in the lower kingdoms of nature, and, accordingly, since spirit is necessarily that which knows itself and must, therefore, recognise its own degrees in its various modes, the spirit in all degrees below that of human personality is bound to respond to itself in that superior degree which constitutes human individuality; and this is the basis of the power of human thought to externalise itself in infinite forms of its own ordering.

But if the subordination of the lower degrees of spirit to the higher is one of the fundamental laws which lie at the bottom of the creative power of thought, there is another equally fundamental law which places a salutary restraint upon the abuse of that power. It is the law that we can command the powers of the universal for our own purposes only in proportion as we first realise and obey their generic character. We can employ water for any purpose which does not require it to run up-hill, and we can utilise electricity for any purpose that does not require it to pass from a lower to a higher potential.

So with that universal power which we call the Spirit. It has an inherent generic character with which we must comply if we would employ it for our specific purposes, and this character is summed up in the one word "goodness." The Spirit is Life, hence its generic tendency must always be lifeward or to the increase of the livingness of every individual. And since it is universal it can have no particular interests to serve, and therefore its action must always be equally for the benefit of all. This is the generic character of spirit; and just as water, or electricity, or any other of the physical forces of the universe, will not work contrary to their generic character, so Spirit will not work contrary to its generic character.

The inference is obvious. If we would use Spirit we must follow the law of the Spirit which is "Goodness." This is the only limitation. If our originating intention is good, we may employ the spiritual power for what purpose we will. And how is "goodness" to be defined? Simply by the child's definition that what is bad is not good, and that what is good is not bad; we all know the difference between bad and good instinctively. If we will conform to this principle of obedience to the generic law of the Spirit, all that remains is for us to study the law of the proportion which exists between the more and less fully integrated modes of Spirit, and then bring our knowledge to bear with determination.

## IV

The law of spirit, to which our investigation has now led us, is of the very widest scope. We have followed it up from the conception of the intelligence of spirit, subsisting in the initial atoms, to the aggregation of this intelligence as the conscious identity of the individual. But there is no reason why this law should cease to operate at this point, or at any point short of the whole. The test of the soundness of any principle is that it can operate as effectively on a large scale as on a small one, that though the nature of its field is determined by the nature of the principle itself, the extent of its field is unlimited. If, therefore, we continue to follow up the law we have been considering, it leads us to the conception of a unit of intelligence as far superior to that of the individual man as the unity of his individual intelligence is superior to that of the intelligence of any single atom of his body; and thus we may conceive of a collective individuality representing the spiritual character of any aggregate of men, the inhabitants of a city, a district, a country, or of the entire world.

Nor need the process stop here. On the same principle there would be a superior collective individuality for the humanity of the entire solar system, and finally we reach the conception of a supreme intelligence bringing together in itself the collective individualities of all the systems in the universe. This is by no means a merely fanciful notion. We find it as the law by which our own conscious individuality is constituted; and we find the analogous principle working universally on the physical plane. It is known to physical science as the "law of inverse squares," by which the forces of reciprocal attraction or repulsion, as the case may be, are not merely equivalent to the sum of the forces emitted by the two bodies concerned, but are equivalent to these two forces multiplied together and divided by the square of the distance between them, so that the resultant power continually rises in a rapidly increasing ratio as the two reciprocally exciting bodies approach one another.

Since this law is so universal throughout physical nature, the doctrine of continuity affords every ground for supposing that its analogue holds good in respect of spiritual nature. We must never lose sight of the old-world saying that "a truth on one plane is a truth on all." If a principle exists at all it exists universally. We must not allow ourselves to be misled by appearances; we must remember that the perceptible results of the working of any principle consist of two factors—the principle itself or the active factor, and the subject-matter on which it acts or the passive factor; and that while the former is invariable, the latter is variable, and that the operation of the same invariable upon different variables must necessarily produce a variety of results. This at once becomes evident if we state it mathematically; for example, $a$, $b$ or $c$, multiplied by $x$ give respectively the results $ax$, $bx$, $cx$, which differ materially from one another, though the factor $x$ always remains the same.

This law of the generation of power by attraction applies on the spiritual as well as on the physical plane, and acts with the same mathematical precision on both; and thus the human individuality consists, not in the mere aggregation of its parts, whether spiritual or corporeal, but in the *unity* of power resulting from the intimate association into which those parts enter with one another, which unity, according to this law of the generation of power by attraction, is infinitely superior, both in intelligence and power, to any less fully integrated mode of spirit. Thus a natural principle, common alike to physical and spiritual law, fully accounts for all claims that have ever been made for the creative power of our thought over all things that come within the circle of our own particular life. Thus it is that each man is the centre of his own universe, and has the power, by directing his own thought, to control all things therein.

But, as I have said above, there is no reason why this principle should not be recognised as expanding from the individual until it embraces the entire universe. Each man, as the centre of his own world, is himself centred in a higher system in which he is only one of innumerable similar atoms, and this system again in a higher until we reach the supreme centre of all things; intelligence and power increase from centre to centre in a ratio rising with inconceivable rapidity, according to the law we are now investigating, until they culminate in illimitable intelligence and power commensurate with All-Being.

Now we have seen that the relation of man to the lower modes of spirit is that of superiority and command, but what is his relation to these higher modes? In any harmoniously constituted system the relation of the part to the whole never interferes with the free operation of the part in the performance of its own functions; but, on the contrary, it is precisely by means of this relation that each part is maintained in a position to discharge all functions for which it is fitted. Thus, then, the subordination of the individual man to the supreme mind, so far from curtailing his liberty, is the very condition which makes liberty possible, or even life itself. The generic movement of the whole necessarily carries the part along with it; and so long as the part allows itself thus to be carried onwards there will be no hindrance to its free working in any direction for which it is fitted by its own individuality. This truth was set forth in the old Hindu religion as the Car of Jaggarnath—an ideal car only, which later ages degraded into a terribly material symbol. "Jaggarnath" means "Lord of the Universe," and thus signifies the Universal Mind. This, by the law of Being, must always move forward regardless of any attempts of individuals to restrain it. Those who mount upon its car move onward with it to endlessly advancing evolution, while those who seek to oppose it must be crushed beneath its wheels, for it is no respecter of persons.

If, therefore, we would employ the universal law of spirit to control our own little individual worlds, we must also recognise it in respect to the supreme centre round which we ourselves revolve. But not in the old way of supposing that this centre is a capricious Individuality external to ourselves, which can be propitiated or cajoled into giving the good which he is not good enough to give of his own proper motion. So long as we retain this infantile idea we have not come into the liberty which results from the knowledge of the certainty of Law. Supreme Mind is Supreme Law, and can be calculated upon with the same accuracy as when manifested in any of the particular laws of the physical world; and the result of studying, understanding and obeying this Supreme Law is that we thereby acquire the power to *use* it. Nor need we fear it with the old fear which comes from ignorance, for we can rely with confidence upon the proposition that the whole can have no interest adverse to the parts of which it is composed; and conversely that the part can have no interest adverse to the whole.

Our ignorance of our relation to the whole may make us appear to have separate interests, but a truer knowledge must always show such an idea to be mistaken. For this reason, therefore, the same responsiveness of spirit which manifests itself as obedience to our wishes, when we look to those degrees of spirit which are lower than her own individuality, must manifest itself as a necessary inflowing of intelligence and power when we look to the infinity of spirit, of which our individuality is a singular expression, because in so looking upwards we are looking for the higher degrees, of *ourself.*

The increased vitality of the parts means the increased vitality of the whole, and since it is impossible to conceive of spirit otherwise than as a continually expanding principle of Life, the demand for such increased vitality must, by the inherent nature of spirit, be met by a corresponding supply of continually growing intelligence and power. Thus, by a natural law, the demand creates the supply, and this supply may be freely applied to any and every subject-matter that commends itself to us. There is no limit to the supply of this energy other than what we ourselves put to it by our thought; nor is there any limit to the purposes we may make it serve other than the one grand Law of Order, which says that good things used for wrong purposes become evil. The consideration of the intelligent and responsive nature of spirit shows that there can be no limitations but these. The one is a limitation inherent in spirit itself, and the other is a limitation which has no root except in our own ignorance.

It is true that to maintain our healthy action within the circle of our own individual world we must continually move forward with the movement of the larger whole of which we form a part. But this does not imply any restriction of our liberty to make the fullest use of our lives in accordance with those universal principles of life upon which they are founded; for there is not one law for the part and another for the whole, but the same law of Being permeates both alike. In proportion, therefore, as we realise the true law of our own individuality we shall find that it is one with the law of progress for the race. The collective individuality of mankind is only the reproduction on a larger scale of the personal individuality; and whatever action truly develops the inherent powers of the individual must necessarily be in line with that forward march of the universal mind which is the evolution of humanity as a whole.

Selfishness is a narrow view of our own nature which loses sight of our place in relation to the whole, not perceiving that it is from this very relation that our life is drawn. It is ignorance of our own possibilities and consequent limitation of our own powers. If, therefore, the evidence of harmonious correlation throughout the physical world leads irresistibly to the inference of intelligent spirit as the innermost within of all things, we must recognise ourselves also as individual manifestations of the same spirit which expresses itself throughout the universe as that power of intelligent responsiveness which is Love.

## V

Thus we find ourselves to be a necessary and integral part of the Infinite Harmony of All-Being; not merely recognising this great truth as a vague intuition, but as the logical and unavoidable result of the universal Life-principle which permeates all Nature. We find our intuition was true because we have discovered the law which gave rise to it; and now intuition and investigation both unite in telling us of our own individual place in the great scheme of things. Even the most advanced among us have, as yet, little more than the faintest adumbration of what this place is. It is the place of *power.* Towards those higher modes of spirit which we speak of as "the universal," the law of man's inmost nature makes him as a lens, drawing into the focus of his own individuality all that he will of light and power in streams of inexhaustible supply; and towards the lower modes of spirit, which form for each one the sphere of his own particular world, man thus becomes the directive centre of energy and order.

Can we conceive of any position containing greater possibilities than these? The circle of this vital influence may expand as the individual grows into the wider contemplation of his unity with Infinite Being; but any more comprehensive law of relationship it would be impossible to formulate. Emerson has rightly said that a little algebra will often do far more towards clearing our ideas than a large amount of poetic simile. Algebraically it is a self-evident proposition that any difference between various powers of $x$ disappears when they are compared with $x$ multiplied into itself to infinity, because there can be no ratio between any determinate power, however high, and the infinite; and thus the relation between the individual and All-Being must always remain the same.*

But this in no way interferes with the law of growth, by which the individual rises to higher and higher powers of his own individuality. The unchangeableness of the relation between all determinate powers of $x$ and infinity does not affect the relations of the different powers of $x$ between themselves; but rather the fact that the multiplication of $x$ into itself to

* $X^2 : X^n :: X^{10} : X^n$.

infinity is mentally conceivable is the very proof that there is no limit to the extent to which it is possible to raise $x$ in its determinate powers.

I trust unmathematical readers will pardon my using this method of statement for the benefit of others to whom it will carry conviction. A relation once clearly grasped in its mathematical aspect becomes thenceforth one of the unalterable truths of the universe, no longer a thing to be argued about, but an axiom which may be assumed as the foundation on which to build up the edifice of further knowledge. But, laying aside mathematical formulæ, we may say that because the Infinite is infinite there can be no limit to the extent to which the vital principle of growth may draw upon it, and therefore there is no limit to the expansion of the individual's powers. Because we are *what* we are, we may *become* what we will.

The Kabbalists tell us of "the lost word," the word of power which mankind has lost. To him who discovers this word all things are possible. Is this mirific word really lost? Yes, and No. It is the open secret of the universe, and the Bible gives us the key to it. It tells us, "The Word is nigh thee, even in thy mouth and in thy heart." It is the most familiar of all words, the word which in our heart we realise as the centre of our conscious being, and which is in our mouth a hundred times a day. It is the word "I AM." Because I am what I am, I may be what I will to be. My individuality is one of the modes in which the Infinite expresses itself, and therefore I am myself that very power which I find to be the innermost within of all things.

To me, thus realising the great unity of all Spirit, the infinite is not the indefinite, for I see it to be the infinite of *Myself.* It is the very same I AM that I am; and this not by any act of uncertain favour, but by the law of polarity which is the basis of all Nature. The law of polarity is that law according to which everything attains completion by manifesting itself in the opposite direction to that from which it started. It is the simple law by which there can be no inside without an outside, nor one end of a stick without an opposite end.

Life is motion, and all motion is the appearance of energy at another point, and, where any work has been done, under another form than that in which it originated; but wherever it reappears, and in whatever new form, the vivifying energy is still the same. This is nothing else than the scientific doctrine of the conservation of energy, and it is upon this well-recognised principle that our perception of ourselves as integral portions of the great universal power is based.

We do well to pay heed to the sayings of the great teachers who have taught that all power is in the "I AM," and to accept this teaching by faith in their bare authority rather than not accept it at all; but the more excellent way is to know *why* they taught thus, and to realise for ourselves this first great law which all the master-minds have realised throughout the ages. It is indeed true that the "lost word" is the one most familiar to us, ever in our hearts and on our lips. We have lost, not the word, but the realisation of its power. And as the infinite depths of meaning which the words I AM carry with them open out to us, we begin to realise the stupendous truth that we are ourselves the very power which we seek.

It is the polarisation of Spirit from the universal into the particular, carrying with it all its inherent powers, just as the smallest flame has all the qualities of fire. The I AM in the individual is none other than the I AM in the universal. It is the same Power working in the smaller sphere of which the individual is the centre. This is the great truth which the ancients set forth under the figure of the Macrocosm and the Microcosm, the lesser I AM reproducing the precise image of the greater, and of which the Bible tells us when it speaks of man as the image of God.

Now the immense practical importance of this principle is that it affords the key to the great law that "as a man thinks so he is." We are often asked why this should be, and the answer may be stated as follows: We know by personal experience that we realise our own livingness in two ways, by our power to act and our susceptibility to feel; and when we consider Spirit in the absolute we can only conceive of it as these two modes of livingness carried to infinity. This, therefore, means infinite susceptibility. There can be no question as to the degree of sensitiveness, for Spirit *is* sensitiveness, and is thus infinitely plastic to the slightest touch that is brought to bear upon it; and hence every thought we formulate sends its vibrating currents out into the infinite of Spirit, producing there currents of like quality but of far vaster power.

But Spirit in the Infinite is the Creative Power of the universe, and the impact of our thought upon it thus sets in motion a veritable creative force. And if this law holds good of one thought it holds good of all and hence we are continually creating for ourselves a world of surroundings which accurately reproduces the complexion of our own thoughts. Persistent thoughts will naturally produce a greater external effect than casual ones not centred upon any particular object. Scattered thoughts which recognise no principle of unity will fail to reproduce any principle of unity. The thought that we are weak and have no power over circumstances results in inability to control circumstances, and the thought of power produces power.

At every moment we are dealing with an infinitely sensitive medium which stirs creative energies that give form to the slightest of our thought-vibrations. This power is inherent in us because of our spiritual nature, and we cannot divest ourselves of it. It is our truly tremendous heritage because it is a power which, if not intelligently brought into lines of orderly activity, will spend its uncontrolled forces in devastating energy. If it is not used to build up, it will destroy. And there is nothing exceptional in this: it is merely the reappearance on the plane of the universal and undifferentiated of the same principle that pervades all the forces of Nature. Which of these is not destructive unless drawn off into some definite direction? Accumulated steam, accumulated electricity, accumulated water, will at length burst forth, carrying destruction all around; but, drawn off through suitable channels, they become sources of constructive power, inexhaustible as Nature itself.

And here let me pause to draw attention to this idea of accumulation. The greater the accumulation of energy, the greater the danger if it be not directed into a proper order, and the greater the power if it be. Fortunately for mankind the physical forces, such as electricity, do not usually subsist in a highly concentrated form. Occasionally circumstances concur to produce such concentration, but as a rule the elements of power are more or less equally dispersed. Similarly, for the mass of mankind, this spiritual power has not yet reached a very high degree of concentration. Every mind, it is true, must be in some measure a centre of concentration, for otherwise it would have no conscious individuality; but the power of the individualised mind rapidly rises as it recognises its unity with the Infinite life, and its thought-currents, whether well or ill directed, then assume a proportionately great significance.

Hence the ill effects of wrongly directed thought are in some degree mitigated in the great mass of mankind, and many causes are in operation to give a right direction to their thoughts, though the thinkers themselves are ignorant of what thought-power is. To give a right direction to the thoughts of ignorant thinkers is the purpose of much religious teaching, which these uninstructed ones must accept by faith in bare authority because they are unable to realise its true import. But notwithstanding the aids thus afforded to mankind, the general stream of unregulated thought cannot but have an adverse tendency, and hence the great object to which the instructed mind directs its power is to free itself from the entanglements of disordered thought, and to help others to do the same. To escape from this entanglement is to attain perfect Liberty, which is perfect Power.

## VI

The entanglement from which we need to escape has its origin in the very same principle which gives rise to liberty and power. It is the same principle applied under inverted conditions. And here I would draw particular attention to the law that any sequence followed out in an inverted order must produce an inverted result, for this goes a long way to explain many of the problems of life. The physical world affords endless examples of the working of "inversion." In the dynamo the sequence commences with mechanical force which is ultimately transformed into the subtler power of electricity; but invert this order, commence by generating electricity, and it becomes converted into mechanical force, as in the motor. In the one order the rotation of a wheel produces electricity, and in the opposite order electricity produces the rotation of a wheel. Or to exhibit the same principle in the simplest arithmetical form, if 10÷2=5 then 10÷5=2. "Inversion" is a factor of the greatest magnitude and has to be reckoned with; but I must content myself here with only indicating the general principle that the same power is capable of producing diametrically opposite effects if it be applied under opposite conditions, a truth which the so-called "magicians" of the middle ages expressed by two triangles, placed inversely to one another. We are apt to fall into the mistake of supposing that results of opposite character require powers of opposite character to produce them, and our conceptions of things in general become much simplified when we recognise that this is not the case, but that the same power will produce opposite results as it starts from opposite poles.

Accordingly the inverted application of the same principle which gives rise to liberty and power constitutes the entanglement from which we need to be delivered before power and liberty can be attained, and this principle is expressed in the law that "as a man thinks so he is." This is the basic law of the human mind. It is Descartes' *"cogito, ergo sum."* If we trace consciousness to its seat we find that it is purely subjective. Our external senses would cease to exist were it not for the subjective consciousness which perceives what they communicate to it.

The idea conveyed to the subjective consciousness may be false, but until some truer idea is more forcibly impressed in its stead it remains a substantial reality to the mind which gives it objective existence. I have seen a man speak to the stump of a tree which in the moonlight looked like a person standing in a garden, and repeatedly ask its name and what it wanted; and so far as the speaker's conception was concerned the garden contained a living man who refused to answer. Thus every mind lives in a world to which its own perceptions give objective reality. Its perceptions may be erroneous, but they nevertheless constitute the very reality of life for the mind that gives form to them. No other life than the life we lead in our own mind is possible; and hence the advance of the whole race depends on substituting the ideas of good, of liberty, and of order for their opposites. And this can be done only by giving some sufficient reason for accepting the new idea in place of the old. For each one of us our beliefs constitute our facts, and these beliefs can be changed only by discovering some ground for a different belief.

This is briefly the rationale of the maxim that "as a man thinks so he is"; and from the working of this principle all the issues of life proceed. Now man's first perception of the law of cause and effect in relation to his own conduct is that the result always partakes of the quality of the cause; and since his argument is drawn from external observation only, he regards external acts as the only causes he can effectively set in operation. Hence when he attains sufficient moral enlightenment to realise that many of his acts have been such as to merit retribution he fears retribution as their proper result. Then by reason of the law that "thoughts are things," the evils which he fears take form and plunge him into adverse circumstances, which again prompt him into further wrong acts, and from these come a fresh crop of fears which in their turn become externalised into fresh evils, and thus arises a circulus from which there is no escape so long as the man recognises nothing but his external acts as a causative power in the world of his surroundings.

This is the Law of Works, the Circle of Karma, the Wheel of Fate, from which there appears to be no escape, because the complete fulfilment of the law of our moral nature to-day is only sufficient for to-day and leaves no surplus to compensate the failure of yesterday. This is the necessary law of things as they appear from external observation only; and, so long as this conception remains, the law of each man's subjective consciousness makes it a reality for him. What is needed, therefore, is to establish the conception that external acts are NOT the only causative power, but that there is another law of causation, namely, that of pure Thought. This is the Law of Faith, the Law of Liberty; for it introduces us to a power which is able to inaugurate a new sequence of causation not related to any past actions.

But this change of mental attitude cannot be brought about till we have laid hold of some fact which is sufficient to afford a reason for the change. We require some solid ground for our belief in this higher law. Ultimately we find this ground in the great Truth of the eternal relation between spirit in the universal and in the particular. When we realise that substantially there is nothing else *but* spirit, and that we ourselves are reproductions in individuality of the Intelligence and Love which rule the universe, we have reached the firm standing ground where we find that we can send forth our Thought to produce any effect we will. We have passed beyond the idea of two opposites requiring reconciliation, into that of a duality in which there is no other opposition than that of the inner and the outer of the same unity, the polarity which is inherent in all Being, and we then realise that in virtue of this unity our Thought is possessed of illimitable creative power, and that it is free to range where it will, and is by no means bound down to accept as inevitable the consequences which, if unchecked by renovated thought, would flow from our past actions.

In its own independent creative power the mind has found the way out of the fatal circle in which its previous ignorance of the highest law had imprisoned it. The Unity of the Spirit is found to result in perfect Liberty; the old sequence of Karma has been cut off, and a new and higher order has been introduced. In the old order the line of thought received its quality from the quality of the actions, and since they always fell short of perfection, the development of a higher thought-power from this root was impossible. This is the order in which everything is seen from *without.* It is an inverted order. But in the true order everything is seen from *within.*

It is the thought which determines the quality of the action, and not *vice versa,* and since thought is free, it is at liberty to direct itself to the highest principles, which thus spontaneously reproduce themselves in the outward acts, so that both thoughts and actions are brought into harmony with the great eternal laws and become one in purpose with the Universal Mind. The man realises that he is no longer bound by the consequences of his former deeds, done in the time of his ignorance, in fact, that he never was bound by them except so far as he himself gave them this power by false conceptions of the truth; and thus recognising himself for what he really is—the expression of the Infinite Spirit in individual personality—he finds that he is free, that he is a "partaker of Divine nature," not losing his identity, but becoming more and more fully himself with an ever-expanding perfection, following out a line of evolution whose possibilities are inexhaustible.

But there is not in all men this knowledge. For the most part they still look upon God as an individual Being external to themselves, and what the more instructed man sees to be unity of mind and identity of nature appear to the less advanced to be an external reconciliation between opposing personalities. Hence the whole range of conceptions which may be described as the Messianic Idea. This idea is not, as some seem to suppose, a misconception of the truth of Being. On the contrary, when rightly understood it will be found to imply the very widest grasp of that truth; and it is from the platform of this supreme knowledge alone that an idea so comprehensive in its adaptation to every class of mind could have been evolved. It is the translation of the relations arising from the deepest laws of Being into terms which can be realised even by the most unlearned; a translation arranged with such consummate skill that, as the mind grows in spirituality, every stage of advance is met by a corresponding unfolding of the Divine meaning; while yet even the crudest apprehension of the idea implied is sufficient to afford the required basis for an entire renovation of the man's thoughts concerning himself, giving him a standing ground from which to think of himself as no longer bound by the law of retribution for past offences, but as free to follow out the new law of Liberty as a child of God.

The man's conception of the *modus operandi* of this emancipation may take the form of the grossest anthropomorphism or the most childish notions as to the satisfaction of the Divine justice by vicarious substitution, but the working result will be the same. He has got what satisfies him as a ground for thinking of himself in a perfectly new light; and since the states of our subjective consciousness constitute the realities of our life, to afford him a convincing ground for *thinking* himself free, is to make him free.

With increasing light he may find that his first explanation of the *modus operandi* was inadequate; but when he reaches this stage, further investigation will show him that the great truth of his liberty rests upon a firmer foundation than the conventional interpretation of traditional dogmas, and that it has its roots in the great laws of Nature, which are never doubtful, and which can never be overturned. And it is precisely because their whole action has its root in the unchangeable laws of Mind that there exists a perpetual necessity for presenting to men something which they can lay hold of as a sufficient ground for that change of mental attitude, by which alone they can be rescued from the fatal circle which is figured under the symbol of the Old Serpent.

The hope and adumbration of such a new principle has formed the substance of all religions in all ages, however misapprehended by the ignorant worshippers; and, whatever our individual opinions may be as to the historical facts of Christianity, we shall find that the great figure of liberated and perfected humanity which forms its centre fulfils this desire of all nations in that it sets forth their great ideal of Divine power intervening to rescue man by becoming one with him. This is the conception presented to us, whether we apprehend it in the most literally material sense, or as the ideal presentation of the deepest philosophic study of mental laws, or in whatever variety of ways we may combine these two extremes. The ultimate idea impressed upon the mind must always be the same: it is that there is a Divine warrant for knowing ourselves to be the children of God and "partakers of the Divine nature"; and when we thus realise that there is solid ground for *believing* ourselves free, by force of this very belief we *become* free.

The proper outcome of the study of the laws of spirit which constitute the inner side of things is not the gratification of a mere idle curiosity, nor the acquisition of abnormal powers, but the attainment of our spiritual liberty, without which no further progress is possible. When we have reached this goal the old things have passed away and all things have become new. The mystical seven days of the old creation have been fulfilled, and the first day of the new week dawns upon us with its resurrection to a new life, expressing on the highest plane that great doctrine of the "octave" which the science of the ancient temples traced through Nature, and which the science of the present day endorses, though ignorant of its supreme significance.

When we have thus been made free by recognising our oneness with Infinite Being, we have reached the termination of the old series of sequences and have gained the starting-point of the new. The old limitations are found never to have had any existence save in our own misapprehension of the truth, and one by one they fall off as we advance into clearer light. We find that the Life-Spirit we seek is *in ourselves;* and, having this for our centre, our relation to all else becomes part of a wondrous living Order in which every part works in sympathy with the whole, and the whole in sympathy with every part, a harmony wide as infinitude, and in which there are no limitations save those imposed by the Law of Love.

I have endeavoured in this short series of articles to sketch briefly the principal points of relation between Spirit in ourselves and in our surroundings. This subject has employed the intelligence of mankind from grey antiquity to the present day, and no one thinker can ever hope to grasp it in all its amplitude. But there are certain broad principles which we must all grasp, however we may specialise our studies in detail, and these I have sought to indicate, with what degree of success the reader must form his own opinion. Let him, however, lay firm hold of this one fundamental truth, and the evolution of further truth from it is only a question of time—that there is only One Spirit, however many the modes of its manifestations, and that "the Unity of the Spirit is the Bond of Peace."

II

# THE PERVERSION OF TRUTH

THERE IS a very general recognition, which is growing day by day more and more widespread, that there is a sort of hidden power somewhere which it is within our ability, somehow or other, to use. The ideas on this subject are exceedingly vague with the generality of people, but still they are assuming a more and more definite form, and that which they appear to be taking with the generality of the public is the recognition of the power of suggestion. I suppose none of us doubts that there is such a thing as the power of suggestion and that it can produce very great results indeed, and that it is *par excellence* a hidden power; it works behind the scenes, it works through what we know as the subconscious mind, and consequently its activity is not immediately recognisable, or the source from which it comes. Now there is in some aspects, its usefulness, its benefit, but in other aspects there is a source of danger, because a power of this kind is obviously one which can be used either well or ill; in itself it is perfectly neutral, it all depends on the purpose for which it is used, and the character of the agent who employs it.

This recognition of the power of suggestion is in many instances taking a most undesirable form, and I commend to your notice, in support of this observation, numerous advertisements in certain classes of magazines—many of you must have seen many specimens of that kind—offering for a certain sum of money to put you in the way of getting personal influence, mental power, power of suggestion, as the advertisements very unblushingly put it, for any purpose that you may desire. Some of them even go into further particulars, telling you the particular sort of purposes for which you can employ this, all of them certainly being such uses as no one should ever attempt to make of it.

Therefore, this recognition of the power of suggestion, say even as a mere money-making power, to leave alone other misapplications of it, is a feature which is taking hold, so to say, of certain sections of the public who do not realise a higher platform in these things. It is deplorable that it should be so, but it is in the nature of things unavoidable. You have a power which can be used affirmatively, and which can be used negatively, which can be used for higher purposes, and can be used for lower purposes, and consequently you will find numbers of people who, as soon as they get hold of it, will at once think only of the lower purposes, not of the higher.

In support of what I say—although this is by no means, I suppose, intended as a low application, probably it is intended as a high application, but I cannot say I agree with it—but to show you that I am talking from actual facts I will read you a note which I have made from the *Daily Mail*, of the 20th January, that I daresay some of you may have seen. It is an article headed "Killing by Prayer," and the article goes on to say that a certain circular has been sent round to the different hospitals and other places where the study of vivisection goes forward to this effect. In this circular, signed with the letters "M. C.," the writer says that he accidentally heard of a person who was in the habit of praying from time to time for the death of one of our leading vivisectors and that always the man indicated died. That is what M. C. heard by chance during conversation at a hotel dinner. Then thinking over this, M. C. goes on to say that he (or she) tried praying that the man most likely to cause suffering to innocent subjects by his experiments might be removed, and the consequence was that about a fortnight later one of our most distinguished medical scientists died.

I do not know who the scientist in question was; I daresay some of you may be aware of the name. However, that is what the *Daily Mail* tells us, and it also states that the Anti-Vivisection Societies were unanimous in condemning this circular, and very properly so. Now you see the sender of that circular, whoever he was, obviously thought he was doing a very good piece of work. I myself am by no means any friend of vivisection. I do not think any one can have a real knowledge of the truth and remain in touch with it, but I certainly agreed with the Anti-Vivisection Societies in condemning such a circular as that. You see there is the assumption that prayer, or mental power, can be used to remove a person from the stage of life, and M. C. claims that he did it in the case of this particular scientist.

That brings back another parallel, almost, I might say, an historical parallel, to our mind; that of Dr. Anna Kingsford, taking place perhaps some forty years ago, who claimed—of course she was a very strong anti-vivisectionist—that by thought-power she caused the death of Claude Bernard, the great vivisection scientist of France. Certainly at the time that she put out her forces he did die, but on the other hand, it has been remarked that it was from that very date that her own break-up commenced, and never ceased till she herself passed into the other world. So you see these actions are likely to revert to the sender, even if they are successful.

Now in these two cases the ultimate object was not a low one, it was one which was supposed to be for the benefit of humanity and of the dumb creation. But that does not justify the means. The maxim, "The end justifies the means," is the greatest perversion of truth, and still more so if this hidden power, the power of suggestion, is used to injure any one for a more personal motive than in these cases which I have cited. The lower the motive, the lower the action becomes, and to suppose that because mental means are employed they make any difference in the nature of the act is a very great mistake.

It has been sometimes my painful duty to sentence people to death for murder, and therefore I claim that I have a very fair knowledge of what differentiates murder from those cases in which life is taken which do not amount to murder; and speaking from the judicial experience of a great many years, and the trial of a large number of cases which have involved the question whether the death penalty should be passed or not, I have no hesitation in saying that to kill by mental means is just as much murder as to kill by poison or the dagger. Speaking judicially, I should have not the least hesitation in hanging any one who committed murder by means of mental suggestion. Psychological crime, remember, is crime just the same; possibly it is more deeply dyed crime, because of the greater knowledge which must go along with it. I say that the psychological criminal is worse than the ordinary criminal.

One of the teachings of the Master is on this very point. I refer you to the miracle of the fig tree. You know that he exhibited his power of killing not a person, not even an animal, but a tree. And when the disciples said to him, see how this tree which you cursed has withered away, he replied, Well, you can do exactly the same thing, and goes on to say, nothing shall be impossible to you. Therefore if you can kill fig trees, you can kill people, but, "forgive, if you have aught against any," that your heavenly Father may forgive you.

He says in effect: now you have seen that this hidden power can be used to the destruction of life, at your peril use it otherwise than as a Divine power. Use it with prayer to God and with forgiveness of all against whom you have any sort of grudge or ill-feeling, and if its use is always prefaced in this way, according to the Master's directions, then nobody can use it to injure another either in mind, body or estate.

Perhaps some of you may be inclined to smile if I use the word "sorcery," but at the present day, under one name or another, scientific or semi-scientific, it is nothing but the old-world sorcery which is trying to find its way among us as the hidden power. Sorcery is the inverted use of spiritual power. That is the definition of it, and I speak upon authority. I refer you to the Bible where you will find sorcery takes a prominent place among the list of those things which exclude from the heavenly Jerusalem; the heavenly Jerusalem not being a town or a city in this place or that place, but the perfected state of man. Therefore, use sorcery, and you cannot reach that heavenly state.

It is on this account that we find in Revelations that wonderful description of two symbolical women; they represent two modes of the individual soul. Of course they go further, they indicate national things, race evolution and so on. Why? Because all national movements, all race evolutions, have their root in the development of the individual. A nation or a race is only a collection of individuals, and therefore if a principle once spreads from one individual to another, it spreads to the nation, it spreads to the race. So, therefore, these two symbolical women represent primarily two modes of soul, two modes of thought. You know perfectly well the description of the two women. One, the woman clothed with the sun, standing with the moon under her feet, and with a diadem of stars about her head; the other seated upon an earthly throne, holding a golden cup, and the cup is full of abominations. Those are the two women, and we know that one of them is called in the Scripture, Babylon, and we know which one that is. One of the marks of this woman—mind you that means the class of individuality—is the mark of sorcery, the mark of the inverted use of spiritual and mental powers.

But what is the end of it? The end is that this Babylon becomes the habitation of devils, the hold—or, as the original Greek has it, the prison of evil, an unclean spirit, the cage of every unclean bird. That is the development which takes place in each individual who sets out to misuse this mental power. The misuse may have a very small beginning, it may be such as is taught in a certain school, which I am told exists in London, where shop assistants are trained in the use of magnetic power, in order to decoy or compel unknowing purchasers into buying what they do not want. I am told there is such a school; I cannot quote you my authority. That is a trifling matter. I go into a shop and spend two or three shillings in buying something which, when I get home, I find absolutely useless, and I say, "How in the name of fortune did I come to buy this rubbish?" Well, I must have been hypnotised into it. It does not make much difference to me, but it makes a great deal of difference to the young man or young woman who has hypnotised me, because it is the first step on the downward path. It may be only a matter of sixpence, but it leads on step by step, and unless that path is retraced, the final end is that of Babylon. Therefore it is that St. John says, "I heard a voice from Heaven saying, 'Come forth, my people, out of her'"—and that is out of Babylon—"come forth, my people, out of her"—that is out of this inverted mode of using spiritual power—"come forth, my people, out of her, that ye have no fellowship with her sins and that ye shall receive not of her plague." Therefore, against this inverted use of the hidden power I warn every one from the first day when he begins to realise that there is such a thing as mental or spiritual power which can be exercised upon other persons.

Are we then on this account to go continually in terror of suffering from malicious magnetism, fearing that some enemy here, or some enemy there, is turning on this hidden power against us? If so, we should go in trepidation continually. No, I do not think there is the least reason for us to go in fear in this way. To begin with there are comparatively few who know the law of suggestion sufficiently well to use it either affirmatively or negatively, and of those who do know it sufficiently to make use of it, I am convinced that the majority would wish only to use it in all kindness, and for the benefit of the person concerned. That, I am confident, is the attitude of nine-tenths, or I might perhaps say ninety-nine hundredths, of the students of this subject. They wish to do well, and look upon their use of mental power as an additional means of doing good. But after all, human nature is human nature, and there remains a small minority who are both able and willing to use this hidden power injuriously for their own purposes.

Now how are we to deal with this minority? The answer is simple. Just see them in their true light, see them for what they really are, that is to say, persons who are ignorant of the real spiritual power. They think they have it, and they have not. That is what it is. See them in their true light and their power will fall away from them. The real and ultimate power is that of the affirmative; the negative is destructive, the affirmative is constructive. So this negative use of the hidden power is to be destroyed by the use of the affirmative, the constructive power. The affirmative destroys the negative always in one way, and that is not by attacking it, not by running at it like a bull in a china shop; but by building up life. It is always a building power—it is building, building, building life and more life, and when that life comes in, the negative of necessity goes out.

The ultimate affirmative position is that of conscious union with the source of life. Realise this, and you need not trouble yourself about any action of the negative whatever. Seek conscious union with the ultimate, the first cause, that which is the starting point of all things, whether in the universe or in yourself as the individual. That starting point is always present; it is the same yesterday, to-day and forever, and you are the world and the universe in miniature, and it is always there working in you if you will recognise it. Remember the reciprocity between yourself and this truly hidden power. The power of suggestion is *a* hidden power, but the power which creates all things is *the* hidden power which is at the back of all things. Now realise that it is in yourselves and you need trouble about the negative no longer. This is the Bible teaching regarding Christ; and that teaching is to bring about this conscious personal union with the Divine All-creating Spirit as a present living power to be used day by day.

The Bible tells us there is such a thing as the mystery of iniquity, that is to say, the mystery of the spiritual power used invertedly, used from the diabolical stand-point; and when the Bible speaks of the mystery of iniquity, it means what it says. It tells us there are powers and principalities in the invisible world which are using precisely these same methods on an enormous scale; because, remember one thing, there is never any departure in any part of the Universe from the universal rule of law; what is law upon earth is law in Heaven, law in Hell, law in the invisible and law in the visible; that never alters. What is done by any spiritual power, whether it is a spiritual power of evil or of good, is done through the mental constitution which you have. No power alters the law of your own mind, but a power which knows the law of your mind can use it.

Therefore, it is so essential that you should know the law of your own mind and realise its continual amenability to suggestion. That being so, the great thing is to get a standard for fundamental, unchangeable, and sufficient suggestion to which you can always turn, and which is automatically impressed upon your subconscious mind so deeply that no counter-suggestion can ever take its place; and that is the mystery of Christ, the Son of God. That is why we are told of the mystery of Christ, the mystery of godliness in opposition to the mystery of iniquity; it is because both the mystery of the Divine and the mystery of the diabolical are seeking to work through you, and they can only work through you by the law of your own mental constitution, that is to say, by the law of subconscious mind acting and re-acting upon your conscious mind and upon your body, and so upon your circumstances.

The mystery of Christ is no mere ecclesiastical fiction. People have distorted it, and made it not clear, by trying to explain what at that time and in those days was not properly known, by trying to explain what they did not know; because what is commonly now known regarding the laws of mind was unknown then. But now this light has come we begin to see that the Bible teaching regarding Christ has a great and a deep meaning, and it is for these reasons St. Paul said to the Corinthians: "Little children of whom I travail again in birth, until Christ be formed in you." That is why he speaks of "Christ in you the hope of glory," that is to say, the Christ conception, the realisation of the Christ principle as exhibited in the Christ person, brings you in touch with the personal element in the Universal Spirit, the divine creative, first moving Spirit of the Universe.

Then you see that realising this as your fundamental fact, it is continually impressed upon your subconscious mind, even when you are not thinking of it, because that is the action of the subconscious mind to take in and reason and argue in its own deductive way upon things of which you are not at the moment consciously thinking. Therefore it is that the realisation of that great promise of redemption, which is the backbone of the Bible from the first chapter of Genesis to the last chapter of Revelations, is according to a scientific law. It is not a hocus-pocus business, it is not a thing which has been arranged this way and might just as well have been arranged in some other; it is not so because some arbitrary Authority has commanded it, and the Authority might just as well have commanded it some other way.

No, it is so because the more you examine it, the more you will find that it is absolutely scientific; it is based upon the natural constitution of the human mind. And it is therefore that "Christ," as set forth in the Bible—whether in the Old Testament symbology, or in the New Testament personality—"is the fulfilling of the law," in the sense of specialising in the highest degree that which is common to all humanity. As we realise this more and more, and specialise it more and more, so we shall rise to higher and higher intercourse and more and more consciousness of reciprocal identity, reciprocal life with the Universal Power, which will raise us above any possibility of being touched by any sort of malicious suggestion.

If anybody should be, then, so ill-willed towards us and so lamentably ignorant of spiritual truth himself as to seek to exercise the power of malicious suggestion against us, I pity the person who tries to do it. He will get nothing out of it, because he is firing peas out of a pea-shooter against an iron-clad war vessel. That is what it amounts to; but for himself it amounts to something more. It is a true saying that "Curses return home to roost." I think if we study these things, and consider that there is a reason for them, we need not be in the least alarmed about negative suggestion, or malicious magnetism, of being brought under the power of other minds, of being got over in some way, of being done out of our property, of being injured in our health, or being hurt in our circumstances, and so on.

Of course if you lay yourself open to that kind of thing, you will get it. "Knock, and it shall be opened unto you." That is why the Scripture says, "He that breaketh through a hedge, a serpent shall bite him." That is the serpent that some of us know something about, that is our old enemy Nahash. Some of you, at any rate, are sufficiently trained in the inner sciences to know the serpent Nahash. Break down the hedge, that is to say, the conscious control of your own mind, and above all the hedge of the Divine love and wisdom with which God himself will surround you in the personality of His Son, break down this hedge and of course Nahash comes in. But if you keep your hedge—and remember the old Hebrew tradition always spoke of the Divine Law as "the hedge"—if you keep your hedge unbroken, nothing can come in except by the door. Christ said, "I am the door, by me if any man enter in, he shall be saved."

I have spoken of the two great mysteries, the mystery of godliness and the mystery of iniquity, the mystery of Christ and the mystery of anti-Christ. Now, it is not necessary, mind you, that you should understand these mysteries in full in order to get into your right position. If it were necessary that we should fully understand these mysteries, either to get away from the one or to get into the other, I think all of us would have an uncommonly bad chance. I certainly should. I can touch only the fringe of these things, but we can realise the principle of the affirmative and the principle of the negative which underlies them both; one is the mystery of light, the other is the mystery of darkness.

I do not say do not study these mysteries; they are exactly what we ought to study, but do not think that you remain in a state of danger until you have completely fathomed the mystery. Not a bit of it. You can quite get on the right side without understanding the whole thing, exactly as you travel on a railway without understanding the mechanism of the engine which takes you along.

So then we have these two mysteries, that of light and that of darkness, and therefore what we have to do is to exercise our will to receive the mystery of light, and then that will make for itself a centre in our own hearts and beings, and you will become conscious of that centre. Whether you understand it or not, you will become conscious of it—and then from that centre, that centre of light in yourself, you can start everything in your life, whether spiritual or temporal. You do not have to go further back; you do not have to analyse the why and the wherefore of these things in order to get your starting point. It may interest you afterwards, it may strengthen you afterwards to do so, but for a practical starting point you must realise the Divine presence in yourself, which is the son of God manifested in you, that is the Divine principle of personality speaking within yourself.

So then, having realised this as your centre, you carry the all-originating affirmative power with you, all through everything that you do and everything that you are; day and night it will be there, it will protect you, it will guide you, it will help you. And when you want to do so you can consciously apply to it and it will give you assistance, and because you take this as your starting point, it will manifest itself in all your conditions; because, remember, it is a very simple law of logic that whatever you start with will manifest itself all down the sequence which comes from it. If you start with the colour red you can make all sorts of modifications and bring out orange, purple and brown, but the red basis will show itself all down the scale of colour, and so if you start with a basis of blue, blue will show itself all down the scale of various colours.

Therefore, if you start with the affirmative basis, the one starting point of the Divine spirit, not taking it lower down the stream, but going to the fountain head, that affirmative principle of life will flow all through, showing its own quality to the very tips of your fingers and beyond that out into all your circumstances. So that the divine presence will be continuously with you, not as a consequence of your joining this Church or that, following this idea, or that teacher, but because you know the truth for yourselves, and you have realised it as an actual living experience in your own mind and in your own heart; and therefore it is that this personal recognition of the Divine love and wisdom and power is what St. Paul calls "Christ in you, the hope of glory."

Each one who recognises this, is one who answers the Biblical description of a true Israelite indeed. That word "Israelite" in the Bible is a very deeply symbolical word, and carries an immense amount of meaning with it. So get this recognition as the real working fact that each one of you is an Israelite indeed, and if so, then make yourselves perfectly happy with the everlasting statement, which is as true now as it was on the day on which it was uttered: "There is no divination or enchantment against Israel."

*1909.*

III

## THE "I AM"

We often do not sufficiently recognise the truth of Walt Whitman's pithy saying, "I am not all contained between my hat and my boots," and forget the twofold nature of the "I AM," that it is at once both the manifested and the unmanifested, the universal and the individual. By losing sight of this truth we surround ourselves with limitations; we see only part of the self, and then we are surprised that the part fails to do the work of the whole. Factors crop up on which we had not reckoned, and we wonder where they come from, and do not understand that they necessarily arise from that great unity in which we are all included.

It is the grand intelligence and livingness of Universal Spirit continually pressing forward to manifestation of itself in a glorious humanity.

This must be effected by each individual's recognition of his power to co-operate with the Supreme Principle through an intelligent conception of its purpose and of the natural laws by which that purpose is accomplished—a recognition which can proceed only from the realisation that he himself is none other than the same Universal Principle in particular manifestation.

When he sees this he sees that Walt Whitman's saying is true, and that his source of intelligence, power, and purpose is in that Universal Self, which is his as well as another's just because it is universal, and which is therefore as completely and entirely identified with himself as though there were no other expression of it in the world.

The understanding which alone gives value to knowledge is the understanding that, when we employ the formula "I am, therefore I can, therefore I will," the "I AM" with which the series starts is a being who, so to speak, has his head in heaven and his feet upon the earth, a perfect unity, and with a range of ideas far transcending the little ideas which are limited by the requirements of a day or an hour. On the other hand, the requirements of the day and the hour are real while they last, and since the manifested life can be lived only in the moment that now is, whether it be to-day or ten thousand years hence, our need is to harmonise the life of expression with the life of purpose, and by realising in ourselves the source of the highest purposes to realise also the life of the fullest expression.

This is the meaning of prayer. Prayer is not a foolish seeking to change the mind of Supreme Wisdom, but it is an intelligent seeking to embody that wisdom in our thoughts so as more and more perfectly to express *it* in expressing *ourselves.* Thus, as we gradually grow into the habit of finding this inspiring Presence *within ourselves,* and of realising its forward movement as the ultimate determining factor in all true healthful mental action, it will become second nature to us to have all our plans, down to the apparently most trivial, so floating upon the undercurrent of this Universal Intelligence that a great harmony will come into our lives, every discordant manifestation will disappear, and we shall find ourselves more and more controlling all things into the forms that we desire.

Why? Because we have attained to *commanding* the Spirit and making it obey us? Certainly not, for "if the blind lead the blind both shall fall into the ditch"; but because we are *companions* of the Spirit, and by a continuous and growing intimacy have changed, not "the mind of the Spirit," but our own, and have learned to think from a higher standpoint, where we see that the old-world saying "know thyself" includes the knowledge of all that we mean when we speak of God.

## I Am Is One

This may seem a very elementary proposition, but it is one of which we are too apt to lose sight. What does it mean? It means everything; but we are most concerned with what it means in regard to ourselves, and to each of us personally it means this. It means that there are not two Spirits, one which is myself and one which is another. It means that there is not some great unknown power external to myself which may be actuated by perfectly different motives to my own, and which will, therefore, oppose me with its irresistible force and pass over me, leaving me crushed and broken like the devotee over whom the car of Jaggarnath has rolled. It means that there is only one mind, one motive, one power—not two opposing each other—and that my conscious mind in all its movements is only the one mind expressing itself as (not merely through) my own particular individuality.

There are not two I AMs, but one I am. Whatever, therefore, I can conceive the Great Universal Life Principle to be, that I am. Let us try fully to realise what this means. Can you conceive the Great Originating and Sustaining Life Principle of the whole universe as poor, weak, sordid, miserable, jealous, angry, anxious, uncertain, or in any other way limited? We know that this is impossible. Then because the I AM is one it is equally untrue of ourselves. Learn first to distinguish the true self that you are from the mental and physical processes which it throws forth as the instruments of its expression, and then learn that this self controls these instruments, and not vice versa. As we advance in this knowledge we know ourselves to be unlimited, and that, in the miniature world, whose centre we are, we ourselves are the very same overflowing of joyous livingness that the Great Life Spirit is in the Great All. The I AM is One.

IV

# AFFIRMATIVE POWER

THOROUGHLY TO REALISE the true nature of affirmative power is to possess the key to the great secret. We feel its presence in all the innumerable forms of life by which we are surrounded and we feel it as the life in ourselves; and at last some day the truth bursts upon us like a revelation that we can wield this power, this life, by the process of Thought. And as soon as we see this, the importance of regulating our thinking begins to dawn upon us. We ask ourselves what this thought process is, and we then find that it is thinking affirmative force into forms which are the product of our own thought. We mentally conceive the form and then think life into it.

This must always be the nature of the creative process on whatever scale, whether on the grand scale of the Universal Cosmic Mind or on the miniature scale of the individual mind; the difference is only in degree and not in kind. We may picture the mental machinery by which this is done in the way that best satisfies our intellect—and the satisfying of the intellect on this point is a potent factor in giving us that confidence in our mental action without which we can effect nothing—but the actual externalisation is the result of something more powerful than a merely intellectual apprehension. It is the result of that inner mental state which, for want of a better word, we may call our emotional conception of ourselves. It is the "self" which we *feel* ourselves to be which takes forms of our own creating. For this reason our thought must be so grounded upon knowledge that we shall *feel* the truth of it, and thus be able to produce in ourselves that mental attitude of feeling which corresponds to the condition which we desire to externalise.

We cannot think into manifestation a different sort of life to that which we realise in ourselves. As Horace says, *"Nemo dat quod non habet,"* we cannot give what we have not got. And, on the other hand, we can never cease creating forms of some sort by our mental activity, thinking life into them. This point must be very carefully noted. We cannot sit still producing nothing: the mental machinery *will* keep on turning out work of some sort, and it rests with us to determine of what sort it shall be. In our entire ignorance or imperfect realisation of this we create negative forms and think life into them. We create forms of death, sickness, sorrow, trouble, and limitation of all sorts, and then think life into these forms; with the result that, however non-existent in themselves, to us they become realities and throw their shadow across the path which would otherwise be bright with the many-coloured beauties of innumerable flowers and the glory of the sunshine.

This need not be. It is giving to the negative an affirmative force which does not belong to it. Consider what is meant by the negative. It is the absence of something. It is not-being, and is the absence of all that constitutes being. Left to itself, it remains in its own nothingness, and it only assumes form and activity when we give these to it by our thought.

Here, then, is the great reason for practising control over our thought. It is the one and only instrument we have to work with, but it is an instrument which works with the greatest certainty, for limitation if we think limitation, for enlargement if we think enlargement. Our thought as feeling is the magnet which draws to us those conditions which accurately correspond to itself. This is the meaning of the saying that "thoughts are things." But, you say, how can I think differently from the circumstances? Certainly you are not required to say that the circumstances *at the present moment* are what they are not; to say so would be untrue; but what is wanted is not to think from the standpoint of circumstances at all. Think from that interior standpoint where there are no circumstances, and from whence you can dictate what circumstances shall be, and then leave the circumstances to take care of themselves.

Do not think of this, that, or the other particular *circumstances* of health, peace, etc., but of health, peace, and prosperity themselves. Here is an advertisement from *Pearson's Weekly:*—"Think money. Big moneymakers *think* money." This is a perfectly sound statement of the power of thought, although it is only an advertisement; but we may make an advance beyond thinking "money." We can think "Life" in all its fulness, together with that perfect harmony of conditions which includes all that we need of money and a thousand other good things besides, for some of which money stands as the symbol of exchangeable value, while others cannot be estimated by so material a standard.

Therefore think Life, illumination, harmony, prosperity, happiness—think the things rather than this or that condition of them. And then by the sure operation of the Universal Law these things will form themselves into the shapes best suited to your particular case, and will enter your life as active, living forces, which will never depart from you because you know them to be part and parcel of your own being.

# V

## SUBMISSION

THERE ARE TWO kinds of submission: submission to superior force and submission to superior truth. The one is weakness and the other is strength. It is an exceedingly important part of our training to learn to distinguish between these two, and the more so because the wrong kind is extolled by nearly all schools of popular religious teaching at the present day as constituting the highest degree of human attainment. By some this is pressed so far as to make it an instrument of actual oppression, and with all it is a source of weakness and a bar to progress. We are forbidden to question what are called the wise dispensations of Providence and are told that pain and sorrow are to be accepted because they are the will of God; and there is much eloquent speaking and writing concerning the beauty of quiet resignation, all of which appeals to a certain class of gentle minds who have not yet learnt that gentleness does not consist in the absence of power but in the kindly and beneficent use of it.

Minds cast in this mould are peculiarly apt to be misled. They perceive a certain beauty in the picture of weakness leaning upon strength, but they attribute its soothing influence to the wrong element of the combination. A thoughtful analysis would show them that their feelings consisted of pity for the weak figure and admiration for the strong one, and that the suggestiveness of the whole arose from its satisfying the artistic sense of balance which requires a compensation of this sort. But which of the two figures in the picture would they themselves prefer to be? Surely not the weak one needing help, but the strong one giving it. By itself the weak figure only stirs our pity and not our admiration. Its form may be beautiful, but its very beauty only serves to enhance the sense of something wanting—and the something wanting is strength. The attraction which the doctrine of passive resignation possesses for certain minds is based upon an appeal to sentiment, which is accepted without any suspicion that the sentiment appealed to is a false one.

Now the healthful influence of the movement known as "The Higher Thought" consists precisely in this—that it sets itself rigorously to combat this debilitating doctrine of submission. It can see as well as others the beauty of weakness leaning upon strength; but it sees that the real source of the beauty lies in the strong element of the combination. The true beauty consists in the power to confer strength, and this power is not to be acquired by submission, but by the exactly opposite method of continually asserting our determination not to submit.

Of course, if we take it for granted that all the sorrow, sickness, pain, trouble, and other adversity in the world is the expression of the will of God, then doubtless we must resign ourselves to the inevitable with all the submission we can command, and comfort ourselves with the vague hope that somehow in some far-off future we shall find that

"Good is the final goal of ill,"

though even *this* vague hope is a protest against the very submission we are endeavouring to exercise. But to make the assumption that the evil of life is the will of God is to assume what a careful and intelligent study of the laws of the universe, both mental and physical, will show us is not the truth; and if we turn to that Book which contains the fullest delineation of these universal laws, we shall find nothing taught more clearly than that submission to the evils of life is not submission to the will of God. We are told that Christ was manifested for this end, that he should destroy him that hath the power of death—that is, the devil. Now death is the very culmination of the Negative. It is the entire absence of all that makes Life, and whatever goes to diminish the living quality of Life reproduces, in its degree, the distinctive quality of this supreme exhibition of the Negative. Everything that tends to detract from the fulness of life has in it this deathful quality.

In that completely renovated life, which is figured under the emblem of the New Jerusalem, we are told that sorrow and sighing shall flee away, and that the inhabitant shall not say, I am sick. Nothing that obscures life, or restricts it, can proceed from the same source as the Power which gives light to them that sit in darkness, and deliverance to them that are bound. Negation can never be Affirmation; and the error we have always to guard against is that of attributing positive power to the Negative. If we once grasp the truth that God is life, and that life in every mode of expression can never be anything else than Affirmative, then it must become clear to us that nothing which is of the opposite tendency can be according to the will of God. For God (the good) to will any of the "evil" that is in the world would be for Life to act with the purpose of diminishing itself, which is a contradiction in terms to the very idea of Life. God is Life, and Life is, by its very nature, Affirmative. The submission we have hitherto made has been to our own weakness, ignorance, and fear, and not to the supreme good.

But is no such thing as submission, then, required of us under any circumstances? Are we always to have our own way in everything? Assuredly the whole secret of our progress to liberty is involved in acquiring the habit of submission; but it is submission to superior Truth, and not to superior force. It sometimes happens that, when we attain a higher Truth, we find that its reception requires us to re-arrange the truths which we possessed before: not, indeed, to lay any of them aside, for Truth once recognised cannot be again put out of sight, but to recognise a different relative proportion between them from that which we had seen previously. Then there comes a submitting of what has hitherto been our highest truth to one which we recognise as still higher, a process not always easy of attainment, but which must be gone through if our spiritual development is not to be arrested. The lesser degree of life must be swallowed up in the greater; and for this purpose it is necessary for us to learn that the smaller degree was only a partial and limited aspect of that which is more universal, stronger, and of a larger build every way.

Now, in going through the processes of spiritual growth, there is ample scope for that training in self-knowledge and self-control which is commonly understood by the word "submission." But the character of the act is materially altered. It is no longer a half-despairing resignation to a superior force external to ourselves, which we can only vaguely hope is acting kindly and wisely, but it is an intelligent recognition of the true nature of our own interior forces and of the laws by which a robust spiritual constitution is to be developed; and the submission is no longer to limitations which drain life of its livingness, and against which we instinctively rebel, but to the law of our own evolution which manifests itself in continually increasing degrees of life and strength.

The submission which we recognise is the price that has to be paid for increase in any direction. Even in the Money Market we must invest before we can realise profits. It is a universal rule that Nature obeys us exactly in proportion as we first obey Nature; and this is as true in regard to spiritual science as to physical. The only question is whether we will yield an ignorant submission to the principle of Death, or a joyous and intelligent obedience to the principle of Life.

If we have clearly grasped the fact of our identity with Universal Spirit, we shall find that, in the right direction, there is really no such thing as submission. Submission is to the power of another—a man cannot be said to submit to himself. When the "I AM" in us recognises a greater degree of I AM-ness (if I may coin the word) than it has hitherto attained, then, by the very force of this recognition, it *becomes what it sees,* and therefore naturally puts off from itself whatever would limit its expression of its own completeness.

But this is a natural process of growth, and not an unnatural act of submission; it is not the pouring-out of ourselves in weakness, but the gathering of ourselves together in increasing strength. There is no weakness in Spirit, it is all strength; and we must therefore always be watchful against the insidious approaches of the Negative which would invert the true position. The Negative always points to some external source of strength. Its formula is "I AM NOT." It always seeks to fix a gulf between us and the Infinite Sufficiency. It would always have us believe that that sufficiency is not our own, but that by an act of uncertain favour we may have occasional spoonfuls of it doled out to us. Christ's teaching is different. We do not need to come with our pitcher to the well to draw water, like the woman of Samaria, but we have *in ourselves* an inexhaustible supply of the living water springing up into everlasting life.

Let us then inscribe "No Surrender" in bold characters upon our banner, and advance undaunted to claim our rightful heritage of liberty and life.

VI

# COMPLETENESS

A POINT ON WHICH students of mental science often fail to lay sufficient stress is the completeness of man—not a completeness to be attained hereafter, but here and now. We have been so accustomed to have the imperfection of man drummed into us in books, sermons, and hymns, and above all in a mistaken interpretation of the Bible, that at first the idea of his completeness altogether staggers us. Yet until we see this we must remain shut out from the highest and best that mental science has to offer, from a thorough understanding of its philosophy, and from its greatest practical achievements.

To do any work successfully you must believe yourself to be a *whole* man in respect of it. The completed work is the outward image of a corresponding completeness in yourself. And if this is true in respect of one work it is true of all; the difference in the importance of the work does not matter; we cannot successfully attempt *any* work until, for some reason or other, we believe ourselves able to accomplish it; in other words, until we believe that none of the conditions for its completion is wanting in us, and that we are therefore complete in respect of it. Our recognition of our completeness is thus the measure of what we are able to do, and hence the great importance of knowing the fact of our own completeness.

But, it may be asked, do we not see imperfection all around? Is there not sorrow, sickness, and trouble? Yes; but why? Just for the very reason that we do not realise our completeness. If we realised *that* in its fulness these things would not be; and in the degree in which we come to realise it we shall find them steadily diminish. Now if we really grasp the two fundamental truths that Spirit is Life pure and simple, and that external things are the result of interior forces, then it ought not to be difficult to see why we should be complete; for to suppose otherwise is to suppose the reactive power of the universe to be either unable or unwilling to produce the complete expression of its own intention in the creation of man.

That it should be unable to do so would be to depose it from its place as the creative principle, and that it should be unwilling to fulfil its own intention is a contradiction in terms; so that on either supposition we come to a *reductio ad absurdum.* In forming man the creative principle therefore *must* have produced a perfect work, and our conception of ourselves as imperfect can only be the result of our own ignorance of what we really are; and our advance, therefore, does not consist in having something new added to us, but in learning to bring into action powers which already exist in us, but which we have never tried to use, and therefore have not developed, simply because we have always taken it for granted that we are by nature defective in some of the most important faculties necessary to fit us to our environment.

If we wish to attain to these great powers, the question is, where are we to seek them? And the answer is *in ourselves.* That is the great secret. We are not to go outside ourselves to look for power. As soon as we do so we find, not power, but weakness. To seek strength from any outside source is to make affirmation of our weakness, and all know what the natural result of such an affirmation must be.

We are complete *in ourselves;* and the reason why we fail to realise this is that we do not understand how far the "self" of ourselves extends. We know that the whole of anything consists of *all* its parts and not only of some of them; yet this is just what we do not seem to know about ourselves. We say rightly that every person is a concentration of the Universal Spirit into individual consciousness; but if so, then each individual consciousness must find the Universal Spirit to be the infinite expression of *itself.* It is *this* part of the "Self" that we so often leave out in our estimate of what we are; and consequently we look upon ourselves as crawling pygmies when we might think of ourselves as archangels. We try to work with the mere shadows of ourselves instead of with the glorious substance, and then wonder at our failures. If we only understood that our "better half" is the whole infinite of Spirit—that which creates and sustains the universe—then we should know how complete our completeness is.

As we approach this conception, our completeness becomes a reality to us, and we find that we need not go outside ourselves for anything. We have only to draw on that part of ourselves which is infinite to carry out any intention we may form in our individual consciousness; for there is no barrier between the two parts, otherwise they would not be a whole. Each belongs perfectly to the other, and the two are one. There is no antagonism between them, for the Infinite Life can have no interest against its individualisation of *itself.* If there is any feeling of tension it proceeds from our not fully realising this conception of our own wholeness; we are placing a barrier somewhere, when in truth there is none; and the tension will continue until we find out where and how we are setting up this barrier and remove it.

This feeling of tension is the feeling that we are *not using our Whole Being.* We are trying to make half do the work of the whole; but we cannot rid ourselves of our wholeness, and therefore the whole protests against our attempts to set one half against the other. But when we realise that our concentration *out of* the Infinite also implies our expansion *into* it, we shall see that our *whole* "self" includes both the concentration and the expansion; and seeing this first intellectually we shall gradually learn to use our knowledge practically and bring our whole man to bear upon whatever we take in hand. We shall find that there is in us a constant action and reaction between the infinite and the individual, like the circulation of the blood from the heart to the extremities and back again, a constant pulsation of vital energy quite natural and free from all strain and exertion.

This is the great secret of the livingness of Life, and it is called by many names and set forth under many symbols in various religions and philosophies, each of which has its value in proportion as it brings us nearer the realisation of this perfect wholeness. But the thing itself is Life, and therefore can only be suggested, but not described, by any words or symbols; it is a matter of personal experience which no one can convey to another. All we can do is to point out the direction in which this experience is to be sought, and to tell others the intellectual arguments which have helped us to find it; but the experience itself is the operation of definite vital functions of the inner being, and no one but ourselves can do our living for us.

But, so far as it is possible to express these things in words, what must be the result of realising that the "self" in us includes the Infinite as well as the Individual? All the resources of the Infinite must be at our disposal; we may draw on them as we will, and there is no limit save that imposed by the Law of Kindness, a self-imposed limitation, which, because of being *self*-imposed, is not bondage but only another expression of our liberty. Thus we are free and all limitations are removed.

We are also no longer ignorant, for since the "self" in us includes the Infinite we can draw thence all needed knowledge, and though we may not always be able to formulate this knowledge in the mentality, we shall *feel* its guidance, and eventually the mentality will learn to put this also into form of words; and thus by combining thought and experience, theory and practice, we shall by degrees come more and more into the knowledge of the Law of our Being, and find that there is no place in it for fear, because it is the law of perfect liberty. And knowing what our whole self really is, we shall walk erect as free men and women radiating Light and Life all round, so that our very presence will carry a vivifying influence with it, because we realise ourselves to be an Affirmative Whole, and not a mere negative disintegration of parts.

We know that our whole self includes that Greater Man which is back of and causes the phenomenal man, and this Greater Man is the true human principle in us. It is, therefore, universal in its sympathies, but at the same time not less individually *ourself;* and thus the true man in us, being at once both universal and individual, can be trusted as a sure guide. It is that "Thinker" which is behind the conscious mentality, and which, if we will accept it as our centre, and realise that it is not a separate entity but *ourself,* will be found equal to every occasion, and will lead us out of a condition of servitude into "the glorious liberty of the sons of God."

VII

# THE PRINCIPLE OF GUIDANCE

If I were asked which of all the spiritual principles ranked first, I should feel inclined to say the Principle of Guidance; not in the sense of being more essential than the others, for *every* portion is equally essential to the completeness of a perfect whole, but in the sense of being first in order of sequence and giving value to all our other powers by placing them in their due relation to one another. "Giving value to our *other* powers," I say, because this also is one of our powers. It is that which, judged from the standpoint of personal self-consciousness, is above us; but which, realised from the point of view of the unity of all Spirit, is part and parcel of ourselves, because it is that Infinite Mind which is of necessity identified with all its manifestations.

Looking to this Infinite Mind as a Superior Intelligence from which we may receive guidance does not therefore imply looking to an external source. On the contrary, it is looking to the innermost spring of our own being, with a confidence in its action which enables us to proceed to the execution of our plans with a firmness and assurance that are in themselves the very guarantee of our success.

The action of the spiritual principles in us follows the order which we impose upon them by our thought; therefore the order of realisation will reproduce the order of desire; and if we neglect this first principle of right order and guidance, we shall find ourselves beginning to put forth other great powers, which are at present latent within us, without knowing how to find suitable employment for them—which would be a very perilous condition, for without having before us objects worthy of the powers to which we awake, we should waste them on petty purposes dictated only by the narrow range of our unilluminated intellect. Therefore the ancient wisdom says, "With all thy getting, get understanding."

The awakening to consciousness of our mysterious interior powers will sooner or later take place, and will result in our using them whether we understand the law of their development or not, just as we already use our physical faculties whether we understand their laws or not. The interior powers are natural powers as much as the exterior ones. We can direct their use by a knowledge of their laws; and it is therefore of the highest importance to have some sound principle of guidance in the use of these higher faculties as they begin to manifest themselves.

If, therefore, we would safely and profitably enter upon the possession of the great inheritance of power that is opening out before us, we must before all things seek to realise in ourselves that Superior Intelligence which will become an unfailing principle of guidance if we will only recognise it as such. Everything depends on our recognition. Thoughts are things, and therefore as we *will* our thoughts to be so we *will* the thing to be. If, then, we will to use the Infinite Spirit as a spirit of guidance, we shall find that the fact is as we have willed it; and in doing this we are still making use of our own supreme principle. And this is the true "understanding" which, by placing all the other powers in their correct order, creates one grand unity of power directed to clearly defined and worthy aims, in place of the dispersion of our powers, by which they only neutralise each other and effect nothing.

This is that Spirit of Truth which shall guide us into all Truth. It is the sincere Desire of us reaching out after Truth. Truth first and Power afterwards is the reasonable order, which we cannot invert without injury to ourselves and others; but if we follow this order we shall always find scope for our powers in developing into present realities the continually growing glory of our vision of the ideal.

The ideal is the true real, but it must be brought into manifestation before it can be shown to be so, and it is in this that the *practical* nature of our mental studies consists. It is the *practical* mystic who is the man of power; the man who, realising the mystical powers within, fits his outward action to this knowledge, and so shows his faith by his works; and assuredly the first step is to make use of that power of infallible guidance which he can call to his aid simply by desiring to be led by it.

## VIII

# DESIRE AS THE MOTIVE POWER

THERE ARE CERTAIN Oriental schools of thought, together with various Western offshoots from them, which are entirely founded on the principle of annihilating all desire. Reach that point at which you have no wish for anything and you will find yourself free, is the sum and substance of their teaching; and in support of this they put forward a great deal of very specious argument, which is all the more likely to entangle the unwary, because it contains a recognition of many of the profoundest truths of Nature. But we must bear in mind that it is possible to have a very deep knowledge of psychological facts, and at the same time vitiate the results of our knowledge by an entirely wrong assumption in regard to the law which binds these facts together in the universal system; and the injurious results of misapprehension upon such a vital question are so radical and far-reaching that we cannot too forcibly urge the necessity of clearly understanding the true nature of the point at issue. Stripped of all accessories and embellishments, the question resolves itself into this: Which shall we choose for our portion, Life or Death? There can be no accommodation between the two; and whichever we select as our guiding principle must produce results of a kind proper to itself.

The whole of this momentous question turns on the place that we assign to desire in our system of thought. Is it the Tree of Life in the midst of the Garden of the Soul? or is it the Upas Tree creating a wilderness of death all around? This is the issue on which we have to form a judgment, and this judgment must colour all our conception of life and determine the entire range of our possibilities. Let us, then, try to picture to ourselves the ideal proposed by the systems to which I have alluded—a man who has succeeded in entirely annihilating all desire. To him all things must be alike. The good and the evil must be as one, for nothing has any longer the power to raise any desire in him; he has no longer any feeling which shall prompt him to say, "This is good, therefore I choose it; that is evil, therefore I reject it"; for all choice implies the perception of something more desirable in what is chosen than in what is rejected, and consequently the existence of that feeling of desire which has been entirely eliminated from the ideal we are contemplating.

Then, if the perception of all that makes one thing preferable to another has been obliterated, there can be no motive for any sort of action whatever. Endue a being who has thus extinguished his faculty of desire with the power to create a universe, and he has no motive for employing it. Endue him with all knowledge, and it will be useless to him; for, since desire has no place in him, he is without any purpose for which to turn his knowledge to account. And with Love we cannot endue him, for that is desire in its supreme degree. But if all this be excluded, what is left of the man? Nothing, except the mere outward form. If he has actually obtained this ideal, he has practically ceased to be. Nothing can by any means interest him, for there is nothing to attract or repel in one thing more than in another. He must be dead alike to all feeling and to all motive of action, for both feeling and action imply the preference for one condition rather than another; and where desire is utterly extinguished, no such preference can exist.

No doubt some one may object that it is only evil desires which are thus to be suppressed; but a perusal of the writings of the schools of thought in question will show that this is not the case. The foundation of the whole system is that *all* desire must be obliterated, the desire for the good just as much as the desire for the evil. The good is as much "illusion" as the evil, and until we have reached absolute indifference to both we have not attained freedom. When we have utterly crushed out *all* desire we are free. And the practical results of such a philosophy are shown in the case of

Indian devotees, who, in pursuance of their resolve to crush out *all* desire, both for good and evil alike, become nothing more than outward images of men, from which all power of perception and of action has long since fled.

The mergence in the universal, at which they thus aim, becomes nothing more than a self-induced hypnotism, which, if maintained for a sufficient length of time, saps away every power of mental and bodily activity, leaving nothing but the outside husk of an attenuated human form—the hopeless wreck of what was once a living man. This is the logical result of a system which assumes for its starting-point that desire is evil in itself, that every desire is *per se* a form of bondage, independently of the nature of its object. The majority of the followers of this philosophy may lack sufficient resolution to carry it out rigorously to its practical conclusions; but whether their ideal is to be realised in this world or in some other, the utter extinction of desire means nothing else than absolute apathy, without feeling and without action.

How entirely false such an idea is—not only from the standpoint of our daily life, but also from that of the most transcendental conception of the Universal Principle—is evidenced by the mere fact that anything exists at all. If the highest ideal is that of utter apathy, then the Creative Power of the universe must be extremely low-minded; and all that we have hitherto been accustomed to look upon as the marvellous order and beauty of creation, is nothing but a display of vulgarity and ignorance of sound philosophy.

But the fact that creation exists proves that the Universal Mind thinks differently, and we have only to look around to see that the true ideal is the exercise of creative power. Hence, so far from desire being a thing to be annihilated, it is the very root of every conceivable mode of Life. Without it Life could not be. Every form of expression implies the selection of all that goes to make up that form, and the passing-by of whatever is not required for that purpose; hence a desire for that which is selected in preference to what is laid aside. And this selective desire is none other than the universal Law of Attraction.

Whether this law acts as the chemical affinity of apparently unconscious atoms, or in the instinctive, if unreasoned, attractions of the vegetable and animal worlds, it is still the principle of selective affinity; and it continues to be the same when it passes on into the higher kingdoms which are ruled by reason and conscious purpose. The modes of activity in each of these kingdoms are dictated by the nature of the kingdom; but the activity itself always results from the preference of a certain subject for a certain object, to the exclusion of all others; and all action consists in the reciprocal movement of the two towards each other in obedience to the law of their affinity.

When this takes place in the kingdom of conscious individuality, the affinities exhibit themselves as mental action; but the principle of selection prevails without exception throughout the universe. In the conscious mind this attraction towards its affinity becomes desire; the desire to create some condition of things better than that now existing. Our want of knowledge may cause us to make mistakes as to what this better thing really is, and so in seeking to carry out our desire we may give it a wrong direction; but the fault is not in the desire itself, but in our mistaken notion of what it is that it requires for its satisfaction. Hence unrest and dissatisfaction until its true affinity is found; but, as soon as this is discovered, the law of attraction at once asserts itself and produces that better condition, the dream of which first gave direction to our thoughts.

Thus it is eternally true that desire is the cause of all feeling and all action; in other words, of all Life. The whole livingness of Life consists in receiving or in radiating forth the vibrations produced by the law of attraction; and in the kingdom of mind these vibrations necessarily become conscious out-reachings of the mind in the direction in which it feels attraction; that is to say, they become desires. Desire is therefore the mind seeking to manifest itself in some form which as yet exists only in its thought. It is the principle of creation, whether the thing created be a world or a wooden spoon; both have their origin in the desire to bring something into existence which does not yet exist. Whatever may be the scale on which we exercise our creative ability, the motive power must always be desire.

Desire is the force behind all things; it is the moving principle of the universe and the innermost centre of all Life. Hence, to take the negation of desire for our primal principle is to endeavour to stamp out Life itself; but what we have to do is to acquire the requisite knowledge by which to guide our desires to their true objects of satisfaction. To do this is the whole end of knowledge; and any knowledge applied otherwise is only a partial knowledge, which, having failed in its purpose, is nothing but ignorance. Desire is thus the sum-total of the livingness of Life, for it is that in which all movement originates, whether on the physical level or the spiritual. In a word, desire is the creative power, and must be carefully guarded, trained, and directed accordingly; but thus to seek to develop it to the highest perfection is the very opposite of trying to kill it outright.

And desire has fulfilment for its correlative. The desire and its fulfilment are bound together as cause and effect; and when we realise the law of their sequence, we shall be more than ever impressed with the supreme importance of Desire as the great centre of Life.

## IX

# TOUCHING LIGHTLY

WHAT IS our point of support? Is it in ourselves or outside us? Are we self-poised, or does our balance depend on something external? According to the actual belief in which our answer to these questions is embodied so will our lives be. In everything there are two parts, the essential and the incidental—that which is the nucleus and *raison d'être* of the whole thing, and that which gathers round this nucleus and takes form from it. The true knowledge always consists in distinguishing these two from each other, and error always consists in misplacing them.

In all our affairs there are two factors, ourselves and the matter to be dealt with; and since *for us* the nature of anything is always determined by our thought of it, it is entirely a question of our belief which of these two factors shall be the essential and which the accessory. Whichever we regard as the essential, the other at once becomes the incidental. The incidental can never be absent. For any sort of action to take place there must be *some* conditions under which the activity passes out into visible results; but the same sort of activity may occur under a variety of different conditions, and may thus produce very different visible results. So in every matter we shall always find an essential or energising factor, and an incidental factor which derives its quality from the nature of the energy.

We can therefore never escape from having to select our essential and our incidental factor, and whichever we select as the essential, we thereby place the other in the position of the incidental. If, then, we make the mistake of reversing the true position and suppose that the energising force comes from the merely accessory circumstances, we make *them* our point of support and lean upon *them,* and stand or fall with them accordingly; and so we come into a condition of weakness and obsequious waiting on all sorts of external influences, which is the very reverse of that strength, wisdom, and opulence which are the only meaning of Liberty.

But if we would ask ourselves the common-sense question Where can the centre of a man's Life be except in himself? we shall see that in all which pertains to us the energising centre must be in ourselves. We can never get away from ourselves as the centre of our own universe, and the sooner we clearly understand this the better. There is really no energy in *our* universe but what emanates from ourselves in the first instance, and the power which appears to reside in our surroundings is derived entirely from our own mind.

If once we realise this, and consider that the Life which flows into us from the Universal Life-Principle is at every moment *new* Life entirely undifferentiated to any particular purpose besides that of supporting our own individuality, and that it is therefore ours to externalise in any form we will, then we find that this manifestation of the eternal Life-Principle *in ourselves* is the standpoint from which we can control our surroundings. We must lean firmly on the central point of our own being and not on anything else. Our mistake is in taking our surroundings too much *"au grand sérieux."* We should touch things more lightly. As soon as we feel that their weight impedes our free handling of them they are mastering us, and not we them.

Light handling does not mean weak handling. On the contrary, lightness of touch is incompatible with a weak grasp of the instrument, which implies that the weight of the tool is excessive relatively to the force that seeks to guide it. A light, even playful handling, therefore implies a firm grasp and perfect control over the instrument. It is only in the hands of a Grinling Gibbons that the carving tool can create miracles of aerial lightness from the solid wood. The light yet firm touch tells not of weakness, but of power held in reserve; and if we realise our own out-and-out spiritual nature we know that behind any measure of power we may put forth there is the whole reserve of the infinite to back us up.

As we come to know this we begin to handle things lightly, playing with them as a juggler does with his flying knives, which cannot make the slightest movement other than he has assigned to them, for we begin to see that our control over things is part of the necessary order of the universe. The disorder we have met with in the past has resulted precisely from our never having attempted consciously to introduce this element of our personal control as part of the system.

Of course, I speak of the *whole* man, and not merely of that part of him which Walt Whitman says is contained between his hat and his boots. The *whole* man is an infinitude, and the visible portion of him is the instrument through which he looks out upon and enjoys all that belongs to him, his own kingdom of the infinite. And when he learns that this is the meaning of his conscious individuality, he sees *how* it is that he is infinite, and finds that he is one with Infinite Mind, which is the innermost core of the universe. Having thus reached the true centre of his own being, he can never give this central place to anything else, but will realise that relatively to this all other things are in the position of the incidental and accessory, and growing daily in this knowledge he will learn so to handle all things lightly, yet firmly, that grief, fear, and error will have less and less space in his world, until at last sorrow and sighing shall flee away, and everlasting joy shall take their place. We may have taken only a few steps on the way as yet, but they are in the right direction, and what we have to do now is to go on.

## X

# PRESENT TRUTH

If thought power is good for anything it is good for everything. If it can produce one thing it can produce all things. For what is to hinder it? Nothing can stop us from thinking. We can *think* what we please, and if to think is to form, then we can form what we please. The whole question, therefore, resolves itself into this: Is it true that to think is to form? If so, do we not see that our limitations are formed in precisely the same way as our expansions? We think that conditions outside our thought have power over us, and so we think power into them. So the great question of life is whether there is any *other* creative power than Thought. If so, where is it, and what is it?

Both philosophy and religion lead us to the truth that "in the beginning" there was no other creative power than Spirit, and the only mode of activity we can possibly attribute to Spirit is Thought, and so we find Thought as the root of all things. And if this was the case "in the beginning" it must be so still; for if all things originate in Thought, all things must be modes of Thought, and so it is impossible for Spirit ever to hand over its creations to some power which is not itself—that is to say, which is not Thought-power; and consequently all the forms and circumstances that surround us are manifestations of the creative power of Thought.

But it may be objected that this is God's Thought; and that the creative power is in God and not Man. But this goes away from the self-evident axiomatic truth that "in the beginning" nothing could have had any origin except Thought. It is quite true that nothing has any origin except in the Divine Mind, and Man himself is therefore a mode of the Divine Thought. Again, Man is self-conscious; therefore Man is the Divine Thought evolved into *individual* consciousness, and when he becomes sufficiently enlightened to realise this as his origin, then he sees that he is a reproduction *in individuality* of the *same* spirit which produces all things, and that his own thought in individuality has exactly the same quality as the Divine Thought in universality, just as fire is equally igneous whether burning round a large centre of combustion or a small one, and thus we are logically brought to the conclusion that our thought must have creative power.

But people say, "We have not found it so. We are surrounded by all sorts of circumstances that we do not desire." Yes, you *fear* them, and in so doing you *think* them; and in this way you are constantly exercising this Divine prerogative of creation by Thought, only through ignorance you use it in a wrong direction. Therefore the Book of Divine Instructions so constantly repeats "Fear not; doubt not," because we can never divest our Thought of its inherent creative quality, and the only question is whether we shall use it ignorantly to our injury or understandingly to our benefit

The Master summed up his teaching in the aphorism that knowledge of the Truth would make us free. Here is no announcement of anything we have to do, or of anything that has to be done for us, in order to gain our liberty, neither is it a statement of anything *future.* Truth *is* what is. He did not say, you must wait till something becomes true which is not true *now.* He said: "Know what *is* Truth now, and you will find that the Truth concerning yourself is Liberty." If the knowledge of Truth makes us free it can only be because in truth we are free already, only we do not know it.

Our liberty consists in our reproducing on the scale of the individual the same creative power of Thought which first brought the world into existence, "so that the things which are seen were not made of things which do appear." Let us, then, confidently claim our birthright as "sons and daughters of the Almighty," and by habitually thinking the good, the beautiful, and the true, surround ourselves with conditions corresponding to our thoughts, and by our teaching and example help others to do the same.

XI

# YOURSELF

I WANT TO TALK to you about the livingness there is in being yourself. It has at least the merit of simplicity, for it must surely be easier to be oneself than to be something or somebody else. Yet that is what so many are constantly trying to do; the self that is their own is not good enough for them, and so they are always trying to go one better than what God has made them, with endless strain and struggle as the consequence. Of course, they are right to put before them an ideal infinitely grander than anything they have yet attained—the only possible way of progress is by following an ideal that is always a stage ahead of us—but the mistake is in not seeing that its attainment is a matter of growth, and that growth must be the expansion of something that already exists in us, and therefore implies our being what we are and where we are as its starting point. This growth is a continuous process, and we cannot do next month's growth without first doing this month's; but we are always wanting to jump into some ideal of the future, not seeing that we can reach it only by steadily going on from where we are now.

These considerations should make us more confident and more comfortable. We are employing a force which is much greater than we believe ourselves to be, yet it is not separate from us and needing to be persuaded or compelled, or inveigled into doing what we want; it is the substratum of our own being which is continually passing up into manifestation on the visible plane and becoming that personal self to which we often limit our attention without considering whence it proceeds. But in truth the outer self is the surface growth of that individuality which lies concealed far down in the deeps below, and which is none other than the Spirit-of-Life which underlies all forms of manifestation.

Endeavour to realise what this Spirit must be in itself—that is to say, apart from any of the conditions that arise from the various relations which necessarily establish themselves between its various forms of individualisation. In its homogeneous self what else can it be but pure life—Essence-of-Life, if you like so to call it? Then realise that as Essence-of-Life it exists in the innermost of *every one* of its forms of manifestation in as perfect simplicity as any we can attribute to it in our most abstract conceptions. In this light we see it to be the eternally self-generating power which, to express itself, flows into form.

This universal Essence-of-Life is a continual becoming (into form), and since we are a part of Nature we do not need to go further than ourselves to find the life-giving energy at work with all its powers. Hence all we have to do is to allow it to rise to the surface. We do not have to *make* it rise any more than the engineer who sinks the bore-pipe for an artesian well has to make the water rise in it; the water does that by its own energy, springing as a fountain a hundred feet into the air. Just so we shall find a fountain of Essence-of-Life ready to spring up in ourselves, inexhaustible and continually increasing in its flow, as One taught long ago to a woman at a wayside well.

This up-springing of Life-Essence is not another's—it is our own. It does not require deep studies, hard labours, weary journeyings to attain it; it is not the monopoly of this teacher or that writer, whose lectures we must attend or whose books we must read to get it. It is the innermost of *ourselves,* and a little common-sense thought as to how anything comes to be anything will soon convince us that the great inexhaustible life must be the very root and substance of us, permeating every fibre of our being.

Surely to be this vast infinitude of living power must be enough to satisfy all our desires, and yet this wonderful ideal is nothing else but what we already are *in principio*—it is all there in ourselves now, only awaiting our recognition for its manifestation. It is not the Essence-of-Life which has to grow, for that is eternally perfect in itself; but it is our recognition of it that has to grow, and this growth cannot be forced. It must come by a natural process, the first necessity of which is to abstain from all straining after being something which at the present time we cannot naturally be. The Law of our Evolution has put us in possession of certain powers and opportunities, and our further development depends on our doing just what these powers and opportunities make it possible for us to do, here and now.

If we do what we are able to do to-day, it will open the way for us to do something better to-morrow, and in this manner the growing process will proceed healthily and happily in a rapidly increasing ratio. This is so much easier than striving to compel things to be what they are not, and it is also so much more fruitful in good results. It is not sitting still doing nothing, and there is plenty of room for the exercise of all our mental faculties, but these faculties are themselves the outcome of the Essence-of-Life, and are not the creating power, but only that which gives direction to it. Now it is this moving power at the back of the various faculties that is the true innermost self; and if we realise the identity between the innermost and the outermost, we shall see that we therefore have at our present disposal all that is necessary for our unlimited development in the future.

Thus our livingness consists simply in being ourselves, only more so; and in recognising this we get rid of a great burden of unnecessary straining and striving, and the place of the old *sturm und drang* will be taken, not by inertia, but by a joyous activity which knows that it always has the requisite power to manifest itself in forms of good and beauty. What matters it whither this leads us? If we are following the line of the beautiful and good, then we shall produce the beautiful and good, and thus bring increasing joy into the world, whatever particular form it may assume.

We limit ourselves when we try to fix accurately beforehand the particular form of good that we shall produce. We should aim not so much at having or making some particular thing as at expressing all that we are. The expressing will grow out of realising the treasures that are ours already, and contemplating the beauty, the affirmative side, of all that we are *now,* apart from the negative conceptions and detractions which veil this positive good from us. When we do this we shall be astonished to see what possibilities reside in ourselves as we are and with our present surroundings, all unlovely as we may deem them: and commencing to work at once upon whatever we find of affirmative in these, and withdrawing our thought from what we have hitherto seen of negative in them, the right road will open up before us, leading us in wonderful ways to the development of powers that we never suspected, and the enjoyment of happiness that we never anticipated.

We have never been out of our right path, only we have been walking in it backwards instead of forwards, and now that we have begun to follow the path in the right direction, we find that it is none other than the way of peace, the path of joy, and the road to eternal life. These things we may attain by simply living naturally with ourselves. It is because we are trying to be or do something which is not natural to us that we experience weariness and labour, where we should find all our activities joyously concentrated on objects which lead to their own accomplishment by the force of the love that we have for them. But when we make the grand discovery of how to live naturally, we shall find it to be all, and more than all, that we had ever desired, and our daily life will become a perpetual joy to ourselves, and we shall radiate light and life wherever we go.

XII

# RELIGIOUS OPINIONS

THAT GREAT AND WISE writer, George Eliot, expressed her matured views on the subject of religious opinions in these words: "I have too profound a conviction of the efficacy that lies in all sincere faith, and the spiritual blight that comes with no faith, to have any negative propagandism left in me." This had not always been her attitude, for in her youth she had had a good deal of negative propagandism in her; but the experience of a lifetime led her to form this estimate of the value of sincere faith, independently of the particular form of thought which leads to it.

Tennyson also came to the same conclusion, and gives kindly warning:—

*"O thou who after toil and storm*
*May'st seem to have reached a purer air,*
*Whose faith has centred everywhere,*
*Nor cares to fix itself to form.*
*Leave thou thy sister when she prays*
*Her early heaven, her happy views,*
*Nor thou with shadowed hint confuse*
*A life that leads melodious days."*

And thus these two great minds have left us a lesson of wisdom which we shall do well to profit by. Let us see how it applies more particularly to our own case.

The true presentment of the Higher Thought contains no "negative propagandism." It is everywhere ranged on the side of the Affirmative, and its great object is to extirpate the canker which gnaws at the root of every life that endeavours to centre itself upon the Negative. Its purpose is constructive and not destructive. But we often find people labouring under a very erroneous impression as to the nature and scope of the movement, and thus not only themselves deterred from investigating it, but also deterring others from doing so. Sometimes this results from the subject having been presented to them unwisely—in a way needlessly repugnant to the particular form of religious ideas to which they are accustomed; but more often it results from their prejudging the whole matter, and making up their minds that the movement is opposed to their ideas of religion, without being at the pains to inquire what its principles really are. In either case a few words on the attitude of the New Thought towards the current forms of religious opinion may not be out of place.

The first consideration in every concern is, What is the object aimed at? The end determines the means to be employed, and if the nature of the end be clearly kept in view, then no objectless complications will be introduced into the means. All this seems too obvious to be stated, but it is just the failure to realise this simple truth that has given rise to the whole body of *odium theologicum,* with all the persecutions and massacres and martyrdoms which disgrace the pages of history, making so many of them a record of nothing but ferocity and stupidity. Let us hope for a better record in the future; and if we are to get it, it will be by the adoption of the simple principle here stated.

In our own country alone the varieties of churches and sects form a lengthy catalogue, but in every one of them the purpose is the same—to establish the individual in a satisfactory relation to the Divine Power. The very fact of any religious profession at all implies the recognition of God as the Source of life and of all that goes to make life; and therefore the purpose in every case is to draw increasing degrees of life, whether here or hereafter, from the Only Source from which alone it is to be obtained, and therefore to establish such a relation with this Source as may enable the worshipper to draw from It all the life he wants. Hence the necessary preliminary to drawing consciously at all is the confidence that such a relation actually has been established; and such a confidence as this is exactly all that is meant by Faith.

The position of the man who has not this confidence is either that no such Source exists, or else that he is without means of access to It; and in either case he feels himself left to fight for his own hand against the entire universe without the consciousness of any Superior Power to back him up. He is thrown entirely upon his own resources, not knowing of the interior spring from which they may be unceasingly replenished. He is like a plant cut off at the stem and stuck in the ground without any root, and consequently that spiritual blight of which George Eliot speaks creeps over him, producing weakness, perplexity, and fear, with all their baleful consequences, where there should be that strength, order, and confidence which are the very foundation of all building-up for whatever purpose, whether of personal prosperity or of usefulness to others.

From the point of view of those who are acquainted with the laws of spiritual life, such a man is cut off from the root of his own Being. Beyond and far interior to that outer self which each of us knows as the intellectual man working with the physical brain as instrument, we have roots penetrating deep into that Infinite of which, in our ordinary waking state, we are only dimly conscious; and it is through this root of our own individuality, spreading far down into the hidden depths of Being, that we draw out of the unseen that unceasing stream of Life which afterwards, by our thought-power, we differentiate into all those outward forms of which we have need. Hence the unceasing necessity for every one to realise the great truth that his whole individuality has its foundation in such a root, and that the ground in which this root is embedded is that Universal Being for which there is no name save that of the One all-embracing I AM.

The supreme necessity, therefore, for each of us is to realise this fundamental fact of our own nature, for it is only in proportion as we do so that we truly live; and, therefore, whatever helps us to this realisation should be carefully guarded. In so far as any form of religion contributes to this end in the case of any particular individual, for him it is true religion. It may be imperfect, but it is true so far as it goes; and what is wanted is not to destroy the foundation of a man's faith because it is narrow, but to expand it. And this expanding will be done by the man himself, for it is a growth from within and not a construction from without.

Our attitude towards the religious beliefs of others should, therefore, not be that of iconoclasts, breaking down ruthlessly whatever from *our* point of view we see to be merely traditionary idols (in Bacon's sense of the word), but rather the opposite method of fixing upon that in another's creed which we find to be positive and affirmative, and gradually leading him to perceive in what its affirmativeness consists; and then, when once he has got the clue to the element of strength which exists in his accustomed form of belief, the perception of the contrast between that and the non-essential accretions will grow up in his mind spontaneously, thus gradually bringing him out into a wider and freer atmosphere. In going through such a process as this, he will never have had his thoughts directed into any channel to suggest separation from his spiritual root and ground; but he will learn that the rooting and grounding in the Divine, which he had trusted in at first, were indeed true, but in a sense far fuller, grander, and larger every way than his early infantile conception of them.

The question is not how far can another's religious opinions stand the test of a remorseless logic, but how far do they enable him to realise his unity with Divine Spirit? That is the living proof of the value of his opinion to himself, and no change in his opinions can be for the better that does not lead him to a greater recognition of the livingness of Divine Spirit in himself. For any change of opinion to indicate a forward movement, it must proceed from our realising in some measure the true nature of the life that is already developed in us. When we see *why* we are *what* we are *now,* then we can look ahead and see what the same life principle that has brought us up to the present point is capable of doing in the future. We may not see very far ahead, but we shall see where the next step is to be placed, and that is sufficient to enable us to move on.

What we have to do, therefore, is to help others to grow from the root they are already *living* by, and not to dig their roots up and leave them to wither. We need not be afraid of making ourselves all things to all men, in the sense of fixing upon the affirmative elements in each one's creed as the starting-point of our work, for the affirmative and life-giving is always true, and Truth is always *one* and consistent with itself; and therefore we need never fear being inconsistent so long as we adhere to this method. It is worse than useless to waste time in dissecting the negative accretions of other people's beliefs. In doing so we run great risks of rooting up the wheat along with the tares, and we shall certainly succeed in brushing people up the wrong way; moreover, by looking out exclusively for the life-giving and affirmative elements, we shall reap benefit to ourselves. We shall not only keep our temper, but we shall often find large reserves of affirmative power where at first we had apprehended nothing but worthless accumulations, and thus we shall become gainers both in largeness of mind and in stores of valuable material.

Of course we must be rigidly unyielding as regards the *essence* of Truth—*that* must never be sacrificed—but as representatives, in however small a sphere, of the New Thought, we should make it our aim to show others, not that their religion is wrong, but that all they may find of life-givingness in it is life-giving because it is part of the One Truth which is always the same under whatever form expressed. As half a loaf is better than no bread, so ignorant worship is better than no worship, and ignorant faith is better than no faith. Our work is not to destroy this faith and this worship, but to lead them on into a clearer light.

For this reason we may assure all inquirers that the abandonment of their customary form of worship is no necessity of the New Thought; but, on the contrary, that the principles of the movement, correctly understood, will show them far more meaning in that worship than they have ever yet realised. Truth is one; and when once the truth which underlies the outward form is clearly understood, the maintenance or abandonment of the latter will be found to be a matter of personal feeling as to what form, or absence of form, best enables the particular individual to realise the Truth itself.

XIII

## A LESSON FROM BROWNING

PERHAPS YOU KNOW a little poem of Browning's called "An Epistle Containing the Strange Medical Experiences of Karshish, the Arab Physician." The somewhat weird conception is that the Arab physician, travelling in Palestine soon after the date when the Gospel narrative closes, meets with Lazarus whom Jesus raised from the dead, and in this letter to a medical friend describes the strange effect which his vision of the other life has produced upon the resuscitated man. The poem should be studied as a whole; but for the present a few lines selected here and there must do duty to indicate the character of the change which has passed upon Lazarus. After comparing him to a beggar who, having suddenly received boundless wealth, is unable to regulate its use to his requirements, Karshish continues:—

*"So here—we call the treasure knowledge, say,*
*Increased beyond the fleshly faculty—*
*Heaven opened to a soul while yet on earth,*
*Earth forced on a soul's use while seeing heaven:*
*The man is witless of the size, the sum,*
*The value in proportion of all things."*

In fact he has become almost exclusively conscious of

*"The spiritual life around the earthly life:*
*The law of that is known to him as this,*
*His heart and brain move there, his feet stay here,"*

and the result is a loss of mental balance entirely unfitting him for the affairs of ordinary life.

Now there can be no doubt that Browning had a far more serious intention in writing this poem than just to record a fantastic notion that flitted through his brain. If we read between the lines, it must be clear from the general tenor of his writings that, however he may have acquired it, Browning had a very deep acquaintance with the inner region of spiritual causes which give rise to all that we see of outward phenomenal manifestation. There are continual allusions in his works to the life behind the veil, and it is to this suggestion of some mystery underlying his words that we owe the many attempts to fathom his meaning expressed through Browning Societies and the like—attempts which fail or succeed according as they are made from "the without" or from "the within." No one was better qualified than the poet to realise the immense benefits of the inner knowledge, and for the same reason he is also qualified to warn us of the dangers on the way to its acquisition; for nowhere is it more true that

"A little knowledge is a dangerous thing,"

and it is one of the greatest of these dangers that he points out in this poem.

Under the figure of Lazarus he describes the man who has practically grasped the reality of the inner side of things, for whom the veil has been removed, and who knows that the external and visible takes its rise from the internal and spiritual. But the description is that of one whose eyes have been so dazzled by the light that he has lost the power of accommodating his vision to the world of sense. He now commits the same error from the side of "the within" that he formerly committed from the side of "the without," the error of supposing that there is no vital reality in the aspect of things on which his thoughts are not immediately centered. This is want of mental balance, whether it shows itself by refusing reality to the inward or the outward. To be so absorbed in speculative ideas as to be unable to give them practical application in daily life, is to allow our highest thoughts to evaporate in dreams.

There is a world of philosophy in the simple statement that there can be no inside without an outside, and no outside without an inside; and the great secret in life is in learning to see things in their wholeness, and to realise the inside and the outside simultaneously. Each of them without the other is a mere abstraction, having no real existence, which we contemplate separately only for the purpose of reviewing the logical steps by which they are connected together as cause and effect. Nature does not separate them, for they are inseparable; and the law of nature is the law of life. It is related of Pythagoras that, after he had led his scholars to the dizziest heights of the inner knowledge, he never failed to impress upon them the converse lesson of tracing out the steps by which these inner principles translate themselves into the familiar conditions of the outward things by which we are surrounded. The process of analysis is merely an expedient for discovering what springs in the realm of causes we are to touch in order to produce certain effects in the realm of manifestation. But this is not sufficient. We must also learn to calculate how those particular effects, when produced, will stand related to the world of already existing effects among which we propose to launch them, how they will modify these and be modified by these in turn; and this calculation of effects is as necessary as the knowledge of causes.

We cannot impress upon ourselves too strongly that reality consists of both an inside and an outside, a generating principle and a generated condition, and that anything short of the reality of wholeness is illusion on one side or the other. Nothing could have been further from Browning's intention than to deter seekers after truth from studying the principles of Being, for without the knowledge of them truth must always remain wrapped in mystery; but the lesson he would impress on us is that of guarding vigilantly the mental equilibrium which alone will enable us to develop those boundless powers whose infinite unfolding is the fulness of Life. And we must remember above all that the soul of life is Love, and that Love shows itself by service, and service proceeds from sympathy, which is the capacity for seeing things from the point of view of those whom we would help, while at the same time seeing them also in their true relations; and therefore, if we would realise that Love which is the inmost vitalising principle even of the most interior powers, it must be kept alive by maintaining our hold upon the exterior life as being equally real with the inward principles of which it is the manifestation.

1902.

XIV

# THE SPIRIT OF OPULENCE

It is quite a mistake to suppose that we must restrict and stint ourselves in order to develop greater power or usefulness. This is to form the conception of the Divine Power as so limited that the best use we can make of it is by a policy of self-starvation, whether material or mental. Of course, if we believe that some form of self-starvation is necessary to our producing good work, then so long as we entertain this belief the fact actually is so *for us.* "Whatsoever is not of faith"—that is, not in accordance with our honest *belief*—"is sin"; and by acting contrary to what we really believe we bring in a suggestion of opposition to the Divine Spirit, which must necessarily paralyse our efforts, and surround us with a murky atmosphere of distrust and want of joy.

But all this exists in, and is produced by, our *belief;* and when we come to examine the grounds of this belief we shall find that it rests upon an entire misapprehension of the nature of our own power. If we clearly realise that the creative power in ourselves is *unlimited,* then there is no reason for limiting the extent to which we may enjoy what we can create by means of it. Where we are drawing from the *infinite* we need never be afraid of taking more than our share. That is not where the danger lies. The danger is in not sufficiently realising our own richness, and in looking upon the externalised products of our creative power as being the true riches instead of the creative power of spirit itself.

If we avoid this error, there is no need to limit ourselves in taking what we will from the infinite storehouse: "All things are yours." And the way to avoid this error is by realising that the true wealth is in identifying ourselves with the *spirit* of opulence. We must be opulent in our *thought.* Do not "think money," as such, for it is only one means of opulence; but *think opulence,* that is, largely, generously, liberally, and you will find that the means of realising this thought will flow to you from all quarters, whether as money or as a hundred other things not to be reckoned in cash.

We must not make ourselves dependent on any particular *form* of wealth, or insist on its coming to us through some particular channel—that is at once to impose a limitation, and to shut out other forms of wealth and to close other channels; but we must enter into the *spirit* of it. Now the spirit is Life, and throughout the universe Life ultimately consists in *circulation,* whether within the physical body of the individual or on the scale of the entire solar system; and circulation means a continual flowing around, and the *spirit* of opulence is no exception to this universal law of all life.

When once this principle becomes clear to us we shall see that our attention should be directed rather to the giving than the receiving. We must look upon ourselves, not as misers' chests to be kept locked for our own benefit, but as centres of distribution; and the better we fulfil our function as such centres the greater will be the corresponding inflow. If we choke the outlet the current must slacken, and a full and free flow can be obtained only by keeping it open. The spirit of opulence—the opulent mode of thought, that is—consists in cultivating the feeling that we possess all sorts of riches which we can *bestow upon others,* and which we can bestow *liberally* because by this very action we open the way for still greater supplies to flow in. But you say, "I am short of money, I hardly know how to pay for necessaries. What have I to give?"

The answer is that we must always start from the point where we are; and if your wealth at the present moment is not abundant on the material plane, you need not trouble to start on that plane. There are other sorts of wealth, still more valuable, on the spiritual and intellectual planes, which you can give; and you can start from this point and practise the spirit of opulence, even though your balance at the bank may be nil. And then the universal law of attraction will begin to assert itself. You will not only begin to experience an inflow on the spiritual and intellectual planes, but it will extend itself to the material plane also.

If you have realised the *spirit* of opulence you *cannot help* drawing to yourself material good, as well as that higher wealth which is not to be measured by a money standard; and because you truly understand the *spirit* of opulence you will neither affect to despise this form of good, nor will you attribute to it a value that does not belong to it; but you will *co-ordinate* it with your other more interior forms of wealth so as to make it the material instrument in smoothing the way for their more perfect expression. Used thus, with understanding of the relation which it bears to spiritual and intellectual wealth, material wealth becomes *one with them,* and is no more to be shunned and feared than it is to be sought for its own sake.

It is not money, but the *love* of money, that is the root of evil; and the *spirit* of opulence is precisely the attitude of mind which is furthest removed from the love of money for its own sake. It does not believe in money. What it does believe in is the generous feeling which is the intuitive recognition of the great law of circulation, which does not in any undertaking make its first question, How much am I going to *get* by it? but, How much am I going to *do* by it? And making *this* the first question, the getting will flow in with a generous profusion, and with a spontaneousness and rightness of direction that are absent when our first thought is of receiving only.

We are not called upon to give what we have not yet got and to run into debt; but we are to give liberally of what we *have,* with the knowledge that by so doing we are setting the law of circulation to work, and as this law brings us greater and greater inflows of every kind of good, so our outgiving will increase, not by depriving ourselves of any expansion of our own life that we may desire, but by finding that every expansion makes us the more powerful instruments for expanding the life of others. "Live and let live" is the motto of the true opulence.

## XV

# BEAUTY

DO WE SUFFICIENTLY direct our thoughts to the subject of Beauty? I think not. We are too apt to regard Beauty as a merely superficial thing, and do not realise all that it implies. This was not the case with the great thinkers of the ancient world—see the place which no less a one than Plato gives to Beauty as the expression of all that is highest and greatest in the system of the universe. These great men of old were no superficial thinkers, and, therefore, would never have elevated to the supreme place that which is only superficial. Therefore, we shall do well to ask what it is that these great minds found in the idea of Beauty which made it thus appeal to them as the most perfect outward expression of all that lies deepest in the fundamental laws of Being. It is because, rightly apprehended, Beauty represents the supremest living quality of Thought. It is the glorious overflowing of fulness of Love which indicates the presence of infinite reserves of Power behind it. It is the joyous profusion that shows the possession of inexhaustible stores of wealth which can afford to be thus lavish and yet remain as exhaustless as before. Read aright, Beauty is the index to the whole nature of Being.

Beauty is the externalisation of Harmony, and Harmony is the coordinated working of all the powers of Being, both in the individual and in the relation of the individual to the Infinite from which it springs; and therefore this Harmony conducts us at once into the presence of the innermost undifferentiated Life. Thus Beauty is in most immediate touch with the very arcanum of Life; it is the brightness of glory spreading itself over the sanctuary of the Divine Spirit. For if, viewed from without, Beauty is the province of the artist and the poet, and lays hold of our emotions and appeals directly to the innermost feelings of our heart, calling up the response of that within us which recognises itself in the harmony perceived without, this is only because it speeds across the bridge of Reason with such quick feet that we pass from the outmost to the inmost and back again in the twinkling of an eye; but the bridge is still there and, retracing our steps more leisurely, we shall find that, viewed from within, Beauty is no less the province of the calm reasoner and analyst. What the poet and the artist seize upon intuitionally, he elaborates gradually, but the result is the same in both cases; for no intuition is true which does not admit of being expanded into a rational sequence of intelligible factors, and no argument is true which does not admit of being condensed into that rapid suggestion which is intuition.

Thus the impassioned artist and the calm thinker both find that the only true Beauty proceeds naturally from the actual construction of that which it expresses. It is not something added on as an afterthought, but something pre-existing in the original idea, something to which that idea naturally leads up, and which presupposes that idea as affording it any *raison d'être.* The test of Beauty is, What does it express? Is it merely a veneer, a coat of paint laid on from without? Then it is indeed nothing but a whited sepulchre, a covering to hide the vacuity or deformity which needs to be removed. But is it the true and natural outcome of what is beneath the surface? Then it is the index to superabounding Life and Love and Intelligence, which is not content with mere utilitarianism hasting to escape at the earliest possible point from the labour of construction, as though from an enforced and unwelcome task, but rejoicing over its work and unwilling to quit it until it has expressed this rejoicing in every fittest touch of form and colour and exquisite proportion that the material will admit of, and this without departing by a hairbreadth from the original purpose of the design.

Wherever, therefore, we find Beauty, we may infer an enormous reserve of Power behind it; in fact, we may look upon it as the visible expression of the great truth that Life-Power is infinite. And when the inner meaning of

Beauty is thus revealed to us, and we learn to know it as the very fulness and overflowing of Power, we shall find that we have gained a new standard for the guidance of our own lives. We must begin to use this wonderful process which we have learnt from Nature. Having learnt how Nature works—how God works—we must begin to work in like manner, and never consider any work complete until we have carried it to some final outcome of Beauty, whether material, intellectual, or spiritual. Is my intention good? That is the initial question, for the intention determines the nature of the essence in everything. What is the most beautiful form in which I can express the good I intend? That is the ultimate question; for the true Beauty which our work expresses is the measure of the Power, Intelligence, Love—in a word, of the quantity and quality of our own life which we have put into it. True Beauty, mind you—that which is beautiful because it most perfectly expresses the original idea, not a mere ornamentation occupying our thoughts as a thing apart from the use intended.

Nothing is of so small account but it has its fullest power of expression in some form of Beauty peculiarly its own. Beauty is the law of perfect Thought, be the subject of our Thought some scheme affecting the welfare of millions, or a word spoken to a little child. True Beauty and true Power are the correlatives one of the other. Kindly expression originates in kindly thought; and kindly expression is the essence of Beauty, which, seeking to express itself ever more and more perfectly, becomes that fine touch of sympathy which is artistic skill, whether applied in working upon material substances or upon the emotions of the heart. But, remember, first Use, then Beauty, and neither complete without the other. Use without Beauty is ungracious giving, and Beauty without Use is humbug; never forgetting, however, that there is a region of the mind where the use is found in the beauty, where Beauty itself serves the direct purpose of raising us to see a higher ideal which will thence-forward permeate our lives, giving a more living quality to all we think and say and do.

Seen thus the Beautiful is the true expression of the Good. From whichever end of the scale we look we shall find that they accurately measure each other. They are the same thing in the outermost and the innermost respectively. But in our search for a higher Beauty than we have yet found we must beware of missing the Beauty that already exists. Perfect harmony with its environment, and perfect expression of its own inward nature are what constitute Beauty; and our ignorance of the nature of the thing or its environment may shut our eyes to the Beauty it already has. It takes the genius of a Millet to paint, or a Whitman in words, to show us the beauty of those ordinary work-a-day figures with which our world is for the most part peopled, whose originals we pass by as having no form or comeliness. Assuredly the mission of every thinking man and woman is to help build up forms of greater beauty, spiritual, intellectual, material, everywhere; but if we would make something grander than Watteau gardens or Dresden china shepherdesses, we must enter the great realistic school of Nature and learn to recognise the beauty that already surrounds us, although it may have a little dirt on the surface. Then, when we have learnt the great principles of Beauty from the All-Spirit which is it, we shall know how to develop the Beauty on its own proper lines without perpetuating the dirt; and we shall know that all Beauty is the expression of Living Power, and that we can measure our power by the degree of beauty into which we can transform it, rendering our lives,

"By loveliness of perfect deeds,
More strong than all poetic thought."

## XVI

# SEPARATION AND UNITY

## I

THE PRINCE OF this world cometh, and hath nothing in Me" (John xiv, 30). In these words the Grand Master of Divine Science gives us the key to the Great Knowledge. Comparison with other passages shows that the terms here rendered "prince" and "world" can equally be rendered "principle" and "age." Jesus is here speaking of a principle of the present age so entirely opposed to that principle of which he himself was the visible expression, as to have no part in him. It is the utter contradiction of everything that Jesus came to teach and to exemplify. The account Jesus gave of himself was that he came "to bear witness to the Truth," and in order that men "might have life, and that they might have it more abundantly"; consequently the principle to which he refers must be the exact opposite of Truth and Life—that is, it must be the principle of Falsehood and Death.

What, then, is this false and destructive principle which rules the present age? If we consider the gist of the entire discourse of which these are the concluding words, we shall find that the central idea which Jesus has been most strenuously endeavouring to impress upon his disciples at their last meeting before the crucifixion, is that of the absolute identity and out-and-out oneness of "the Father" and "the Son," the principle of the perfect unity of God and Man. If this, then, was the great Truth which he was thus earnestly solicitous to impress upon his disciples' minds when his bodily presence was so shortly to be removed from them—the Truth of Unity—may we not reasonably infer the opposing falsehood to be the assertion of separateness, the assertion that God and man are not one? The idea of separateness is precisely the principle on which the world has proceeded from that day to this—the assumption that God and man are not one in being, and that the matter is of a different essence from spirit. In other words, the principle that finds favour with the intellectuality of the present age is that of duality—the idea of two powers and two substances opposite in kind, and, therefore, repugnant to each other, permeating all things, and so leaving no wholeness anywhere.

The entire object of the Bible is to combat the idea of two opposing forces in the world. The good news is said to be that of "reconciliation" (2 Cor. v. 18), where also we are told that "all things are from God," hence leaving no room for any other power or any other substance; and the great falsehood, which it is the purpose of the Good News to expose, is everywhere in the Bible proclaimed to be the suggestion of duality, which is some other mode of Life, that is not the One Life, but something separate from it—an idea which it is impossible to state distinctly without involving a contradiction in terms. Everywhere the Bible exposes the fiction of the duality of separation as the great lie, but nowhere in so emphatic and concentrated a manner as in that wonderful passage of Revelations where it is figured in the mysterious Number of the Beast. "He that hath understanding let him count the number of the Beast . . . and his number is six hundred and sixty and six" (Rev. xiii, 18, R.V.). Let me point out the great principle expressed in this mysterious number. It has other more particular applications, but this one general principle underlies them all.

It is an established maxim that every unity contains in itself a trinity, just as the individual man consists of body, soul, and spirit. If we would perfectly understand anything, we must be able to comprehend it in its threefold nature; therefore in symbolic numeration the multiplying of the unit by three implies the completeness of that for which the unit stands;

and, again, the threefold repetition of a number represents its extension to infinity. Now mark what results if we apply these representative methods of numerical expression to the principles of Oneness and of separateness respectively. Oneness is Unity, and 1 × 3=3, which, intensified to its highest expression, is written as 333. Now apply the same method to the idea of separateness. Separateness consists of one and another one, each of which, according to the universal law, contains a trinity. In this view of duality the totality of things is two, and 2 × 3=6, and, intensifying this to its highest expression, we get 666, which is the Number of the Beast.

Why of the Beast? Because separateness from God, or the duality of opposition, which is also a duality of polarity, which is Dual-Unity, recognises something as having essential being, which is not the One Spirit; and such a conception can be verbally rendered only by some word that in common acceptance represents something, not only lower than the divine, but lower than the human also. It is because the conception of oneself as a being apart from God, if carried out to its legitimate consequences, must ultimately land all who hold it in a condition of things where open ferocity or secret cunning, the tiger nature or the serpent nature, can be the only possible rule of action.

Thus it is that the principle of the present age can have no part in that principle of Perfect Wholeness which the Great Master embodied in His teaching and in Himself. The two ideas are absolutely incompatible, and whichever we adopt as our leading principle, it must be to the entire exclusion of the other; we cannot serve God and Mammon. There is no such thing as partial wholeness. Either we are still in the principle of Separateness, and our eyes are not yet open to the real nature of the Kingdom of Heaven; or else we have grasped the principle of Unity without any exception anywhere, and the One Being includes all, the body and the soul alike, the visible form and the invisible substance and life of all equally; nothing can be left out, and we stand complete here and now, lacking no faculty, but requiring only to become conscious of our own powers, and to learn to have confidence in them through "having them exercised by reason of use."

The following communication from "A Foreign Reader," commenting on the Number of the Beast, as treated by Judge Troward in "Separation and Unity," is taken from *EXPRESSION* for 1902, in which it was first published. Following is Judge Troward's reply to this letter.

Dear Mr. Editor.—

A correspondent in the current number of *Expression* points out the reference in the Book of Revelation to the number 666 as the mark of the Beast, because the trinity of mind, soul, and body, if considered as unity, may be expressed by the figures 333, and therefore duality is $333 \times 2 = 666$.

I think the inverse of the proposition is still more startling, and I should like to point it out. Instead of multiplying let us try dividing. First of all take unity as the unit one and divide by three (representing of course the same formula, viz., mind, soul and body). Expressed by a common fraction it is merely 1/3, which is an incomplete mathematical figure. But take the decimal formula of one divided by three, and we arrive at .3 circulating, i.e., .3333 on to infinity. In other words, the result of the proposition by mathematics is that you divide this formula of spirit, soul, and body into unity, and it remains true to itself ad infinitum.

Now we come to consider it as a duality in the same way. Expressed as a vulgar fraction it is 2/3; but as a decimal fraction it is .6666 ad infinitum. I think this is worth noting.

Yours very faithfully,
A Foreign Reader.
*Brussels, Aug. 14, 1902.*

Dear Editor.—

I return with many thanks the very interesting letter received with yours, and I am very glad that my article should have been instrumental in drawing forth this further light on the subject.

This, moreover, affords an excellent illustration of one great principle of Unity, which is that the Unity repeats itself in every one of its parts, so that each part taken separately is an exact reproduction (in principles) of the greater Unity of which it is a portion. Therefore, if you take the individual man as your unit (which is what I did), and proceed by multiplication, you get the results which were pointed out in my article. And conversely, if you take the Great Unity of All-Being as your unit, and proceed by division, you arrive at the result shown by your foreign correspondent. The principle is a purely mathematical one, and is extremely interesting in the present application as showing the existence of a system of concealed mathematics running through the whole Bible. This bears out what I said in my article that there were other applications of the principle in question, though this one did not at the time occur to me.

I am much indebted to your correspondent for the further proof thus given of the correctness of my interpretation of the Number of the Beast. Both our interpretations support each other, for they are merely different ways of stating the same thing, and they have this advantage over those generally given, that they do hot refer to any particular form of evil, but express a general principle applicable to all alike.

Yours sincerely,
T.
*London, Aug. 30, 1902.*

## II

It may perhaps emphasize my point if I remind my readers that it was the conflict between the principles of Unity and separation that led to the crucifixion of Jesus. We must distinguish between the charge which really led to his death, and the merely technical charge on which he was sentenced by the Roman Governor. The latter—the charge of opposition to the royal authority of Cæsar—has its significance; but it is clear from the Bible record that this was merely formal, the true cause of conviction being contained in the statement that of the chief priests: "We have a law, and by our law he ought to die, because he made himself the Son of God."

The antagonism of the two principles of Unity and separation had first been openly manifested on the occasion when Jesus made the memorable declaration, "I and my Father are one." The Jews took up stones to stone him. Then said Jesus unto them, "Many good works have I shown you from my Father; for which of those works do ye stone Me?" The Jews replied,

"For a good work we stone thee not; but for blasphemy; and because that thou, being a man, makest thyself God." Jesus said, "Is it not written in your law, I said ye are gods? If He called them gods, unto whom the Word of God came (and the Scriptures cannot be broken), say ye of him, whom the Father hath sanctified, and sent into the world, thou blasphemest; because I said, I am the Son of God?" Here we have the first open passage of arms between the two opposing principles which led to the scene of Calvary as the final testimony of Jesus to the principle of Unity. He died because he maintained the Truth; that he was one with the Father. That was the substantive charge on which he was executed. "Art thou the son of the Blessed?" he was asked by the priestly tribunal; and the answer came clear and unequivocal, "I am." Then said the Council, "He hath spoken blasphemy, what further need have we of witnesses?" And they all condemned him to be worthy of death.

Jesus did not enter into a palpably useless argument with judges whose minds were so rooted in the idea of dualism as to be impervious to any other conception; but with a mixed multitude, who were not officially committed to a system, the case was different. Among them there might be some still open to conviction, and the appeal was, therefore, made to a passage in the Psalms with which they were all familiar, pointing out that the very persons to whom the Divine word was addressed were styled "gods" by the Divine Speaker Himself. The incontrovertibleness of the fact was emphasised by the stress laid upon it as "Scripture which cannot be broken;" and the meaning to be assigned to the statement was rendered clear by the argument which Jesus deduced from it. He says in effect, "You would stone me as a blasphemer for saying of myself what your own Scriptures say concerning each of you." The claim of unity with "the Father," he urges, was no unique one, but one which the Scripture, rightly understood, entitled every one of his hearers to make for himself.

And so we find throughout that Jesus nowhere makes any claim for himself which he does not also make for those who accept his teaching. Does he say to the Jews, "Ye are of this world; I am not of this world?" Equally he says of his disciples, "They are not of the world, even as I am not of the world." Does he say, "I am the light of the world?" Equally, he says, "Ye are the light of the world." Does he say, "I and my Father are one?" Equally he prays that they all might be one, even as we are one. Is he styled "the Son of God?" Then St. John writes, "To them gave he power to become sons of God, even to as many as believe on his name"; and by belief on the name we may surely understand belief in the principle of which the name is the verbal representation.

The essential unity of God and man is thus the one fact which permeates the whole teaching of Jesus. He himself stood forth as its living expression. He appealed to his miracles as the proofs of it: "it is the Father that doeth the works." It formed the substance of his final discourse with his disciples in the night that he was betrayed. It is the Truth, to bear witness to which, he told Pilate, was the purpose of his life. In support of this Truth he died, and by the living power of this Truth he rose again. The whole object of his mission was to teach men to realise their unity with God and the consequences that must necessarily follow from it; to draw them away from that notion of dualism which puts an impassable barrier between God and man, and thus renders any true conception of the Principle of Life impossible; and to draw them into the clear perception of the innermost nature of Life, as consisting in the inherent identity of each individual with that Infinite all-pervading Spirit of Life which he called "the Father."

"The branch cannot bear fruit except it abide in the vine"; the power of bearing fruit, of producing and of giving forth, depends entirely on the fact that the individual is, and always continues to be, as much an organic part of Universal Spirit as the fruit-bearing branch is an organic part of the parent stem. Lose this idea, and regard God as a merely external Creator who may indeed command us, or even sometimes be moved by our cries and entreaties, and we have lost the root of Livingness and with it all possibility of growth or of liberty. This is dualism, which cuts us off from our Source of Life; and so long as we take this false conception for the true law of Being, we shall find ourselves hampered by limitations and insoluble problems of every description: We have lost the Key of Life and are consequently unable to open the door.

But in proportion as we abide in the vine, that is, consciously realise our perpetual unity with Originating Spirit, and impress upon ourselves that this unity is neither bestowed as the reward of merit, nor as an act of favour—which would be to deny the Unity, for the bestowal would at once imply dualism—but dwell on the truth that it is the innermost and supreme principle of our own nature; in proportion as we consciously realise this, we shall rise to greater and greater certainty of knowledge, resulting in more and more perfect externalisation, whose increasing splendour can know no limits; for it is the continual outflowing of the exhaustless Spirit of Life in that manifestation of itself which is our own individuality.

The notion of dualism is the veil which prevents men seeing this, and causes them to wander blindfolded among the mazes of endless perplexity; but, as St. Paul truly says, when this veil is taken away we shall find ourselves changed from glory to glory as by the Lord the Spirit. "His name shall be called Immanuel," that is "God *in* us," not a separate being from ourselves. Let us remember that Jesus was condemned by the principle of separation because he himself was the externalisation of the principle of Unity, and that, in adhering to the principle of Unity we are adhering to the only possible root of Life, and are maintaining the Truth for which Jesus died.

XVII

# EXTERNALISATION

WHO WOULD NOT be happy in himself and his conditions? That is what we all desire—more fulness of life, a greater and brighter vitality in ourselves, and less restriction in our surroundings. And we are told that the talisman by which this can be accomplished is Thought. We are told, Change your modes of thought, and the changed conditions will follow. But many seekers feel that this is very much like telling us to catch birds by putting salt on their tails. If we can put the salt on the bird's tail, we can also lay our hand on the bird. If we can change our thinking, we can thereby change our circumstances.

But how are we to bring about this change of cause which will in its turn produce this changed effect? This is the practical question that perplexes many earnest seekers. They can see their way clearly enough through the whole sequence of cause and effect resulting in the externalisation of the desired results, if only the one initial difficulty could be got over. The difficulty is a real one, and until it is overcome it vitiates all the teaching and reduces it to a mere paper theory. Therefore it is to this point that the attention of students should be particularly directed. They feel the need of some solid basis from which the change of thought can be effected, and until they find this the theory of Divine Science, however perfect in itself, will remain for them nothing more than a mere theory, producing no practical results.

The necessary scientific basis exists, however, and is extremely simple and reasonable, if we will take the pains to think it out carefully for ourselves. Unless we are prepared to support the thesis that the Power which created the universe is inherently evil, or that the universe is the work of two opposite and equal powers, one evil and the other good—both of which propositions are demonstrably false—we have no alternative but to say that the Originating Source of all must be inherently good. It cannot be partly good and partly evil, for that would be to set it against itself and make it self-destructive; therefore it must be good altogether. But once grant this initial proposition and we cut away the root of all evil. For how can evil proceed from an All-originating Source which is good altogether, and in which, therefore, no germ for the development of evil is to be found? Good cannot be the origin of evil; and since nothing can proceed except from the one Originating Mind, which is only good, the true nature of all things must be that which they have received from their Source—namely, good.

Hence it follows that evil is not the true nature of anything, and that evil must have its rise in something external to the true nature of things. And since evil is not in the true nature of the things themselves, nor yet in the Universal Mind which is the Originating Principle, there remains only one place for it to spring from, and that is our own personal thought. First we suppose evil to be as inherent in the nature of things as good—a supposition which we could not make if we stopped to consider the necessary nature of the Originating Principle. Then, on this entirely gratuitous supposition, we proceed to build up a fabric of fears, which, of course, follow logically from it; and so we nourish and give substance to the Negative, or that which has no substantial existence except such as we attribute to it, until we come to regard it as having Affirmative power of its own, and so set up a false idea of Being—the product of our own minds—to dispute the claims of true Being to the sovereignty of the universe.

Once assume the existence of two rival powers—one good and the other evil—in the direction of the universe, and any sense of harmony becomes impossible; the whole course of Nature is thrown out of gear, and, whether for ourselves or for the world at large, there remains no ground of certainty anywhere. And this is precisely the condition in which the majority of people live. They are surrounded by infinite uncertainty about everything, and are consequently a prey to continual fears and anxieties; and the only way of escape from this state of things is to go to the root of the matter, and realise that the whole fabric of evil originates in our own inverted conception of the nature of Being.

But if we once realise that the true conception of Being necessarily excludes the very idea of evil, we shall see that, in giving way to thoughts and fears of evil, we are giving substance to that which has no real substance in itself, and are attributing to the Negative an Affirmative force which it does not possess—in fact, we are creating the very thing we fear. And the remedy for this is always to recur to the original nature of Being as altogether Good, and then to speak to ourselves thus: "My thought must continually externalise something, for that is its inherent quality, which nothing can ever alter. Shall I, then, externalise God or the opposite of God? Which do I wish to see manifested in my life—Good or its opposite? Shall I manifest what I know to be the reality or the reverse?" Then comes the steady resolve always to manifest God, or Good, because that is the only true reality in all things; and this resolve is with power because it is founded upon the solid rock of Truth.

We must refuse to know evil; we must refuse to admit that there is any such thing to be known. It is the converse of this which is symbolised in the story of the Fall. "In the day that thou eatest thereof thou shalt surely die" was never spoken of the knowledge of Good, for Good never brought death into the world. It is eating the fruit of the tree of a so-called knowledge which admits a second branch, the knowledge of evil, that is the source of death. Admit that evil has a substantive entity, which renders it a subject of knowledge, and you thereby create it, with all its consequences of sorrow, sickness and death. But "be sure that the Lord He is God"—that is, that the one and Only Ruling Principle of the universe, whether within us or around us, is Good and Good only—and evil with all its train sinks back into its original nothingness, and we find that the Truth has made us free. We are free to externalise what we will, whether in ourselves or our surroundings, for we have found the solid basis on which to make the needed change of mental attitude in the fact that the Good is the only reality of Being.

*1902.*

## XVIII

# ENTERING INTO THE SPIRIT OF IT

"ENTERING INTO the spirit of it." What a common expression! And yet how much it really means, how absolutely everything! We enter into the spirit of an undertaking, into the spirit of a movement, into the spirit of an author, even into the spirit of a game; and it makes all the difference both to us and to that into which we enter. A game without any spirit is a poor affair; and association in which there is no spirit falls to pieces; and a spiritless undertaking is sure to be a failure. On the other hand, the book which is meaningless to the unsympathising reader is full of life and suggestion to the one who enters into the spirit of the writer; the man who enters into the spirit of the music finds a spring of refreshment in some fine recital which is entirely missed by the cold critic who comes only to judge according to the standard of a rigid rule; and so on in every case that we can think of. If we do not enter the spirit of a thing, it has no invigorating effect upon us, and we regard it as dull, insipid and worthless. This is our everyday experience, and these are the words in which we express it. And the words are well chosen. They show our intuitive recognition of the spirit as the fundamental reality in everything, however small or however great. Let us be right as to the spirit of a thing, and everything else will successfully follow.

By entering into the spirit of anything we establish a mutual vivifying action and reaction between it and ourselves; we vivify it with our own vitality, and it vivifies us with a living interest which we call its spirit; and therefore the more fully we enter into the spirit of all with which we are concerned, the more thoroughly do we become *alive.* The more completely we do this the more we shall find that we are penetrating into the great secret of Life. It may seem a truism, but the great secret of Life is its Livingness, and it is just more of this quality of Livingness that we want to get hold of; it is that good thing of which we can never have too much.

But every fact implies also its negative, and we never properly understand a thing until we not only know what it is, but also clearly understand what it is not. To a complete understanding the knowledge of the negative is as necessary as the knowledge of the affirmative; for the perfect knowledge consists in realising the relation between the two, and the perfect power grows out of this knowledge by enabling us to balance the affirmative and negative against each other in any proportion that we will, thus giving flexibility to what would otherwise be too rigid, and form to what would otherwise be too fluid; and so, by uniting these two extremes, to produce any result we may desire. It is the old Hermetic saying, *"Coagula et solve"*—"Solidify the fluid and dissolve the solid"; and therefore, if we would discover the secret of "entering into the spirit of it," we must get some idea of the negative, which is the "not-spirit."

In various ages this negative phase has been expressed in different forms of words suitable to the spirit of the time; and so, clothing this idea in the attire of the present day, I will sum up the opposite of Spirit in the word "Mechanism." Before all things this is a mechanical age, and it is astonishing how great a part of what we call our social advance has its root in the mechanical arts. Reduce the mechanical arts to what they were in the days of the Plantagenets and the greater part of our boasted civilisation would recede through the centuries along with them. We may not be conscious of all this, but the mechanical tendency of the age has a firm grip upon society at large. We habitually look at the mechanical side of things by preference to any other. Everything is done mechanically, from the carving on a piece of furniture to the arrangement of the social system. It is the mechanism that must be considered first, and the spirit has to be fitted to the mechanical exigencies. We enter into the mechanism of it instead of into the Spirit of it, and so limit the Spirit and refuse to let it have its own way; and then, as a consequence, we get entirely mechanical action, and complete our circle of ignorance by supposing that this is the only sort of action there is.

Yet this is not a necessary state of things even in regard to "physical science," for the men who have made the greatest advances in that direction are those who have most clearly seen the subordination of the mechanical to the spiritual. The man who can recognise a natural law only as it operates through certain forms of mechanism with which he is familiar will never rise to the construction of the higher forms of mechanism which might be built up upon that law, for he fails to see that it is the law which determines the mechanism and not vice versa. This man will make no advance in science, either theoretical or applied, and the world will never owe any debt of gratitude to him. But the man who recognises that the mechanism for the application of any principle grows out of the true apprehension of the principle studies the principle first, knowing that when *that* is properly grasped it will necessarily suggest all that is wanted for bringing it into practical use.

And if this is true in regard to so-called physical science, it is *a fortiori* true as regards the Science of Spirit. There is a mechanical attitude of mind which judges everything by the limitations of past experiences, allowing nothing for the fact that those experiences were for the most part the results of our ignorance of spiritual law. But if we realise the true law of Being we shall rise above these mechanical conceptions. We shall not deny the reality of the body or of the physical world as facts, knowing that they also are Spirit, but we shall learn to deny their power as causes. We shall learn to distinguish between the *causa causata* and the *causa causans,* the secondary or apparent physical cause and the primary or spiritual cause, without which the secondary cause could not exist; and so we shall get a new standpoint of clear knowledge and certain power by stepping over the threshold of the mechanical and entering into the spirit of it.

What we have to do is to maintain our even balance between the two extremes, denying neither Spirit nor the mechanism which is its form and through which it works. The one is as necessary to a perfect whole as the other, for there must be an *outside* as well as an *inside;* only we must remember that the creative principle is always *inside,* and that the outside only exhibits what the inside creates. Hence, whatever external effect we would produce, we must first enter into the spirit of it and work upon the spiritual principle, whether in ourselves or others; and by so doing our insight will become greatly enlarged, for from without we can see only one small portion of the circumference, while from the centre we can see the whole of it. If we fully grasp the truth that Spirit is Creator, we can dispense with painful investigations into the mechanical side of all our problems. If we are constructing from without, then we have to calculate anxiously the strength of our materials and the force of every thrust and strain to which they may be subjected, and very possibly after all we may find that we have made a mistake somewhere in our elaborate calculations. But if we realise the power of creating from within, we shall find all these calculations correctly made for us; for the same Spirit which is Creator is also that which the Bible calls "the Wonderful Numberer." Construction from without is based upon analysis, and no analysis is complete without accurate quantitative knowledge; but creation is the very opposite of analysis, and carries its own mathematics with it.

To enter into the spirit of anything, then, is to make yourself one in thought with the creative principle that is at the centre of it; and therefore why not go to the centre of all things at once, and enter into the Spirit of Life? Do you ask where to find it? *In yourself;* and in proportion as you find it there, you will will find it everywhere else. Look at Life as the one thing that is, whether in you or around you; try to realise the livingness of it, and then seek to enter into the Spirit of it by affirming it to be the whole of what you are. Affirm this continually in your thoughts, and by degrees the affirmation will grow into a real living force within you, so that it will become a second nature to you, and you will find it impossible and unnatural to think in any other way; and the nearer you approach this point the greater you will find your control over both body and circumstances, until at last you shall so enter into the Spirit of it—into the Spirit of the Divine creative power which is the root of all things—that, in the words of Jesus, "nothing shall be impossible to you," because you have so entered into the Spirit of it that you discover yourself to be *one with it.* Then all the old limitations will have passed away, and you will be living in an entirely new world of Life, Liberty and Love, of which you yourself are the radiating centre. You will realise the truth that your Thought is a limitless creative power, and that you yourself are behind your Thought, controlling and directing it with Knowledge for any purpose which Love motives and Wisdom plans. Thus you will cease from your labours, your struggles and anxieties, and enter into that new order where perfect rest is one with ceaseless activity.

*1902.*

## XIX

# THE BIBLE AND THE NEW THOUGHT

### 1.

### THE SON

A DEEPLY INTERESTING SUBJECT to the student of the New Thought movement is to trace how exactly its teaching is endorsed by the teaching of the Bible. There is no such thing as new thought in the sense of new Truth, for what is truth now must have been truth always; but there is such a thing as a new presentment of the old Truth, and it is in this that the newness of the present movement consists. But the same Truth has been repeatedly stated in earlier ages under various forms and in various measures of completeness, and nowhere more completely than in the Scriptures of the Old and New Testaments. None of the older forms of statement is more familiarly known to our readers than that contained in the Bible, and no other is entwined around our hearts with the same sacred and tender associations: therefore, I have no hesitation in saying that the existence of a marked correspondence between its teaching and that of the New Thought cannot but be a source of strength and encouragement to any of us who have been accustomed in the past to look to the old and hallowed Book as a storehouse of Divine wisdom. We shall find that the clearer light will make the rough places smooth and the dim places luminous, and that of the treasures of knowledge hidden in the ancient volume the half has not been told us.

The Bible lays emphatic stress upon "the glorious liberty of the sons of God," thus uniting in a single phrase the twofold idea of filial dependence and personal liberty. A careful study of the subject will show us that there is no opposition between these two ideas, but that they are necessary correlatives to each other, and that whether stated after the more concentrated method of the Bible, or after the more detailed method of the New Thought, the true teaching proclaims, not our independence of God, but our independence in God.

Such an enquiry naturally centres in an especial manner around the sayings of Jesus; for whatever may be our opinions as to the nature of the authority with which he spoke, we must all agree that a peculiar weight attaches to those utterances which have come down to us as the *ipsissima verba* from which the entire New Testament has been developed; and if an identity of conception in the New Thought movement can be traced here at the fountain-head, we may expect to find it in the lower streams also.

The Key to the Master's teaching is to be found in his discourse with the Woman of Samaria, and it is contained in the statement that "the Father" is Spirit, that is, Spirit in the absolute and unqualified sense of the word, as appears from the original Greek, and not "A Spirit" as it is rendered in the Authorised Version: and then as the natural correlative to "the Father" we find another term employed, "the Son." The relation between these two forms the great subject of Jesus' teaching, and, therefore, it is most important to have some definite idea of what he meant by these terms if we would understand what it was that he really taught.

Now if "the Father" be Spirit, "the Son" must be Spirit also; for a son must necessarily be of the same nature as his father. But since "the Father" is Spirit, Absolute and Universal, it is evident that "the Son" cannot be Spirit, Absolute and Universal, because there cannot be two Universal Spirits, for then neither would be universal. We may, therefore, logically infer that because "the Father" is Universal Spirit, "the Son" is Spirit not universal; and the only definition of Spirit not-universal is Spirit individualised and particular. The Scripture tells us that "the Spirit is Life," and taking this as the definition of "Spirit," we find that "the Father" is Absolute, Originating, Undifferentiated Life, and "the Son" is the same Life differentiated into particular forms. Hence, in the widest sense of the expression, "the Son" stands for the whole creation, visible or invisible, and in this sense it is the mere differentiation of the universal Life into a multiplicity of particular modes. But if we have any adequate idea of the intelligent and responsive nature of Spirit*—if we realise that because it is Pure Being it must be Infinite Intelligence and Infinite Responsiveness—then we shall see that its reproduction in the particular admits of innumerable degrees, from mere expression as outward form up to the very fullest expression of the infinite intelligence and responsiveness that Spirit is.

The teachings of Jesus were addressed to the hearts and intelligences of men, and therefore the grade of sonship of which he spoke has reference to the expression of Infinite Being in the human heart and intellect. But this, again, may be conceived of in infinite degrees; in some men there is the bare potentiality of sonship entirely undeveloped as yet, in others the beginnings of its development, in others a fuller development, and so on, until we can suppose some supreme instance in which the absolutely perfect reproduction of the universal has been attained. Each of these stages constitutes a fuller and fuller expression of sonship, until the supreme development reaches a point at which it can be described only as the perfect image of "the Father"; and this is the logical result of a process of steady growth from an inward principle of Life which constitutes the identity of each individual.

It is thus a necessary inference from Jesus' own explanation of "the Father" as Spirit or Infinite Being that "the Son" is the Scriptural phrase for the reproduction of Infinite Being in the individual, contemplated in that stage at which the individual does in some measure begin to recognise his identity with his originating source, or, at any rate, where he has capacity

* *Intelligence and Responsiveness* is the Generic Nature of Spirit in *every* Mode, and it is the *concentration* of this into centres of consciousness that makes personality, i.e., *self*-conscious individuality. This varies immensely in degree, from its first adumbration in the animal to its intense development in the Great Masters of Spiritual Science. Therefore it is called "The Power that Knows Itself"—It is the power of *Self*-recognition that makes *personality,* and as we grow to see that our personality is not all contained between our hat and our boots, as Walt Whitman says, but *expands* away into the Infinite, which we then find to be *the Infinite of ourselves,* the *same* I AM that I am, so *our personality* expands and we become conscious of ever-increasing degrees of Life-in-ourselves.

for such a recognition, even though the actual recognition may not yet have taken place. It is very remarkable that, thus defining "the Son" on the direct statement of Jesus himself, we arrive exactly at the definition of Spirit as "that power which knows itself." In the capacity for thus recognising its identity of nature with "the Father" is it that the potential fact of sonship consists, for the prodigal son was still a son even before he began to realise his relation to his "Father" in actual fact. It is the dawning of this recognition that constitutes the spiritual "babe," or infant son; and by degrees this consciousness grows till he attains the full estate of spiritual manhood. This recognition by the individual of his own identity with Universal Spirit is precisely what forms the basis of the New Thought; and thus at the outset the two systems radiate from a common centre.

But I suppose the feature of the New Thought which is the greatest stumbling-block to those who view the movement from the outside is the claim it makes for Thought-power as an active factor in the affairs of daily life. As a mere set of speculative opinions people might be willing to pigeon-hole it along with the philosophic systems of Kant or Hegel; but it is the practical element in it which causes the difficulty. It is not only a system of Thought based upon a conception of the Unity of Being, but it claims to follow out this conception to its legitimate consequences in the production of visible and tangible external results by the mere exercise of Thought-power. A ridiculous claim, a claim not to be tolerated by common sense, a trespassing upon the Divine prerogative, a claim of unparalleled audacity: thus the casual objector. But this claim is not without its parallel, for the same claim was put forward on the same ground by the Great Teacher Himself as the proper result of "the Son's" recognition of his relation to "the Father." "Ask what ye will, and it shall be done unto you"; "Whatsoever you shall ask in prayer, believing, you shall receive, and nothing shall be impossible unto you"; "All things are possible to him that believeth." These statements are absolutely without any note of limitation save that imposed by the seeker's want of faith in his own power to move the Infinite. This is as clear a declaration of the efficacy of mental power to produce outward and tangible results as any now made by the New Thought, and it is made on precisely the same ground, namely, the readiness of "the Father" or Spirit in the Universal to respond to the movement of Spirit in the individual.

In the Bible this movement of individualised Spirit is called "prayer," and it is synonymous with Thought, formulated with the intention of producing this response.

> "Prayer is the heart's sincere desire,
> Uttered or unexpressed,"

and we must not let ourselves be misled by the association of particular forms with particular words, but should follow the sound advice of Oliver Wendell Holmes, and submit such words to a process of depolarisation, which brings out their real meaning. Whether we call our act "prayer" or "thought-concentration," we mean the same thing; it is the claim of the man to move the Infinite by the action of his own mind.

It may be objected, however, that this definition omits an important element of prayer, the question, namely, whether God will hear it. But this is the very element that Jesus most rigorously excludes from his description of the mental act. Prayer, according to the popular notion, is a most uncertain matter. Whether we shall be heard or not depends entirely upon another will, regarding whose action we are completely ignorant, and therefore, according to this notion, the very essence of prayer consists of utter uncertainty. Jesus' conception of prayer was the very opposite. He bids us believe that we have already in fact received what we ask for, and makes this the condition of receiving; in other words, he makes the essential factor in the mental action to consist in Absolute Certainty as to the corresponding response in the Infinite, which is exactly the condition that the New Thought lays down for the successful operation of Thought-power.

It may, however, be objected that if men have thus an indiscriminate power of projecting their thought to the accomplishment of anything they desire, they can do so for evil as easily as for good. But Jesus fully recognised this possibility, and worked the only destructive miracle recorded of him for the express purpose of emphasising the danger. The reason given by the compilers of the Gospel for the destruction of the fig-tree is clearly inadequate, for we certainly cannot suppose Jesus so unreasonable as to curse a tree for not bearing fruit out of season. But the record itself shows a very different purpose. Jesus answered the disciples' astonished questioning by telling them, that it was in their own power, not only to do what was done to the fig-tree, but to produce effects upon a far grander scale; and he concludes the conversation by laying down the duty of a heart-searching forgiveness as a necessary preliminary to prayer. Why was this precept so particularly impressed in this particular connection? Obviously because the demonstration he had just given of the valency of thought-power in the hands of instructed persons laid bare the fact that this power can be used destructively as well as beneficially, and that, therefore, a thorough heart-searching for the eradication of any lurking ill-feeling became an imperative preliminary to its safe use; otherwise there was danger of noxious thought-currents being set in motion to the injury of others. The miracle of the fig-tree was an object-lesson to exhibit the need for the careful handling of that limitless power which Jesus assured his disciples existed as fully in them as in himself. I do not here attempt to go into this subject in detail, but enough has, I think, been shown to convince us that Jesus made exactly the same claim for the power of Thought as that made by the New Thought movement at the present day. It is a great claim, and it is, therefore, encouraging to find such an authority committed to the same assertion.

The general principle on which this claim is based by the exponents of the New Thought is the identity of Spirit in the individual with spirit in the universal, and we shall find that this, also, is the basis of Jesus' teaching on the subject. He says that "the Son can do nothing of himself, but what he seeth the Father do these things doeth the Son in like manner." It must now be sufficiently clear that "the Son" is a generic appellation, not restricted to a particular individual, but applicable to all; and this statement explains the manner of "the Son's" working in relation to "the Father." The point this sentence particularly emphasises is that it is what he sees the Father doing that the Son does also. His doing corresponds to his seeing. If the seeing expands, the doing expands along with it. But we are all sufficiently familiar with this principle in other matters. What differentiates an Edison or a Marconi from the apprentice who knows only how to fit up an electric bell by rule of thumb? It is their capacity for seeing the universal principles of electricity and bringing them into particular application. The great painter is the one who sees the universal principles of form and colour where the smaller man sees only a particular combination; and so with the great surgeon, the great chemist, the great lawyer—in every line it is the power of insight that distinguishes the great man from the little one; it is the capacity for making wide generalisations and perceiving far-reaching laws that raises the exceptional mind above the ordinary level. The greater working always results from the greater seeing into the abstract principles from which any art or science is generated; and this same law carried up to the universal principles of Life is the law by which "the Son's" working is proportioned to his seeing the method of "the Father's" work. Thus the source of "the Son's" power lies in the contemplation of "the Father," the endeavour, that is, to realise the true nature of Being, whether in the abstract or in its generic forms of manifestation.* This is Bacon's maxim, "Work as God works"; and similarly the New Thought consists before all things in the realisation of the laws of Being.

And the result of the seeing is that "the Son" does the same things as "the Father" "in like manner." The Son's action is the reproduction of the universal principles in application to specific instances. The principles remain unaltered and work always in the same manner, and the office of "the Son" is to determine the particular field of their operation with regard to the specific object which he has in view; and therefore, so far as that object is concerned, the action of "the Son" becomes the action of "the Father" also.

Again, there is no concealment on the part of "the Father." He has no secrets, for "the Father loveth the Son, and showeth him all things that himself doeth." There is perfect reciprocity between Spirit in the Universal and in Individualisation, resulting from the identity of Being; and "the Son's" recognition of Love as the active principle of this Unity gives him an intuitive insight into all those inner workings of the Universal Life which

---

* Everything depends on this principle of Reciprocity. By contemplation we come to realize the true nature of "Spirit" or "the father." We learn to disengage the *variable* factors of particular *Modes* from the *invariable* factors which are the essential qualities of Spirit underlying *all* Modes. Then when we realize these essential qualities we see that we can apply them under any mode that we will: in other words *we* supply the *variable* factor of the combination by the action of our Thought, as Desire or Will, and thus combine it with the *invariable* factor or "constant" of the *essential* law of spirit, thus producing what result we will. This is just what we do in respect to physical nature—e.g., the electrician supplies the *variable* factor of the particular Mode of application, and the *constant* laws of Electricity *respond* to the nature of the invitation given to them. This *Responsiveness* is *inherent* in Spirit; otherwise Spirit would have no means of expansion into manifestation. Responsiveness is the principle of Spirit's Self-expression. We do not have to create responsive action on the part of electricity. We can safely take this Responsiveness for granted as pure natural law. Our desire first works on the Arupa level and thence concentrates itself through the various Rupa levels till it reaches complete external manifestation.

we call the arcana of Nature. Love has a divine gift of insight which cannot be attained by intellect alone, and the old saying, "Love will find out the way," has greater depths of meaning than appear on the surface. Thus there is not only a seeing, but also a showing; and the three terms—"looking, seeing, showing"—combine to form a power of "working" to which it is impossible to assign any limit.

Here, again, the teaching of Jesus is in exact correspondence with that of the New Thought, which tells us that limitations exist only where we ourselves put them, and that to view ourselves as beings of limitless knowledge, power, and love is to become such in outward manifestation of visible fact. Any objections, therefore, to the New Thought teaching regarding the possibilities latent in Man apply with equal force to the teachings of Jesus. His teaching clearly was that the perfect individuality of Man is a Dual-Unity, the polarisation of the Infinite in the Manifest; and it requires only the recognition of this truth for the manifested element in this binary system to demonstrate its identity with the corresponding element which is not externally visible. He said that He and his Father were One, that those who had seen him had seen the Father, that the words which he spoke were the Father's, and that it was the Father who did the works. Nothing could be more explicit. Absolute unity of the manifested individuality with the Originating Infinite Spirit is asserted or implied in every utterance attributed to Jesus, whether spoken of himself or of others. He recognises only one radical difference, the difference between those who know this truth and those who do not know it. The distinction between the disciple and the master is one only of degree, which will be effaced by the expansive power of growth; "the disciple, when he is perfected, shall be as his Master."

All that hinders the individual from exercising the full power of the Infinite for any purpose whatever is his lack of faith, his inability to realise to the full the stupendous truth that he himself is the very power which he seeks. This was the teaching of Jesus as it is that of the New Thought; and this truth of the Divine Sonship of Man once taken as the great foundation, a magnificent edifice of possibilities which "eye hath not seen, nor ear heard, neither hath entered into the heart of man to conceive," grows up logically upon it—a glorious heritage which each one may legitimately claim in right of his common humanity.

## 2.
## THE GREAT AFFIRMATION

I take it for granted that my readers are well acquainted with the part assigned to the principle of Affirmation in the scheme of the New Thought. This is often a stumbling-block to beginners; and I feel sure that even those who are not beginners will welcome every aid to a deeper apprehension of this great central truth. I, therefore, purpose to examine the Bible teaching on this important subject.

The professed object of the Bible is to establish and extend "the Kingdom of God" throughout the world, and this can be done only by repeating the process from one individual to another, until the whole mass is leavened. It is thus an individual process; and, as we have seen in the last chapter, God is Spirit and Spirit is Life, and, therefore, the expansion of "the Kingdom of God" means the expansion of the principle of Life in each individual. Now Life, to be life at all, must be Affirmative. It is Life in virtue of what it is, and not in virtue of what it is not. The quantity of life in any particular case may be very small; but, however small the amount, the quality is always the same: it is the quality of Being, the quality of Livingness, and not its absence, that makes it what it is. The distinctive character of Life, therefore, is that it is Positive and not Negative; and every degree of negativeness, that is, every limitation, is ultimately traceable to deficiency of Life-power.

Limitations surround us because we believe in our inability to do what we desire. Whenever we say "I cannot" we are brought up sharp by a limitation, and we cease to exercise our thought-power in that direction because we believe ourselves stopped by a blank wall of impossibility; and whenever this occurs we are subjected to bondage. The ideal of perfect Liberty is the converse of all this, and follows a sequence which does not thus lead us into a *cul-de-sac.* This sequence consists of the three affirmations: I am—therefore I can—therefore I will; and this last affirmation results in the projection of our powers, whether interior or external, to the accomplishment of the desired object. But this last affirmation has its root in the first; and it is because we recognise the Affirmative nature of the Life that is in us, or rather of the Life which we are, that the power to will or to act positively has any existence; and, therefore, the extent of our power to will and to act positively and with effect, is exactly measured by our perception of the depth and livingness of our own Being. Hence the more fully we learn to affirm that, the greater power we are able to exercise.

Now the ideal of perfect Liberty is the entire absence of all limitation, and to have no limitation in Being is to be co-extensive with All-Being. We are all grammarians enough to know that the use of a predicate is to lead the mind to contemplate the subject as represented by that predicate; in other words, it limits our conception for the time being to that particular aspect of the subject. Hence every predicate, however extensive, implies some limitation of the subject. But the ideal subject, the absolutely free self, is, by the very hypothesis, without limitation; and, therefore, no predicate can be attached to it. It stands as a declaration of its own Being without any statement of what that Being consists in, and therefore it says of itself, not "I am this or that," but simply I am. No predicate can be added, because the only commensurate predicate would be the enumeration of Infinity. Therefore, both logically and grammatically, the only possible statement of a fully liberated being is made in the words I am.

I need hardly remind my readers of the frequency with which Jesus employed these emphatic words. In many cases the translators have added the word "He," but they have been careful, by putting it in italics, to show that it is not in the original. As grammarians and theologians they thought something more was wanted to complete the sense, and they supplied it accordingly; but if we would get at the very words as the Master himself spoke them, we must strike out this interpolation. And as soon as we have done so there flashes into light the identity of his statement with that made to Moses at the burning bush, where the full significance of the words is so obvious that the translators were compelled to leave the place of the predicate in that seeming emptiness which comes from filling all things.

Seen thus, a marvellous light shines forth from the instruction of the Great Teacher: for in whatever sense we may regard him as a Great Exception to the weak and limited aspect of humanity with which we are only too familiar, we must all agree that his mission was not to render mankind hopeless by declaring the path of advance barred against them, but "to give light to them that sit in darkness," and liberty to them that are bound, by proclaiming the unlimited possibilities that are in man waiting only to be called forth by knowledge of the Truth. And if we suppose any personal reference in his words, it can, therefore, be only as the Great Example of what man has it in him to become, and not as the example of something which man can never hope to be; an Exception, truly, to mankind as we see them now, but the Exception that proves the rule, and sets the standard of what each one may become as he attains to the measure of the stature of the fulness of Christ.

Let us, therefore, by striking out this interpolation, restore the Master's words as they stand in the original: "Except ye believe that I am, ye shall die in your sins." This is an epitome of his teaching.

"The last enemy that shall be overcome is death," and the "sting," or fatal power, of death is "sin." Remove that, and death has no longer any dominion over us; its power is at an end. And "the strength of sin is the Law": sin is every contradiction of the law of Being; and the law of Being is infinitude; for Being is Life, and Life in its innermost essence is the limitless I am. Dying in our sins is thus not a punishment for doubting a particular theological dogma, but it is the unavoidable natural consequence of not realising, not believing in, the I am. So long as we fail to realise its full infinitude in ourselves, we cut ourselves off from our conscious unity with the Infinite Life-Spirit which permeates all things. Without this principle we have no alternative but to die—and this because of our sin, that is, because of our failure to conform to the true Law of our Being, which is Life, and not Death. We affirm Death and Negation concerning ourselves, and therefore Death and Negation are externalised, and thus we pay the penalty of not believing in the central Law of our own Life, which is the Law of all Life. The Bible is the Book of Principles, and therefore by "dying" is meant the acceptance of the principle of the Negative which culminates in Death as the sum-total of all limitations, and which introduces at every step those restrictions which are of the nature of Death, because their tendency is to curtail the outflowing fulness of Life.

This, then, is the very essence of the teaching of Jesus, that unbelief in the limitless power of Life-in-ourselves—in each of us—is the one cause of Death and of all those evils which, in greater or lesser measure, reproduce the restrictive influences which deprive Life of its fulness and joy. If we would escape Death and enter into Life, we must each believe in the I am in ourselves. And the ground for this belief? Simply that nothing else is conceivable. If our life is not a portion of the life of Universal Spirit, whence comes it? We are because that is. No other explanation is possible. The unqualified affirmation of our own livingness is not an audacious self-assertion: it is the only logical outcome of the fact that there is any life anywhere, and that we are here to think about it. In the sense of Universal Being, there can be only One I am, and the understanding use of the words by the individual is the assertion of this fact. The forms of manifestation are infinite, but the Life which is manifested is One, and thus every thinker who recognises the truth regarding himself finds in the I am both himself and the totality of all things; and thus he comes to know that in utilising the interior nature of the things and persons about him, he is, in effect, employing the powers of his own life.

Sometimes the veil which Jesus drew over this great truth was very transparent. To the Samaritan woman he spoke of it as a spring of Life forever welling up in the innermost recesses of man's being; and again, to the multitude assembled at the Temple, he spoke of it as a river of Life forever gushing from the secret sources of the spirit within us. Life, to be ours at all, must be ourselves. An energy which only passed through us, without being us, might produce a sort of galvanic activity, but it would not be Life. Life can never be a separate entity from the individuality which manifests it; and therefore, even if we conceive the life-principle in a man so intensified as to pulsate with what might seem to us an absolutely divine vitality, it would still be no other than the man himself. Thus Jesus directs us to no external source of life, but ever teaches that the Kingdom of Heaven is within, and that what is wanted is to remove those barriers of ignorance and ill-will which prevent us from realising that the great I am, which is the innermost Spirit of Life throughout the universe, is the same I am that I am, whoever I may be.

On another memorable occasion Jesus declared again that the I am is the enduring principle of Life. It is this that is the Resurrection and the Life; not, as Martha supposed, a new principle to be infused from without at some future time, but an inherent core of vitality awaiting only its own recognition of itself to triumph over death and the grave. And yet, again hear the Master's answer to the inquiring Thomas. How many of us, like him, desire to know the way! To hear of wonderful powers latent in man and requiring only development is beautiful and hopeful, if we could only find out the way to develop them; but who will show us the way? The answer comes with no uncertain note. The I am includes everything. It is at once "the Way, the Truth, and the Life": not the Life only, or the Truth only, but also the Way by which to reach them. Can words be plainer? It is by continually affirming and relying on the I am in ourselves as identical with the I am that is the One and Only Life, whether manifested or unmanifested, in all places of the universe, that we shall find the way to the attainment of all Truth and of all Life. Here we have the predicate which we are seeking to complete our affirmation regarding ourselves. I am—what? the Three things which include all things; Truth, which is all Knowledge and Wisdom; Life, which is all Power and Love; and the unfailing Way which will lead us step by step, if we follow it, to heights too sublime and environment too wide for our present juvenile imaginings to picture.

As the New Testament centres around Jesus, so the old Testament centres around Moses, and he also declares the Great Affirmation to be the same.* For him God has no name, but that intensely living universal Life which is all in all, and no name is sufficient to be its equivalent. The emphatic words I am are the only possible statement of the One-Power which exhibits itself as all worlds and all living beings. It is the Great I am which forever unfolds itself in all the infinite evolutionary forces of the cosmic

---

* The Old Testament and the New treat the I AM from its opposite poles. The Old Testament treats it from the relation of the *Whole to the Part,* while the New Testament treats it from the relation of the *Part to the Whole.* This is important as explaining the relation between the Old and New Testaments.

(a) "My Word shall not return unto me void but shall accomplish that whereunto I send it."

(b) The Principle here indicated is that of the Alternation and Equation between Absorption and Radiation—a taking-in before, and a giving-out.

(c) *"Order"*—Whatever betrays this is "Disorder."

(d) *"Conscious"*—It is the degree of *consciousness* that always marks the transition from a lower to a higher Power of Life. The *Life* of *All Seven* Principles *must* always be present in us, otherwise we should not exist at all; therefore it is the degree in which we learn to *consciously* function in each of them that marks our advance into higher kingdoms within ourselves, and frequently outside ourselves also.

(e) The Central Radiating Point of our Individuality is *One* with All-Being.

(f) *Equilibrium*—Note the difference between the Living Equilibrium of Alternate Rhythmic *Pulsation* (the whole Pulsation Doctrine) and the dead equilibrium of merely *running down* to a *dead level.* The former implies the Doctrine of the Return, the Upward Arc compensating the Downward Arc—The deadness of the latter results from the absence of any such compensation. The Upward Arc results from the contemplation of the Highest Ideal.

(g) Spirit cannot leave any portion of its Nature behind it. It *must* always have *all* the qualities of Spirit in it, even though the lower parts of the individuality are not yet conscious of it.

(h) The Great Affirmation is The Guide to the whole Subject.

scheme, and which, in marvellous onward march, develops itself into higher and higher conscious intelligence in the successive races of mankind, unrolling the scroll of history as it moves on from age to age, working out with unerring precision the steady forward movement of the whole towards that ultimate perfection in which the work of God will be completed. But stupendous as is the scale on which this Providential Power reveals itself to Moses and the Prophets, it is still nothing else than the very same Power which Jesus bids us realise in ourselves.

The theatre of its operations may be expanded to the magnificent proportions of a world-history, or contracted to the sphere of a single individuality: the difference is only one of scale; but the Life-principle is always the same. It is always the principle of confident Affirmation in the calm knowledge that all things are but manifestations of itself, and that, therefore, all must move together in one mighty unity which admits of no discordant elements. This "unity of the spirit" once clearly grasped, to say I am is to send the vibrations of our thought-currents throughout the universe to do our bidding when and where we will; and, conversely, it is to draw in the vitalising influences of Infinite Spirit as from a boundless ocean of Life, which can never be exhausted and from which no power can hold us back. And all this is so because it is the supreme law of Nature. It is not the introduction of a new order, but simply the allowing of the original and only possible order to flow on to its legitimate fulfilment. A Divine Order, truly, but nowhere shall we find anything that is not Divine; and it is to the realisation of this Divine and Living Order that it is the purpose of the Bible to lead us. But we shall never realise it around us until we first realise it within us. We can see God outside only by the light of God inside; and this light increases in proportion as we become conscious of the Divine nature of the innermost I am which is the centre of our own individuality.

Therefore, it is that Jesus tells us that the I am is "the door." It is that central point of our individual Being which opens into the whole illimitable Life of the Infinite. If we would understand the old-world precept, "know thyself," we must concentrate our thought more and more closely upon our own interior Life until we touch its central radiating point, and there we shall find that the door into the Infinite is indeed opened to us, and that we can pass from the innermost of our own Being into the innermost of All-Being. This is why Jesus spoke of "the door" as that through which we should pass in and out and find pasture. Pasture, the feeding of every faculty with its proper food, is to be found both on the within and the without. The livingness of Life consists in both concentration and externalisation: it is not the dead equilibrium of inertia, but the living equilibrium of a vital and rhythmic pulsation. Involution and evolution must forever alternate, and the door of communication between them is the I am which is the living power in both. Thus it is that the Great Affirmation is the Secret of Life, and that to say I am with a true understanding of all that it implies is to place ourselves in touch with all the powers of the Infinite.

This is the Universal and Eternal Affirmation to which no predicate is attached; and all particular affirmations will be found to be only special differentiations of this all-embracing one. I will this or that particular thing because I know that I can bring it into externalisation, and I know that I can because I know that I am, and so we always come back to the great central Affirmation of All-Being. Search the Scriptures and you will find that from first to last they teach only this: that every human soul is an individualisation of that Universal Being, or All-Spirit, which we call God, and that Spirit can never be shorn of its powers, but like Fire, which is its symbol, must always be fully and perfectly itself, which is Life in all its unlimited fulness.

In assigning to Affirmation, therefore, the importance which it does, the New Thought movement is at one with the teaching of Jesus and Moses and of the entire Bible. And the reason is clear. There is only one Truth, and therefore careful seeking can bring men only to the same Truth, whether they be Bible-writers or any other. The Bible derives its authority from the inherent truth of the things it tells of, and not vice versa; and if these things be true at all, they would be equally true even though no Bible had ever been written. But, taking the Great Affirmation as our guide, we shall find that the system taught by the Bible is scientific and logical throughout, and therefore any other system which is scientifically true will be found to correspond with it in substance, however it may differ from it in form; and thus, in their statements regarding the power of Affirmation, the exponents of the New Thought broach no new-fangled absurdity, but only reiterate a great truth which has been before the world, though very imperfectly recognised, for thousands of years.

## 3.
## THE FATHER

If, as we have seen, "the Son" is the differentiating principle of Spirit, giving rise to innumerable individualities, "the Father" is the unifying principle by which these innumerable individualities are bound together into one common life, and the necessity for recognising this great basis of the universal harmony forms the foundation of Jesus' teaching on the subject of Worship. "Woman, believe me, the hour cometh, when neither in this mountain, nor yet at Jerusalem, shall ye worship the Father. Ye worship that which ye know not; we worship that which we know; for salvation is from the Jews. But the hour cometh and now is when the true worshippers shall worship the Father in spirit and truth" (Revised Version). In these few words the Great Teacher sums up the whole subject. He lays particular stress on the kind of worship that he means. It is, before all things, founded upon knowledge.

"We worship that which we know," and it is this knowledge that gives the worship a healthful and life-giving quality. It is not the ignorant worship of wonderment and fear, a mere abasement of ourselves before some vast, vague, unknown power, which may injure us if we do not find out how to propitiate it; but it is a definite act performed with a definite purpose, which means that it is the employment of one of our natural faculties upon its proper object in an intelligent manner. The ignorant Samaritan worship is better than no worship at all, for at least it realises the existence of some centre around which a man's life should revolve, something to prevent the aimless dispersion of His powers for want of a centripetal force to bind them together; and even the crudest notion of prayer, as a mere attempt to induce God to change his mind, is at least a first step towards the truth that full supply for all our needs may be drawn from the Infinite. Still, such worship as this is hampered with perplexities, and can give only a feeble answer to the atheistical sneer which asks, "What is man, that God should be mindful of him, a momentary atom among unnumbered worlds?"

Now the teaching of Jesus throws all these perplexities aside with the single word "knowledge." There is only one true way of doing anything, and that is knowing exactly what it is we want to do, and knowing exactly why we want to do it. All other doing is blundering. We may blunder into the right thing sometimes, but we cannot make this our principle of life to all eternity; and if we have to give up the blunder method eventually, why not give it up now, and begin at once to profit by acting according to intelligible principle? The knowledge that "the Son," as individualised Spirit, has his correlative in "the Father," as Universal Spirit, affords the clue we need.

In whatever way we may attempt to explain it, the fact remains that volition is the fundamental characteristic of Spirit. We may speak of conscious, or subconscious or super-conscious action; but in whatever way we may picture to ourselves the condition of the agent as contemplating his own action, a general purposeful lifeward tendency becomes abundantly evident on any enlarged view of Nature, whether seen from without or from within, and we may call this by the general name of volition. But the error we have to avoid is that of supposing volition to take the same form in Universal Spirit as in individualised Spirit. The very terms "universal" and "individual" forbid this. For the universal, as such, to exercise specific volition, concentrating itself upon the details of a specific case, would be for it to pass into individualisation, and to cease to be the Absolute and Infinite; it would be no longer "the Father," but "the Son." It is therefore exactly by not exercising specific volition that "the Father" continues to be "the Father," or the Great Unifying Principle. But the volitional quality is not on this account absent from Spirit in the Universal; for otherwise whence would that quality appear in ourselves? It is present; but according to the nature of the plane on which it is acting. The Universal is not the Specific, and everything on the plane of the Universal must partake of the nature of that plane. Hence volition in "the Father" is not specific; and that which is not specific and individual must be generic. Generic volition, therefore, is that mode of volition which belongs to the Universal, and generic volition is tendency. This is the solution of the enigma, and this solution is given, not obscurely, in Jesus' statement that "the Father" seeks those true worshippers who worship Him in spirit and in truth.

For what do we mean by tendency? From the root of tendere, to stretch; it signifies a pushing out in a certain definite direction, the tension of some force seeking to expand itself. What force? The Universal Life-Principle, for "the Spirit is Life." In the language of modern science this "seeking" on the part of "the Father" is the expansive pressure of the Universal Life-Principle seeking the line of least resistance, along which to flow into the fullest manifestation of individualised Life. It is a tendency which will take manifested form according to the degree in which it meets with reception.

St. John says, "This is the boldness that we have towards him, that if we ask anything according to His will, He heareth us; and if we know that He heareth us whatsoever we ask, we know that we have the petitions that we have asked of Him" (1 John v. 14). Now according to the popular notion of "the will of God," this passage entirely loses its value, because it makes everything depend on our asking "according to His will," and if we start with the idea of an individual act of the Divine volition in each separate case, nothing short of a special revelation continually repeated could inform us what the Divine will in each particular instance was. Viewed in this light, this passage is a mere jeering at our incapacity. But when once we realise that "the will of God" is an invariable law of tendency, we have a clear standard by which to test whether we may rightly expect to get what we desire. We can study this law of tendency as we would any other law, and it is this study that is the essence of true worship.

The word "worship" means to count worthy; to count worthy, that is, of observation. The proverb says that "imitation is the sincerest form of flattery"; more truly we may say that it is the sincerest worship. Hence the true worship is the study of the Universal Life-Principle "the Father," in its nature and in its modes of action; and when we have thus realised "the Law of God," the law that is inherent in the nature of Infinite Being, we shall know that by conforming our own particular action to this generic law, we shall find that this law will in every instance work out the results that we desire. This is nothing more or less miraculous than what occurs in every case of applied science. He only is the true chemist or engineer who, by first learning how to obey the generic tendency of natural laws, is able to command them to the fulfilment of his individual purposes; no other method will succeed. Similarly with the student of the divine mystery of Life. He must first learn the great laws of its generic tendency, and then he will be in a position to apply that tendency to the working of any specific effect he will.

Common sense tells us what the law of this tendency must be. The Master taught that a house divided against itself cannot stand; and for the Life-Principle to do anything restrictive of the fullest expansion of life, would be for it to act to its own destruction. The test, therefore, in every case, whether our intention falls within the scope of the great law, is this: Does it operate for the expansion or for the restriction of life? and according to the answer we can say positively whether or not our purpose is according to "the will of God." Therefore so long as we work within the scope of this generic "will of the Father" we need have no fear of the Divine Providence, as an agency, acting adversely to us. We may dismiss this bugbear, for we ourselves are manifestations of the very power which we call "the Father." The I am is one; and so long as we preserve this unity by conforming to the generic nature of the I am in the universal, it will certainly never destroy the unity by entering upon a specific course of action on its own account.

Here, then, we find the secret of power. It is contained in the true worship of "the Father," which is the constant recognition of the lifegivingness of Originating Spirit, and of the fact that we, as individuals, still continue to be portions of that Spirit; and that therefore the law of our nature is to be perpetually drawing life from the inexhaustible stores of the Infinite—not bottles of water-of-life mixed with other ingredients and labelled for this or that particular purpose, but the full flow of the pure stream itself, which we are free to use for any purpose we desire. "Whosoever will, let him take the water of life freely." It is thus that the worship of "the Father" becomes the central principle of the individual life, not as curtailing our liberty, but as affording the only possible basis for it. As a planetary system would be impossible without a central controlling sun, so harmonious life is impossible without the recognition of Infinite Spirit as that Power, whose generic tendency serves to control each individual being into its proper orbit. This is the teaching of the Bible, and it is also the teaching of the New Thought, which says that life with all its limitless possibilities is a continual outflow from the Infinite which we may turn in any direction that we desire.

But, it may be asked, what happens if we go counter to this generic law of Spirit? This is an important question, and I must leave the answer for further consideration.

## 4.
## CONCLUSION

I concluded my last chapter with the momentous question, What happens if we go counter to the generic law of Spirit? What happens if we go counter to any natural law? Obviously, the law goes counter to us. We can use the laws of Nature, but we cannot alter them. By opposing any natural law we place ourselves in an inverted position with regard to it, and therefore, viewed from this false standpoint, it appears as though the law itself were working against us with definite purpose. But the inversion proceeds entirely from ourselves, and not from any change in the action of the law. The law of Spirit, like all other natural laws, is in itself impersonal; but we carry into it, so to speak, the reflection of our own personality, though we cannot alter its generic character; and therefore, if we oppose its generic tendency towards the universal good, we shall find in it the reflection of our own opposition and waywardness.

The law of Spirit proceeds unalterably on its course, and what is spoken of in popular phraseology as the Divine wrath is nothing else than the reflex action which naturally follows when we put ourselves in opposition to this law. The evil that results is not a personal intervention of the Universal Spirit, which would imply its entering into specific manifestation, but it is the natural outcome of the causes that we ourselves have set in motion. But the effect to ourselves will be precisely the same as if they were brought about by the volition of an adverse personality, though we may not realise that in truth the personal element is our own. And if we are at all aware of the wonderfully complex nature of man, and the various interweavings of principles which unite the material body at one end of the scale to the purely spiritual Ego at the other, we shall have some faint idea of on how vast a field these adverse influences may operate, not being restricted to the plane of outward manifestation, but acting equally on those inner planes which give rise to the outer and are of a more enduring nature.

Thus the philosophic study of Spirit, so far from affording any excuse for laxity of conduct, adds an emphatic definiteness to the Bible exhortation to flee from the wrath of God. But, on the other hand, it delivers us from groundless terrors, the fear lest our repentance should not be accepted, the fear lest we should be rejected for our inability to subscribe to some traditional dogma, the fear of utter uncertainty regarding the future—fears which make life bitter and the prospect of death appalling to those who are in bondage to them. The knowledge that we are dealing with a power which is no respecter of persons, and in which is no variableness, which is, in fact, an unalterable Law, at once delivers us from all these terrors.

The very unchangeableness of Law makes it certain that no amount of past opposition to it, whether from ignorance or wilfulness, will prevent it from working in accordance with its own beneficent and life-giving character as soon as we quit our inverted position and place ourselves in our true relation towards it. The laws of Nature do not harbour revenge; and once we adapt our methods to their character, they will work for us without taking any retrospective notice of our past errors. The law of Spirit may be more complex than that of electricity, because, as expressed in us, it is the law of conscious individuality; but it is none the less a purely natural law, and follows the universal rule, and therefore we may dismiss from our minds, as a baseless figment, the fear of any Divine power treasuring up anger against us on account of bygones, if we are sincerely seeking to do what is right now. The new causes which we put in motion now will produce their proper effect as surely as the old causes did; and thus by inaugurating a new sequence of good we shall cut off the old sequence of evil. Only, of course, we cannot expect to bring about the new sequence while continuing to repeat the old causes, for the fruit must necessarily reproduce the nature of the seed. Thus we are the masters of the situation, and, whether in this world or the next, it rests with ourselves either to perpetuate the evil or to wipe it out and put the good in its place. And it may be noticed in passing that the great central Christian doctrine is based upon the most perfect knowledge of this law, and is the practical application to a profound problem of the deepest psychological science. But this is a large subject, and cannot be suitably dealt with here.

Much has been written and said on the origin of evil, and a volume might be filled with the detailed study of the subject; but for all practical purposes it may be summed up in the one word limitation. For what is the ultimate cause of all strife, whether public or private, but the notion that the supply of good is limited? With the bulk of mankind this is a fixed idea, and they therefore argue that because there is only a certain limited quantity of good, the share in their possession can be increased only by correspondingly diminishing some one else's share. Any one entertaining the same idea, naturally resents the attempt to deprive him of any portion of this limited quantity; and hence arises the whole crop of envy, hatred, fraud, and violence, whether between individuals, classes, or nations. If people only realised the truth that "good" is not a certain limited quantity, but a stream continuously flowing from the exhaustless Infinite, and ready to take any direction we choose to give it, and that each one is able by the action of his own thought to draw from it indefinitely, the substitution of this new and true idea for the old and false one of limitation would at one stroke remove all strife and struggle from the world; every man would find a helper instead of a competitor in every other, and the very laws of Nature, which now so often seem to war against us, would be found a ceaseless source of profit and delight.

"They could not enter into rest because of unbelief," "they limited the Holy One of Israel": in these words the Bible, like the New Thought, traces all the sorrow of the world—that terrible *Weltschmerz* which expresses itself with such direful influence through the pessimistic literature of the day—to the one root of a false belief, the belief in man's limitation. Only substitute for it the true belief, and the evil would be at an end. Now the ground of this true belief is that clear apprehension of "the Father" which, as I have shown, forms the basis of Jesus' teaching. If, from one point of view, the Intelligent Universal Life-Principle is a Power to be obeyed, in the same sense in which we have to obey all the laws of Nature, from the opposite point of view, it is a power to be used. We must never lose sight of the fact that obedience to any natural law in its generic tendency necessarily carries with it a corresponding power of using that law in specific application. This is the old proverb that knowledge is power. It is the old paradox with which Jesus posed the ignorant scribes as to how David's Lord could also be his Son. The word "David" means "Beloved" and to be beloved implies that reciprocal sympathy which is intuitive knowledge. Hence David, the Beloved, is the man who has realised his true relation as a Son to his Father and who is "in tune with the Infinite." On the other hand, this "Infinite" is his "Lord" because it is the complex of all those unchangeable Laws from which it is impossible to swerve without suffering consequent loss of power; and on the other, this knowledge of the innermost principles of All-Being puts him in possession of unlimited powers which he can apply to any specific purpose that he will; and thus he stands towards them in the position of a father who has authority to command the services of his son. Thus David's "Lord" becomes by a natural transition his "Son."

And it is precisely in this that the principle of "Sonship" consists. It is the raising of man from the condition of bondage as a servant by reason of limitation to the status of a son by the entire removal of all limitations. To believe and act on this principle is to "believe on the Son of God," and a practical belief in our own sonship thus sets us free from all evil and from all fear of evil—it brings us out of the kingdom of death into the kingdom of Life. Like everything else, it has to grow, but the good seed of liberating Truth once planted in the heart is sure to germinate, and the more we endeavour to foster its growth by seeking to grasp with our understanding the reason of these things and to realise our knowledge in practice, the more rapidly we shall find our lives increase in livingness—a joy to ourselves, a brightness to our homes, and a blessing expanding to all around in ever-widening circles.

Enough has now been said to show the identity of principle between the teaching of the Bible and that of the New Thought. Treated in detail, the subject would extend to many volumes explanatory of the Old and New Testaments, and if that great work were ever carried out I have no hesitation in saying that the agreement would be found to extend to the minutest particulars. But the hints contained in the foregoing papers will, I hope, suffice to show that there is nothing antagonistic between the two systems, or, rather, to show that they are one—the statement of the One Truth which always has been and always will be. And if what I have now endeavoured to put before my readers should lead any of them to follow up the subject more fully for themselves, I can promise them an inexhaustible store of wonder, delight, and strength in the study of the Old Book in the light of the New Thought.

*1902.*

## XX

# JACHIN AND BOAZ

"AND HE REARED up the pillars before the temple, one on the right hand, and the other on the left; and called the name of that on the right hand Jachin, and the name of that on the left Boaz." (II Chron. iii, 17.)

Very likely some of us have wondered what was the meaning of these two mysterious pillars set up by Solomon in front of his temple, and why they were called by these strange names; and then we have dropped the subject as one of those inexplicable things handed down in the Bible from old time which, we suppose, can have no practical interest for us at the present day. Nevertheless, these strange names are not without a purpose. They contain the key to the entire Bible and to the whole order of Nature, and as emblems of the two great principles that are the pillars of the universe, they fitly stood at the threshold of that temple which was designed to symbolise all the mysteries of Being.

In all the languages of the Semitic stock the letters J and Y are interchangeable, as we see in the modern Arabic "Yakub" for "Jacob" and the old Hebrew "Yaveh" for "Jehovah." This gives us the form "Yachin," which at once reveals the enigma. The word Yak signifies "one"; and the termination "hi," or "hin," is an intensitive which may be rendered in English by "only." Thus the word "Jachin" resolves itself into the words "one only," the all-embracing Unity.

The meaning of Boaz is clearly seen in the book of Ruth. There Boaz appears as the kinsman exercising the right of pre-emption so familiar to those versed in Oriental law—a right which has for its purpose the maintenance of the Family as the social unit. According to this widely-spread custom, the purchaser, who is not a member of the family, buys the property subject to the right of kinsmen within certain degrees to purchase it back, and so bring it once more into the family to which it originally belonged. Whatever may be our personal opinions regarding the vexed questions of dogmatic theology, we can all agree as to the general principle indicated in the role acted by Boaz. He brings back the alienated estate into the family—that is to say, he "redeems" it in the legal sense of the word. As a matter of law his power to do this results from his membership in the family; but his motive for doing it is love, his affection for Ruth. Without pushing the analogy too far we may say, then, that Boaz represents the principle of redemption in the widest sense of reclaiming an estate by right of relationship, while the innermost moving power in its recovery is Love.

This is what Boaz stands for in the beautiful story of Ruth, and there is no reason why we should not let the same name stand for the same thing when we seek the meaning of the mysterious pillar. Thus the two pillars typify Unity and the redeeming power of Love, with the significant suggestion that the redemption results from the Unity. They correspond with the two "bonds," or uniting principles spoken of by St. Paul, "the Unity of the Spirit which is the Bond of Peace," and "Love, which is the Bond of Perfectness."

The former is Unity of Being; the latter, Unity of Intention: and the principle of this Dual-Unity is well illustrated by the story of Boaz. The whole story proceeds on the idea of the Family as the social unit, the root-conception of all Oriental law, and if we consider the Family in this light, we shall see how exactly it embodies the two-fold idea of Jachin and Boaz, unity of Being and unity of Thought. The Family forms a unit because all the members proceed from a common progenitor, and are thus all of one blood; but, although this gives them a natural unity of Being of which they cannot divest themselves, it is not enough in itself to make them a united family, as unfortunately experience too often shows. Something more is wanted, and that something is Love. There must be a personal union brought about by sympathetic Thought to complete the natural union resulting from birth. The inherent unity must be expressed by the Individual volition of each member, and thus the Family becomes the ideally perfect social unit; a truth to which St. Paul alludes when he calls God the Father from Whom every family in heaven and on earth is named. Thus Boaz stands for the principle which brings back to the original Unity that which has been for a time separated from it. There has never been any separation of actual Being—the family right always subsisted in the property even while in the hands of strangers, otherwise it could never have been brought back; but it requires the Love principle to put this right into effective operation.

When this begins to work in the knowledge of its right to do so, then there is the return of the individual to the Unity, and the recognition of himself as the particular expression of the Universal in virtue of his own nature.

These two pillars, therefore, stand for the two great spiritual principles that are the basis of all Life: Jachin typifying the Unity resulting from Being, and Boaz typifying the Unity resulting from Love. In this Dual-Unity we find the key to all conceivable involution or evolution of Spirit; and it is therefore not without reason that the record of these two ancient pillars has been preserved in our Scriptures. And finally we may take this as an index to the character of our Scriptures generally. They contain infinite meanings; and often those passages which appear on the surface to be most meaningless will be found to possess the deepest significance. The Book, which we often read so superficially, hides beneath its sometimes seemingly trivial words the secrets of other things. The twin pillars Jachin and Boaz bear witness to this truth.*

---

* The following comment was made by Judge Troward, after the publication of this paper in *Expression:*

"*The Two Pillars* of the Universe are Personality and Mathematics, represented by Boaz and Jachin respectively. This is the broadest simplification to which it is possible to reduce things. Balance consists in preserving the Equilibrium or Alternating Current between these two Principles. Personality is the Absolute Factor. Mathematics are the Relative Factor, for they merely Measure different Rates or Scales. They are absolute in this respect. A particular scale having been selected all its sequences will follow by an inexorable Law of Order and Proportion; but the selection of the scale and the change from one scale to another rests entirely with Personality. What Personality can not do is to make one Scale produce the results of another, but it can set aside one scale and substitute another for it. Hence Personality contains in itself the Universal Scale, or can either accommodate itself to lower rates of motion already established, or can raise them to its own rate of motion. Hence Personality is the grand Ultimate Fact in all things.

"Different personalities should be regarded as different degrees of consciousness. They are different degrees of emergence of The Power that knows Itself."

## XXI

# HEPHZIBAH

"THOU SHALT no more be termed Forsaken; neither shall thy land any more be termed Desolate; but thou shalt be called Hephzibah, and thy land Beulah: for the Lord delighteth in thee, and thy land shall be married" (Isaiah lxii, 4). The name Hephzibah—or, as it might be written, Hafzbah—conveys a very distinct idea to any one who has lived in the East, and calls up a string of familiar words all containing the same root *hafz,* which signifies "guarding" or "taking care of," such as *hafiz,* a protector, *muhafiz,* a custodian, as in the word *muhafiz daftar,* a head record-keeper; or again, *hifazat,* custody, as *bahifazat polis,* in custody of the police; or again, *daim-ul-hafz,* imprisonment for life, and other similar expressions.

All words from this root suggest the idea of "guarding," and therefore the name Hephzibah at once speaks its own meaning. It is "one who is guarded," a "protected one." And answering to this there must be some power which guards, and the name of this power is given in Hosea ii, 16, where it is called "Ishi." "And it shall be at that day, saith the Lord, that thou shalt call me Ishi; and thou shalt call me no more Baali." "Baali" means "lord," "Ishi" means "husband," and between the two there is a whole world of distinction.

To call the Great Power "Baali" is to live in one world, and to call it "Ishi" is to live in another. The world that is ruled over by Baali is a world of "miserable worms of the dust" and such crawling creatures; but the world that is warmed and lightened by "Ishi" is one in which men and women walk upright, conscious of their own divine nature, instead of dodging about to escape being crushed under the feet of Moloch as he strides through his dominions. If the name Baali did not suggest a wrong idea there would be no need to change it for another, and the change of name therefore indicates the opening of the mind to a larger and sounder conception of the true nature of the Ruling Principle of the universe. It is no imperious autocrat, the very apotheosis of self-glorification, ill-natured and spiteful if its childish vanity be not gratified by hearing its own praises formally proclaimed, often from lips opened only by fear; nor is it an almighty extortioner desiring to deprive us of what we value most, either to satisfy its greed or to demonstrate its sovereignty. This is the image which men make of God and then bow terrified before it, offering a worship which is the worship of Baal, and making life blank because all the livingness has been wiped out of it.

Ishi is the embodiment of the very opposite conception, a wise and affectionate husband, instead of a taskmaster exploiting his slaves. In its true aspect the relation of husband and wife is entirely devoid of any question of relative superiority or inferiority. As well ask whether the front wheel or the back wheel of your bicycle is the more important. The two make a single whole, in which the functions of both parts are reciprocal and equally necessary; yet for this very reason these functions cannot be identical.

In a well-ordered home, where husband and wife are united by mutual love and respect, we see that the man's function is to enter into the larger world and to provide the wife with all that is needed for the maintenance and comfort of the home, while the function of the woman is to be the distributor of what her husband provides, in doing which she follows her own discretion; and a sensible man, knowing that he can trust a sensible wife, does not want to poke his finger into every pie. Thus all things run harmoniously—the woman relieved of responsibilities which are not naturally hers, and the man relieved of responsibilities which are not naturally his. But let any perplexity or danger arise, and the woman knows that from her husband she will receive all the guidance and protection that the occasion may require, he being the wise and strong man that we have supposed him, and having this assurance she is able to pursue the avocations of her own sphere undisturbed by any fears or anxieties.

It is this relation of protection and guidance that is implied by the word Hephzibah. It is the name of those who realise their identity with the all-ordering Divine Spirit. He who realises this unity with the Spirit finds himself both guided and guarded. And here we touch the fringe of a deep natural mystery, which formed the basis of all that was most valuable in the higher mysteries of the ancients, and the substance of which we must realise if we are to make any progress in the future, whatever form we may adopt to convey the idea to ourselves or others. It is the relation of the individual mind to the Universal Mind, the combination of unity with independence which, though quite clear when we know it by personal experience, is almost inexpressible in words, but which is frequently represented in the Bible under the figure of the marriage relations.

It is a basic principle, and in various modes pervades all Nature, and has been symbolised in every religion the world has known; and in proportion as the individual realises this relation he will find that he is able to *use* the Universal Mind, while at the same time he is guided and guarded by it. For think what it would be to wield the power of the Universal Mind without having its guidance. It would be the old story of Phaeton trying to drive the chariot of the Sun, which ended in his own destruction; and limitless power without corresponding guidance would be the most terrible curse that any one could bring upon his head.

The relation between the individual mind and the Universal Mind, as portrayed in the reciprocally connected names of Hephzibah and Ishi, must never be lost sight of; for the Great Guiding Mind, immeasurably as it transcends our intellectual consciousness, is not another than *ourselves.* It is The One Self which is the foundation of all the individual selves, and which is, therefore, in all its limitlessness, as entirely one with each individual as though no other being existed. Therefore we do not have to go out of ourselves to find it, for it is the expansion to infinity of all that we truly *are,* having, indeed, no place for those negative forms of evil with which we people a world of illusion, for it is the very Light itself, and in it all illusion is dispelled; but it is the expansion to infinity of all in us that is Affirmative, all that is really living.

Therefore, in looking for its guiding and guarding we are relying upon no borrowed power from *without,* held at the caprice and option of another, but upon the supreme fact of our own nature, which we can use in what direction we will with perfect freedom, knowing no limitation save the obligation not to do violence to our own purest and highest feelings. And this relation is entirely *natural.* We must steer the happy mean between imploring and ignoring. A natural law does not need to be entreated before it will work; and, on the other hand, we cannot make use of it while ignoring its existence.

What we have to do, therefore, is to take the working of the law for granted, and make use of it accordingly; and since that is the law of Mind, and Mind is Personality, this Power, which is at once *ourselves* and above ourselves, may be treated as a Person and may be spoken with, and its replies received by the inner ear of the heart. Any scheme of philosophy that does not result in this personal intercourse with the Divine Mind falls short of the mark. It may be right so far as it goes, but it does not go far enough, and fails to connect us with our vital centre. Names are of small importance so long as the intercourse is real. The Supreme Mind with which we converse is only to be met in the profoundest depths of our own being, and, as Tennyson says, is more perfectly ourselves than our own hands and feet. It is our natural Base; and realising this we shall find ourselves to be in very truth "guarded ones," guided by the Spirit in all things, nothing too great and nothing too trivial to come within the great Law of our being.

There is another aspect of the Spirit in which it is seen as a Power to be used; and the full flow of life is in the constant alternation between this aspect and the one we have been considering, but always we are linked with the Universal Mind as the flower lives by reason of its root. The connection itself is intrinsic, and can never be severed; but it must be consciously realised before it can be consciously used. All our development consists in the increasing consciousness of this connection, which enables us to apply the higher power to whatever purpose we may have in hand, not merely in the hope that it *may* respond, but with the certain knowledge that by the law of its own nature it is bound to do so, and likewise with the knowledge that by the same law it is bound also to guide us to the selection of right objects and right methods.

Experience will teach us to detect the warning movement of the inner Guide. A deepseated sense of dissatisfaction, an indescribable feeling that somehow everything is not right, are the indications to which we do well to pay heed; for we are "guarded ones," and these interior monitions are the working of that innermost principle of our own being which is the immediate outflowing of the Great Universal Life into individuality. But, paying heed to this, we shall find ourselves guarded, not as prisoners, but as a loved and honoured wife, whose freedom is assured by a protection which will allow no harm to assail her; we shall find that the Law of our nature is Liberty, and that nothing but our own want of understanding can shut us out from it.

XXII

# MIND AND HAND

I HAVE BEFORE ME a curious piece of ancient Egyptian symbolism. It represents the sun sending down to the earth innumerable rays, with the peculiarity that each ray terminates in a hand. This method of representing the sun is so unusual that it suggests the presence in the designer's mind of some idea rather different from those generally associated with the sun as a spiritual emblem; and, if I interpret the symbol rightly, it sets forth the truth, not only of the Divine Being as the Great Source of all Life and of all Illumination, but also the correlative truth of our individual relation to that centre. Each ray is terminated by a hand, and a hand is the emblem of active working; and I think it would be difficult to give a better symbolical representation of innumerable individualities, each working separately, yet all deriving their activity from a common source. The hand is at work upon the earth, and the sun, from which it is a ray, is shining in the heavens; but the connecting line shows whence all the strength and skill of the hand are derived.

If we look at the microcosm of our own person we find this principle exactly reproduced. Our hand is the instrument by which all our work is done—literary, artistic, mechanical, or household—but we know that all this work is really the work of the mind, the willpower at the centre of our system, which first determines what is to be done, and then sets the hand to work to do it; and in the doing of it the mind and hand become one, so that the hand is none other than the mind working. Now, transferring this analogy to the microcosm, we see that we each stand in the same relation to the Universal Mind that our hand does to our individual mind—at least, that is our normal relation; and we shall never put forth our full strength except from this standpoint.

We rightly realise our will as the centre of our individuality, but we should do better to picture our individuality as an ellipse rather than a circle, a figure having two "conjugate foci," two equilibrated centres of revolution rather than a single one, one of which is the will-power or faculty of *doing,* and the other the consciousness or perception of *being.* If we realise only one of these two centres we shall lose both mental and moral balance. If we lose sight of that centre which is our personal will, we shall become flabby visionaries without any backbone; and if, in our anxiety to develop backbone, we lost sight of the other centre, we shall find that we have lost that which corresponds to the lungs and heart in the physical body, and that our backbone, however perfectly developed, is rapidly drying up for want of those functions which minister vitality to the whole system, and is only fit to be hung up in a museum to show what a rigid, lifeless thing the strongest vertebral column becomes when separated from the organisation by which alone it can receive nourishment. We must realise the one focus of our individuality as clearly as the other, and bring both into equal balance, if we would develop all our powers and rise to that perfection of Life which has no limits to its glorious possibilities.

Keeping the ancient Egyptian symbol before used, and considering ourselves as the hand, we find that we derive all our power from an infinite centre; and because it is infinite we need never fear that we shall fail to draw to ourselves all that we require for our work, whether it be the intelligence to lay hold of the proper tool, or the strength to use it. And, moreover, we learn from the symbol that this central power is generic. This is a most important truth. It is the centre from which all the hands proceed, and is as fully open to any one hand as to any other. Each hand is doing its separate work, and the whole of the central energy is at its disposal for its own specific purpose. The work of the central energy, as such, is to supply vitality to the hands, and it is they that differentiate this universal power into all the varied forms of application which their different aptitudes and opportunities suggest. We, as the hands, live and work because the Central

Mind lives and works in us. We are one with it, and it is one with us; and so long as we keep this primal truth before us, we realise ourselves as beings of unlimited goodness and intelligence and power, and we work in the fulness of strength and confidence accordingly; but if we lose sight of this truth, we shall find that the strongest will must get exhausted at last in the unequal struggle of the individual against the universe.

For if we do not recognise the Central Mind as the source of our vitality, we are literally "fighting for our own hand," and all the other hands are against us, for we have lost the principle of connection with them. This is what must infallibly happen if we rely on nothing but our individual will-power. But if we realise that the will is the power by which we give out, and that every giving out implies a corresponding taking in, then we shall find in the boundless ocean of central living Spirit the source from which we can go on taking in *ad infinitum,* and which thus enables us to give out to any extent we please. But for wise and effective giving out a strong and enlightened will is an absolute necessity, and therefore we do well to cultivate the will, or the active side of our nature. But we must equally cultivate the receptive side also; and when we do this rightly by seeing in the Infinite Mind the one source of supply, our will-power becomes intensified by the knowledge that the whole power of the Infinite is present to back it up; and with this continual sense of Infinite Power behind us we can go calmly and steadily to the accomplishment of any purpose, however difficult, without straining or effort, knowing that it shall be achieved, not by the hand only, but by the invincible Mind that works through it. "Not by might, nor by power, but by My Spirit, saith the Lord of hosts."

*1902.*

## XXIII

# THE CENTRAL CONTROL

IN CONTEMPLATING the relations between body, soul, and spirit, between Universal Mind and individual mind, the methodised study of which constitutes Mental Science, we must never forget that these relations indicate, not the separateness, but the unity of these principles. We must learn not to attribute one part of our action to one part of our being, and another to another. Neither the action nor the functions are split up into separate parts. The action is a whole, and the being that does it is a whole, and in the healthy organism the reciprocal movements of the principles are so harmonious as never to suggest any feeling than that of a perfectly whole and undivided self. If there is any other feeling we may be sure that there is abnormal action somewhere, and we should set ourselves to discover and remove the cause of it. The reason for this is that in any perfect organism there cannot be more than one centre of control.

A rivalry of controlling principles would be the destruction of the organic wholeness; for either the elements would separate and group themselves round one or other of the centres, according to their respective affinities, and thus form two distinctive individualities, or else they would be reduced to a condition of merely chaotic confusion; in either case the original organism would cease to exist. Seen in this light, therefore, it is a self-evident truth that, if we are to retain our individuality; in other words, if we are to continue to exist, it can be only by retaining our hold upon the central controlling principle in ourselves; and if this be the charter of our being, it follows that all our future development depends on our recognising and accepting this central controlling principle. To this end, therefore, all our endeavours should be directed; for otherwise all our studies in Mental Science will only lead us into a confused labyrinth of principles and counter-principles, which will be considerably worse than the state of ignorant simplicity from which we started.

This central controlling principle is the Will, and we must never lose sight of the fact that all the other principles about which we have learnt in our studies exist only as its instruments. The Will is the true self, of which they are all functions, and all our progress consists of our increased recognition of the fact. It is the Will that says "I AM"; and therefore, however exalted, or even in their higher developments apparently miraculous, our powers may be, they are all subject to the central controlling power of the Will. When the enlightened Will shall have learnt to identify itself perfectly with the limitless powers of knowledge, judgment, and creative thought which are at its disposal, then the individual will have attained to perfect wholeness, and all limitations will have passed away for ever.

And nothing short of this consciousness of Perfect Wholeness can satisfy us. Everything that falls short of it is in that degree an embodiment of the principle of Death, that great enemy against which the principle of Life must continue to wage unceasing war, in whatever form or measure it may show itself, until "death is swallowed up in victory." There can be no compromise. Either we are affirming Life as a principle, or we are denying it, no matter on how great or how small a scale; and the criterion by which to determine our attitude is our realisation of our own Wholeness. Death is the principle of disintegration; and whenever we admit the power of any portion of our organism, whether spiritual or bodily, to induce any condition *independently of the intention of the Will,* we admit that the force of disintegration is superior to the controlling centre in ourselves, and we conceive of ourselves as held in bondage by an adversary, from which bondage the only way of release is by the attainment of a truer way of thinking.

And the reason is that, either through ignorance or carelessness, we have surrendered our position of control over the system as a whole, and have lost the element of *Purpose,* around which the consciousness of individuality must always centre. Every state of our consciousness, whether active or passive, should be the result of a distinct *purpose* adopted by our own free will; for the passive states should be quite as much under the control of the Will as the active. It is the lack of *purpose* that deprives us of power. The higher and more clearly defined our purpose, the greater stimulus we have for realising our control over *all* our faculties for its attainment; and since the grandest of all purposes is the strengthening and ennobling of Life, in proportion as we make this our aim we shall find ourselves in union with the Supreme Universal Mind, acting each in our individual sphere for the furtherance of the same purpose which animates the ruling principle of the Great Whole, and, as a consequence, shall find that its intelligence and powers are at our disposal.

But in all this there must be no strain. The true exercise of the Will is not an exercise of unnatural force. It is simply the leading of our powers into their natural channels by intelligently recognising the direction in which those channels go. However various in detail, they have one clearly defined common tendency towards the increasing of Life—whether in ourselves or in others—and if we keep this steadily in view, all our powers, whether interior or exterior, will be found to work so harmoniously together that there will be no sense of independent action on the part of any one of them. The distinctions drawn for purposes of study will be laid aside, and the Self in us will be found to be the realisation of a grand ideal being, at once individual and universal, consciously free in its individual wholeness and in its joyous participation in the Life of the Universal Whole.

XXIV

# WHAT IS HIGHER THOUGHT?

Resolution Passed October, 1902,
by the Kensington Higher Thought Centre.

*"That the Centre stands for the definite teaching of absolute Oneness of Creator and Creation—Cause and Effect—and that nothing which may contradict or be in opposition to the above principles be admitted to the 'Higher Thought' Centre Platform.*

*"By Oneness of Cause and Effect is meant, that Effect (man) does consist only of what Cause is; but a part (individual personality) is not therefore co-extensive with the whole."*

This resolution is of the greatest importance. Once admit that there is *any* Power outside yourself, however beneficent you may conceive it to be, and you have sown the seed which must sooner or later bear the fruit of *"Fear"* which is the entire ruin of Life, Love and Liberty. There is no *via media.* Say we are only reflections, however accurate, of The Life, and in the admission we have given away our Birthright. However small or plausible may be the germ of thought which admits that we are anything less in principle than The Life Itself, it must spring up to the ultimate ruin of the Life-Principle itself. We *are* It itself. The difference is only that between the generic and the specific of the *same* thing. We must contend earnestly, both within ourselves and outwardly, for the *one great foundation* and never, now on to all eternity, admit for a single instant any thought which is opposed to this, the Basic Truth of Being.

The leading ideas connected with Higher Thought are (I) That Man controls circumstances, instead of being controlled by them, and (II) as a consequence of the foregoing, that whatever teaches us to *rely* on power *borrowed* from a source *outside* ourselves is *not* Higher Thought; and that whatever explains to us the *Infinite* source of *our own inherent* power and the consequent *limitless* nature of that power *is* Higher Thought. This avoids the use of terms which may only puzzle those not accustomed to abstract phraseology, and is substantially the same as the resolution of October, 1902.

## XXV

# FRAGMENTS

1. God is Love.

   Man, having the understanding of God, speaks the Word of Power.

2. Man gives utterance to God.
3. The Father is Equilibrium.

   The Son is Concentration of the *same* Spirit.

   The Spirit is Projection.

***The Tri-une Relation*—always consists of these Three:**

**(I) THE POTENTIAL—(II) THE IDEAL—(III) THE CONCRETE.**

(I) The Potential is Life in its most highly abstract mode not yet brought into Form even as Thought. Not particularised in *any* way.

(II) The Ideal is the particularising of the Potential into a certain Formulated Thought.

(III) The Concrete is the Manifestation of the Formulated Thought in Visible Form.

What everybody wants is to become *more alive*—as Jesus said, "I am come that they might have Life and might have it more abundantly"—and it is only on the basis of realising ourselves as a *perfect unity throughout,* not made up of opposing parts, and that unity *Spirit,* that we can realise in ourselves the *Livingness* which *Spirit is,* and which we *as Spirit* ought to be.

## Hence Perfect Demonstration.

"The Truth shall make you Free"

Life :

Love : = The Truth

Liberty :

The Ultimate Truth will always be found to consist of these three, and anything that is contrary to them is contrary to Fundamental Truth.

## Worship

Worship consists in the recognition of the *Personal* Nature of Holy Spirit, and in the Continual Alternation (Pulsation) between the two positions of "I am the Person that Thou art," and "Thou art the Person that I am." The Two Personalities are One.

# Troward's Teachings in Condensed Form

by Harry Gaze,
from *My Personal Reflections of Thomas Troward* (Booklet Three)

1958

# TROWARD'S TEACHINGS IN CONDENSED FORM

1. First of all Judge Troward teaches that there are higher and deeper definitions of Spirit and so-called matter. Life's intelligence and life's livingness are one. Spirit's essential quality is thought, and form is the quality of "matter."
2. The form we see extends in space, and its borders are of a limited nature. Thought, on the other hand, is not limited by boundaries and is everywhere, or to quote Troward, "at every point of space simultaneously." Spirit is thought and equally present everywhere.
3. As we increase our perception and awareness, this higher development controls lesser-developed intelligence.

*Author's Note: These techniques are given in abbreviated form to enable the reader to make a brief survey of the highlights of his teaching. I trust that when read it will lead each student to secure the books from which the ideas are culled. Literal quotations are so marked.*

4. The distinction between Universal Intelligence and individual intelligence concerns the will of the individual. The work of New Thought is to learn to know the relations of our will to the Universal Will.
5. Developing the power of abstract reasoning, we grow to see the truth of the principle of evolution. This is now reaching the higher stage of

evolution, which Troward describes as "intelligent, individual evolution." Up to this time we have evolved unconsciously. Now we become interested and participate in evolution from this time forward.

6. Though from the standpoint of the five physical senses there seems to be a definite line of separation between things, there is always a fundamental unity. The basic principle of the New Thought is that there is just One Power.
7. It is possible for us to use our intelligence and volition to condense Spirit into any point, anywhere, any time, and individualize or specialize it as we desire.
8. Troward, like Hudson, taught the control of the subjective by the objective mind. Today we would express this modern vocabulary by saying *The control of the subconscious mind by the power of the conscious mind.* The subjective mind has remarkable psychic powers, telepathy, or thought-reading; clairvoyance, or clear-seeing, independent of time and space.
9. The subjective mind knows infinitely more about the conditions under which disease develops, and can accurately diagnose, and excel the most intelligent and skillful doctors, and reveal the true and perfect remedy.
10. The subjective mind is the chemist and the builder of the body. Because of its amenability to thought patterns, it will manufacture the desired chemistry and build the personality that we learn to impress upon it.
11. Before this knowledge has fully developed in the mind and secured adequate realization, wisely selected medicine will serve a good purpose. On the other hand, when we have trained our minds and learned to coordinate these spheres of the One Mind, we will have discovered the true fountain of everlasting life. We must think of the mind as such a fountain of perpetual livingness and health.
12. Judge Troward taught that the individual subjective mind (or subconscious mind) is our share of the Universal Mind.
13. As Universal Mind, this Cosmic Mind does not, in itself, work on the individual plane, but when we are working for some definite purpose, we are using the power of the Universal Mind to do so.
14. To control conditions, we must learn to control the relative by the Absolute.

15. The first step in making any attainment, or securing any good, is to construct a spiritual prototype, archetypal idea, or mental equivalent. This, if faithfully practiced, will come into the practical world of visible form and use.
16. These correspondences or prototypes must be good and constructive, for the Law will work out for the manifestation of the undesirable as well as the desirable. Each seed will bring forth "after its kind."
17. The desirable thoughts of health and healing, or success and prosperity, can be aided by the trained power of imagination and visualization.
18. Judge Troward carefully explained how the Universal Mind does not have a self-recognition of personality in itself, yet must have the quality of personalness, or we could not be centers of personal intelligence. He made a distinction between personality and individuality.
19. "The Infinite, Underlying, All-producing Mind is ready immediately to respond to all who realize their true relation to it." Troward emphasizes the wonderful power of deep, heart-felt feeling.
20. The whole position, summed up, is that we do not want to run the whole Universe, but draw particular results of a happy nature, spiritual, mental, physical, social. In regard to your own individual requirements, face the Universal Subjective Power, and "make up its mind for it." When its mind is thus made up, it continues to exercise its creative power, and sets to work to carry out the purpose for which you have concentrated it.
21. Carefully distinguish between the Universal First Cause, on the one hand, and secondary causes on the other. The understanding and use of this Power is the whole object of Mental Science. A condition, whether positive or negative, is never primary cause, and the primary cause of any series can never be negative, for negation is the condition which arises from the absence of active causation.

    It will be seen that all error or inharmony is typified by darkness. You do not have to turn out the darkness. You simply turn on the light, for where there is light, there is no darkness.
22. Secondary causes are mere reflections. Image the desired idea, in the realm of the absolute, and you can cheerfully await the desired results.
23. As Spirit operates independently of space and time, the work cannot be formed in the future. It must be accomplished *here and now.*
24. There should be no fearful, anxious thought about the conditions to be

replaced with the desirable. You must work, but take no anxious thought. "We must not fly in the face of the Law by expecting it to do *for* us what it can only do *through* us; and we must therefore use our intelligence with the knowledge that it is acting as *the instrument of a greater intelligence* . . . Anxiety and 'toilsome labor' will be replaced by states that are a permanent source of all that is good."

25. Intuitive power, by which we perceive Truth, is the right path to travel in. For this, we have to be trained in the right way. It is very important to have a real understanding of intuition and to distinguish real intuition from groundless fears and distorted imagination. Before the conscious or objective mind starts to argue or object, the mind is like the waters of a still lake. With fear, the image is blurred as when a stone is thrown into the lake.
26. The basic principle of all New Thought, and mental and spiritual healing, is a change of belief— from falsity to faith in Truth. "The wrong belief which externalizes as sickness is the belief that some secondary cause, which is really only a condition, is a primary cause."
27. The healer tells the patient to take a receptive attitude. The healer also relaxes, but for the purpose of "flowing out": and the patient relaxes to permit a "flowing in."
28. Realize the importance of the will. While imagination is of a creative nature, the will does the work of keeping it to a given path or center. The will guides your faculty of imagination rightly.
29. The power of concentration is not a strenuous proceeding. The law of force is not to be used. "From this standpoint we see that all is Life, and all is Good. Nature is one vast storehouse of Life and Good entirely devoted to our individual use. We have the key to all her treasures. . . . Realizing this, we shall draw from it streams of vital energy which will make the very sensation of livingness a joy."
30. To get into a state of attunement with the Universal Mind, we should think of ourselves as pure Being. We are spiritual beings in a spiritual universe, here and now. We are expressions of the Infinite Mind, sons of God. We must make a proper identification of ourselves.
31. The conscious mind reasons by all methods of reasoning, but not always correctly. The subconscious reasons deductively only, and its deductions are perfect. That is, they are true to the major premise laid down by the conscious mind.

32. The master teacher, Jesus, has given rules which, *rightly interpreted and applied,* solve all our problems, whether they are business, health, love, marriage, or abilities.
33. The old Elizabethan poet says, "The soul is form and doth the body make." The body must be included in complete integration. Only so can we have wholeness of personality.
34. The evolution of the individual wholly depends on the Universal Mind working on the plane of the individual. The Supreme All-originating Spirit is essentially creative, in the Eternal Now. The Life Spirit seeks expression of its perfect and everlasting livingness. Beauty is eternally in the Divine Mind. We are here to give it expression.
35. "Principle is not bound by precedent." The future is in no way limited by the past and the present. The multitudes know that certain good things are utterly impossible, but fortunately someone is always born who does not know they are impossible, so this one goes ahead and does them.
36. There is always a new order in which things can be arranged. This is familiar to us, but what is now known is that the Personal Factor can be introduced. We can always make something better. Our manifest life is a process of becoming, and we can move on to new excellence.
37. "We have now got at some reason why concrete material form is a necessity of the Creative Process. Without it the perfect Self-recognition of Spirit from the individual standpoint, which we shall presently find is the means by which the Creative Process is to be carried forward, would be impossible. . . . Here we find the *initial* polarity of Universal Spirit and Universal Substance, each being the complementary of the other. . . . Spirit supplies Selection and Motion. Substance supplies something from which selection can be made and to which Motion can be imparted, so it is a *sine qua non* for the Expression of Spirit."
38. "Spirit wants to enjoy the reality of its own life—not merely to vegetate. This Spirit does by Self-contemplation. . . . Thinking of itself as having the enjoyment it wishes gives it Reality." When we contemplate the Spirit doing this, we have more and more joy in our lives. Think of the All-originating mind as the Great Artist creating through us.
39. Let your mind dwell on the relationship between the Universal Manifesting Principle and its individual manifestation. This is the essence of the matter. We may contemplate Spirit and re-orient ourselves in

true creative fashion. The Creative Power is the Spirit of the Affirmative. The Divine Ideal is that of individuality which recognizes its Source. We are to become channels of its inexhaustible supply of life, love, wisdom, joy, youth, and beauty.

40. We should not be so interested in transferring ourselves to other planets. There is infinitely more life and goodness in this planet than anyone has ever discovered. Understanding this, old age can be prevented, even cured. Life can be made perpetual.
41. Unless we get the good results, we have introduced interferences by our thought. We have brought in the negative element of wrong thinking.
42. "Spirit creates by Self-contemplation; therefore, what it contemplates itself as being, that it becomes. You are individualized Spirit: therefore, what you contemplate as the Law of your being becomes the Law of your being. Hence contemplate a law of death," and you die. . . . "Contemplate a Law of Life as inherent in the very Being of the Spirit. . . . [and you are] building up a healthier and happier personality in mind, body, and circumstances." Express this by Initiative and Selection. There is an eternal principle, as active as ever. It is available now. Like God, we must express the pure Affirmative Spirit.
43. We are to evolve from the necessary race thought to individually practiced initiative. Race thought would let us become ill, grow aged, and die. We must saturate ourselves with the Spirit and really, truly live.
44. When we are open to the Spirit, vivifying thoughts, ideas, and feelings will flow in.
45. There will be eternal progress through more highly developed form of expression in man. People read and interpret the Bible imperfectly and imagine it teaches inevitable death. This arises through careless reading. "These are good, well-meaning people with a limited idea which they read into the Bible. Man possesses a joyous and immortal Life-permeating spirit, soul, and body." Life is a gay adventure and God is on our side!
46. Regeneration can be accomplished here and now.* We are to keep a free, full circulation between us and God. Creation is produced by the action of Divine will upon Nature. "Death will sometime cease to be

* Read the author's *How to Live Forever: The Secret of Longevity* (Brooklyn, N.Y.: Revisionist Press).

for the simple reason that Life alone can be the enduring principle." True worship is communion with the Supreme Life of the Universe. Jesus said, "I am the resurrection and the life." We, too, must learn to say it, and mean it.

47. The Divine Power is the "I am." This is *the* Word which we read of in the Gospel of St. John which is also the Light. "And the Word was with God and was God." "The Light that lighteth every man that cometh into the world." The Light (the Word) that was with God and was God is our divine light.
48. Knowing, then, that the Divine Word within us is God Himself, we will speak our words with divine authority, knowing that these words are conceived and spoken by the God in us. "Life and Death are in the power of the tongue."
49. Although the Law is Immutable, and we cannot change it, we can introduce the personal factor. By changing our word, we can change our relationship to the Law. "The Law itself never changes, but we can specialize it by realizing the principle involved." "The Law cannot be changed, and the Word can."
50. From the Law and the Word we should secure: (1) Freedom from worry and anxiety, (2) "Something to look forward to and feel an interest in." Granted that these two conditions be fulfilled, I think we should all be well pleased to go on living *ad infinitum.*
51. The way to fulfill these two conditions is to use the Word with confidence, constructiveness, and in perfect harmony. Be sure it is the right word in harmony with the principle of Unity. This will give freedom from anxiety. Then if we always have a succession of new ideals, we will have a continual interest in life. New vision is new life.
52. The promises of the Bible comprise all sorts of desirable things: health of body, peace of mind, earthly prosperity, prolongation of life, and finally even the conquest of death itself; but always on one condition: "perfect confidence in the power of the All-originating Spirit in response to our reliance on the Word." There must be true quality of faith.
53. "We must always bear in mind that the Law is set in motion by the Word. The Word does not make the Law, but it gives it something to work on." This is true of the negative as well as the positive, so we have the power of choice.

54. "Death and taxes" are typical expressions of the race mind, but it is not true that they are inevitable, certainly not in the eternal plan of things.
55. "How can I know that I am not speaking my own Word instead of that of the Creative Spirit? The Word of the Spirit is always based on the idea of Becoming. The word of the smaller personality is always based on the idea of possessing. . . . If we base our speaking of the Word on the Promise of Spirit, we may be sure that we are on the right track."
56. The true interpretation of the Bible is within us. The True Word will make us free, the quality of that freedom being the "Liberty of the Sons and Daughters of God."
57. "The great Truth concerning Man is that he is the image and likeness of God. Man is at first ignorant of this Truth, and this ignorance is his Fall. Man at last comes to the perfect knowledge of this Truth, and this knowledge is his Rising-again, and these principles will expand until they bring us to the Life that is in us all."
58. Distinguish between the personal name of Jesus and the Christ. The Christ is within all men. The word *Man* means the Measurer. Consciousness is the cup which measures the degree of love, wisdom, joy, power, life, and peace we pour out for ourselves.

## ABOUT THE AUTHOR

THOMAS TROWARD (1847–1916) inspired many of the twentieth century's leading lights of New Thought and positive thinking. A British judge in colonial India who dedicated himself to metaphysical and esoteric studies, Troward crafted the most rigorous philosophical arguments in support of the contention that our thoughts are causative. His six classic books, each collected in this volume, are required reading for any serious student of metaphysics.